Cinema Arthuriana

Cinema Arthuriana
Twenty Essays

REVISED EDITION

Edited by Kevin J. Harty

McFarland & Company, Inc., Publishers
Jefferson, North Carolina, and London

ALSO BY KEVIN J. HARTY
AND FROM MCFARLAND

*The Reel Middle Ages: American, Western and
Eastern European, Middle Eastern and Asian Films
About Medieval Europe* (1999; paperback 2006)

*King Arthur on Film: New Essays
on Arthurian Cinema* (1999)

Frontispiece: Richard Harris as King Arthur
in Joshua Logan's 1967 film *Camelot*.

*The present work is a reprint of the illustrated case
bound edition of* Cinema Arthuriana: Twenty Essays,
first published in 2002 by McFarland.

LIBRARY OF CONGRESS CATALOGUING-IN-PUBLICATION DATA

Cinema Arthuriana : twenty essays / edited by
Kevin J. Harty.— Rev. ed.
p. cm.
Includes bibliographical references and index.

ISBN 978-0-7864-4683-4
softcover : 50# alkaline paper ∞

1. Arthurian romances in motion pictures. 2. Arthurian romances —
Adaptations — History and criticism. 3. Kings and rulers in motion pictures.
4. Medievalism — History — 20th century. 5. Middle Ages in motion pictures.
I. Harty, Kevin J.
PN1995.9.A75 C5 2010   791.43'651— dc21   2002003335

British Library cataloguing data are available

©2002 Kevin J. Harty. All rights reserved

*No part of this book may be reproduced or transmitted in any form
or by any means, electronic or mechanical, including photocopying
or recording, or by any information storage and retrieval system,
without permission in writing from the publisher.*

Cover photograph: Emmett J. Flynn's 1921 film *A Connecticut Yankee
in King Arthur's Court* (courtesy of the Museum of Modern Art)

Manufactured in the United States of America

*McFarland & Company, Inc., Publishers
Box 611, Jefferson, North Carolina 28640
www.mcfarlandpub.com*

In memory of
Jamie, Jim, Chuck, Jim,
Richard and Yves, and Adam
and for
Jeff, John and Russell, and Matt and Charlie

You may grow old and trembling in your anatomies, you may lie awake at night listening to the disorder of your veins, you may miss your only love, you may see the world about you devastated by evil lunacies, or know your honor trampled in the sewers of baser minds. There is only one thing for it then — to learn. Learn why the world wags and what wags it. That is the only thing which the mind can never exhaust, never alienate, never be tortured by, never fear or distrust, and never dream of regretting. Learning is the thing for you.

— T. H. White, *The Once and Future King*

Acknowledgments

In putting together this revised edition of *Cinema Arthuriana*, I have been helped and encouraged by many people. I wish first to thank collectively all those who contributed their essays to this new edition and Gary Kuris, who was the guiding force behind the original edition.

I owe a special debt to librarians and archivists at a number of research centers. At La Salle University, Stephen Breedlove and Nancy Tresnan tirelessly (and cheerfully?) filled what must at times have seemed like thousands of interlibrary loan requests. Their colleagues in the Reference Department of La Salle's Connelly Library also readily answered questions and queries that always seemed to pop up at the last minute or at odd times, and Georgina Murphy helpfully ordered books for the Connelly Collection to meet my own research, as well as more general, interests. Madeline F. Matz, Reference Librarian in the Library of Congress's Motion Picture, Broadcasting and Recorded Sound Division, also responded to queries by fax, telephone, and e-mail and helped me to arrange screenings of rare films in the Library's collection. I am indebted, for their assistance, to Nancy Goldman at the Pacific Film Archive and to the staffs of the Theater and Film Collection of the New York Public Library, of the corresponding collection at the Philadelphia Free Library, and of the Film Library and Stills Archive at the Museum of Modern Art in New York. Courtesy lines in the captions to the stills used throughout this volume further record my debts to a number of institutions who generously supplied me with materials for this revised edition.

For research matters, my biggest debt remains to the Library of the British Film Institute (especially David Sharp) and the National Film and Television Archive (especially Olwen Terris) in London, where everyone from staff in reception to librarians, pages, archivists, researchers, and their assistants readily made me feel at home over the many years I have been studying cinema Arthuriana. In London, I am also grateful for the assistance (and wonderful company) provided by Rick Fisher, Sheena Napier, David Barrable, Simon Cunniffe, Judith Greenwood, Gary Yershon, and Gordon Terris.

Since 1982, La Salle University, through its Committee on Leaves and Grants, has provided me with released time and financial support to pursue my studies of cinema Arthuriana, and I am especially grateful to a succession of deans and provosts for their encouragement of this and other projects, especially Brother Emery Mollenhauer, F.S.C. My colleague, former chair, and good friend James A. Butler has been unstinting in his advice and counsel. And I have benefited too from the assistance of a number of former and present colleagues, especially Robert T. Fallon, Linda Merians, William Eiler Hall, Bill Wine, John Keenan, George B. Stow, John Christopher Kleis, Helena White, Francine Lottier, and Brother Gabriel Fagan, F.S.C. For assistance and encouragement, I also want to thank Kathleen Harty,

Matt McCabe and Charlie Wilson, Eleanore Samarzes, Richard Meiss and Peter Rudy, Russell Leib, Jeff Petraco, and most especially Donald Burns.

Not the least of the joys that working in the field of Arthuriana affords are the friendships one develops with like-minded scholars (many of whom contributed to this volume) from across the globe. For much good cheer at scholarly conferences and elsewhere, I am especially grateful to Bonnie Wheeler, Jo Goyne, Norris J. Lacy, Joan Grimbert, Donald Hoffman, Barbara and Alan Lupack, Jacqueline de Weever, François de la Bretèque, Jeffrey Richards, Stephen Knight, Richard F. Green, Jacqueline Jenkins, Elizabeth Sklar, Michael Salda, Arjo Vanderjagt, Sandra Gorgievski, Laura Kendrick, and Leo Carruthers.

Kevin J. Harty
Philadelphia
Summer 2002

Contents

Preface	1
The Contributors	3
1. Cinema Arthuriana: An Overview Kevin J. Harty	7
2. Mythopoeia in *Excalibur* Norris J. Lacy	34
3. Fire, Water, Rock: Elements of Setting in John Boorman's *Excalibur* and Steve Barron's *Merlin* Muriel Whitaker	44
4. Morgan and the Problem of Incest Jacqueline de Weever	54
5. An Enemy in Our Midst: *The Black Knight* and the American Dream Alan Lupack	64
6. *Tortilla Flat* and the Arthurian View John Christopher Kleis	71
7. The Retreat from Camelot: Adapting Bernard Malamud's *The Natural* to Film Barbara Tepa Lupack	80
8. Cinematic American Camelots Lost and Found: The Film Versions of Mark Twain's *A Connecticut Yankee in King Arthur's Court* and George Romero's *Knightriders* Kevin J. Harty	96
9. The Ironic Tradition in Four Arthurian Films Raymond H. Thompson	110
10. Two Films That Sparkle: *The Sword in the Stone* and *Camelot* Alice Grellner	118
11. *Monty Python and the Holy Grail*: Madness with a Definite Method David D. Day	127
12. Not Dead Yet: *Monty Python and the Holy Grail* in the Twenty-first Century Donald L. Hoffman	136

13. The Arthurian Legend in French Cinema: Robert Bresson's
    Lancelot du Lac and Eric Rohmer's *Perceval le Gallois*   149
    Jeff Rider, Richard Hull, and Christopher Smith; with Michael Carnes,
    Sasha Foppiano, and Annie Hesslein

14. From Stage to Screen: The Dramatic Compulsion in French
    Cinema and Denis Llorca's *Les Chevaliers de la table ronde* (1990)   163
    Sandra Gorgievski

15. Blank, Syberberg, and the German Arthurian Tradition   177
    Ulrich Müller (translated by Julie Giffin)

16. Gawain on Film (The Remake): Thames Television Strikes Back   185
    Robert J. Blanch and Julian N. Wasserman

17. Will the "Reel" Mordred Please Stand Up? Strategies for
    Representing Mordred in American and British Arthurian Film   199
    Michael A. Torregrossa

18. Filming the Tristan Myth   211
    Meradith T. McMunn

19. *Fable* and *Poésie* in Cocteau's *L'Éternel Retour* (1943)   220
    Joan Tasker Grimbert and Robert Smarz

20. Arms and Armor in Arthurian Films   235
    Helmut Nickel

21. Cinema Arthuriana: A Comprehensive Filmography
    and Bibliography   252
    Kevin J. Harty

Index   303

Preface

> Few legends have been recast more often or in more forms than that of Arthur. From *dux bellorum* to immortal king, from medieval romance to Broadway stage, from Malory to Monty Python and Tennyson to television, Arthur has been familiar to many centuries and in numerous languages and media. The Arthurian tradition is rich and complex, with every generation, indeed every writer and artist, reinterpreting the material in light of contemporary conceptions of the King or current artistic, ideological, or even political views. In part, it is this "transposability" of the legend that explains, or at least permits, its popularity.
> — Norris J. Lacy, "Preface,"
> *The Arthurian Encyclopedia* (1986)

The original edition of *Cinema Arthuriana*, published in 1991 and sadly long out of print, broke new ground. It was the first comprehensive examination of the long history of film and television versions of the legend of King Arthur. That edition offered fifteen essays and a complete filmography and bibliography.

This second edition reprints four of the essays from the first edition in their original form. To these four essays, it adds eleven substantially revised essays from the original edition, and six new essays for an even more comprehensive overview of cinema Arthuriana from 1904 (the date of the release of Edison's *Parsifal*) to 2001, when Summer audiences in America were offered a television version of Marion Zimmer Bradley's *The Mists of Avalon*. In all, this revised edition contains twenty essays written (and a filmography and bibliography compiled) by Arthurian and film specialists from across the United States, Canada, and Europe. (For a complementary collection of essays, readers may want to consult the 1999 collection I edited entitled *King Arthur on Film: New Essays on Arthuriana Cinema*.)

This revised edition begins with an overview of cinema Arthuriana that catalogues feature and made-for-television films whose plots are substantially indebted to some version of the legend of Arthur. Essays by Norris J. Lacy, Muriel Whitaker, and Jacqueline de Weever that focus on John Boorman's 1981 film *Excalibur* follow. Boorman's film is arguably one of the most discussed examples of cinema Arthuriana, and these three critics analyze the film's successes and failures in handling Arthurian materials and the ways that other directors have approached these same materials in contrast to Boorman.

The Arthurian legend has found a ready home in America — and in the American cinema as the essays by Alan Lupack, John Christopher Kleis, Barbara Tepa Lupack, and Kevin J. Harty make clear. But as these different critics demonstrate, there is no one American cinematic approach to the Arthurian legend. Rather, the legend's continuing adaptability has allowed it to find its way into a variety of American films.

Comedy in all its forms has long been a hallmark of cinema Arthuriana as essays by Raymond H. Thompson, Alice Grellner, David D. Day, and Donald L. Hoffman make clear, the latter two focusing on *Monty Python and the Holy Grail*, a perennial favorite rereleased in 2001 with new footage and an assortment of product tie-ins.

While the origins of the Arthurian legend lie in fifth century Britain, that legend crossed the English channel in the twelfth century to find a ready home first in France and then in Germany. In essays on the French tradition of cinema Arthuriana, Jeff Rider and his students and Sandra Gorgievski discuss films directed by Robert Bresson, Eric Rohmer, and Denis Llorca. Complementing these essays, Ulrich Müller examines the use of the Arthurian legend in two German screen versions of the legend of Parsifal.

Within the early Arthurian literary tradition, the characters of Gawain and Mordred figure prominently. Robert J. Blanch and Julian N. Wasserman survey film Gawains, while Michael A. Torregrossa surveys film Mordreds. In medieval times, the story of the star-crossed lovers Tristan and Isolde came to be attached to that same early Arthurian literary tradition, and essays by Meradith T. McMunn and by Joan Grimbert and Robert Smarz trace how directors have transposed the legend of these two lovers to the screen.

Helmut Nickel, writing from his unique point of view as former head of the Department of Arms and Armor at New York's Metropolitan Museum of Art, rounds out this collection of essays with a comprehensive overview of arms and armor in Arthurian films. This new edition of *Cinema Arthuriana* then concludes with an expanded comprehensive filmography and bibliography.

The Contributors

Robert J. Blanch is Professor of English at Northeastern University in Boston. He is editor of *Sir Gawain and Pearl: Critical Essays* (1966), author of *Sir Gawain and the Green Knight: A Reference Guide* (1983) and *The Gawain Poems: A Reference Guide, 1978-1993* (2000), co-editor of *Chaucer in the Eighties* (1986) and *Text and Matter: New Critical Perspectives of the Pearl-Poet* (1991), and co-author of *From Pearl to Gawain: Forme to Fynisment* (1995).

Michael Carnes received his bachelor of arts in English and Film Studies from Wesleyan University in 2002.

David D. Day has been Lecturer in Literature and Communications at the University of Houston at Clear Lake since completing his doctorate in English from Rice University in 1992. His primary research field is law and literature in the early Middle Ages, and he has published articles on legal issues in Old English and medieval Latin literature.

Jacqueline de Weever is Professor of English (now retired) at Brooklyn College of the City University of New York. She is the author of *Mythmaking and Metaphor in Black Women's Fiction*, *The Chaucer Name Dictionary*, and *Sheba's Daughters, Whitening and Demonizing Saracen Women in Medieval French Epic*.

Sasha Foppiano received her bachelor of arts in English and French Studies from Wesleyan University in 2002. Her senior thesis was on bread production in medieval France.

Julie Giffin, who holds bachelor's and master's degrees in German from the University of Vermont and from Bowling Green State University respectively, has been a Fulbright Teaching Assistant in English as a Second Language in Austria and a teacher of German at the Burke Mountain Academy in Vermont. She currently lives and works as a physical therapist in Plattsburgh, New York.

Sandra Gorgievski holds a doctorate from the University of Paris IV-Sorbonne and is lecturer in English at the University of Toulon in France. Her research interests include the use of the Arthurian myth in film, literature, and comics. She has published articles on *Beowulf*, angels and demons, and films about the Middle Ages. She is also author of a grammar book, *Les temps* (1999).

Alice Grellner is Professor Emerita at Rhode Island College where she taught Arthurian Literature, among other things, for twenty-five years.

Joan Tasker Grimbert, Professor of French at The Catholic University of America, has served as secretary-treasurer of the International Arthurian Society, North American Branch. Her publications include *Songs of the Women Trouvères* (2001), *Tristan and Isolde: A Casebook* (1995), *Yvain dans le miroir: Une Poétique de la réflexion dans le*

"*Chevalier au lion*" *de Chrétien de Troyes* (1988), and articles on medieval romance, medieval lyric, and film.

Kevin J. Harty is Professor in and Chairman of the Department of English at La Salle University in Philadelphia. An associate editor of *Arthuriana*, he is also the editor or author of nine books including *King Arthur on Film, New Essays on Arthurian Cinema* and *The Reel Middle Ages*, both published in 1999.

Annie Hesslein received her B.A. in Anthropology from Wesleyan University in 2001. Her senior thesis was a study of the evolution of the concept of race.

Donald L. Hoffman is a long-time Arthurian who has published on Arthurian topics in twelfth-century Italy and twentieth-century African American and Caribbean Literature. He has most recently co-edited with Elizabeth S. Sklar a collection of essays on *King Arthur in Popular Culture* (2002).

Richard Hull received his bachelor of arts in Film Studies from Wesleyan University in 1990. His animated film, *Eat or Be Eaten*, won the 1990 Frank Capra Prize. He currently lives in Massachusetts, where he continues to work in animation.

John Christopher Kleis is retired Associate Professor of English at La Salle University. He was editor of the literary quarterly *Four Quarters* for eight years and has published in *Victorian Newsletter, Texas Studies in Literature and Language,* and *Arthuriana*. His critique of Hans-Jürgen Syberberg's film *Parsifal* appeared in *King Arthur on Film, New Essays on Arthurian Cinema* (1999).

Norris J. Lacy is the Edwin Erle Sparks Professor of French at Pennsylvania State University. He is past President (now Honorary President) of the International Arthurian Society. His publications deal largely with medieval narrative literature, especially Arthurian romance and fabliau, but he has also published on modern literature and film. He is author, editor, or translator of over twenty books, including *The Craft of Chrétien de Troyes, The New Arthurian Encyclopedia, The Arthurian Handbook, Béroul's Tristan, Reading Fabliaux,* and *The Old French Arthurian Vulgate and Post-Vulgate Cycles in Translation*.

Alan Lupack, currently President of the North American Branch of the International Arthurian Society and Director of the Robbins Library at the University of Rochester, has written numerous essays on medieval and modern Arthurian literature. He has also edited medieval English Arthurian romances and four volumes of modern Arthurian literature, is co-author of *King Arthur in America*, and is the author of a volume of Arthurian poetry.

Barbara Tepa Lupack has published extensively on American literature, film, and culture. Her most recent books include *Nineteenth-Century Women at the Movies: Adapting Classic Women's Fiction to Film* and, with Alan Lupack, *King Arthur in America* and *Arthurian Literature by Women*. Forthcoming is *Literary Adaptations in Black American Cinema: From Micheaux to Morrison*.

Meradith T. McMunn is Professor of Medieval Literature in the Department of English at Rhode Island College in Providence. Her publications include *Beasts and Birds of the Middle Ages: The Bestiary and Its Legacy* with Willene B. Clark and numerous articles on the secular literature of the Middle Ages, text and illustration in medieval manuscripts, and the manuscripts of the *Roman de la Rose*. She is now completing a decade-long project to locate and describe the corpus of more than 9,000 illustrations in the manuscripts of the *Roman de la Rose* for a forthcoming descriptive catalogue and study.

Ulrich Müller is Professor of Medieval German Literature at the University of Salzburg in Austria. His special fields of interest, besides medieval literature, are medievalism and musical theatre (especially that of Mozart and Wagner), topics on which he has written extensively and organized many academic conferences.

Helmut Nickel received his Ph.D. from the Free University of Berlin in 1958 with a thesis on the equestrian shield in Medieval Western Europe. In 1960, he joined the Department of Arms and Armor at New York's Metropolitan Museum of Art, from which he retired as Curator Emeritus in 1989.

Jeff Rider is Professor of French and Medieval Studies at Wesleyan University. He has published essays on medieval literature and history, and he is the author, editor, or translator of four books. His most recent publication is *God's Scribe, The Historiographical Art of Galbert of Bruges* (2001).

Robert Smarz has a lifelong interest in film and photography.

Christopher Smith is a graduate of Wesleyan University.

Raymond H. Thompson is Professor of English (now retired) at Acadia University in Wolfville, Nova Scotia. He is the author of *The Return from Avalon: A Study of the Arthurian Legend in Modern Fiction* (1985); an Associate Editor of *The New Arthurian Encyclopedia* (1991; 1996); and consulting editor of Pendragon Fiction, published by Green Knight. He has also conducted a series of interviews, *Taliesin's Successors: Interviews with Authors of Modern Arthurian Literature,* which are available at http://www.lib.rochester.edu/camelot/intrvws/contents.htm.

Michael A. Torregrossa received a master of arts in Medieval Studies in 1999 from the University of Connecticut, where he is presently pursuing a second master's degree in English. His publications include articles on Arthurian film, television, and comic books.

Julian N. Wasserman is Provost Distinguished Professor of English at Loyola University in New Orleans. He has published widely on medieval and modern literature.

Muriel Whitaker is Professor Emerita of English, University of Alberta, Edmonton, Canada. She has published two Arthurian studies, *Arthur's Kingdom of Adventure: The World of Malory's Morte Darthur* (1984) and *The Legends of King Arthur in Art* (1990; pbk. 1995). In addition, she has edited eight books of collected stories and critical essays and contributed extensively to books, journals, and encyclopedias in the areas of medieval, Victorian, Arthurian, and Canadian literature and art.

1

Cinema Arthuriana: An Overview

Kevin J. Harty

Since at least 1904, the legend of King Arthur has produced a complicated film legacy that others and I continue to call cinema Arthuriana.[1] Unlike films we classify as films noirs or westerns or road pictures, films about King Arthur do not easily fit into any one cinematic genre. Rather cinema Arthuriana is a form of medievalism, the attempt as old as the birth of the early modern or Renaissance period to revisit or reinvent the medieval world for contemporary purposes.

Explanations for the persuasive influence and continued popularity of the medieval vary, although the semiotician and cultural critic Umberto Eco has pointed out that people simply seem to like the Middle Ages (61). We see in the medieval a world at once distant from yet related to our own. Interest in Arthurian medievalism is further encouraged by the promise that Arthur will come again, that he is once and future king. Contemporary retellings of the legend of Arthur, on film or in other media, only serve in part as self-fulfilling prophecies of Arthur's promised return, a key element in versions of the Arthurian legend since at least the early twelfth century.

Thomas Edison is responsible for the oldest surviving example of cinema Arthuriana.[2] In 1904, Edison commissioned his principal director and cameraman at the time, Edwin S. Porter, to bring a version of Wagner's Grail opera, *Parsifal,* to the screen.[3] However, Edison and Porter were less interested in the matter of Arthur than they were in capitalizing on the huge success of the New York production of Wagner's opera after it opened at the Metropolitan Opera House on Christmas Eve 1903. Wagnerian acolytes back in Germany may have viewed this production (or any other production of the opera outside of Germany) as sacrilegious, but New York critics and audiences alike declared *Parsifal*, which was sung in German, the highlight of the year's opera season. A second production sung in English opened in Boston in October 1904, moved to New York two weeks later, and then went on tour.[4]

In the Edison-Porter film, a group of actors using a highly exaggerated style of acting, interspersed with trick camera effects, present a series of scenes from Wagner's opera. Porter's camera technique is fairly simple. He positioned his camera so that all shots are from the audience's point of view, and the highly exaggerated acting style suggests that the actors are singing as they stand or move about the set. The film, which runs for over 600 feet, proved to be the most ambitious and costly film that Porter ever made for Edison (Niver 74). But, despite Porter's considerable talents and Edison's best intentions, their *Parsifal* was not a success. The technology to synchronize phonographic recordings with film did not yet exist (Bush 607–08). And Edison had to withdraw the film from distribution because of legal proceedings: the copyright owner successfully sued Edison for using the script of the opera without permission (Spears 226).

But the technical and legal problems experienced by Edison and Porter did not dissuade other directors from attempting to film stage, or create original, productions of operas for the screen. In 1909, Albert Capellani directed a well-received film of *Tristan et Yseult* for the Pathé Frères Company in Paris,[5] and Mario Caserini directed screen versions of *Siegfried* and *Parsifal* in 1912 for Turin's Ambrosio Company. Caserini's *Parsifal* is more elaborate and detailed than Porter's, but it is again hampered by the director's inability to combine camera and gramophone successfully.[6] And while the works of Wagner proved popular with filmmakers and audiences, other directors, especially in Italy, brought operas by Donizetti and Verdi to the screen throughout the teens despite continuing technical problems with synchronization of sound to film.

In 1911, Ugo Falena, who had already helmed a number of historical films, directed *Tristano e Isotta* for Pathé's Italian subsidiary, a film indebted to both Wagner and to the medieval legend as retold by Bédier. But Falena also adds details to the story of the star-crossed lovers, including a role for Morgan Le Fay and a second love triangle involving Tristan, Isolde, and Tristan's female servant.[7] In 1920, the French director Maurice Mariaud attempted a more elaborate version of *Tristan et Yseut* based solely on Wagner for the Louis Nalpas Company. This film featured six song segments, each 650 meters long, set against the cliffs of the Riviera, which stand in for those of Cornwall and Ireland.[8] Despite location shots and other attempts to convey the grandeur of the story of two star-crossed lovers, Mariaud failed to capture on film the alternating desperation and ardor of the two title characters. Less static than Porter's film, but less complex than Caserini's, Mariaud's film reveals him to be one of the earliest in a long line of directors overwhelmed by the Arthurian story they attempt to bring to the screen (Fescourt 193).

Cinema Arthuriana and opera would not prove a successful mix for many years.[9] A not widely distributed 1953 film version of Wagner's *Parsifal* directed by Daniel Mangrane combined elements from the opera with medieval legends and literature about the Grail. Much better known and much more controversial, Hans-Jürgen Syberberg's 1982 screen version of Wagner's *Parsifal* remains for many *the* most successful film version of any opera (Kroll 49). Running a total of 255 minutes, Syberberg's film presents Wagner's opera in a claustrophobic labyrinth constructed out of the cracks and crevices of an enormous model of the composer's death mask. The film's final scene takes place before a double cave entrance eventually revealed to be the nostrils of that mask.

While inadequate technology had hindered the first efforts to bring Wagner's opera successfully to the screen, Syberberg's production succeeds by using elaborate sets (some oversized, others miniature), puppets, expert dubbing, and the daring conceit of having the title character played alternately by a man and a woman. Parsifal, the savior, is, as Thomas Elsaesser points out in his review of the film for *Monthly Film Bulletin*, "male *and* female, and his saving grace [is] the recognition of both as parts of the same self" (50 [May 1983]: 137–38).

Literature also readily afforded filmmakers with plot lines for early examples of cinema Arthuriana. In *Launcelot and Elaine,* a 1909 production for Vitagraph, Charles

Kent turned to Tennyson's poem of the same title as his source. Kent's free rendering of the poem afforded him opportunities to display cinematic innovations while also doing justice to his poetic subject matter. The film includes scenes in a dark cave and close-ups of the tournament in which Launcelot fights to win the queen's favor. Both critics and movie-goers responded positively to the film's use of elaborate scenic displays to heighten its narration of the events drawn from Tennyson's poem. A note in the trade papers praised the film pointing out that

> with the aid of half a dozen captions the entire story of King Arthur's most famous knight is told so simply to be within the mental grasp of the unthinking, while the rich poetic atmosphere of the poem is fully preserved for those to whom Tennyson is an open book.[10]

To promote the film on the day of its release, Vitagraph ran an advertisement in *Moving Picture World* which practically gushed in its assertions that *Launcelot and Elaine*

> was a thoroughly artistic production of Sir Alfred Tennyson's most charming poem. The highest developments of photography, the vast resources of the producing plant and the very acme of pantomimic acting combine in this subject to establish a new standard [13 November 1909: 672].

When *Launcelot and Elaine* was rereleased in January 1914, a note in *Bioscope* declared the film was "one of the finest productions, and greatest of successes, in poetical pictures" (15 January 1914: suppl. xxxi).

Not much information survives about Giuseppe de Liguoro's 1910 film for Milano *Il Re Artù e i cavalieri della tavola rotonda,* which was released in Great Britain by New Agency Films under the title *King Arthur; or, The Knights of the Round Table.* But a brief note in *Bioscope* (15 September 1910: 39) indicates that the film was lavishly produced and featured a cast of almost 100, and D'Heur and De Groeve suggest that the film's source may have been Sir Thomas Malory's fifteenth century Arthuriad, *Le Morte d'Arthur* (423).

We know more about two American films that incorporate the figure of Sir Galahad into their otherwise non–Arthurian plots. The 1914 film *Sir Galahad of Twilight* sets a love triangle on Twilight Mountain where two rivals for the hand of a young girl try to prove who is her true Galahad. The 1915 film *The Grail* directed by and starring William Worthington presents a dishonest banker who embezzles funds and lays the blame for the crime on his own daughter's fiancé. When the daughter and father are stranded in the desert, the fiancé comes to their rescue in a series of scenes that draw clear parallels to Galahad's quest for the Holy Grail.[11]

In 1917, Thomas Edison teamed up with the Boy Scouts of America to produce his second Arthurian film, *The Knights of the Square Table; or, The Grail.* The film's plot reflects earlier attempts by Lord Robert Baden-Powell, the founder of scouting, to model his organization in part on the fellowship of the Round Table.[12] The film can be read as part of the attempt in America to link the story of Arthur with the issue of the proper education of young boys.[13] With a screenplay by National Field Scout Commissioner James A. Wilder, *Knights of the Square Table* skillfully tells parallel stories of two groups of boys, one a troop of scouts and the other a gang of delinquents, whose leader's prize possession is a copy of Howard Pyle's *The Story of King Arthur and His Knights* (first published in 1903). After a series of misadventures, the leader of the delinquents is seriously wounded in a robbery in which he is forced to participate. The Grail Knight appears to him and heals his wounds, after which he and the members of his gang agree to join the Boy Scouts.

The most interesting cinematic Arthurian project of the decade was never completed. In 1916, D. W. Griffith announced plans for a spectacle, *The Quest of*

Arthur Dennis as Sir Launfal (left) and Charles Mussett as King Arthur in Alan Crosland's 1917 film *Knights of the Square Table*. (Still courtesy of the Library of Congress.)

the Holy Grail, to be based on the famous series of fifteen murals by Edwin Austin Abbey that decorate the Book Delivery Room in the Boston Public Library.[14] After obtaining the rights from Abbey's widow, Griffith, for reasons never explained, abandoned the project.

The Grail did, however, make its way to New York in the 1922 film *The Light in the Dark* directed by Clarence Brown and starring Lon Chaney. In the film, a wealthy playboy finds the sacred cup, which a film title refers to as "Tennyson's Grail," in the ruins of an English church and brings it home to New York where its healing powers cure a critically ill young girl whom the playboy earlier jilted. A sequence in the middle of the film transports the two back to the Middle Ages and reenacts an elaborate Grail ceremony in which the faithful are healed of a variety of ailments and infirmities. The inspirational message of the film led to its being rereleased in a shorter version entitled *The Light of Faith* that was shown in churches and schools across America later in the 1920s.

Cinema Arthuriana took a more comic literary turn in 1920 with Emmett J. Flynn's production for Fox of *A Connecticut Yankee at King Arthur's Court,* the first of many screen adaptations of Twain's novel. Flynn's film established an unfortunate tradition in which filmmakers deleted any hint of misanthropy or social criticism from the novel and turned its plot into a romantic comedy, so much so that Twain himself, had he still been alive when it was released, might not have acknowledged the film (or any subsequent screen or television adaptation) as based on his novel. Where Twain presented his readers with Hank Morgan, the quintessential self-reliant New Englander—"a Yankee of the Yankees"—Flynn presented his viewers with Martin Cavendish (played by Harry Myers after Douglas Fairbanks turned down the role), a wealthy young man whose mother wants him to marry Lady Grey Gordon. Cavendish in turn wants to marry his mother's secretary, Betty. One night, while reading about the Age of Chivalry, Cavendish is knocked unconscious by a burglar. In a dream, he finds himself in sixth-century England at King Arthur's court. Thereafter, the film's plot follows the general outlines of Twain's novel, although it omits the massive carnage with which the novel ends. Cavendish instead simply awakens from his dream and elopes with Betty.[15]

Despite the liberties the film takes with the plot and the tone of Twain's novel, Flynn's *Connecticut Yankee* garnered much critical praise. In his review of the film for *Photoplay*, Burns Mantle called the film the second best screen comedy of the year, after Charlie Chaplin's *The Kid* (June 1921: 51), and Francis Taylor Patterson saw the film's success as proof of the screen's potential for intelligent comedy rather than only for slapstick (143–44). Flynn also established another pattern for film adaptations of Twain's novel; he missed no opportunity to add contemporary touches to the screenplay. References abound to the Volstead Act, Tin Lizzies, and the Battle of Argonne; the titles rely heavily upon current American slang and colloquialisms; and the army of knights, who arrive at the end of the film to rescue the Yankee, do so on motorcycles rather than on bicycles as they do in the novel. Subsequently, Flynn's film was adapted by Richard Rodgers and Lorenz Hart into a Broadway musical, *A Connecticut Yankee,* in 1927–28. The musical moved to London in 1929, and it was revived in 1943 with some minor changes for a second run on Broadway.

Flynn's film also inspired a talking remake in 1931 directed by David Butler and released under the title of *A Connecticut Yankee.* Butler, like Flynn, softens his source's dark side by once again turning Twain's novel into romantic comedy, though here Hank Martin, played by Will Rogers (who would seem to have been a natural spokesperson for some of Twain's social commentary and barbs), brings about a reconciliation of two lovers rather than elopes with the girl of his own dreams. Knocked unconscious by an armored figure while trying to repair a radio for a slightly crazed customer who believes he can use the radio to listen in on conversations from Arthur's Round Table, Martin awakens to find himself in England in the year 528, where he amazes the court and confounds Merlin with his cigarette lighter. Motorcycles again replace bicycles when the knights come to the rescue. Martin's army also uses a fleet of automobiles, machine guns, sawed-off shotguns, and several tanks and airplanes, yet, despite these massive armaments, the final battle remains fairly bloodless. The film, which also features Myrna Loy as Morgan Le Fay and Maureen O'Sullivan as Alisande, proved such a critical and commercial success that it was rereleased in 1936.

In 1949, Tay Garnett directed a third film of Twain's novel for Paramount with Bing Crosby in the title role. The film, romantic comedy now turned into a musical as well, was not, because of problems with copyright, based on the Rodgers and Hart Broadway show. Unfortunately, the method used throughout by Garnett, usually a more accomplished director, calls for the plot to advance not by dramatic interaction but rather by song mixed with silly dialogue.

Garnett's film was followed by several adaptations of Twain for television. Franklin Schaffner directed a sixty minute version of the novel for CBS in 1952, noteworthy only because Boris Karloff played King Arthur to Thomas Mitchell's Yankee. Fielder Cook's 1954 adaptation for Kraft Theatre and ABC turned Twain's novel into a farce, portraying Merlin (Victor Jory) as a comical character and shifting the eclipse to the end of the narrative. A 1955 version for NBC directed by Max Liebman featured Eddie Albert as the Yankee and Boris Karloff once again as Arthur. Liebman's more immediate source was the 1943 revival of the Rodgers and Hart Broadway musical: this production has Martin Barrett ready to marry Fay Morgan until he runs into his former fiancée, Alice Carter. The enraged Fay, upon finding the two together, knocks Barrett unconscious. In a dream, he then imagines that he is in Arthur's court rescuing Lady Alisande from Queen Morgan Le Fay. In 1960, the novel's satiric and comic edges were reduced to the home-spun in the 1960 Ford Startime production *Tennessee Ernie Ford Meets King Arthur*, a curiosity of interest only for the fact that it was directed by Lee J. Cobb in a rare stint behind, rather than in front of, the camera.

In 1970, Australian television presented an animated feature-length version of Twain's novel punctuated with updated contemporary gadgetry. In the final climactic battle, the Yankee harmlessly routs an army of 50,000 using compressed air and water cannons. In 1978, another sixty minute adaptation of Twain's novel for PBS's *Once Upon a Classic* series at least nodded obliquely in the direction of its source's dark conclusion: the Yankee shoots a knight dead with his revolver, and all Camelot recoils in horror at the homicide.

Russ Mayberry's 1979 film for Disney *The Unidentified Flying Oddball* (released in England as *The Spaceman and King Arthur*) turns the Yankee into reluctant astronaut Tom Trimble who arrives in Camelot with a look-alike humanoid robot in tow thanks to a NASA mishap. Once there, Trimble battles Merlin (Ron Moody), who is out to destroy him, and Morgan, who is out to destroy Arthur. Again, there is no final carnage; the Yankee even returns to Camelot a second time, though some of the novel's humor survives in this unlikely film adaptation.

A Russian adaptation of Twain's novel, *The New Adventures of a Connecticut Yankee in King Arthur's Court,* directed by Viktor Gres (1987) makes Lancelot the hero. Hank Morgan is here an American Air Force pilot who crashes his plane in a desert and awakens in Camelot. In a bit of Cold War propaganda, Hank sets out to introduce the age of chivalry to the wonders of modern American technology. Arthur's world is less than enthusiastic about accepting what Hank has to offer, so Hank challenges the knights of the Round Table to trial by combat. In the final battle, Lancelot defeats Hank, chivalric values are protected, and Hank returns to the twentieth century.

Further distancing themselves from Twain's novel have been three more recent films in which the Yankee is turned into a youngster or teenager. In 1989, Mel Damski directed a version of *Connecticut Yankee* for NBC that featured Keshia Knight Pulliam from *The Cosby Show* as the Yankee, Karen Jones, and Michael Gross from *Family Ties* as Arthur. Karen introduces Camelot to karate, aerobics, Polaroid cameras, Walkmans, and tape recorders, while the telemovie scrupulously avoids any of the substantive or controversial issues raised by its source.

In Michael Gottlieb's 1995 *A Kid in King Arthur's Court* for Disney, Calvin Fuller, a California Little Leaguer with low self-esteem, finds himself transported back to Camelot when an earthquake — the film is, after all, set in California — opens a fissure in the earth into which he falls. (Perhaps in a nod toward Malamud's *The Natural*, Calvin plays baseball for the Reseda Knights.) Once he arrives at Arthur's court, Calvin finds a befuddled Merlin and a hapless Arthur harassed by the evil Lord Belasco, who has designs on Arthur's older daughter, Princess Sarah, and the throne. Calvin himself is smitten with the king's younger daughter, Princess Katey. Dubbed Sir Calvin of Reseda by Arthur, the Little Leaguer helps the king, Merlin, and Sarah defeat Belasco. The film's only potentially interesting addition to the Arthuriad is its ultimately feeble attempt to counter the largely misogynic Arthurian tradition in having Princess Sarah, disguised as the Black Knight, save rather than threaten the day.

Also in 1995, R. L. Thomas directed *A Young Connecticut Yankee in King Arthur's Court* for Canada's Filmline International. Here Hank is a teenager who is nearly electrocuted when his guitar amplifier shorts out. He awakens to find himself in Camelot where he helps Merlin (played by a miscast Michael York) and Arthur defeat Morgan. The 1998 *A Knight in Camelot* for ABC television's *The Wonderful World of Disney* turns the Yankee into Dr. Vivien Morgan, a Connecticut scientist (played by Whoopi Goldberg, no less), transported back into Arthur's world for an improbable series of adventures more or less — actually less — indebted to Twain's novel than some earlier screen or television adaptations had been.

The 1940s saw not only the Bing Crosby *Connecticut Yankee* but also a number of other examples of cinema Arthuriana. In 1942, John Steinbeck's *Tortilla Flat*, one of a number of the author's works which critics and Steinbeck himself have linked to the Arthuriad, came to the screen in a humdrum adaptation directed by Douglas Shearer and starring Spencer Tracy, John Garfield, and Hedy Lamarr. Comedy combined with the British War effort in Marcel Varnel's *King Arthur Was a Gentleman* (also

Evelyn Dall as Susan Ashley and Arthur Askey as Arthur King examining "Excalibur" in Marcel Varnel's 1942 film *King Arthur Was a Gentleman*. (Still courtesy of the British Film Institute.)

released in 1942), starring the popular comic actor Arthur Askey as a Chaplinesque sad sack named Arthur King. Assigned to a desk job in the War Office, King wants instead to join the troops at the front. Finally conscripted, he is presented with a sword that friends convince him is Excalibur. Ordered to the front, King, believing in the sword's power as talisman, performs a series of heroic acts only to have his faith in magic and his courage shattered when his friends tell him that the sword is not really Excalibur.

More disturbingly, the Second World War influenced another example of cinema Arthuriana, *L'Éternel Retour*, Jean Cocteau's 1943 modernized version of the story of Tristan and Isolde directed by Jean Delannoy. Made during the German Occupation, the film can be viewed at times as less than subtle in its racism. Cocteau's screenplay adds to the Tristan story a sinister, if not pathological, family, the Frossins: Marc's sister-in-law Gertrude, her deranged husband Amédée, and their adult dwarf son Achille. These three join with Marc to subvert at every turn the uncontrollable love that Patrice (Tristan) and Natalie (Iseult) have for each other. Unfortunately, as a review of the film in *Monthly Film Bulletin* points out, "the hero and the heroine in their blond supremacy may represent the Teutonic herrenvolk, whilst the Frossins are the degenerate products of the lower Romance races, the offal of a culture the Teutons would destroy, the Aryan burden" (13 [28 February 1946]: 22–23).

Properly, the first Arthurian "art film," *L'Éternel Retour* streamlines the Tristan story while suggesting, almost Nietzsche-like, that legends live on reborn without the knowledge of their principals — hence the significance of the film's title. Indeed, as the final credits appear, the film also notes: "And so begins their real life...." (Cocteau 99). The main incidents of the legend are all present in the film in updated form, although the presence of Achille drew mixed responses from critics. Some reviews saw him as one of the film's outstanding features, "A concentrated symbol of the world's evil and conventional hypocrisy" (*Variety* 17 December 1947: 8, 22), while others saw him as "just plainly ghastly" and a major flaw (*New York Times* 5 January 1948: 15). The film also ran afoul of the Catholic Church. The Legion of Decency banned *L'Éternel Retour* by placing the film in its Class C, or Condemned, category because the film "presents a glorification of immoral actions" and "contains suggestive sequences" (*New York Times* 29 March 1948: 18).

More benign examples of cinema Arthuriana appeared in 1948 and 1949. In their 1948 comedy *Squareheads of the Roundtable* (remade in 1954 with additional footage as *Knutzy Knights*), the three Stooges brought their unique brand of mayhem to Camelot. And in 1949, the Hollywood serial weighed in with an Arthurian cliffhanger, Columbia's *The Adventures of Sir Galahad*. True to its genre, this fifteen-part serial presents a convoluted plot indebted to bits and pieces of the legend of Arthur.[16] Galahad, played by television's Superman, George Reeves, must retrieve the missing Excalibur as Saxons invade England. Merlin's role is ambivalent. Modred, disguised as the Black Knight, is clearly the villain, but Merlin at first uses his magic to harass Galahad, and Morgan Le Fay helps the hero counter Merlin's magic and defeat the Saxons. Once the Saxons unite with Modred to kidnap Guinevere, Merlin joins with Galahad to retrieve Excalibur from the Lady of the Lake and to rescue the queen. As a reward for his bravery, Galahad is then made a knight of the Round Table.

While the medieval setting for *Sir Galahad* allowed for some variation from the stock scenes typical of cliffhangers, this serial set a pattern for Arthurian films made in the 1950s and the early 1960s. Despite the armor and the swordplay, characters in examples of cinema Arthuriana made during the next two decades usually became little more than cowboys chasing each other across medieval versions of the Great Plains of the American Old West. The tradition of the film western in fact combined with the new technical possibilities afforded by CinemaScope to produce three Arthurian films: MGM's 1953 *Knights of the Round Table*, 20th Century–Fox's *Prince Valiant*, and Warwick and Columbia's *The Black Knight* (both released in 1954).[17]

Although MGM claimed that its researchers in Hollywood and in England had stuck "close to the facts," basing their script on Malory's "studious work,"[18] *Knights of the Round Table* presents a curious jumble of Arthurian legend. As the film opens, Morgan Le Fay, Arthur's stepsister, and Modred, who is either her husband or her paramour, dispute the king's claim to the throne. When Arthur does assume the throne, Morgan and Modred continue to plot against him. *Knights* clearly presents a Lancelot and Guinevere infatuated with each other, but their passion is limited to longing glances and one brief kiss; Jerry Zucker's more recent *First Knight* (1995) repeats this innocent exchange. Modred and Morgan, however, witness the kiss, and when they accuse the two of treason, Lancelot is banished. In a quick series of events, Modred rebels against and kills Arthur, and Lancelot casts Excalibur into the sea, kills Modred, pays a visit to a now-cloistered Guinevere, and pledges his life and that of his son, Galahad, to securing peace for all of England.

In its general outline, some details in *Knights* do bear a resemblance to earlier versions of the legend of Arthur, but the performances in the film are, as a review in the *New York Times* pointed out, on the level of "Sir Lancelot went thataway" and "The rest of you knights follow me" (8 January 1954: 17). The film presents a *Classics Illustrated* version of the legend of Arthur in which the good guys wear white armor and the bad guys wear black.[19] With charging armies, clashing swords, and colorful pageantry displayed in full wide-screen spectacle, the film is more notable for its use of CinemaScope than for its use of Arthurian materials.

The funny papers proved another source for cinema Arthuriana when 20th Century–Fox hired Henry Hathaway to direct a version of Hal Foster's long-running comic strip, *Prince Valiant*. (The strip had first appeared in print on 13 February 1937.) Again, CinemaScope provided viewers with spectacular interior and exterior shots, including a climactic fire that engulfs and destroys a castle, but the plot of the film is fairly wooden. As in the original comic strip, Valiant, a Viking prince unjustly driven into exile, comes to Arthur's court and fights renegade Vikings under the leadership of Sir Brack to regain his throne and to help Arthur secure his. As a reward for his courage, Arthur makes Valiant a Knight of the Round Table. Both *Prince Valiant* and *Knights* reflect Hollywood's continued fascination with medieval themes, although American directors especially have often been unable to do justice to a period of history so obviously rich in film possibilities. In an interview, Hathaway later disavowed *Prince Valiant*, claiming that he had simply made the film as a favor to Darryl Zanuck at Fox (Eyman 11).

Slightly more successful in its attempt to translate the Arthurian legend to the screen is Tay Garnett's 1954 film for Warwick and Columbia, *The Black Knight*, with Alan Ladd in the title role. Here the Black Knight, whose character the film critic for the *New York Times* compared to Hopalong Cassidy (29 October 1954: 27), is the hero rather than the stock villain. The film's plot is certainly original: to overthrow Arthur, King Mark is in league with a band of Saracens intent upon carrying out human sacrifices at Stonehenge. The story of the central character, John, who advances from

Arthur and the Knights of the Round Table gather in Cornel Wilde's 1963 film *The Sword of Lancelot*.

the rank of commoner to that of knight and savior of the Round Table, may owe a slight debt to the medieval traditions of the young Perceval and the so-called "Fair Unknown," who despite their youth and inexperience succeed eventually in performing deeds of derring-do.[20]

Continued interest in the legend of Arthur led to four examples of cinema Arthuriana being released in 1963. Independent filmmaker Bruce Baillie's *To Parsifal* is a typically 1960s meditation on the environment and the role of myth in the modern world. Inspired as much by T. S. Eliot's *The Wasteland* as by Wagner's opera, *To Parsifal* is set in and around San Francisco. The director described his film as being about the legendary figure of Parsifal, who does not appear on screen, in this way: "It is a tribute ... to the hero and to the opera, although it is not an attempt to reproduce or 'cover' the opera itself" (Polt 51).

The Sword of Lancelot, released in Great Britain as *Lancelot and Guinevere*, retains some of the influence of the movie western that can be seen in examples of cinema Arthuriana made in the 1950s. CinemaScope once again afforded ample opportunity for spectacle, but Cornel Wilde, who wrote, directed and also played the role of Lancelot, chose to concentrate less on swordplay and chase scenes and more on the tragic consequences of the love between Lancelot and Guinevere. Indeed, Wilde was disappointed in the way that the film was released by the studio, which advertised *Sword* simply as a swashbuckler, despite the film's having won a prize in an Italian film festival and its having garnered positive reviews both in England and in the United States (Coen 57–58).

Loosely based on Malory's *Le Morte d'Arthur*, Wilde's film is the first to treat unhesitatingly the adultery between Lancelot and Guinevere. The film's Arthur, however, is much older than his counterpart in Malory, another feature Jerry Zucker's 1995 film *First Knight* would borrow. In *Sword*, Arthur is in fact an old man married to a much younger woman, so the film cannot fairly balance the conflict among the principals in the love triangle. Central to this conflict is the tension between love and loyalty, marriage and friendship. While loyalty is a central theme in many of Wilde's films (Kaminsky 23), *Sword* so clearly favors the two lovers that a review of the film in *Films and Filming* argued that "this Lancelot and Guinevere deserved a happy ending" (9 [July 1963]: 24). Instead, Wilde has Lancelot first win Guinevere from Mordred for Arthur, then later rescue her from the stake, only finally to lose her to the convent.

In Nathan Juran's *Siege of the Saxons,* released in Great Britain as *King Arthur and the Siege of the Saxons,* Arthur is ailing as Saxon armies eagerly await his death so that they may overrun England unopposed. The king foolishly entrusts his safety to a former champion, Edmund of Cornwall, who is secretly in league with the Saxons. Earlier in the film, with unexpected assistance from the outlaw Robert Marshall, Arthur and his daughter, Katherine, escape safely from a Saxon ambush. A second attack on Arthur's life led by Edmund is, however, successful, although Marshall is at least able to rescue Katherine. Edmund proposes to marry Katherine, who refuses his offer, but her refusal does not keep Edmund from claiming the throne, as Katherine and Marshall seek out Merlin for assistance. The wizard arrives to interrupt Edmund's coronation by demanding he pull Excalibur from its scabbard. Edmund fails to do so, but Katherine succeeds. In the civil war that follows, Katherine and Robert handily defeat Edmund and the Saxons, restore order to the kingdom, marry, and rule over an England finally at peace.

Obviously, *Siege* presents a rather unorthodox version of Arthurian legend, and despite the film's being British, its debt to the movie western is apparent in its many chase scenes and in the stock footage it shares with *The Black Knight.* The film also has an oblique connection to the legend of a later medieval hero, Robin Hood. While Robert Marshall does not steal from the rich to give to the poor, his status as an outlaw nonetheless loyal to the true king echoes the legendary loyalty of Robin Hood to the absent Richard I, often chronicled on film and television.

According to legend, Excalibur is usually embedded in a stone, not sheathed in a scabbard, and the story of the sword in the stone and of its role in Arthur's early childhood provides the plot for the first full-length animated version of the legend of Arthur, Disney's 1963 film *The Sword in the Stone.* Loosely based on the first book of T. H. White's *The Once and Future King,* this Disney film recounts the education of Arthur, known as Wart, a young boy intent on training to become a squire to his loutish older foster brother Kay. Wart's education takes an unexpected turn when he meets Merlin and his talking owl, Archimedes. Merlin soon takes charge of Wart's education, turning him in quick succession into a fish, a squirrel, and a sparrow to teach the boy firsthand a series of valuable lessons about life.[21]

Merlin's nemesis is Mad Madame Mim, a witch whom Merlin eventually defeats in a magical battle of wits. Wart, meanwhile, still a would-be squire, forgets Kay's sword and pulls Excalibur from the stone for Kay to use in a tournament. At first, no one believes Wart's feat, but when he repeats the deed, he is proclaimed king. *The Sword in the Stone* is a rarity among examples of cinema Arthuriana in its portrayal of Arthur's childhood, a topic murky in medieval versions of the legend. Its treatment of that topic is limited to some degree by the film's genre, but as a cartoon *Sword* is vintage Disney.[22]

A second feature-length animated version of Arthur's childhood was released in France in 1980 under the title *Le Roi Arthur.* But the film is really a cobbled together version of several of the thirty episodes of the popular Japanese animated television series *Moero Arthur,* directed by Masayuki Akehi and originally televised in 1979–80.[23]

White's *The Once and Future King* is also the source for Joshua Logan's 1967 film version of the Broadway musical *Camelot.* Both the original stage play and Logan's film are generic oddities. They are musical tragedies, not musical comedies, a point White himself made in reacting with considerable annoyance to negative reviews of the play from critics who wanted something more akin to *My Fair Lady* (White, "What It's Like" 117). The film explores a wide range of ideas with mixed success: the frailty of romantic love, marital infidelity, the betrayal of friendship, the destruction of ideals, and the triumph of right over might. As in the original stage musical, the downfall of Camelot is clearly caused by the tension created in Arthur's court by the Arthur-Guinevere-Lancelot love triangle.

While admitting to some dissatisfaction with the Broadway play, Logan failed to add any depth to the story he transferred to the screen. His film simply presents, rather than explains or examines, the issues it raises. To his credit, Logan rejected the usual gloomy Hollywood backlots for the spectacle afforded by location shots in Spain. But, following White's lead, Logan also tinkered with his sources. While White had made Lancelot ugly — "He looked like an African ape" (White, *The Once and Future* 317) — Logan's Lancelot, Franco Nero, is an overly fastidious, sanctimonious cad who beds Guinevere only minutes after raising a knight he has just killed from the dead. For screen audiences, Wilde's earlier *The Sword of Lancelot* had brought the adultery of Lancelot and Guinevere out into the open; Logan's film continues to focus on that love and its tragic consequences, but in a one-dimensional way.[24]

In the 1970s, cinema Arthuriana continued to be popular as no fewer than nine directors attempted screen versions of the legend. In 1972, the French director Yvan Lagrange went to Iceland to film an operatic version of the story of Tristan and Isolde, *Tristan et Iseult,* which adds nothing new to the legend of the doomed lovers. But Lagrange had a different purpose in mind in making the film. He subtitled the film an "opera en scope-coleurs" to signal his interest in harmonizing the conflicting artistic demands, and in exploring the conflicting artistic subtleties, afforded by working simultaneously in several media. Such a multimedia approach focuses the viewer's attention on the conflict between love and war that Lagrange sees at the heart of the oft-told legend (Cornand 103–04). While not always successful, the film is nonetheless an interesting attempt to retell an old tale in a new way.

A more original attempt to retell an old tale in a new way had already occurred in Luis Buñuel's 1970 film *Tristana,* where the young hero finds herself in the care of the much older Don Lope when she is really in love with the much younger Horacio. Unwilling to make a commitment to Horacio, Tristana returns instead to the care of Don Lope. When she loses a leg because of cancer, Tristana marries Don Lope, but remains in love with Horacio. From the novel by Benito Pérez Galdós, Buñuel's film has a complicated political subtext about power and gender. In addition, it represents a contemporary revision of the Tristan legend, one of several which see Tristan as a woman.[25]

Less successful in its attempt to retell a well-known Arthurian tale is Stephen Weeks's *Gawain and the Green Knight*, released in 1973. Anyone even vaguely familiar with the plot of the anonymous fourteenth century poem *Sir Gawain and the Green Knight*, arguably the finest Arthurian romance written in Middle English, will find little to recognize in the film. Those more widely read in Arthuriana will find a seemingly mindless pastiche of elements drawn from the medieval legends of Yvain, Gawain, Perceval, and others.

In handling medieval sources, Weeks, like many of his Hollywood counterparts, is unable to tell a straight story and instead tries to conflate several unrelated plots into one whose whole is greater than the sum of its parts. The result is either ludicrous or ponderous, depending upon the viewer's background or point of view. Weeks himself blamed United Artists for the film's final messy state (Berry 7), but, not content to leave bad enough alone, Weeks directed a bigger budgeted remake ten years later, *Sword of the Valiant*, with Sean Connery as an iridescent Green Knight and Trevor Howard as a very weary Arthur, that again has little relationship to the poem that is his putative source and that again proves the director incapable of handling the complexities of one of the masterpieces of medieval literature.

More successful in translating the medieval poem to the screen is a 1991 Thames made-for-British-television version of *Gawain and the Green Knight*, directed by John Michael Phillips from a script by David Rudkin. The telefilm, copies of which are now marketed to secondary school and college and university viewers, uses voice-overs and flashbacks to recount Gawain's encounters with the Green Knight and Lady Bercilak. The result is an at times effective cinematic gloss of the poem, although Morgan Le Fay's character gets lost in the transition from page to screen and the poem's moral lesson ends up being diluted in the film's final frames.

A more interesting and successful film, from a decidedly more skilled director, is Robert Bresson's *Lancelot du Lac* (1974), one of the better examples of cinema Arthuriana. For the general outlines of its plot, Bresson's film owes much to the *Mort Artu*, the final section of the Vulgate Cycle, the influential thirteenth century French prose retelling of the Arthuriad.[26] But Bresson is interested in doing more than simply charting the fall of Camelot. Originally entitled *The Grail*, the film is an apocalyptic meditation on the downfall of the Middle Ages because of the era's loss of a sense of the spiritual, symbolized by the Grail which is intentionally absent from the film (Williams 10–13).

In *Lancelot,* Bresson turns the traditional Arthurian triangle into a rectangle. Gawain's love of Guinevere, Lancelot, and Arthur suggests a deeper pattern of conflicting loyalties. Lancelot's unsuccessful return from the quest for the Grail sets into motion a pattern of events that will bring about the downfall of Camelot. No one finds salvation, not Arthur, not his court, especially not Lancelot, who dies in the final battle staring heavenward but murmuring Guinevere's name. And thanks to Bresson's conscious use of anachronisms (Estève 102–08), the film is strikingly modern in its concerns: both the medieval and the modern world repeatedly fail in their attempts to attain the spiritual.

In light of the seriousness with which Bresson approaches the Arthurian legend, *Monty Python and the Holy Grail*, released in 1975, might suggest that cinema Arthuriana was in the 1970s moving from the sublime to the ridiculous. There is, however, more to the Python film than slapstick. What the troupe lampoons is not the legend of Arthur, but rather earlier treatments (cinematic and otherwise) of that legend. Against carefully chosen authentic backdrops of castles and their ruins and with the incorporation of manuscript illuminations both real and faux,[27] the film presents what may at first appear only to be the broad satire and farce that became the Python trademark: holy hand grenades, killer rabbits, fear inducing shrubbery, a castle of maidens begging for X-rated punishment for the sin of lighting a Grail-shaped beacon in the tower, and so on. But there is clearly method to the madness here. The film abounds in conventions from and threads of the Arthurian legend, as well as in take-offs on Hollywood-esque swashbuckling adventures, spectacles, and fights to the death — and just a note or two of Bresson's doom and gloom sent up, of course, comically.

In the 1975 *King Arthur: The Young Warlord,* the Celtic warrior Arthur, here brother to Kai and son to Llud, fights

Saxons, Picts and Jutes, as well as King Mark of Cornwall, to protect his people and the integrity of his homeland. Never commercially released, this film is a videotape of three episodes of *Arthur of the Britons,* a twenty-four half-hour episode British television series that originally aired on the Harlech Television Channel in 1972–73. The series presents Arthur as a "warrior in a time of tribal dissension and battle whose legend surpassed his deeds," thus reflecting the fact that Arthur's possible historicity has a basis in Celtic attempts in the fifth century to repel successive waves of Saxon invaders.[28]

The most authentically medieval example of cinema Arthuriana remains Eric Rohmer's 1978 film *Perceval le Gallois,* in which the director consciously set out to make a different kind of film on a medieval theme. Rejecting earlier attempts by Bresson, Olivier (in *Henry V*), and Hollywood directors in general as unrealistic in their portrayals of the Middle Ages, Rohmer sought to "rediscover the vision of the Medieval period as it saw itself" (Tesich-Savage 51–52). Unlike many previous examples of cinema Arthuriana, Rohmer's *Perceval* carefully follows a medieval text, Chrétien de Troyes's twelfth century poem *Le Conte du Graal,* in its treatment of the story of Perceval.

Rohmer, however, cuts from Chrétien's unfinished text the final adventures of Gawain in order to focus on Perceval. Where Chrétien concludes his narrative about Perceval with a comment that Perceval simply learned that Christ was crucified on Good Friday, Rohmer has Perceval take the central role in a version of a medieval passion play, where the hero's spiritual rebirth is shown as a true union with Christ. While Bresson had shown the spiritual bankruptcy of the Middle Ages, Rohmer finds the soul of the medieval period and in it a lesson for the present.

In contrast, the 1979 film *Tristan and Isolt* (released on videotape as *Lovespell*) strays very far from any recognizable source, medieval or otherwise. Directed by Tom Donovan for Clar Productions, the film stars Richard Burton as Mark, in one of a series of roles Burton took at the time to earn money at the expense of his reputation as a serious actor. But cinema Arthuriana's nadir in the 1970s must surely be Bruno Gantillo's 1971 *Morgaine et ses nymphes,* an inane soft-core pornographic romp in which Morgan Le Fay, Queen of the Fairies, obtains the souls of young women who pass through her kingdom by promising them endless sexual pleasures.

In the 1980s, the tradition of cinema Arthuriana continued, with some of the most notable films coming from German directors (most notably Hans-Jürgen Syberberg's *Parisfal,* which I discussed earlier). In 1980, Richard Blank directed a ninety-minute version of *Parzival* for (what was then) West German television. Blank's film differs from earlier screen versions of the Grail in two ways. First, Blank used Wolfram von Eschenbach's *Parzival,* written sometime after 1200, as his source.[29] Second, through his use of abundant references to the modern world, Blank provides a straightforward and accessible reading of the Grail legend as a group of actors in a windowless attic, employing puppets and toy props, stage a much condensed version of Wolfram's poem.

In 1981, a second German director, Veith von Fürstenberg, made his debut with *Feuer und Schwert— Die Legende von Tristan und Isolde.* Von Fürstenberg's source is the much distilled medieval tale of fated lovers. To his medieval sources, themselves often a jumble of conflicting details, von Fürstenberg adds some personal touches. In the film, Isolde knowingly gives Tristan the love potion to drink. Isolde bears Tristan a child, and Tristan, once rejected by Isolde, who hopes to end the civil war in Cornwall between forces loyal to Mark and those loyal to Tristan, turns marauder pillaging the countryside. While not a commercial success, the film is notable for the poetry of its visual images.[30]

Even more innovative in its treatment of the legend of Tristan and Isolde is Hrafn Gunnlauggson's 1988 film *In the Shadow of the Raven* (*I Skugga Hrafnsina*), which resets that story in the director's native Iceland. In medieval times as Christianity spreads throughout the Scandinavian region, two rival tribes continue their long standing family feud. Trausti, a young warrior, kills the leader of the rival tribe, whose daughter Isold vows revenge. A powerful bishop tries to arrange a marriage between Trausti and Isold, but the two are not united before their familial feud plays itself out in further death and bloodshed.

In Arthur Joffe's *Merlin, ou le cours de l'or*, the jealous devil, Merlin, shares an apartment with a rich old lady. She lusts after him; he, after her gold. Trading upon the tradition of Merlin's demonic links, this film won the Golden Palm Award for Best Short at Cannes in 1982.

Critical reaction to John Boorman's 1981 film *Excalibur* has, on the other hand, been sharply divided. Pauline Kael dismissed the film's dialogue as "near-atrocious" (146), while Michael Ciment, in a long survey of Boorman's career, saw the film as the culmination of Boorman's own cinematic quest (179–201). Boorman himself indicated that he was determined "to tell the whole story of *Le Morte d'Arthur*," although he saw Malory as "the first hack writer" (Kennedy 33).

Boorman's comments notwithstanding, *Excalibur* is not a cinematic translation of Malory. Boorman has, instead, been free with his sources, conflating materials as is general directorial practice, to suit his needs. Arthur is the Grail King, but the Grail is stripped of any Christian associations. In a film where the king and the land are one, the Grail is the central symbol of a murkily defined pagan fertility ritual. Boorman's vision of the Grail owes more to Jessie Weston than it does to Malory (Shichtman 35–48). The central character in the film is Merlin, whose "charm of making" links the past and the future.[31] Events in the film revolve around the complex relations between Arthur, Lancelot, and Merlin and a corresponding trinity of women: Igrayne, Guinevere, and Morgana (Boorman's conflation of the traditionally separate characters of Morgawse, Nimue, and Morgan Le Fay).

George Romero's *Knightriders*, which had the misfortune to be released in a limited market during the same week as Boorman's *Excalibur*, offers a different vision of the quest, a quest not for the Grail but for the American dream. Set in western Pennsylvania, *Knightriders* examines the values of Arthurian society as practiced by a group of motorcycle stunt riders. Romero's film presents the usual Arthurian characters (although Morgan here is a man in the traditional roles of both Morgan Le Fay and Mordred) along with a Friar Tuck, a Pippin, and an assortment of stock heavies and bad guys. Romero's surface debt is to the film western's subgenre, the biker film, but Romero's deeper debt is, as he indicated in an interview, to the tradition that sees Arthur as once and future king:

> The motorcycle culture seemed to fit the Arthurian story. The bikers are a romanticized image, at least in this country. They have their own culture and attitude of this is us, and the rest of the world is you. That made sense on a pure story level, and as allegory [Burke-Block 25].

Knightriders presents a utopic quest, a meditation on the possibility of recreating the Arthurian ideal in a troubled and fractured contemporary America.

Dorian Cowland's *Excalibur: The Raising of the Sword*, which premiered at the 1983 Welsh International Film Festival, tells the story of a youthful Merlin's search for Excalibur. It is a credible amateur production. A little more credible and less-amateurish was Vic Hughes's 1978 *The Boy Merlin,* part of a series for children about magic and the supernatural produced in Great Britain for Thames Television.

On the other hand, Clive Donner's three-hour version of the legend of Arthur entitled *Arthur the King* is truly amateurish. Made in 1982, the telefilm was shelved until it finally aired on CBS in 1985. Somewhat Alice-in-Wonderland–like, Katherine, a tourist in modern-day England, stumbles into a hole while wandering around Stonehenge, where she encounters King Arthur and his knights. Camelot is in chaos. The wine cellar is empty, hundreds of Vikings are expected for dinner, and the Romans have abandoned England. Even worse, the countryside is overrun with dragons and brigands, and the ever present fog just will not lift. With Katherine's assistance, Merlin and his beloved Niniane restore order to the kingdom by challenging Morgan Le Fay and her ally, Mordred. Everything about the film — acting, dialogue, settings, costumes — is simply dreadful.

Much more interesting, if not always successful, is a BBC "silent version" of Malory, which aired in 1984 as *The Morte d'Arthur.* Part drama, part dance piece, part mime, the telefilm stars the Royal Shakespeare Company's John Barton as the knight-prisoner Sir Thomas Malory, who narrates the events of the last two books of *Le Morte.* As Barton speaks, Malory's narrative comes to life in a series of choreographed scenes re-enacting the collapse of the Arthurian ideal.

Cinema Arthuriana proved it could be both traditional and modern in Jytte Rex's 1989 film *Isolde.* In Rex's retelling, the standard triangle is played out among Isolde and two characters simply identified as the Warrior and the Husband in a film that successfully balances action with metaphysical speculation. Less successful in attempting to balance medieval and modern, action and speculation, is Ingemo Engström's 1992 film *Ginevra,* in which a screen actor, who likes to call herself Guinevere, suffers a mental breakdown and then races across Europe torn between her two lovers, Luc, a doctor, and Arthur, a painter. The obvious Arthurian triangle here — for Luc read Lancelot — gets buried in a convoluted and ultimately monotonous plot.

A different kind of feminine focus informs Jud Taylor's *Guinevere* (1994), a made-for-cable-television retelling of the legend of Arthur as "her"-story very loosely based on the series of popular novels written during the 1980s by Persia Woolley. In the film, the young Guinevere receives the kind of education usually reserved for a man. She can fight with a sword and negotiate skillfully. When her father meets an untimely death, she is thrust into the role of ruler which requires her to abandon her affection for Lancelot.[32]

An attempt to link medieval and modern is also apparent in François Truffaut's 1981 film *La Femme d'à côté (The Woman Next Door)* and Barry Levinson's 1984 film *The Natural.* In Truffaut's film — the more original of the two — Mathilde and Bernard, formerly lovers and now each married to another, become obsessed with each other again. Their rekindled love affair becomes increasingly violent and ends with Mathilde shooting first Bernard and then herself. Truffaut offers up here what some have seen as a contemporary reworking of the legend of Tristan and Isolde.[33]

In Levinson's film, Roy Hobbs, an aging baseball player, returns at the invitation of Pop Fisher to play for the New York Knights, but his past, which the film explores in terms of the Arthurian legend, comes to haunt him. Based on Bernard Malamud's novel of the same title, *The Natural,* Levinson's film lacks the ironic tone of its source and changes the novel's ending. Because the film is clearly meant to be a star-vehicle for Robert Redford rather than a faithful adaptation of a literary text, the novel's connections to the Arthurian legend are not unexpectedly obscured in its translation from page to screen.

Two additional French films, neither widely distributed, attempted with mixed results to make parts of the Arthurian legend accessible to modern audiences. In Louis Grospierre's *Connemara* (1989), an impetuous young man named Loup is sent by his uncle Mark to fetch his fiancée, Sedrid of the long red tresses. They attempt to remain loyal to Mark, who nonetheless discovers that the two have fallen in love with each other. The plot of the film is obviously an analogue — although not a very well made one — to the oft-told medieval tale of Tristan, Isolde, and Mark. More successful is Denis Llorca's *Les Chevaliers de la table ronde* (1990). In its retelling of scenes selected from the thirteenth century French prose Vulgate cycle, Llorca's film, originally a marathon stage play, presents the stories of Arthur and Guinevere, of Morgan and her jealousy, of Merlin and his enchantment by Vivien, and of the Fisher King Bron, his daughter, and her son, Galahad.

Film directors returned to the Arthurian legend again in Steven Spielberg's *Indiana Jones and the Last Crusade* (1989), Terry Gilliam's *The Fisher King* (1991), and Jerry Zucker's *First Knight* (1995). Spielberg and Gilliam revisit the legend of the Grail by situating that legend in the modern world, but in very different ways. *The Last Crusade* is the third film in Spielberg's Indiana Jones trilogy, but it is the first chronologically in its recounting of the hero's life and adventures. In the film, archaeologist Indiana Jones joins with his father, Dr. Henry Jones, to keep the Holy Grail from falling into the hands of the Nazis. In some ways the most successful and best made of the Indiana Jones trilogy, *Last Crusade* borrows heavily from Joseph Campbell in its approach to myth and effectively combines comic wit with special effects and action-adventure scenes.

Spielberg's approach to the Grail is less serious than Gilliam's. For Spielberg, the quest for the Grail, which in the film does have the power to heal physically, is simply the impetus for an action-adventure yarn. In *Fisher King*, Jack Lucas, a radio "shock-jock," is in part responsible for the death of the wife of a professor of medieval history. Parry, the professor, goes insane and thinks he is on a quest to find the Holy Grail. His quest leads to an encounter with the DJ, whom Richard Homan sees as a contemporary Everyman (21–30). Both Jack and Parry find redemption from their guilt and their pain. Gilliam's film offers one of the more effective modern retellings of the Grail myth, seeing both Jack and Parry as twin Parsifal-like characters. Unlike in *Last Crusade*, here the healing is spiritual, and in *The Fisher King*, New York becomes an urban wasteland in as much need of healing as the wounded central characters.

Zucker's *First Knight* examines the passionate, rather than the spiritual, side of the Arthurian legend. The aging Arthur decides to marry the much younger Guinevere, in part to protect her kingdom. But the peace of Camelot is shattered when Malagant tries to kidnap Guinevere, who is rescued by Lancelot, an itinerant knight and n'er-do-well. Lancelot joins the knights of the Round Table and conducts a passionate, though chaste, affair with Guinevere. Arthur discovers them in an embrace and orders them tried for adultery. The trial is interrupted when Malagant's forces attack Camelot. In the ensuing battle, Arthur and Malagant are killed, and Camelot and Guinevere pass into Lancelot's hands for safekeeping.

Given that there is no one version of the tale of Arthur, Lancelot and Guinevere, filmmakers can be granted some license in their interpretation of that legend. But nothing in *First Knight* quite works. Clearly, Zucker intends his film to be an Arthuriad for the 1990s: Richard Gere's

Sean Connery (left) as Dr. Henry Jones and Harrison Ford as his son and the title character in Steven Spielberg's 1989 film *Indiana Jones and the Last Crusade*.

Lancelot seems cast in a post–*Iron John* mold. But the film fails to capture the spirit of the original legend or to make a case for its contemporary translation of the oft-told story of the Arthur-Lancelot-Guinevere love triangle.

If Zucker's *First Knight* is problematic in its treatment of the Arthurian legend, Paul Hunt's *October 32nd* (1992) is downright ludicrous in its approach. In the film, a California businessman named Pendragon turns out to be an ageless medieval tyrant intent upon seizing Excalibur from Merlin's conveniently equally ageless disciple Loong Tao. Pendragon hopes to use the sword to make time stand still and plunge the world into chaos on October 32nd. His plans are thwarted by Christy Lake, a reporter who is the reincarnation of Merlin's daughter, the Lady of the Lake, and by geologist John Pope, who is her eternal protector. This perfectly silly film, which understandably was dumped directly to video in 1994 with the title *Merlin*, owes a debt to a variety of film traditions, including the kung fu action yarn and the western. Less clear is its debt to anything recognizably Arthurian.

Richard Kurti's 1994 *Seaview Knights* casts a bungling bank robber as a modern-day Arthur finding Britain in need of a savior. The robber's transformation is accomplished by a blow to the head that convinces him he is Arthur reincarnated. The film's plot waivers between the contrived and the inane. In a slap at Tory indifference to the plight of the British poor and middle class, the would-be Arthur sets out for London to do battle with the Gray Knight, clearly meant to be John Major, but ends up instead unexpectedly foiling an attempt by unidentified but decidedly swarthy-looking Arabs to blow up Parliament, proving that a film can always sink to ethnic stereotype when its attempts at humor fail. In the 1994 Welsh film, *Ymadawiad Arthur,* the rulers of an independent Wales located far in the future find themselves in a crisis and decide to travel back in time to find Arthur. Unfortunately, they mistake a teenage Welsh rugby player named David Arthur for the once and future king, and much confusion ensues.

A 1995 Czech film, *Artus, Merlin a Prichlíci,* directed by Vera Simková-Plívová from her juvenile novel of the same title, borrows the names of two Arthurian figures and assigns them to two dogs owned by a poor peasant family. The dogs run amuck involving the Prichlíci children in a series of misadventures.[34]

Four subsequent examples of cinema Arthuriana are clearly intended for younger audiences, Robert Tinnell's *Kids of the Round Table* (1995), Peter Werner's *Four Diamonds* (1995), Kenneth J. Burton's *Merlin's Shop of Magical Wonders* (1996), and Peter Chelsom's *The Mighty,* which premiered at the 1998 Cannes Film Festival.

In *Kids,* a group of children, whose leader, Alex, is an Arthurian enthusiast, are terrorized by three bullies. While running through the woods to escape these bullies, Alex stumbles upon Excalibur and meets Merlin. Warned only to use the power of Excalibur for the good, Alex summons its power to defeat a new boy in town, Luke, with whom Alex's girlfriend, Jenny, has fallen in love. Alex loses Excalibur and Merlin's counsel, but finds both restored when he single-handedly captures three armed bank robbers who hold his friends hostage. *Kids* attempts to trade on the legend of the return of Arthur, but the acting — especially that of the adult characters — is terrible, and the plot drags. Even children, the intended audience here, are likely to find the film boring.

Four Diamonds is a very different kind of film. Fourteen year old Chris Millard is dying from a rare form of nasal cancer. To distract himself from his illness and its treatment as well as to find some courage to cope with what he faces, Chris imagines an Arthurian world in which he is a squire in search of four diamonds (courage, wisdom, honesty, and strength) that he must find in order to become a knight of the Round Table. A contemporary examination of the theme of the return to Camelot, this made-for-television movie is one of the better cinematic uses of the Arthurian legend. The film is based on a short story written by the real Chris Millard, who died in 1972.

Peter Chelsom's *The Mighty,* loosely based on Rodman Philbrick's popular juvenile novel *Freak the Mighty,* (1993) also uses the Arthurian legend in a therapeutic way. Here a copy of Sir James Knowles's 1862 book *King Arthur and His Knights* so fascinates an illiterate teenager that he determines to learn to read. Eventually he teams up with his tutor, a younger boy crippled by a terminal disease, to do deeds of derring-do on the streets of present-day Cincinnati. The film is especially notable for its expansion of the Arthurian materials found in its source.

In *Merlin's Shop of Magical Wonders,* a retired scriptwriter (played by veteran actor Ernest Borgnine) tells his grandson two bedtime stories about Merlin. In the first, Merlin opens a magic shop in modern-day California and teaches an arrogant, doubting journalist a lesson. In the second, an analogue to the tale of the monkey's paw, a mechanical monkey stolen from the shop wreaks havoc in the lives of those with whom it comes into contact. But this silly anthology piece wastes Borgnine's talents, and its production values are so inept that it is little wonder that the film was released directly to video.

Little better can be said of noted horror-film director Anthony Hickox's *Prince Valiant* (1997), in which Morgan Le Fey steals Merlin's book of spells from his coffin and sends Viking warriors to Camelot to steal Excalibur. The wounded Gawain's squire, Valiant, sets out to retrieve the sword and to rescue Princess Ilene of Wales. His quest takes him from Wales to Thule, where he is recognized as rightful heir to the throne. In a final battle, Morgan and Thagnar, the Viking leader, are killed, as is Ilene.

But she is brought back to life by the Lady of the Lake, and Valiant rescues Excalibur and returns it to a grateful Arthur, who makes him a knight of the Round Table.

In this unintentionally comic remake of the 1954 film, Conan the Barbarian meets Foster's comic strip characters. Missing are the Hollywood touches that at least made the 1954 film visually spectacular. In its more interesting scenes, Hickox's film fades to panels from the original strip, but there is little else to recommend it, except perhaps Joanna Lumley's over-the-top portrayal of Morgan in full-length black leather gown and chain-mail headdress. Edward Fox plays an aging Arthur (cf. *First Knight*), whose haircut and beard would also easily allow him to portray Charles I if anyone wants to remake *Cromwell.*

In April 1998, Hallmark and NBC television teamed up to present *Merlin*, a four hour mini-series which cost nearly $30 million to make and which drew large audiences among television viewers. The half-mortal Merlin (Sam Neill) spends his life longing to be with his beloved Nimue and battling short-sighted mortals and his magical nemeses, Queen Mab (the mini-series' original and unexplained addition to the Arthurian legend) and Morgan Le Fey. (Both Mab and Morgan, for reasons also never explained, have severe speech impediments.) The story of Arthur, the love triangle with Lancelot and Guinevere, and the quest for the Holy Grail are all treated almost as afterthoughts. Director Steve Barron concentrates instead on Merlin's battles with Mab and Morgan, who are aided by Mordred and the gnome Frik. When this mini-series trusts the basic Arthurian story, *Merlin* works; more often than not, however, its plot bogs down. The writers have enough good material to spin an interesting two-hour film, but the production plods along for almost twice as long for no ostensible reason.

In Frederik Du Chau's animated 1998 *Quest for Camelot,* when the evil Ruber steals Excalibur in an attempt to seize Camelot, Kayley, the young daughter of Sir Lionel whom Ruber previously killed, and the blind Garrett come to Arthur's aid. They venture through the Forbidden Forest where they encounter a variety of mythical beasts, including a helpful two-headed dragon named Devon and Cornwall. Kayley and Garrett finally retrieve Excalibur, and save Arthur and Camelot. *Quest*, Warner Bros.' first fully animated feature, lacks the sharpness of Disney's trademark animation and further suffers from a consistently bland score. Slightly indebted to, rather than, as Warner publicity claims, actually based on Vera Chapman's novel *The King's Damosel*, in which the title character Lynett seeks the Grail, *Quest* does place an active Kayley at its center at least for a while. The film's plot, however, proves formulaic: the bad guys wear black armor and eventually Kayley has to settle for the more traditional role of damosel, while Garrett is rewarded with knighthood.

Paul Matthews's 2000 film *Merlin: The Return* uses a traditional Arthurian cinematic plot device, time travel, but in reverse. Here Arthur and his knights travel to the twentieth century in an ineptly directed sword-and-sorcery exercise whose plot makes no sense.[35] Sounding another familiar Arthurian note, Jon Jacobs' 1999 *Lucinda's Spell* appropriates Boorman's charm of making from *Excalibur* in telling the story of a descendant of Merlin who must couple with a "sex witch" before the Feast of Beltane, an ancient Celtic holy day. The film flirts with being pornographic almost as much as it flirts with having an understandable plot.

The Feast of Beltane is the occasion for the coupling of Morgaine and Arthur in Uli Edel's 2001 two-part telefilm of Marion Zimmer Bradley's massive *The Mists of Avalon*. That coupling sets into motion events that will eventually destroy both

Haley Joel Osment as Cole in the role of the Boy Arthur in his school play in M. Night Shyamalan's 1999 film *The Sixth Sense*.

Avalon and Camelot. Bradley's novel certainly contains enough material for a film or a television miniseries, and screenwriter Gavin Scott did not claim, as did Boorman and his co-writer Rospo Pallenberg, that he would retell the entire story of his source. But what viewers see spread over four hours is Bradley much condensed with great numbers of subplots and characters simply missing, yet at a pace that is at times mind numbingly slow. The male characters are, as in the novel, the bit players. They are reduced in the miniseries to being little more than Arthurian boy toys in Edward Atterton's Arthur, Michael Vartan's Lancelot, and Hans Matheson's Mordred. Stage center stand three women: Anjelica Huston's Viviane, Julianna Margulies's Morgaine, and Joan Allen's Morgause. Samantha Mathis's Gwenhwyfar continues the screen tradition of Arthur's queen as a marginalized character, though here she is marginalized by almost everyone, male and female.

Huston and Allen seem at least to be having fun with their parts. Huston maintains a gyno-sacerdotal demeanor appropriate to the Lady of the Lake, and Allen plays the vamp as heavy in a throwback to an acting style that seems inspired by Theda Bara. Margulies, try as she might, simply lacks *gravitas*— her still-intact-television *ER* midwestern accent making the telefilm's already tinny dialogue sound only worse. Present in the miniseries is the novel's battle between pagan-feminine-nurturing and Christian-masculine-destructive, with the Saxons thrown in for good measure as enemies to all. The time frame is correct, and some of the costuming and sets are close enough, but overall a great deal of talent, time, money, and effort seems to have been for naught.

Unexpectedly, the Arthurian myth is also central to the plot of M. Night Shyamalan's *The Sixth Sense,* the much-acclaimed sleeper of 1999. The film advances the trope familiar enough from such different films as *Equus, The Elephant Man,* and *Agnes of God* of having a doctor as much in need of healing as his or her patient. The impasse central to the film's plot between the boy Cole and his psychiatrist Malcolm is finally broken when Cole confides his full secret to the psychiatrist: he sees dead people who do not know they are dead. The boy asks Malcolm (who we will eventually learn is himself dead) to help him no longer be afraid. Cole in turn elicits from Malcolm the confession that he is feeling estranged from his wife, that he too is unhappy.

Having confronted his fear, Cole seems changed and finds himself cast in the central role of a school play. Actually, this play is the second staged in the film. The first stars a pompous and over-acting classmate, Tommy Tammisimo, as a Doctor Dolittle–like character who talks to the animals. Cole has only a bit part in this first play. The second play is, however, the story of the sword in the stone, and here Cole is cast in the central role, while, in a nice touch, Tommy plays the village idiot. As a narrator solemnly intones, "only the pure of heart can take the sword from the stone," Cole as the boy Arthur easily pulls Excalibur free. Cole is cheered by his classmates who carry him on their shoulders in triumph. Malcolm and the other members of the audience join in the acclamation for what is clearly now a reborn Cole.

Cole and Malcolm then meet for their last session, in front of a faux medieval stained glass window. As Cole waves Excalibur, he tells Malcolm to talk to his wife when she is asleep so that she can listen to him "without hearing." Patient and doctor have clearly switched roles. Cole as Arthur has healed himself and will soon heal others, including his mother, who has her own unresolved issues with her dead mother.

The Sixth Sense, a film that on its surface seems far removed from the world of Camelot, nonetheless marks an Arthurian return. The boy Arthur returns, here as Cole Sear—whose surname surely cannot be accidental—to heal himself, to heal his mother, and, most importantly, to heal Malcolm Crowe, a man who thinks it is his responsibility to heal Cole. As a "see-r," Cole finds himself cast both in the role of Merlin and in that of the boy Arthur, though at first he seems much less than he turns out to be, a trope readily found in any number of earlier versions of Arthur's childhood. He also has a connection to the once and future since Cole helps the dead, haunted by their pasts, and he uses his ability to communicate with the past to lay out the future for himself, for his mother, and even for Malcolm, who initially also serves as a kind of Merlin figure, a supernatural guide, it turns out, who helps Cole to understand the unique role he is called upon to play.[36]

Other recent youthful visitors to Camelot have not fared as well. In both the 1998 *The Excalibur Kid* and the 2000 *Arthur's Quest* (neither released commercially), there are nods to Twain. In *The Excalibur Kid*, a boy named Zack, upset that his family is about to move to a new city, wishes he were back in Arthurian times— and ends up there helping Merlin thwart Margause's plans to overthrown Arthur. Crucial to her defeat is a spell of making that seems to echo Boorman's charm of making in *Excalibur*. In *Arthur's Quest*, Merlin sends the boy Arthur forward in time to save him, only to find that he is reluctant to return to medieval times. In the 1999 *Lancelot: Guardian of Time*, it is the eponymous hero who is sent into the present to ensure the survival of Camelot, in a film whose plot defies even easy synopsis because it is so ridiculously convoluted.

As this overview of cinema Arthuriana suggests, there has been almost a century-long tradition of film versions of the legend of King Arthur: some good, some bad, some serious, some more lighthearted. (Unfortunately, quantity and quality do not always go hand in hand.) Any imaginative response to return to Arthur is a reimagining of the medieval, and as Umberto Eco has pointed out contemporary Americans and Europeans have gotten into the habit of "dreaming" the Middle Ages. Indeed, Eco suggests there are at least ten separate modern dreams of the medieval (61–72). The relationship between these dreams and whatever reality the Middle Ages may have once had is constantly shifting. Few legends have been retold as often or in as many ways as that of Arthur, King of the Britains, and the long tradition of cinema Arthuriana clearly documents Arthur's continuing role as once and future king.

Perhaps in our search for a true cinematic translation of the Arthurian myth, we have been looking in all the wrong places. We may never get a definitive screen version of the Arthuriad set in medieval (or modern) times, although great numbers of Arthurians clearly have their own personal favorite films. But films such as *The Sixth Sense* surprise and tease us: they attest to the continuing viability of the Arthurian legend, especially in terms of its ability to heal. Arthur is indeed once and future king who returns on the page, on the screen, or in other ways, when needed, in various guises to aid those in need of his help. As Raymond H. Thompson has noted: "The need for Arthur to ride yet again against the eternal foe is as eternal as the human failings that foment strife, and as long as we continue to yearn for a better world, so will Arthur's return be assured" (11). In *The Sixth Sense*, a frightened eight-year-old with a symbolic surname becomes the boy Arthur, wise beyond his years, bringing healing to himself and to those around him. What more can Arthurian scholars and enthusiasts ask for from an example of cinema Arthuriana!

NOTES

1. I coined the phrase *cinema Arthuriana* as part of the title for a brief filmography published

1. in 1987. See Harty, "Cinema Arthuriana: A Filmography" 5–8.

2. Early films, like medieval manuscripts, often survive as much by accident as by design. There may, therefore, be lost earlier examples of cinema Arthuriana. Edison's interest in the cinematic possibilities of the medieval period dates from as early as 1895 when his company made what must be the first film about Joan of Arc. The sole surviving copy of this film, alternately entitled *Joan of Arc* or *[The] Burning of Joan of Arc*, is housed in the David Flaherty Collection of the Canadian National Archives in Ottawa. Other films on medieval themes were also made before 1904 by other directors and production companies. See Harty, *The Reel Middle Ages* passim.

3. The Grail entered the Arthuriad simply as a mysterious vessel at the end of the twelfth century in Chrétien de Troyes's unfinished *Le Conte du Graal*. But, from the early thirteenth century onward, the Grail continued to fascinate writers who later identified it with the sacred vessel which first held the wine at the Last Supper and then collected the blood of Christ at the disposition from the Cross. For his opera, Wagner transformed the Grail into the central symbol in an elaborate set of Christian rituals.

4. On the German reaction to the New York production of *Parsifal*, the production's positive critical reception in America, and the touring production in English, see *New York Times* 27 December 1903: 12; 28 August 1904: 13; 14 September 1904: 9; 18 October 1904: 6; 23 October 1904: 4. 6; and 30 October 1904: 4. 3.

5. Arguably the most famous and enduring love story that has come down to us from the Middle Ages, the legend of Tristan and Isolde has long been popular with filmmakers. Celtic in its origins, the Tristan legend in verse form seems to have passed through Brittany to France in the middle of the twelfth century, spreading thereafter to Germany and Norway. Separately, a prose tradition of the legend developed in the second half of the thirteenth century that saw Tristan as a member of Arthur's court, often second in prowess only to Lancelot. Twentieth-century versions of the legend often owe a debt to Wagner's opera, to Joseph Bédier's conflation of the medieval versions of the legend first published in 1900, or to both. (For Bédier's version of the medieval legend, see *The Romance of Tristan and Iseult as Retold by Joseph Bédier*. Trans. by Hilaire Belloc. 1945. rpt. New York: Vintage Books, 1965.)

6. For a summary of the plot of the Caserini *Parsifal*, see *Moving Picture World* 28 December 1912: 1307–08.

7. For further details on and analysis of Falena's *Tristano e Isotta*, see Harty, "A Note on Maureen Fries" 313–18.

8. For information concerning Mariaud's *Tristan et Yseut*, see Abel 17, 162, and 557.

9. Olton provides an extensive list of televised productions of Arthurian operas. See his *Arthurian Legends on Film and Television* passim.

10. *Moving Picture World* 23 October 1909: 565. For reviews of Kent's *Launcelot and Elaine*, see *Moving Picture World* 27 November 1909: 759; and *New York Dramatic Mirror* 20 November 1909: 16.

11. Despite its title and its religious themes, the 1923 western also called *The Grail*, which starred the popular actor Dustin Farnum, is not an example of cinema Arthuriana.

12. For Baden-Powell's successive statements, beginning in 1904, linking the Scouting movement with the legend of Arthur, see Rosenthal 603–17.

13. On the connection between the Arthurian legend and the proper education of boys, see Alan Lupack, "Visions of Courageous Achievement" 50–68.

14. For a brief discussion of the Abbey murals, see Alan Lupack and Barbara Tepa Lupack, *King Arthur in America* 279–80.

15. For a complete summary of the plot of Flynn's *Connecticut Yankee*, see O'Dell 248–49. Unfortunately, no complete copy of the film seems to have survived. It originally ran about 100 minutes. Approximately thirty minutes of the film consisting of scenes spliced together in random order are stored in the Film Archive at the Museum of Modern Art in New York. The Library of Congress owns an additional five minutes from the film with scenes also spliced together in no particular order.

16. The series with individual screenplays by George H. Plympton and others included the following episodes varying in length from 15 to 25 minutes: "The Stolen Sword," "Galahad's Daring," "Prisoners of Ulric," "Attack on Camelot," "Galahad to the Rescue," "Passage of Peril," "Unknown Betrayers," "Perilous Adventure," "Treacherous Magic," "The Sorcerer's Spell," "Valley of No Return," "Castle Perilous," "The Wizard's Vengeance," "Quest for the Queen," and "Galahad's Triumph."

17. Cinema Arthuriana in the 1950s and 1960s in many ways replicated the film western, showing that things have come full circle in the American view of the relationship between the knight in shining armor and the cowboy. In the July 1895 issue of *Harper's*, Owen Wister, whose 1902 *The Virginian* is the quintessential western novel, published an essay entitled "The Evolution of the Cow-Puncher" in which he argued that the ancestor of the cow-puncher was the Knight of the Round Table. For more on Wister's views, see Lukacs 52–57, which was adapted from his

Philadelphia, Patricians & Philistines 1900–1950 (New York: Farrar, Straus, Giroux, 1981).

18. MGM documented the extensive research that supposedly made *Knights* possible in an unpaginated souvenir booklet distributed when the film was released, *The Knight of the Round Table* (New York: Al Greenstone, 1954).

19. A fuller discussion of *Knights* as a *Classics Illustrated* Arthuriad can be found in a review of the film in *Films and Filming* when it was rereleased (5 [June 1963]: 37).

20. The story of the Fair Unknown is a fixture in medieval French, Italian, German, and English literature, having been first told by Renault de Beaujeu in a late twelfth century verse romance, *Le Bel inconnu*. In class-bound medieval society, advancing from commoner to a member of the nobility may be acceptable to our modern sensibilities, as the non–Arthurian 2001 film *A Knight's Tale* proves. But there is often a gap between historical fact and modern prejudices that leads to the re-creation of history as it should have been or as we wish it had been. The Fair Unknown does not really advance beyond any class barrier in medieval literature; he is noble by birth, a fact at first unknown to him and to others.

21. In the original novel, Arthur is turned into a fish, an ant, a wild goose, and a badger.

22. This view of the film was not shared by all critics when *Sword* was released in 1963. See the excerpts from reviews reprinted in *Film Facts* 6 (December 1963): 286–87.

23. For information about the film and the television series, see Leguèbe 918 and Baricordi 114. I am grateful to Professor Toshiyuki Takamiya of Keio University for additional information about the television series.

24. The principals were, one might argue, all badly cast. Harris badgered Logan to get the part, and while Logan was adamant about not casting Julie Andrews as Guinevere, the role she played in the Broadway musical, he was also ambivalent about replacing her with Vanessa Redgrave. See Smith 97–105 and Logan 194–210.

25. Tristan is a woman in Buñuel's source, in John Updike's novel *Brazil*, and in the comic book series *Camelot 3000*. On Buñuel's reworking of the Tristan story, see Hoffman 167–82.

26. Sloan presents a detailed synopsis of the film's screenplay but wrongly identifies the film's source as Chrétien de Troyes's *Le Chevalier de la charette* (83–88).

27. See Meuwese 2–13 for a comparison of the film's illuminations with those in medieval manuscripts.

28. The eight-episode 1979 Australian and British television series, *The Legend of Arthur*, presents a better and more straightforward retelling of the rise and fall of the Round Table because of Morgan's jealousy of Arthur and the continuing passion of Lancelot and Guinevere. For a novelization based on the series, see Davies, *The Legend of King Arthur*.

29. Wolfram's poem, which runs to nearly 25,000 lines in rhymed couplets, is the acknowledged masterpiece of German literature of the High Middle Ages. Wolfram obviously knew Chrétien, but in Wolfram's version, the court of Arthur and the Grail legend are clearly linked in the character of Parzival, who is related through his father to Arthur and through his mother to the Grail society.

30. A 1998 German-Italian coproduced telefilm (alternately entitled *Il Cuore e la spade* and *Tristan und Isolde, Eine Liebe für die Ewigkeit*) drew mixed critical response. Directed by Fabrizio Costa for Italy's Canale 5, the two-part miniseries is more or less indebted to the medieval legend of Tristan and Isolde, but ends with a jarring scene in which Isolde impales herself on the dead Tristan's sword.

31. Perhaps no topic related to Boorman's film has been more discussed on ArthurNet than the charm of making, with more scholarly subscribers generally holding the charm is gibberish and their less scholarly counterparts arguing for its authenticity. For the latter view, see Monroe (246 ff.), whose book claims (on the back cover of the paperback edition) to be "the complete course in authentic Druidism."

32. Despite its title, Audrey Wells' 1998 *Guinevere* is not an Arthurian film. Indeed, it bears no relation to the Arthurian legend at all. The central male character simply nicknames his much younger girlfriend "Guinevere."

33. On whether or not Truffaut's film is indeed indebted to the Tristan legend, see Grimbert 183–201.

The question of what is and what is not a Tristan film — or for that matter what is and what is not an example of cinema Arthuriana — is not always easy to answer. Ingmar Bergman's 1964 comedy *För atte inte talla om alla dessa Kvinnor* (alternately released in English as *Now About These Women* or *All These Women*) includes among its cast characters named Tristan and Isolde, but they do not bear much relation to the medieval lovers, though Olton tries (I think unconvincingly) to make the case that the film is connected to the legend (18–19). André Zwobada's 1948 *Noces de Sable* (*Daughters of the Sands*), with a screenplay by Jean Cocteau, is, according to reviews in *Variety* (20 February 1952: 18) and *Monthly Film Bulletin* (19 [October 1952]: 140), an unsuccessful attempt to present an allegorical Arabic version of the legend of Tristan and Isolde.

34. I am indebted to Professors Barbara Tepa Lupack and Helena White for translating infor-

mation about this film for me from Czech into English.

35. Time travel in cinema Arthuriana is usually backwards not forwards, as the many screen adaptations of Twain show. The model here is probably Jean-Marie Poiré's 1992 *Les Visiteurs* (*The Visitors*), which remains the highest grossing film comedy ever released in France and which spawned two inferior sequels. In Poiré's film, a twelfth-century knight and his squire wreak havoc in modern France when they encounter their twentieth-century descendants.

36. For further discussion of the Arthurian elements in *The Sixth Sense*, see Harty, "Looking for Arthur in All the Wrong Places" 57–62.

WORKS CITED

Abel, Richard. *French Cinema, The First Wave, 1915–1929.* Princeton: Princeton University Press, 1984.
Baricordi, Andrea, and others. *Anime: A Guide to Japanese Animation (1958–1988).* Trans. Adeline D'Opera. Montréal: Protoculture, 2000.
Berry, Dave. "Stephen Weeks." *Film* 37 (May 1976): 6–7.
Burke-Block, Candace. "The *Film Journal* Interviews George Romero on 'Knightriders.'" *Film Journal* 84 (4 May 1981): 25.
Bush, W. Stephen. "Possibilities of Synchronization." *Motion Picture World* 2 September 1911: 607–08.
Ciment, Michel. *John Boorman.* Trans. Gilbert Adair. London: Faber, 1986.
Cocteau, Jean. *Three Screenplays.* Trans. Carol Martin-Sperry. New York: Grossman, 1972.
Coen, John. "Producer/Director: Cornel Wilde." *Film Comment* 6 (Spring 1970): 52–61.
Cornand, André. Review of *Tristan et Iseult. Image et son* 284 (May 1974): 103–04.
Davies, Andrew. *The Legend of King Arthur.* London: Armada, 1979.
D'Heur, J. M. and J. De Groeve. "Arthur, Excalibur and the Enchanter Boorman." *Studia in honorem prof. M. de Riquer, III.* Barcelona: Quaderns Crema, 1988.
Eco, Umberto. *Travels in Hyperreality.* Trans. William Weaver. San Diego: Harvest Books, 1983.
Estève, Michel. *Robert Bresson.* Rev. ed. Paris: Éditions Seghers, 1974.
Eyman, Scott. "'…I Made Movies…' An Interview with Henry Hathaway." *Take One* 5 (February 1976): 6–12.
Fescourt, Henri. *Le Foi et les montaignes.* Paris: Montel, 1959.
Grimbert, Joan Tasker. "Truffaut's *La Femme d'à côté* (1981): Attenuating a Romantic Archetype — Tristan and Iseult?" In Kevin J. Harty, ed. *King Arthur on Film: New Essays on Arthurian Cinema.* Jefferson, N.C.: McFarland, 1999.
Harty, Kevin J. "Cinema Arthuriana: A Filmography." *Quondam et futurus* 7 (Spring 1987): 5–8; 7 (Summer 1987): 18.
_____. "Looking for Arthur in All the Wrong Places: A Note on M. Night Shyamalan's *The Sixth Sense.*" *Arthuriana* 10 (Winter 2000): 57–62.
_____. "A Note on Maureen Fries, Morgan Le Fay, and Ugo Falena's 1911 Film *Tristano e Issota.*" In Bonnie Wheeler and Fiona Tolhurst, eds. *On Arthurian Women: Essays in Memory of Maureen Fries.* Dallas: Scriptorium Press, 2001.
_____. *The Reel Middle Ages, American, Western and Eastern European, Middle Eastern and Asian Films About Medieval Europe.* Jefferson, N.C.: McFarland, 1999.
Hoffman, Donald L. "Tristan la Blonde: Transformations of Tristan in Buñuel's *Tristana.*" In Kevin J. Harty, ed. *King Arthur on Film: New Essays on Arthurian Cinema.* Jefferson, N.C.: McFarland, 1999.
Homan, Richard. "The Everyman Movie, Circa 1991." *Journal of Popular Film & Television* 25 (Spring 1997): 21–30.
Kael, Pauline. "Boorman's Plunge." *New Yorker* 58 (20 April 1981): 146–51.
Kaminsky, Stuart. "Getting Back to Basics with Cornel Wilde." *Take One* 5 (October 1976): 22–24.
Kennedy, Harlan. "The World of King Arthur According to John Boorman." *American Film* 6 (March 1981): 30–37.
Kroll, Jack. Review of *Parsifal. Newsweek* 101 (31 January 1983): 49.
Leguèbe, Éric. *Cinéguide 2001.* Paris: Omnibus, 2000.
Logan, Joshua. *Movie Stars, Real People, and Me.* New York: Delacorte, 1978.
Lukacs, John. "From Camelot to Abilene." *American Heritage* 32 (February-March 1981): 52–57.
Lupack, Alan. "Visions of Courageous Achievement: Arthurian Youth Groups in America." In Kathleen Verduin, ed. *Medievalism in North America.* Studies in Medievalism VI. Cambridge, Eng.: D. S. Brewer, 1994.
_____, and Barbara Tepa Lupack. *King Arthur in America.* Cambridge, Eng.: D. S. Brewer, 1999.
Mantle, Burns. Review of *A Connecticut Yankee at King Arthur's Court. Photoplay* 20 (June 1921): 51.
Meuwese, Martine. "De Animatie van Margedecoratie in *Monty Python and the Holy Grail.*" *Madoc* [The Netherlands] 12.1 (1998): 2–13.

Monroe, Douglas. *The 21 Lessons of Merlyn.* St. Paul, Minn.: Llewellyn Publications, 1997.

Niver, Kemp R. *The First Twenty Years: A Segment of Film History.* Los Angeles: Locare Research Group, 1968.

O'Dell, Scott. *Representative Photoplays Analyzed.* Hollywood, Calif.: Palmer Institute of Authorship, 1924.

Olton, Bert. *Arthurian Legends on Film and Television.* Jefferson, N.C.: McFarland, 2000.

Patterson, Frances Taylor. *Cinema Craftsmanship.* New York: Harcourt, 1921.

Polt, Harriet. "The Films of Bruce Baillie." *Film Comment* 2 (Fall 1964): 50–53.

Rosenthal, Michael. "Knights and Retainers: The Earliest Version of Baden-Powell's Boy Scout Scheme." *Journal of Contemporary History* 15 (October 1980): 603–17.

Shichtman, Martin B. "Hollywood's New Weston: The Grail Myth in Francis Ford Coppola's *Apocalypse Now* and John Boorman's *Excalibur.*" *Post Script* 4 (Autumn 1984): 35–48.

Sloan, Joan. *Robert Bresson: A Guide to References and Resources.* Boston: Hall, 1983.

Smith, Gus. *Richard Harris: Actor by Accident.* London: Robert Hale, 1990.

Spears, Jack. "Edwin S. Porter." *Films in Review* 21 (June–July 1970): 327–54.

Tesich-Savage, Nadja. "Rehearsing the Middle Ages." *Film Comment* 14 (September–October 1978): 50–56.

Thompson, Raymond H. "Introduction: Does One Good Return Deserve Another?" In Debra N. Mancoff, ed. *King Arthur's Modern Return.* New York: Garland, 1998.

White, T. H. *The Once and Future King.* 1958. rpt. New York: Berkeley, 1966.

_____. "What It's Like to Be Translated into 'Camelot.'" *Vogue* 15 February 1961: 117.

Williams, Alan. "On the Absence of the Grail." *Movietone News* 47 (January 1976): 10–13.

2
Mythopoeia in Excalibur

Norris J. Lacy

Mythopoeia, not only the creation but also the renewal of myth, has from the beginning been a part of Arthurian literature and art. Reinterpretations and modifications of the legend are inevitable, and by ensuring its vitality and currency, they are its lifeblood as well. Especially in England and North America, where enthusiasm for Arthuriana has often approached the level of a cult, hundreds of literary and visual artists have reworked the story of the Once and Future King, drawing most often from Sir Thomas Malory's monumental *Le Morte d'Arthur* (1485), less often from Alfred, Lord Tennyson's *Idylls of the King*, for which Malory was in turn a primary source. In the process, many of them have invented new characters and events, have suppressed (or occasionally censored) others, and have otherwise modified the shape and meaning of the original.

But Malory's work itself is the "original" in a very limited sense: to compose his text, he adapted a number of sources, especially the thirteenth-century French Vulgate Cycle, including the *Queste du Saint Graal*, while those texts in turn went far beyond the first great French Arthurian poet, Chrétien de Troyes (late twelfth century). Chrétien departed strikingly from Geoffrey of Monmouth's Latin chronicle of Arthur (*Historia Regum Britanniae*, ca. 1136), which itself was formed out of oral legends, fragmentary written references, and especially Geoffrey's own imagination. In other words, the Arthurian myth, for better or for worse, is constantly being remade.

A number of recent authors and filmmakers, having transformed the temporal or cultural context of the Arthurian story, have shown themselves to be far more radically innovative than John Boorman.[1] However, among retreatments of the legend that maintain a more or less traditional context (knights, ladies, and castles in either Dark Age or medieval settings), Boorman's film *Excalibur* must surely be counted as one of the most original. On the face of it, that originality may not be entirely apparent, for Boorman himself claimed to tell "the whole story" of *Le Morte d'Arthur* (Kennedy 33), and his closing credits inform us that he and Rospo Pallenberg adapted the text of Malory, the quintessential Arthurian story for anglophones. While most viewers may accept such claims uncritically, even the briefest comparison of the film and the medieval text reveals that Boorman modifies the story in substantial and significant ways, innovating in fact and detail alike, in an evident if not entirely successful attempt to enhance the cinematic impact of his presentation.[2]

Indeed, if the film was based at all on Malory, the English author provided at most a source of inspiration rather than an actual model. The viewer who knows Malory reasonably well will find that the film produces shocks, large and small, all along the way. The fact is that, despite the claim made in his credits, Boorman makes only general use of Malory, and Shichtman has persuasively argued that the English text is not even his primary source, that his film is instead "pure Jessie Weston."[3] Consequently, there is little point in assembling a catalog of Boorman's departures from Malory: the result would be too extensive to be of value, and it would demonstrate little beyond Boorman's independence from his putative source. A few examples will suffice, and those I offer here are mostly drawn from the early part of the story, since my larger discussion to follow will deal with later stages.

- In Malory, Uther lies with Igrayne (begetting Arthur) several hours after her husband the duke was killed: "The duke himself was slain ere ever the king came to the castle of Tintagel" (5).[4] In the film, the duke dies at the very instant of Arthur's conception. The juxtaposition of life ending and life beginning, emphasized by intercutting scenes of death agony and sexual intensity, produces a striking scene out of a small change from Malory.

- Boorman has Excalibur belong originally to Uther, who received it from Merlin. Before his death, according to the film, Uther plunges the sword into the stone, from which Arthur later withdraws it. In Malory, the Sword in the Stone is not mentioned until long after Uther's death, when "there was seen in the churchyard opposite the high altar a great stone ...; in the middle thereof was an anvil of steel a foot in height, and therein stuck a fair naked sword by the point" (8). Arthur draws the sword and eventually is declared king.

- For Boorman, the Round Table is Arthur's inspiration and invention. In Malory (63), it existed prior to Arthur's birth; it was originally a gift from Uther to Lodegraunce, Guinevere's father, who offers it to Arthur as a wedding present.

- Boorman makes Mordred the son of Morgana (the film's recasting of the traditional character of Morgan Le Fay), not of her sister Morgause, as in Malory.

Of course, a good many of Boorman's departures from the "orthodox" legend have precedents in texts, medieval or modern, other than Malory's. Boorman is not the first to conflate the figures of Morgan and Morgause, nor is he alone in simply doing away with the third sister, Elayne. And if he has Arthur invent the Round Table or replaces Galahad by Perceval as the Grail knight,[5] he has company in those changes as well. Consequently, my comments concerning innovations or departures from tradition are not intended to suggest that he is in every case creating something entirely new, only that his reliance on Malory is sporadic at best.

While Boorman simplifies a great deal by conflating some characters and motifs and by eliminating others, he also redefines some crucial elements of the traditional Arthurian story, especially the wasteland and the Grail quest, and creates at the same time a very complex vision. One of his more successful sequences (inspired, as noted, more by Weston than by Malory) involves the presentation of the wasteland, the causes and symptoms of which are traced in relentless detail and with memorable imagery. That wasteland is literal, of course, as the country is devastated and infertile, but as in Arthurian tradition it is also moral and perhaps even religious. The moral dimension is underlined by Lancelot when he defines Camelot's decadence ("We have lost our way, Arthur"), and it will be expressed clearly in the Grail scene discussed below.

Although a moral failure is the ultimate cause of the wasteland, Boorman presents a complicated cluster of causes, symptoms, and additional effects of that failure. Whether as cause or effect — and the distinction is not in every case clear — the crisis of the Arthurian world in Boorman's vi-

Nigel Terry as the Young Arthur pulls Excalibur from the stone in John Boorman's 1981 film *Excalibur*.

sion involves Arthur's ineffectiveness (and the later decline of his health and vigor), the lassitude and indolence of the knights, Lancelot and Guinevere's fall into adultery, Merlin's departure, Morgana's treachery, and Mordred's eventual treason.

Lancelot's reaction to the crisis of the court is to withdraw in order to rediscover his way alone, in the wilderness. His departure proves, however, to be an ironically destructive course, for Guinevere follows him into the forest. There they meet and yield, apparently for the first time, to their temptation. Their illicit love, emblematic of the decay of the Arthurian court, sows the seed of its ultimate destruction in a specific way, for Arthur discovers them together, sleeping nude in each other's embrace.

The scene is fascinating for reasons other than its eroticism and its destructive effect. Guinevere's flight into the woods in pursuit of Lancelot is accompanied by music from the prelude to Wagner's *Tristan und Isolde*. For viewers who do not recognize it, it is simply lush romantic music appropriate to the scene. For those many who do, it is a startling development implying some kind of parallel or conjunction of the two pairs of ill-fated lovers, or rather of two corresponding and equally destructive love triangles: Lancelot/Guinevere/Arthur and Tristan/Isolde/Mark. Love and the announcement of impending tragedy are united in the music.

This music also prepares, very subtly, the next step in the wasteland spiral, for Boorman employs a motif without parallel in Malory's account of Lancelot and Guinevere, but drawn instead from the Tristan story.[6] Finding the sleeping lovers in the forest, Arthur leaves his sword between them (plunging it into the ground in a scene visually reminiscent of Uther's thrusting it into the stone). Upon awakening, they realize with horror that they have been discovered by the King. The scene is doubly catastrophic, however: not only is their sin revealed to her husband and his king, but, more important, Arthur loses Excalibur.

The consequence of the sword's loss is explained by Lancelot, who exclaims: "The King without a sword — the land without a king!" This loss is a symbolic manifestation of Arthur's failing powers — Excalibur is the "symbol and sceptre" of leadership (Haller 2) — but it is also a precise, literal cause of what is to come. As is traditional, in accounts from Chrétien de Troyes to Jessie Weston, there is an immediate link between the king's health and virility and the fertility, or infertility, of the land; here, there is an additional link, between the king's sword and his virility. Arthur is without the sword created by Merlin, left to him by Uther, and accepted as the symbol and instrument of his authority.

The Arthurian world's decline into impotence is both hastened and signaled powerfully by Merlin's withdrawal from the world. Arthur is deprived not only of the power and authority associated with Excalibur, but also of the guidance provided by Merlin. Moreover, Merlin's withdrawal is all the more tragic because it is followed by Morgana's apprenticeship, by her success in extracting from Merlin the incantation that will effectively transfer his power to her. Thereupon, she, Arthur's sister, uses an enchantment to seduce the King and conceive Mordred, who will later kill his father.

Mordred's birth is followed by a curious scene in which Arthur is struck by lightning. The immediate cause of this physical disability is thus a physical event, but one that crystallizes the moral developments traced here. While the lightning strike may appear to be an unnecessary physical elaboration of the King's decline and Camelot's decadence, it is consistent with Boorman's method, which provides parallel sequences on the physical and moral levels. On the physical level, Arthur loses his strongest support when Lancelot and Merlin are separated from the court; he loses the instrument of his authority when he leaves Excalibur in the forest; and he is literally struck down by the lightning. The second, moral, level is no less clearly delineated: the demoralization of his knights, betrayal by his wife, and his own incest. The wasteland is established with chilling thoroughness.

But not, of course, with finality. There is one solution, a solution familiar to every reader of Arthurian fiction. The Grail is their last hope, and Arthur announces: "We must find what was lost: the Grail. Only the Grail can restore leaf and flower.... Only the Grail can redeem us." Viewers even remotely familiar with the Arthurian story will doubtless not be surprised that the Grail is the remedy, although they must surely be struck by the fact that it has not been mentioned before and that, now that it is evoked, there is no explanation. Neither the identity nor the nature of the Grail is discussed; nor does Arthur explain how the Grail was lost, how he knows that it will redeem them, or, since he does know that, why he did not suggest its recovery earlier.

Boorman's inadequate preparation for the scene — a charge sometimes leveled at Malory as well — and his lack of explanation weaken a crucial sequence, almost suggesting that the Grail theme was an afterthought,[7] rather than the climax and centerpiece of the Arthurian story. Yet that sequence, although less than entirely satisfying, includes what is surely the most remarkable set of innovations in the film, and it is here that *Excalibur* raises, as a result, the most complex questions of meaning and filmic vision, and moreover of viewer response.

In the quest episodes, Boorman's method of conflating characters and events from tradition is pursued almost to its logical conclusion. Most significant are the changes in the Grail imagery and, especially, in the identity of the Grail king. Specifically, Arthur himself replaces two or even three characters from more traditional accounts. In addition to being the king who directs the Grail quest, Arthur here also takes the role traditionally given to the wounded and disabled Fisher King, the restoration of whose health, and that of the land, depends on the quest's successful conclusion. This is a significant innovation — Shichtman notes (43) that this is the only treatment of the legend in which "Arthur himself becomes the helpless lord of the Wasteland" — and a major departure from Malory, where the quest occurs not when the realm is wasted, but instead when it is prospering (Shichtman 48, n. 22). And, most spectacularly, in the complex scene that depicts the culmination of the quest, Arthur also appears to replace Christ. That scene merits some detailed discussion.

When Perceval first has an opportunity to complete the quest, he has a vision of the Grail, an elevated chalice glowing in an ethereal light. A disembodied voice asks, "What is the secret of the Grail? Whom does it serve?" Perceval flees without responding and later confesses, "Arthur, the secret was in my grasp. I failed you."

There is nothing in Malory or in the tradition of Grail lore in general that could prepare viewers for Boorman's highly original treatment of Perceval's second Grail vision. On that second occasion, the question is repeated, this time answered by Perceval:

— What is the secret of the Grail? Whom does it serve?
— You, my lord.
— Who am I?
— You are my lord and king. [Pause] You're Arthur.
— Have you found the secret that I have lost?
— Yes: you and the land are one.

During this exchange, the Grail is transmuted from a chalice into a luminous vision of an Arthur in armor, and then back into the chalice, but this time it is not an image but the object itself: the vessel that can be grasped by Perceval and brought to Arthur.

Here, Boorman is faithful to his earlier method of maintaining parallel physical and moral, or real and symbolic, lines. As noted, however, that method here involves dividing Arthur into two. On the one hand, he is the disabled king who directed the Grail quest and who awaits its conclusion. On the other hand, he is the Grail King himself. He is both a real king of flesh and blood and the spiritual being that, in a curiously self-reflexive development, provides for the restoration of his own physical incarnation. One Arthur-figure has the power to redeem the other, healing himself, as it were, but through the mediation of Perceval.

The episode raises other questions, concerning both meaning and method. Perceval reaches out and is able to seize the Grail, which had just taken Arthur's form; he then takes it to Arthur and announces, "You and the land are one. Drink." His next statement is the only instance in which the Grail is specifically called a chalice, and the intent is clear: "Drink from the chalice and you will be reborn, and the land with you." Not simply healed or restored: *reborn*. Arthur replies, "I didn't know how empty was my soul — until it was filled." Thereupon, his strength and the land are restored, and soon after, Arthur visits Guinevere, who returns Excalibur, still instrument and symbol of his power, to him.

Haller comments about Boorman's Grail that "Christian significance is never suggested" (3), and Harty concurs that "the Grail is stripped of any Christian associations" (108). While it is correct that Boorman establishes no explicit connection with traditional Christian interpretations of the Grail, he does on the other hand provide hints that we can hardly ignore. The references to a chalice, to rebirth, to emptiness of soul not only confirm that this is a mystical vision but also imbue the episode with a fundamentally religious resonance, and it is inconceivable that viewers will not supply the associations at which Boorman only hints.

Indeed, this is one of the points in the film where a "naive" (i.e., fully uninformed) viewing is virtually impossible, for the association of Grail with Chalice of the Last Supper, firmly established during the Middle Ages, has become so thoroughly entrenched, even in the popular mind, that reference to the Grail inevitably evokes Christian themes. Only more knowledgeable viewers will be able to appreciate fully the eccentricities of Boorman's presentation, but both his "hints" and our usual assumptions surely make it impossible to exclude all Christian associations.

And yet the filmmaker, all the while forging dialogue and images to encourage such associations, manages to subvert them. Everything in the scene seems to have pointed toward a traditionally religious interpretation of the events surrounding the Grail, and indeed Perceval's response to the disembodied voice — "you are my lord" — appears to confirm that interpretation. But then, startlingly, he adds, after a slight pause, "You're Arthur." This substitution is a stunning and daring innovation, one of the larger shocks of the film.

On the face of it, the effect of combining King, Fisher King, Grail King, and, by implication, Christ into a single person concentrates extraordinary symbolic import in the figure of Arthur. He is the center of his world, whereas traditional Grail texts had largely displaced him as focus, in order to replace Arthurian chivalry by a higher order, a celestial chivalry based on devotion to a moral and religious purpose. Undeniably, Boorman produces a more concentrated if unconventional vision, with Arthur as sender and receiver, as director of the Grail quest and as its principal recipient, and as the character whose physical and moral health remains closely linked to, and directly responsible for, the state of his land.

But a more concentrated vision is not necessarily a more effective one, and the value of this conflation still bears consider-

Lancelot (Nicholas Clay) and Guinevere (Cherie Lunghi) embrace in John Boorman's 1981 film *Excalibur*.

ation. Is the film symbolically impoverished because Boorman diminishes the connection of the Grail to Christ, and therefore that of Arthur to sacred history? Or, conversely, is it enriched by the apotheosizing of Arthur? In other words, is Boorman brilliantly innovative or hopelessly muddled?

One defensible reaction is that Boorman has largely trivialized the legend by severing it from one of its most productive elements: its explicit relationship to sacred history. Medieval versions of the Grail story, as far back as the twelfth century, tended to open it up "vertically," adding layers of symbolic and mystical meaning by setting it within universal history and by pointing not only toward a physical restoration and a moral rebirth but also toward a spiritual ascension.[8] Arthur is a significant part of that process, but his role is simply an aspect of the historical process working toward a triumphant redemption.

In fact, it could be argued that the mythic appeal of the Grail legend derives precisely from the complex association of an ancient myth, the identity of land with its ruler, with the central religious beliefs of the West. Boorman intimates a tenuous connection with the latter beliefs, in his references (for example) to an empty soul, but without establishing them with the clarity they may call for; and Arthur's supplanting the deity at the conclusion of the quest appears to obscure the meaning of the Grail.

On the other hand, the result of that substitution is the apotheosizing of Arthur: Boorman raises him beyond the status of wise ruler and able soldier, even beyond the status he could attain with Merlin's magic. Instead of being a pawn, albeit a key one, in the quest ordained by God, he is central to the quest in every sense: he conceives and orders it, he (along with the land in general) is the beneficiary of it, and — most important — he is finally the power behind it. From this point of view, the figure of Arthur is expanded, both horizontally, in that he subsumes identities and roles elsewhere taken by others, and vertically, in that his role transcends the usual limits of his humanity. In other words, Boorman is in effect expanding the *Arthurian* legend at the expense of the *Grail* legend.

Ultimately, while we can easily enough identify Boorman's innovations, we can make no objective evaluation of their effectiveness. Along with other variables, such as personal taste and appreciation of cinematic technique, that influence the reaction to any film, the level of knowledge a viewer is likely to bring to *Excalibur* is a crucial determinant of response. This principle logically holds for any retreatment of tradition: obviously, only those conversant with the tradition can fully appreciate and evaluate a work of art that exploits it. But Boorman's film constitutes a particular problem, owing both to the ubiquity of the legend and to his radical departures from earlier accounts of Arthur. The Arthurian story is so firmly established in Western, especially anglophone, culture and in the popular mind that everyone has at least a vague notion of how it is supposed to "go."[9] Beyond the most basic response, however, our evaluation of Boorman's vision and of the strengths or flaws of his film will naturally vary a good deal with the extent of our acquaintance with Malory, with Jessie Weston, or with Arthurian tradition in general.

To offer a simple example of the relationship of response to knowledge of the tradition: viewers unfamiliar with earlier texts will surely find nothing amiss when Arthur asks Perceval to throw the sword into the lake. Yet those who know Arthurian legend reasonably well must wonder why Perceval replaces the Bedivere of English tradition (who incidentally replaced Girflet in the French account).[10] This is a question with a perfectly good answer — eliminating Bedivere, Girflet, and even such characters as Galahad helps to concentrate the film's focus — but few are the viewers able to supply or appreciate that answer. Similarly, as I noted above, whether the use of Wagner's *Tristan und Isolde* simply sets a romantic mood or instead establishes a complex overlay of themes prefiguring both passion and death depends quite simply on the viewer's recognition of the music.

But the most complicated problems of response in this film are related to the Grail and to Arthur's multiple roles: as the impotent or "maimed" king, the instigator of the quest, and the image that implicitly replaces Christ. At least in the case of the Grail, even a rudimentary awareness of precedents, such as almost everyone has, transforms the viewer into an active participant, who brings some degree of knowledge and experience to the viewing. In regard to other sequences and themes, viewers' knowledge of Arthuriana, and thus their responses to the film, are likely to vary from the most informed readings of medieval literature and modern fiction to the vaguest associations drawn from popular culture.

By no means has it been my intent to criticize Boorman for his originality. He cannot be faulted for having modified the legend he inherited from others, for, as I suggested, Malory and most of the others did no less; in fact, only constant renewal can ensure the continued vitality of the Arthurian story. If Boorman is to be either praised or faulted, it must be for the effect of his innovations and for the overall quality of his creation. I do indeed find the film deeply flawed in a number of ways, but I also consider it to be among the most fascinating treatments of the legend. Boorman is highly original in his conception but far less successful in his execution. For those who have seen it, and especially for those who know the tradition reasonably well, it is material for a case study in cinematic response, and in any event it provides a singular illustration of the power cinema has to remake even our most profoundly held myths.

NOTES

I wish to express my gratitude to Kevin J. Harty, who facilitated the preparation of this essay by providing valuable advice and bibliographical assistance.

1. Examples are transpositions into the sports or motorcycle culture. George Romero's film *Knightriders* (which appeared in 1981, the same year as Boorman's) depicts modern Arthurian "knights" on motorcycle. The best-known, and most subtle, retreatment of Arthurian legend in the context of sport is Bernard Malamud's *The Natural* (1952), which uses the Perceval story as underlying structure. Babs Deal, in *The Grail: A Novel* (1963), relates the Grail quest to the endeavors of an American football team.

2. Although the film has a good many champions, particularly among French critics, it had an equal number of detractors, one of the most severe of whom was Vincent Canby, who described *Excalibur* as a "gigantic, overblown, overlong, pompous, essentially boorish reworking of the Arthurian legends" (Canby, "Of a Hit" 13). Although Canby's judgment is harsh, I agree that the film is far from flawless: it is overlong, often structurally unclear, at times thematically confused. While problems of clarity and meaning are the crucial matters, the film is also frequently jarring by its anachronisms and other distractions, which sometimes border on silliness. Examples are Mordred's gold armor and pseudoclassical mask, which appear (as Canby notes, 10 April 1981: 3. 11) "left over from Mr. Boorman's science-fiction film 'Zardoz.'" Boorman himself admitted the resemblance of Mordred's mask to those of *Zardoz,* commenting that "perhaps there was a lack of imagination on our part!" (Ciment 201).

3. Shichtman 41; the reference is to Weston's *From Ritual to Romance*, a study in cultural anthropology that is best known as the primary inspiration for T.S. Eliot's *The Waste Land*. Weston links Grail themes to ancient nature rituals; the specific connection to Boorman's film is provided by her consideration of "the intimate relation at one time held to exist between the ruler and his land" (114). It must be noted that Boorman himself has acknowledged his debt to authors other than Malory; they include Weston, T. H. White, John Cowper Powys, T. S. Eliot, Chrétien de Troyes, and "the most fascinating and modern of them all," Wolfram von Eschenbach (Ciment 185, 192).

4. For convenience and clarity, I quote Malory in Lumiansky's modernized edition; for the original text, see the edition by Vinaver.

5. In Boorman's mind this was not a substitution but an additional conflation, the combining of Perceval and Galahad to permit the solution of a number of cinematic problems; see Tessier 31.

6. For Béroul's Old French treatment of this motif, in his *Tristan* (late twelfth century), see Lacy, ed. (97). The Tristan legend is evoked elsewhere in the film, both by the use of Wagner's music and, as Jessica Yates (30) notes, by the sequence in which Lancelot, escorting the Queen to Arthur's wedding, falls in love with her.

7. Canby ("Of a Hit") notes that Boorman "introduces the search for the Holy Grail very late in the film as if the Grail were some misplaced lunchbox, not worth anything in itself but possessing sentimental value" (10). Canby is in my view mistaken about the lack of worth Boorman ascribes to the Grail, but his objection about the suddenness and lateness of its introduction is irrefutable. Yates acknowledges that the Grail episode is "fairly incomprehensible" but then defends Boorman's treatment by adding, "but then, so is the Grail legend" (30); it is hardly necessary to respond that incomprehensibility arising from divine inspiration is quite unlike incomprehensibility due to inadequate artistic preparation.

8. The most dramatic example of this approach is the *Roman du Graal* (also known as the *Joseph d'Arimathie*) of Robert de Boron, a French poet writing at the end of the twelfth century or during the very first years of the thirteenth. It was Robert who first connected the Grail with the Chalice of the Last Supper; he also presented the Round Table as the third in a series that included the table of the Last Supper and a table established by Joseph of Arimathea, at the direction of the Holy Spirit, to celebrate the service of the Grail. Arthurian legend is thus linked to sacred history, and the Grail to the chalice of Christ.

9. As Charles Champlin put it, the Arthurian legend "sticks like lint to generations of schoolboys and girls" (1).

10. This role, incidentally, seems to be assignable to almost anyone. In the 1953 film *Knights of the Round Table*, it is Lancelot who returns Excalibur to the sea.

WORKS CITED

Béroul. *The Romance of Tristran*. Ed. and trans. Norris J. Lacy. New York: Garland, 1989.

Canby, Vincent. "Of a Hit, a Series and the Word." *New York Times* 10 May 1981: D13.

———. Review of Boorman's *Excalibur*. *New York Times* 10 April 1981: 3. 11.
Champlin, Charles. Review of Boorman's *Excalibur*. *Los Angeles Times* 17 June 1981: Calendar 1.
Ciment, Michel. *John Boorman*. Trans. Gilbert Adair. London: Faber, 1986.
Haller, Robert A. "Excalibur and Innovation." *Field of Vision* 13 (Spring 1985): 2–3.
Harty, Kevin J. "Cinema Arthuriana." *Arthurian Interpretations* 2 (Fall 1987): 95–113.
Kennedy, Harlan. "The World of King Arthur According to John Boorman." *American Film* 6 (March 1981): 30–37.
Malory, Sir Thomas. *Le Morte d'Arthur*. Ed. R. M. Lumiansky. New York: Collier, 1982.
———. *The Works of Thomas Malory*. Ed. Eugène Vinaver. London: Oxford University Press, 1954.
Robert de Boron. *Le Roman de l'Estoire du Graal*. Ed. William A. Nitze. Paris: Champion, 1927.
Shichtman, Martin B. "Hollywood's New Weston: The Grail Myth in Francis Ford Coppola's *Apocalypse Now* and John Boorman's *Excalibur*." *Post Script* 4 (Autumn 1984): 35–48.
Tessier, Max. "Entretien avec John Boorman (sur *Excalibur*)." *Revue du cinéma* 363 (July–August 1981): 31–34.
Weston, Jessie L. *From Ritual to Romance*. 1920. rpt. Garden City, N.Y.: Doubleday, 1957.
Yates, Jessica. "Boorman's Arthur." *Mythlore* 31 (Spring 1982): 29–30.

3

Fire, Water, Rock: Elements of Setting in John Boorman's Excalibur *and Steve Barron's* Merlin

Muriel Whitaker

When the fifteenth-century knight-prisoner Sir Thomas Malory wrote *Le Morte d'Arthur*, few doubted that Arthur was a real king who had unified Britain, led an army to the continent and become Roman emperor. William Caxton, who published *Le Morte* in 1485, pointed in a prologue to the tomb at Glastonbury, his seal in Westminster Abbey, and his Round Table at Winchester as evidences that "there was suche a noble kynge named Arthur." In the text, references to architecture, costume, arms and armor, to the military campaigns of the Hundred Years' War and the Wars of the Roses, to commercial details, and to the use of cannon fix Arthurian society in the late Middle Ages. Lacking the concept of historical perspective, author and audience visualized the past in contemporary terms. Because *Le Morte d'Arthur* is the definitive English version, modern audiences accept this fifteenth century world as the conventional Arthurian milieu.

In the late twentieth century, however, the question of Arthur's historicity is also relevant to visualization. Archaeological excavations such as those at South Cadbury in Somerset[1] have popularized the idea that Arthur was a sixth-century *dux bellorum* who led the Britons against invading Saxons. Novelists like Rosemary Sutcliff, Henry Treece, and Victor Canning have striven to recreate a wild and barbarous land in which a few Britons, galvanized by a hero Arthur, struggle to maintain the fading Roman culture.[2] Romance and history, then, project conflicting visions.

When Orion offered the British film director John Boorman the chance of making an Arthurian film in 1979, he had at his disposal still another model, one developed by the Victorians. Approved by Queen Victoria and Prince Albert and promoted by Alfred, Lord Tennyson in *Idylls of the King* was an English historical myth which treated King Arthur not as historical reality or romantic hero but as the progenitor of a relevant "national identity." Tennyson gave Boorman a way of combining the primitive world of Dark Age Britain with the myth of a hero who for a brief period established peace, truth, and justice. Though doomed to defeat, the hero survives in the imagination as an ideal of human achievement.

Tennyson saw Arthur as "a man who spent himself in the cause of honour, duty and self-sacrifice, who felt and aspired with his nobler knights, though with a stronger and clearer conscience" (Hallam Tennyson I, 193). For both Tennyson and Boorman, myth is didactic: "Listen carefully to the echoes of myth. It has much more to tell us than the petty lies and insignificant truths of recorded history," the director said on the set of *Excalibur* (Strick 168).

Tennyson provided a mythic time scheme that links the progress of Arthur's life to a seasonal cycle, making it possible to use the world of nature as a source of mood and symbol. Winter signifies the barbarous world into which Arthur is born, to be carried off immediately through a treacherous forest of twisted roots, bare branches, muddy banks, and thorny thickets. Boorman's visualisation of the Perilous Forest is one that Arthur Rackham established in illustrating *The Romance of King Arthur and His Knights of the Round Table* of 1917.[3] At Easter (eighteen years later in linear time) the hero succeeds in the sword test, flourishing Excalibur in a leafy forest hung with banners. Guenevere comes to Camelot amid the flowers of May. The chivalric summer finds Lancelot riding through a sunlit glade carpeted with bluebells. He and Guenevere consummate their love to the accompaniment of birdsong. Mordred's milieu is the dark world of autumn where bare branches and brown bogs signify oppression and sterility. The last battle takes place at the year's end in a setting that Boorman seems to have based closely on Tennyson's lines:

Then rose the King and moved his host by
   night,
And ever push'd Sir Mordred, league by
   league,
Back to the sunset bound of Lyonness –
A land of old upheaven from the abyss
By fire, to sink into the abyss again;
Where fragments of forgotten peoples dwelt,
And the long mountains ended in a coast ...

And there, that day when the great light of
   heaven
Burn'd at his lowest in the rolling year,
On the waste sand by the waste sea they closed
...
A deathwhite mist slept over sand and sea:
Whereof the chill, to him who breathed it,
   drew
Down with his blood, till all his heart was cold
With formless fear; and ev'n on Arthur fell
Confusion, since he saw not whom he fought.
    ["The Passing of Arthur" ll. 80–99]

Both productions conclude with the image of the barge sailing into light as "the new sun rose bringing the new year." Cyclical time allows for the possibility that Arthur will return. Though Malory's *Le Morte d'Arthur* is *Excalibur*'s credited source, the *Idylls of the King* was equally influential in shaping the imaginative construct.

In addition to the myth of sovereignty, Boorman is fascinated by the myth of the Holy Grail. He ignores Malory's hero Sir Galahad, a representation of thirteenth-century Cistercian mysticism, preferring to reach back through T. S. Eliot, Jessie L. Weston, Wagner, Wolfram von Eschenbach, and Chrétien de Troyes to the primitive vegetation myth which related the prosperity of a land and its people to the health of the ruler. In the earliest medieval adaptations, Perceval is the saviour who, by finding his way to the Grail Castle and asking the right question, restores the Maimed King and his wasted land. The secret that the film Perceval learns from the Grail and carries back to Arthur is "You and the land are one." When Arthur (Nigel Terry) drinks from the chalice (both a pagan vessel of healing and a Christian symbol of grace), he is physically and psychologically revitalized. Boorman equates the "achievement" of the Grail with man's repossession of ancient magic through a transcendent experience independent of the materialistic world (Yakir 49).

The film's aesthetic patterning depends on a series of polarities explored through aspects of setting. A state of barbarism is briefly ameliorated by a golden age of chivalry. The powers of ancient, pagan magic, which Merlin (Nicol Williamson) and Morgana (Helen Mirren) can tap, are diminished by the newly established Christianity to which Arthur, Lancelot, Perceval, and Guenevere adhere. The world of pristine nature is modified by the "emerging world of man." Fire, water, rock, dragon, sword, and chalice — these are motifs within the matrix of forest, the perilous realm of romance.

Tennyson commenced "The Coming of Arthur" with a scene of desolation, rapine, and confusion as "a heathen horde/Reddening the sun with smoke and earth with blood" lays waste the land. *Excalibur*'s opening scene shows bare-branched trees and black knights in pig-snout helms (a fifteenth-century style) silhouetted against a lurid sky. Steam from the horses' nostrils condenses in the frosty air. Torches flicker in the hands of knights who charge into misty battle behind a wall of flame. Few subsequent scenes lack their fires. Balls of flame hurtle through the air as knights attack. Gas-fed jets enclose the bed where Uther (Gabriel Byrne) engenders Arthur on Igrayne (Katrina Boorman), shoot from the cauldron in the lair of Morgana, flare on the battlements where Arthur learns of his queen's adultery. Dragon flames synthesize the lovers' embraces, which rob Arthur of his power, and Merlin's submission, which allows Morgana to claim the dragon's power. Fire is an essential element in the aesthetic of violence and of magic, evoking the primitive, the destructive, and the passionate.

Fire can be used apocalyptically, too. Merlin's brightening staff symbolizes the light of civilization, a significance reinforced by the curtain of white candles which illuminates the Round Table in Arthur's new hall and the bright knights who sit down to feast wearing complete plate armor. The lights dim as the King's power fades.

Believing that the Arthurian world should be pristine and magical, Boorman chose to film the movie in Ireland, that misty, moisty country with a mythology that lies at the heart of Arthurian legend. Rain endows grass, leaves and mosses with a luminosity which the technicians enhance by using filters and green gel. Green is the faerie color.

In Irish myth and medieval romances with Celtic motifs, water in some form — lakes, rivers, fountains, ocean, mist, rain, fog — marks the boundary between the mundane world and the magical Otherworld. Boorman uses the association between water and the supernatural to point up scenes of heightened experience which transcend everyday life. The sea pounds on Tintagel's cliffs when Uther, magically changed to Cornwall's appearance, approaches Igrayne. Arthur, about to be knighted, stands knee-deep in a castle moat — the parallel to Christ's baptism is probably intentional. The young Guenevere (Cherie Lunghi) tends the young king beside a clear pool, bathing his wounds with water from a fountain. Arthur meets Lancelot for the first time beside a waterfall and sparkling stream. Filled with envy and anger, he insists on fighting, with the result that he breaks Excalibur. It slips away into the pool. In the underwater world which represents in Jungian terms Arthur's subconscious, the sword is mended and restored by the Lady of the Lake to symbolize the King's suppression of anger, pride, and envy.

In the Waste Land, Perceval's Jungian victory over doubt and fear is conveyed when he emerges from the perilous underwater passage, clean and almost naked, to enter the Grail Castle. Mist is the sign of Morgana's magic, rising from her cauldron to obscure Merlin. The wizard's taunt, "I see no mist," forces her to chant for the last time the spell of change which transmutes her into a hag while filling the battlefield with fog to Mordred's chagrin, as Morgana had promised him a clear day. The film's most magical scene shows Excalibur breaking through the water to hover, a shimmer of blue and green, in the pure white of off-stage lights. The simulated magic depended on shooting the sword from an underwater platform with a charge that sent it speedily into the air. A special camera recording 280 frames a second caught the images.

While the lakes, waterfalls, and rushing streams are real, the castles are not. They are incomplete constructions of timber, plywood, polystyrene, and paint representing bits of battlement, cavernous passageways between stone slabs, some ceremonial staircases, and Romanesque pillars with zoomorphic designs on the capitals. Like Malory, Boorman recreates only the castle parts that are relevant to the action. Great blocks of "stone" oppose attacking knights, enclose devious intruders or, shaped grotesquely into stalagmites and stalactites, incarcerate Merlin. Beyond the castles, County Wicklow's boulder strewn landscape evokes the primitive world of the ancient Britons, as do the Stonehenge monoliths[4] which Boorman cannot resist when he composes a setting for Merlin's return to "the land of dreams." The blood-caked stones of the ultimate battleground demonically represent Malory's "colde erthe."

After Boorman's original title "Merlin Lives" had to be abandoned because of copyright problems, other familiar "icons" — Excalibur, the Grail, the Round Table — were "juggled into juxtapositions that might attract success at the world's box office" (Strick 168). The choice of *Excalibur* was an inspired one. The sword image dominates the film by combining history and myth, reality and fantasy, water and rock. A gift from the underwater world, it is held in rock to await its destined possessor. Because it represents sovereignty, it must be returned to the Otherworld when the King's reign ends. Boorman expands the significance by relating the sword to Arthur's moral and spiritual condition. Broken in anger and envy of Lancelot, "the best knight in the world," it is restored when the king regains a virtuous equilibrium. It is lost, however, when overcome again by anger and envy, Arthur plunges it between Guenevere and her lover. Lancelot runs through the forest crying, "The king without a sword! The land without a king!" The cross-shaped Excalibur pierces rock to "the coils of the dragon," the source of life.

Like so many of *Excalibur*'s archetypes, the dragon is ambivalent. It is the personal symbol of Uther and his son Arthur. In medieval chronicle, it derives from the victorious red dragon under Vortigern's tower which foretells Uther's defeat of the Saxons. Like Tennyson, the movie director turns the dragon to gold, embossing it on Arthur's shield and on the great scarlet banners which fly above the king's victorious army. A dragon sculpture guards Camelot's entrance, as in Tennyson's construct where

> both the wings are made of gold, and flame
> At sunrise till the people in far fields,
> Wasted so often by the heathen hordes,
> Behold it, crying, "We have still a King."
> ["The Holy Grail" ll. 242–45]

At the heart of the rock, and the heart of Boorman's myth, lies a more ancient dragon, the primal source of life. It represents the spirit of nature in all its forms — the snake descending from the branch, the owl, the centipede, the lizard, the fire, the rock. While the adolescent Arthur fears this spirit's manifestations, Merlin and then Morgana draw power from it. Merlin releases the dragon's breath so that Uther can lie with Igrayne and so that Lancelot can be healed. When Arthur, betrayed, drives Excalibur between Guenevere and Lancelot, the sword pierces through rock to "the coils of the dragon," causing a transfer of power from the forces of good (Merlin and Arthur) to the forces of evil (Morgana and Mordred). Only when Merlin, renewed by Arthur's love, challenges Morgana to "call the dragon; mend the sword; speak the spell of making" can the dragon's power end the fée's supernatural youth and beauty, restore Excalibur to Arthur's use, and release Merlin into Arthur's dream.

Excalibur is flawed by a lack of consistency which Boorman defends by asserting that "the film has to do with mythical truth, not historical truth" (Yakir 49). Yet it is his treatment of myth that causes the problems. In mingling the Celtic mythology from which Arthurian romance derives and the Teutonic mythology which Boorman imposes by way of Tolkien and Wagner, the director sets up irreconcilable patterns of allusion. He sees Arthurian England as "a kind of Middle Earth in Tolkien terms" (Kennedy 33), ignoring the fact that Middle Earth is an Anglo-Saxon construct inappropriate both to the "historical" Arthurian sixth century, when the Saxons were the enemy, and to the French dominated High Middle Ages when Arthurian literatures evolved. Merlin is presented as an Odin-Gandalf type, complete with ravens. Worst of all, musical quotations from Richard Wagner's *Ring* Cycle, *Parsifal* and *Tristan und Isolde* as well as from Carl Orff's *Carmina Burana* underline the false analogy between Arthurian romance and Teutonic hero tales.

Another kind of inconsistency occurs when the director interrupts the cyclical time scheme that he has adopted from Tennyson's *Idylls*. Though there is too much water in evidence, the Waste Land images of snow, brown grass, and grey trees from which dangle the bodies of hanged knights are appropriate to the season of late autumn, with its resonances of approaching death. But after drinking from the Grail, the invigorated Arthur with his loyal followers rides through blossoming apple orchards on his way to Almesbury and the last battle. True, the scene conveys both the physical and psychological restoration which Perceval's achievement of the Grail

Keith Buckley (left) as Uryens and Robert Addie as Mordred in John Boorman's 1981 film *Excalibur*.

quest has effected, while referring obliquely to Glastonbury's identification with Avalon, the *insula pomorum*, but it is an inappropriate prelude to the day of doom which swiftly follows. Perhaps it is intended as a promise that the "fair time may come again." Boorman has commented that "a filmmaker functions as a Merlin in the sense that he tries to organize the world" (Yakir 50). Whether the motifs of fire, water and rock are sufficient to provide unity, only the viewer can judge.

Steve Barron's *Merlin* (1998), a made-for-TV Hallmark Entertainment film, is the biography of the Arthurian magician, or, perhaps one should say, the autobiography since Merlin is intermittently the narrator. It begins in the pseudo-historical fifth century of Geoffrey of Monmouth's *Historia Regum Britanniae* (ca. 1137) when the Christian king Constant (played by a Lear-like Sir John Gielgud) is murdered and the pagan Vortigern (Rutger Hauer) literally picks up his crown. Merlin is the boy without a father whose blood mixed with mortar will, according to the soothsayer, end the repeated collapsing of Vortigern's tower.[5] Geoffrey's Merlin was the offspring of a royal nun and an incubus appearing as a handsome young man. Later medieval versions such as the thirteenth century *Suite du Merlin*[6] and the English *Prose Merlin* (ca. 1450) presented an assembly of devils who plot to damn the human race by creating a prophet half human, half devil to rival Christ.[7] This idea seems to be the film's inspiration for its antagonist, Queen Mab, who, determined to destroy Christianity and restore the old religion, conceives Merlin in a glowing crystal and incarnates him in a peasant girl's womb.

Behind Mab stand several mythic figures — the demonic engenderer of a strange male child on a mortal mother; Shakespeare's Queen Mab, "the fairies' midwife," a tiny mischiefmaker and dream merchant (*Romeo and Juliet* I. iv. 53–94); the Irish Queen Medb of Connacht, ambitious, ruthless, exemplifying the power of women in the heroic society (Dillon and Chadwick 125); and the Irish goddess the Morrigan, often cited as a forefunner of Morgan Le Fay (Paton 148-53). Here, with her murderous proclivities, shapeshifting, battle lust, prophetic skill, storm-making power and hateful laugh, she is the prototype of Merlin's and Arthur's chief enemy. Miranda Richardson, featuring the jet black hair, waxy face and glassy eyes of a doll, plays the husky-voiced mistress of black magic. The adult Merlin (Sam Neill), because of his dead mother's goodness and foster mother's nurturing, refuses to be Mab's agent. No effort is made to present Merlin or Arthur as defenders of Christianity; the hostility is personal and not philosophical.

To fit the multifarious Matter of Britain into two hours necessitates simplifications, conflations and exclusions. Nimue (Isabella Rosellini), Merlin's beloved, is a young aristocrat with no supernatural powers. Vortigern holds her hostage to ensure her father's loyalty. Mab promises that sacrificing her to the dragon will bring about Vortigern's victory over the invading Uther. Later Mab bargains to heal the girl's fire-scarred face in return for luring Merlin to a place of no return. The Lady of the Lake (also played by Richardson) is the dark queen's beneficent sister, possessor of Excalibur and Merlin's confidant. The ugly child Morgan is sufficiently sighted to recognize that the shape-shifted Uther is not her father, the Duke of Cornwall. Through Mab's gnome Frick (Martin Short), Morgan learns magic, is transformed into a beauty (Helena Bonham Carter), seduces Arthur, and trains her son Mordred in the ways of ambitious revenge. The eventless Quest of the Holy Grail is introduced only to remove Arthur from the scene so that the adultery of Lancelot and Guinevere may occur. Elaine of Corbenec (here Joyous Gard), Lancelot's wife

Sam Neill (left) as Merlin and Paul Curran as Arthur in Steve Barron's 1998 telefilm *Merlin*. (Still courtesy of NBC.)

and Galahad's mother, assimilates Elaine of Astolat so that, dying of a broken heart, she may float down the river in a pre–Raphaelite manner, visually replicating the last voyage of numerous Elaines and Ladies of Shalott (Whitaker 217–22, 289–91).

Scenes are shifted like a pack of cards, repetitiously and sometimes rapidly to produce simultaneity or suspense. Variety is the spice of televised life. The wooden fortresses of Vortigern and Uther resemble nineteenth-century fur-trading posts. Tintagel, the castle of Igraine (a Howard Pyle beauty), venomous Morgan and vicious Mordred, on its sea-girt headland is like a picturesque watercolor produced by an amateur Victorian artist. Romanesque Camelot, which Arthur describes as a golden city devoted to peace and charity, overlooks a placid lake and valley but its interior has little to distinguish it, unlike the shining splendor of Boorman's construct.

Several settings suggest the two versions of the Celtic Otherworld which was located on an island or within a mountain or hollow hill (Patch 27–59). The island of Avalon, ringed with azure and silver, is paradisal. Its convent of white-robed nuns offers Nimue protection and healing though it cannot exclude Mab's intrusions. Her castle and Nimue's cottage in the Land of Dreams lie deep within the hollow hills. The place where Merlin and, one assumes, Arthur grow up is a peasant hut of bentwood and thatch construction set in a forest of bare trees on ground thickly strewn with dry leaves. The imagery suggests the season of Samain (November Eve) when the Celts believed the walls between the mundane world and fairyland were down so that fairies became active, witches worked charms, and chaos was let loose (Rees and Rees 89–92). Here Mab kills Merlin's mother and foster mother, Ambrosia, on whose snow-covered graves the youth swears vengeance. From this place in autumn, he is taken to learn magic and will later take Arthur to claim Excalibur. Mab actively participates in each event.

Some scenes are filmed in the Welsh countryside. Some are constructed in the studio. Some are produced by the technique of matting, and some are computer generated. The integration is not flawless; patchwork is the word that comes to mind. Seldom does the viewer have the sense of actuality that Boorman sometimes achieves.

As in *Excalibur*, fire characterizes scenes of violence and destruction, but it also serves as a vehicle of Mab's power. With it, she punishes Ambrosia and attacks Merlin in the wizardly competition that recalls the battle between Madame Mim and Merlin in the Disney *The Sword in the Stone*. But rock is Mab's true element, to which her heart is likened by Ambrosia, Merlin and even Frick. She makes her entrances by erupting from a megalith. She caresses rocks, uses fiery crystals for prophecy, injects a black stone with evil so that through the child Morgan's agency she can curse Arthur in his cradle. Megaliths, stone circles, and crags (icons of the old religion) are her sites for accosting mortals. She uses rocks to kill Morgan and, by shifting mountains, imprisons Nimue inside "the land of magic" while closing the entrance to exclude her lover. Her castle within a mountain can only be reached by following a treacherous waterway, littered with rocks, through caverns obscured by stalagmites and stalactites and buzzing with malevolent fairies. A stone drawbridge and steep ascending stairway end in a pillared doorway.[8]

Water is the necessary antithesis to demonic rock and fire. Not only does it facilitate transitions between this world and the Otherworld, but, according to Irish poets, the brink of water is the place where knowledge and wisdom are revealed (Rees and Rees 345). In a winter landscape, Merlin stands on the edge of a lake to summon the Lady of the Lake with her spray-fashioned gown and necklace of swimming fish. To aid the "red dragon" Uther against Mab's ally Vortigern, she provides Excalibur, "the sword of the just" which rises through snow and ice (an original touch). In the subsequent battle (shades of Eisenstein's *Alexander Nevsky*), the wizard, plunging the sword into the ice-bound river, creates a crevice which causes the villain to drown. Later Excalibur's power facilitates the shapeshifting that brings Uther to Igraine's bed.

Water is the medium of the hero's "hand magic" from his revelation of the stream and dragons destabilizing the king's building program to his production of a cataract to save Nimue from another dragon. His summoning of rain quenches the fires about Guenevere in time for Lancelot to rescue her.

But he is a rather unsatisfactory magician; unlike Boorman's image, he lacks a primal source of power comparable to the ancient dragon. One might have expected Barron to use Excalibur, the Lady of the Lake's Otherworld gift to Merlin, as an effective weapon for good in opposition to Mab's evil. Yet it remains morally ambiguous, allowing one villain, Uther, to defeat another villain, Vortigern, and to sate his lust on an ally's wife after killing the husband (who goes into battle wearing a cross!). Arthur, on a rocky mountainside, having drawn the sword from the stone where Merlin has set it to await a just king, uses it only to separate flames from candles at the beginning of his reign and kill Mordred at the end.

Despite a leather and metal casque, feathered cape and bifurcated staff, Sam Neill cannot match Nicol Williamson's aura of gravity and intelligence. He is powerless to free himself from Vortigern's prison where lack of air and space inhibit his dreams and visions. He cannot restore Nimue's beauty. His prescience is spacial rather than temporal, preventing him from warning Arthur in advance about Morgan or Guenevere. He misunderstands the Lady of the Lake's advice to find a saviour at Joyous Gard, choosing Lancelot rather than Galahad. He defeats Mab by neglect, not action. When Mordred's plots succeed, Merlin leaves the king's side, only returning in time to take Excalibur from his dying friend and throw it into the lake. Then he supports himself not as a soothsayer or magician but as a storyteller.

A major difference between *Excalibur* and *Merlin* is the degree to which the directors make magic seem credible. Boorman effects a willing suspension of disbelief on the part of the viewers when they see Excalibur breaking through the water, the Grail Castle's opening to Perceval and the release of the dragon's power. Magic in *Merlin* is mere trickery (to use the wizard's own term), the trickery not of dramatic illusion but of technology. "Frame Store creates over 550 shots," a promotional blurb trumpets. A dragon by Henson's Creature Shop, griffins courtesy of Buf, Paris, and live action blue screen dancers with tacked on wings fail to arouse either wonder or fear. Mab's croaky voice hurling imprecations, the ridiculous dragon flapping its wings, the griffins leaping like cougars from trees, the quivering mountain speaking with James Earl Jones' voice to tell Arthur, Merlin and Morgan, "I cannot die. I am the Rock of Ages. I will live forever on the edge of dream" — these sights and sounds may cause the viewer to quake — but with laughter, not fear. Not to mention such unintentional comedy as Frick's retort to Mab, "May God have mercy on your soul."

The tragic sense of life inherent in medieval Arthurian romance and retained in *Excalibur* is vitiated by television's demand for a happy ending. Lancelot and Guenevere ride "out of my story and into legend." Arthur sails off into the wide blue yonder. England under Galahad enjoys a golden age which smiling children validate. And Merlin with Nimue, perpetually youthful, retire into a land of dreams glowing with artificial radiance, a fairy tale ending for the poor but honest boy who, after numerous vicissitudes, wins the beautiful princess. In a film where the dialogue plunges to the depths of banality, the plot lacks convincing motivation and the underlying myth is fragmented, what one remembers may, after all, be the settings — Avalon rising from its silvery waters, the river-ice showing Vortigern's drowned face, the rocky pillar shattering to eject Mab, Stonehenge in moonlight where Mab interprets the soothsayer's stones, and the desolate field of the last battle where Arthur is dying in his bespattered golden armor.

NOTES

1. See Leslie Alcock, '*By South Cadbury is that Camelot ...*': *Excavations at Cadbury Castle 1966–70* (London: Thames and Hudson, 1972).

2. See Raymond H. Thompson, *The Return to Avalon: A Study of the Arthurian Legend in Modern Fiction* (Westport, Conn.: Greenwood, 1985), especially chapter 3.

3. The composition and imagery of this scene almost certainly are derived from Arthur Rackham's black-and-white illustration, "Sir Beaumains espied upon great trees how there hung full goodly armed knights by the neck" in Alfred W. Pollard, *The Romance of King Arthur and His Knights of the Round Table Abridged from Malory's Morte d'Arthur* (London: Macmillan, 1917), 97. Compare also "How Queen Guenevere rode a–Maying into the woods and fields beside Westminster" (opp. 420) as a source of Guenevere's wedding procession and "How Mordred was slain by Arthur, and how by him Arthur was hurt to the death" (opp. 490) as a source of the last battle. For a study of Arthurian illustration, see Muriel Whitaker, "The Illustration of Arthurian Romance" in Valerie M. Lagorio and Mildred Leake Day, eds. *King Arthur through the Ages* (New York: Garland, 1990), 2, 123-48; and Muriel Whitaker, *The Legends of King Arthur in Art* (Cambridge, Eng.: D. S. Brewer, 1990 and Rochester, N.Y.: Boydell & Brewer, 1991; pbk. 1995).

4. In Geoffrey of Monmouth's *Historia Regum Britanniae* (ca. 1137), Merlin is credited with moving the stone circle known as the Giant's Dance to the present location of Stonehenge.

5. The story first appeared in Nennius' *Historia Brittonum* where the boy is called Ambrosius.

6. This is Malory's source for the revelation of Arthur's parentage, the acquisition of Excalibur from the Lady of the Lake, the installation of the Round Table order, the birth of Mordred, and Vivian's (Nimue's) bespelling and incarceration of Merlin.

7. Some illustrated Arthurian manuscripts show Merlin's sleeping mother being mounted by a devil characterized by a hairy face, bulbous nose and horns; for example, London, British Library, Add. 10292 and London, British Library, Egerton 3028.

8. Although the Celtic Otherworld is usually designed to satisfy all the hero's desires, in some Irish stories such as *The Wooing of Emer* and *The Adventure of Art Son of Conn,* it is demonic, and the approach to it is hazardous.

WORKS CITED

Dillon, Myles, and Nora Chadwick. *The Celtic Realms.* London: Weidenfeld and Nicolson, 1967.

Geoffrey of Monmouth. *Historia Regum Britanniae*

of *Geoffrey of Monmouth*. Ed. Neil Wright. Cambridge, Eng.: D. S. Brewer, 1985.

Kennedy, Harlan. "The World of King Arthur According to John Boorman." *American Film* 6 (March 1981): 30–37.

Malory, Sir Thomas. *Le Morte d'Arthur*. Ed. James W. Spisak. 2 vols. Berkeley: University of California Press, 1983.

Patch, Howard Rollin. *The Otherworld According to Descriptions in Medieval Literature*. 1950. rpt. New York: Octagon, 1970.

Paton, Lucy A. *Studies in the Fairy Mythology of Arthurian Romance*. 1903. rpt. New York: Franklin, 1960.

Rees, Alwyn, and Brinley Rees. *Celtic Heritage: Ancient Tradition in Ireland and Wales*. London: Thames and Hudson, 1961.

Strick, Philip. "John Boorman's Merlin." *Sight and Sound* 49 (Summer 1980): 168-71.

Tennyson, Alfred. *The Idylls of the King*. Ed. J. M. Gray. New Haven: Yale University Press, 1983.

Tennyson, Hallam. *Alfred Lord Tennyson, a Memoir*. 2 vols. New York: Macmillan, 1897.

Whitaker, Muriel. *The Legends of King Arthur in Art*. Cambridge, Eng: D. S. Brewer, 1990 and Rochester, N.Y.: Boydell and Brewer, 1991; pbk. 1995.

Yakir, Dan. "The Sorcerer." *Film Comment* 17 (May-June 1981): 49–53.

4

Morgan and the Problem of Incest

JACQUELINE DE WEEVER

Morgan le Fay, Arthur's sister, challenges his court in several ways and may be said to inhabit the margins of the Arthurian canon, even when she is the cause and mover of the action, as in *Sir Gawain and the Green Knight* (c. 1375–1400). Although absent from earlier versions of the Arthuriad, the incest theme has become an important part of later retellings of the story. Appearing first in Malory's *Le Morte d'Arthur*, it is treated variously in film versions of the legend of the once and future king. In John Boorman's 1981 film *Excalibur*, Morgana, as she is called, destroys Arthur's realm by oblique means. In disguise as Guinevere, she seduces Arthur and bears Mordred, the son who will be the agent of the unraveling of the Arthurian ideals and of the kingdom itself. In the 2001 telefilm based on Marion Zimmer Bradley's novel, *The Mists of Avalon*, Viviane manipulates Morgaine and Arthur into an incestuous episode, neither participant knowing the identity of the partner. Incest and its concomitant doubling become the agents of Camelot's destruction.

From the beginning, Morgan is a character who may or may not be included in the Arthurian story. She is absent from Geoffrey of Monmouth's *History of the Kings of Britain* (ca. 1136) but appears in his *Vita Merlini* (ca. 1150) as the wisest and fairest of the nine maidens who rule the Island of Apples. To this island Arthur is brought after the battle of Camlann to be healed. "Morgen" receives him with honor and agrees to tend his wounds (Jarman 97). Geoffrey imputes to her neither jealousy, animus, nor incestuous plans. She is also absent from Wace's *Roman de Brut* (1155) and Layamon's *Brut* (ca. 1180–1204), a retelling of Wace. By the fourteenth century, however, Morgan grows more powerful. In *Sir Gawain and the Green Knight*, she sends the Green Knight to challenge the court and to frighten Guinevere to death; although she does not kill the Queen, she succeeds because Gawain fails the tests of the castle of Hautdesert. In the fifteenth century, Malory portrays her as a constant irritant to Arthur and his knights: some she entraps, others she enchants, always seeking Arthur's death and Camelot's destruction. Tennyson pays her no attention in his *Idylls of the King*, and T. H. White ignores her in *The Once and Future King* (1939). Wherever she does appear, she is a challenge to the court, and, in later versions of the Arthuriad, she is one of the causes of Camelot's fall when she reveals the love affair between Lancelot and Guinevere.

In film, with its need for contrasting characters to represent good and evil, Morgan makes her most dramatic and important appearances. Several films have emphasized in different ways Morgan's role as an opponent of Camelot, whether or not they make explicit the relationship between Arthur and Mordred. This depiction of Morgan as destroyer of the court of the Round Table appears, for example, in Richard Thorpe's *Knights of the Round Table* (1953) and in John Boorman's *Excalibur* (1981).

Bound up in the theme of Morgan's destruction of Arthur's court is the theme of incest. In both Wace and Layamon, the incest occurs between Mordred, the king's nephew, and Guinevere, the king's wife. In Wace's *Roman de Brut*, Mordred is

> a marvellously hardy knight, whom Arthur loved passing well. Mordred was a man of high birth, and of many noble virtues, but he was not true. He had set his heart on Guenevere, his kinswoman, but such a love brought little honour to the queen. Mordred had kept this love close, for easy enough it was to hide, since who would be so bold as to deem he loved his uncle's dame? The lady on her side had given her love to a lord of whom much good was spoken; but Mordred was of her husband's kin! This made the shame more shameworthy. Ah, God, the deep wrong done in this season by Mordred and the queen [Wace and Layamon 79].

Lancelot, a creation of romance, does not appear, and the dishonor of the court is created by the liaison between Mordred and Guinevere. Wace does not name Mordred's mother, except to say that she is the King's sister. Layamon, however, says that Walwain or Gawain, King Loth's eldest son, is Mordred's brother. This makes Morgawse his mother (Wace and Layamon 214–215, 260). Malory picks up this part of the genealogy and makes Morgawse Mordred's mother by her brother, Arthur.

By the time that films began to be made, the focus of Arthur's incest has shifted from Morgawse to Morgan. Directors have developed several ways to deal with this troubling subject. They can remove it to the background, as Thorpe does in his *Knights of the Round Table*, where Mordred is Morgan's "champion," implying that he fights her battles since, as a woman, she cannot fight her own. They can name Mordred's mother but not explain that she is Arthur's sister, as in *Camelot* (1967). They can ignore it altogether, as in the satirical *Monty Python and the Holy Grail* (1975). They can make Morgan a man and thus eliminate the possibility of incest, as in George Romero's *Knightriders* (1981). And they can meet the challenge head-on, as Boorman does in *Excalibur*.

The dates of these films are important. Given the cultural and political climate of 1953, a director could not deal honestly with a source that included incest, especially with a subject of such popular interest as King Arthur and the Round Table. Richard Thorpe, however, states the issues at the very beginning of *Knights of the Round Table*. Morgan demands the kingdom because she is the rightful heir and Arthur is not, given that, technically, he is a bastard by birth. The issues are clearly drawn. Arthur has to prove that he is the heir by drawing the sword out of the stone twice. The great battle of Badon Hill, by which in the chronicles Arthur establishes peace in the kingdom, is fought at the beginning of the film also, but it is a battle demanded by Mordred. Arthur defeats him and accepts his allegiance, so Mordred lives to sow dissension in the kingdom and indeed becomes Morgan's champion as he carries out her schemes. She is determined to expose Lancelot's love for Guinevere, and thus she is at the very heart of the film.

The development of the plot hinges on her machinations. To escape Morgan, Lancelot leaves the court to fight the Picts. He marries Elaine to save the Queen's honor and moves with her to the Scottish border. But Elaine dies in childbirth; Mordred encourages the Picts to sue for peace because peace would force Lancelot back to Camelot, back to Guinevere, and back into Morgan's power. Merlin is against the plan, but Morgan kills him in his cell. Peace is declared, and Lancelot returns to court. Knowing that he is in danger, Lancelot avoids Guinevere, but she visits him at night, and they are discovered. Arthur sends Guinevere to a convent and banishes Lancelot. Morgan and Mordred declare war, which brings about the destruction of the kingdom and Arthur's death. Lancelot returns to fight for the King and kills Mordred. Mordred's parentage is never revealed.

The film is singularly devoid of magic. Morgan is not Merlin's apprentice, nor a sorceress. Merlin performs no magic. The only supernatural occurrence is the vision of the Grail, near the end of the film.

The musical *Camelot*, based on T. H. White's *The Once and Future King* (1939), also ignores the incest theme. White follows Malory in making Morgawse, Arthur's elder sister, Mordred's mother, and he repeats Malory's statement that Arthur did not know that Morgawse was his sister when he accepted her invitation to share her bed. (We must remember also that Oedipus did not know that Jocasta was his mother when he married her, but ignorance of the true relationship does not make the deed incestuous.) Lerner and Loewe, the lyricist and composer of Camelot, follow White in making Morgawse Mordred's mother but do not state that she is Arthur's sister. Arthur accepts Mordred as his son when the youth arrives from Scotland and tries to change his character, but Mordred refuses to adopt Arthur's ideals. The destruction of Camelot follows through Mordred's machination.

Knightriders, released the same year as *Excalibur*, 1981, is an inversion of the Morgan story found in Malory. Here, Morgan is a man, and the knights are part of a motorcycle-stunt circus. The magic is the result of the stunts. Like Malory's Morgan, a woman of many lovers, Romero's leaves his faithful girlfriend to go off with different women, though he always returns to her. Morgan's ambition is at the heart of the film (his refrain is "I want to be king"), and no Mordred is necessary to fight for him since he is well able to fight for himself. In all the motorcycle tournaments, he defeats Billy (the king) decisively, yet Billy will not give up the rule of the group. Morgan leaves to form his own traveling show with some of the group, but he returns when the group falls apart because of internal battles. Billy finally yields to Morgan, and when he is killed by a truck on the highway, Morgan's rule becomes total and legitimate. Morgan in this film is thus a combination of Morgan le Fay and Mordred, and the incest theme is bypassed altogether.

Excalibur's credits tell us that the film is based on Malory's account (Kennedy 30–37). Malory mentions Morgan briefly in book I.2, where he tells us that Morgan le Fay is one of three daughters of Queen Igraine. The eldest, Morgawse, marries King Lot and is Gawain's mother; the second, Elaine, marries King Nentres; and the third, Morgan, is sent to a nunnery, where she learns necromancy, and afterward marries King Uriens of Gore. She next appears in Book IV.6–16, an extended episode that shows her hatred of the King. She sends a hart to lure Arthur, King Uriens, and Sir Accolon of Gaul, who have been hunting in a great forest. When their horses die of exhaustion, the men follow on foot until Arthur kills the hart. Suddenly, on the edge of a lake, a ship appears, and the three men board. Twelve fair damsels appear and entertain the King and his men until they fall into a deep sleep. They awake in separate cells of a dark prison, held by Morgan le Fay. Arthur is told by one of the ladies that he can deliver himself and the knights whose moans he hears by fighting a joust. He agrees and prepares for the contest. At the same time, a dwarf sent by Morgan delivers the same message to Sir Accolon. To ensure his victory, Morgan has sent him Excalibur, the King's sword, while sending Arthur only a copy of his sword. The joust goes ill for Arthur until he retrieves the real

Excalibur. Accolon's life is forfeit, but the combatants reveal themselves to each other, and Arthur forgives Accolon, who later dies of his wounds. Morgan is later able to steal Excalibur's scabbard. Arthur pursues her, but she turns herself and her knights into huge stones to escape. She again makes an attempt on his life through the gift of a poisoned robe.

Three things are emphasized in Malory's Book IV: Morgan hates Arthur, her half-brother; she is a shape-changer who can turn herself into stone if she so wishes; and she is determined to kill Arthur one way or another. The one thing Morgan does not do in Malory's version of the Arthurian story is seduce the King and bear him Mordred, a role filled by Morgan's sister Morgawse (Book I.19).

John Boorman's film is a variant of Malory's narrative. Boorman supplies his own motive for Morgana's actions, actions that are directed mostly against Merlin for his creation of Arthur and thus for depriving her of her rightful inheritance. Malory's Morgan also becomes Boorman's Morgana.

Boorman's film becomes a revenge tragedy, as Sara Boyle has argued (42–43). Boyle suggests that in *Excalibur* Merlin's plan to give the Britons the ideal king does not take Morgana into account. Morgana is helpless against the forces unleashed by Merlin, "a woman shaped by treachery, twisted at the root, and determined to wield power" (Boyle 43). We do not know her exact age when her father dies, but she appears to be about eight years old when Gorlois dies in battle with Uther Pendragon. Maureen Fries suggests that she is seven years old, the age of reason (Fries 76). She possesses second sight, and at the moment of her father's death, she cries out to her mother, "My father is dead." But almost immediately Uther in the form of Gorlois arrives, and Igraine says to Morgana: "No. See, your father is here." The child Morgana gives this "Gorlois" a knowing stare. She watches as Uther copulates with her mother, who cries out more in pain than in pleasure. When the real Gorlois is brought home dead, Morgana caresses his face, her own face expressionless as she seems to put the events together. When Arthur is born, Merlin appears to take him away, and Morgana asks him, "Are you the mother and the father of the baby now, Merlin?" Her question is merely rhetorical because she knows that Merlin is Arthur's creator. Igraine and Uther are only agents of his will.

Morgana's revenge is carefully planned. She next appears at Arthur's marriage to Guinevere. She leaves the ceremony to follow Merlin into the woods. In surprise, he asks her why she has left the wedding, and she replies, "I am a creature like you," and asks to be his pupil. The more Morgana learns from him, however, the more she wants to learn, and Merlin begins to fall in love with her.

The plan for revenge centers at first on the court, and particularly on Merlin. After returning to Arthur's court, where she sows dissension by revealing Lancelot's love for Guinevere, Morgana leaves for her cavern. She wants desperately to learn the "charm of making," the secret of creation, which Merlin possesses. He finally agrees to teach her, but he tells her, "Here is desire and regret, knowledge and oblivion, in the total knowledge including love and hate." He warns her that such knowledge would burn. "Then burn me," she replies. As he speaks the charm, she takes it from his lips and traps him in his own cave. "You fool," she exults. "You are trapped with the same sorcery you used to deceive my mother. You are nothing. You are not a man. I shall find a man and give birth to a god."

With these words, Morgana makes clear that her motives are threefold: to avenge her mother's rape by Uther Pendragon, to produce a god-king who will displace Arthur, and to achieve power. She

Helen Mirren as Morgana and Nicol Williamson as Merlin in John Boorman's 1981 film *Excalibur*.

puts a spell on Arthur and appears to him as Guinevere while she seduces him. Just as she snatches the charms of making from Merlin, she snatches Arthur's seed from him to create Mordred, Arthur's nemesis. In all these scenes, Morgana is the actor: she creates opportunities to work her will; she controls events more than Merlin does. But her power is used to destroy, not to create, as is illustrated most vividly by the Grail episode. Morgana sends the boy Mordred to lure the Grail knights to her castle, where she seduces them, then hangs them in trees for birds to pick out their eyes and the vultures to tear their flesh.

Arthur and his knights age throughout, but Morgana keeps her beauty. Nothing touches her, neither experience, nor emotion, nor events. She is an unearthly creature, and Merlin acknowledges her power when he returns from his cave. "You, madam, flow into a dream, a shadow — that comes and goes." He taunts her into speaking the charm of making, and as she speaks it, he takes it back, and her breath becomes a fog that clouds the battlefield as Mordred faces Arthur's army. Mordred comes to her tent before the battle and, terrified, strangles the hag who says she is his mother.

By suppressing the love affair of Lancelot and Guinevere as the main cause of the Round Table's fall, Boorman enhances Morgana's role as a destroyer. Indeed, he frames the story with Morgana's presence: at the beginning, she witnesses Uther's rape of her mother, which leads to Arthur's birth; she seduces Arthur precisely to create Mordred; she is present before the fatal battle, where Arthur and his kingdom perish; and in bringing down the kingdom, she destroys herself.

Boorman is not the first to project the figure of Morgan in some guise into a primary role in the Arthurian story. Morgan is also the instigator of the action in the fourteenth-century poem *Sir Gawain and the Green Knight*. Sheila Fisher (who cites the few scholarly articles devoted to Morgan's role in the poem) contends that despite her power Morgan is relegated to the margins of the poem, appearing as an old hag sitting at the highest place at table with the lady of the castle. The Lady is Morgan's agent in Gawain's testing, not her husband's, as the poem at first suggests (79–80). Both Morgan and the Lady are, therefore, dangerous to Gawain. Fisher argues: "Proprietor of her castle, generator of the contracts and exchanges forming the poem's plot, Morgan has the power to displace both Bishop Bawdewyn and Bertilak, ecclesiastical and secular authority. In her powers of displacement lies the danger the narrative needs to displace. For this poem's particular construction of female sexuality and subjectivity inscribes a threatening otherness that is not only, and perhaps not primarily, sexual" (80). It is this enormous power that Bertilak acknowledges to Gawain at the end of the poem:

I was entirely transformed and made terrible of hue
Through the might of Morgan le Fay, who remains in my house.
Through the wiles of her witchcraft, a lore well learned,
Many of the magical arts of Merlin has she acquired,
For once she lavished her love delightfully
On that susceptible sage, a sorcerer your knights know
        By name.
  So "Morgan the goddess"
  She accordingly became;
  The proudest she can oppress
  And to her purpose tame.
    [Fitt 4.XIX, Stone 122]

And yet, Fisher argues, this power, which displaces both chivalry and Christianity, is itself displaced, as the poem places Morgan in the margin. She continues: "Morgan's subsequent motivations ... become increasingly dubious and increasingly trivial, because they are represented as increasingly dissociated from the values intrinsic to feudal, Christian ideology" (95). The poem's ambivalence toward its first cause, Morgan, is evident in the outcome:

> The poem concludes by linking the green girdle with betrayal, and specifically with the betrayal generated by women. The green girdle stands, then, as a warning against women and the currency of their tokens and even of their tokenism within the court....
> ... For if Morgan could be effectively marginalized and if Guenevere could be reduced to permanent absence, the Round Table would not fall [99].

The theme that Fisher exposes in her discussion of *Sir Gawain and the Green Knight*, the marginalization of the power of women to bring down the carefully constructed kingdom of Camelot, Boorman confirms in his treatment of Morgana in his film. Morgana does not reside in the margins but in the center. She deliberately sets out to destroy Camelot and succeeds. But she does not escape. The internecine strife that she engenders with her conception of Mordred also causes her death. By emphasizing her power and her hatred, Boorman suggests that her death at Mordred's hands is deserved. She dies by what she has created. Boorman thus joins the tradition of antifeminist interpretations of *Sir Gawain and the Green Knight*, that women's power is to be feared because it produces only evil.

A secondary theme not fully developed but only hinted at in Morgana's seduction of Arthur is the theme of doubling, generally linked with the theme of incest. Morgana transforms herself into a likeness of Guinevere, Arthur's wife, when she enters his bedroom to seduce him. Why Guinevere specifically and not just another beautiful woman? The double usually denotes another side of the character for whom it is the double and suggests that certain qualities belonging to Guinevere may also be found in Morgana. The film implies that Morgana would like to change places with Guinevere in Arthur's bed, although Morgana is given no overt longing for or sexual fascination with Arthur. The seduction is the only scene in which Morgana doubles as Guinevere. Short and decisive, it adds another dimension to Morgana's character.

In discussing doubling and incest in the *Mabinogi*, Andrew Welsh writes: "A purely psychological view of doubling in literature, such as Otto Rank's, explains it in terms of 'projection': unwanted instincts and desires, rejected aspects of the inner life (of a character or of the author, depending on the critic's focus), are dissociated from the self and then personified in the outer world" (347–48). Welsh goes on to caution, however, that doubling in literature is not as simple as implied in Rank's explanation, a point explored in Welsh's discussion of the two Isoldes in the Tristan romance.

In *Excalibur*, Morgana's seduction of Arthur adds an unsuspected depth to the incest motif, something not found in any of the Arthurian legends, and is thus a decidedly post–Freudian addition, one that lends credence to Freud's statement that aberration is part of family romance. Arthur succumbs to Morgana's advances and is then horrified when she reveals her true self with a laugh as she leaves the room. Morgana is here a diabolical figure, powerful as the shape-shifter Malory describes, wholly focused on destroying her brother, Arthur, who has robbed her of her kingdom, because incest, as Welsh writes, "creates serious confusion in social structures." He continues:

> Incest is not ... a sign of familial unity or social vitality in *Oedipus Rex*, *Paradise Lost*, *Wuthering Heights*, or *Absalom, Absalom!* but of complex conditions of familial and social crisis: irruptions into the social order of the destructive will, defiant irrationality, or individual self-absorption; and the denial or disintegration of communal roles, duties, and bonds; or catastrophic intrusions into the world of nature and mankind by metaphysical evil or perverse fate [357–58].

Morgana's cold-blooded seduction of Arthur, involving no buildup of conflicting emotions or psychological torment, may be viewed as one of "irruptions" into the social order of Camelot, a defiant will to power through the son she would conceive and bear. The film makes it clear from the beginning that Morgana is older than Arthur but that a son would inherit Uther Pendragon's kingdom. Were there no Arthur, Morgana would still be near to power through the husband chosen for her by her parents. With Arthur's birth, she loses any hope of even the appearance of wielding power. Arthur is an intruder sired by magic.

Maureen Fries has suggested that Lacan's theory of the gaze may be applied to Boorman's presentation of Morgana in this film. At the film's beginning, Morgana witnesses Uther's rape of her mother, and what she sees determines her later actions. Fries makes the point that, at the end of the film, Merlin is Morgana's destroyer, just as at the beginning he is Arthur's creator. The scene in which Merlin reclaims the charm of making that Morgana had stolen from him in a previous encounter is the pivotal scene in this interpretation. As Fries points out, Lacan's theory was "initalliy applied to his concept of the mirror stage in child development," and Fries defines that theory as "what emanates from [the object viewed] capturing the viewer" (75). Fries argues that this theory of the gaze is particularly pertinent to this scene of Merlin's recapturing of his charm which, it appears, has kept Morgana "looking" young because Morgana "is in command of the deceitful possibilities of sight by the Other" (78). Mordred's strangling of Morgana now forms "a distorted mirror of [the film's] beginning, by the bedside of a woman besieged by an aggressive male." Fries concludes that by fully "using the technique of the gaze Boorman has restored Morgan le Fay fully to Arthurian history" (79).

Excalibur's feminist subtext emerges as readers and viewers ponder its meanings. Men cannot deny women their rightful inheritances and expect the world to live happily ever after. *Excalibur* makes a point Boorman may not have intended in depicting Arthur's creation so specifically as Merlin's attempt to provide a good king for the Britons, to the exclusion of Morgana. Music from Wagner's *Götterdammerung* is used in the film to herald the end of one kind of world, the world of many gods, as Merlin calls it, but does not hint at what kind of new world will eventually emerge. The unintended point is that a world created upon a deliberate exclusion of a rightful claimant is just as doomed as the world it is intended to replace. Lerner and Loewe's *Camelot*, not brave enough to face the incest motif, places the blame for the destruction of the kingdom on Mordred as an embodiment of evil, as he taunts the King: "Kill the Queen or kill the Kingdom." *Excalibur* suggests a tantalizing paradox: that Camelot cannot stand, despite the power of the ideal king, because the seeds of its destruction have been sown at the beginning, when Arthur is only an idea of Merlin's, created to save the social order, which is nevertheless doomed by his birth.

The meddler with destiny in the latest film version of the Arthurian story, Turner Network Television's *The Mists of Avalon*, is Viviane, the Lady of the Lake. The 2001 telefilm is based on Marion Zimmer Bradley's 1982 novel of the same title. Viviane, like Merlin, seeks to create a hero who will free Britain from the Saxons' continuous ravages. Merlin's role, so essential in the Arthurian canon, is here given to Viviane. Since Bradley's novel is a feminist retelling, Morgaine, the main character, is presented sympathetically. She does have the sight and knows that her father Gorlois is dead; she recognizes the dragon tattooed on Uther Pendragon's hand when he comes to her castle, and almost immediately after she tells Igraine, "My father is dead," the men bring Gorlois's body into the forecourt.

Uli Edel, the telefilm's director, follows Bradley's conception of the incest at the heart of the story. Bradley locates the incest episode in the myth of the Great Marriage, in which the hunter who kills the stag mates with the young priestess. In this case, the successful hunter is Arthur, who is then brought to the cave in which Morgaine waits for the mating. Each young person is heavily masked so that each does not know the identity of the other participant. In this way, Viviane hopes to create a successor to Arthur who will continue to keep the Saxons at bay. At the end of the telefilm, Mordred joins the Saxons, and in the final battle, Arthur kills him. The focus is, however, on Morgaine, who loves her brother and does not seek his destruction. When she discovers she is carrying Arthur's child, she is determined to drink the potion Morgause has prepared when Viviane intervenes. Out of anger with Viviane, she decides to bear the child, but to allow Morgause to bring him up. And that decision is the basis for all the trouble that will ensue. Morgause is determined to have power; she boasts that through her magic Guinevere is barren. Arthur will have no heir except Mordred, whom she will educate to hate his father.

The machinations within the family give this version of the Arthurian story a more complicated context with which to understand the fall of Camelot. The brother-sister incest is not a deliberate act on Morgaine's part, but a manipulation of the High Priestess of Avalon to bend events to her will. Following the traditions of Western tragedy as first laid out by the Greek dramatists of the fifth century before

From left to right, Joan Allen as Morgause, Julianna Margulies as Morgaine, and Anjelica Huston as Viviane, the Lady of the Lake, in Uli Edel's 2001 mini-series *The Mists of Avalon*. (Still courtesy of Turner Network Television.)

our time, this sort of manipulation is bound to backfire.

In her novel, Bradley reclaims the original Morgan of Geoffrey of Monmouth's *Vita Merlini*, the Morgan who receives the king with honor. As mentioned above, the early versions of the story do not include a motif of brother-sister incest. Malory's invention of the incest with Morgause, who does not know that the young man she has invited to her bed is her brother, itself captures the filmmaker's imagination, which transforms Morgause into Morgan. Malory's accidental incest becomes deliberate incest in Boorman's film, which becomes in turn sacred incest in the rites of the goddess in Bradley-Edel. In this recension, the attempt to control and order events, using the same means of incest, destroys the very ideals this attempt is intended to nurture. So, although the motivations in Malory's version and Bradley's version differ, the result is the same. Contrary to Boorman's exposition in *Excalibur*, where women are denied their rights, Bradley-Udel's feminist reading shows that, even when women exercise their rights, discernment and judgment need to be exercised, or disaster will result.

WORKS CITED

Boyle, Sara. "From Victim to Avenger: The Women in John Boorman's *Excalibur*." *Avalon to Camelot* 1 (Summer 1984): 42–43.

Bradley, Marion Zimmer. *The Mists of Avalon*. New York: Knopf, 1982.

Fisher, Sheila. "Taken Men and Token Women in *Sir Gawain and the Green Knight*." In Sheila Fisher and Janet E. Halley, eds. *Seeking the Woman in Late Medieval and Renaissance Writings*. Knoxville: University of Tennessee Press, 1989.

Fries, Maureen. "How to Handle a Woman, or Morgan at the Movies." In Kevin J. Harty, ed. *King Arthur on Film: New Essays on Arthurian Cinema*. Jefferson, N.C.: McFarland, 1999.

Geoffrey of Monmouth. *The History of the Kings of Britain*. Trans. Lewis Thorp. Harmondsworth: Penguin, 1966.

Jarman, A. O. H., ed. and trans. *Geoffrey of Monmouth*. Cardiff: Wales, 1966.

Kennedy, Harlan. "The World of King Arthur According to John Boorman." *American Film* 6 (March 1981): 30–37.

Malory, Sir Thomas. *Le Morte d'Arthur*. ed. Janet Cowen. 2 vols. Harmondsworth: Penguin, 1969.

Sir Gawain and the Green Knight. Ed. and trans. Brian Stone. Harmondsworth: Penguin, 1959.

Wace and Layamon. *Arthurian Chronicles*. Trans. Eugene Mason. 1912. New York: Dutton, 1962.

Welsh, Andrew. "Doubling and Incest in the *Mabinogi*." *Speculum* 65 (April 1990): 344–62.

White, T. H. *The Once and Future King*. 1958. New York: Putnam, 1965.

5

An Enemy in Our Midst: The Black Knight and the American Dream

ALAN LUPACK

Of the many film versions of the matter of Britain, one of the most unusual is the 1954 production *The Black Knight*. Other Arthurian movies generally have a firm foundation in traditional stories, even when they alter and reshape those stories fairly radically. *Lancelot and Guinevere*, for instance, deals with the love affair that Malory and others make central to the downfall of Arthur's kingdom, even though the movie allows itself cinematic license in the treatment of that love. *Sword of the Valiant* is a modern retelling of *Sir Gawain and the Green Knight*, although it takes its hero into realms of which the medieval author did not conceive. *Camelot* is consciously based on T. H. White's *The Once and Future King*. Rohmer's *Perceval* takes its inspiration from Chrétien de Troyes. And the 1949 version of *A Connecticut Yankee in King Arthur's Court*, directed by Tay Garnett, who also directed *The Black Knight*, is obviously rooted in Twain's novel, even if Bing Crosby as Hank Morgan is more crooner than crusader.

While these films contain elements or episodes that are unknown to medieval legend, all of them appear familiar to anyone versed in Arthurian tradition. Garnett's *The Black Knight*, however, hardly seems cut from the same cloth. Though Arthur and his knights reside at Camelot and gather around the Round Table and some familiar characters appear, there is little else in this film that is traditional. Certainly, there is no medieval or modern version of the story that one could point to as a source or even an analogue. As the review in the *Monthly Film Bulletin* observed, "The film is gleefully disrespectful of history and tradition...." (147).

Even the hero of *The Black Knight* is unlike the usual hero of Arthurian romance. The film is the story of John, a blacksmith in the service of the Earl of Yeonil. John loves the earl's daughter Linet but is told by the earl that no relationship can develop between him and Linet because of the difference in their stations. The threat to John's personal happiness is paralleled by a threat to Camelot. John learns that Palamides and his Saracens, who are in league with King Mark's Cornishmen in a plot to take over Arthur's kingdom, have been masquerading as Viking raiders to create panic and instability in Britain. In order to prove his accusation of treason against Palamides, John must acquire the skills of a knight and adopt a secret identity as the Black Knight. Ultimately, through his ability and with a sword he made with his own hands, John saves both the woman he loves and the kingdom from the foreign threat. As a result, he is knighted and is granted the hand of Lady Linet in marriage.

Arthurian romance — and medieval romance in general — abounds with examples of men and women who initially perform menial tasks but who turn out in the end to be noble. However, these characters, like Malory's Sir Gareth, who works in Kay's kitchen, are noble by birth, and the normal pattern of a romance is a revelation of that nobility rather than an actual change in station. (The only example of a commoner's rising to knighthood that comes to mind is in the non–Arthurian poem *Rauf Coilyear*, in which a collier gives shelter to Charlemagne on a cruelly stormy night and is later rewarded with knighthood.)

The unprecedented plot of *The Black Knight* is clearly something other than the kind of spectacular cinematic adaptation of Arthurian material that took place a year before its release in another Arthurian film, *Knights of the Round Table*. Though there is no dearth of spectacle in *The Black Knight*, that particular spectacle is very strange spectacle indeed in an Arthurian context. A routing of pagans about to sacrifice Christians at Stonehenge, the defeat of Saracens attacking Camelot — what have these to do with Arthur? Or even with each other? As the *New York Times* review noted, "One wonders how Saracens happened to be in England when ritual sacrifices were being made at Stonehenge or at Camelot, for that matter" (27). The reviewer for *Commonweal* made a similar observation: "I could never quite figure out what the Saracens were doing in olde England; but there are many other odd things in this movie including a wild bacchanal at Stonehenge that had me baffled" (188). Either such unusual elements as these and the rise of a blacksmith to knighthood and nobility must be considered a hodgepodge of absurdities, or some justification or at least explanation must be offered for linking them in an Arthurian movie. The explanation seems to be that director Tay Garnett was creating a thoroughly Americanized version of the Arthurian legends, a version that reflects perennial American values and ideals as well as specific American concerns of the 1950s.

Though *The Black Knight* was produced by Warwick, a British company, Garnett, the director, and Alec Coppel, the screenwriter, were both Americans, as was the star, Alan Ladd. The basic story they combine to create has been common in American literature ever since Benjamin Franklin wrote about his rise from poverty to power. Having arrived in Philadelphia with almost no money, Franklin tells us in his *Autobiography*, he reached a point, through industry and ingenuity, where he met with kings and even sat down to dinner with one. This was and still is for many the American Dream.

In *The Black Knight*, that dream is realized by John the blacksmith. In fact, from beginning to end, the film's plot focuses the viewer's attention on his rise. Even the opening sequence wherein a minstrel sings a song to a ballad tune defines the protagonist's task. The words of the song do not tell the traditional ballad tale of death or tragic love. Rather, they are about a brave young man who must earn the right to be a knight and win his lady.

The question of John's station is central throughout the movie. When he tells Linet, played by Patricia Medina, that their love is impossible because "You're the earl's daughter," she responds, "That doesn't make me any better than you are. A birthright's an accident, nothing more." Of course, the plot demands an obstacle to their love. The earl, who does not share his daughter's democratic views, dismisses the blacksmith from his service.

Thus far, the plot is fairly standard stuff, but what follows is far less predictable. John is comforted by the earl's friend Sir Ontzlake, who says to him, "You made spurs here; apply them to yourself. You have ambition; fashion it like a suit of armor." While the earl's reaction is just what might be expected in a hierarchic society, Sir Ontzlake's could only come from someone who believes that ability and hard work are more important than inherited titles or the trappings of knighthood. And the notion that ambition can become the "armor" that John needs to prove himself worthy of a noblewoman is reminiscent of another American author who saw knighthood as something symbolic rather than as a literal condition of birth or wealth. In *The Story of King Arthur and His Knights*, Howard Pyle, after telling of Arthur's drawing the sword from the stone, writes, "Thus Arthur achieved the adventure of the sword that day and entered into his birthright of royalty. Wherefore, may God grant His Grace unto you all that ye too may likewise succeed in your undertakings. For any man may be a king in that life in which he is placed if so be he may draw forth the sword of success from out of the iron of circumstance" (35).

I am not suggesting a borrowing from Pyle, but it does seem clear that *The Black Knight*, with its armor of ambition, is in the same tradition as Pyle's sword of success. The symbolic nature of the knight's equipment extends even further in Garnett's film. After the minstrel's song, which precedes the opening credits, and a brief scene showing a column of knights riding to a castle, the setting shifts to the blacksmith's forge where John is fashioning a sword that he intends to give to the Earl of Yeonil. The viewer sees various stages in the production of the sword until, at last, a fine weapon is raised with pride by its fashioner.

This emphasis on the making of the sword seems strange at first. Should not an Arthurian tale tell how a sword is used rather than how it is made? But in actuality the way John obtains his sword is as important as the way Arthur receives his in more traditional versions of the matter of Britain. Because of his dismissal from the earl's service, the gift is never given to the one for whom it is intended. But Sir Ontzlake, who has seen a demonstration of the quality and keenness of the sword, tells John, "You made it with your own hands. Now let it make you." The sword wrought by John's industry and skill becomes symbolic of those qualities. The fact that he made it indicates that he will be a self-made man. As Ontzlake advises him, "Knighthood is a flower to be plucked." While such a statement could not have been made when knighthood was in flower, it is a clear indication that the Arthurian legend has been translated into a different mythical realm. This is no sword destined for a hero by a fairy power; it is one the hero must hammer and temper and sweat over. As he shapes the sword, he shapes his destiny.

Ontzlake's training of John is depicted in a series of short scenes showing the two practicing with lance, sword, knife, and then lance again. The collage effect parallels that of the scenes of the making of the sword and once again suggests the industry and hard work of the future knight. The viewer sees how, with practice, the foolish mistakes of the beginner are corrected and ultimately the skill of the accomplished knight is acquired.

Sir Ontzlake himself is important to the thematic statement of the movie. He not only becomes an adviser and a teacher for John but is also an example of what can be achieved. Though now a knight of the Round Table, he was, as he tells John, "not always a knight. Some are born to it; I was not." After teaching John about the possibilities of life, he helps him learn how to use a sword to save Arthur's kingdom.

The choice of Ontzlake's name may be an intentional allusion to Malory. In Caxton's edition of Malory (but not in the Winchester manuscript, where the name is Outlake or some variation thereof), Ontzlake is the name of the knight in the Arthur and Accolon episode whose patrimony has been taken from him by his brother Damas. Though the character of Ontzlake and his role are very different in *Le Morte d'Arthur*, the name does seem appropriate to the person who teaches John to use the sword fashioned with his own hands. Damas will give him none of his inheritance except what "Ontzlake kepeth thorow prowesse of his handes" (Malory I:127). But whereas Ontzlake achieves justice only when Arthur defeats Damas's champion, Accolon, and gives Ontzlake his due, in *The Black Knight* Arthur's lands must be saved for him by John with Ontzlake's assistance.

If this analysis is correct, John embodies the American Dream. Perhaps this explains the lack of any attempt to make him act like a British knight. Though many of the cast members are British and speak with decidedly British accents, Ladd does not even try to sound as if he comes from anywhere outside the United States. The reviewer for *Time* comments, "Nor kann this knight e'en parler ye Englysshe langue, bot muttereth mayhappe in Frensshe, as, 'Yagottalissena me. Englans gonnabeen vaded'" (110).

A striking visual image that marks John as the American hero is the heraldic device he wears: an eagle with wings spread wide, or "displayed." This is the same position in which the American eagle is portrayed, as on the dollar bill. It is not, of course, the American eagle; but it might well pass for a medievalized version. And, interestingly, John wears the eagle, as a medallion, even before he adopts the identity of the Black Knight. The suggestion is therefore that those qualities that make John a worthy knight were inherent in him before he received training from Sir Ontzlake. As in the popular notion of the American Dream, his native ability rather than any advantage of birth leads to his success.

In the end, John does achieve what he desires when he is rewarded for his service with knighthood and Lady Linet. Thus, he completes the rags-to-riches pattern. That this is not a fanciful interpretation is confirmed by a statement made by the director in his autobiography: "Fundamentally, the plot was one of those bootblack-to-President things. Alan, as a kid, worked in a blacksmith's shop, hammering out armor. With diligence, courage, and lots of help from Coppel's script, he worked his way up to a fiery sword" (Garnett 286).

But more is going on in *The Black Knight* than a simple rags-to-riches or "bootblack-to-President" story. If John is symbolically representative of American values, there is a threat to those values, indeed to the stability of Arthur's kingdom. The danger comes from a foreign invader, from treason within, and from an attack on Christianity. Given this combination and the mood of America in the fifties, it seems plausible that the threat to Camelot may be seen as a thinly disguised allegory of what was perceived at the time as the Communist threat to America.

Though not directly relevant to my thesis, it is interesting that, on the same page of the 27 November 1954 edition of *America* on which a brief review of *The Black Knight* appears, there is also an advertisement for a book called *America Faces World Communism* (259). The advertisement quotes a general who says the book "Presents ... the methods of the greatest conspiracy against mankind that history records." Another endorsement in the advertisement says that the author "sees clearly the Communist threat and helps his readers to see its magnitude."

Ironically, it is Palamides in the film who says, "Certainly there is an enemy in our midst." Actually, there are two. Palamides himself is the representative of the foreign power, the Saracens, who are in league with one of Arthur's own subjects,

Alan Ladd in the title role in Tay Garnett's 1954 film *The Black Knight*.

King Mark. The danger is all the greater because those who would defend Arthur's kingdom are "looking across the sea."

John is the first to recognize the nature of the threat. When the Earl of Yeonil's castle is sacked and burned, he follows one of the pillagers, Palamides' servant Bernard, to Camelot. But since the raiders were disguised as Vikings, he is not believed and is under sentence of death unless he can prove his accusation. Ontzlake later recognizes the magnitude of the danger and tells John that "there is treason all about us and it must be stamped out before all of us — you and I and King Arthur himself — are overwhelmed."

Perhaps most prominent in this context is the threat to Christianity. In fact, much of the movie is devoted to documenting this threat. As Nora Sayre has pointed out in her book on the cold-war films of the fifties, Churchill defined Communism as a "peril to Christian civilization" and many clergymen preached that "the Communists were going to destroy Christianity and morality" (10–11).

The Black Knight depicts the forces seeking to undermine Arthur's rule as such a threat to Christian civilization. There is none of the religious ambiguity about Arthur's realm that is sometimes found in Arthurian story. The kingdom is undoubtedly Christian. Early in the movie, when Sir Hal is being knighted, he must vow to be in all things a Christian gentleman. John, like his father before him, proves himself a supporter of the church. His father had made a cross of peace, formed from the weapons thrown down by defeated invaders. John gives the cross to the local abbot, who tells him that he, like his father, is a good Christian.

In contrast, the hostile forces are intent on destroying Christianity. When the raiders masquerading as Vikings attack and burn the abbey, one of them rips a cross from around the neck of a monk, looks at it scornfully, then spits on it before hurling it to the ground. Coming shortly after John has given the cross to the abbot, this scene puts John in opposition to these pagans. After setting fire to the abbey, Mark and Palamides' minions line up many of the monks to be executed, as Palamides asks with a wry smile, "Are Christians invincible against arrows?"

Mark, the other enemy within, is worse than his accomplice. He is, as we are told, "a baptized Christian king." But this is only "to deceive Arthur." Actually, he believes that "there's danger in this Christianity," a statement that almost parallels Marx's well-known statement that "religion is the opiate of the masses." In this context, it would be difficult to present a character who espouses atheism, but Mark is an advocate of what is depicted as a particularly debauched style of paganism. He wants the high priest at Stonehenge to be the religious leader of Britain.

Just what that would mean is demonstrated by a fascinating scene set among Stonehenge's megaliths. The abbot and some of his monks have been brought to Stonehenge along with Lady Linet, all of whom are to be sacrificed to the sun god in a pagan ritual. There is heavy drinking and much of what passed in the fifties for sensuous dancing. Of course, the Black Knight arrives just in time to save Linet from the descending sacrificial sword and to free the monks from the cages in which they are suspended and under which fires have been lit. He is followed by Arthur and his knights, who disperse the pagans and, at the King's command, topple the megaliths as a sign of "heaven's wrath against the evil practiced here."

The cliché of the last-minute rescue of the damsel in distress is repeated when Linet is saved from the other enemy within. She has been taken to Palamides' castle so that she can be questioned about the Black Knight. The Saracen turns her over to his servant Bernard so he can "persuade her to talk." In this scene, the servant clearly represents a foreign threat. Bare-chested and dark-featured, he is willing, even delighted, to torture the heroine.

Aside from the features of Bernard and Palamides, also dark and foreign-looking, there are other striking visual representations of the Saracens' foreignness and of the danger they embody. In the room in Palamides' castle where Linet is held captive and then rescued, there is a mural in the background depicting a Satanic figure, a sort of demonic hell-mouth, which marks the villains as more than believers in a different religion; it shows them to be agents of the devil.

Given the importance of the sword in the symbolic framework of the movie, it seems quite significant that Palamides does not have a broadsword of the type forged by John. Rather, he wields a scimitar. The alien sword marks him as a character at odds with the good and true knights of Arthur's court. But even without such a marker, Palamides must be looked on with some suspicion. He is traditionally Tristan's rival in love for Isolde. Never quite able to win her or to best Tristan in any way, he has moments of weakness but generally remains noble and, in Malory, is converted in the end. The treacherous, scheming, deceitful, and haughty Palamides of *The Black Knight* is quite a different person. And his failings are emphasized by being divorced from the courtly love context of medieval romance. The best of knights can be driven to temporary insanity by unrequited love, but without his passion for Isolde (a character who does not appear in the film) to mitigate or at least explain his actions, Palamides appears to practice evil for its own sake. He becomes a figure as satanic as the mural in his castle suggests.

One other visual symbol has unavoidable significance. In the mass assault by the Saracens at the end of the movie, all of the attackers wear red tunics, making them almost literally a "red horde." Since John's intelligence-gathering has resulted in the nullification of the Cornish threat, the attackers are left without their allies. This allows for a fairly easy victory by the forces from Camelot and leads to John's knighting because he has saved the kingdom.

The mood of the country and of much of Hollywood in particular in the fifties had a tremendous influence on the types of films made. It has become a commonplace of film criticism that movies like *Invasion of the Body Snatchers* (made just two years after

The Black Knight) and other science-fiction films that describe a threat to humanity are allegories for the dangers of Communism. As Peter Biskind has observed, "It has long been evident, in fact from the moment the first blob oozed its way across the screen, that the little green men from Mars stood in the popular imagination for the clever red men from Moscow. The media portrayed Russians in such lurid fashion that the connection was inevitable, even if unintended by writers and directors" (185).

A similar dynamic seems to be at work in *The Black Knight*. The threat is not from an alien planet but from an alien nation and an alien philosophy. There is surely the kind of "Us/Them" framework that Biskind defines, in which "that which threatened consensus was simply derogated as 'Other.'" And, as he goes on to say, "The Other was indeed communism" (186). The dark and treacherous Saracens and the pagan religion of the Cornishmen are as great a danger to Western civilization as the pods of *Invasion of the Body Snatchers*. When *The Black Knight* is seen as an allegory for the triumph of American values over a Communist threat, the strange and untraditional elements make perfect sense. Forming a familiar pattern, they mark *The Black Knight* as a work in the tradition of Lowell's *Vision of Sir Launfal* and Twain's *A Connecticut Yankee in King Arthur's Court*. Like them, the film departs radically from standard Arthurian story in order to create a tale that is thoroughly a product of its time and thoroughly American.

WORKS CITED

Biskind, Peter. "Pods, Blobs, and Ideology in American Films of the Fifties." In Al LaValley, ed. *Invasion of the Body Snatchers.* New Brunswick, N.J.: Rutgers University Press, 1989.

Garnett, Tay, and Fredda Dudley Balling. *Light Your Torches and Pull Up Your Tights.* New Rochelle, N.Y.: Arlington House, 1973.

"The Jones Girl and the Alan Lad." *Commonweal* 61 (19 November 1954): 188–89.

Malory, Sir Thomas. *Le Morte d'Arthur: The Original Edition of William Caxton.* Ed. H. Oskar Sommer. 4 vols. London: Nutt, 1889.

Pyle, Howard. *The Story of King Arthur and His Knights.* New York: Scribner, 1905.

Review of *The Black Knight. Monthly Film Bulletin* 21 (October 1954): 147.

Review of *The Black Knight. Time* 64 (8 November 1954): 110.

Sayre, Nora. *Running Time: Films of the Cold War.* New York: Dial, 1982.

W., A. "'The Black Knight' Wins His Spurs at Globe." *New York Times* 29 October 1954: 27.

6

Tortilla Flat *and the Arthurian View*

John Christopher Kleis

To consider the importance of an Arthurian component in John Steinbeck's 1935 novel *Tortilla Flat* is to entertain a number of issues. The first is whether there *is* an Arthurian element. Others are the ways in which the myth has been used in American literature, the puzzle of why Steinbeck's brand of left-wing thinking has so appealed to American middle-class readers, and the question of why critics sometimes believe anything they read. The 1942 film version,[1] devoid of any explicit traces of the myth, gives additional pause. As usual, Hollywood was ready to subordinate Arthurian associations to conventional bourgeois ideals.

Steinbeck invites such speculation. In a Preface added later to the novel (Lupack and Lupack 191), he sets forth the parallel:

> For Danny's house was not unlike the Round Table, and Danny's friends were not unlike the knights of it. And this is the story of how that group came into being, of how it flourished and grew to be an organization beautiful and wise. This story deals with the adventuring of Danny's friends, with the good they did, with their thoughts and their endeavors. In the end, this story tells of how the talisman was lost and how the group disintegrated [1].

Steinbeck explicitly connects this myth with male bonding ("a unit in which the parts are men") and the "Mystic sorrow" associated with the end (indeed with the whole) of the Arthur story. A page later, he places the story and its connotations in direct contrast with American life in 1935: "The paisanos are clean of commercialism, free of the complicated systems of American business, and, having nothing that can be stolen, exploited, or mortgaged, that system has not attacked them very vigorously" (2).

Steinbeck also uses chapter headings that are reminiscent of Malory and Caxton (Fontenrose 24–25; Lupack and Lupack 191). At first, critics took Steinbeck at his word, but even granting the leeway that the ambiguous "not unlike" construction allows, it is difficult to identify exactly what Arthurian parallels there are. Is the Arthur figure Danny or Pilon? What is the talisman — Danny's houses, the watch he inherits from his grandfather, the St. Francis candlestick? Which episodes in the novel parallel incidents in Malory? There is no agreement on any of these points. As early as 1957, W. M. Frohock was suspicious: "[Steinbeck] is the only person ... who affirmed that the [Arthur-based] unity was there" (130). Fontenrose made the first serious attempt at tracing literal parallels, and the Lupacks and Owens make the most convincing cases. But many of the later commentators have been much more cautious. At the same time that the whole proposition has become more and more dubious, more convoluted and questionable attempts have been made to sustain it.

In the second edition of his Twayne study, Warren French withdraws most of the speculations about the Arthurian parallels in *Tortilla Flat* that he made in the first edition (71), although his vagueness about what he would keep and what he would reject is eloquent testimony to how hard it is to dislodge critical truisms once they have been enshrined. Critics sometimes believe anything they read: in his first stab at this effort ("Arthurian Cycle"), Arthur Kinney starts out by making all sorts of claims, but has to abandon the attempt in the end, where he starts making a brand-new case for the novel as a "mock-epic" treatment of the legend (20). Owens picks up on the reference to the death of Arthur Morales (*Flat* 9), and makes a case for a "post–Arthurian" reading set in a fallen Californian Eden, where capitalism is corrupting the natural order of things. Danny is a Lancelot figure, "unable to move back into the freer, more natural past and unable to go forward into the economic structure of the present and future" (206).

As if this sort of grasping for parallels is not enough, Owens follows Kinney in another failed attempt to take on this topic ("Revisited" 12–13). Despite Steinbeck's specific stricture that the paisanos are a contrast to the bourgeois ethic, Kinney makes them "Capitalists at heart" (Owens 207). While they might in some respects be satirical versions of bourgeois capitalists (they are greedy and selfish), they lack most of the qualities of the type (they do not think in the long term; they have no highly articulated set of values). The Arthurian knights, on the other hand, distinctly do possess these latter qualities. Peter Lisca is more on the mark when he observes that the paisanos "temporarily accept" bourgeois conventions when it suits them (82). In any event, it is difficult to accept Owens' view of Danny as a tragic figure (206), or French's picture of the passive Danny as an "epic hero" or a "wild man," who "confronts civilization too long and tries to make it come to terms with him" (71–72). Danny may indeed succumb "to the responsibility of property" (Owens 168), but it is Pilon who makes Danny come to terms with him. French would like to make the novel a critique of the "hypocritical highmindedness" of "respectable Americans" (71), but we see almost nothing of this type of American — except as the paisanos' victims.

As a youthful writer, Steinbeck had personal reasons for evoking Arthur's knights. Throughout his life, and culminating in his last, unfinished work, *The Acts of King Arthur and His Noble Knights*, Steinbeck bore witness to how his childhood reading of the Arthurian stories (Malory via Caxton) formed his taste for reading, his interest in storytelling, his "sense of right and wrong" and "any thought [he] might have had against the oppressor and for the oppressed," not to mention (a nice touch of modesty here) for his "feeling of noblesse oblige" (xii), in his 1930s-style sympathy for the "little people" who are oppressed by the social order.

But the account of his work on *Acts* twenty-five years later "despite discouragement from publishers and friends who saw little value in the pursuit" (Kiernan 15) bears witness to a continuing uncertainty about what the Arthurian stories might mean,[2] an uncertainty that is evident in *Tortilla Flat*. It is hard to see how his interest in Arthur jibes in most ways with the content of the novel. Pilon, Danny, and the paisanos who cluster around them barely — with one exception, their brief encounter with the Pirate — exemplify a social conscience at all. At best, they are a bunch of alcoholics whose prime concern is pulling various scams in order to get food, drink, sex, and other necessities without working for them. For all their creator's assertions, their group hardly seems an "organization" at all, let alone one that is "beautiful and wise." Just as surely as they are not oppressed by the capitalist system, they seem short on real "sweetness and joy" or "philanthropy" and on the capacity for "mystic sorrow" (a quality not to be confused with self-pity, a quality they do possess).

In any event, Arthur does not go down to destruction because his mission has been taken away, let alone been fulfilled. He goes down trying to rescue it, with dignity. Danny, on the other hand, dies in alcohol-induced despair over the emptiness of his life. At the end of Malory, we sense the end of something basically good (despite the imperfections of the participants); at the end of Steinbeck's novel, we sense in Danny's fate the end of something childish (not childlike, as Steinbeck probably intended) and morally bankrupt.

What the group mostly does do is indulge itself in a series of highjinks that are characteristic of American Arthurian treatments best known in the work of Twain.[3] Steinbeck's Camelot is the boy's-book Camelot, albeit with grown-up elements such as alcohol and sex. Its themes — male bonding, adventure, and the inhibiting effect of institutionalism — are, to be sure, characteristics of the Arthurian myth, but here they are presented without any serious underpinnings. Women in this world are threatening; social conscience is a meaningless concept that the outside (read adult) world wants to impose on them and that they are duty-bound to resist; practical joking (sometimes very cruel) is the central activity of life.

Pilon resembles Tom Sawyer and Merlin; Steinbeck's *Acts* is much more interested in the trickster Merlin than in Arthur, and Danny occupies the same secondary position here that Arthur does in *The Acts*. The sole exception to the group's irresponsibility is the aid that they give to the Pirate, but they see no qualitative difference between aiding the Pirate and their usual behavior. Their association with him begins as a scam, results in no real social value (let alone revolutionary value), and has no permanent effect on the paisanos' basic attitude toward life. One thinks of Huck Finn's conversion to racial enlightenment and his subsequent reversion to racism under the guidance of Tom Sawyer and the Connecticut Yankee's assumption that Arthur's Court is just a venue to show how "cool" he is.

According to Kiernan, "Steinbeck tended to remember his childhood in romantic, Tom Sawyer–like terms," even though it was not much like that (20). The Caxton-Malory volume young Steinbeck encountered was part of a series edited by Sidney Lanier (Prindle 26). Lanier was a contemporary of Twain's who shared a revulsion against the middle class values of his day and a predisposition to the alleged pastoral values of the pre–Civil War South. Twain presents Tom's childhood as a nostalgic Golden-Age alternative to the Gilded Age; it is likely that Lanier's very popular "Boy's Library of Legend and Chivalry" was intended — and accepted — in the same spirit. Prindle also points out that there was another medieval revival just as Steinbeck began writing and that it too was part of a reaction against contemporary mores (25). The same phenomenon is occurring today. There is a strong nostalgic component to this aspect of the story; the end of the youthful idyll is cause for great sorrow, as it often is in American myth.

The group more often resembles another pseudo-medieval boy's-book favorite, *Robin Hood's Merry Men*. This source has traditionally allowed for more horseplay and less social responsibility. But as an American Robin Hood tale, *Tortilla Flat* suffers (as it does in the Arthurian interpretation) from the typically American inability to acknowledge the more sophisticated social, economic, and moral issues (including morally ambiguous behavior) that English and European sources exploit. Mizener points out that Steinbeck draws heavily on the pastoral genre, another source that emphasizes eternal youth (*Sense* 20). The group also resembles the characters of the picaresque tale, with its emphasis on living by one's wits and "the delights of poverty and lawlessness" (Yarmus 82). Steinbeck later compared the Arthurian stories to the Western genre (*Acts*, Appendix 314), another boy's-book favorite. The paisanos resemble, however, more the Western's secondary comic characters, often ethnically stereotyped ones, of the Western than they do the main characters.[4]

The young Steinbeck may have also evoked Camelot because of his interest in Jungian archetypes (evident throughout his career), to give the appearance of unity to a bunch of sketches,[5] or to lift what is basically regionalism to a more universal level,[6] albeit one that smacks of adolescence.

In any event, it is hard to follow Steinbeck through the tonal and thematic melange that is *Tortilla Flat* with its uneasy mixture of high seriousness and low humor.[7] By hook or by crook, though, he did find a way to appeal to a lot of readers, especially male ones.[8] His message is often left-wing and anti-establishment — not one that middle-class readers would normally have any use for. But it is couched in terms so far removed from the real world of adult responsibility and so close to mainstream male conditioning that it becomes defanged and therefore tolerable.

The Film

In forging a screenplay from Steinbeck's novel, John Lee Mahin and Benjamin Glazer created an odd combination of slavish fidelity and almost complete thematic violation of Steinbeck's material.[9] The fidelity is perhaps a touching reminder that people used to read the book before they saw the film and expected to see what they knew. Absent is any sort of Arthurian reference, despite the fact that the film, like the novel, has a little preface ("a warmhearted people of laughter and kindness") that oversimplifies the moral issues we have seen. Present, however, are all the Arthurian boy's-book highjinks, hearty humor, obsessive self-serving of most of the characters most of the time, and emphasis on the mechanics of male bonding (including the implied homophobic caveats of such endeavors — Danny will share everything with his buddies except his bed). Even the episodes that are extremely episodic — the anecdote about the little boy who thrives on a diet of tortillas and beans and the story of the corporal and his son — are there,[10] even if their thematic value is altered significantly.

Some of that alteration is tonal. For instance, the Pirate episodes are swathed in religious soft-focus (including musical soft focus) in a way that sets them farther apart from the other doings of the characters than they are in the novel. But a larger change is substantive: the film's heart is in its endorsement of the bourgeois values of marriage and the economic life rather than in the free life that Steinbeck advocates. (Again, note the resemblance to *Camelot*.) In aesthetic terms then, the screenplay is an attempt to have it both ways: to preserve the episodic quality of the novel with its stress on the existential quality of the paisanos' life *and* to achieve unity of plot and theme. Visually, the film shifts back and forth between fairly realistic sets and mildly stylized ones; again, it is not quite sure what effect it wants to create.

The screenplay's fidelity to much of Steinbeck's detail caused many of the critics to overestimate the fidelity of the whole to the novel. For instance, while Scheer recognizes "the abandonment of the novel's loose and rambling structure," he still believes that changing Sweets from a "homely, simple-minded girl of easy virtue" into "an independent, intelligent, respectable woman" who wants conventional marriage does not "upset the intent or spirit" of the novel (34). It certainly makes her into less of the Guinevere figure that Olton sees her as (289). Crowther and Faber note that fear of the Hays Office resulted in the studio's reducing some of the paisanos' material and sexual exploitation of women, but the fact that some of the misogyny is suggested in the film (mostly on the level of chicken-stealing symbolism) bears witness to the film's ambivalence, not its fidelity.

Pilon (the Spencer Tracy character and Merlin parallel) does retain his substantial presence in the film. For the most part, he serves again as the exponent of boy's-book freedom, though in the end he serves also as the voice of conventional values. Two of the characters in the novel — Sweets and the Priest — have a much expanded presence that points toward the film's quite different outcome: Danny converts to the bourgeois values of work and marriage rather than dying in despair over the emptiness of the carefree life. The Priest and Sweets's neighbor both see Danny's new-found wealth as a qualification for marriageability, and Danny himself, in Garfield's performance, from the start seems prone to the possibility of deserting the carefree life; he and Lamarr do achieve some nice chemistry. Garfield made a name playing bad boys, but here, running to fat and sporting a goofy smile, he looks like a sitting duck for domestication, not in any way like French's "wild man."[11] The funniest scene in the novel — Danny's purchase of the vacuum cleaner as a gift to Sweets even though she has no electricity — therefore comes across in the film more as prefiguring Danny's future as a married man than as symbolizing his freedom from earthbound reality.

Mahin and Glazer manufacture a new, stronger central conflict in the movie — the plot becomes a series of hostile encounters between Sweets and Pilon. The prize is Danny's soul, and it is clear from the start that Sweets is going to win.

For one thing, from the start, Hedy Lamarr looks much more comfortable playing Sweets than Spencer Tracy does playing Pilon. Tracy's Irish eyes are positively bizarre looking out from beneath Jack Dawn's heavy, almost black-face, makeup, and the Spanglish dialogue gives him trouble. Millichap says he looks like he is still playing the Portuguese ship captain in his earlier hit *Captains Courageous*, also directed by Victor Fleming (66). On the other hand, Lamarr's heavier features look entirely appropriate to her Hispanic character, and her dialogue is more in colloquial English.

Tracy did make a career playing smart-guy characters, and as long as he can play Pilon that way, he is all right. He is convincing as he talks Danny into "renting" his second house to him, often using guilt as a weapon. He is also quite believable when he first senses that Sweets might pose a threat to him. Their conflict begins when Danny wants to buy Sweets some candy; Tracy's Pilon gives him the full scale treatment — how could he sell the brotherhood out by actually going to work to pay for the candy? That, plus Danny's social ineptitude — his bullying of Sweets's gentleman caller and his genuine shock when he discovers that she believes in working for a living — would seem to guarantee that Pilon, the boy's book Merlin, will prevail.

At this point, however, the paisanos encounter the corporal and his baby, and the screenplay radically alters Steinbeck; the whole emphasis of the scene — the critique of the ruling class — shifts to something else entirely. Sweets has a big role here (she has none in the book), and for her the issue is one of child custody, not of class. She directly confronts Pilon with the allegation that someone as irresponsible as he has no business taking care of a child. Lamarr is lit like a Madonna as she lights into him; there is no question as to who is right and who is stronger here.

The Tracy smart-guy persona is also effective at the start of the Pirate's role in the film, for his appearance is taken by Pilon as an opportunity for another scam. But again the screenwriters shift the emphasis. Some critics of the novel see the Pirate episodes as intensifying the paisano brotherhood and deepening the moral tone of the whole novel. Owens asserts that he "breaks the chain of irresponsibility" (169). But there is room to doubt that he has such a lasting effect on the brotherhood, or that the acquisition of the St. Francis candlestick in any way benefits the community. In the film, however, there is no doubt: the Pirate changes everything completely. The Priest makes the case that religion and socioeconomic convention go hand in hand early in the film. The Pirate episodes nail down that theme, and we know that Pilon is doomed. It is probably not coincidental that Danny's disruptive visit to Sweets in the factory takes place at this moment. No such scene exists in the book. Far from interrupting the flow of the film, the scene supports it. This event gets Danny to thinking that maybe he could work for a living too (and that he could use some of the money which they want to con from the Pirate to buy a boat, a speculation that predictably upsets Pilon).

The subsequent winning-over of the paisanos by the Pirate is treated in the best Hollywood-religious manner. The classy music (from Mendelssohn's "Midsummer Night's Dream," not so very appropriate really, but obviously an indicator of serious intent), the angelic choirs, the saintly lighting, the shamelessly sentimental performance of Frank Morgan (which elicited raves from the critics!), the cute animals, the Priest's sermon about how the community has benefited from the Pirate and his

Akim Tamiroff as Pablo (left), John Garfield as Danny (center), and Spencer Tracy as Pilon in Victor Flemming's 1942 film *Tortilla Flat*.

friends — all of these details make Steinbeck's boy's-book sentimentality look mild by comparison, and inverts his themes totally. Danny's behavior at this point in the film — his drunkenness, his buying of the vacuum cleaner — no longer reflects the weightiness of property; it suggests anxiety that he is not part of the bourgeois ethic. Even less convincingly, Pilon undergoes a change of heart, and starts implementing Danny's entrance into the bourgeoisie.

"If Danny could only see this," Pilon says of the religious-social fusion at the ceremony where the St. Francis candlestick is donated. Indeed Danny — and Pilon —*are* beginning to "see" it, as we see in two subsequent scenes, neither of which appears in the book: Danny's second drunken visit to Sweets at her factory job, in the course of which he is injured, and the following scene at the hospital. At the end of the latter, Sweets accuses Pilon of being responsible for Danny's reckless behavior and worthless life. And Pilon takes her at her word — she has won.

So have Mahin and Glazer, who now begin to reorient and refashion Steinbeck radically. The St. Francis miracle in the forest (which Pilon witnesses) further convinces him of the errors of his ways. Pilon goes directly to the church, where (thanks to Mahin and Glazer, not to Steinbeck), he — to the accompaniment of angelic choirs! — promises to get a job himself if St. Francis will cure Danny (i.e., cause him to marry Sweets). The Priest, once again acting in his social as well as religious capacity, witnesses this scene, and takes full advantage of it in the scenes that follow. The next we see of Pilon he is actually working (though he tries to hide the fact from his pals). We know that his prayers have been answered, for we are told that Sweets has forgiven him. The triumph of social responsibility is complemented by economic respectability — at the Priest's urging (practically blackmail), Pilon organizes a raffle to finance a boat for Danny. The sentimental wedding scene once again tells us that, although wedding bells are breaking up this aging Tom Sawyer's gang, Pilon is curiously acquiescent.

There is an epilogue in which Pilon burns down the second house (which he blames for Danny's problems) and concludes the film with a paean to the carefree life (sleeping under the sky). But this reversion to Steinbeck's boy's-book Arthurianism is highly unconvincing after the resolution of the plot. Pilon's reference to the weightiness of property is an especially bizarre turnabout here, for we have already gotten the message: the end of the boy's-book idyll is a positive thing. Yet somehow it will also continue. Even though the original is less than a triumph of consistency, one might indeed wonder what Steinbeck thought of the strange inversions Hollywood imposed on his work.

NOTES

1. Metro-Goldwyn-Mayer, directed by Victor Fleming. Originally filmed in sepia; videotape in black and white.

2. It is painful to see Steinbeck still at this late date trying to put his finger on what is timeless about the Arthurian stories, and determining what sort of tone, shape, and thematic perspective this material should have. Accordingly, the results are choppy, shapeless, and overladen with detail, with a strong emphasis on slam-bang violence. See the letters to his agent Elizabeth Otis and his editor Chase Horton published as an Appendix to this long-gestating and unfinished last work.

3. See the Lupacks on the links with Twain (183–86).

4. Millichap dismisses the parallelism as Steinbeck's "condescension," "sentimentality," and insincere ennobling of proletarian "little people" (62).

5. Lisca, one of the most articulate skeptics of the Arthurian parallels, asserts that Steinbeck used his alleged parallels to convince his early publisher, Robert S. Ballou, and his agent that the novel was unified (74).

6. Northern Californians seem in particular need of this sort of universalization. As a visitor to the region in Armistead Maupin's *Significant Others* puts it, "You demand adoration for the place.

You're not happy until *everybody* swears undying love for every nook and cranny...." (96).

7. If Steinbeck is unsure about the contemporary applicability of Arthur, he is not alone, as the countless medieval updates of our day bear evidence. Later, he could see that Twain, White, and Alan Jay Lerner had similar difficulties (*Acts,* Appendix 345). Lerner deprives Arthur of stature by turning him into a bourgeois CEO and family man, who does not dirty his hands with the more suspect actions of his knights. In Joshua Logan's bizarre film version of *Camelot*, this middle class behavior sits uneasily with the fantasy-like sets, which suggest an aristocratic and other-worldly aura. Of course, the tonal transitions that came so naturally to White on the page proved impossible for Lerner to unify in dramatic terms.

8. Levant suggests that Steinbeck always had problems with reconciling "structure" with "materials" and that the public acceptance of his sentimental, short-term solution to unification in *Tortilla Flat* blinded him to the problem for the rest of his career (52, 68-73). At times, one is tempted to agree with Mizener that Steinbeck is "an incurable amateur philosopher" whose "real but limited talent is, in his best works, watered down by tenth-rate philosophizing" ("Moral Vision" 4, 45).

9. Steinbeck kept his reaction to the finished product to himself. But he had reason to be suspicious of adaptation. The film is not the first adaptation of the novel. Jack Kirkland did a Broadway version in 1938 that is clearly an attempt to follow up on his success with *Tobacco Road* by emphasizing the down-and-dirty regionalism in the source. It only had a five-performance run. Brooks Atkinson's review in the *New York Times* (13 January 1938: 16) is a prime example of his and his paper's moralistic criticism — the play is bad because the characters are. His colleague Bosley Crowther calls the film "propaganda for common vagrancy" (27). *Time* calls the Kirkland version a "dirty, dismal" play ("Cinema" 84); Kirkland punched out another critic who faulted him (Kiernan 226). Steinbeck hated the adaptation, and this unhappy experience may have prompted his later attempt to buy back the film rights (*Time* 84). The film does not credit Kirkland.

10. This little story may, however, not be quite so integral as it seems. Linda Gordon notes that a prejudice against tortillas and beans is a typical Anglo attitude, similar to the one against garlic in Italian food (75). Steinbeck may be identifying the doctor's astonishment that the little boy could be perfectly healthy on such a diet as an example of prejudice. Even though Millichap is probably right about Steinbeck's condescension toward the paisanos (see note 4 above), this would be an instance where he is perfectly sincere about the value of their lifestyle. Lisca reads the episode of the corporal as a radical critique of the "predatory social system which the paisanos have successfully avoided" (9). The film presents it in a completely different, indeed establishment, light.

11. A much more likely candidate for a "wild man"/Arthur figure is Doc (based on Steinbeck's friend Ed Ricketts), the marine biologist who is the central figure in Steinbeck's related Monterey novels *Cannery Row* and *Sweet Thursday*. The Arthurian preface in *Tortilla Flat* would make much more sense in one of those books. Doc is much more concerned for the welfare of his ragtag friends than Danny is. Nick Nolte's performance as Doc in the 1982 film from these two novels, *Cannery Row*, is truly moving because he finds a way to combine the high and low elements of the character, a synthesis that eludes the cast of *Tortilla Flat*. The Lupacks make a good case for Steinbeck's anti-capitalism in these later novels (199). The visual combination of realism and symbolism in this later film is, however, even more uneasy than that in the 1942 film.

WORKS CITED

"Cinema: The New Pictures." *Time* 39 (18 May 1942): 84.

Crowther, Bosley. "The Screen in Review." *New York Times* 22 May 1942: 27.

Farber, Manny. "Not by the Book." *New Republic* 106 (1 June 1942): 766.

Fontenrose, Joseph. *John Steinbeck: An Introduction and Interpretation.* New York: Barnes and Noble, 1965.

French, Warren. *John Steinbeck.* 2nd ed. rev. Boston: Twayne/G. K. Hall, 1975.

Frohock, W. M. *The Novel of Violence in America.* Dallas: Southern Methodist University Press, 1957.

Gordon, Linda. *The Great Arizona Orphan Abduction.* Cambridge: Harvard University Press, 1999.

Kiernan, Thomas. *The Intricate Muse: A Biography of John Steinbeck.* Boston: Little, Brown, 1979.

Kinney, Arthur F. "The Arthurian Cycle in *Tortilla Flat.*" *Modern Fiction Studies* 11 (Spring 1965): 11-20.

———. "*Tortilla Flat* Revisited." In Testumaro Hayashi, ed. *Steinbeck and the Arthurian Theme,* Steinbeck Monograph Series 5. Muncie, Ind.: Ball State University/John Steinbeck Society of America, 1975.

Levant, Howard. *The Novels of John Steinbeck: A Critical Study.* Columbia: University of Missouri Press, 1974.

Lisca, Peter. *The Wide World of John Steinbeck.* Rev.

ed. New York: Gordian Press, 1981. [Originally published New Brunswick: Rutgers University Press, 1958.]

Lupack, Alan, and Barbara Tepa Lupack. *King Arthur in America*. Cambridge, Eng.: D. S. Brewer, 1999.

Maupin, Armistead. *Significant Others*. New York: Harper and Row, 1987.

Millichap, Joseph R. *Steinbeck and Film*. New York: Frederick Ungar, 1983.

Mizener, Arthur. "Does a Moral Vision of the Thirties Deserve a Nobel Prize?" *New York Times Book Review* 9 December 1962: 4, 43–45.

———. *The Sense of Life in the Modern Novel*. Boston: Houghton Mifflin, 1964.

Olton, Bert. *Arthurian Legends on Film and Television*. Jefferson, N.C.: McFarland, 2000.

Owens, Louis. *John Steinbeck's Re-Vision of America*. Athens: University of Georgia Press, 1985.

Prindle, Dennis. "The Pretexts of Romance: Steinbeck's Allegorical Naturalism from *Cup of Gold* to *Tortilla Flat*." In Donald R. Noble, ed. *The Steinbeck Question: New Essays in Criticism*. Troy, N.Y.: Whitson Publishing, 1993.

Scheer, Ronald D. "Steinbeck into Film: The Making of *Tortilla Flat*." *Philological Papers* 26 (August 1980): 30–36.

Steinbeck, John. *The Acts of King Arthur and His Noble Knights*. Ed. Chase Horton. New York: Farrar, Strauss, Giroux, 1976.

———. *Tortilla Flat*. New York: Penguin, 1977; 1981.

Yarmus, Marcia. "The Picaresque Novel and John Steinbeck." In Cliff Lewis and Carroll Britch, eds. *Rediscovering Steinbeck: Revisionist Views of His Art*. Lampeter, Dyfed, Wales: Mellen, 1989.

7

The Retreat from Camelot: Adapting Bernard Malamud's The Natural *to Film*

Barbara Tepa Lupack

Hit or myth? Bernard Malamud's first novel *The Natural* (1952) was both: a bestseller and an important work of literary fiction with Arthurian and other mythic undertones. Almost from the time of its publication, the novel seemed a natural for cinematic adaptation; but, in fact, more than thirty years passed before a director — Barry Levinson, the writer and director of the engagingly successful film *Diner*— took up the challenge of translating it to the screen. In the process of adaptation, Levinson turned Malamud's decidedly dark and cynical parable of baseball and of American life into an entertaining but familiar and formulaic film with an upbeat Hollywood-style ending. With Levinson's embrace of Hollywood, however, came a retreat from Camelot and a reduction or elimination of most of the novel's Arthurian themes and images.

Malamud's *The Natural* is the story of Roy Hobbs, an exceptional ballplayer who at nineteen is invited to try out as pitcher for the Cubs. But en route to Chicago, he is seduced and almost killed by a dark, mysterious woman named Harriet Bird, who hunts down star athletes and shoots them with silver bullets. Fifteen years pass before Roy's near-lethal groin wounds heal and he regains his former prowess. Now the oldest rookie player, he makes it to the big leagues again — this time, however, with the New York Knights, the worst team in the National League. Roy instantly perceives that he has a "mission": to lead his fellow Knights to victory. That mission becomes particularly urgent when the Knights' manager, Pop Fisher, is forced into a deal with the team's majority owner, Judge Goodwill Banner: unless the Knights have a winning year, Pop stands to lose his job, his financial stake in the team, and the single dream he ever had, of capturing the pennant. Roy promises to play his best for Pop, and for a while that is precisely what he does. After Bump Baily, the Knights' star player, dies while attempting the catch of his life, Roy takes over Bump's role — both on the team and in the affection of Bump's girlfriend Memo Paris (Pop's wayward niece) — and guides the team toward its best season ever.

Roy's intimacy with Memo, however, causes the worst slump of his career, a slump that has deleterious consequences for all of the Knights. Even after the earth-motherly Iris Lemon, a woman who "hate[s] to see heroes fail" and who appreciates that "without heroes we're plain people and don't know how far we can go" (154), helps to restore his status as a popular idol, Roy cannot seem to resist Memo. Before a crucial game near the end of the season, he attends a party in Memo's hotel room. In contrast to the obligatory fasting of the Grail knight the night before his vigil, Roy over-indulges his gluttonous appetite, just as he had indulged a different appetite years earlier in Harriet's hotel room on the eve of his tryout with the Cubs — an indulgence that had earned him his first terrible blow to the gut. He lands in the hospital, where he is visited by the Judge, who tempts him to throw the last game.

Roy realizes that, by taking the bribe, he can afford the kind of life Memo desires, and it seems that he is ready to accept the money, even though it means disappointing Pop and the rest of his teammates. The next day, during his first couple of attempts at the plate, a weak Roy intentionally hits foul balls and then strikes out; but in his final try at bat, after another encounter with Iris (during which she reveals that she is pregnant with his child), he finds a fresh energy and purpose. Unfortunately, it is too little, too late: he strikes out again, on a "bad ball" from the Pirates' young replacement pitcher, aptly named Youngberry, who — in the cyclic pattern of the novel and of Arthurian mythology, especially the legends of the Fisher King — becomes the new hero who displaces the aging one, much as Roy did fifteen years earlier when he struck out Walter the Whammer Wambold, the leading hitter and three times Most Valuable Player of the American League.

Roy, however, is more than just an ordinary "hero" (32) in the novel; from the beginning, he is described as a "bewitched" (14) and mystical figure, a contemporary knight who, Malamud repeats, could even have been "king" (156, 237), as his name suggests (Roy=*roi*).[1] Moreover, he is a "natural" not only in the modern sense of possessing an outstanding innate talent but also in the medieval sense of being an innocent fool. As Jeffrey Helterman explains, "The natural [of the Middle Ages], touched by God, retained his Edenic nature and seemed a fool to the rest of mankind. Though armed with a natural goodness, the natural was easy prey to the worldly-wise if he strayed from his God-given intuitions" (24).[2] At nineteen, Roy is talented enough to strike out the legendary Whammer, but he is not sufficiently worldly-wise to keep from succumbing to the charms of the mysterious Harriet, a Morgan Le Fay figure who, suggests Sidney Richman, "in the tradition of grail literature, has been sent to test the hero's worthiness and exact punishment when he fails" (32).

Nor is Roy sufficiently self-aware to grasp that it is not enough for a hero simply to have talent; he must also have a purpose in life. When Harriet asks what he hopes to accomplish, he replies that he wants people to say of him, "there goes Roy Hobbs, the best there ever was in the game." Harriet assumes there must be more to the nature of his quest, "something over and above earthly things — some more glorious meaning to one's life and activities ... perhaps if you understood that our values must derive from —" (33–34). Not understanding "what she's been driving at," Roy feels "curiously deflated and a little lost, as if he had just flunked a test" (34). Fifteen years after his disastrous encounter with Harriet, he is certainly less innocent although not much wiser. He ignores Iris's important lesson about redemption through suffering, the lesson that people have two lives, "the life we learn with and the life we live with after that" (158); persists in chasing records rather than values; and continues to be distracted from virtue (Iris) by duplicity (Memo).

Roy's first publicly heroic feat, "the inspiring sight" of his victory over Whammer, is likened to "Sir Percy lancing Sir Maldemar" (32–33). Malamud's allusion,

Joe Don Baker as the American League's greatest hitter, The Whammer, in Barry Levinson's 1984 film *The Natural*.

while humorous, is not spurious, for Roy is indeed much like the Percival of Arthurian legend, the sometimes foolish but ultimately heroic knight who fails to ask the correct question of the Fisher King and who, therefore, cannot achieve his quest — at least not until a subsequent attempt, which Percival earns through his persistence. Roy, too, is both fool and hero; and Roy, too, is persistent. As Jonathan Baumbach notes, even Roy's name — "linguistically, king rustic" — is "an analogue of Percival" (107). Like his medieval counterpart, Roy engages in games that are "contests of skill" (26) or "tourneys" (31). Although the team to which he has been signed consists of little more than a bunch of "cripples" (5), denizens of a modern wasteland, he wears their uniform with great pride; the first time he dons it, in fact, tears come to his eyes. In uniform, Roy takes on "a warrior's quality" (152). Despite the Knights' reputation, Roy immediately determines to apply all of his "magic" (119) to winning the contemporary Grail of the pennant. His "undeniable destiny," it seems, is to "lead the Knights" (168) to victory; so "even when no enemy was visible ... he roused himself to do battle" (190). Without him, as the Judge recognizes, "the Knights are demoralized" (209) and unable to beat even a sandlot team.

At first, it seems as if nothing can distract Roy from his goal. Other teams unsuccessfully try "probing his armor" (83); but Roy refuses to let anything bother him, "not sun, shadow, nor smoke-haze... [H]e was good at gauging slices and knew when to charge" (84), his stride "smooth," and his wrists ready to "slash" out at the necessary moment. Even after he becomes physically and ethically debilitated, he still makes a powerful impression: Vogelman, the opposing pitcher, imagines an invincible "Roy, in full armor, mounted on a black charger" (231) coming directly at him, and he passes out from fright, forcing the younger, more fearless Youngberry to replace him.

Roy's "foolproof lance" (11) is Wonderboy, a naturally white bat hewn by Roy's hands from a lightning-felled tree near his childhood home.[3] Like Arthur's Excalibur, Roy's Wonderboy does not fail him; in fact, only when he corrupts the ideal for which Wonderboy stands by trying to foul out in the final game — a particularly passive and cowardly way of keeping his bargain with the Judge — does it lose its magic and break irreparably into several pieces. Earlier, however, when Roy used Wonderboy to play with honor, it "flashed in the sun" (80), so blindingly golden that "some of the opposing pitchers complained that it shone in their eyes" (90–91). During Roy's first time at bat, Wonderboy "cracked the sky. There was a strange, ripping sound and a few drops of rain spattered to the ground" (80), delivering the first signs of life to the parched wasteland of Knights Field. With the magical bat but with "nothing of value yet to show for what he was accomplishing" (91), Roy feels strangely unsatisfied. When he begins to focus more on Memo than on the game, Pop urges him to break his slump by trying a different bat. But Roy realizes that, while Wonderboy shines whenever he does, "whatever is wrong is wrong with me and not my bat" (135). And, in the final game, even after Wonderboy is broken, Roy knows he can still "cure what ailed him" with a single hit or "truly redeem" himself with "a homer, with himself scoring the winning run" (230). It is worth noting that, like Arthur returning Excalibur to the lake after the final battle, Roy, after the last game, carefully buries Wonderboy in the earth, "wishing it would take root and become a tree" again (234).

Like Sir Percival and other heroes of medieval romance, Roy Hobbs is a figure very much out of time. On the novel's opening page, he is described as "having no timepiece" (9). By returning to the game as the oldest rookie, he indeed tries to erase the damage done by Harriet's bullet and by the intervening years. And for most of the season, Roy is quite successful. During one game, he even smashes a ball into the outfield clock, shattering it and scattering time everywhere, in "a symbolic gesture" that Helterman (32) notes is ultimately as futile as his desire to achieve a kind of immortality by fathering a child with the barren Memo. But Roy's past soon catches up with him, in turn obliterating his present triumphs. He realizes that Memo is not his girl but the girl of "the dead man," Bump; he is implicated by Max Mercy not only in the earlier scandal with Harriet but also in the current "sell-out"; and in the novel's final paragraphs, as Malamud suggests, he "will be excluded from the game and his records forever destroyed" (237). Thus, what is expunged is not the past that Roy has tried to repress but rather his glorious moment in the sun of Knights Field.

Distracted too long by a false Grail, symbolized by the sterile Memo, whose "sick breast" reveals her inability to nurture the hero or bear her own offspring and makes her "inimical to life in every way" (Helterman 28), Roy overlooks the redeeming fecundity of the true Grail, symbolized by Iris Lemon, whose very name reinforces her fertility and vitality. Nowhere is the contrast between the two women more vivid than in the scenes involving children and automobile accidents. In the first of those scenes, after Roy's abortive attempt at lovemaking, Memo takes the wheel and drives his new white Mercedes away at more than ninety miles an hour. At the side of the road, Roy glimpses what he believes to be a boy and his dog; then he hears a thud, but Memo refuses to stop to investigate. Although there is no blood on the car, Roy is convinced that they have killed the child, and he suffers tremendous guilt over his complicity in the crime. As several critics have demonstrated, the boy is likely more symbolic than real, an emblem of Roy's lost hopes and innocence, while Memo — like Harriet before her — is an agent of that loss and destruction.

By contrast, Iris is connected with Roy's first selfless act, which also involves a boy injured in a car accident. As Babe Ruth actually did, Roy promises to hit a home run for a hospitalized boy who has lost his will to live. It is the first time that he attempts to assume any responsibility for someone other than himself. But his guilt over the boy he might have killed and his frustration over his affair with Memo leave him unable to concentrate on the game. When Iris, white rose in hand, stands up in the bleachers in a show of support, Roy responds by hitting the ball so hard that it shoots through the second baseman's "astounded" legs and up to the very spot where Iris is standing. It is Iris, an inspiring vision, therefore, who helps him to fulfill his promise.

Iris, it turns out, is Roy's spiritual counterpart in many ways. She too has suffered: like Roy, she was the youthful victim of an unknown assailant, a man who had "pounced like a tiger" and raped her. At thirty-three, Iris decides (just as Roy does) to begin her life again — or more literally, to resurrect it at the point at which she had abandoned it years before. When she and Roy swim by moonlight in the waters of Lake Michigan — a contrast to the stagnant pool that Roy visits with Memo — Iris offers Roy an opportunity for rebirth and regeneration through commitment. He leaps to the lake bottom, and according to Stanley Richman, as he ascends, Roy sees the form of Iris "floating beyond his head in the emblem of the Grail, luminously gold and charged with love" (38). After they make love and she admits to him that she is a grandmother, Iris appears as another archetype, "a form of the ancient hag whom the knight must marry in order to attain his goal" (Richman 38) — although, ultimately, Iris is more of a fecund vegetation goddess than a hag, and such a "marriage" offers the fertility that is lacking in Roy's life.

But Roy can neither see Iris's real beauty nor accept the opportunity for rejuvenation she offers; after their evening together, he neglects her and continues to pursue Memo. And shortly before the crucial game, when Memo is dispatched to enjoin Roy to take part in the conspiracy against Pop, he even proposes marriage to her. Roy's moral blindness is shared by several other characters in the novel, who, as Jeffrey Helterman (32–33) and others have demonstrated, are afflicted with various disorders of the eye. "In the Knot Hole" columnist Max Mercy, who in fact shows no mercy at all, has a "one-eyed obsession with finding the worst in anyone"; the myopic Judge Goodwill Banner, whose name belies his satanic nature, prefers to sit in rooms so dark that they suggest his own spiritual state; the glass-eyed gambler Gus Sands, who manipulates events for his own greedy purposes, is blind to nobler causes.

Because of his own blindness, Roy fails both in his quest for Knightly fame and in his quest to help others, including the Fisher King, Pop Fisher (and his subordinate, the aptly named Knights' coach Red Blow).[4] A former ballplayer, Pop once played in the World Series against the Athletics, but, as he was circling the bases in the crucial seventh game, "his legs got tangled under him and he fell flat on his stomach, the living bejesus knocked out of him" (62); ever since, he has lived with the painful memory of what the newspapers called "Fisher's Famous Flop." When Roy first meets him, Pop — now the team's manager and part owner — is seated at the edge of a "dusty field" complaining, literally and metaphorically, that "it's been a blasted dry season. No rains at all. The grass is worn scabby in the outfield and the infield is cracking. My heart feels as dry as dirt" (45). And he has a wound — athlete's foot on his hands—that will not heal. As Roy begins winning games for the Knights, the rains come; Knights Field grows green again; and even Pop "got into the spirit.... He unwound the oily rags on his fingers and flushed them down the bowl. His hands healed and so did his heart" (93). But when Roy, distracted by Memo, goes into a slump, Pop again feels the pain of his wounds and restores the bandages to "his pusing fingers" (138). Nevertheless Pop maintains his faith in Roy, believing that he alone will deliver Pop's lifelong dream of a pennant. During the final game, however, after Roy deliberately strikes out, "there were no Knight hits after [that;] ... a breeze blew dust all over the place" (221); and Pop recognizes that his last hope is gone. Removing his false teeth, which felt like rocks in his mouth, Pop "swayed on the bench, drooling a little out of the corners of his puckered mouth" (228), his eyes ringed in black, his voice broken. The prospect of achieving the Knights' Grail —the league pennant—had been within Roy's reach; but Roy reduces to dust not only his own dream but Pop's as well.

Critics have commented on various aspects of Malamud's Grail story.[5] Sidney Richman, for instance, identified the "pattern of the grail-quest" (33) underlying the novel, especially in incidents such as the trip to the netherworld-like nightclub, the Pot of Fire. According to Richman, Roy fails because "he hides the secrets of his past from all eyes ... unlike the grail knight who bore the evidence of his perfidy for all to see in a gesture of humility." The secrecy breeds such guilt that Roy "not only suffers on the field but must encounter, like knights in the Chapel Perilous, the visitations of bats, monsters and formless spectres" (35). Robert Ducharme, on the other hand, links each of the characters in *The Natural* to the Grail stories of Frazer, Weston, and Eliot: Roy as "a modern Sir Percival in quest of the major league pennant," Gus as Merlin, Iris as the Lady of the Lake, Memo as Morgan, and the derisive fan in the bleachers Otto Zipp "as the Arthurian dwarf who taunts and scourges the questing hero" (9). John Kimsey asserts that *The Natural* draws on Chrétien's *Perceval* and Malory's *Balin, or the Knight with the Two Swords* (allegories "of the male quest for individuation" and essays "on the meaning of heroism" [103]), while Peter L. Hays tries to find the origins of *The Natural* and Malamud's other "medieval stories" in another of Chrétien's works, *Lancelot, or the Knight of the Cart*.

Jonathan Baumbach also identifies Hobbs with Percival; he concludes, though, that while the notion of "Sir Percival as baseball star is a witty idea," the pleasure of the novel is not in its Arthurian allegory but rather "in the hallucinated and idiomatic particulars of its narrative" (111). Earl R. Wasserman, however, argues just the opposite: in perhaps the most perceptive essay of all on *The Natural*, he writes that Malamud avoided the risk of contrived allegory that lurks in inventing a fiction in order to carry a meaning precisely by drawing on memorable real events; yet "the clean surface of this baseball story ... repeatedly shows beneath its translucency another myth of another culture's heroic ritual by which man once measured the moral power of his humanness." Roy at bat "is every quester who has had to shape his own character to fulfill his goal"; by drawing his material from actual baseball lore and yet fusing it with baseball legend, "Malamud sustains his novel in a region that is both real and mythic, particular and universal" (47).

The film adaptation of *The Natural*, directed by Barry Levinson and released by Tri-Star in 1984, turned Malamud's dense and darkly comic tale into an old-fashioned, inspirational, and largely formulaic entertainment. Levinson's film featured solid performances by Robert Redford as baseball legend Roy Hobbs[6] and a stellar supporting cast (including Robert Duvall, Wilford Brimley, Richard Farnsworth, Robert Prosky, and Darren McGavin); meticulously re-created period detail; and impressive, evocative cinematography by Caleb Deschanel. But the simplification of the plot, the recasting of the major characters into opposing types (saints and sinners), and the addition of a Hollywood happy ending reduced most of the novel's Arthurian elements and transformed Malamud's incisive examination of the mythology of the American hero into a celebration of an idealized and idealistic America.

As *Cineaste* reviewer Rob Edelman observed, Levinson's film is not only simple; it is also somewhat simplistic because it suggests that "there is good, and there is evil, and good is destined to triumph over evil; you can go home again, you can rediscover, and recapture, your innocence; if you struggle courageously, you will surely overcome all adversity, win the Big Game and be rewarded with a happy-ever-after future" (45). Motivated by the memory of his father and inspired by the girl he loves, Redford's all–American farmboy Roy leaves his heartland home to try out for the Cubs. After striking out the legendary but arrogant Whammer, a Babe Ruth–like character played by Joe Don Baker, Roy seems well on his way to success — until he is critically wounded by a silver bullet fired by mysterious seductress Harriet Bird (Barbara Hershey). When Roy finally returns to the big leagues sixteen years later, he must overcome the ridicule of his fellow Knights and the resentment of manager Pop Fisher (Wilford Brimley); but given the opportunity, Roy proves himself to be a natural who leads the team within sight of the pennant. When sportswriter Max Mercy (Robert Duvall) tries to dig up news of the reticent rookie's past and Memo Paris (Kim Basinger) — at the instigation of Pop's unwanted partner, the Judge (Robert Prosky) — attempts to divert him from his game, Roy's fortunes change; only his longtime love Iris (Glenn Close), rising suddenly like a beatific vision from the ballpark stands, breaks his losing streak and guides him to his greatest triumph.

In translating the novel to the screen, Levinson and screenwriters Robert Towne and Phil Dusenberry eliminated virtually all of the secondary and supporting story lines; gone are the subplots involving Roy's complicity (imagined or actual) in the criminal car accident, his occasional willful cruelty (e.g., crushing a bird to death in his hands), his visiting of the New Jersey fortuneteller, even his promise to hit a home run for the injured, hospitalized boy who has lost his will to live. More importantly, by manipulating certain plot events, Levinson infused the film with a sunny optimism that supplanted the novel's cynicism.[7] Malamud's Roy, for instance, is a jaded young man who comes from a sad and broken home. Roy tells Memo that his mother was "a whore [who] spoiled my old man's life" (185). To Harriet, he confirms that sometimes he wanted "to skull" his father. "After my grandma died, the old man dumped me in one orphan home after the other, wherever he happened to be working — when he did" (32). Not only does his dysfunctional early family life cause Roy to reenact his failed father-son relationship by disappointing his surrogate father figures, scout Sam Simpson and team manager Pop Fisher; but it also disinclines Roy from committing to family life — as a husband, father, and instant grandfather — to such a degree that even the news of Iris's pregnancy is not enough to restore him at the end.

By contrast, Levinson's Roy is innocent and uncorrupted. As a boy, he outfits his bedroom with pennant flags from the various baseball teams he admires, and — hoping himself to become a ballplayer — practices pitches with his father on the golden wheat fields of the family farm. When his father dies suddenly, Roy tries to honor his memory by pursuing their shared dream. Becoming "the best there ever was" in baseball is not just Roy's selfish goal, as in the book; it was also Ed Hobbs's greatest hope for his son. As Roy tells Pop just before the final game, "My dad [always] wanted me to be a baseball player."[8] Out of the wood of the lightning-felled tree under which Ed died, Roy carves the magical bat that he carries with him even to the majors and that connects him to his happy youth.[9] The glove and ball that Roy sees years later in Iris's apartment are a further reminder of those special years; Roy even affirms to Iris that "a father makes all the difference" in a boy's life.[10]

When Iris appears at his hospital bed (situated, significantly, on the maternity ward, where Roy experiences another rebirth) intending to disclose her son's paternity, he speaks warmly of his own father and expresses his regret that the elder Hobbs never witnessed his success. The next day, at the pennant game itself, Roy is rejuvenated by Iris's revelation that he is the father of her adolescent son, who is in the stadium watching with great expectation and admiration. The immediate connection Roy feels to his son mirrors the continuing connection he feels to his late father; even the names of Roy's father and son — Ed Hobbs (Alan Fudge) and Ted Hobbs (Robert Rich III) — reinforce that connection.[11] With the help of the Knights' batboy Bobby Savoy (George Wilkosz) — depicted throughout the film as a kind of surrogate son[12] — Roy replaces the cracked, split Wonderboy with the "Savoy Special" (hand-crafted by Bobby at Roy's urging and with Roy's assistance) and hits the winning home run, to the cheers of his many young fans.[13] Roy's son having restored power to the aging king (and thus allowing Roy to restore power to the aging Fisher King, Pop), Roy retires with his new family to the farm, where he again becomes one with the land and where he re-creates the idyll of his youth; only this time, it is he who is pitching to his son as Iris looks on.

Roy's relationship with Iris is another important aspect of the novel's plot that Levinson reworked and ultimately enhanced. In the novel, Iris Lemon was a young but worldly-wise grandmother, whose fecundity simultaneously attracts and repels Roy. When she first appears, dark-haired and red-clad, more than halfway into the book, she offers Roy the hope of new life through love and commitment; but her earth-motherliness is insufficient to distract Roy from the charms of the wanton Memo. At the crucial pennant game, after Iris rises in the stands a second time to offer Roy support, he responds not with a game-winning run (as he did the first time) but with a foul ball that bounces off Otto Zipp, the heckling dwarf, and strikes Iris in the face, knocking her unconscious. Even after Iris informs him of her pregnancy and is removed from the stadium by ambulance, Roy strikes out at his next at-bat and loses both the game and the pennant. Afterwards, feeling "old and grimy" and filled with "overwhelming self-hatred," he remembers various "disgusting happening[s] of his life" and realizes "now I have to suffer again" (236–37). Ultimately, therefore, Roy's love affair with Iris — if indeed it can be called such — brings him little consolation and no redemption.

On the other hand, the film's Iris — now surnamed Gaines, to highlight the symbolic "gains" that she offers Roy to compensate for his many losses — is an important and ongoing part of his life. She first appears early in the film as the young Roy, waiting in the station to board the train to his try-out with the Cubs, flashes back to his boyhood. That flashback merges into Roy's memory of the previous evening, when he spirited Iris from her home to celebrate the news that he had been called up to the majors. In the wheat fields at daybreak, they consummate their relationship only hours before Roy departs, promising that he will send for Iris so they can be married. But sixteen years pass before they see each other again, after Iris seeks Roy out at Wrigley Field, where the Knights are playing the Cubs. The event is especially symbolic, since — had Roy's life not been so radically altered by Harriet's bullet — he would have been a Cub rather than a Knight. Even though by then Iris is a mother, the film depicts her as ethereal and virginal, the link to all the innocent pleasures that Roy has had to foresake. After all, as Kevin Thomas Curtin observed, "someone named Iris might be expected in this film to embody clear vision" (238). Iris's love thus redeems Roy and allows him to fulfill his dream and his promise.

In addition to paring down the novel's plot so that he could emphasize Roy's relationships with his father and Iris, Levinson transformed Malamud's complex and intricately shaded characters into simple, opposing types: light and dark, good and evil.[14] Blond-haired Roy is literally and metaphorically a golden boy; like the film's other fundamentally decent characters, including the gruff but likeable Pop and the empathetic coach Red (Richard Farnsworth), he seems to thrive in the light. When Roy and Red sit together at the shoeshine stand and talk admiringly about Pop, they are illuminated from behind by a large Palladian window that frames their images like an enormous halo. By contrast, the shady, dishonest figures like the Judge, Max Mercy, and Gus Sands are usually enveloped by darkness. The power-mad Judge (Robert Prosky) prefers rooms as dark as his sinister nature. It is, he tells Roy, a habit he acquired in childhood as a way of overcoming his fear of the dark. The Judge even tries to draw Roy into his dark world by urging him to betray Pop and later by offering him a bribe to throw the crucial game, an offer that Roy immediately rejects. (The opposition between Roy and the Judge is best illustrated in the scene that occurs the first time Roy visits the Judge's office: Roy seats himself near the only bright lamp, while the Judge appears largely in silhouette; after refusing to support the Judge in his attempt to "steal" the team from Pop, Roy walks out — but not before flipping on the office lights and symbolically exposing the Judge for the criminal that he is. "You could use a little more light," Roy tells him.) Similarly, as Krey and Haney note, Max Mercy devolves into an increasingly reptilian character and is depicted accordingly: "in dark rooms, the tunnels under the stadiums, and in a glass booth that looks rather like an aquarium" (62). And another of the Judge's unscrupulous accomplices, glass-eyed Gus Sands (an unbilled Darren McGavin), inhabits a world as shadowy and clouded as his own vision.

If the film's men are all clearly defined villains or heroes, then the women, as Rob Edelman writes, "are either temptresses or angels" (46); they are dichotomized, according to the *Variety* reviewer, "schematically and simplistically" into the "archaic" categories of whores or angels.[15] The angelic Iris, swathed in white or floral pastels, essentially floats across the screen; like a heavenly apparition, she appears at the ballpark at precisely the moment that Roy most needs her intervention.[16] Memo, on the other hand, is as evil as Iris is saintly. An associate of the dishonest Judge and the mistress of the shady Gus, she too is a creature of the night who is most comfortable in darkened or artificially-lit surroundings like the Judge's smoke-filled box or her own lavish apartment, which Gus helped purchase. On their first date together, Roy and Memo stay out so late that he — presumably for the first time — misses his curfew, causing Pop to predict that Memo will only bring trouble. And in diametrical opposition to the angelic Iris, the diabolical Memo typically wears black. Interestingly, only when she is trying to seduce Roy or to insinuate herself further into his life does Memo change to white clothing. For example, she appears in Roy's hotel room after their first evening together wearing only a white fur coat; and on another occasion in his bed she sports a white silk nightgown. Later, after reading a newspaper story about "The Knight and the Lady in White," Memo tries to imitate Iris: she telephones him in Chicago to tell him that she is thinking about him and that she is wearing only a white slip when in fact she is clad in her usual black. And again after Roy's return to New York, she tries to win back Roy's affection by donning, uncharacteristically, a pure white formal gown.

The dark-haired, dark-eyed Harriet Bird — like Memo, a woman of evil nature — also wears black, sometimes with a red accent. The red rose that Harriet carries and that correctly suggests she is a dangerous and scarlet woman contrasts with the white flower that the good-hearted Iris pins to the bosom of her white dress. The two "dark" women in Roy's life, in fact, are linked visually as well as symbolically in the film. On the beach during their first evening together, for example, in a scene original to the film, Memo suggests that she and Roy have met before. Just before the big game, when Memo takes a gun out of the Judge's drawer and fires it at him, Roy confirms, "You were right, Memo. We *have* met before."[17] Memo, therefore, is a reincarnation of Harriet; but Roy is no longer her unsuspecting victim.

The delineation of both male and female characters into good or evil is reinforced throughout by the pervasive use of light and dark imagery. Believing that Malamud's novel, "in its simplest form based on Arthurian Legend," contained "all these wonderful black and white characters," cinematographer Caleb Deschanel decided "to stylize each character in terms of how they're lit" and to move "everything as much as possible towards black and white" (Krey and Haney 60). Indeed, the consistently white lighting of Iris, most memorably the backlighting of her wide-brimmed halo-like white hat when she first stands up to cheer on Roy, suggests her purity and reflects her beneficial place in Roy's memory.[18] As Deschanel affirmed, she is always "in this pure light. She has an iridescent quality. We wanted to create the sense of her always being aglow. If it wasn't the light in her face, it was the light which lit the hat."[19]

Harriet and Memo, on the other hand, are often cast in shadows. Only moments before she shoots Roy, Harriet obscures her own face with a lacy black widow's veil. Similarly, when Roy bursts unannounced into the Judge's private office to reject the bribe, he finds the compromised Memo hovering in the darkness behind the corrupt Judge. The locations in which the women are placed not only are revealing in themselves but also correspond to the film's light/dark imagery. Iris "is always 'at home' — whether she is in her own comfortable apartment or in a similarly familial setting in Chicago, the soda fountain. Memo, on the other hand, inhabits sleazier spaces; dark offices, glittery nightclubs and sultry bedrooms" (Krey and Haney 62).

Light and dark also work in other ways throughout the film: to underscore key moments and to evoke certain emotions. The opening section depicting Roy's boyhood, for instance, is inspired by the early autochrome process that combined color and black and white technology to yield color prints of low saturation that are similar to hand-tinted black and white photos. And when Roy leaves the farm, Deschanel used special gels to give the interior shots a warm amber tone that evoked the nostalgic past. By contrast, the daytime baseball scenes of Roy at practice and at play on Knights Field were slightly overexposed to enhance the feeling of bright sun and to suggest the equally bright future of Roy, the game's newest golden boy.[20] Moreover, specific recurring images like lightning, as Sally Hibbin notes, emphasize particular themes "in Hobbs' life: he fashioned his faithful bat from a tree split by it and whenever it appears wondrous things result." When Roy replaces Bump Bailey and hits his first home run, for instance, lightning strikes and brings on the rain that restores life to Knights Field; later, when Roy encounters Mercy on the way out of the stadium, lightning brightens the evening sky. When teammate John Olsen (Jon Van Ness)—in imitation of Roy's success with Wonderboy, which is emblazoned with a symbol of a lightning bolt—sews a lightning bolt patch onto his uniform, uncharacteristically he starts hitting the ball; soon all the Knights are sporting similar patches—and winning ballgames. And when, in the pennant game, an injured but unbowed Roy slams another home run, lightning strikes yet again.[21]

The imagery of light and dark extends even to the ending of the film, which marks a change from the novel so fundamental that, according to Vincent Canby, it transforms Malamud's brooding moral fable into a sunny fairy tale. Malamud's Roy accepts the Judge's bribe, changes his mind, and then tries unsuccessfully to win the crucial game that is being pitched by replacement Pirate Herman Youngberry, who, as his name suggests, in the cycle of Arthurian and specifically Fisher King mythology is the new hero displacing the old; but Levinson's Roy rejects the bribe and decides to play, even after being poisoned by Memo, who acts on the Judge's instruction, and learning that the damage from Harriet's silver bullet, lodged for sixteen years in his body, could cause a lethal explosion of his stomach. Struck out during his first attempt at bat, a renewed Roy smashes the ball first into the glass window of Mercy's press booth and then into the stadium lights, causing them to rain down like fireworks past the Judge's box and to explode into the infield. In contrast to the pessimistic conclusion of Malamud's novel, in which Roy's dreams are shattered, his scandals—past and present—are exposed, and his records are "forever destroyed," Levinson's Roy is hailed as the hero he had always hoped to be. Moreover, the exertion of slamming the game-winning run does not cause him mortal injury, as the film's doctors had earlier predicted it might. Instead, consistent with Hollywood's feel-good formulas, Roy not only survives but, in a closing scene that brings the film full circle, plays again—with his son, on the sunlit farm fields of his idyllic youth.

Just as Levinson radically modified the ending of the novel and recast many of its characters and plot elements, he downplayed most of the novel's Arthurian elements. The mythic resonances are still evident in the film, but only in bare outline—and only to the viewer who is searching for them. Underlying the novel was the Grail quest, with Roy cast simultaneously as a King Arthur, leading his Knights to victory and wielding his Excalibur-like weapon Wonderboy, and as a modern Sir Percival, trying to redeem his original failed quest by asking the correct questions that will ensure the healing of the wasteland (Knights Field); Iris as Blanchefleur; Pop as the injured Fisher King; and the league pennant as the Grail.

Malamud's novel makes clear Roy's connection to Percival in several ways, most explicitly when Harriet likens Roy's defeat of Whammer to "Sir Percy's" defeat of Sir Maldemar. In the film, Harriet uses a similar allusion; but instead of likening Roy to Percival, she alludes to a more familiar knight, "Sir Lancelot jousting Sir Turquine—or was it Maldemar?" Nonetheless, Levinson's Roy is portrayed as both a Percival-like natural and a naif, whose closeness to the parched land that he ultimately revives is reinforced by his habit of rubbing dirt from the field onto his hand each time he steps up to bat. Having fallen short in his first quest for glory, Roy determines not to fail again; as he reminds both Pop and the Judge, he has waited too long to get back to the majors to give any less than his best. And, indeed, it is his single-minded pursuit of his ideal that allows the Knights to achieve their quest.

The wasted land that Roy restores is the domain of Pop Fisher, the central Fisher King figure of both the novel and the film. But contrary to the novel, Levinson's Pop is neither a failed former player nor a severely injured old man, whose oozing wounds begin to heal after Roy's appearance at Knights Field and reopen after Roy betrays his team's trust.[22] Rather he is, as Red tells Roy, a sincere albeit occasionally gruff individual who "gave his heart and soul to the game, only to get it trampled on." Pop's hope is to win a pennant and to retire to a farm; like the Fisher King, he wants to become one with the land again. Just as Pop is renewed by the promise of a winning season, Knights Field itself, the arid dusty wasteland over which Pop presides, is brought back to life by the rains (preceded by symbolic lightning) that accompany Roy's appearances at the stadium. "It didn't start to rain," Chicago candy shop owner Al tells a customer, "until after he [Roy] hit the ball." The references to Knights Field's aridity, however, are generally more oblique than in the novel and not tied as directly to Arthurian story: the malfunctioning water fountain near the dugout, for instance; the long losing streak that persists until Roy replaces the corrupted Bump; the dearth of fans in the stands.

For Roy, the game of baseball becomes a kind of contemporary chivalric ritual. Harriet, in the film as in the novel, realizes that fact when she calls the match-up between him and Whammer a "contest of skill"; and when Whammer awaits Roy's pitch in the film, he holds his bat aloft like a jousting lance to fend off his opponent's assault. Levinson's Roy is victorious, in that and other encounters, because he follows a knightly code. "I thought I could rely on your honor," the Judge tells Roy, who refuses to accept his bribe. "You're about to," Roy replies.

Certainly, however, the most obvious use of Arthurian mythology in the film is

Robert Redford as Roy Hobbs in Barry Levinson's 1984 film *The Natural*.

the fabled pristine bat Wonderboy, crafted by Roy out of wood that he cut from the heart of a tree, much as the young King Arthur retrieved the legendary sword from the stone, and that he wields as magically as Arthur wielded Excalibur. As Kevin Thomas Curtin writes, Wonderboy thus "becomes a phallic fertility totem from the heartland of America. Roy's instrument will help him to bring new life to an urban wasteland that is being sucked dry by evil forces" (230).[23] A brief flashback sequence early in the film illustrates how Roy acquires Wonderboy. Young Roy stares out of his bedroom window; a storm rages outside; flashes of lightning illuminate various objects in his room, especially the beloved baseball team pennants on his wall. The camera pauses prophetically on one particular pennant: "NY Knights." As a bolt of lightning fells the tree under which his father died, Roy notices a single piece of white wood protruding, almost gleaming, from the tree's base — an image visually reminiscent of the anvil on the stone from which Arthur pulls his sword. Roy sculpts and sands and hones that wood into a singular bat that he uses to defeat all of his opponents. So long as he acts honorably, the magical instrument does not fail him.

In the novel, when Roy accepts money to throw the pennant game, Wonderboy cracks and splits; in the film, even though Roy (who admits that he "does not give [money] much thought") refuses the Judge's bribe, the bat cracks anyway. But instead of burying it in the ground (as Malamud's Roy did) so that it can "take root" again — the way that Arthur returned Excalibur to the lake after the final battle — the film's Roy engages in a different symbolic, cyclical ritual: he uses batboy Bobby Savoy's special bat, a kind of regenerated Excalibur that he helped to fashion, for his final slam. In this way, it could be argued, the aging hero passes his strength and his ideal to a new generation, "all of the young boys" — as Iris tells him — whom he has influenced over the years.[24] Furthermore, it is in this more subtle and at times more oblique way that the film incorporates the novel's Arthurian mythology.

Malamud, as Jerry Tallmer writes, was not willing to talk about the film adapted from his first and best-known novel. He was, however, "thought to be disgruntled. Certainly his novel was a pessimistic view of American heroism; certainly the movie is not" (27). In a comment to *Sports Illustrated*, Robert Redford also recognized and remarked on the differences between the film adaptation and its source: since film is not a literary medium, he suggested, much of the novel's symbolism simply could not be transferred to the screen (71). Yet, even though the film marked a retreat from Camelot by its deemphasis of the novel's Arthurian resonances, it captured a different magic — the magic of baseball as a national experience — and evoked a new mythic hero for a new era.

NOTES

1. There are numerous references in the novel to Roy as royalty in the world of baseball. For instance, he is called "King of the Klouters" (164), but soon he becomes "the Clown Prince" (170).

John Kimsey also provides another interpretation of Roy as king. Kimsey writes that Roy Hobbs's "name — in a narrative full of archly symbolic names — suggests a king (roi) who is lame (hobbled)" (107). Though Kimsey's inference that Roy is lame is largely inaccurate, his suggestion that Roy is injured ("hobbled") certainly offers an interesting reading.

2. Earl R. Wasserman suggests another perspective on Roy as the natural. He notes that "Roy, the questing Knight, by access to the sources of life, has restored virility to his community and the vegetative process to nature. In this radical sense of the word, he is the 'natural'" (48).

Other critics have also commented on Roy as the natural. For instance, Ellen Pifer (139–40), basing her definition on a listing in the *OED*, sees Roy as "a man who rejects moral knowledge and, for most of his career, remains blind to moral responsibility." And John Kimsey (106), in explaining and contextualizing Roy's "feeble-mindedness," reaches back to Locke's *Essay Concerning Human Understanding* and Shakespeare's *The Tempest*.

3. Wonderboy is a talisman of Roy's potency, according to Wasserman, just as Harriet's hatbox is a talisman of female potency. "The two objects — bat and hat — correspond to the Arthurian symbols, sword and chalice, which Jessie Weston and others have identified as talismans of male and female potency. Each has selfishly made the talisman for himself and will not relinquish it to others" (52). Wasserman also offers an excellent analysis of Harriet's role as "terrible mother" and of Roy's groping

of Harriet's breast and his other acts of infantilism, especially in the absence of a father figure.

4. Although Pop Fisher is clearly the Fisher King figure of the novel, it is worth noting the existence of a secondary Fisher King — Happy Pellers, the groundskeeper of Knights Field. And Pop's assistant is Knights' coach Red Blow, who — as Bert Olton has observed — is also part of the novel's Grail mythology: "Pop Fisher — The Fisher King, Red Blow — the Wound, the Dolorous Stroke" (215).

5. Malamud also incorporated aspects of Arthurian myth in works other than *The Natural*. For a brief discussion of Malamud's Ladies of the Lake, Fisher King figures, wasteland motifs, and Percival allusions, see Lupack and Lupack 219–20.

6. Vincent Canby writes that at times Redford's "legendary presence as a major movie star perfectly fits the character of Roy, who is as much of a legend as the actor" (15). That presence is enhanced by the fact that the part of Roy Hobbs marked a return to the screen for Redford after a four-year absence.

7. Levinson, with screenwriters Roger Towne and Phil Dusenberry, also made other, less significant alterations to the characters and plot. Bump Baily becomes Bump Bailey, whose ashes are scattered symbolically over Knights Field; Judge Goodwill Banner becomes simply "The Judge"; the period of Roy's convalescence and absence from the game is changed from fifteen to sixteen years; the pitcher in the final pennant game is Nebraska farmboy John Rhoades, who replaces Herman Youngberry during Roy's final at-bat. (In the novel, it is the rising star Youngberry who replaces Vogelman after Vogelman passes out from fright at the sight of an invincible Roy at the plate.) Dialogue is often shifted. Iris's observation that people live "two lives," for example, occurs soon after she meets Roy in the book; in the film, however, Iris utters these words after she visits him in the hospital the day before the big game.

8. In the opening sequences of the film, as Roy flashes back to a memory of playing baseball on the family farm, he recalls his father's words: "You've got a gift, Roy. But it's not enough. You've got to develop yourself. If you rely too much on your gift, you'll fail." Just moments before the final game, Roy is reminded of those words. Ironically, it is Gus Sands who warns him, "You've got a great gift, a talent. But it's not enough." This time, however, Roy neither squanders his gift nor commits the same mistake again.

9. In the novel, Roy carves the bat out of wood from a tree downed by lightning. In the film, however, the lightning-felled tree is special: it is the tree under which Roy's father died. The film thus creates another connection between Roy and his father that is absent from the book.

10. The film's Iris recognizes the significant role of the elder, now-deceased Hobbs in Roy's life. When Roy informs her that he has been called up to the Cubs, she immediately replies, "Oh, your dad would be proud!" Even the film's Memo alludes to the father-child relationship when she confesses to Roy that many of her own troubles began after her father's departure: "My father walked out when I was a little girl."

11. It is important to appreciate that, while the novel's Roy feels repulsed by the fact that marriage to Iris would make him a grandfather and give him an instant family, the film's Roy is delighted — and rejuvenated — by the fact of his instant fatherhood and reconnection to Iris.

12. Roy, as Curtin observes, is "father to Bobby Savoy — the chunky batboy, a sort of Everybody" (239). Roy's "roots in rural America and his years in exile have given him a depth of character that most people cannot have, and through all the suffering he sustains a quality of generosity that might have come as a gift from his fathers. And thus when [surrogate son] Bobby Savoy, clearly in awe of Hobbs, approaches him and in a shy, squeaky voice asks Roy to show him how to carve out a bat like 'Wonderboy,' a hero takes time and care to pass on some hard-won knowledge to the next generation" (239). Tina Washburn also explores the film's seminal relationship between Roy and Bobby. "The fact," she writes, "that Bobby — an over-all quiet, shy, and unathletic boy — feels he can approach Roy and that Roy is genuinely concerned about him contributes to Levinson's shaping of his Roy's more sympathetic and glorified character. Roy shares his knowledge with the boy, teaches him. Roy is willing to do what the other players don't seem to do very much of, namely, spend time with Bobby, time Roy could have devoted to practicing his catching, throwing, batting, or for that matter pursuing Memo. By offering to help Bobby make the bat, Roy becomes the boy's friend, maybe even a father figure, one who helps a child grow and live some of his dreams" (90).

13. Notably, in the film, Roy enjoys a strong relationship with the young boys — and young girls — who idolize him. In news footage, he is seen signing balls and offering supportive advice to admiring youngsters; and his heroism, like his failure, on the field is reflected in the faces of the young boys in the stands. ("The children's cheers," as Tina Washburn has demonstrated, "are often audible over the rest of the crowd" [91]. And, unlike his adult fans, Roy's younger fans are consistent in their support of him, even when he is losing.) Moreover, as Kevin Thomas Curtin suggests, Roy's experience and extraordinary power make him a kind of father figure to "thousands of kids every-

where": "he inspires positively, as no doubt the film makers hope their movie might do for our cynical republic" (239). In the book, after Roy has disgraced himself and the game, it is a young boy who offers the last word on his dishonorable conduct: "Say it ain't true, Roy" (237).

14. Nowhere is this more evident than in the depiction of Roy. As Jeffrey Saperstein writes, "Because Roy is elevated to sainthood in the film, his complexity is diminished. Whereas Malamud's character is impatient, undisciplined, proud, and lustful — in other words, deeply flawed — Redford's Hobbs is merely 'nice'.... Indeed, the film version portrays a passively noble hero who is up against an evil that is outside of himself. In the more ambiguous source, the major conflict is internal" (85).

15. The *Variety* reviewer also observes that "whenever he [Hobbs] goes for harlots like Hershey or Basinger, Redford is in big trouble, from which he must be rescued by Close." He concludes that, "even as a convention from the era depicted, this doesn't go down too well" (10).

16. Moreover, according to Saperstein, "Levinson wipes out Iris's past and reduces her to a cliché: the ever-patient childhood sweetheart" (86).

17. On another occasion, when they are in bed together, Memo touches the wound that he sustained from Harriet's silver bullet. In that instant, the sleeping Roy has a nightmarish vision of Harriet smiling coyly at him, and he awakens from the nightmare badly shaken.

18. The film makes an interesting visual association between memory and time. When Iris rises in the stands to show support for Roy, he responds by slamming a ball into the stadium clock, shattering it — and symbolically shattering the gulf of sixteen years that separated them. Thus, the film suggests, Iris is as much a part of Roy's future as she was of his past.

19. Quite literally," as Robert Krey and Michael Haney (61) write, "Iris is lit by a less diffuse and more brilliant light."

20. For a detailed examination of the uses of light and lighting, see Krey and Haney (58–63).

21. Indeed, as Sally Hibbin concludes, "each flash [of lightning] leads to greater deeds" (44).

22. Tom Milne writes that "of course the Fisher King's pursuit of the Holy Baseball Grail cannot be attended by anything so nasty as a skin disease." According to Milne, the absence of the Fisher King's injuries, like the other significant departures from the novel, helps to turn *The Natural* into what he calls "an embarrassingly arch message film for all aspiring Reagan *wunderkinds*" (38).

23. Thus, as Malamud does, Curtin conflates the image of Roy as Arthur and as Percival.

24. Earlier in the film, in newsreel footage, Roy is portrayed as "Hero to Young." But he is also admired by the old-timers. In fact, after Roy's successes at bat, the camera often pans the stands, moving from the cheering faces of the young boys to the wizened visages of old men and back again. The image of youth giving way to age and then to youth again reinforces the thematic notion of cyclicality that is central to both novel and film.

WORKS CITED

Baumbach, Jonathan. *The Landscape of Nightmare: Studies in the Contemporary American Novel.* New York: New York University Press, 1965.

Canby, Vincent. Review of *The Natural. New York Times* 11 May 1984: C-15.

Champlin, Charles. "The Way We Were." *San Francisco Chronicle* 18 May 1984: 66.

Curtin, Kevin Thomas. "*The Natural*: Our Iliad and Odyssey." *The Antioch Review* 43 (Spring 1985): 225–41.

Ducharme, Robert. *Art and Idea in the Novels of Bernard Malamud.* The Hague: Mouton, 1974.

Edelman, Rob. Review of *The Natural. Cineaste* 13 (October 1984): 45–46.

Hays, Peter L. "The Complex Pattern of Redemption." In Leslie A. Field and Joyce W. Field, eds. *Bernard Malamud and the Critics.* New York: New York University Press, 1970.

Helterman, Jeffrey. *Understanding Bernard Malamud.* Columbia: University of South Carolina Press, 1985.

Hibbin, Sally. Review of *The Natural. Films and Filming* 357 (October 84): 44.

Kimsey, John. "Dolorous Strokes, or Balin at the Bat: Malamud, Malory, and Chrétien." In Donald E. Morse, Marshall B. Tymn, and Csilla Bertha, eds. *The Celebration of the Fantastic: Selected Papers from the Tenth Anniversary International Conference on the Fantastic in the Arts.* Westport, Conn.: Greenwood Press, 1989.

Krey, Robert, and Michael Haney. "Caleb Deschanel, ASC, and *The Natural.*" *American Cinematographer* 66 (April 1985): 58–63.

Lupack, Alan, and Barbara Tepa Lupack. *King Arthur in America.* Cambridge: D. S. Brewer, 1999.

Malamud, Bernard. *The Natural.* New York: Harcourt, Brace, 1952.

Milne, Tom. Review of *The Natural. Monthly Film Bulletin* 51 (November 1984): 37–38.

Olton, Bert. *Arthurian Legends on Film and Television.* Jefferson, N.C.: McFarland, 2000.

Pifer, Ellen. "Malamud's Unnatural *The Natural.*" *Studies in American Jewish Literature* 7 (Fall 1988): 138–52.

Review of *The Natural. Motion Picture Product Digest* 11 (30 May 1984): 94.

Review of *The Natural*. *Sports Illustrated* 7 May 1984: 71.

Review of *The Natural*. *Variety* 9 May 1984: 10.

Richman, Sidney. *Bernard Malamud*. New York: Twayne, 1966.

Saperstein, Jeffrey. "Irony and Cliché: Malamud's *The Natural* in the 1980s." *Literature/Film Quarterly* 24.1 (1996): 84–87.

Siskel, Gene. "An Interview." *Daily News* [New York] 11 May 1984: 5.

Tallmer, Jerry. "Now at Bat: '*The Natural*.'" *New York Post* 10 May 1984: 27.

Washburn, Tina. "Levinson's Roy: A Child's Hero." *Literature/Film Quarterly* 24.1 (1996): 88–91.

Wasserman, Earl R. "The Natural: World Ceres." In Leslie A. Field and Joyce W. Field, eds. *Bernard Malamud and the Critics*. New York: New York University Press, 1970.

8

Cinematic American Camelots Lost and Found: The Film Versions of Mark Twain's A Connecticut Yankee in King Arthur's Court *and George Romero's* Knightriders

KEVIN J. HARTY

The legend of King Arthur and the Knights of the Round Table has readily found a home in the American imagination. As Alan and Barbara Tepa Lupack point out in their comprehensive study of the American Arthuriad, "the central literary text in American Arthuriana" remains Mark Twain's *A Connecticut Yankee in King Arthur's Court* (35), the only version of the legend "that fully realises the social and historical forces of its period" (Knight 187). But Twain's novel has always proven problematic. Its initial intent seemingly parodic, the novel starts off as what Justin Kaplan calls "an avowedly sweet-natured takeoff on ... Malory" and the "high sentiment" of Tennyson, to which American and British readers responded with such enthusiasm. "But once Hank Morgan realizes that cruelty, ignorance, and superstition are the driving forces in this picturesque society, his mild exasperation turns into rage, and Mark Twain's sweet-natured parody turns into anarchic rampage" (Kaplan 97–98).

Twain began the novel in part out of an impulse to spoof Malory's *Le Morte d'Arthur*, a book he liked. "Dream of being a knight errant in armour in the middle ages," he wrote in his notebook. "Have the notion & habits of thought of the present day mixed with the necessities of that. No pockets in the armor. No way to manage certain requirements of nature. Can't scratch.... Make disagreeable clatter when I enter church.... See Morte DArthur" (Clemens 291). As this notebook entry from 1885 suggests, Twain's original plan was somehow to introduce a contemporary American to European feudal society in order to ridicule the tendency to worship the past. But the story took shape over the next four years in a decidedly different form. As Lou Stanek notes:

While the balance of the comparison between past and present remained heavily in favor of contemporary American liberalism and innovation, the basic plot of his story caused a shift in mood. The satire of *A Connecticut Yankee* was ultimately directed against what Mark Twain would later call "the damned human race," not simply against Scott's or Tennyson's idealization of the past. While the Yankee's time travel to sixth-century England produced humorous, even light-hearted adventures, it ended on a darker note, with a cataclysmic battle using weapons of "modern" warfare [1].

Twain's novel becomes in the final analysis such a polemic against American idealism that it fails to strike a balance between the meliorism and the pessimism inherent in the Arthurian myth. It is curious, therefore, that it has been so popular with filmmakers. Indeed, it may have inspired more Arthurian films than any other literary work, though with decidedly curious results. Film audiences looking for a more balanced cinematic adaptation of the Arthurian myth in American terms will have to look elsewhere, to George Romero's 1981 *Knightriders*, as I will show below.

Actually, Twain's works have been a favorite of filmmakers in search of good plot lines since at least 1907, when Vitagraph made a one-reeler called *A Curious Dream* from the Twain short story. Twain, who gave permission for Vitagraph to make the film and who lived to see it, wrote that he found the film "frightfully and deliciously humorous" (Roman 20). A half-dozen other films based on Twain's works found appeared between 1907 and 1920, when Fox made the first film version of Twain's tale of Hank Morgan, a silent feature entitled *A Connecticut Yankee at King Arthur's Court.*[1]

Twain might not at first have recognized many of the details of this 1920 film as being inspired by his novel, had he lived long enough to see the Fox production.[2] (He died in 1910.) And this film set an unfortunate precedent. While Twain's novel offers a satire of both medieval and nineteenth-century Britain and an at times "disturbing picture of American and human ideals" (Lupack and Lupack 47), the 1920 and subsequent film versions of *A Connecticut Yankee* move further and further away from their source's biting edge. Filmmakers seem to have found Twain's message too bleak if not even inherently anti–American, so in adapting the novel to the screen they have made radical changes to their source.

In the 1920 Fox film, Twain's hero, Hank Morgan, "a Yankee of the Yankees" (Clemens 8), has become Martin Cavendish (played by Harry Myers[3]), a wealthy young man who is in love with his mother's secretary, Betty, though his socially conscious mother wants him to marry Lady Gray Gordon.

One night, while reading in his home library, Cavendish becomes fascinated by a suit of armor. As his mind wanders back to the days when knighthood was in flower, a burglar quietly enters the house. Cavendish discovers him, the two scuffle, and Cavendish is knocked unconscious as the thief stands over him, threatening him with a lance. When Cavendish opens his eyes, he has somehow traveled more than twelve hundred years back in time and finds himself lying under a tree, as a mounted Sir Sagramore is jabbing him with a lance. Except for the Yankee's time travel, there is so far not much Twain in this film.

As in the novel, Sagramore marches Cavendish off to Camelot, where linguistic confusion ensues. Cavendish is bewildered by the archaic English spoken by his captors, while his use of the latest American slang puzzles them. But all linguistic confusion is soon resolved when Cavendish begins adding *-eth* as a suffix to his nouns and verbs: "Cans't telleth me where the helleth I am?" he asks of a suddenly comprehending member of Arthur's court. Condemned to death, Cavendish saves himself in the well-known scene involving Merlin and the solar eclipse.[4]

Dubbed Sir Boss by a now grateful Arthur, Cavendish proceeds to modernize Camelot with the latest inventions, including telephones, electric lights, indoor plumbing, and automobiles manufactured from discarded suits of armor. The knights themselves soon punch time clocks and spend their lunch hours shooting craps. Impressed by Sir Boss's ingenuity, Arthur sends him to rescue the beautiful Lady Alisande ("Sandy") who is being held captive by the King's half-sister the wicked and, as portrayed by Rosemary Theby, the vampish Morgan Le Fay. The rescue is successful, but only after Cavendish rejects Morgan's amorous overtures and makes good use of his trusty six-shooter. (Like any red blooded American, Cavendish prefers violence to lust any day.)

Back at Camelot, Cavendish accepts a challenge to meet Sir Sagramore in the lists, but, instead of wearing armor and using a lance, he appears dressed as a cowboy armed with only a lariat. Cavendish soon yanks Sagramore from his horse and chases the rest of the armor-clad knights from the tournament field. Convincing Arthur to disguise himself, Cavendish conducts him on a tour of the domain so that the King can see for himself that "all this nobility stuff is bunk" (whereas, of course, naive Americanism is the real thing). When Arthur and Cavendish are captured by "the four horsemen of the eucalyptus" in the employ of Morgan, they are rescued by Sandy and Sir Lancelot. Finally, Cavendish comes to, discovers his experiences have been nothing but a dream, and, to settle matters, elopes with Betty.

In adapting Twain's novel, those responsible for the film missed no opportunity to add touches of contemporaneity to Bernard McConville's screenplay. When he is about to be burned at the stake, Cavendish, knowing that there will be a total solar eclipse within minutes, needs a diversion. Lighting a cigarette provides just the right diversion, and a film title cleverly announces "Finding his pack of Camels was a lucky strike," reflecting the intense competition between Camels and Lucky Strikes in the 1920s to corner the American male smoking market. Later in the film, while locked with Arthur in Morgan's prison, the ever-resourceful Yankee shows no fear. Examining the lock on their cell door, he tells the King not to worry: "I'm a Harvard man, and I just love to pick on a Yale lock!"—the best selling brand at the time.

Despite the liberties the film takes with its source in reducing any attempt at social satire to what is little more than romantic comedy, the 1920 Fox *Connecticut Yankee* garnered much critical praise. Burns Mantle declared the film the second-best screen comedy of the year, right behind Chaplin's *The Kid* (51),[5] while other critics commented that the film, directed by Emmett J. Flynn, proved the screen's potential for intelligent comedy rather than only for simple-minded slapstick (Patterson 143–44).

In the film's titles, references abound to the Volstead Act, Tin Lizzies, and the Battle of Argonne. Headed by Lancelot driving a flivver, the army of rescuing knights arrives on motorcycles (in an obviously unintended anticipation of George Romero's 1981 *Knightriders*), rather than on bicycles as they do in the novel. The film was made on a lavish scale. An announcement in the program for the film stated that "every available motorcyclist around Los Angeles was drafted for the big rescue scene, that 370 pounds of nitroglycerin were used to destroy a castle built in the hills, and that two miles of roadway were constructed for the march of the motorcycle army" (Review, *New York Times* 14). In addition, the film required sets big enough to support scenes in which as many as 1,000 people appeared" ("Special Service" 1673).

The plot of both novel and film is built around a dream, but the 1920 Fox film is a dream story with an unexpected twist. In

Harry C. Meyers as the Yankee and Rosemary Theby as Queen Morgan Le Fay in Emmett J. Flynn's 1920 film *A Connecticut Yankee at King Arthur's Court*. (Still courtesy of the Film Archive of the Museum of Modern Art.)

order to ensure moviegoers a surprise ending, contemporary cinematic practice dictated that screenplays offer no early hint that events in a film were fantastic or related to a dream sequence. The Fox *Connecticut Yankee* never deludes the viewer into believing that any of the fantastic things it presents ever took place, and yet, as one contemporary critic noted, "the effect is as enjoyable as if they *had* actually happened" (O'Dell 249–50).

The artistic and commercial success of this 1920 silent version of Twain's novel doubtless contributed to Fox's decision to remake the film eleven years later.[6] This second screen version of the novel, simply entitled *A Connecticut Yankee*, with Will Rogers as the Yankee, Myrna Loy as Morgan, and Maureen O'Sullivan as Sandy again takes considerable liberties with Twain's plot.[7] Here, the Yankee becomes Hank Martin, a repairman called in by a slightly crazed listener who thinks his radio is broadcasting discussions from King Arthur's court. Knocked out when a suit of armor falls on him, Martin awakens to find himself in Camelot. Events more or less familiar from Twain's novel follow. Martin's incantations "to bring on" the eclipse begin with the line "Prosperity! Farm relief! Freedom for Ireland—and light wines and beer!" and end with an invocation of "Coolidge, Hoover, and Al Smith!" And William Conselman's screenplay is filled with dialogue rich in other contemporary references. Hank uses a cigarette lighter rather than a match to outwit Merlin, telephone switchboards are staffed by flirtatious operators, messengers ply their trade on roller skates, and, in a variation on a dry cleaners, Martin opens a business that cleans and oils armor.

A joust once again matches Sir Sagramore in armor against Martin dressed as a cowboy. The contest is even broadcast on radio, sponsored by the "Camelot Iron Works — Builder of Lanceproof Armor." In a nice combination of cinematic special effects and realism, Morgan becomes enamored of the Yankee, whose innocence and shyness are emphasized when he blushes scarlet on the screen as she flirts with him. The film was of course released in black-and-white, but David Butler, the director, had each frame in this scene tinted progressively darker shades of pink (Sterling and Sterling 113). The final battle scene used a fleet of automobiles —174 Austins in all ("Will Rogers" 8. 7) — plus machine guns, sawed-off shotguns, tanks, helicopters, and airplanes that level a castle and knock out Martin, who then awakens in the present where a contemporary Clarence and Sandy need help in eloping. The film ends with Martin gladly lending a hand to assist young love.

The Will Rogers *A Connecticut Yankee* cost almost $750,000 to make (Review, *Variety* 20), a considerable sum for a film in its day, and proved a critical and commercial success despite its lack of fidelity to its source; Depression era America was in no mood for Twain's social satire. The *New York Times* selected the film as one of the year's ten best, and it was successfully rereleased in 1936.

Perhaps better known than either the 1920 or the 1931 screen versions of Twain's novel is Paramount's *A Connecticut Yankee in King Arthur's Court*, directed by Tay Garnett[8] with a screenplay by Edmund Beloin and starring Bing Crosby in the title role, William Bendix as Sir Sagramore, Sir Cedric Hardwicke as a buffonish King Arthur, and Rhonda Fleming as Sandy. As the film opens, Hank Martin visits Pendragon Castle and meets the present lord, a descendant of Arthur, to whom he tells in a flashback his time-travel adventure. In that story, Hank (again Martin rather than Morgan), a happy-go-lucky New England blacksmith, is knocked unconscious when he and his horse collide with a tree during a violent thunderstorm. Martin awakens to find himself face to face with Sir Sagramore, here cast as Martin's eventual apprentice in the role of Clarence from the novel.

Crosby as Martin has the expected run-ins with Merlin, but thanks to a pocketful of kitchen matches he is able to get the better of his sixth-century rival and to unnerve Arthur and his court sufficiently that they leave him alone to open a small blacksmith shop on the outskirts of Camelot. In the next plot complication, Martin becomes infatuated with Sandy (Crosby is no blushing Rogers), and despite the fact that she is betrothed to Sir Lancelot, Sandy returns Martin's affection. Once Lancelot finds out about this mutual attraction, he challenges the peace-loving Martin to a joust. Given permission by Arthur to choose his own weapon, Martin renders Lancelot helpless by entangling him in a lasso. Sandy, upset that Martin would use such an unchivalric tactic, rushes to Lancelot's side to comfort him.

Merlin and his accomplice, Sir Logris, then try to take over the kingdom by kidnapping Sandy and holding her prisoner. Martin goes to her rescue but receives a blow on the head in the process that transports him back to the present. Martin's arrival at Pendragon castle occurs several months later. After he tells his tale to the castle's current lord, the old man suggests that Martin visit the castle's garden to meet his niece before he leaves to return to America. Martin is both surprised and delighted to discover that the girl is the image of his beloved Sandy.

Truer in detail to the plot of its source than either the 1920 or the 1931 screen adaptations, Garnett's film is nonetheless the least successful of the three. Crosby's many fans may applaud the star's amply displayed musical talents — indeed, the film seems primarily a vehicle for showcasing his vocal abilities — but Garnett makes little use of the cinematic possibilities of his source.[9] The directorial method used throughout the film calls for the plot to advance not by dramatic interaction but rather by snappy tunes mixed with bits of rather silly dialogue: in attempting to instruct a sixth-century orchestra in some musical fine points, Martin exclaims for instance, "Puteth in the brass and taketh out the lead"[10] — in what seems like a comment taken from Martin Cavendish's 1920 dialogue.

Twain's novel returned to the screen in 1979 in the largely ignored *The Unidentified Flying Oddball*[11] directed for Disney by Russ Mayberry from a screenplay by Don Tait. With this cinematic adaptation, Twain's novel has become the stuff of children's film. In *Oddball*, a freak accident causes robotics engineer Tom Trimble to be launched along with a look-alike humanoid robot, Hermes, in the inaugural flight of a new spacecraft. Since the spacecraft travels faster than the speed of light, the reluctant astronaut finds himself, thanks to a NASA malfunction, traveling backward in time to the sixth century, where he meets a peasant girl, Alisande, and a goose, which she is convinced is her magically transformed father.

Captured by the evil Sir Mordred and taken before Arthur's court, Tom is unable to explain to the court where he has come from, despite his rambling synopsis of world history. Imprisoned and condemned to be burned at the stake, Tom is saved by his heat-resistant spacesuit. Later in the film, he uses magnets to disarm an array of foes. After accusing Mordred of treachery — the knight is trying to corner the real estate market in Camelot — Tom is obliged to fight him in a joust. Tom substitutes Hermes for himself in the lists, and Alisande looks on in horror as the figure she assumes to be Tom is cut to pieces. Hermes continues to fight despite multiple wounds and amputations, in a scene reminiscent of the battle between Arthur and the knight at the bridge in *Monty Python and the Holy Grail*. When Tom exposes Mordred's scheme, he is rewarded with a seat at the Round Table. He is, however, obliged to return to the present, although the film's closing scene has him turning the spacecraft's clock back so he can return to Camelot for Sandy.

At first glance, nothing could seem further from Twain's novel than this Disney film. Closer examination, however, shows that the novel and the film do have a number of points in common. In the novel, Sandy is convinced that a herd of swine are really enchanted princesses, whom she requires Hank to treat royally (Chapter 20). In the film, Sandy is convinced the goose is her father. Twain's novel uses language, especially German, which he regularly took to task in the novel and elsewhere in his writings, as the basis for much of its humor. So does the film. Tom's rambling survey of Western civilization delivered in schoolboy slang clearly baffles Arthur and his court, whose number includes a Sir Winston who looks, talks, and carries himself like Churchill. Finally, Twain's novel examines what happens when modern technology is imposed on medieval England. *The Unidentified Flying Oddball* carries this point further by widening the gap: here space-age technology meets medieval England with repeatedly comic results. If not always the most successful screen adaptation of Twain's novel, *The Unidentified Flying Oddball* may be closer in spirit to its source than the 1920, the 1931, and the 1949 films, while also being the most genuinely funny of the four.

Funny turns into silly in a made-for television version of Twain's novel that aired on NBC as a Christmas special in 1989[12] — the hundredth anniversary of the publication of the novel. In this telefilm directed by Mel Damski from a script by Pulitzer-prize winning dramatist Paul Zindel, the Yankee becomes Karen Jones, a Connecticut schoolgirl played by Keisha Knight Pulliam from *The Cosby Show*; Michael Gross from *Family Ties* plays Arthur. Knocked unconscious in a fall from a horse, Karen awakens in Camelot and undergoes some of the Yankee's usual adventures. Here her "magic" weapons are a Polaroid camera, a Walkman, and a tape recorder. She teaches aerobics and karate to Guinevere and the ladies of the court, whom she also encourages to develop a concern for endangered species. Previously, they carved ivory figures from elephant tusks; their consciousness having been raised by Karen, they now embroider pillows that read "Save the Elephants." Some of the novel's dialogue does survive in this telefilm, but too much of what Karen says ranges from the border-line obnoxious to the overly cute. And the weak environmentalist message is at best a superficial attempt to touch on the serious side of both the Arthurian myth and Twain's novel.

Late twentieth century youngsters continue to drop into Camelot by way of adaptations of Twain's novel in a film and another made-for-television special, both released in 1995: *A Kid in King Arthur's Court* directed by Michael Gottlieb from a screenplay by Michael Part and Robert Levy for Disney; and a Canadian telefilm *A Young Connecticut Yankee in King Arthur's Court* directed by R. L. Thomas from a screenplay jointly penned by Thomas and Frank Encarnacao. The Canadian made-for-television movie sends a shy suburban teenager jolted by a short in his electric guitar's amplifier back to King Arthur's Court. Once there, teenage Hank retraces, with some 1990s' updates, the misadventures of Twain's eponymous hero. Dubbed Sir Dude, Hank saves Camelot from the wiles of Morgan Le Faye in an adaptation dismissed by a critic from the *Toronto Star* as "an embarrassment to Canadian filmmaking, a fiasco from start to finish" (Quill B8).

In *A Kid in King Arthur's Court*, Twain's Hank Morgan becomes Calvin Fuller, an awkward fourteen-year-old Southern Californian who dreams of success on the Little League field. (In a possible nod to Bernard Malamud's *The Natural*, Calvin's team is called the Knights.) An earthquake conveniently opens a fissure in the middle of the baseball diamond into which Calvin slides; he emerges equally conveniently in sixth century England in Merlin's cave. Merlin,[13] here reduced to the disembodied ghost of the once-powerful mage, seeks a champion to defeat Lord Belasco, who is attempting to overthrow the ineffectual Arthur.

In *A Kid*, Calvin has, like a number of his cinematic predecessors, a love interest. Arthur has two daughters, Princess Sarah, whom Belasco wishes to marry, and Princess Katey, whom Camelot's twentieth-century visitor introduces to Bull Dog Double Bubble Gum, Sony Discmans, Big Macs, Swiss Army Knives, roller blades, a rock-and-roll battle of the bands, mountain bikes, and karate. In a nice initial twist, Sarah fights to defend Camelot disguised as the Black Knight, but the Disney film has no real feminist brief. The screenplay eventually settles for traditional gender roles.[14]

There is, of course, a long tradition of children's literature about Arthur, but the superimposition of the cinematic upon the juvenile in adapting Twain's novel for screen and television has in many ways produced even worse results than earlier attempts to turn the novel into a love story or a musical comedy. None of these genres is an appropriate vehicle for social commentary, let alone social criticism. As Elizabeth S. Sklar points out:

> where romance narrative is sociable, optimistic, and integrative, Twain's novel is antisocial, pessimistic, and violently disintegrative; things come together in romance, blow apart in Twain. Twain's bitter apocalypticism, as well as his premises, are diametrically opposed to, and completely incompatible with, the standard

Whoopi Goldberg as Dr. Vivien Morgan in Roger Young's 1998 telefilm *A Knight in Camelot*.

components of romance narrative (or juvenile text for that matter). In short, these [juvenile cinematic versions of Twain's novel] should never have been undertaken in the first place: they were doomed from the start [106].

In the most recent made-for-television version of Twain's novel, the 1998 Disney-ABC *A Knight in Camelot* directed by Roger Young, Hank changes gender and race, becoming Dr. Vivien Morgan (played by Whoopi Goldberg in full dreadlocks). Guinevere becomes the film's villain: she is jealous of the attention that Arthur pays to Vivien. Such tinkering with characters and their motivations does, as Barbara Tepa Lupack points out, provide Joe Wiesenfield's screenplay with perhaps a veneer of social concern, but with a decidedly mixed message. On one hand, Arthur gives voice to the quintessential American belief in democracy and equality, while Goldberg's Vivien seems at times willing to sacrifice the rights and needs of the individual for some greater societal good (Review 168–69).

But ultimately, as with earlier film and

television adaptations of Twain's novel, *A Knight in Camelot* advances any note of greater social concerns very, very quietly and unobtrusively. Taken as a group, these film adaptations can at times be funny, and Twain's novel is, among other things, a comic tour de force. But it is also much more. In writing the novel, Twain pulled together several strands of plot material: the Arthurian legend, the international novel depicting the confrontation between American and European cultures, the idea of time travel, barbed satire against the established Church and the monarchy, and finally the attack on what Twain came to call "the damned human race."[15]

This consistent failure of film to match the critical complexities of Twain's novel is one of the frustrations those who study cinema Arthuriana must confront: quantity and quality do not go hand and hand. What is at least the quintessential nineteenth century American literary recreation of the Arthuriad cannot, somehow, make its way to the screen or television intact. Directors and their screenwriters seemed to have decided that biting satire, misanthropy, and the carnage made possible by modern methods of warfare do not play well in Peoria — or anywhere else.[16] By watering down the novel, these films ultimately eliminate Twain's social critique and the ways in which he uses the novel to wrestle with a curious American dualism. In the novel, Hank Morgan, that "Yankee of the Yankees," is alternately chauvinistic and doubtful, optimistic and misanthropic.

There is, however, a successful, cinematic counterpart to Twain that seeks to present a genuinely American reworking of the Arthuriad. Where Twain can be read as essentially anti–American, this film can be read in just the opposite way. George Romero's 1981 film *Knightriders* had the bad luck to be given a limited original release during the same week as John Boorman's *Excalibur* and disappeared from movie screens within a few weeks.[17] A second release on the midnight circuit and on video has given the film a loyal, if limited, second audience, especially among fans of Romero's *Night of the Living Dead* classic horror series. But *Knightriders* has still not attracted nearly the audience and the critical attention it deserves. Unlike the film adaptations of Twain, Romero's film does not avoid social criticism, but unlike Twain's novel, it finds a balance between the meliorism and the pessimism of the Arthurian myth.

Romero's surface debt in *Knightriders* is to the American film western by way of its subgenre the biker film. The film's deeper debt is to the long tradition that sees Arthur as once and future king. Romero's earlier work as a director would at first suggest that he would be the last person to be interested in making an Arthurian film. But, like most directors of his generation, Romero grew up watching films: "I loved all genre films — horror films as well as war and cowboy films. Whenever one was at a neighborhood theatre or on television, I'd watch it" (Seligson 12). Older genre films also stimulated Romero's interest in the legend of Arthur: "I'd give my eyeteeth to make an *Ivanhoe*. In *Knightriders*, I'm borrowing from all those Cornel Wilde, Robert Taylor movies" (Seligson 16). In addition, *Knightriders*, like other Romero films, examines a community under siege from without. The menace here is not from an army of zombies but rather from the hucksterism and encroaching commercialism that threatens Billy, the film's Arthur, and the community he hopes to create, a community whose survival signals a potential rebirth of the power of the magical.[18] In Twain's novel, Hank Morgan had, of course, little time for Merlin's "magic," but the film adaptations of the novel reduce the magical to the level of the superficial.

Knightriders tells the story of a troupe of dropouts from mainstream American society who travel throughout rural Pennsylvania in the mid 1970s. The troupe consists of assorted artisans and a group of armor-clad motorcycle stuntpeople who travel from county fair to county fair to peddle their arts and crafts and to hold jousting tournaments. The troupe is headed by Billy — Sir William — and his queen, Linet. Around them, Billy has gathered a ragtag group who have adopted Arthurian (and some not so Arthurian) names. While Billy's troupe include Sirs Ban (of Boston), Hector (of Newark), Ewain, Bors, Marhalt, and Morgan (the film's conflation of the traditional characters of Morgan Le Fay and Mordred), as well as Merlin, there are also Alan, Tuck, and Little John from the legend of Robin Hood, Pippin from the legend of Charlemagne, and Sir Rocky (a woman, though a match to any man with whom she "does battle").

The film's opening sequence is visually striking. Before the initial titles appear, the camera shows a raven in flight — the raven will prove one of the film's central symbols — after which the camera cuts to a naked Billy and Linet lying in the forest. Billy is next shown flagellating himself and then kneeling before his upraised sword. Linet and he then robe, and, just when we assume Billy has mounted his trusty steed, he is shown riding off on his motorcycle with Linet holding on to his waist as the opening titles begin to roll.

While Billy espouses a utopian ideal, *Knightriders* is not always clear about what his vision and what the threats to that vision are. At one point in the film, Merlin links Billy's dream of a raven that will some day defeat him with the notion of destiny by telling Malory's story of Arthur's unsuccessful attempt to avoid his destiny by ordering the slaughter of all male children to eliminate the prophesied threat to his throne from Mordred.[19]

Billy rejects the adulation accorded him by his followers and his fans because he "is not trying to be a hero"— he is trying "to fight the dragon." That dragon takes several forms in the film, each intent upon destroying Billy's utopic vision: a corrupt deputy sheriff named Cook, a slick entertainment promoter, a rapacious television reporter, and eventually even Morgan. Billy with mixed success thwarts their efforts, but the film's central tournament signals the downfall of Billy's Camelot. In the midst of a scene of general mayhem, a Native American bearing a raven on his shield appears to do battle. While Billy does defeat him, he sustains a life-threatening wound as the tournament's spectators turn into a howling mob egging on the increasing violence. Morgan and his followers split with the troupe to follow the promise of riches and slick promotional tours. Alan, the film's Lancelot, also leaves, and Billy's few remaining loyal followers sit and wonder what will happen next.

Eventually, Alan and Morgan and his followers return to Billy's side for a last tournament, at the end of which Morgan rightly wins the crown and Billy entrusts Linet to Alan's care. With only the Native American as his companion, Billy evens the score with Cook and makes amends to a young boy to whom he had previously refused to give an autograph. In a scene reminiscent of the episode between Arthur and young Tom Malory in White's *The Once and Future King* (634–37), he gives the young boy his sword. Then imagining himself transformed into a knight in shining armor riding his charger across a field, Billy rides off down the highway. The fantasy ends abruptly outside Gettysburg when Billy is struck and killed by a truck. The film's final scenes take place at Billy's grave where a saddened troupe gather under Morgan's leadership to mourn Billy. The film's last frames once again show the raven, suggesting that Billy has finally achieved his goal, that he may well be once and future king.

Knightriders is not without its flaws. The film is clearly in need of editing. Originally almost three hours long, the film was released with a running time of 145 minutes — making it even longer than Boorman's too long *Excalibur*. Billy's vision is not, as I have already indicated, always clearly articulated. But that vision is a version of the American dream, a utopian society that accepts all people regardless of race, sex, affectional preference, or disability. *Knightriders* is in many ways a latter day cinematic Arthurian romance. As Sutton notes in his review of the film:

> Romero's central concern has always been with the direction and dilemma of civilisation, and in *Knightriders* he proposes an "optimistic" vision by invoking the rigorous morality, the Edenic virtues of Camelot. The hype of the media, the corruption of the law, the material overindulgence of the average citizen is contrasted with the selfless dreams and organic structure of Arthurian legend [38].

Not only does *Knightriders* find that the Arthurian legend and the American dream are compatible, the film also presents — though it finally dispels — a vision as dark at Twain's.

And the spirit of Malory's *Le Morte d'Arthur* informs the film as well, depending upon what we think that spirit may be. In 1971, Elizabeth T. Pochoda published a study of Malory called *Arthurian Propaganda* in which she argued that *Le Morte d'Arthur* was in part a text grounded in fifteenth century theories of what we would today call political science. In brief, Pochoda argued that Malory saw in the world of Arthur a political ideal gone wrong, which he offered as a corrective to his contemporaries in a country long torn by civil war and political strife. According to Pochoda, what Malory essentially suggests to his contemporaries is a way *not* to go.

While a number of directors and screenwriters have (falsely) claimed Malory

Amy Ingersoll as Lady Linet and Ed Harris as King Billy in George Romero's *Knightriders*.

as their putative source, Romero makes no such claim. But, despite the obvious differences between a literary work set in a fifteenth century conception of a medieval past and a film set in what was then contemporary rural western Pennsylvania, *Knightriders* has much in common with Malory philosophically, at least as Pochoda reads *Le Morte d'Arthur*. Romero argues for a clear fit between somewhat radical contemporary American values and the Arthurian ideal, and *Knightriders* examines that ideal as it is practiced by an itinerant group of motorcycle stunt riders. As Romero indicated in an interview, "The motorcycle culture seemed to fit the Arthurian story. The bikers are a romanticized image, at least in this country. They have their own culture and attitude of this is us, and the rest of the world is you. That made sense on a pure story level, and as allegory" (Burke-Block 25)

In the final analysis, *Knightriders* presents a utopic quest, a Malorian meditation on the possibility of recreating the Arthurian ideal in a troubled and fractured America. Romero's *Knightriders* is clearly not a cinematic retelling of what Malory himself called "the whole book of King Arthur and his noble knights of the Round Table." Nor is it as finely tuned a social commentary as Twain's *A Connecticut Yankee in King Arthur's Court*. The film's distinction lies in the fact that, unlike the many cinematic adaptations of Twain's novel, it rings true to a unified, if flawed, ideal and represents one of the most genuine American cinematic expressions of the Arthuriad that we have had.[20] *Knightriders* embraces America despite all its flaws, something Twain could not or was unwilling to do. In Romero's view, there is no "damned human race." There is simply a flawed dream capable of redemption by one of the most enduring myths of Western civilization.[21]

NOTES

1. Unfortunately, the 1920 Fox *Connecticut Yankee* appears to be lost. No complete copy survives in any of the major film archives in the United States, France, or Great Britain. When it was released, the film was 8,291 feet long on eight reels and ran for slightly more than 100 minutes. The Film Archive at the Museum of Modern Art in New York owns a set of stills and about 30 minutes of footage from the film spliced together on three reels in no particular order. The Library of Congress owns an additional five minutes of footage consisting of random scenes again spliced together in no particular order.

2. Roman quotes an unidentified critic who, when the film was released, remarked that "this *Connecticut Yankee* is William Fox's, not Mark Twain's" (25).

3. The part was originally offered to Douglas Fairbanks, who turned it down. See the review of the film in *Variety* 28 January 1921: 40.

4. Given the American penchant for monolingualism, Cavendish's adding a simple suffix to words to make himself understood remains fairly typical even today whenever an (innocent?) American abroad encounters a language other than (American) English. For the incident involving the eclipse, see chapter 6 in the novel.

5. Mantle's sentiments were echoed by the critic for the *New York Times*, who wrote: "So although there are those who would rather see Charlie Chaplin in 'The Kid' than 'A Connecticut Yankee,' everyone can see both and enjoy both, in different degrees and for different reasons, but with good measure in the case of each" (14).

6. The 1920 film version of the novel was also the inspiration for the very successful 1927 Broadway musical with songs by Rodgers and Hart.

7. Interestingly, in reviewing the 1920 film, the critic for *Exceptional Photoplays* remarked: "Most of the acting comes up to the level of the picture. The role of the Yankee, it is true, simply cries out for Will Rogers (a Yankee from Oklahoma)" (2).

8. In 1954, Garnett directed a second Arthurian film, *The Black Knight*.

9. For legal and financial reasons, the score of the 1949 film owes no debt to that of the 1927 stage musical, which had been revived in 1943. See Nathan (1907) for an explanation of the complications surrounding the screen rights to the 1927 musical.

10. Garnett's film is not, however, without its admirers. Bookbinder praises the "outstanding art direction, set decoration and photography ... and a spectacular studio recreation of Camelot" (184).

11. In Great Britain, the film was released as *The Spaceman and King Arthur*.

12. Other television versions of Twain's novel

include Franklin Schaffner's 60-minute abridged version of the novel for CBS, in which Boris Karloff played Arthur; the 1954 ABC-Kraft Theatre *A Connecticut Yankee*; the 1955 Max Liebman Production of the Rodgers and Hart musical for NBC, in which Boris Karloff again played Arthur; the 1960 *Tennessee Ernie Ford Meets King Arthur*, which did have the distinction of being directed by Lee J. Cobb but which tried unsuccessfully to substitute Ford's homespun wit for Twain's satiric edge; a 1970 feature-length animated version of the novel made for Australian television; and a second 60-minute abridged version of the novel, first broadcast in 1978 as part of the PBS *Once Upon a Classic* series. For further details on these television versions of Twain's novel, see Harty, *The Reel Middle Ages*.

13. Ron Moody, who earlier played Merlin in *The Unidentified Flying Oddball*, returned to the role in this Disney film. *Excalibur*'s Mordred, Robert Addie, plays the film's Sagramore.

14. For the mixed messages sent by screen adaptations of Twain's novel which change Hank into a youngster, see Sklar 97–108.

15. Between 1900 and 1909, Twain worked on the manuscript of a work entitled *The Damn Human Race* (Geismar 534). Publication of the work (text in DeVoto 209–32) was delayed because of the objections of Twain's daughter, Clara Clemens.

16. Neither the 1970 full-length animated version nor the 1978 abridged PBS version of Twain's novel remains any truer to the darker side of Twain's novel.

Despite its title and its anti–American propagandistic intent, the 1987 Russian film directed by Viktor Gres for Dovzhenko Studios, *Novye Prikluchenia Janke pri Dvore Kovola Artura* (*The New Adventures of a Connecticut Yankee at King Arthur's Court*), is, according to a film production location report, "not a screening of Mark Twain's novel, but a fantasy based on all his works" (Basina 18).

The 1989 telefilm purposely softened Twain's message to make the novel more palatable to viewers by eliminating its source's "heavy social satire about the class system" and "propensity for violence" (Knutzen 4–5).

In 1991, Terry Gilliam, who had already directed two Arthurian films (*Monty Python and the Holy Grail* and *The Fisher King*), and screenwriter Robert Mark Kamen began work on a screen version of Twain's novel that would develop the novel's darker side. Gilliam was committed to "tell the tale the way Twain intended, as a cautionary comment on warfare and America's unerring sense of intervention." But eventually both director and screenwriter could not reach agreement on the project's direction — Gilliam would eventually accuse Kamen of selling out — and the film was never made (McCabe 158).

17. The film was originally released in only three major markets, New York, Los Angeles and Florida, overrun at the time with college students on Spring break (Gagne 117).

18. As Gagne points out, Romero's earlier film, *Martin*, also laments the death of the magical in the modern world. In addition, Gagne argues that *Knightriders* is "more than a bit autobiographical" (108).

19. See Malory Book I, Chapter 27 (1: 58–59). The story of the slaughter of the innocents is, of course, Biblical.

20. Other films unexpectedly genuine in their approach to, if not in the particulars of, the Arthuriad include *Four Diamonds*, *The Mighty*, and *The Sixth Sense*. See Harty, "Looking for Arthur in All the Wrong Places" 57–62; and Harty, "'Arthur? Arthur?'—Where Exactly Is the Cinematic Arthur to Be Found?" forthcoming in Alan Lupack, ed. *New Directions in Arthurian Studies*. Cambridge, Eng.: D. S. Brewer, 2002.

21. In writing this essay, I have benefited greatly from the comments of my colleagues John Christopher Kleis and James A. Butler, to whom I am happy to express my thanks.

WORKS CITED

Basina, Natalia. "On the Spot Report." *Soviet Film* 6 (1987): 18–19.

Bookbinder, Robert. *The Films of Bing Crosby*. Secaucus, N.J.: Citadel, 1977.

Burke-Block, Candace. "The *Film Journal* Interviews ... George Romero on 'Knightriders.'" *Film Journal* 84 (4 May 1981): 25.

Clemens, Samuel Langhorne [Mark Twain]. *A Connecticut Yankee in King Arthur's Court*. Ed. Alison R. Esnor. New York: Norton, 1982.

DeVoto, Bernard, ed. *Mark Twain, Letters from the Earth*. New York: Harper and Row, 1962.

Gagne, Paul R. *The Zombies That Ate Pittsburgh: The Films of George Romero*. New York: Dodd, Mead, 1987.

Geismar, Maxwell. *Mark Twain: An American Prophet*. Boston: Houghton Mifflin, 1970.

Harty, Kevin J. "Looking for Arthur in All the Wrong Places: A Note on M. Night Shyamalan's *The Sixth Sense*." *Arthuriana* 10 (Winter 2000): 57–62. [Special issue on *Screening Camelot: Further Studies of Arthurian Cinema*. Ed. Alan Lupack and Kevin J. Harty.]

_____. *The Reel Middle Ages: American, Western and Eastern European, Middle Eastern and Asian Films About Medieval Europe*. Jefferson, N.C.: McFarland, 1999.

Kaplan, Justin. "A Connecticut Yankee in Hell." *American Heritage* 40 (November 1989): 97–104.

Knight, Stephen. *Arthurian Literature and Society.* London: Macmillan, 1983.

Knutzen, Eirik. "Michael Gross in a Royal Role." *Philadelphia Inquirer TV Week* 17–23 December 1989: 4–5.

Lupack, Alan, and Barbara Tepa Lupack. *King Arthur in America.* Cambridge, Eng.: D. S. Brewer, 1999.

Lupack, Barbara Tepa. Review of *A Knight in Camelot. Arthuriana* 9 (Spring 1999): 167–69.

Malory, Sir Thomas. *Le Morte d'Arthur.* Ed. Janet Cowen. 2 vols. 1969. rpt. New York: Penguin, 1977.

Mantle, Burns. Review of *A Connecticut Yankee at King Arthur's Court. Photoplay* 20 (June 1921): 51.

McCabe, Bob. *Dark Knights & Holy Fools: The Art and Films of Terry Gilliam.* New York: Universe Publishing, 1999.

Nathan, Paul S. "Books into Films." *Publisher's Weekly* 153 (1 May 1948): 1907.

O'Dell, Scott. *Representative Photoplays Analyzed.* Hollywood, Calif.: Palmer Institute for Authorship, 1924.

Patterson, Frances Taylor. *Cinema Craftsmanship.* New York: Harcourt, 1921.

Pochoda, Elizabeth T. *Arthurian Propaganda: Le Morte D'Arthur as an Historical Ideal of Life.* Chapel Hill: University of North Carolina Press, 1971.

Quill, Greg. "CBC Critics Best Heed a Warning from the U.S." *Toronto Star* 1 June 1995: B8.

Review of *A Connecticut Yankee. Variety* 15 April 1931: 20.

Review of *A Connecticut Yankee at King Arthur's Court. Exceptional Photoplays* 4 (March 1921): 2.

_____. *New York Times* 15 March 1921: 14.

_____. *Variety* 28 January 1921: 40.

Roman, Robert C. "Mark Twain on the Screen." *Films in Review* 12 (1961): 20–33.

Seligson, Tom. "George Romero: Revealing the Monsters Within Us." *Twilight Zone* 1 (August 1981): 12–17.

Sklar, Elizabeth S. "Twain for Teens: Young Yankees in Camelot." In Kevin J. Harty, ed. *King Arthur on Film: New Essays on Arthurian Cinema.* Jefferson, N.C.: McFarland, 1999.

"Special Service Section on *A Connecticut Yankee in* [sic] *King Arthur's Court.*" *Motion Picture News* 26 February 1921: 1673–82.

Stanek, Lou. *A Teacher's Manual for A Connecticut Yankee in King Arthur's Court.* Berkeley: University of California Press, 1984.

Sterling, Bryan B., and Frances N. Sterling. *Will Rogers in Hollywood.* New York: Crown, 1984.

Sutton, Mark. Review of *Knightriders. Films and Filming* 334 (July 1982): 38.

White, T. H. *The Once and Future King.* 1958. rpt. New York: Berkeley, 1966.

"Will Rogers and King Arthur." *New York Times* 29 March 1931: 8. 7.

9

The Ironic Tradition in Four Arthurian Films

RAYMOND H. THOMPSON

The high-minded ideals of Arthurian romance have over the centuries proven an inspiration not only for chivalrous behavior but also for irony and humor. After all, actions that impress one person as noble and self-sacrificing may strike another as foolish and impractical. The Holy Grail was a source of religious inspiration for Arthur's knights, to whom it represented the highest quest. Yet who in his right mind, one might ask, would spend years seeking an object of such disputed appearance and uncertain location? Hank Morgan, the nineteenth-century protagonist of Mark Twain's *A Connecticut Yankee in King Arthur's Court*, concludes, "There was worlds of reputation in it, but no money" (78).

The ironic tradition in Arthurian literature has remained strong throughout the centuries, from Chrétien de Troyes and the *Gawain*-poet in the Middle Ages to Mark Twain and Thomas Berger in more recent times, and thus it is not surprising to find it intruding into the medium of Arthurian films. Between 1963 and 1989, four films have adopted an ironic approach to Arthurian legend. *The Sword in the Stone*, an animated feature directed by Wolfgang Reitherman for the Disney Studios in 1963, is loosely based upon T. H. White's *The Sword in the Stone* (1938). *Monty Python and the Holy Grail*, directed by Terry Gilliam and Terry Jones for Python Pictures in 1975, draws upon general Arthurian tradition rather than any one source. *The Unidentified Flying Oddball* (released in Great Britain as *The Spaceman and King Arthur*), directed by Russ Mayberry for Disney Studios in 1979, and *A Connecticut Yankee in King Arthur's Court*, directed by Mel Damski for Consolidated Productions and shown on NBC Television as a 1989 Christmas holiday special, are both based on Mark Twain's *A Connecticut Yankee in King Arthur's Court*, published in 1889.

Of the four films, *Monty Python and the Holy Grail* has achieved the most enduring popularity and critical recognition. The passage of time has not been kind to *The Sword in the Stone*, as critics have observed: "Though well-received when it came out, and grossing $4.5 million, *The Sword in the Stone* has sunk out of sight since it came out in the early 1960s. It is seldom mentioned in discussions of Disney's work and no character in it evolved into a Disney favorite" (Nash 7:3250). *The Unidentified Flying Oddball* has received even less critical attention, nor is *A Connecticut Yankee in King Arthur's Court* likely to do any better. By contrast, *Monty Python and the Holy Grail* is recognized as the finest film by the Monty Python troupe and has remained a perennial favorite with the devoted fans of their work (Proudy 4:1633–1637; Burns 86–97). As a study of all four films reveals, their success has depended upon the skill with which they use the ironic techniques so central to their vision of the Arthurian legend.

The failure of the film adaptation of *The Sword in the Stone* to develop into a Disney favorite is disappointing, because the book is well loved by readers and would seem to lend itself readily to the Disney fantasy touch. The film, however, borrows little from the book beyond the basic situation of the young Arthur, or Wart as he is known, learning valuable lessons about life while magically transformed into various creatures by his tutor, Merlin the Magician.

Both Wart's first transformation, into a perch, and the wizard's duel with Madame Mim are also found in the book, but the details are changed. In the former episode, Wart's conversation with the huge pike is replaced by an exciting and at times humorous chase. This change allows the film to replace words with action, yet still make essentially the same point about the dangers of power as does the book. It also provides many opportunities for irony, as the expectation by both pursuer and audience that Wart the perch will be caught is repeatedly, and often comically, frustrated.

Unfortunately, exciting and humorous chases occur both frequently and lengthily in the film, by the wolf, the squirrel, the hawk, and Madame Mim (in various shapes). Consequently, the novelty palls despite the ingenuity of the individual situations depicted. Moreover, because so much time is spent on chases, particular devices recur predictably. Thus, on several occasions, a friendly creature pulls on the pursuing predator's tail, slowing it just enough to allow Wart to evade snapping jaws or clutching talons by inches: Merlin (in the shape of a tench) and the owl Archimedes both hinder the pike, the female squirrel, the wolf, and Archimedes the hawk.

The message of these chase scenes is that smaller creatures can escape and even defeat a physically stronger foe through quick wits and courage. This philosophy is a firm favorite with Disney, dating back to his early cartoons, and it is developed with great success in classics like *Cinderella* and *The Jungle Book*. It is central to *The Sword in the Stone*, however, not only because so much of the film is devoted to chases, but also because of Wart's domestic situation. In White's novel, Wart is loved by everyone, even Kay in his own way, and he enjoys a glorious childhood in a community where everybody is happy. In the film, by contrast, he becomes a Cinderella figure, bullied by both the blustering Ector and the oafish Kay. Yet just as he eludes the larger animal predators, so he confounds Ector and Kay. Despite their low opinion of him, he rises to heights undreamed of, becoming king of England. They, by contrast, discover they have less to be proud of than they think, when they are soundly defeated by the ensorceled kitchen mops and dishes.

Merlin is another example of adult incompetence, setting off in the wrong direction for Ector's castle, and arousing the mirth of Archimedes when he tangles his model airplane in his beard. Yet like Wart he also demonstrates how those discounted by others can achieve more than expected, when he defeats Madame Mim by turning into a tiny but potent germ.

This pattern in which the weak overcome the strong affords ample opportunity for irony, but it does grow tiresome through repetition. Moreover, it obscures other ideas that are present in the film. The transformations teach Wart a number of lessons, but they are forgotten amid the hectic action of chases and neglected in the aftermath. Wart learns the power of love when he is pursued through the trees by an amorous female squirrel, but his vigorous defense of Merlin against the criticism of Ector emphasizes the importance of open-mindedness rather than love for his tutor. And Merlin's transformations in the wizards' duel focus upon the comic effect of his bumbling impracticality, rather than the message that knowledge and wisdom bring power. The result is a film that offers little beyond the one basic message, and through repetition it grows tiresome, despite the charm of individual scenes.

The Disney Studios returned to the Arthurian legend in *The Unidentified Flying Oddball*. Although based upon Twain's *A Connecticut Yankee in King Arthur's Court*, it too borrows little more than the essential situation: in this case, a modern man with advanced technological skills who travels back in time to the days of King Arthur. As in the novel, he survives burning at the stake, is befriended by Clarence the page, makes an enemy of Merlin, and falls in love with Sandy, but that virtually exhausts the similarities. Instead, action centers upon a plot by Mordred and Merlin to usurp Arthur's kingdom. It is foiled because the hero, Tom Trimble, employs such modern devices as rockets and electromagnets to support the King.

The irony in the film arises from a number of sources. There are unexpected parallels with features of the modern age: for example, the speeches of one knight recall those of Winston Churchill, and Merlin's chambers are modeled on a doctor's office, complete with receptionist, who primly announces, "The magician will see you now." There are also examples of naive behavior by the people of Arthur's era: Sandy believes, on dubious circumstantial evidence, that her father has been transformed into a goose; and Arthur, reproving Gawain for unguardedly turning his back on the enemy, commits the same mistake himself while pulling out a spear that has pinned the knight's cloak to a door. Fortunately, the butt of the spear knocks down the onrushing soldier.

Most of the irony, however, is caused by the bewilderment of Arthur and his followers over Tom's modern gadgetry and language usage. Tom survives burning at the stake, thanks to his heat-resistant space suit, and he flies about in a one-man rocket-powered propulsion unit, attacking the enemy where they least expect it. His fondness for jargon based upon such features of contemporary life as fast food and baseball, together with an inability to discern what information is really important for his listeners to know, cause them great confusion.

The problem here, as in *The Sword in the Stone*, is overkill. The idea of magnetizing Mordred's sword and then attaching metal objects to it until it grows too heavy to wield is a clever example of how modern scientific knowledge can defeat physical superiority, in spite of most people's expectation of victory for the latter, but the actual fight scene is prolonged unduly. Moreover, the idea surfaces again at the climax of the action, when Tom's look-alike robot companion uses their spacecraft's electromagnets to immobilize Mordred's armored troops. The scene in which they are drawn back to the craft, one after another, is extended at far too great a length. Once the results of an action cease to be unexpected, there is no longer any irony.

The same failure mars the joust between Mordred and the robot. The ability of the machine to keep functioning despite the loss of an arm certainly confounds the spectators, who believe it is Tom, but the dismemberment continues until the irony becomes merely gruesome. Arthur speaks for us all when he urges Mordred to put an end to the "butchery."

Nor is Tom's use of modern jargon any more successful. People cannot be expected to understand language based upon developments that lie in the future. The audience realizes this after a couple of conversations have taken place, and it is baffled that Tom, for all his mechanical skill, does not.

Sheila White as Alisande and Dennis Dugan as Spaceman Tom Trimble in Russ Mayberry's 1979 film *The Unidentified Flying Oddball.*

Thus, the irony generated by the interaction of ancient and modern attitudes fades as responses become predictable through repetition. The novelty palls rapidly because the individual incidents lack the ingenuity of those found in *The Sword in the Stone*. There just is not enough variety to sustain interest, despite the occasionally funny moment.

The 1989 *A Connecticut Yankee in King Arthur's Court* is one in a continuing series of adaptations of Twain's novel to the screen. Released on television as a Christmas special for younger viewers, it stars Keshia Knight Pulliam, the youngest daughter in *The Cosby Show*, as Karen Jones from Hartford, Connecticut. This version adopts not only the basic idea of a modern person traveling back to Arthur's day but also a number of specific details and incidents, such as Karen's use of the solar eclipse to escape burning at the stake, taking the name Sir Boss, traveling with the King disguised as peasants, and being rescued by knights on bicycles. Here too, however, the action focuses upon a plot by Mordred, Morgana de la Fey, and Merlin to seize Arthur's throne.

Irony again stems from the interaction of modern and Arthurian culture. When Karen teaches aerobic dancing, karate, and the equality of women to Guinevere and her ladies-in-waiting, we relish the incongruity of such elegant aristocrats "working out." The same incongruity is achieved by the sight of Arthur's knights in full armor riding on bicycles.

Yet too often the effect is marred by carrying the superstitious response of Arthur's court to excessive lengths. Their astonishment and fear at such modern inventions as the Polaroid camera and tape recorder, both of which, they believe, trap a part of themselves that can be harmed, seem unwarranted. While Twain's novel also stresses the credulity of people in the sixth century, Hank Morgan has to demonstrate his powers more devastatingly, not only with the eclipse (which occurs at the outset of the story, not near its conclusion as in the film), but also by blowing up buildings and people from time to time.

The contrast can be seen in the episode where the King and the Yankee, disguised as peasants, are attacked by knights for failing to show proper respect to their social superiors. In the novel, Hank blows up the two knights with a dynamite bomb, and "during the next fifteen minutes we stood under a steady drizzle of microscopic fragments of knights and hardware and horse-flesh" (272). In the film, Karen frightens off their single assailant by recording and playing back his speech. He flees, proclaiming that she is a "voice witch." Hank's violence would be out of character in Karen, who encourages the Queen and her ladies to decorate cushions with the motto "Save the Elephants" (in itself an ironic contrast with the views of Hank, who is willing to exploit everything), but it does much more to account for his reputation as a powerful magician who should be treated with healthy respect. Presumably in an attempt to compensate for the lack of convincing motivation, some of the actors compound the problem by overacting (though in fairness it must be admitted that any fear they demonstrate might strike the audience as excessive).

The naivete of the characters is not confined to their response to modern wonders. Arthur trusts Mordred and Morgana, despite warnings from knights such as Lancelot, and he is easily outwitted by the plotters. Without more justification than the script offers, this behavior taxes the belief of the audience. A king unaware that his people are being taxed ninety percent of their income would hardly have survived even as long as he has. But then perhaps it was assumed that only a monarch so out of touch with reality would make a young girl one of his knights. One does not look for reality from a fantasy, especially since it all may be no more than a dream resulting from a blow to the head, but one certainly expects the motivations of the characters to be convincing, even if only in their own terms.

Monty Python and the Holy Grail is the creation of the comedy troupe comprising Graham Chapman, John Cleese, Terry Gilliam, Terry Jones, Eric Idle, and Michael Palin. Their popular comedy series *Monty Python's Flying Circus* ran on British television from 1969 to 1974, and they went on to make a number of films. Their style, which has been described as "comic anarchy" (Proudy 4:1634), is offensive to some, but it has built up a devoted and enthusiastic following. In the film, the Grail quest serves as a narrative frame for a series of comic sketches, in which members of the troupe play several different roles.

As in the other films, the Arthurian borrowing for the narrative frame is confined to the basic situation: this time, the quest by the Knights of the Round Table for the Holy Grail. Although probably borrowed from Malory, at least indirectly, the story is freely adapted, adding, for example, such non-traditional knights as the cowardly Sir Robin. Some of the motifs it employs are found in more than one source. Thus, the voyage of Arthur and Bedevere on the mysterious vessel recalls that of Galahad and his companions, not only in Malory, but in other accounts based on his source, the French Vulgate *Queste del Saint Graal*.

The sources of the comic sketches within the narrative frame are even less easy to identify. The Camelot dance scene evokes Lerner and Loewe's musical *Camelot*, and Castle Anthrax recalls the Castle of Maidens in both Malory and Chrétien de Troyes. Most of the episodes, however, seem to be based upon general romance tradition rather than any one account; for example, Arthur's fight against the Black Knight, who refuses to yield despite the amputation of all his limbs, derides the exaggerations of knightly combat that occur everywhere. Others, like the witch hunt, come from outside Arthurian tradition entirely.

Most of the irony is aimed at the many conventions that occur in medieval romance, especially those connected with deeds of valor. The mindless enthusiasm for fighting is mocked not only in Arthur's encounter with the Black Knight, who dismisses the loss of an entire arm as "just a scratch ... I've had worse," but also in Lancelot's "rescue" of the prince in the tower. "I sometimes get a bit carried away," he confesses, after slaughtering many of the wedding guests, including such inoffensive figures as the garlanded maidens dancing in a circle. The knights are not always so fierce, however. They are forced to beat an ignominious retreat when bombarded with livestock by the French soldiers, and Sir Robin's flight from the three-headed knight is celebrated in song by his accompanying minstrels. Nor do they have much success against the rabbit that guards the cave.

Despite the special attention to knightly combat, few romance conventions are spared the Monty Python irony. Love and the rescue of maidens in distress are mocked in Lancelot's rescue of the prince, whom he mistakes for a princess, in the tower; mysterious and perilous castles, by Castle Anthrax, which is filled with damsels only too eager to be ravished; the imposition of difficult tasks upon the hero, by the demand for a shrubbery by the Knights Who Say "Ni"; religious devotion, by God's irritable command that the knights seek the Holy Grail; magicians, by Tim the Enchanter, who can set off explosions yet fears a rabbit; the unthinking assumptions of feudal authority, by Arthur's argument with a subject from an "anarcho-syndicalist commune."

Nor is the irony confined to romance conventions. The need to answer difficult questions before passing over the Bridge of Death is a motif from folklore and legend; the call to "bring out your dead" is from history; and the commentary of the scholar is from the television documentary (or the university lecture hall).

This variety certainly helps to avoid the predictability that mars the other films. Nevertheless, so wide a range of targets might have caused confusion in the mind of the audience if certain ironic techniques had not been deployed to link the material more closely. First of all, the extensive use of double reversals integrates the action within the individual episodes. When Bedevere reasons with the peasants who accuse a young woman of being a witch on very flimsy evidence, we expect him to expose the folly of their accusations. The charge by one of their number, that he had been turned into a newt but had "got better," seems improbable even to his companions. Instead, Bedevere concludes by proposing the equally ridiculous test of weighing her against a duck. Yet this test does not prove her innocent, as we might confidently assume, for woman and duck turn out to weigh the same: "It's a fair cop," she wryly admits.

In search of the Holy Grail, Galahad pounds at the door of the sinister Castle Anthrax, but expectations of either dire perils or mystical revelations are dispelled by the warm welcome from its nubile inhabitants. Galahad resists their overtures and seeks to escape, until urged to spank them all, then engage in oral sex. At this invitation, his resistance unexpectedly melts, and he decides to "stay a bit longer" after all. Any prospect of an orgy is denied, however, by the arrival of Lancelot and another knight, who rescue him from his "deadly peril."

This series of reversals is further enriched by associations with Arthurian tradition. Recollections of the Castle of Maidens in Chrétien de Troyes's *Conte du Graal*, with roots in tales of the Celtic Otherworld, or of demons in disguise seeking to seduce the Grail knight to his eternal damnation, are contrasted with attitudes that belong in an English girls' school. The tradition of

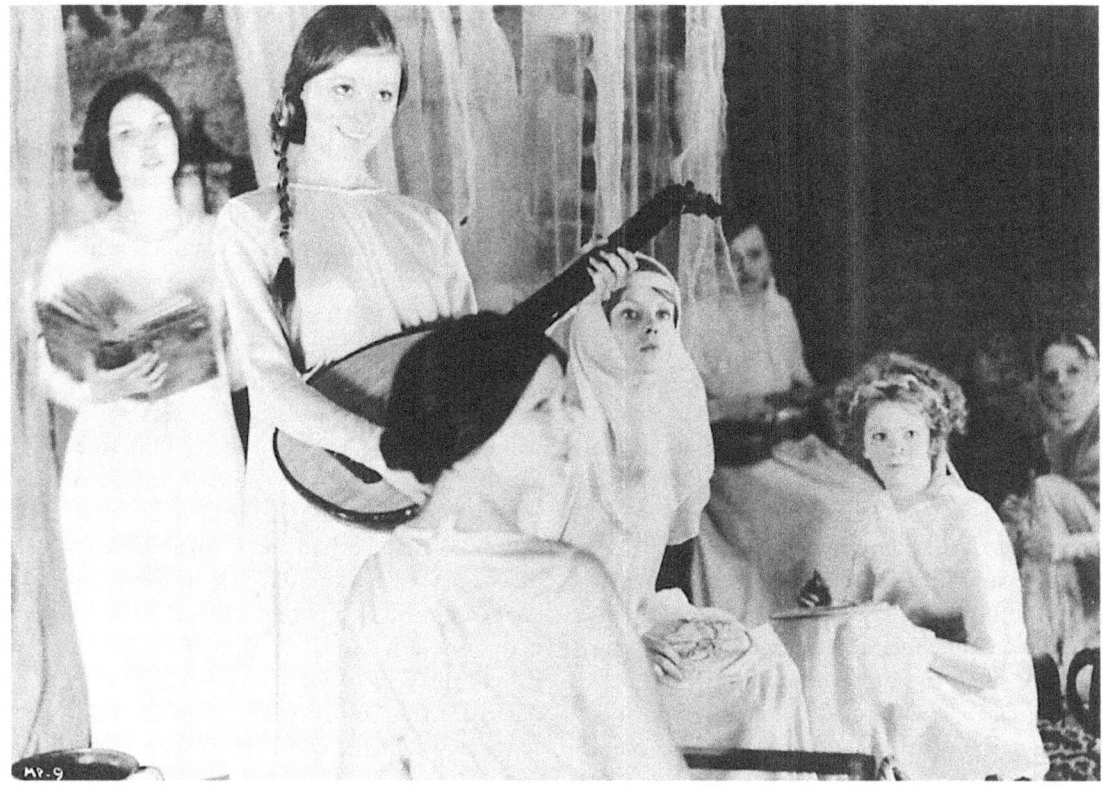

Zoot (with her lute) and "the equally delectable girlies" who inhabit Castle Anthrax in Terry Gilliam and Terry Jones's 1975 film *Monty Python and the Holy Grail*.

purity associated with Galahad's initial resistance contrasts with his eager anticipation of the orgy. And instead of the perfect Galahad defeating all foes, not only is he the one who must be rescued, but he is also the one most reluctant to leave: "I want to face perils and trials," he protests, "I can handle them"; to which the eager damsels chorus, "Yes, handle me, handle me."

At the conclusion of the scene, he accuses his father of homosexual inclinations, and this detail adds irony and humor to Lancelot's embarrassed discovery that the princess whom he comes to rescue from the tower in a later episode is in fact an effeminate young prince. This technique is extended into the running joke in order to link episodes together.

When Arthur engages in the frustrating conversation about the swallow and the coconut with the guards on the castle wall in the opening scene, we enjoy the incongruity of the King of the Britons kept waiting while his social inferiors debate obscure details of natural history. The humor of this exchange is recalled by the allusion to swallows during the narrative bridge between Galahad's adventure at Castle Anthrax and the visit to the soothsayer by Arthur and Bedevere. And when Arthur uses the information he has gained about swallows to outwit the guardian of the Bridge of Death, we not only remember the earlier dialogues, but enjoy the King in the unfamiliar role of trickster.

In the episode where the villagers are summoned to "bring out your dead," one man arrives carrying a body that is still alive. While he tries to persuade the body collector to take this unusual "corpse," very much as a modern British houseowner might cajole a dustman into taking an item barred by regulations, the old man keeps interrupting: "I'm not dead yet.... I'm getting better.... I'm feeling quite well now." Eventually, the body collector knocks him on the head with a club and adds him to his pile. This pattern, in which a "dying" man stages a miraculous and unwelcome recovery, is reenacted several times in the episode where Lancelot rescues the prince: first by Lancelot's servant after he is hit by an arrow; then by the father of the bride after he has been cut down by Lancelot; and finally by the prince himself, who survives a fall from the tower.

The other three films all make the mistake of repeating a particular formula until it becomes predictable, and thus no longer ironic. *The Sword in the Stone* shows how the weak may overcome the strong; *The Unidentified Flying Oddball* and *A Connecticut Yankee in King Arthur's Court* explore the confusion caused by modern technology to people of an earlier age. *Monty Python and the Holy Grail* avoids this trap by tackling a variety of targets. Because one never can be sure what is coming next, the irony retains its force.

At the same time, *Monty Python and the Holy Grail* avoids much of the disjointedness of other films by the Monty Python troupe for two reasons. First of all, it makes effective use of such ironic techniques as the double reversal and running joke to link the material together. Second, it employs a narrative frame that permits the inclusion of a wide variety of episodes while still advancing the story. Indeed, the narrative style of the film is not unlike the interlacing that marks medieval prose romances of the Holy Grail.[1]

It may be that the other three films are assuming that the younger audience at which they were aimed can only understand lessons that are repeated over and over again. If so, it is time filmmakers realized that boredom is as deadly an obstacle to learning as it is to irony. *Monty Python and the Holy* Grail has its faults, as critics have noted: "Ninety minutes is simply a long time to sustain their nonstop goofiness.... The constant flood of absurdity can become wearing" (Proudy 4:1637). Yet its skillful and varied use of irony demonstrates just how effective this approach to the Arthurian legend in film can be, deflating our pretensions by exposing our penchant for romanticizing our heroes — and ourselves.

NOTES

1. For a discussion of interlacing, see, for example, Vinaver, "The Questing Knight" in *The Binding of Proteus* 126–40.

WORKS CITED

Burns, E. Jane. "Nostalgia Isn't What It Used to Be: The Middle Ages in Literature and Film." In George Slusser and Eric S. Rabkin, eds. *Shadows of the Magic Lamp: Fantasy and Science Fiction in Film.* Carbondale: Southern Illinois University Press, 1985.

Nash, Jay Robert, and Stanley Ralph Ross. *The Motion Picture Guide, 1927–1983.* 9 vols. Chicago: Cinebooks, 1987.

Proudy, Howard H. "Monty Python and the Holy Grail." In Frank N. Magill, ed. *Magill's Survey of Cinema: English Language Films.* Series 2. 6 vols. Englewood Cliffs, N.J.: Salem, 1981.

Twain, Mark [Samuel L. Clemens]. *A Connecticut Yankee in King Arthur's Court.* Ed. Bernard L. Stein. Berkeley: University of California Press, 1979.

Vinaver, Eugène. *The Binding of Proteus: Perspectives on Myth and the Literary Process.* Lewisburg, Penn.: Bucknell University Press, 1980.

10

Two Films That Sparkle: The Sword in the Stone *and* Camelot

ALICE GRELLNER

Two musical films, totally different in content, tone, and targeted audience, have drawn their subject matter and inspiration from T. H. White's tetralogy *The Once and Future King*, the one book more responsible than any other for the twentieth-century revival of the popularity of the legend. *The Sword in the Stone* (1963) and *Camelot* (1967) each remain true to at least one aspect or dimension of White's vision, while eliminating or downplaying much of the novel's multifaceted, ambivalent, misogynistic, often contradictory, and darkly pessimistic view of human nature.

The Disney animated film *The Sword in the Stone*, based on White's first Arthurian book, is lively, amusing, fanciful, and wholly optimistic in tone, with wonderfully evocative music by George Bruns. The opening scenes are charming. The pages of an illuminated manuscript are turned while a voice sings a ballad recounting the background of the story. Illuminations shift to illustrations, and when the sword appears on an anvil on top of a stone in the square before the church, a voice takes up the story to describe the Dark Age that fell on England after Uther's death, "without law and without order, when the strong preyed on the weak."

The scene shifts to a forest, where wolves and eagles are preying on the weak, and finally zeroes in on Merlin, a blundering old codger, living in a clearing in the forest conversing with his owl, Archimedes, and waiting for Wart to drop in. Wart, the young Arthur, is at the moment tagging along after Kay, who is trying to kill a deer. Wart climbs out on a limb to see better. When the limb breaks, alerting the deer and causing the arrow to shoot far into the forest, Wart sets out to retrieve it, while Kay stomps off home.

This detail is one of the many minor changes Bill Peet, the animated feature's story writer, makes in White's tale, in the interest of simplicity and visual humor. In White's story, Wart goes after a hawk that Kay had lost through improper handling, and the episode illustrates a crucial difference between the two boys. Kay's behavior demonstrates his petulance, lack of responsibility, and habitual tendency to assert his privilege of birth and to lord it over Wart because of his lowly status in the household. Wart, on the other hand, shows his natural concern, not only for the hawk, Cully, but also for Hob, the falconer who had trained him, and a determination to retrieve the hawk that cannot be thwarted by his fear of the dark forest. Before he meets Merlin in the clearing, he has a brief encounter with King Pellinore, portrayed as an eccentric member of the nineteenth-century English gentry, who has been following the Questing Beast for seventeen years.

In the film, however, Wart simply goes after the arrow, quite unaware that a wolf is dogging his heels, and in a scene reminiscent of a Jacques Tati film innocently thwarts this symbol of evil, until, in trying to pull the arrow from a tree, he quite literally "drops in" through the thatched roof of Merlin's cottage. Merlin presents himself as a soothsayer and prognosticator, a wizard who knows the future because he is living backward and has already been there. Screenwriter Peet preserves and expands on Merlin's magic home, with dishes that not only wash but also pack themselves with the books into a small bag for the trip back to the castle. But Merlin warns Wart not to "get any idea that magic will solve all your problems."

Sir Ector is drawn as a portly, red-haired country squire who gives Wart demerits that he must redeem by doing kitchen duty. He readily hires Merlin (who comes home with Wart after finding Cully with the help of Archimedes, his owl) as a tutor and houses him in a leaking ruin of a tower. When Pellinore turns up in a rainstorm, Merlin sends Archimedes down to spy on him and bring back the news that a tournament will be held and the winner will receive the crown. Wart is told he can go as Kay's squire and becomes more energetic than Kay in practicing the arts of chivalry.

Meanwhile, Wart's "education" continues under Merlin's unorthodox tutelage. Merlin teaches Wart the important lessons of life he will need when he is king: how to use his imagination and how to use his intellect to outwit the strong who "will try to conquer you." Other lessons are "Always look before you leap," "Love is a powerful thing," and "Get an education" by learning to read. Merlin teaches these lessons by turning Wart into a fish, a squirrel, and a bird, and Wart's adventures as these animals parallel Kay's training as a knight. Some of the most delightful artwork in the film is found in these sequences, with the vivid primary colors of Wart's orange jerkin and Merlin's blue magician's cloak preserved in the animal colors, set against the subtle blues, greens, greys, and browns of the moat. When Wart as a squirrel is pursued by a girl squirrel, Merlin tells him, "You're on your own, lad. I'm afraid magic can't solve this." But Merlin's gentle laughter at Wart quickly backfires when he himself becomes the object of unrequited love. Later, the cook complains that the kitchen is bewitched when the dishes wash themselves to music that swings, in a sequence that uses the magic of animation to create a nightclub chorus line out of dishes and tableware, an idea adapted much later for musical numbers in Disney's *Beauty and the Beast*.

One of the charms of the film is the way it plays off of fairy-tale allusions: the wicked wolf pursuing Wart in the woods, the Cinderella image of Wart doing dishes and being told he cannot go to the tournament after all, Wart's falling into the clutches, à la Hansel and Gretel, of Mim, the wicked witch in the woods. This shapeshifter, part Morgan le Fay and part Nimue, changes sizes like Alice in Wonderland, has a temper like the Red Queen, and competes with Merlin in a battle of wits and sexes. A long sequence, for which there is no source in White, allows the animators full scope to indulge in their favorite techniques of rapid movement, impossible situations, astonishing reverses, and the animated-cartoon equivalent of the car chase. Though not my favorite sequence in the film, it is very likely a favorite with children, and the moral Merlin draws from it, one of the several gems scattered throughout the "lessons" of the film, is, "It was worth it, if

The boy Arthur and Merlin in Wolfgang Reitherman's 1963 animated feature *The Sword in the Stone*.

you learned something. Knowledge and wisdom is the real power."

Wart does finally get to go as Kay's squire to London, as we knew all along he would, since it was his fate to draw the sword from the stone. "Let the tournament games begin," the announcer cries out in an anticipatory echo of the opening of the twentieth-century Olympics, just as Wart realizes he has forgotten Kay's sword. Although White put the blame for this oversight on Kay, as he did earlier in losing the hawk, the film writer has made Wart a gawky, slightly clumsy teenager who would be likely to forget things and get into trouble with his elders. It is Archimedes who points out the sword in the churchyard, and when Wart gives it to Kay, it is Kay, portrayed throughout as a big country lout, who tries to take the credit for drawing it from the stone. When everyone returns to the churchyard for a second try, church music swells as Wart draws it out again. The assembled crowd laughs, but Pellinore declares, "It's a miracle," and the solemn voice from the opening scenes announces, "So at last the miracle had come to pass."

A final scene by way of epilogue has Wart sitting alone on a throne wearing a huge crown. He tries to run away, but at every door he tries he meets cries of "Long live the King." In desperation, he calls on Merlin, who had disappeared suddenly just before the trip to London after exclaiming, "Well, blow me to Bermuda." Now he returns wearing Bermuda shorts and a loud touristy-looking modern shirt. But he consoles Wart and tells him that "they'll be writing books and even make a motion picture about you — something like television, without commercials," a wonderful and completely accurate hindsight prophecy.

Madame Mim in Wolfgang Reitherman's 1963 animated feature *The Sword in the Stone*.

The 1967 film *Camelot*, starring Richard Harris, Vanessa Redgrave, and Franco Nero, is based on the 1960 stage musical of the same name by Alan Jay Lerner and Frederick Loewe. Like *The Sword in the Stone*, *Camelot* took its inspiration from T. H. White, but primarily from Books III and IV, *The Ill-Made Knight* and *Candle in the Wind*. There are also references in the dialogue and story to material from the earlier books and to Tennyson's *Idylls of the King*. The musical play was only moderately well received on Broadway. However, by the time the film came out, four years after John F. Kennedy's death, its mystique and lyrics had come to be identified with that "one brief, shining moment," and the public was ready to accept the ideology and the romance, the humor, the satire, and the fantasy of the movie as an escape from the disillusionment of Vietnam, the bitterness and disenchantment of the antiwar demonstrations, and the grim reality of the war on the evening television news.

Americans at home wanted desperately to believe that their involvement in Vietnam was a use of *might* for right, and they were doomed, like Arthur in the play, to ask, "What went wrong?" The movie-going public was also apparently willing to accept the conventional masculine fantasy that all beautiful women secretly dream of being abducted, ravished, tied to a tree, in short, raped. Guinevere is insulted when Arthur assures her that he has no intention of doing these things and petulantly asks him, "Why not?"

Camelot came out on the eve of the woman's liberation movement. It is hard to imagine that this exchange would have been in the film had it been made five years later. It has no basis in the book, and it has nothing to do with subsequent events, except to indicate that Guinevere, like most women, is a wanton lass, who will ultimately succumb to her penchant for illicit adventure. This impression is reinforced later in the film when Vanessa Redgrave and her maidens, wearing filmy garments and dancing with the abandon of Isadora Duncan, sing of the lusty month of May, "when everyone goes blissfully astray." The song foreshadows her infidelity, though her initial reaction to Franco Nero's priggish Lancelot is to try to bring him down from his narcissistic pedestal. The attempt is doomed from the start, for it is an attempt to deny, to herself and to him, their mutual attraction. This characterization too has no basis in White, who depicts her as being kind to Lancelot because Arthur asks her to, and as being hurt by his cruelty and indifference. White's "ill-made knight," whose cruelty to Guinevere turns to love when he sees the hurt in her eyes, becomes in Lerner's version a comically self-adulating perfectionist.

Lerner's Arthur, however, is closer to White's original conception than either Lancelot or Guinevere. A dreamer, a pacifist, somewhat shy, fearful, and unsure of himself in love, because it is the one thing Merlin never taught him anything about, he suffers a Hamlet-like paralysis at the thought of confronting the lovers. This conception of Arthur appears to stem from White's own psyche. Sylvia Townsend Warner in her prologue to *The Book of Merlyn* (1977) says that, throughout his life, White suffered from fears, which he fought with "courage, levity, sardonic wit, and industry" (ix). Lerner captures this perfectly when he has Arthur say, the night before his wedding, "I know what my people are thinking tonight," and answers himself in song: "I wonder what the king is doing tonight? He's scared! He's wishing he were in Scotland fishing tonight!" Arthur is afraid of women, afraid of his own sexuality, and afraid of hurting others. His training by Merlin to think himself into the minds of others is at once his strength and his weakness. Each of these characterizations, whether radically changed or dramatically simplified from its source, works in the film to create an Eden-like Camelot, where "the rain may never fall till after sundown," and where the inhabitants almost achieve earthly perfection.

Lancelot himself is a very different character in the film than the one White conceived. White portrayed him as homely, with a face "as ugly as a monster's in the king's menagerie," and insecure about his looks. Our first view of Lancelot, standing on a parapet of a fairy-tale castle, clutching the parchment calling knights to the Round Table, and singing, "C'est Moi," reinforces this impression. "Had I been made a partner of Eve, we'd be in Eden still," the handsome Franco Nero sings, and it is apparent that Guinevere will not have to fall for him despite his appearance, as she does in White's version.

In the novel, their affair has its roots in Guinevere's response to Arthur's request that she be kind to the young man. White's Lancelot at first treats Guinevere with cold disdain, accepting her kindnesses but hardly noticing that she is there. One day, when she was helping him with his hawk mastery, she wound up the creance wrong, and he scowled at her. Guinevere stood quite still, "hurt in her heart." For the first time, Lancelot saw her as a real person and began to fall in love. Whole sections of the novel are then omitted in the film, especially Lancelot's madness and his affair with Elaine, which in the film would only distract from the central romance.

In the film, even the illicit love is almost hallowed, as long as it is not admitted, because the lovers love Arthur and he loves them and forgives them even as they sin, because Lancelot wins Guinevere's love by working a miracle, and because time seems to stand still. Because the lovers do not grow older, as they do in the novel, they can still hope, and be symbols of hope. Arthur becomes almost godlike, even as his old plan of using might for right, and then replacing might with civil law, begins to fall apart. There is a serpent in the garden, and his name is Mordred, the offspring of a brief, incestuous union between Arthur and his half-sister Morgause long before, a son-nephew whom Arthur must love and accept because he is good, and because he has now rejected might even for right. Mordred insists, with the ruthless honesty of the truly wicked, that Arthur must absent himself from the castle overnight, so that the lovers can fall into his trap. He insists, in White's own summary of Malory's *Le Morte d'Arthur*, "on blowing the gaff on Launcelot and Guinevere's affair, which Arthur was content to overlook, as long as it was not put into words" (Warner in White, *Book*, xi).

From this point on, the action moves with the inevitability of a Greek drama. White himself likened the story to the Orestian trilogy, with the sins of the father not only visited on but replicated in the son. Lerner, however, stops short of having Arthur engage in warfare with Mordred, possibly because it would have complicated the clean romance story line. So the final scene, with Arthur knighting young Tom of Warwick and ordering him to return to Warwick to tell the tales of Camelot, takes place in the predawn preparations for a battle with Lancelot, a scene filled with mist, as vague and confusing as Arthur's anguished efforts to explain what went wrong with his dream. Lancelot and Guinevere come to ask his forgiveness and to say goodbye. Guinevere has cut her glorious hair and is in the care of the "holy sisters," though earlier in the film there were hints, in the May song and the mockery of Lancelot's fanatical religiosity, that she symbolized the earlier pagan religion. Now Guinevere the wanton has become penitent.

Arthur sadly explains that he cannot call off the battle because "they've forgotten justice, they want revenge." There is nothing to be done. They must leave decisions to God. The sense of fatality and doom is enhanced by the music. The dark gloomy tones of the cinematography and costumes are in strong contrast to the virginal white-on-white of Guinevere's first appearance, the soft greens and golds of the tight shots of Guinevere and Arthur or Guinevere and Lancelot singing their loves and their dreams, or the pastel profusion of the May Day dance. The music changes from the lilting, mildly mocking rhythms of the early songs "C'est Moi," "I Wonder What the Common Folk Are Doing Tonight," "Where Are the Simple Joys of Maidenhood?" and "How to Handle a Woman." It becomes slow, sentimental, almost solemn, and helps to seduce the audience into accepting the unlikely premise that wrongdoing becomes wrong only when made public.

The stunning cinematography, along with the catchy lyrics, plays no small part in compressing the action and suggesting the epic sweep of the story. The opening scene is shot in the mist, with Arthur asking Merlin, present only in his imagination and in the camera's eye, how he blundered into this absurdity, a question many Americans were beginning to ask by the end of the sixties, and a question T. H. White tried to grapple with at the end of the thirties. The voice of Merlin tells him to think back, and Arthur recreates himself as Wart, first meeting Merlin. Not that far back, Merlin tells him, but "The day you met Guinevere." The audience is magically transported twice through time, making a quick cinematic allusion to Arthur's boyhood, which is referred to later in the dialogue, when Arthur tells Guinevere how Merlin taught him to think by turning him into animals, "well, by making me believe he turned me into animals."

After a charming but unorthodox wooing scene, the camera shifts to the castle, a long shot of Guinevere riding a white horse led by Arthur, their procession to the altar against a background of lighted candles, and a shot of Arthur slipping a ring on Guinevere's finger. The scene shifts to a map of England, with Arthur's voice explaining to

Vanessa Redgrave as Guinevere and Franco Nero as Lancelot in Joshua Logan's 1967 film *Camelot*.

Guinevere in ponderous logic that it is better to be alive than dead. His monologue continues while he goes behind a curtain and is wheeled out in a bathtub, as he outlines his plan to use might *for* right instead of holding that might *is* right, and to build a table with no head, for knights to talk across. The monologue continues over a montage of shots, giving a flavor of Hollywood's conception of life in this anachronistic, never-never time: Guinevere buying from merchants at a fair, Guinevere currying a horse, and so forth, until finally she responds that her father has just the thing, and he's not using it: the Round Table.

At this point, hundreds of pages of White's text are compressed into a brief cinematic collage. Messengers are sent out to the music of "Camelot," silhouetted against gorgeous sunsets, riding through forests, observed by picturesque peasants. Arthur and Guinevere pore over maps, stamping the places from which knights are beginning to pour in to assemble around the table in shadowy forms; carrier pigeons carry the message overseas, to Lancelot in far-off France. Lancelot is seen riding away to England, leading his horse, singing over a campfire, singing against the sky in a small boat as he crosses a remarkably placid English Channel, riding toward Camelot on a white horse, until he meets Arthur and in the fervor of his unthinking devotion challenges and unseats Arthur himself in the name of Arthur. Arthur, amused, welcomes him to the Round Table, but Lancelot is as excessive in his abject apology as he was in his zeal to defend Arthur's honor.

The cinematic-musical interlude is over and the story resumes, with the unbending, serious Gaul demanding a mission, and being told that nothing much is going on now, the knights are all out with the Queen, who has gone a–Maying. In contrast to the stiff-necked righteousness of Lancelot, the Queen and her maidens appear decked with flowers playing like children on swings and seesaws, being tossed in blankets in a most undignified manner, and generally behaving like the nobility in a picture by Fragonard. In the midst of this spring frolic, King Pellinore appears, the very image of a dotty English gentleman parodying a knight-errant. He once spent a fortnight "here" with Wart, in a real bed, and hopes to be invited again. In White as well as in Malory, Pellinore had a real role in the plot. He killed King Lot, and his son Lamorak had an affair with Morgause, Lot's wife, triggering some of the tragedy. But the film has made him into just a comic but loveable old geezer with mutton chops, spectacles sliding down his nose, and a sympathetic clucking for the wayward youngsters in the court.

The action proceeds in a series of vignettes. Arthur appears with his new friend Lancelot, who condescends to Guinevere. Guinevere coquettishly asks Sir Lionel, Sir Sagramore, and Sir Dinadan each to challenge Lancelot in a tournament.

Arthur soliloquizes in song on how to handle a woman, the first hint of trouble in the marriage, and the scene shifts to a fair with puppets, masks, and acrobats providing visual charm. Then comes the critical scene, the turning point in the romance. Sir Lancelot unseats each of the knights in turn, but Sir Dinadan dies, and Lancelot, seeing the Queen's grief and confident of his own holiness, works a miracle to restore him to life. Though the miracle is in the sources, it comes at the end of the work, is performed in order to restore Sir Urry to health, and is used to reassure Lancelot that his repentance has been acceptable to God. Here, it is used to introduce a recognition scene.

When Guinevere looks into Lancelot's eyes, she sees his love and goodness, and kneels to him, and Arthur sees the look and knows the truth. Later, back in the castle, Lancelot, looking for Arthur, comes upon a disconsolate Guinevere and confesses his love just as Arthur comes upon them both. The second half of the film is filled with pain, the pain of three good people, each in love with the other two. This *ménage à trois* is held in delicate balance until Mordred upsets it. The scene shifts again to the court, but this time the costumes are outlandish and the faces grotesque and evil-looking, reflecting the loss of innocence.

The pageantry of Lancelot's investiture is in long shot, with Arthur and Guinevere stony-faced, formal, and distant. Intimacy and warmth are gone, as well as innocence. Later, Arthur moves in soliloquy from pain to anger to understanding and finally to resolution to *be* a king, to reach for the stars. He responds to the highest law of all, God's law, where vengeance is neither the justification for the taking of a life nor the solution to the problem of pain. Church music swells in the background, and another montage follows: knights assembled around the Round Table, cathedral windows in the background, the King making a progress, being worshiped by a grateful populace, Lancelot defending his honor by might, Guinevere observing all and slipping away to a secret hideaway to meet Lance, to tell him to go away. They sing "If Ever I Would Leave You" while the camera effectively summarizes the passage of time and the intimacy and duration of their affair. But they are never seen unclothed or in more intimate contact than an impassioned kiss, unlike their portrayal in later films.

Meanwhile, back in the throne room, Arthur sits, gloomy and alone. Pellinore enters with two unhappy tasks: to announce Mordred and to warn Arthur of the betrayal by Lancelot and Guinevere. Arthur rejects both messages, but Mordred enters anyway. The effect of Mordred's appearance is twofold: to remind Arthur of his own youthful transgression, increasing his tolerance for the misdeeds of the two people he loves most; and to allow his cherished concept of might for right to prove itself, by permitting his beloved Lance and Jenny to come to trial by law, confident that there will be no proof to condemn them.

But there will be proof, circumstantial and rigged by Mordred, and there is no time for explanations, as Arthur, racing back to warn them, is almost run down by Lance escaping. Arthur's return to the castle to find Guinevere being led away in chains leads into another cinematic montage with the song "Guinevere" being sung softly, plaintively in the background: the trial, the pronouncement of the sentence, the preparation of the stake, Pellinore watching, Arthur on his throne listening to the tolling of the bells, waiting to give the signal for the execution, waiting for Lancelot to rescue her, Mordred taunting him with his dilemma, to kill the Queen or kill the law, the dramatic rescue, and the symbolic splitting of the table. The final scene returns to the opening scene, the dawn before the battle, which both the novel and the film stop short of portraying.

Both films, like the book on which they are based and the characters who inhabit them, are flawed, anachronistic, anarchic, sentimental, and idealized. They are only a few drops in the explosion of novels and films about Arthur, but oh, how they do sparkle.

WORKS CITED

White, T. H. *The Book of Merlyn*. Austin: Shaftesbury, 1977.
_____. *The Once and Future King*. 1958. Austin: Shaftesbury, 1977.

11

Monty Python and the Holy Grail: *Madness with a Definite Method*

David D. Day

Criticism of any comedy as apparently random as the Monty Python troupe's always runs the risk of being caught up in the very absurdity it analyzes. Professorial seriousness and pompousness were always among the troupe's favorite targets, and when writing about their comedy it is hard to avoid sounding exactly like one of the hapless academics they so loved to skewer. When I look candidly at my first essay on the film from the first edition of this volume, now more than ten years old, I find this apprehension grows on me, for reasons obvious to me and probably anyone who reads the essay now.[1] But it is important to resist such self-consciousness. Succumbing to it out of a fear of appearing humorless prevents analysis of some of the smartest comedy to come out of Britain in the 1970s, and misses the possibility that sophisticated comedy is as carefully crafted as any other narrative form, more so than many. Simply put, that Monty Python's humor is very funny makes it no less worthy a subject of serious analysis.

What I would like to attempt here, without becoming too serious myself, is to analyze one of the more notably consistent of Monty Python's comic techniques, one readily found in some of their television programming and repeatedly used in what is probably their most sophisticated work of all, *Monty Python and the Holy Grail*: the juxtaposition of unlikes. Interestingly, given some shifts in academic and critical thinking over the last decade, this technique curiously parallels the concerns of modern medievalists with the ways we try to understand the Middle Ages. Although my position on these questions is not really much different from what it was in my first essay on *Monty Python and the Holy Grail*, I will focus here more precisely on one or two of the ways the Python troupe gets its laughs, and suggest how, even more strikingly than I originally thought, they anticipate, parallel, or mock academic concerns about how we recapture the past.

The best way to illustrate the trademark Python juxtaposition of unlikes is to look at the Python television show. In a sketch from the first series, John Cleese plays a terribly earnest television announcer from BBC "high intellect" programming (a kind of broadcast journalist and a class of programming they repeatedly satirize), who introduces a show called "The Epilogue: A Question of Belief."[2] Cleese is set up as moderator of what we presume will be a debate between two intellectual heavy hitters on the question of God's existence — Monsignor Edward Gay, Visiting Pastoral Emissary at the Somerset Theological College and author of the best seller *My God*, and Dr. Tom Jack, "humanist, broadcaster, lecturer, and author of the book *Hello, Sailor*." But Cleese tells us that rather than debate God's existence, his two guests have decided tonight to wrestle for it, the question to be decided by two falls, two submissions, or a knockout. The studio backdrop then parts to reveal a wrestling ring, where the ringmaster, in a high pitched, nasal, huckster's voice, introduces on his right, "for Jehovah," Monsignor "Eddie" Gay, and on his left, "author of the books *The Problems of Kierkegaard* and *Hello, Sailor*, and Professor of Modern Theological Philosophy at the University of East Anglia, Dr. Tom Jack." The two then start to wrestle, with Cleese providing sportscaster analysis of the match, before the scene changes.

This short sketch nicely illustrates my point in this essay. Theological and metaphysical debates are about as abstruse and rarified as forms of dispute come. By their very nature they involve subtle intellectual distinctions and questions of proof and belief that as a rule cannot be settled finally. Above all, theology and metaphysics are intellectual disciplines. But here, they are unexpectedly juxtaposed with wrestling — and while intending no slight to the complexities of wrestling, compared to metaphysics the sport clearly is not subtle. Rather, it is terribly obvious, and almost altogether physical.

The juxtapositioning of these two kinds of contest is so violent and jarring that it makes us laugh, from surprise and shock as much as from anything else. But the humor is even more subtle — there's a strong satirical edge to the juxtaposition as well. The existence of God is an issue about which many people would like some certainty. And yet as the history of philosophy and theology has shown, these disciplines have been frustratingly unable to answer this extremely difficult question. Sports, on the other hand, almost always produces a clear winner and loser (enough so that when a tie occurs, fans of both sides are often more frustrated than they would be by a clear loss for their side). The sketch thus subtly satirizes a very human desire for certainty — wouldn't it be wonderful if we could answer the question of God's existence as simply as we settle a wrestling match? In fact, Cleese in a voice over at the end of the show tells us that "God exists by two falls to a submission."

Many of the juxtapositions in Monty Python's humor are made much funnier by the anachronism of the two things being put together. Take for example "The Attila the Hun Show."[3] This sketch from the second season starts off with Cleese's voiceover of clips from old Hollywood costume spectaculars, in which he talks of the various barbarian leaders ravaging the Roman Empire in the fifth century, of whom "none surpassed in power and cruelty the mighty Attila the Hun." The scene then cuts to "The Attila the Hun Show," in which we see Cleese as Attila in black leather armor, long hair and mustache, running in slow motion into the arms of Carol Cleveland in a leopard skin bikini, while cheesy sounding background music by "The Hunlets" warbles on about how "all you need is just a little love." Next, Attila — rather like Dick Van Dyke — comes into his blandly decorated suburban home, the only nod to "Hunnish" style a pair of crossed spears on the wall, and gives a present to his two children, Jenny and Robby Attila the Hun — a severed head. Cleese then mugs a huge smile into the camera, saying that he wants his kids to "get aHEAD," followed by a conspicuously canned sounding laugh track.

Again, the humor here depends on the juxtaposition of unlikes — fifth century savagery and violence placed up against twentieth century sitcom banality — and the disjunction between the two gets most of the laughs. But as with "The Epilogue," there is a strong satirical edge here as well — the Python troupe seems to be making fun of the capacity for conventional situation comedy to go for laughs while remaining completely oblivious to the more alarming implications of its subject matter. And the sketch also perhaps ridicules our attempts to imagine or recreate the past. When we in the present try to recapture the essential nature of past figures such as Attila the Hun, we always end up recreating them in ways that reflect our own prejudices, desires, and stupidities. We cannot escape anachronism in our re-creation of the past because we inevitably create the past in our own image.

This anachronistic juxtaposition of unlikes is a major feature of *Monty Python and the Holy Grail*. It can be found hilariously in the confrontation between Arthur and Dennis the peasant. This scene begins with Arthur, wonderfully played by Graham Chapman as a sort of vexed royal straight man, riding over the crest of a hill crowned with a standard that seems to consist of a wagon wheel on top of a pole with a human body stretched over it. (Perhaps as punishment? In any case, the situation is presumably uncomfortable and even fatal. We see the same standard in the film's first scene.) In the camera's foreground two peasants (one of them Dennis, played by Michael Palin, and the other by Terry Jones in drag) are kneeling in the mud, gouging at the ground with sticks and piling up "filth." The angle of the shot changes to show Arthur riding up behind Dennis as he trudges along, pulling a heavy cart. Thanks to the scene's blocking, Dennis and Arthur stand framing a distant castle. Both these shots are ideologically loaded. Their setups in each case present the laboring peasants in the foreground with a symbol of authority placed behind and slightly above them, the standard (and Arthur) in the first shot and the castle in the second.

The scene develops to identify this ideology. Arthur mistakenly accosts Dennis as "old woman," asking who the owner of the castle is. At this point, perhaps because of the scene's setup, but as much because we all have certain ideas (variously derived) about how peasants behaved in the Middle Ages towards their betters, we expect Dennis to show some deference. Dennis is, however, anything but deferential in his response. Instead, he tells Arthur that he and his companion are part of an anarcho-syndicalist commune. Dennis also objects to Arthur's automatic treatment of him "as an inferior," and he accuses Arthur of "exploiting the workers" and "hanging on to outdated imperialist dogma." The conflict intensifies as Arthur becomes increasingly exasperated with Dennis's torrent of quasi-Marxist rhetoric, which grows more impudent and abusive with the arrival of reinforcements. In the middle of their argument, the other peasant intrudes, saying, "Dennis, there's some lovely filth over here." Then, being informed that Arthur is her king, she wants to know how he got to be king — she "didn't vote for him."

Arthur, his eyes turned heavenward, launches into a description of how he received his kingship by the supernatural sanction of "the Lady of the Lake, her arm clad in the purest shimmering samite," who lifted Excalibur "aloft from the bosom of the water, signifying by divine providence" that he, Arthur, "was to carry Excalibur." As he speaks, a choir of angelic voices begins to sing in the background. While Dennis' abrasive repulsiveness makes Arthur a sympathetic character here, Arthur is, nonetheless, abruptly cut short by Dennis' derisive squawk, followed by one of the funniest lines in the movie: "Strange women lying in ponds distributing swords is no basis for a system of government: You can't expect to wield supreme executive power just because some watery tart threw a sword at you!"

The juxtaposition of unlikes is clear here: the dialogue offers two radically different ideas about where the right to rule derives from, each drawn from very different periods in history. Arthur's is the more authentically medieval of the two: he claims to rule by supernatural sanction, reflected by the intervention of the Lady. This is not surprising: medieval political theory saw a reflection of the divine order in the structuring of the monarchical state. As Dante puts it, "When mankind is subject to one Prince it is most like to God and this implies conformity to the divine intention, which is the condition of perfection" (13). Dennis' reply is of course thoroughly modern: political power "derives from the mandate of the masses, not from some farcical aquatic ceremony." As with "The Epilogue" and "The Attila the Hun Show," the juxtapositioning of these two ideas is startling and funny. But the humor becomes much sharper by the presence of anachronism in the juxtaposition. Dennis refers to Arthur's ideas as "outdated." But in the Middle Ages, they would not seem outdated at all, and so Dennis's dismissal of them seems that much more bizarre and jarring. The satire also becomes more incisive. I am putting this crudely, but generally speaking, Marxist theory has tended to see in the "exploitative" medieval social order an earlier form of economic organization later transcended by capitalism, as capitalism would be transcended by communism. There is a sort of self-congratulatory positivism in this stance: we who live at the end of history can afford to patronize a past we have transcended by imagining it any way we want to. Having Dennis anticipate the worker's utopia in this way satirizes the modern tendency to create a past that bolsters our current political self-satisfaction (rather ironically, given the course of political history since the movie came out in 1975).

There are other free standing gems of this kind in the movie — such as the Rambo-esque juxtaposition of modern military hardware and medieval religious relics in the scene involving the Holy Hand Grenade of Antioch with its biblical instruction manual, the Book of Armaments. A much more complicated series of these juxtapositions involves the film's "self-referentiality" — its tendency to call attention to itself as a fictional narrative being made about King Arthur and the Middle Ages more generally, but in our own technologically sophisticated present.

One example of this self-referentiality occurred in the first advertisements for the film: the original 1975 poster for the film proclaimed that it "sets movie making back 900 years." The anachronistic absurdity of the joke — there was no film 900 years ago — nevertheless zeroes in on a very real modern desire to know the past: *if* film making technology had existed in the Middle Ages, wouldn't it now be possible to know that distant time and place much better than we currently do? Film, after all, shows us things as they really are; it is as close as we have come to a truly transparent medium of representation. The problem with this wish, though, is that film is no less crafted than any other narrative mode — and like any such mode, it will show traces of its fictional, manufactured nature in various ways. In films about the past, bad costumes, historical inaccuracies, or stilted, archaic dialogue might be some of the more noticeable features of the film's manufactured nature. Film itself, by the use of camera shots, lighting, and other technical aspects of the "language" of film, will also show up the created nature of the movie. To heighten the sense of realism in the film, movies about the past usually try to avoid these problems by paying very close attention to the minutiae of period representation (as with *The Last of the Mohicans* and *Gladiator*). *Monty Python and the Holy Grail*, though, does just the opposite. Despite a very sophisticated and even evocative visual style, from the film poster on, this film calls attention to its fictive nature by continually juxtaposing the Arthurian illusion with the means necessary to produce it.

The most notorious of these incidents involves the coconut shells, which anyone who has ever seen the film will always mention the first time it comes up in conversation. The film proper starts off (after the fiasco of the credits subtitled in Swedish) with the appearance of large white uncial letters against a black background, reading "England 932 A.D.," accompanied by a rolling flourish of heroic music. The writing and the sound set up an (extremely apprehensive) expectation that the scenes that follow will be "medieval," whatever that means. We have the date, and we have the place (to most Americans, anyway, England and the Middle Ages usually go together); if we have ever heard of the Holy Grail, we know the film has something to do with King Arthur—so we are set up to expect some version of the medieval. And the film cunningly plays on these expectations: there is swirling mist blown on a sighing, ominous wind (England is gray and foggy, right?), and then that cryptic standard from the later scene with Arthur and Dennis appears. It is cryptic, but nonetheless it feeds our preconceptions: people were tortured and executed in the Middle Ages all the time, and while nailing them to wagon wheels and sticking the whole affair on a pole may not be authentic, the scene achieves its intended effect. Then the most important thing happens: we hear the horse's hooves clopping for a second or two before we see what is really making the noise. Most people seeing the movie the first time probably expect to see a knight, on a horse, come out of that mist—few ideas modern people have about the Middle Ages are more omnipresent than the image of the knight. He best represents our mixture of awe at the barbaric splendor of the Middle Ages and revulsion at its violence and hierarchy. But what comes on screen is of course King Arthur and his squire, both on foot, with the squire clicking two coconut shells together to make the sound of the horse's hooves.

This scene is wonderful because it almost impudently insists on the importance of getting the sound of a medieval icon right, even if it denies us (for a while, anyway) the visual representation of that icon. The Python troupe displays a sort of comically misplaced fussiness with getting one detail right while failing to see that leaving another out tends to make the exercise rather pointless (except as self mockery, at which it succeeds brilliantly, of course). And the scene virtually shouts out, "This is a movie, and what's more, a very silly movie that will continually call attention to the fact that it's a silly movie and nothing more. Deal with it."

The scene is perhaps the most memorable example of *Monty Python and the Holy Grail*'s tendency to undercut its illusion by juxtaposing it with the means for creating that illusion. But there are others. One that is especially funny occurs late in the film, as Arthur and his knights are being chased around by the Black Beast of Aaaaarrrrgghh. The sequence is of course animated in Terry Gilliam's wonderful "mock illumination" style, although the Beast itself looks like one of the flabby, rounded grotesques from the animated sequences in the TV series. The narrator (Michael Palin) solemnly intones that the heroes would certainly have perished had not the animator suffered a sudden, fatal heart attack, whereupon the scene cuts briefly to Gilliam having a seizure, then back to the Beast vanishing from the cartoon. Again, illusion is juxtaposed with the means of creating it.

It is probably far too grave to refer to this particular kind of juxtaposition as a theme in *Monty Python and the Holy Grail*. But it probably is not being too serious to refer to it as a major feature of the movie's plot, such as it is, especially considering a thread that starts around halfway through the film, after the failure of the Trojan Rabbit ploy. An elderly, tweed suited, spectacled man, referred to in a subtitle only as "a famous historian," comes on screen to explain Arthur's subsequent strategy for taking the castle. This man is a cartoon example of the sort of academic the Monty Python troupe regularly satirized on television. He looks like the stereotype of the British academic, and sounds like one, too: his English is carefully correct, he has the right accent, and he speaks and gestures with the sort of animation academics famously bring to lectures about subjects most people cannot get that worked up about. Then there is a drum of horse's hooves, followed by the appearance of a knight on a real horse, in full armor, who flashes between the camera and the historian and cuts him down with a single stroke.

The brutality of this scene is shocking but also funny: the historian's explanation is simply unnecessary to follow the film's plot, and we mourn him no more than we might any other big mouth interrupting an amusing story. His wife, or daughter, or some other middle aged female relation is upset, though, and she appears on screen standing over his body before the story moves on to the "Tale of Sir Robin." The narrative again briefly alludes to this new subplot several scenes later, when the episode of the Knights Who Say "Ni" is followed by a brief shot showing the same woman standing over the historian's body with several policemen, plainly telling them what happened. The policemen next appear standing by the shrubbery plot of the Knights Who Say "Ni," following the explosion of the Holy Hand Grenade and alerted to its sound. They appear again after Arthur outwits the Bridge Keeper, shaking Lancelot down as he leans with his hands against the roof of their squad car, the static and scratchy voices of their radios providing the shot's only sound. And their final and most important appearance is of course in the film's last scene, when their car pulls up in front of Arthur's advancing army. The last shot is of Arthur being led away in handcuffs, obliterated finally by a policeman's bark of "that's enough" and his palm covering the camera.

These last juxtapositions of the film's "outside," the means and circumstances of its production, with its fictional medieval "inside," very amusingly tie the film up. When *Monty Python and the Holy Grail* was first released, I remember hearing more than one person remark that the ending was something of a disappointment, and I always wondered if there were any more appropriate way the Python troupe might have ended it. But I have always concluded there was not. In an interview taped at the time the *Fawlty Towers* videotapes were released, John Cleese remarked that people staying in hotels are always under the illusion that they have some ownership of their room, when in reality there is a host of staff who constantly want to get in that room, for various reasons. The situation with *Monty Python and the Holy Grail* is humorously similar: the makers of the medieval fiction may want to have their world, their room, all to themselves as a sort of imaginary space, but modernity intrudes in spite of their best efforts. Sometimes they have to use coconuts to make the sound of horses if they cannot get the real thing; sometimes the animators keel over and die; sometimes the cops break in and stop the party, especially if the film has knights on the set running around killing historical consultants. The film thus satirizes not just particular views and ideas that we have of the Middle Ages, but the modern obsession with mak-

King Arthur and his knights encounter one of the Knights Who Say "Ni" in Terry Gilliam and Terry Jones's 1975 film *Monty Python and the Holy Grail*.

ing and holding them at all. The film seems to say that the enterprise of historical recreation simply cannot be maintained.

Perhaps it is not surprising that *Monty Python and the Holy Grail* is concerned with how the means of fiction impact on its matter: that "the somehow may be thishow," in Browning's phrase. Narrators in various media have been mulling over this problem for centuries. Such a concern is even less surprising in a story about King Arthur, for storytellers have been adapting the Arthurian materials to their own purposes since the Middle Ages — altering the legend to suit their own times and circumstances. Malory combines the medieval French focus on Lancelot and Guenevere with the native English treatment of Arthur as a warrior king, to produce the story of an ideal, chivalrous society standing as an example to his own politically fragmented mid-fifteenth century world. Tennyson writes of a Round Table maintained by united faith in the vision of an ideal leader, an act of will he feared the British Empire of his own day was growing incapable of.

Graham Chapman's Arthur is similarly a man who, in some sense, is let down by the frivolity of his followers and his environment. He is as earnest and serious as we expect Arthur to be, but his Camelot disappoints him, if not us. When he prepares to visit his court, the scene cuts to the knights of the Round Table dancing the Can Can on banqueting tables, playing drums on each others' helmets, and singing about knights in Camelot who eat Spam a lot. Turning to his followers, he says in disgust, "Let's not go to Camelot. It is a silly place." This is truly an Arthur for the post–Vietnam political and social cynicism of the 1970s:

individuals may be fine, but collective institutions disappoint.

Rather surprisingly, and interestingly, this technique of juxtaposing anachronistic unlikes focuses on issues that professional medievalists were only beginning to be aware of when I first wrote on *Monty Python and the Holy Grail* ten years ago. At that time, scholars of medieval literature such as Lee Patterson, David Aers, and Sheila Delaney were actively debating the then tottering methods of the "patristic school" represented by critics such as D. W. Robertson, Jr., which sought to interpret medieval texts according to the models of medieval Biblical exegesis.[4] Patterson and the others essentially argued that patristic scholarship was based on a politically conservative, perhaps even reactionary, idolization of the Middle Ages as an historical period free of textual ambiguity, when the meaning of texts could be neatly discovered by application of a prevailing interpretive template controlled by the medieval church. Rather than try to replace this conservative approach with one more liberal, these scholars argued for a criticism that frankly admitted its ideological motivations and preconceptions even as it used them to interpret the past. As Aers put it, "To acknowledge this [one's ideological stance and the effects it has on one's criticism] is to acknowledge severe problems. But these are simply unavoidable, and they are best confronted openly" (2). Here was a medievalism that tried to acknowledge its means even as it used them to recapture the past, a juxtaposition not unlike that deployed to humorous effect in *Monty Python and the Holy Grail*.

In the decade since, this historiographic sophistication has become much more the norm in medieval studies, not just in literature but in history, enough so that a medieval historian like Norman Cantor can write a fairly popular book on the subject—*Inventing the Middle Ages*. Even more remarkable may be the way this awareness of how means condition product is now all over the historical map. For example, it is of central concern in books on the personality of Hitler, such as Ron Rosenbaum's *Explaining Hitler*, or to the issues of Holocaust denial raised by the David Irving libel trial. But then, this conflict is perhaps not so surprising after all. In both these areas, the political basis of historical interpretation is glaring, much more so than in medieval studies.

I do not wish to suggest for a moment that the Monty Python troupe had any intention of critiquing historiography when they made either their TV series or *Monty Python and the Holy Grail*. To do so would be giving them a sort of intellectual prescience that probably gives them too much credit in one sense and denies them too much in another. It would certainly make them sound like very serious drudges, and would take a lot of the fun out of looking closely at their work. But the way their work parallels (for lack of a better word) the concerns of historians and other academics is interesting. When the troupe satirizes the ways we know the past and our motives in doing so, they seem to be treading the same intellectual path or one very similar to that which the serious academics whom they satirize have since trodden. That the Python troupe got there first is a wryly funny comment on the frequent obtuseness of academic critics, and also the way that witty comics can brilliantly identify the same issues academics do—treating them with a humor and lightness of touch never found in professional criticism. But any critic who has thoughtfully read Swift or Chaucer, or carefully watched *Monty Python and the Holy Grail*, should not be surprised to find his subject anticipating him.

NOTES

1. Day, "Monty Python and the Medieval Other" 84–92.

2. "Sex and Violence." *Monty Python's Flying Circus*. Written and performed by Graham Chapman, John Cleese, Terry Gilliam, Eric Idle, Terry Jones and Michael Palin. 1969. (Videocassette, vol.1 in the collected series. A&E, 1999.)

3. "The Attila the Hun Show." *Monty Python's Flying Circus*. Written and performed by Graham Chapman, John Cleese, Terry Gilliam, Eric Idle, Terry Jones and Michael Palin. 1970. (Videocassette, vol. 10 in the collected series. A&E, 1999.)

4. Probably the best discussions of this problem are still Patterson's *Negotiating the Past: The Historical Understanding of Medieval Literature*, and the essays collected by David Aers in *Medieval Literature: Criticism, Ideology and History*.

WORKS CITED

Aers, David. *Medieval Literature: Criticism, Ideology, and History*. Brighton: Harvester, 1986.

Dante Alighieri. *Monarchy*. Trans. Donald Nicholl. London: Weidenfeld and Nicholson, 1954.

Day, David D. "Monty Python and the Medieval Other." In Kevin J. Harty, ed. *Cinema Arthuriana: Essays on Arthurian Film*. New York: Garland, 1991.

Patterson, Lee. *Negotiating the Past: The Historical Understanding of Medieval Literature*. Madison: University of Wisconson Press, 1987.

12

Not Dead Yet: Monty Python and the Holy Grail *in the Twenty-first Century*

DONALD L. HOFFMAN

Dead parrots and plummeting sheep, to say nothing of Spiny Norman and the Minister of Silly Walks, are at best unlikely companions for the Knights in Quest of the Grail. All, however, feature in the amazingly diverse, inclusive, bizarre, and absurd repertoire of Monty Python, the comedy troupe that dominated Public Television in the seventies. The brilliantly inventive troupe had predecessors in popular culture (Music Hall skits and the British Christmas Pantomime), earlier smart young university wits (citing Christopher Marlowe might claim too prestigious a heritage, but the successful *Beyond the Fringe* group—Peter Cook, Jonathan Miller, Dudley Moore, and Alan Bennett—surely established a precedent), and contemporary theatre practice and theory (both the waning of "Absurdist" theatre and the growing awareness in England of French theory). They had an easy time playing with Existentialism (placing Mrs. Jean Paul Sartre on a sinking submarine, for example), but some of the great experiments in *Monty Python and the Holy Grail* seem to reflect French theory filtered through the practice of French film-makers, like Jean Luc Godard (who made it clear that making a film is a form of film criticism) and Robert Bresson (whose *Lancelot du Lac* seems to have inspired the famous encounter with the Black Knight).

The deconstruction of film tradition, if not film as a medium, begins in *Monty Python and the Holy Grail* with the famous mobile credits. The joke of the credits, to which I shall return, involves the ludicrous Swedish subtitles, but the location of the credits alone raises an interesting issue. These silly subtitles were, when the film was released, placed at the end where an audience ordinarily expects to find them these days. The tape and DVD releases place these credits at the beginning. The original placing of the credits at the end accomplished the useful, if accidental, purpose of encouraging audiences to stay until the end of the film and taught them that finding out who did what can be an informative and entertaining exercise. This placement did, however, undermine the stark ending of the film.

With the credits at the beginning, the film ends not merely with a ridiculous joke, but with cameras stopped by an irate policeman and a few sprockets of empty film. While placing the joking credits at the beginning allows the movie to start with a critique of film tradition, placing them at the end allows a critique of film itself.

Even now the subtitles are funny, but they are funny without resonance, or, at least, without a specific resonance. Most audiences, I imagine, are still familiar with subtitle, despite the relentless marketing of Hollywood product that has rendered foreign films not only unpopular but unfashionable.[1] The Swedish subtitles are not, however, a joke about subtitles in general, but a specific evocation of the time when Ingmar Bergman reigned supreme as the world's most prestigious director of serious films. The subtitles recall a poignantly distant day when serious films in a foreign language could actually attract a significant audience. Monty Python's Swedish subtitles are still funny, but the wit is now generic; it has a specificity lost on and irrelevant to a contemporary audience. As a joke, it's not dead yet, but, unlike the old man in the plague scene, it's not "getting better."

As the credits get sillier and sillier, a placard announces that those responsible have been sacked; not too long after, we learn of the sacking of the sackers. Silliness again, but in a different register. These comments make jokes not on the tradition of film, but on the process of film-making. With these jokes, the Pythons introduce a more complex comedy that begins to deconstruct the process of creating and sustaining illusion. This sort of deconstruction may have begun with the moment Herod left the pageant to rage in the streets in the York Mystery Cycle, continued with the interruptions of the scripted audience in Francis Beaumont's *Knight of the Burning Pestle*, and gone on to erupt in the blurry distinctions between actors and audiences in Tom Stoppard's *The Real Inspector Hound*. The fact that this sort of deconstruction of illusion still shocks an audience is powerful testimony to our desire to be deceived.[2]

The film begins with the title in Gothic script: England, 932 A.D. The most interesting thing about this year is that nothing much happened in it. The Laud Manuscript of the Anglo-Saxon Chronicle skips over it entirely, while the Parker Manuscript notes only: "Her for[th] ferde Fry[th]e stan bisceop" (106).[3] Although we may join in mourning the death of Frithstan out of fellow feeling, we are not likely to be deeply moved by it and even less likely to have any notion of who the old fellow may have been.[4] The year 932 is just not memorable; indeed, for Arthurians it is significantly insignificant. It is roughly four centuries too late for an attempt at pseudo-historicism, an attempt to situate the narrative in the period of the Germanic invasions of England against which a possibly historical Arthur may have fought. It is, on the other hand, more or less three centuries too soon for the efflorescence of Arthurian literature inspired by Geoffrey of Monmouth and slightly more than half a millennium too early for a setting appropriate for Sir Thomas Malory, the most direct Arthurian source for the film. At best, it is more or less accidentally halfway between 1469, when Malory claims to have completed *Le Morte,* and 542, when, according to the Vulgate *Queste del Saint Graal*, the Quest of the Holy Grail was undertaken. The joke is a small one, but it reveals a certain perverse intelligence for the Pythons to have arrived at a date so completely certain to reverberate soundlessly, to evoke so clearly associations with absolutely nothing. It is possible that there have been duller years in English history than 932, but there cannot have been many.

Into this dullest and least Arthurian of years, the Pythons insert Arthur and his coconut horse,[5] a dissertation on the migratory habits of the African swallow, an encounter with the plague, and a commentary on the foundations of British political economy. None of these items has anything to do with the Quest for the Holy Grail, but they do set up a series of references that recur with increasing silliness in the course of the film, from the question about the velocity of the sparrow at the Bridge of Death, to the recurring strains of the *Pie Jesu* punctuated by monks smashing themselves in the head with planks, to the poignant refrain of the fragile and disposable, "I'm not dead yet." What does not recur is the brief but brilliant commentary on Arthurian politics — from the famous observation that the king is easily recognizable, because he is the only one not covered in shit, to the uncertainty over whether Britain is a monarchy or an autonomous collective. Above all, there is the famous demystification of Arthur's authority when his vision of the Lady of the Lake, her arm clothed in purest white samite, who bestows on him the destined sword Excalibur, is countered by Dennis's celebrated view that "strange women lying about in ponds distributing swords is no basis for a system of government." A less intense critique of the Arthurian system, but one that penetrates deeply into the roots of the definition of Arthur's historical role, is Dennis's elderly companion's response to Arthur's announcement that he is "King of the Britons" with the query "King of the who?" "King of the Britons?" he replies as the inquiry shifts from the governed to the governor and the questioning of kingship as an institution. After all, as the Old Lady points out, she did not vote for him.

These three first scenes are silly in themselves, but, as did the credits, they begin to mock and deconstruct certain film conventions. As the credits parodied the conventions of subtitles and the Swedish chic of Bergman films, the coconut horses attack a prime feature of the medieval cinematic epic, and also undermine the basis of medieval chivalry. There may well have been some compelling practical reasons for cutting out the horses, coconuts are cheaper and easier to train, for example, and the Pythons may not have been particularly expert horsemen. Whatever the reason, there is a brilliant confusion of genres, as the coconut horse hooves, so effective on radio and soundtracks, are shown to be absurd when made apparent and visual. The device also, whether intentionally or not, cuts to the heart of that notion of knighthood rooted in the *chevalier* and his *cheval*. Once that glorious *cheval* has become a coconut, the basis of aristocratic privilege has been erased, and it is only a short step to Dennis and his Marxist analysis of feudalism.

A few short scenes involving witches, ducks, and God follow, but first Arthur encounters the Black Knight, an episode that, interesting problems of dating aside, is most probably a parody of the battles in Bresson's *Lancelot du Lac*. While the too easily lopped off limbs comically echo Bresson's treatment of battle, particularly in the mass quantities of blood that issue from cavernous wounds, the scene also reduces the notion of chivalric heroism to the very bottom line of absurdity, as the armless, legless stump of a knight screams at his "cowardly" foe to return and fight to the finish. Silly as it appears to be, this deconstruction of a chivalric ethos is as implicitly powerful as Dennis's deconstruction of feudal power. The absurdity at the heart of both chivalry and monarchy is made visible and, consequently, made ridiculous. At the same time, the foreign-language art film also finds itself the target. Like the Swedish subtitles in the opening credits, the Bresson-like dismemberment of the feisty torso punctures the high style artsiness of the French film. Ultimately, Bresson and the Pythons may, in fact, tend toward a very similar ideological analysis of feudalism and chivalry, but their methods are as unlike as a comic book from a Sorbonne dissertation.

The encounter with the hyper-heroic Black Knight is followed by the Scene of the Witch Test in which it is proved that a witch weighs the same as a duck, because of course witches are made out of wood, and wood, like a duck, floats. There are logical flaws here, but they are, perhaps, not greater than the notorious ontological leap in Anselm's proof of God. More serious than the critique of scholastic logic, however, is the realization that a mob intent on murdering witches is more than happy to accept a faulty argument. The victim, however, is equally complicit with the Inquisition. "Fair cop," she says, suspended in her little cage balancing the equal and opposite weight of the complacent fowl. The unruly mob joyously pursues the witch, its faith in logic amply rewarded. And her Inquisitor turns out to be Bedivere, who is dubbed a knight and becomes the first of Arthur's companions on the quest.[6]

Graham Chapman (left) as King Arthur and Terry Gilliam as "his trusty steed" Patsy in Terry Gilliam and Terry Jones's 1975 film *Monty Python and the Holy Grail.*

The film then takes up the cinematic equivalent of *occupatio* by telling rather than showing Arthur's acquisition of knights. We are shown, as is the feature of pseudo-historical and story book films, the illustrated ancient book whose pages are turned by a manicured hand. We are given nine pages with lovely Gothic lettering on the *verso* and scenes from the film in place of illuminations on the *recto*. As with the Swedish credits, this parody of another feature of film tradition begins as silly and grows sillier by repetition and excess. The nine chapter headings are:

The Book of the Film
Sir Lancelot the Brave
Sir Galahad the Pure
Sir Robin-the-not-quite-so-brave-as-Sir-Lancelot...
Who had nearly fought the Dragon of Angnor...
Who nearly stood up to the vicious Chicken of Bristol...
And who personally wet himself at the Battle of Badon Hill[7]
Sir Not-Appearing-in-this-Film
Together they formed a band whose names and deeds were to be retold throughout the centuries.

And as the page turner prepares to turn the final page, a hairy bearlike claw emerges slowly from the right-hand corner of the frame and closes over the manicured hand. It is again a moment of purely Python silliness, but it reflects film conventions, such as all those storybook pages turned in the classic Disney features from *Snow White* on. Those relentless chapter headings also recall serious film as well, such as the title cards in the silent film era, while also recalling medieval traditions as well in its evocation of the chapter headings familiar from Caxton's *Malory*.

At last, after six scenes of parodic riffs critiquing and reorienting our expectations of the Middle Ages and modern cinema, the witch test and the book lead to the initiation of the titular quest, and the knights' approach to the legendary castle of Camelot. Unhappily, this is not the moment of grandeur the knights and the audience may have anticipated, for as Patsy (of the clopping coconuts) points out, "It's only a model" (deconstructing illusion once again) and, after the Round Table knights break into a chorus celebrating themselves as "knights of Camelot / who eat ham and jam and Spam a lot," even Arthur is forced to conclude, "It's a silly place."

Turning from Camelot and riding (coconutting?) on, the knights come face to face with God Himself, or, at least, with a wonderful Terry Gilliam drawing of Him, as He sends the knights to find the Grail. This version of the initiation of the quest varies significantly from any of the medieval sources. It may, in fact, fit in quite nicely with many assumptions about the quest as a divine mission, but it is both a little more mysterious and a little less divine in the Vulgate or in Malory, who is the most likely source for the Pythons (although it is more than likely some of the troupe were acquainted with the Vulgate as well). The scene is then more a parody of the audience's expectations than it is of the actual source. What the Pythons have eliminated is the Pentecostal imagery of the first appearance of the Grail at Camelot, the prophecies of Siege Perilous, the Loathly Lady,[8] and all the machinery preparing for the supplanting of Lancelot and his earthly chivalry by his own son Galahad and his new institution of spiritual chivalry. But, since the knights had already turned away from Camelot as a "silly place," they would not be there to see the Grail even if it had appeared. In lieu of this interior setting, God speaks to the questers in an open space that reproduces a certain kind of Moses on Sinai sublimity, but then undercuts that sublimity completely by reducing God to a cartoon.

Now that the Quest has begun, the first stop is at a castle inhabited by Frenchmen. In the universe of comedy, there is probably nothing as funny as a Monty Python Frenchman played by John Cleese. From his response to Arthur's earnest announcement, "We have come to seek the Grail" ("We've already got one"), to his concluding insult ("I fart in your general direction"), Cleese's amazing accent raises the silly to the stupendous, turns a parody of the French into the birth of a new race of creature, vulgar, pretentious, violent, outrageous, and sublimely comic. The voluble Frenchman, sort of a Cyrano on crack, is funnier than a flying cow, although the Pythons give us that, too, by the end of the scene. Most will agree that this transcendently inane moment has just about nothing to do with the Holy Grail, except ... never underestimate the deviousness of Frenchmen (maybe they did have a Grail) or the French origins of the Vulgate quest. The silliness of the scene evokes serious reflections, after all. It certainly calls upon England's traditional difficulty in dealing with France, an issue that probably predates 1066, but was certainly raised to the level of the permanently problematic in that critical year. The scene also suggests that, if you are planning to look for a Grail, you had best begin with the French. Cathars, Celts, Sarmatians, and who knows who else have their supporters as the original keepers of the Grail, but no one has quite gotten around the fact that the earliest texts that claim to be Grail texts are in French. From Robert de Boron to the Vulgate *Queste* to the massive *Continuations*, the Grail Castle is a French Castle. So the silly knights of Camelot may be looking in the wrong place, but they at least started on the right track. They also discover what most researchers into the history of the Grail discover, that one must start with the French, but will be led down a number of disappointing paths. The Grail Quest is the quintessentially French quest, the search for origins, for a transcendent signifier that leads relentlessly to ruptures, gaps, and the inevitable *mise en abîme*. The search for origins, in other words, dissipates, is as irrecoverable as a "fart in your general direction."

The search for origins is complicated by the siege of the French Castle in the following scene, a siege accomplished by the epic machinery of the Trojan Rabbit, which harkens back to the siege of Troy and forward to Arthur's encounter with Caerbannog, the killer rodent. As before, the prime function of the Trojan Rabbit is to be supremely silly. This, it accomplishes both visually (it is quite a magnificent instrument) and diegetically (since the invaders neglect to get inside the thing). At the same time, the Trojan Rabbit inserts the *matière de Rome* into the *matière de Bretagne*, an amalgamation of periods, persons and genres that is entirely medieval. Think, for example, of the famous anachronisms of *The Second Shepherd's Play* where the Nativity seems to have taken place in the West Midlands, or, perhaps more to the point, of all those echoes of the myth of Theseus in the tale of Tristan: the tribute to the Morholt, for example, which is like that paid to the Minotaur, or the white sails exchanged for black.[9] This free appropriation of materials reflects a thoroughly medieval sort of *bricolage*. In addition, and accidentally or not, there is no ancient legend more implicated in Arthurian history than the story of the fall of Troy. After all, as Geoffrey of Monmouth tells us, Britain was founded by the son of Aeneas, the Trojan prince who escaped the Fall. And London was, after all, referred to as New Troy. Intentionally or not, much of this Troiano-Romano-Britonic tradition is encapsulated in the image of the Trojan Rabbit.

On the other hand, it is a rabbit, isn't it? No tradition remains intact in the presence of the Pythons' quest for silliness. Replacing the Horse by the Rabbit may be the most devastating burlesque of the Trojan legend since Chaucer compared the squawking of the hens when Chanticleer was captured by the fox to the lamentations of the Trojan women at Pyrrhus' murder of Priam at the Fall of Ilium.

Abandoning the siege, the knights return to the quest, and, following the ancient principle of *entrelacement*, the tale leaves off recounting the travails of the group and focuses for the first time on the individual adventures of one knight. The "Book" returns and brings us to "The Tale of Sir Robin." Although hitherto unknown, it would not be correct to think of Sir Robin as an unsung hero. He is accompanied by his own minstrel who relentlessly burbles the "Ballad of Sir Robin." This ballad may not be specifically derived from Chaucer's *Tale of Sir Thopas*, but its heart and spirit are direct descendants of the utter silliness of Chaucer's pre–*Melibee* performance. Like *Sir Thopas,* "Sir Robin" imitates the remorseless rhymes and rhythms of the form, and, like *Sir Thopas,* "Sir Robin" celebrates the defects of a not too effective knight, whose most successful combat technique is "to bravely run away."

The Pythons then continue yet another tradition, if not an Arthurian one, with its roots in the Middle Ages,[10] and also helpfully contribute to the expansion of the Arthurian company which had been lacking its full complement of cowards.[11] Sir Robin's main adventure involves a three-headed knight, who has no counterpart in Arthurian legend, but may, minus the canine features, owe something to Cerberus. The heads argue over whether to have tea or kill Sir Robin first. They decide to kill Robin and then have tea and biscuits, but fall into dissension about biscuits, and by the time they are ready to kill Sir Robin, they look down to discover, as the minstrel tells us, he had "bravely turned his tail and fled."

The jaunty strains of the ballad turn to a reiteration of the *Pie Jesu*, this time in the margins of an animated manuscript, another stroke of Terry Gilliam's genius. The monks proceed liturgically along the foliate curves of the illustration, banging themselves on the head, as they did in the "Bring Out Your Dead" scene, and sort of plunge into white space as their leafy support comes to a finial finale. While Gilliam probably did not intend some sort of reference to a leap of faith in this brilliant manuscript joke, there is, in addition to a cynical comment on the monks' lemminglike willingness to follow and imitate the unthinking leaders of an unthoughtout ritual, a kind of innocent faith in the assumption that the leap into the blankness of the page is not, in fact, a leap into mere emptiness. There is, perhaps, also a faith in the vocation and industry of the monks who preserved classical learning in spite of their own beliefs, and a faith that what they labored to preserve will preserve them. The leap into the abyss also brings us back to the *mise en abîme* that continues to thwart scholarly attempts to get to the heart of the Grail business. Modern scholars, indeed, are not unlike these pathetic little hero monks who fall or leap into the blankness of the page, hoping for a revelation that is inevitably deferred, perhaps denied.

It is not inappropriate, perhaps, that the monks fall into the space surrounding the title of the next episode: "The Tale of Sir Galahad." One would not expect the Pythons' Galahad to be the ascetic knight of the legend, and one would certainly not expect the Pythons to approve of the *Queste*'s rigorous ascetic monastic values. Oddly, however, the bizarre, almost anti–*Queste* episode of the lusty maidens luring knights to their castle does have some precedent in the Vulgate. There is an obvious connection to Maiden Castle, a site that figures prominently in the *Queste*, although there do not seem to be a great many maidens in Maiden Castle. There is also an episode in the Vulgate in which, as with the nervous Sir Galahad, a virgin knight is surrounded by desperately lusty ladies. In that text, Sir Bors finds himself in a castle ruled by an impetuous damsel, who demands that he make love to her. If not, all her companions will throw themselves from the tower with her. Sir Bors declines, disappointing the damsel and, undoubtedly, her plummeting companions.

Like Sir Bors, the Pythons' Sir Galahad remains chaste despite temptation, and the ladies remain unsatisfied, but alive. The effectiveness of the scene, in part, depends, most likely, on a certain misrecognition of the medieval depiction of women. While the medievalists among the Pythons should know that there are a number of aggressive women in medieval literature, it seems a good deal of the comedy of the scene depends on the simple fact that the castle of women is also a castle of horny women. As its complement, the comedy also depends on the presence of non-horny men,[12] which does have a precedent in the original, but is comic here where it is not, or at least not intentionally so, in the original, because the chastity is not based so much on an ascetic ideal as it is on the men's squeamishness; Galahad seems less chaste than frightened. Gawain, as one might expect, is quite ready for action, but dissuaded by Galahad. There are then elements of this deceptive Grail Castle that can be traced to the original, but the Pythons have no precedent for the castle as a lure, a conscious snare set out for Grail knights. Like the Bat Signal well known to denizens of Gotham, the ladies of the castle have their Grail signal all set to deceive knights. Naughty, naughty Zoot claims responsibility; she also claims the needs to be spanked by the knights, a penitence the other ladies eagerly claim the right to share. Alas, these knights are unable or unwilling to satisfy either desire: lust and justice are equally unfulfilled.

The quest continues with a visit to a craggy gentleman who prophesies the Bridge of Death and an encounter with the famous Knights Who Say "Ni" and who are, for inscrutable reasons, in serious need of a shrubbery. The first episode, which calls itself "Scene 24" is, if you are counting, actually scene 13.[13] It is almost redundant of the Pythons to call attention to the episodic structure of the narrative. It is in no small measure a structure that reflects the origins of the Pythons in television sketch comedy and it is easy enough to view the film as a series of sketches roughly grouped around a theme. What the Pythons do, however, is incorporate a deconstruction of their method within the film. "Scene 24" interrupts sequence, even an episodic sequence, and calls attention to the arbitrary nature of these sequences. Episodes could be shuffled, reorganized, rearranged with no loss of meaning, and possibly an increase in texture and suggestion for the new and accidental arrangement. It is a gesture toward the sort of experimentation of Italo Calvino or Julio Cortazar. Again, however, this parodic post-modernism of the Pythons remains anchored in the Middle Ages, where episodic structures are not uncommon, especially in chivalric romances, and, as students of manuscript tradition can attest, episodes are migratory, can change position at the whim of a scribe. As so often happens, the Pythons are most surprising when they are most medieval.

Subject as well as technique might be seen as a reflection of medieval tradition. While neither a monk nor a Loathly Lady, the Loathly cave dweller does prophesy and give obscure directions like so many of the white hermits in the Vulgate *Queste*. The explications are less complex and the moral dimension pretty much neglected, but insofar as they operate as plot devices the Pythons' craggy caveman serves the same purpose, to simultaneously surprise and predict — by the time the prophesy comes to be fulfilled we have pretty much forgotten it was made. On the other hand, the Knights Who Say "Ni" serve no purpose at all, except to be enormously silly and to remind us yet again that in the world of Monty Python anything can happen.

Returning to the book, we take up "The Tale of Sir Lancelot," one of the more extended sequences. While there is no specific precedent for this sequence, the basic plot is familiar. It is the tale of the princess locked in a tower and forced to marry against her will. Into her lonely life, a hero arrives to rescue her from her sad and lonely fate. It is that sort of story the Pythons tell us, except that the sad and lonely princess turns out to be Prince Herbert. And Sir Lancelot is confused. This gender-bending moment does, in fact, have some precedent in medieval texts, particularly in Malory. The pseudo-seduction in which Lancelot hastens to aid what he thinks is a lamenting woman only to discover the whining Prince Herbert has a sort of precedent in Lancelot's encounter with Sir Belleus, who is surprised to feel a beard when he embraces what he thought had been his paramour. Fortunately, the Pythons' Lancelot discovers his error before he accidentally embraces the unappetizing Prince Herbert. The cross-dressing Prince may also owe something to the episode when Lancelot forces Dinadan to dress as a woman at the conclusion of the Tournament at Surluse. Neither of these precedents, however, does quite the damage the Pythons do to the pattern of the romance. The Prince is not so much unmasked as massacred: the Prince tries to escape by making a ladder of the bedsheets. Lancelot slices them to let the Prince plunge to an uncertain, but certainly unhappy, fate. In this rough dismissal of the transgressive prince, the Pythons raise issues of cross-dressing and deviance, only to ruthlessly restore a brutal heteronormativity. On the other hand, the masculine norm may be undercut by its own excess, for Lancelot's subsequent escape involves a sweeping slaughter of the wedding guests. It is hard to explain why bridesmaids splattered with the blood of decapitated relatives is funny. And perhaps for many it isn't. But one does react to the excess and the sheer outrageousness of the slaughter as if it were funny, and it may be so, perhaps, because it is so uncalled for, so unreal, and so over the top. Lancelot cancels the threat of homosexuality (effeminacy perhaps) represented by Prince Herbert (and Sir Belleus in Malory[14]) by first assisting in the Prince's murder, and then by senseless slaughter. The butchery at the banquet, in a way, restores his reputation for heroism, for machismo, but at the same time destroys it. By being so much the macho hero, Lancelot drains the concept of both sense and sensibility.

From this parodic romance interlude, the tale returns to the Grail quest. Like that primordial quest narrative, the "Tale of Culhwch and Olwen," the film makes use of the structure of the intercalated quest. The Grail knights do, in fact, return to the Knights Who Say "Ni" bearing the desired shrubbery. As this sort of story demands, the fulfillment of one quest merely motivates the initiation of another quest, so the Knights are requested to perform another quest, which is to fetch another shrubbery ... "a little higher and to the left." They are, however, spared this arduous task when the Knights Who Say "Ni" (now the Knights Who Used to Say "Ni") are reduced to helpless lumps by the sudden speaking of the unbearable word (apparently the reckless use of "it").

Entrelacement reigns as Sir Robin returns, an ill-fated professor, whose accidental and anachronistic death brings contemporary policemen into the Arthurian corpus, is recalled, and Terry Gilliam provides a glorious interlude based on the Duc de Berry's *Book of Hours*. The famous Limburg brothers illustrations are parodied, but also imitated with a certain affection. It is a subtle manuscript parody that is also a manuscript tribute.

The manuscript tour through the seasons leads into the encounter with Tim the Enchanter and the film's closest approach to the cliché image of medieval knights, the dragon fight. There are, in fact, few dragon fights in Arthurian literature, but there is the story of St. George which, for England, in particular, fixed the image of the knight for the later Middle Ages, although the later Middle Ages in this case should probably be defined as the Age of Victoria. While there are few dragons in Arthurian literature, the Questing Beast plays a significant, if largely inscrutable, role in Arthurian legend, primarily in the prose *Tristan* where he is pursued by Palomede. There is also the enigmatic Welsh kitty, the Cath Pulag, that seems to have engaged in battle with Arthur somewhere in Switzerland. It seems unlikely, however, that these obscure beasts were the direct sources of the extraordinary creations of the Monty Pythons, the deadly Caerbannog and the Beast of Arrrghhh. Like Cath Pulag, the killer kitty, Caerbannog appears to be a cuddly little rodent, continuing the rabbit theme introduced in the device of the Trojan Rabbit. He is, however, a deadly Killer Rabbit who returns us to the grim comedy of gore and corpses. The Beast of Arrghhh allows Terry Gilliam at last to exercise the power of the pen in imaging a truly fanciful monster. He is a cartoon, but an exuberantly grotesque creature, with hints of Cerberus, Argus, Hydra, and other mythical monsters. He also, in a wittily post-modern sort of touch, inscribes the death of the artist into the work of art. The beast is named Arrghh because before his plot is complete, before his story is entirely drawn, the artist himself dies and his final spasms scribble the monster into scraggly fragments and name him in his dying gasps, "Arrghh!"

Escaping from the monster, the knights arrive at the Bridge of Death. This is the same bridge that had been prophesied in Scene 24, which was, of course, Scene 13. Riddles and questions have always been a crucial motif in Arthurian legend. Indeed, the entire quest, with its origins in Chrétien's *Perceval*, depends on the answer to the question, "Whom does one serve with the Grail?" Questions and riddles are, then, implicated in the very earliest texts of the quest. They are rarely, however, connected with peculiar ridges that throw visitors in crevasses and threaten them with questions, such as "What is the capital of Assyria?" "What is your favorite color?" "What is the airspeed velocity of an unladen swallow?" The last question in a masterpiece of farcical *entrelacement* loops back to the initial discussion of the coconut horses and the theory of the migration of coconuts via African swallows. The questioner at the Bridge of Death is unprepared for Arthur's question, its legitimacy prepared for a dozen or more scenes earlier, "African or European swallow." The questioner unprepared for this question cannot answer, so he himself, in the venerable tradition of the trickster tricked, plunges to his own death. The remaining questers cross the bridge in safety.

But not before the questers are interrupted by a new peril, one unknown to the original Knights of the Holy Grail, but familiar to anyone exposed to the mammoth epics of the sixties, or anything shown in Italy, the dreaded "Intermission." The epic Hollywood film of the fifties, like *Around the World in Eighty Days*, is probably the model for the sudden intrusion of the "Intermission" notice in the midst of the challenge of the Bridge of Death. Those old epics did, however, usually have some sense of when a break would be appropriate. While the Pythons seem less likely to have had an Italian model in mind, it in many ways seems more apposite. The sudden, unexpected, intrusive "Fine Primo Tempo," to which Italian audiences are subjected, parallels the absurd timing of the Pythons' "Intermission." It is shocking and absurd, coming, as it does, in the midst of an episode that could easily have been allowed to complete itself before the break, and that is also situated something like three-quarters of the way into the film. As with the subtitles at the beginning of the film, this is the sort of reference that has nothing to do with the Arthurian legend, but with the conventions of film. The absurdities of cinematic practice, American, English, Swedish, and, in this case, Italian, are called attention to. These sorts of devices, while not precisely derived from Brecht's theatre, are clearly allied to Brecht's theory, a theory the Pythons surely knew. His famous, if ambiguous (*i.e.* multi-valenced) theory of the *Verfremdungseffekt* would embrace precisely these sorts of devices that shock us out of our cinematic complacency to force us to consider the nature of film and demystify the medium. This demystifying could be Marxist, serious, and revolutionary, or, as in the case of the Pythons, it could be silly. As the Pythons make clear, however, beginning with the brilliant social analysis of Dennis the peasant, it is entirely possible to be very silly and very Marxist simultaneously. Indeed, if the condition of man under capitalism is essentially alienated and absurd, silliness becomes the most appropriate and accurate response.

The Pythons, then, are true Brechtians and true Marxists not in spite of their silliness, but because of it. Even if the object of their demystification is trivial (such as the cinematic Intermission), it provides the basis for the questioning of systems and media that are too often assumed to be eternal and unchanging. Teaching us to laugh at an oddly placed intermission is a minor triumph. Teaching us to see through the absurdities and deceits of conventions (conventions that include intermissions, and extend to other media events, like press conferences and Tom Brokaw) is of considerably more value. Silliness may not win the war, but it's not a bad way to begin the battle.

The battle begins to begin in earnest once the Pythons more or less cross the Bridge of Death. They arrive at a Grail Castle. While we are spared the endless explications that Perceval's sister inflicts on the Grail knights

King Arthur and his knights seek advice from the Mighty Wizard Tim in Terry Gilliam and Terry Jones's 1975 film *Monty Python and the Holy Grail*.

and their readers in the *Queste*, the Pythons approach the castle by sea in a mysterious dragon-shaped ship. The ship may look a little more Scandanavian than Norman, a bit more suited to Beowulf than Bedivere, but it, nevertheless, recalls the magical ships which recur in the *Queste*. When the ship arrives at the last of the illusory Grail Castles, it turns out to be occupied by the marvelously silly Frenchmen we encountered at the beginning of the film. They remain absurd, and they remain a dead end.

In this relentless circling to return to the beginning, perhaps the essential meaning of a "cycle," the film ends with a deconstruction of film more absolute than the Swedish nonsense at the beginning. The motif of the lecturing professor, the twentieth-century Academic murdered by the tenth-century Lancelot, returns in the arrival of the police investigating his death. The last frames of the film are the hand of an infuriated policeman blocking the camera in a move familiar from contemporary investigative documentaries. The investigation and the quest[15] both end abruptly, both incomplete and cancelled by the constable's hand.

The Pythons are primarily playing with the anachronism of the intrusion of the twentieth century on the fifteenth, and commenting on the chronic violence inherent in the practice of chivalry, commenting as well on the ironic lawlessness of a quest dedicated to the recovery of a spiritual order. This inconclusive conclusion is, however, a strange replication of the original quest narratives. From Chrétien's uncompleted *Perceval* on to the extraordinary regenerating series of incomplete conclusions (Manessier, etc.) that followed, it is almost a feature of the Quest that it remains unachieved.[16]

The conclusion of the Pythons' quest narrative is abrupt and shocking, although the end may not be the end. Those Swedish credits at the beginning of the VHS and DVD followed the view of the canceling hand when the film was originally released. This change in order, moving the credits from the beginning to the end, is almost certainly an order determined by producers who feared that audiences would be enraged and impatient with a list of credits (however hilarious) being placed in such a shocking position as the beginning of the film. There are some advantages to getting the audience into the action sooner, but they are more than outweighed by the brilliant abruptness of the film ending with the interruption of the police and the canceling, censoring, hand of ultimate authority. This Brechtian refusal of a complacent climax comments on the insidious easiness of the traditional Hollywood film. It is an ending, however, that is probably far more accurately medieval than the Pythons may have had in mind, for it reminds us that the Quest is a process more than a goal.

It may be an accident that the meaning of *Monty Python and the Holy Grail* seems so accurately to reflect in a modern context that sense of the quest as an ongoing process, a becoming, but what is true is that this silly film is by no means a trivial one. It remains strangely true to its origins, and, as it touches both irreverently and poignantly on issues of justice, violence, and desire, it remains amazingly funny and pertinent nearly thirty years on. In its interpenetration of the medieval and the modern, the Pythons vitalize and question both. They give new life to the Middle Ages and at the beginning of the twenty-first century, the film makes one powerful statement about the Pythons and about the quest for the Holy Grail. Both the Middle Ages and the Monty Pythons retain their potential to entertain and delight. Like the energetic, life-affirming, plague-resisting ancient, the Middle Ages and the Monty Pythons are demonstrably "not dead yet."

NOTES

1. A change in this perspective may have been accomplished by the remarkable success of *Crouching Tiger, Hidden Dragon*, which achieved, somewhat surprisingly, both critical and popular acclaim.

2. This sort of deconstruction is similar to the work of Penn and Teller in a slightly different medium.

3. "In this year, Frythstan the Bishop died."

4. The notes do record the tradition (via Bede) of Frithstan's death in the act of prayer (II, 136). This tradition was most likely not a factor in the Pythons' decision to choose 932 as the date of the narrative.

5. The opening scene is also, as McCabe has noted, remarkably beautiful. He comments on the "visual splendor" of the scene and adds a perceptive commentary on the opening: "But amongst the grey skies and dark, satanic hills, amid the early morning fog, lies the heart of the movie, its humor and its subversion. Into such a visually redolent background, complete with a suitably ornate orchestral score, the Pythons send a noble king ... and a guy named Patsy banging two coconut shells together to make up for the lack of a horse. This one scene typifies the nature of the movie and, indeed, a good deal of Python humor. It is not so much parody as the constant undercutting of expectation: knowing the route but taking the surreal off-ramp" (55).

6. Again by a circuitous route, the Pythons have echoed a traditional element of the Arthurian tradition. Bedivere (along with Gawain/Gwalchmai) is one of the earliest heroes to be associated with the King.

7. The Battle of Badon Hill is hardly an obscure reference for Arthurians, but it is another allusion to key features of the legend, in this case to one of the few actual historical battles in which (an) Arthur may have participated.

8. Could the witch be a much reinvented version of the Loathly Lady?

9. The similarities are developed in detail in Sigmund Eisner's *The Tristan Legend*. While his speculations on how those elements arrived in Cornwall and into the story of Tristan have not met

with wide approval, the similarities are certainly there.

10. "The Tournament at Tottenham" would also be an example of this anti-heroic and mock-heroic tradition and usefully complements the high-style Chaucer with a more popular example.

11. One might argue for a precedent in the figure Malory names Sir Brewnys Saunz Pitee. While not quite as egregious a coward as Sir Robin, he shares his penchant for running away. Sir Brewnys has the habit of trampling fallen knights a few times and then fleeing on the speediest horse in Christendom.

12. Men unwilling to take advantage of available women are almost always comic characters in English literature. There is even Biblical precedent. Joseph running barely clothed from Potiphar's wife heads a comic tradition that culminates, if it does not conclude, with Fielding's Joseph Andrews.

13. To be precise, it is chapter 13, according to the listing on the DVD.

14. There is also the even more complicated situation of Sir Lavain, which is investigated by Gretchen Mieszkowski; see esp. pp. 45–47.

15. A similar, if subtler, connection is made between quest text and inquest by Howard R. Bloch (108). In the film, the climax cuts between the failed end of the quest and the beginning of the investigation and inquest into the death of the contemporary professor.

16. The Vulgate Quest is, of course, a significant exception to the rule, but if it was intended to impose closure on Quest narratives, to provide a final and unarguable conclusion, it was not a success.

WORKS CITED

Bloch, Howard R. "The Text as Inquest: Form and Function in the Pseudo-Map Cycle." *Mosaic* 8.4 (1975): 107–119.

Eisner, Sigmund. *The Tristan Legend*: A Study in Sources. Evanston, Illinois: Northwestern University Press, 1969.

McCabe, Bob. *Dark Knights and Holy Fools: The Art and Films of Terry Gilliam*. New York: Universe Publishing, 1999.

Mieszkowski, Gretchen. "The Prose Lancelot's Galahad, Malory's Lavain, and the Queering of Late Medieval Literature." *Arthuriana* 5 (1995): 21–51.

The Tournament of Tottenham. In *Middle English Metrical Romances*. 2 vols. Ed. Walter Hoyt French and Charles Brockway Hale. 1930; rpt. New York: Russell & Russell, 1964.

Two of the Saxon Chronicles Parallel. Vol. I. ed. Charles Plummer. 1892; rpt. Oxford: Clarendon, 1929.

13

The Arthurian Legend in French Cinema: Robert Bresson's Lancelot du Lac *and* Eric Rohmer's Perceval le Gallois

JEFF RIDER, RICHARD HULL, AND
CHRISTOPHER SMITH; WITH MICHAEL CARNES,
SASHA FOPPIANO, AND ANNIE HESSLEIN

This essay seeks to explain the common significance of the Arthurian legend for Robert Bresson and Eric Rohmer and to situate *Lancelot du Lac* (1974) and *Perceval le Gallois* (1978) within their bodies of work. We begin by considering the place of the Arthurian legend in modern French culture and go on to discuss the legend's appeal to these directors. The second part of this essay identifies the uniquely "Bressonian" and "Rohmerian" elements of the two films. The essay's third part explores the directors' reasons for adapting two literary models, the *Mort Artu* (or *Mort le Roi Artu*)[1] and Chrétien de Troyes's *Conte du Graal*,[2] and suggests why they diverged widely from these models in the conclusions to their films.

The Arthurian legend fascinated both Bresson and Rohmer. Bresson began laying plans for *Lancelot* as early as 1953 and had drawn up a detailed outline for the film by 1956 (Prédal, "Bresson" 6; A[mengual] 55; Estève, *Robert Bresson: La passion* 75; Sémolué 203–4; Ehrenstein 103; Reader 116–17). Rohmer, who had taught Chrétien de Troyes's *Conte du Graal* to his students while he was a high school teacher, adapted the story for television in 1964. He filmed illustrations from "thirteenth-, fourteenth-, and fifteenth-century manuscripts, and then add[ed] a commentary which explained the story" (Tesich-Savage 51). Dissatisfied with the result, he began planning the film version of the romance, which he realized fourteen years later (Tesich-Savage 51; Magny and Rabourdin 10; Angeli 34; Tortajada 116–20). Both films were thus long-term projects conceived years before they were realized, and both were kept alive until the directors were able to raise the money to make them.[3]

Bresson and Rohmer were attracted to these Arthurian projects by the strangeness of the Arthurian world for modern audiences, especially for modern French audiences, and by the role and associations of the Arthurian legend in French culture. For contemporary audiences, the world of the Arthurian legend is strange historically, materially, and culturally. Its inhabitants dress, talk, act, and think differently. But for the French, the legend is also cinematically strange, having appeared only rarely in French-language films. In 1979, Jacques Durand published a list of fifty-seven chivalric films made between 1910 and 1978 (39); only four of these films were French.[4] Of the thirty-four films that Kevin J. Harty listed in his original 1989 filmography and bibliography of Arthurian films made between 1904 and 1984 (119–37), only five are French.[5] No chivalric or Arthurian films were made in French between Jean Delannoy's *L'Éternel Retour* and Bernard de la Tour's *Du Guesclin* in the 1940s and the films made in the 1970s by Yvan Lagrange, Bresson, Frank Cassenti, and Rohmer, a gap of almost twenty-five years. Rohmer, at least, was clearly aware of this hiatus (see his remarks cited in Magny and Rabourdin 15).

This cultural and cinematic strangeness was seductive to directors as self-consciously independent and artistic as Bresson and Rohmer. As Jacques Fieschi notes, a "process of distancing … lies at the foundation of all [Rohmer's] cinema" (5), and Rohmer himself acknowledges that "making *Perceval* was … a means of getting off certain well-trodden paths" (Adair 231). His much-discussed fidelity to Chrétien's text, his use of medieval music for the sound track, and his imitation of the visual style of medieval manuscript illuminations in an effort "to rediscover the vision of the medieval period as it saw itself" (Tesich-Savage 51)[6] may all be seen as efforts to take full advantage of his subject's potential strangeness.[7] The strangeness of Bresson's *Lancelot du Lac* lies more in the camera than in front of it,[8] and his film has impressed French critics as "a most singular work" (Vitoux 73) whose "composition … is unique, totally specific" (G[uiguet] 29). In this film, notes Capdenac, Bresson takes us into a "'strange/foreign [*étrange*] country' … inhabited by the armed phantoms of anxiety and the unconscious" (59).

The two directors were also intrigued by the role and associations of the Arthurian legend in contemporary France. In Anglo-American culture, the Arthurian legend serves as a means of quasi-historical reflection. For a modern English-speaking audience, that is, every treatment of the Arthurian legend, in whatever medium and however patently fictitious or inaccurate, refers to a dim, mythological past, and is thus a statement about the way things were, might have been, or should have been — and is also, therefore, a statement about the way present-day Anglo-American culture is, might be, or should be.

The Arthurian legend plays an altogether different role in France. The past to which modern French treatments of the legend refer is not shadowy and mythological but datable and literary. The principal referent is not a pseudo-historical recollection of archaic military glory and political ascendancy, but some of the greatest works of medieval literature: above all, the twelfth-century verse romances of Chrétien de Troyes, like the *Conte du Graal*, and the thirteenth-century prose romances of the Vulgate (or Lancelot-Grail) cycle, like the *Mort Artu*.[9] A French audience today associates the Arthurian legend with artistic greatness rather than with the thwarted imperial destiny of a pseudo-historical king.[10]

The different expectations with which French- and English-speaking audiences approach modern treatments of the Arthurian legend, and the different contexts in which they interpret and judge them, are neatly emblematized in the initial reactions of reviewers to Rohmer's casting of Fabrice Luchini in the role of Perceval. In an interview recorded while he was still at work on *Perceval*, Rohmer states that he chose Luchini for the role before he wrote the script, that he wrote the script with Luchini in mind, and that there was only one way, Luchini's, to play the role. For Rohmer, Luchini's wide-eyed innocence and boyish figure capture Perceval's inexperience and naiveté. His entire persona embodied Rohmer's directorial intentions perfectly — Luchini was Perceval, and Perceval was Luchini (Tesich-Savage 54–55).

In general, French reviewers applauded his choice. Mireille Amiel wrote that the character Perceval "cannot be disassociated from the actor (Fabrice Luchini) playing the role (and this [brilliant bit of casting] is not the least of the *auteur*'s merits)" (7). Danièle Dubroux thought that the casting, along with everything else in the film, was absolutely true to Chrétien's text and that the actors played their roles "perfectly"; she further noted that Luchini's "hallucinatory stare [*regard*] ... reproduces the stare of a child who has been quieted by reality" and attributed the film's "oneiric dimension" to this "illuminated stare, of a waking dreamer or a sleepwalker [that] guides the vision [*regard*] of the spectator, making him or her discover the world of chivalry at the same time as [Perceval]" (43). Max Tessier observed that "the dumbfounded air of Fabrice Luchini/Perceval is not the least surprising element of this unusual work, and, through him, more than through any other [element], Rohmer plays on a distancing humor which is constantly present" (72).

English and American reviewers generally had a different reaction. Stanley Kauffman thought that Luchini was "goofy" (31). Andrew Sarris said that Luchini's Perceval reminded him of the "bemused ultra-Catholic bourgeois played by Jean-Louis Trintignant in [Rohmer's] *My Night at Maud's* (1969), but without Trintignant's charm" (76). Gerald Clarke wrote that "Luchini is more a suggestion of a knight than a knight himself. With a receding chin, concave chest, and dangling, half-open mouth, he looks as if he would be afraid to kill a mouse with a trap, much less joust with a man in armor" (104). Marsha McCreadie observed that, as Perceval, Luchini was the "dopiest looking of all [the "silly looking" characters] ... we're meant to chuckle, perhaps, at the *naif*, but here the hero has clearly been chosen to look ludicrous and baffled" (54).

The French appreciation and Anglo-American depreciation of Luchini — reactions that echo critics' response to the film in general[11] — can be attributed to essentially different attitudes towards the Arthurian legend. The English and American critics, viewing the film as a treatment of a mythological past, as a pseudo-historical reflection, compared Luchini to their concept of an "authentic" (i.e., mythological) knight and found him ludicrous. For French critics, viewing the film as an artistic adaptation of a work of medieval literature, Luchini's conformity to a modern concept of knighthood was unimportant: they were more interested in what the casting revealed about the *auteur*'s understanding of his material.[12]

The literary associations of the Arthurian legend in French culture made the legend an attractive point of departure for Bresson and Rohmer, and the influence of these associations on the two directors is evident when one compares their choice and treatment of their narrative models with those of, say, John Boorman. Linguistic limitations,[13] considerations of target audiences, and cultural chauvinism all undoubtedly played a part in Bresson's decision to base his film on the *Mort Artu*[14] and Rohmer's to base his on the *Conte du Graal*, just as they did in Boorman's choice of Malory's *Le Morte d'Arthur* as a source — albeit a loose one — in making *Excalibur*. Boorman's invocation of *Le Morte d'Arthur*, however, was also shaped by the Anglo-American associations of the Arthurian legend: he was interested in the mythological impact of the entire legend, and this inter-

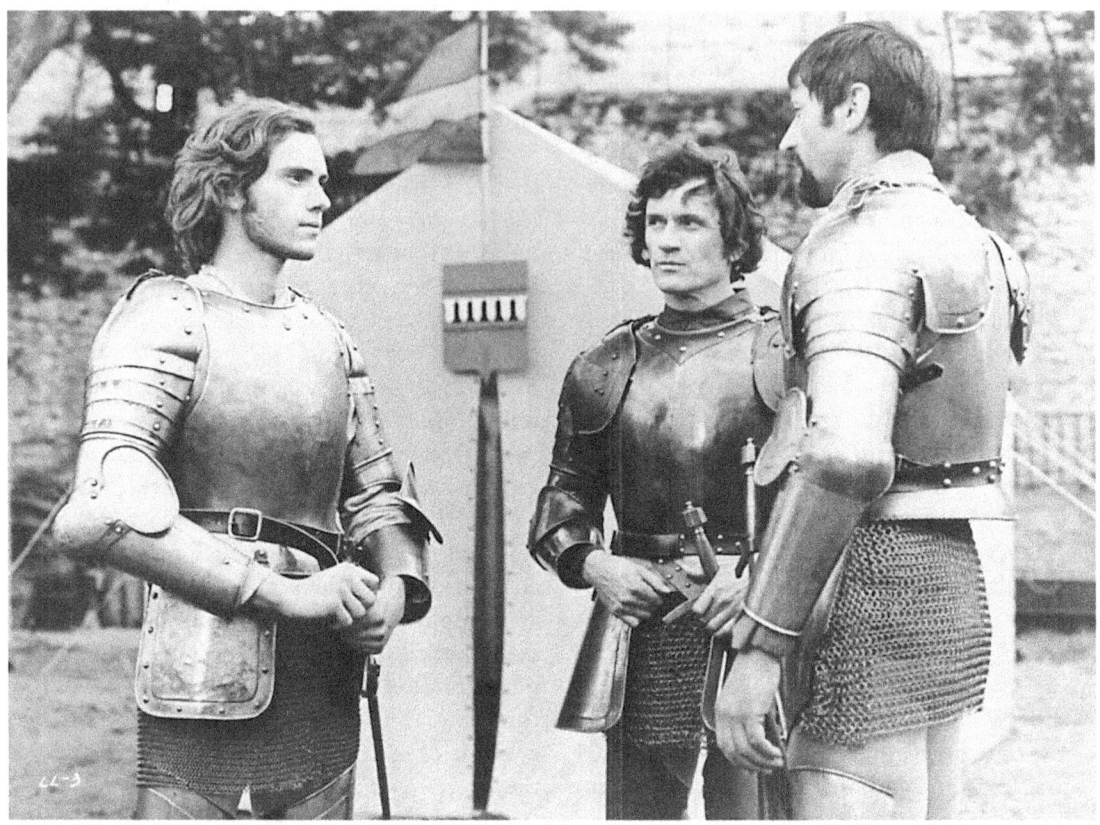

From left to right, Patrick Bernard as Gauvain, Luc Simon as Lancelot, and Vladimir Antolek as Arthur in Robert Bresson's 1974 film *Lancelot du Lac*.

est led him to invoke a comprehensive literary model that relates Arthur's entire career.[15] Bresson and Rohmer chose literary models of more limited scope, with greater unity of action, time, and place.

The same biases are evident in the directors' differing degrees of fidelity to their literary models. Rohmer is the most faithful; Boorman, the least. Rohmer and Bresson abridge but follow their model narratives reasonably closely, except at the very end of their films; Boorman does not. The French directors adhere more closely to their sources because these stories *are* the inspirations for their films: the films are an important manifestation of the reception of medieval French literature in modern French culture.[16] The inspiration for Boorman's film, on the other hand, is not Malory's narrative, not a literary past, but the mythological past of the Arthurian legend. Ultimately, because his film stands in the same relation to that mythological past as the medieval literary work — they are treatments of a common legend, reflections on the same moment of the pseudo-past — Boorman felt less obliged to follow his model.[17]

The Arthurian legend, in sum, offered Bresson and Rohmer an aura of "strangeness" coupled with an atmosphere of "great literary art." Such a combination was irresistible and immensely valuable to such doggedly original arch-*auteurs*.[18] This combination gave them the opportunity and the freedom to create two highly personal visions of the Middle Ages, and explains their enduring desires to make films based on parts of that legend. Let us turn now to those visions and the ways they exploited the "strangeness" and prestige of their literary models.

Lancelot du Lac is a thickly constructed film whose narrative is propelled by a number of formal devices. To begin with, Bresson uses sound effects to create the illusion of a natural setting. The audience hears horses whinny and gallop, hears the knights' armor clanking as they walk, hears a vessel being emptied. Some of these sounds are anchored visually; others are not. This off camera sound extends the world of the film beyond what can be seen on the screen — the creaking armor or stomping hooves, for example, alert the audience to a knight's approach — but it also creates a mood of expectation and anxiety because one hears actions one cannot see. Despite their use to invoke a naturalistic ambience, moreover, many of these sound effects are so elaborate that they take on a life and a significance of their own. After a time, the constant clanking cacophony of armor or the whinnies one hears off-screen start to seem hyperreal and to hint at hidden meanings.[19]

The lighting in *Lancelot* is likewise both naturalistic and significant. Generally low-key (dim and subdued) and diffused, it is punctuated with certain high-key scenes (scenes with bright, even lighting) in the corridors and rooms of the castle and just before and during the tournament. These high-key scenes are the visual opposites of the dark forest in which the knights meet their fated end. This tension between light and dark is most evident in the courtyard of Arthur's castle where the red glow from the knights' tents and the unattainable beacon of Guenièvre's window shine in a darkness that has not yet overcome them.

The earth, to which everything will eventually fall, is the visual leitmotif of the film, and many shots appear aimed at reducing space to a two-dimensional plane. There are no establishing shots or wide angles. Shots and scenes often begin and end with the camera pointing at the ground, and the audience sees a great many high-angle shots of the ground as feet and hooves move over it. These shots inform the audience that people are moving through space without showing the actual space. Bresson also uses the black, green, and brown colors of the earth to set off, and to contrast with, the brighter, artificial shades of human tissues, artifacts, and constructions. This concentration on the earth thematizes the film's vertical dimension and knighthood's descent through it. In the opening scenes, the mounted knights cut a swathe of destruction through the dark forest, and their collective death is predicted by an old woman hunched on the ground. At the end of the film, one sees the same knights, ambushed by archers hiding in the trees above them, falling into a pile of armor on the same dark forest floor.[20]

Bresson's objective visual presentation of his material prevents the audience from identifying strongly with any of the characters.[21] The only action sequences are the tournament and the final battle. The tournament is Lancelot's finest moment, but Bresson presents it as a repetition of the same action: Lancelot reaches for his lance, the bagpipe skirls, a pennant is raised, Lancelot charges, his opponent falls from his horse. This repetition dulls any excitement the audience may feel and suggests the violence is meaningless. Even the shots from horseback at the tournament are too steady to be point-of-view shots that might communicate the inner experience of the characters. Bresson adopts the same approach to the "climactic" battle at the end of the film. There are repeated shots of riderless horses running through the woods, dead or dying knights, and archers firing down from trees until Bresson ends the loop in a pile of armed bodies. The battle has neither narrative structure nor clues as to who killed whom or which side won. The knights' deaths are meaningless.

Bresson's habitual casting of non-professional actors in the starring roles likewise prevents the audience from identifying with them on the basis of experience. The audience thus has no reason to empathize with Lancelot, for example, when he is injured in the tournament. They have not had enough screen time with the hero at this point to feel any particular sympathy for him, and his injury seems inevitable in the context of the general fate of knighthood in the film. The unindividuated destroyers of the film's opening scenes are thus reflected in the heap of anonymous armor with which the film closes. The knights are as constrained by the thematization of the space they occupy and by the formal devices used to portray them as they are by their armor, which none of them ever completely removes. Guenièvre is the only character in the film who bares more than her face and hands. When juxtaposed with the knights' metal shells, this human softness gives her an air of vulnerability — particularly in the scene where her bare hand rests on Lancelot's mailed wrist as he escorts her back to Arthur[22] — but Guenièvre, too, is cold. Her lighted bedroom window is more inviting than her unreadable face.

Laura Duke Condominas as Guenièvre in Robert Bresson's 1974 film *Lancelot du Lac*.

Visually, Rohmer's *Perceval le Gallois* is theatrical and distant. No effort is made to create a sense of filmed history, an impression that one is watching something that really happened, or that could have happened. Rohmer establishes this distance between film and audience in several ways. The props and set are stagelike and highly stylized. Modeled on illuminations found in medieval manuscripts, the set consists principally of reflective silver trees and uniformly beige castles. The actors' gestures are likewise modeled on gestures found in these illuminations and seem stiff and artificial.[23] All of the sound is anchored visually: everything one hears originates from something on the screen. The script (essentially Chrétien's text, edited and modernized by Rohmer),[24] the period music, the sung narration, and the visibility of the chorus and musicians also create a stagelike feel.[25] Rohmer increases, or at least does nothing to soften, the theatricality of what he has assembled in front of his camera by making that camera as inconspicuous as possible throughout the film: the camera movements, when they occur, are practical and functional, the shots are long, the cuts straightforward and unobtrusive. This "invisible" camera allows the director to focus the audience's attention on other things.

Rohmer goes to great lengths to emphasize the theatricality of the film, its production, and the mechanics of "performing" the story. In Chrétien's romance, this performance is divided between the narrator, who addresses the audience and describes what the characters feel and think as well as what happens, and the characters, who think aloud or speak to one another. Rohmer, interestingly, does not assign the role of the narrator to a single voice, character or set of characters, such as the chorus, but divides this role between the chorus and the characters. Perceval, for example, may narrate his own thoughts and actions in the third person as well as speak his "lines." The distinction between narrator and character is further effaced when the members of the chorus leave their conventionally removed space and participate in the action as speaking characters. The disintegration or dispersion of the narrative voice prevents the audience from identifying with the characters or even focusing exclusively on them. It invites the audience to concentrate instead on the manner in which the tale is told.[26]

Rohmer thus takes an already culturally distant story and removes it farther from his audience through its staging, camera work, and an unconventional redistribution of the narration. His presentation of Chrétien's text encourages the audience to focus on the cinematic renarration, both visual and aural, of the tale, a renarration that is ultimately the film's major theme.

The situation of the Arthurian legend in French culture offered common advantages to Bresson and Rohmer and permitted them to create perhaps the most formally "Bressonian" and "Rohmerian" of all their films. However, the Arthurian legend, and the particular narrative that each director used as a model, also offered them particular advantages and opportunities related to their individual styles and themes.

"In the sparse, medieval world of Camelot where everything from battle to bath to bed takes on the air of a formal ritual," as Fred Barron observes, "Bresson is in his element. His cinematic style and the content of the story are in perfect harmony...." (34). Jean Delmas and Frédéric Vitoux point out that Bresson's trademark anti-psychologism, anti-theatricalism, and depersonalization of the actors are made less remarkable and less disconcerting by the archaic strangeness of the legendary material (Delmas 21; Vitoux 73). "By picking out such a well-known tale as the legend of Camelot," Fred Barron further notes, "Bresson has freed himself totally from the narrative: a liberation he has long sought" (34). This tale — especially the love of Lancelot and Guenièvre which, Bresson states, "give[s] the film its movement" ("*Lancelot du Lac*: Un film de Robert Bresson" 48) — also offers Bresson the advantage of a ready-made emotional response in his audience with, and against, which he can play. The passionate emotion traditionally associated with this love and the utter dispassion of the actors create a self-reflexive tension in the minds of the audience and is perhaps the primary source of the impression that the film has a metaphorical or metaphysical dimension.[27] Observing that Bresson's major theoretical reflection, *Notes sur le cinématographe* — on which he worked for thirty years — appeared just after the production of *Lancelot*[28] — on which he had likewise been at work for twenty of those years — Prédal suggests that the film can "legitimately be seen as the realization of his own artistic quest" ("Poétique" 109; compare Rosenbaum 201, Thompson 289–90, Sémolué 226).

The *Conte du Graal*, too, offered Rohmer particular advantages and continuities with his earlier work. The narration of the film, even if it is divided among the various actors, recalls the narrators of Rohmer's earlier series of six films, the *Contes Moraux*. *Perceval* also contains, as Fieschi notes, "an adolescent eroticism" reminiscent of these earlier films (5). There is, moreover, a substantial thematic continuity between the *Contes Moraux* and *Perceval*. Perceval, as both Tom Milne and George Morris point out, is a typically Rohmerian hero (Milne 193–94; Morris 10), and Lucy Fischer observes that "the themes of the romance are relevant to the sensibility of the director's six ... 'Moral Tales' ... a romance like Chrétien's *Perceval and the Grail* contains the ideological roots of Rohmer's world-view" (21). Amiel (7), Williams (71–72), Wise (2410) and Crisp (84) likewise remark on the continuity of "the underlying moral values" (Crisp 84) of *Perceval* and the *Contes Moraux*, and Rohmer says that he was intrigued "less by the magic [of the *Conte du Graal*] than by the moral, less by the esoteric tale than by the *roman d'apprentissage*" (Rohmer 7): he may have left out some of the "fantastic and magical aspects" of the text, but he "kept everything having to do with the moral theme: the simultaneously moral and amorous apprenticeship of Perceval" (Magny and Rabourdin 16).[29]

Having followed their medieval narrative models faithfully for most of their films, however, Bresson and Rohmer break cleanly away from these models at the end in order to draw their own starkly moral conclusions. The ultimate attraction of the *Mort Artu* and the *Conte du Graal* for Bresson and Rohmer seems indeed to have been the authority these works would confer by association on the directors' inventions. The subject of *Lancelot du Lac*, in Capdenac's terms, is "the collapse of a world in fury and ferocity," "the end of a world and a legend sinking in the horror and cruelty of a general disaster" (57, 59). In the *Mort Artu*, Bresson found what is arguably the greatest representation of such a disaster in Western literature, one that also possesses what Delmas calls a "fecund uncertainty that permits [one] to make a metaphor of it" (21). The two things that drew him to the *Mort Artu*, Bresson tells us, were a desire "to draw it from what is our mythology," to make it accessible to a modern audience, or, in other words, to make a metaphor of it, and "a situation, that of the knights who return to Arthur's castle without the Grail. The Grail, which is to say the absolute, God...." ("*Lancelot du Lac*: Un film de Robert Bresson" 48). The film is thus the metaphorical representation of the collapse of a godless world.[30]

The one problem with the *Mort Artu*, from Bresson's point of view, is that it is insufficiently grim and pessimistic: the collapse is gradual and never total. Arthur, Lucan the Butler, and Girflet all survive the battle against Mordred on Salisbury Plain, and although we later discover Arthur's tomb in the Black Chapel and may presume that he has died of his wounds, we are never sure: we last see him alive in Morgan's boat and care, his death is not described, and we never see the corpse. Guenièvre enters a convent after the battle and dies there a short time later: "but never," the medieval author tells us, "had a high-born lady had a finer and more repentant end to her life, or more tenderly begged Our Lord for forgiveness." Lancelot and his kinsmen Bors, Lionel, and Hector are not even present at the final battle. They return to England only after they have heard of Arthur's death and defeat, and they kill Mordred's sons in a subsequent conflict. Lionel dies in this later battle, but Hector, Bors and Lancelot all end their days as saintly hermits. The Archbishop of Canterbury, one of Lancelot's two companions in his final days, is sleeping at the moment of Lancelot's death, and in a dream he sees "a great company of angels ... carrying to heaven the soul of our brother Lancelot." The body is returned to the castle of Joyeuse Garde where it is placed in a magnificent tomb in the main church (Cable 191–235).

This ending was far too cheerful and hopeful for Bresson, so he changed it and had Arthur, Lancelot, and all their knights die together on the scrap heap of godless passion and ambition in what Reader has called "the most cosmically pessimistic of Bresson's endings" (120)[31]. What *Lancelot du Lac* shows us is not cinema in the service of medieval literature, but medieval literature transformed into a cinematic mask for twentieth-century alienation.

The conclusion to *Perceval le Gallois* departs more sharply still from its narrative model. The Passion play is simply not in Chrétien's romance, which leaves Perceval taking communion with his hermit uncle on Easter morning, goes on at some length to relate the further adventures of Gawain, and breaks off in the middle of one of these adventures. This lack of satisfactory conclusions to both Perceval's and Gawain's ad-

Fabrice Luchini (left) as Perceval and Michel Etchverry as King Arthur watch the procession of the Grail maidens in Eric Rohmer's 1978 film *Perceval le Gallois*.

ventures makes the romance enigmatic and has provoked a great deal of critical attention. Rohmer's departure from his model at this point is all the more surprising because of his scrupulous fidelity to Chrétien's romance up to this point.[32] The Passion play is a "tearing rupture," moreover, not only with the preceding portions of this film,[33] but with all of Rohmer's preceding films: here, "for the first time in his work," writes Fieschi, "the filmmaker attains a direct pathos" (6). Rohmer adduces three reasons for this ending. First, "I wanted a brilliant ending, [a] surprise ending [that would] bring out strong emotions ... the audience should be carried away by it." Second, "If I represented the Passion, it's also because it is an important motif for the Middle Ages and very tempting for a cinéaste.... But the essential reason," third, "is that it is in the logic of Perceval's search.... Perceval, in the beginning, believes that God is a warrior, and in the end he realizes that God is a victim, a man humiliated, beaten.... It very much seems that the text is centered on the Christian, Christly, idea that God is Christ.

I did nothing more," concludes Rohmer, "than be faithful to Chrétien de Troyes" (Magny and Rabourdin 16–17; Tesich-Savage 55, 56).

The notions that Chrétien's text is centered on a "Christly idea" and that the Passion was "in the logic" of Perceval's search are highly debatable. It is undoubtedly true, however, that the Passion was a temptation to both the Catholic moralist and the filmmaker in Rohmer, and it is very much "in the logic" of his reading and adaptation of the romance. What Rohmer has filmed, in other words, is not Chrétien's romance, but his, Rohmer's, profoundly Catholic, highly moralized interpretation of Chrétien's romance. The Passion is not a particularly apt or likely conclusion to the medieval romance, but it is an apt and likely conclusion to Rohmer's interpretation of the romance.[34]

The conclusions to both films, then, are less "in the logic" of their medieval narrative models than they are "in the logic" of Bresson's and Rohmer's readings and interpretations of those narratives as moralistic,

Catholic, French filmmakers. In both cases, the medieval narrative served as a means of grasping and expressing an individual's thoroughly contemporary concerns. And is it not in this way and for this purpose that these works, the Arthurian legend, and indeed the entire Middle Ages, remain a viable part of modern-day culture?

NOTES

We would like to thank Professors John Frazer, Kevin J. Harty, and Norris J. Lacy for their helpful comments on the first version of this essay. We would also like to thank Steven Lebergott, Connie Fraser, Kathy Stefanowicz, and Kate Wolfe of the Olin Library Interlibrary Loan Office for their extensive help in acquiring secondary materials. We are likewise grateful for a grant from the Office of Academic Affairs of Wesleyan University which permitted us to screen these two films while preparing the first version of the essay.

All translations are ours unless otherwise noted.

1. *La Mort le Roi Artu*, ed. Jean Frappier (Geneva: Droz; Paris: Minard, 1954); trans. James Cable, *The Death of King Arthur* (Harmondsworth: Penguin, 1971).

2. Chrétien de Troyes, *Le Roman de Perceval ou le Conte du graal*, ed. Keith Busby (Tübingen: Max Niemeyer, 1993); *The Complete Romances of Chrétien de Troyes*, trans. David Staines (Bloomington, Indiana: Indiana University Press, 1990), 339–449.

3. Rosenbaum writes that "one indication of the sustaining power of [Bresson's] dream — a blend of chance and predestination oddly echoing the metaphysics of his fictional world — can be seen in his selection of Laura Duke Condominas to play Guenièvre, a decision initially reached when he came across a photograph of her, with no prior information about who she was. It was only afterward that he discovered she was the daughter of Niki de St. Phalle ... his original choice for Guenièvre some two decades ago" (202).

4. The four films are *Du Guesclin* (dir. Bernard de la Tour, 1948), *Lancelot du Lac, La Chanson de Roland* (dir. Frank Cassenti, 1978), and *Perceval le Gallois*.

5. The five films are: *Tristan et Yseut* (dir. Maurice Mariaud, 1920), *L'Éternel Retour* (dir. Jean Delannoy, 1943), *Tristan et Iseult* (dir. Yvan Lagrange, 1972), *Lancelot du Lac*, and *Perceval le Gallois*.

6. As Donald Hoffman points out, however, "Rohmer's geometric trees and foil castles may evoke the look of a manuscript illumination, but the effect of naive quaintness is surely not the effect for which the original illustrators were aiming" (45; compare Cormier 392–93).

7. Chrétien de Troyes likewise sought to maintain an "aesthetic distance" between his audience and his work, and Rohmer, as Joan Tasker Grimbert puts it, was perhaps "drawn instinctively to an artist in whom he recognized a kindred spirit" (34). On the ways in which both Chrétien and Rohmer distance their audiences from their works, see Beatie 253–55, Tortajada, Grimbert 33–44, and Hoffman 45–47. Williams writes that Rohmer embraced and cultivated the "strange" aesthetic qualities of his medieval textual and visual sources to suggest "the possibility of an aesthetic system that can, like the inconsistent perspectives of medieval art, accommodate contradiction," and his sources' "affinities with a post-modern aesthetic which, for very different reasons, values these same qualities.... Rohmer's special insight with *Perceval*," she concludes, "has been to demonstrate the extent to which the purging of the usual 'modern' interpretation of a medieval, 'pre-modern' text can produce a 'post-modern' work of dazzling originality" (77, 78, 81).

8. According to Bertin-Maghit, Bresson deliberately refused the "false realism" of an "American-style Middle Ages" (*un 'Moyen Age à l'américaine'*) that is "so reassuring for the spectator" (53–54). Angeli suggests, in fact, that "Bresson tries to reduce the distance between us and the Middle Ages as much as possible.... By filming obstinately the details, the fragments of a chivalric universe whose materiality denies the fact that it no longer exists, the director seems to affirm that the Middle Ages are with us" (42). Compare Rosenbaum 203–04; Thompson 289, 296–97, 304–11; Prédal, "Poétique" 104; and Reader 117–18. Bresson himself said that the film "exists neither in time nor space. As I worked on it, it never occurred to me that armor wasn't contemporary. It was simply metal clothing, which made noises, music, rhythms" (Baby 4). With respect to his earlier historical film, the *Procès de Jeanne d'Arc* (1962), Bresson remarked that "'it is the privilege of cinematography to reinsert the past in the present'" (Estève, *Robert Bresson* 29; compare 32–33).

9. For an introduction to the twelfth- and thirteenth-century Arthurian romances, see Norris J. Lacy, ed., *The New Arthurian Encyclopedia*, updated paperback ed. (New York: Garland, 1996).

10. On the role of the Arthurian tradition in the Anglo-American and the French cultures, see also Burns 86–90 and Prédal, "Poétique"103–04.

11. On the difference between the Anglo-American and the French critical reactions to the film, see also Beatie 249–51.

12. The difference between the Arthurian legend's associations and situation in the two cultures — mythic, historical, and popular in Anglo-American culture, literary, scholarly and elite in French culture — is also evident in the numbers of chivalric and Arthurian films made in French and in English (see notes 4 and 5 above); in the fact that at least six of the seven French films listed in notes 4 and 5 are based on distinct, famous literary models (three are based on the legend of Tristan and Iseult, one on the *Mort Artu*, one on the *Chanson de Roland*, and one on the *Conte du Graal*); and in the difficulty Bresson and Rohmer encountered in raising the money they needed to make their films (Crisp 85; Hanlon 187; and Magny, *Eric Rohmer* 156).

13. When Rohmer was asked if he might consider making a film based on a work of English literature, for example, he replied that it was unlikely because "there is the problem of language.... Unfortunately, I have no knowledge of English at all" (Adair 234).

14. It has sometimes been said that Bresson had no precise literary model for *Lancelot*, and Bresson himself said, "I prefer to invent, as I did in this film, characters which are slightly different from those of rather imprecise legends, and give them a voice of my own choosing, rather than be faithful to even great writers like Dostoievski and Bernanos, which I already did in several films…. In the past, I approached great works of literature with enormous precaution and respect, whereas today [1974] I feel that I am most faithful to them by being unfaithful, and that the only thing to use from them is the enlightenment which I experience when I read them" (Baby 5).

The film's narrative is nonetheless clearly based on the *Mort Artu*, and Paquette even suggests that it is probably based on a résumé of the story by Jean Frappier that Bresson could have found in the introduction to Frappier's 1936 edition of the *Mort* or in his *Étude sur La Mort le Roi Artu* published in the same year (114, 115). Given that Bresson's desire to direct a *Lancelot* dates to 1953–54, it is interesting that Frappier's edition of the *Mort* was republished in 1954. For an analysis of Bresson's adaptation of the *Mort*, see Paquette 114–15 and Thompson 290–95.

It is also interesting to note that, in 1964, Bresson, in a letter to George Cukor, expressed the desire to make *Lancelot* in English with Burt Lancaster and Natalie Wood in the roles of Lancelot and Guenièvre. Lancaster, Bresson wrote, "'is exactly Lancelot…. No one will ever be able to incarnate him as well'" (Ehrenstein 103; compare Rosenbaum 202). It is hard to imagine how this transcultural experiment would have turned out.

15. "I think of the story, the history," says Boorman, "as a myth. The film has to do with mythical truth, not historical truth…." He goes on to add that he "was determined … to tell the whole story of the *Morte d'Arthur*…" (cited in Kennedy 31, 33).

16. Jean-Pierre Lefebvre writes that "*Lancelot du lac* does not belong to objective history but instead to the heroic and chivalric (and mystical) literature of the twelfth century" (34), and Dubroux notes similarly that "*Perceval le Gallois* … is based in large measure on the scholastic memories of our [French] childhood"(42); Fabrice Luchini called Perceval "a scholarly project" (*Cinématographe* 44 [February 1979], 15, cited in Crisp 86) and Huchet notes that a substantial "pedagogical operation" was mounted to encourage the use of the film in French classrooms (85, n. 33; see also Tortajada 116–20). On the literary and scholastic associations of the two films for a French audience, see also Prédal, "Bresson" 8; Armes 82; Adair 230–31; Tesich-Savage 51; Amiel 7–8; Magny, "Eric Rohmer ou la quête du graal" 26; Magny and Rabourdin 10; Rohmer 6–7; and Cugier 119.

17. Boorman says that he told "the actors that they are not reenacting a legend. They are creating it…." He felt free, for example, "to have Uther Pendragon, Arthur's real father and the 'primogenitor' of the whole saga, if you like, drive the sword into the stone, rather than Merlin, as in Malory…. The thing about myths," he remarks, "is that they're a body of stories completely homogeneous and interrelated, yet also completely flexible. You can rearrange or extend or elide the order of events quite liberally without destroying the meaning" (Kennedy 33, 34).

In his article "Arthurian Film and the Tyranny of Tradition," Norris Lacy identifies "two opposing impulses" at work in film versions of the Arthurian legend: "on the one hand, the natural desire to innovate; on the other, the need to tell a story that corresponds at least in major respects to the audience's understanding of orthodox Arthurian fact" (76). If the former impulse predominates in *Perceval* and *Lancelot* (although their innovations are more cinematographic than narrative) while the latter is stronger in *Excalibur*, it is because an Anglo-American audience approaches an Arthurian film with stronger and better defined expectations than a French one does and is, therefore, less likely to approve any innovations introduced by the director. The common text from which all directors of an Arthurian film aimed at an Anglo-American audience have to start, the text that they all have to adapt regardless of their apparent sources, is that audience's received understanding of the legend. Boorman may follow his literary source less closely than Bresson or Rohmer, but Bresson's method for handling his sources does not mean that he is freer to innovate than they are; he is, on the contrary, obliged to deviate from his source in order to satisfy his audience.

18. The literary aspect of the Lancelot legend perhaps held a particular appeal for Bresson. Five of the eleven films he directed before *Lancelot* were likewise adaptations of literary works—*Les Dames du Bois de Boulogne* (1945), *Journal d'un curé de campagne* (1951), *Mouchette* (1967), *Une Femme Douce* (1969), *Quatre nuits d'un rêveur* (1972)—and Estève observes that Bresson "first became known as a filmmaker capable of transposing very different sorts of novelistic works onto the screen" (*Robert Bresson* 17; compare Rosenbaum 202–3). On Bresson's awareness of the treatment of the Arthurian legend in the Middle Ages, see Baby 4–5 and Sémolué 205.

19. On the sound of Lancelot, see Rosenbaum 206–07; Thompson 303–04 and Bartone 147.

20. See also Bartone 147–48.

21. See Margetts 610; Prédal, "Poétique" 111–13; and Bartone 146–47.

22. According to Sémolué, Bresson's first concept of Guenièvre in *Lancelot* was of "a very young woman, frail, surrounded by broad-chested men, locked in their armor. This founding image contained all the sensuality and all the violence of the future film" (211). Compare Rosenbaum 206.

23. On Rohmer's medieval visual models and his interpretation of them, see Smith 62–63, Williams 78–79, and Angeli 46–48.

24. Rohmer's script has been printed in *l'Avant-scène cinéma* 221 (Feb. 1979), 9–64. On his revision of Chrétien's text, see Smith 61–62 and Beatie 251–53.

25. On the music of *Perceval*, see Beatie 253 and Grimbert 35–36.

26. On this "relay-style of exposition" (Grimbert), see Smith 62, Williams 75–76, Beatie 254, and Grimbert 36–37.

27. See Bertin-Maghit 55–56.

28. *Notes sur le cinématographe* (Paris: Gallimard, 1975); *Notes on Cinematography*, trans. Jonathan Griffin (New York: Urizen, 1977).

29. Angeli points out that in general the Middle Ages has a nostalgic attraction for modern audiences as if it "were in fact the memory of our childhood," and she suggests that Rohmer was drawn to the *Conte du Graal* precisely because it is a medieval *Bildungsroman* with an adolescent hero, an aspect of the romance that he emphasizes in the film (34–36, 45).

30. Prédal calls the film a "parable ... set outside of History and reality" ("Poétique" 104); see also Bertin-Maghit 54; Dempsey 7; Cugier 124; and Prédal, "Poétique" 104–07).

31. On Bresson's departures from the ending of the *Mort Artu*, see also Margetts 616. Reader points out that the only three women who have speaking roles in "the bleakly androcentric world" of *Lancelot* are Guenièvre, "the old peasant and the young girl in the woods." The world of the film, he concludes, seems to lack "the wherewithal for its biological as well as its cultural and symbolic renewal" (123). According to Thompson, this pessimistic ending marks a turning point in Bresson's oeuvre and introduces "the increasingly bleak outlook of Bresson's later films; rather than finding a religious or moral grace, as in the earlier ones, the characters now lose the grace they have in the face of a corrupt society's pressures" (299). Dempsey notes the same turn in Bresson's oeuvre and includes *Lancelot* in the later, pessimistic films, but he dates the shift to *Une Femme Douce*, which appeared in 1969 (2–3).

32. As Beatie points out (257–58) and Grimbert reminds us (44 n. 26), moreover, the Passion play represents a very substantial addition to Chrétien's text, taking up over thirteen percent of the film's running time.

33. On the way in which this scene runs counter to everything in the film up to this point, see Hoffman 47.

34. For other reactions to the Passion play, see Smith 64, Huchet 87–89, Williams 77–88, Wise 2411–12, Tigoulet 25, Lacy 79, Beatie 258–63, and Grimbert 39–41. Huchet suggests that Rohmer's interpretation of the *Conte du Graal* was influenced by "the medieval reading of the *Conte de [sic] Graal* that was carried out in the thirteenth century by the authors of the Lancelot-Grail cycle" (88). Gérard Genette likewise situates Rohmer's Passion play in a general tendency to "christianize" the Grail story dating back to "Robert de Boron ... the *Didot-Perceval* [and] especially the *Lancelot-Grail*," but he finds the play "highly abusive and highly ridiculous"(217–18).

WORKS CITED

Adair, Gilbert. "Rohmer's Perceval." *Sight and Sound* 47 (Autumn 1977): 230–34.

A[mengual], B[arthélemy]. Review of *Lancelot du Lac*. *Positif* 162 (October 1974): 55–56.

Amiel, Mireille. "*Perceval le Gallois*: Des arts, des armes et des lois...." *Cinéma* 242 (February 1979): 7–9.

Angeli, Giovanna. "Perceval le Gallois d'Eric Rohmer et ses sources." *Cahiers de l'association internationale des études françaises* 47 (1995): 33–48.

Armes, Roy. *The Ambiguous Image: Narrative Style in Modern European Cinema*. Bloomington: Indiana University Press, 1976.

Baby, Yvonne. "Metal Makes Sounds. An Interview with Robert Bresson." Trans. Nora Jacobson. *Field of Vision* 13 (Spring 1985): 4–5. [First published in *Le Monde* (24 September 1974).]

Barron, Fred. "Robert Bresson's Lancelot du Lac: That Hollow Ring." *Take One* 7 (December 1974): 34.

Bartone, Richard C. "Variations on Arthurian Legend in Lancelot du Lac and Excalibur." In Sally K. Slocum, ed. *Popular Arthurian Traditions*. Bowling Green, Ohio: Bowling Green State University Popular Press, 1992.

Beatie, Bruce A. "The Broken Quest: The 'Perceval' Romances of Chrétien de Troyes and Eric Rohmer." In Debra N. Mancoff, ed. *The Arthurian Revival. Essays on Form, Tradition*, and *Transformation*. New York: Garland, 1992.

Bertin-Maghit, Jean-Pierre. "De l'écran à la classe. Lancelot du Lac de Robert Bresson." *Pédagogie* 31 (1976): 53–64.

Burns, E. Jane. "Nostalgia Isn't What It Used To Be: The Middle Ages in Literature and Film." In George Slusser and Eric S. Rabkin, eds. *Shadows of the Magic Lamp, Fantasy and Science Fiction in Film*. Carbondale, Illinois: Southern Illinois University Press, 1985.

Capdenac, Michel. Review of *Lancelot du Lac*. *Écran* 29 (October 1974): 57–59.

Clarke, Gerald. "Knight Errant." *Time* 114 (20 November 1978): 104.

Cormier, Raymond J. "Rohmer's Grail Story: Anatomy of a French Flop." *Stanford French Review* 5 (1981): 391–96.

Crisp, C[olin]. G. *Eric Rohmer: Realist and Moralist*. Bloomington, Indiana: Indiana University Press, 1988.

Cugier, Alphonse. "'Lancelot du Lac' de Robert Bresson. Le Moyen Age revisité ou la dimension tragique du XXe siècle." *Les Cahiers de la cinémathèque* 42–43 (Summer 1985): 119–24.

Delmas, Jean. "Robert Bresson et ses armures." *Jeune cinéma* 82 (November 1974): 19–24.

Dempsey, Michael. "Despair Abounding: The Recent Films of Robert Bresson." *Film Quarterly* 34.1 (Fall 1980): 2–15.

Dubroux, Danièle. "Le rêve pédagogique." *Cahiers du cinéma* 299 (April 1979): 42–43.

Durand, Jacques. "La Chevalerie à l'écran." *l'Avant-scène cinéma* 221 (1 February 1979): 29–40.

Ehrenstein, David. "Bresson et Cukor. Histoire d'une correspondance." *Positif* 430 (December 1996): 103.

Estève, Michel. *Robert Bresson*. Paris: Seghers, 1962.

_____. *Robert Bresson: La passion du cinématographe*. Paris: Albatros, 1983.

Fieschi, Jacques. "Une innocence mortelle." *l'Avant-scène cinéma* 221 (1 February 1979): 4–6.

Fischer, Lucy. "Roots: The Medieval Tale as Modernist Cinema." *Field of Vision* 9–10 (Winter-Spring 1980): 21–25, 33.

Genette, Gérard. *Palimpsestes. La Littérature au second degré*. Paris: Seuil, 1982.

Grimbert, Joan Tasker. "Distancing Techniques in Chrétien de Troyes's *Li Contes del Graal* and Eric Rohmer's *Perceval le Gallois*." *Arthuriana* 10 (Winter 2000): 33–44.

G[uiguet], J[ean]-C[laude]. Review of *Lancelot du Lac*. *Image et Son* 285 (June-July 1974): 29.

Hanlon, Lindley. *Fragments: Bresson's Film Style*. Cranbury, New Jersey: Fairleigh Dickinson University Press, 1986.

Harty, Kevin J. "Cinema Arthuriana: A Bibliography of Selected Secondary Materials." *Arthurian Interpretations* 3 (Spring 1989): 119–37.

Hoffman, Donald L. "Re-Framing Perceval." *Arthuriana* 10 (Winter 2000): 45–56.

Huchet, Jean-Charles. "Merceval." *Littérature* 40 (1980): 69–94.

Kauffman, Stanley. Review of *Perceval le Gallois*. *New Republic* 179 (21 October 1978): 30–31.

Kennedy, Harlan. "The World of King Arthur According to John Boorman." *American Film* 6 (March 1981): 30–37.

Lacy, Norris J. "Arthurian Film and the Tyranny of Tradition." *Arthurian Interpretations* 4 (Fall 1989): 75–85.

"Lancelot du Lac: Un film de Robert Bresson." *l'Avant-scène cinéma* 155 (1 February 1975): 47–49.

Lefebvre, Jean-Pierre. "Le cinéma de derrière l'émulsion." *Cinéma Québec* (May 1975): 34–36.

McCreadie, Marsha. Review of *Perceval le Gallois*. *Films in Review* 76 (January 1979): 53–54.

Magny, Joël. *Eric Rohmer*. Paris: Rivages, 1986.

_____. "Eric Rohmer ou la quête du graal." *Cinéma* 242 (February 1979): 19–31.

_____, and Dominique Rabourdin. "Entretien avec Eric Rohmer." *Cinéma* 242 (February 1979): 10–18.

Margetts, John. "Robert Bressons 'Lancelot du Lac.' Monotonie und Depression." In Jürgen Kühnel and others, eds. *Mittelalter—Rezeptions II. Gesammelte Vorträge des 2. Salzburger Symposions "Die Rezeption des Mittelalters in Literatur, Bildener Kunst und Musik des 19. und 20. Jahrhunderts."* Göppingen: Kümmerle, 1982.

Milne, Tom. "Rohmer's Siege Perilous." *Sight and Sound* 50 (Summer 1981): 192–95.

Morris, George. Review of *Perceval le Gallois*. *Take One* 7 (January 1979): 10.

Paquette, Jean-Marcel. "La Dernière métamophose de Lancelot." *Les Cahiers de la cinémathèque* 42–43 (Summer 1985): 113–18.

Prédal, René. "Bresson et son temps." *Cinéma* 294 (June 1974): 4–11.

———. "Poétique de Robert Bresson: Expression plastique et approche de l'indicible dans *Lancelot du Lac.*" *Recherches et travaux* 37 (1989): 103–16.

Reader, Keith. *Robert Bresson.* Manchester: Manchester University Press. 2000.

Rohmer, Eric. "Note sur la traduction et sur la mise en scène de *Perceval.*" *l'Avant-scène cinéma* 221 (1 February 1979): 6–7.

Rosenbaum, Jonathan. "The Rattle of Armor, the Softness of Flesh." *Sight and Sound* 43 (Summer 1974): 128–30. [Rpt. in Rosenbaum. *Movies as Politics.* Berkeley, California: University of California Press, 1997.]

Sarris, Andrew. Review of *Perceval le Gallois. Village Voice,* 23 October 1978: 75–76.

Sémolué, Jean. *Bresson ou L'acte pur des métamorphoses.* Paris: Flammarion, 1993.

Smith, Sarah W. R. "Rohmer's *Perceval* as Literary Criticism." In Maud Walther, ed. *Proceedings of the Purdue University Fifth Annual Conference on Film.* West Lafayette, Indiana: Dept. of Foreign Languages and Literatures, 1980.

Tesich-Savage, Nadja. "Rehearsing the Middle Ages." *Film Comment* 14.5 (September-October 1978): 50–56.

Tessier, Max. Review of *Perceval le Gallois. Écran* 76 (15 January 1979): 71–72.

Thompson, Kristin. *Breaking the Glass Armor, Neoformalist Film Analysis.* Princeton: Princeton University Press, 1988.

Tigoulet, Marie-Claude. "Note sur *Perceval le Gallois.*" In Michel Estève, ed. *Eric Rohmer 2.* Etudes cinématographiques 149–52. Paris: Minard, 1986.

Tortajada, Maria. "L'Exception médiévale. *Perceval le Gallois* d'Eric Rohmer." *Equinoxe* 16 (1996): 115–30.

Vitoux, Frédéric. "L'armure sied à Bresson." *Positif* 163 (November 1974): 72–73.

Williams, Linda. "Eric Rohmer and the Holy Grail." *Literature-Film Quarterly* 11 (April 1983): 71–82.

Wise, Naomi. "Perceval (Perceval le Gallois)." *Magill's Survey of Cinema, Foreign Language Films.* Vol. 5. Englewood Cliffs, New Jersey: Salem Press, 1985.

14

From Stage to Screen: The Dramatic Compulsion in French Cinema and Denis Llorca's Les Chevaliers de la table ronde *(1990)*

SANDRA GORGIEVSKI

Denis Llorca's *Les Chevaliers de la table ronde*, produced by Pierre Braunberger (Les Films du Jeudi), was born out of a challenging creative process. It was shot during the performances of the 12–hour play *Quatre Saisons pour les chevaliers de la table ronde*, written by Denis Llorca and Philipe Vialèles (performed in 1989 and 1990 in Besançon, Dijon, Saint-Etienne, Marseilles, Albe-la-Romaine, Paris). The film condenses the play's convenient frame for the Arthurian cycle, with each of the four seasons centering on a character—*Spring or Merlin, Summer or Lancelot, Autumn or Gauvain, Winter or the Grail*. The actors from the Centre Dramatique National de Franche-Comté (Besançon) acted in front of the camera by day, while performing on stage at night. The intense work thus involved and the two overlapping stages and techniques were no doubt a strain and limitation in terms of acting, location and props, yet then infused the film with the richness of Llorca's long time stagecraft as an immoderately ambitious theater director.

Llorca has worked with other mythical material, including the Bible. He has also staged the history of the kings of England (*Kings*, 10 hours) as well as adaptations of literary masterpieces like Dostoevski's *The Possessed* (8 hours) and Victor Hugo's *Les Misérables* (3.5 hours). His *Les Chevaliers de la table ronde* is inordinately long (3.5 hours) not only because this fresco, like Boorman's 2.5 hour-long *Excalibur* (1981), ventures on encompassing the whole Arthurian legend, but also because of his own idiosyncrasies. Llorca was unhindered by the earlier French cinematic versions of arch-*auteurs* Robert Bresson and Eric Rohmer, who concentrated on a single episode (the failure of the Grail Quest in *Lancelot du Lac*, 1974) or a single character's adventures (*Perceval le Gallois*, 1979). If Llorca stands no comparison with either Rohmer, Bresson or John Boorman as a film director, he is nonetheless no amateur. His movie *L'Orage en colère brise la voix de la forêt* (1984), already dealing with the medieval period, was selected for the competition (*Caméra d'or*) in the Cannes Film Festival.

Llorca's film is devoid of the epic breadth one finds in *Excalibur,* with its association of glamour and clamor of battles and the marvelous, no doubt shaped by the Anglo-Saxon tradition inherited from Malory's prose narrative. Like the two other French directors, Llorca relied on the carefully crafted, courtly poetry of Chrétien de Troyes; hence the film's contemplative mood, the emphasis on text rather than narrative dynamism. The French directors do not so much focus on the mythological impact of the matter of Britain as reflect about ways of reworking the mythic using distancing techniques, stylization, and the concept of passive heroism.

Before tackling these three aspects of *Les Chevaliers*, one must acknowledge Llorca's work on the script. Llorca sets the legend into motion with clever narrative inventions in much the way Boorman did, mainly enhancing the role of female characters and values.

Igerne (Nadine Darmon), not Uther, strikes a bargain with young Merlin (Jean-François Prévaud), defending the driving force of love as a fusion of souls against the magician's cynical view of lust as an attraction of cells and chemical union of bodies. But Igerne is a victim of appearances: she makes love with Uther, who is disguised as her husband, the Duke of Tintagel, and gives birth to twins Arthur and Morgane. The latter deliberately begets an incestuous son on blissfully unaware Arthur, and plots against Lancelot and Guenièvre, working for the kingdom's downfall — a figure of evil in the wake of Boorman's Morgana, condensing the wicked aspects of legendary Morgause and Morgane le Fay.

Young Viviane (Catherine Rétoré) involuntarily defeats arch-seducer Merlin who renounces his experiments to run after her. She is more prescient than the powerful alchemist working on the creation of a human body (a testimony to the new genetic version of the mad scientist), informing him about the Sword in the Stone, witnessing Arthur's drawing of Excalibur, and designating him to an unbelieving assembly.

Whereas powerless, aging Merlin (Alain Cuny) ultimately deserts Arthur (only to reappear by the side of the mystical Fisher King), aged Viviane (Maria Casarès) actively works for Arthur's kingdom. She convinces her son Lancelot, maddened by his entrapment with Guenièvre, to come to the king's rescue against Mordret. Guenièvre's (Valérie Durin) enthusiasm and resilience stand in contrast with wishy-washy, self-depreciating Arthur (Alain Macé). Her brilliant speech in vindication of the Queen is opposed to Arthur's view of both King and Queen as puppets in the hands of fate. Even Amythe, the Fisher King's daughter, tries to resist the orders of her unflagging father.

All these women work as female counterparts to the Grail Knights Gauvain (Benoit Brione), Perceval (Gilles Geisweiller), Lancelot (Denis Llorca) and Galaad (François Berreur).

Distancing Techniques

The film displays a complex treatment of time and diegesis, far from any continuous, chronological unfolding, as shown in the structure of the narrative in the layout below:

BIBLE	FOREST	LAKE/TINTAGEL/KAMAALOT	GRAIL CASTLE
Crucifixion Deposition Origin of the Holy Grail			
	Galaad has visions (night)		

		Lady of the Lake's prophecy: Viviane
		Viviane and Merlin's affair (Tintagel)
		Igerne cheated by Merlin, gives birth
		  to twins Arthur and Morgane
		Viviane raises young Lancelot (Lake)
		Sword in the Stone — Coronation of
		  Arthur
		Merlin's prophecies: Round Table and
		  Grail Castle	

			Gauvain: Bed Adventurous, fight against Yvain and lion

		Foundation of the Round Table
		Merlin's prophecy: Siege Perilous
		Lancelot leaves his mother Viviane to
		  become a knight
		Arthur cheated by incestuous Morgane
		Arthur and Guenièvre's wedding
		Lancelot's adventures: Knight of the
		  Cart, Sword Bridge, Guenièvre rescued
		  from Mélégant. Adultery
		Morgane raises Mordret	

			Lancelot cheated by Fisher King's daughter Amythe.
		Merlin takes leave of Arthur Amythe reveals Galaad's existence Gauvain remembers: Perceval remembers: Galaad sits on Siege Perilous	*Flashbacks*: Gauvain at the Grail Castle Perceval with young Galaad
	Galaad remembers (night)		
		Knights depart for Grail Quest Entrapment scene of the lovers Lancelot's madness Lancelot, warned by his mother, joins Arthur's army Final battle Mordret/Arthur Death of Lancelot The queen returns to the king Arthur's corpse departs for Avallon Excalibur returns to the Lake	
	Galaad wakes up (morning)		
			Fisher King and Merlin waiting Despair Galaad's voice is heard.

The narration moves on four levels. The entire story of the Round Table is framed by Galaad's night in the forest with his visions, dreams or recollections, which is but a sequel to the opening section on Christ's Crucifixion. As in response to the sacred episode, Galaad is the medium through which flashbacks and memories are presented to the viewer. This indirect presentation is interrupted by the interpolated, apparently disconnected stories of the Grail Knights. Except in Lancelot's adventures at the Grail Castle following chronologically his adventures at Arthur's court, there is no continuity, either in time or location, between Gawain's tale and the two reported tales of Gawain and Perceval — a testimony to Chrétien's *récits enchassés*. But the Grail section finally merges into the main diegesis when Galaad, who has awakened from his night in the forest, is heard arriving at the Grail Castle. The expected healing of the Fisher King symbolically transcends Christ's wounds seen in the opening shots. The prophecy of the Grail Quest is thus fulfilled along with the structural unifying of all the threads of the narrative.

The mythical discourse of the prodigal son's return is superimposed, as Galaad is made into the Fisher King's grandson, in a decisively opimistic, if not miraculous ending. Such an ending is closer to Rohmer's redeeming Passion Play in which Perceval reenacts Christ's sufferings, than to the dire shot of a heap of dead corpses in Bresson's pessimistic statement about the fall of guilt-ridden chivalry. In Llorca, the whole Arthurian myth seems directed at the Grail Quest in a kind of reenactment of Christ's story. The opening Deposition with the Virgin Mary cradling Christ's corpse finds visual echoes when Lancelot is cradled by Amythe, then by his mother Viviane, and when Guenièvre is later cradled by a dying Arthur.

The viewer first gets the impression of filmed theater rather than cinematic recreation, hence the divided critical recep-

Alain Cuny as Merlin takes leave of Alain Macé as King Arthur in Denis Llorca's 1990 film *Les Chevaliers de la table ronde*. (Still courtesy of Les Films du Jeudi.)

tion — cinema reviews like *Positif* and *Les Cahiers du cinéma* depreciated the film while other reviews applauded.[1] Outdoors locations are rare, the minimalist props and set are clearly taken from the stage, and spaces on screen seem to be filled with an elaborate text often delivered with high-sounding, theatrical diction. But the numerous allusions to silent films, with their theatrical conventions, often static camera and emotional impact of the close-ups give a more complex account of Llorca's goal. Insert titles even open and close the film: when a biblical reference to Christ riding an ass to Jerusalem opens the narrative, and when the final section involving the Fisher King portrays silent actors on a boat, the dialogue is provided by insert titles. In the middle of the film, a fake intermission is provided by another, self-reflexive insert title directed at the audience: "Here the dreamer will wake up from his dream."

These ironic references provide deflation as to the apparent supremacy of the inflated text over images, stressing the originality of the film which questions the Arthurian myth as well as the language in which it might be transmitted, what Roland Barthes called "métalangage" (Barthes 199). Llorca's technique is close to the interrogations in Rohmer's "conscientious theatricality of the devices, willingness to use the possibilities of film that forces the viewer to consider rather than to sink into the spectacle" (Hoffman 51). The camera seems invisible with practical and functional long shots and straightforward cuts, just as in Rohmer (Rider 49). Furthermore, the camera is often static, as in the love scene between Lancelot and the Fisher King's daughter Amythe: a slow, almost unobtrusive traveling backwards gradually frames the couple within the rectilinear lines of the bed, then stops still — a sacred icon because Galaad is to be born of this union. Consequently, any blatant use of camera movement arouses the viewer's attention, taking on greater importance precisely because it strikes the viewer as artificial. The very cinematic devices (traveling, slow motion, repetitive shots) participate in the distancing techniques.

The overlapping of visual and verbal data to fulfill the narrative function creates distance. In Rohmer, the network of voices — the chorus, the mixture of direct and indirect discourse — for instance underlines Perceval's difficulty reconciling what he sees with what he hears, thus failing to speak in the Grail Castle as he was advised not to talk too much (Grimbert 37–38). Gauvain frequently speaks of himself in the third person then enacts what he has just said (a testimony to the almost magical power of designation of words), while continuing to narrate in the third person the fight he is engaged in. In Llorca, Gauvain reports his adventure at the Grail Castle to the knights at Kamaalot in a kind of flashback, as the tale has already been presented to the viewer. Gawain's story is thus told twice, perhaps in accordance with the medieval use of repetition: the first, complete version is strictly filmic, while the second version begins with Gauvain's oral report in the first person but is interrupted, then replaced by a selection of cuts from the first version. The rhythm of the cutting is accelerated to make the story shorter of course, but that rhythm also underlines the repetitive patterns. Perceval reports his adventures at the Grail Castle to Arthur and his knights in the same way, except that the condensed filmed version is all the viewer will have access to, with the same motifs highlighted.

The very process of storytelling is thus underlined, with a complex structure of *mise en abyme*. Within Gauvain's tale, Gauvain is seen telling the story of his journey to the Fisher King, with the cold and the rain and all the illnesses he was subjected to, a tale that will find no visual equivalent, perhaps a nod to the fourteenth-century Middle English poem *Sir Gawain and the Green Knight*. In the entrapment scene, Arthur brandishes his sword Excalibur and hesitates before killing Lancelot and Guenièvre. His internal debate is conveyed by another flashback, a condensed version of the former sequence of the Sword in the Stone. Lancelot's departure from his mother before his initiatory journey to become a knight is an interesting mixture of close-ups on Viviane's face (Maria Casarès) reciting and cuts on Lancelot (Denis Llorca) on his horse. Her fading voice and final disappearance from the screen, as the narration is taken on by images only, objectify the mother's obliteration from her son's memories.

Off-voices are heard when supernatural or unfathomable elements are involved, identified as those of the two magicians who are pulling the strings behind the curtains, all the more recognizable as they are played by two superstars from the French theater and cinema. The mysterious voices of the tree and the wind on water heard by Galaad in the forest at night are later identified as aged Merlin's (Alain Cuny) and aged Viviane's. Off-screen Merlin delivers prophecies of the Round Table, the Grail Quest and the Siege Perilous, comments on the silent Grail procession, giving narrative and interpretative clues to both the characters and the viewer. But the height of the marvelous is indirectly conveyed at the end of the film when Galaad's off-voice is heard on a pictureless white screen. The fulfillment of the quest remains veiled, unvoiced and unseen, as if it were reserved for higher vision. The white screen, preventing the viewer from witnessing the miracle, lays the emphasis on the quest itself rather than on its object, as the Fisher King acknowledges.

Sound is particularly significant in Llorca's film. In Rohmer, the musicians narrating the story, commenting on the actions of the characters and playing music for them, toning down their artificial verse, provide links between the historical minute details and the artificial elements (Gorgievski, "Réalisme" 207). In Llorca, music is reduced to three instrumental sounds — a gong stroke, a short organ tune and a tiny bell tinkling, which set brief auditory links, narrative connections, as they punctuate the major scenes. They structure the film, emphasize key moments in the action like the Wagnerian extracts of Siegfried's Funeral March in *Excalibur*, also underlining the discontinuity between the four levels of narration, either to guide or puzzle the viewer. The gong signals a disquieting, appalling event or danger: it can be heard during Gauvain's adventure at the Grail Castle, when an unworthy knight is burnt on the Siege Perilous or when Galaad ultimately sits down on it, when Merlin reveals Morgane's incestuous plans to Arthur who then turns his lover out, when Mélégant challenges the queen at court and later wounds Lancelot, when Merlin announces the renewal of the quest at the deserted Round Table, and when Arthur is on the verge of killing the sleeping lovers during the entrapment scene.

The solemnity of the organ tune is more ceremonious, conveying a sense of impending doom, or underlining fateful events. It seems to interrupt the course of events when young Viviane surprises Merlin with another woman. Viviane's hand is seen in close-up holding a skeleton's hand just after the birth of the twins Arthur and Morgane, implicitly making the viewer understand that the die is cast and the legend can begin. When aged Viviane tells her son Lancelot about the duties of knighthood, the organ punctuates her dire warning that a knight should "fear shame more than death." As in response, the organ is heard again at Arthur's wedding while Lancelot is made a knight by Arthur and first catches sight of Guenièvre, when he answers Mélégant's challenge, penetrates into the forest, succeeds in uplifting the stone from the magic grave that leads him to the queen and finally comes to her chamber at night. The warning sound is heard when the lovers argue before the entrapment scene, when Viviane lulls guilt-ridden Lancelot in his cave and goads him into action, and when dying Arthur takes Guenièvre in his arms.

The bell tinkling underlines all the archetypal Arthurian motifs when Arthur draws the sword, is crowned, and dies in a metonymous shot of his crown falling, and when the boat carrying his corpse departs for Avallon. The tinkling sound also characterizes the adventures of Gauvain, Perceval and Lancelot at the Grail Castle, following each step of the ritual: when the knight's feet are washed during the Grail procession, when the Fisher King wakes up at night and, significantly, when Lancelot sleeps with Amythe. Llorca works numerous variations when the mysterious, magical tinkle turns into a light, joyous one signaling Galaad's arrival to the Grail Castle, along with Amythe's singing, which she had not done with the other Grail Knights. Bells ring more solemnly during the farewell scene between Merlin and Arthur. Even when Galaad sits down on the Siege Perilous, the organ tune sounds less frightening, as it acknowledges his victory.

Llorca also resorts to naturalistic sounds such as off-screen birds singing. When Lancelot and Guenièvre wake up in the shed, bird singing marks the loss of innocence as the next cut shows them discovering Excalibur stuck between their naked bodies. When a little boy walks into the peaceful lake to throw Excalibur back to where it came from, birdcalls underline a possible return to innocence thanks to an eschatological ending, with the undelivered, yet well-known prophecy of the king's return. Birdcalls accompany and amplify images contrary to their function as substitutions for a scene in Bresson: birdcalls are heard each time Lancelot and Guenièvre meet in the forest shed, but they are substitutes for the lovers' unseen reunion after the rescue of the queen. Cawing sounds work as forebodings that culminate in the final ghastly shot when crows circle in the sky above the heap of dying knights (Thompson 304). In Llorca, the soundtrack also incorporates seemingly realistic sounds. Lancelot bending his bow sounds odd and surprisingly muffled in the otherwise silent scene, signaling the fact that he has grown into a mature archer and knight, ready to leave his mother. Llorca reworks Bresson's technique of using sound effects as half-concrete, half-fantasmatic, such as the haunting sound of horses' hooves and whinnies, the clanking of armor that stands in for an entire battle that is not screened, or the sounds of footsteps, slammed doors and clattering windows in the ghost-like, deserted castle, enhancing the impression of "hyperreality" (Rider 45).

Intertextual references also create aesthetic distance. The myth of eternal love and fateful passion between Tristan and Iseult is superimposed on Lancelot and Guenièvre in the entrapment scene. Just as in Boorman's *Excalibur*, Arthur plays the part of King Mark refraining from killing the lovers but leaving his sword as a sign of curse or pardon. Llorca's play had openly acknowledged his debt not only to Chrétien de Troyes, but also to Shakespeare and Molière. The film retains some of these elements, with mad Lancelot in the cavern torn because of the discrepancy between words and deeds—a typical issue in Molière's *Le Misanthrope* or *Le Médecin malgré lui*. Shakespearean undertones can be found in Arthur's difficult handling of power, as his crown and mantle seem too large for him, in a visual translation of Macbeth's words.

But even more surprising is Llorca's unacknowledged reference to Beckett. In the fourth act of Llorca's play (*Winter or the Grail*) and in the Grail sections of the film, the main issue of the Fisher King helplessly waiting for a Grail Knight to cure him is staged or screened in a way strongly reminiscent of Beckett's somber, static *Waiting for Godot*. The absurdity that is at the core of the modern play is of course absent in the film. The Fisher King keeps justifying waiting as God's sacred design and is ultimately rewarded, but his doctrine is momentarily shaken at the end of the film, when he undergoes a crisis of faith, even getting angry at his own daughter. The viewer experiences the lengthy, repetitive waiting sequences involving Merlin and the Fisher King in the boat, with the same painful impression of suspended time, the same resignation yet unbearable monotony as in *Waiting for Godot*.

A boring ritual, an empty verbal game, is created to kill time: as Vladimir repeatedly asks Estragon how he spent the night, if he was beaten again, if it hurts, Merlin keeps asking the Maimed King if he suffered during the night. Then the old man is seen suffering and waking up a number of times, or uttering the same sentence: "I have to be taken away." Intertextuality heightens the strained waiting experience for the viewer, but provides a kind of comic relief thanks to the improbable reworking of Merlin and Fisher King as burlesque Gogo and Didi. In the final mock-scene taken from the technique of a silent film, no word is uttered. The insert titles display the dialogue in short sentences, almost monosyllabic words, like Estragon and Vladimir's sterile dialogues. The process of endless waiting is ironically underlined by intertextuality just before Galaad's miraculous, reassuring arrival, his mellifluous voice calling "Grandpa?"—thus replacing the tantalizing M. Godot.

STYLIZATION

The French directors achieve a striking synthesis between stylization and historical realism—the minute thirteenth-century details in Rohmer, disenchantment stemming from both neorealistic elements and the fourteenth-century decline of chivalry in Bresson. Into his film's narrative, Llorca weaves highly stylized, anachronistic *tableaux vivants*, offering contemplative moments suggesting a timeless mythical dimension. These visual references to painting, especially sixteenth-century Mannierism, give the film universality. The opening shots on Crucifixion are formalized, lit by a sophisticated *chiaroscuro*, the static camera focusing on a detail before traveling backwards, thus revealing progressively the whole scene and stopping to frame it. In the Deposition, Christ's lying corpse is thus framed at the bottom of the screen, after the manner of Rosso Fiorentino's *Deposizione* (Volterra). In the morbid, carnivalesque scene of the Bed Perilous, Gauvain and his torturers are lit from above, light falling bluntly on them, as in Caravaggio's paintings. Young Viviane's face is lit by the candle in a *chiaroscuro* reminiscent of George de la Tour, while she is marveling at something off-screen, as if enlightened by Merlin's knowledge and arts. Nineteenth-century Pre-Raphaelite painting also comes to mind when dejected, melancholy King Arthur and his court are waiting for the rescue of Guenièvre. They are all moving on the rectilinear plane of a terrace, with moody, ethereal and fixed looks, wearing the typical dark violet heavy robes found in Edward Burne-Jones. These *tableaux vivants* are moments of internal focalization. A similar effect is hinted at in Bresson in the unique, Degas-like scene of Guenièvre having a bath, with the color gradation of roses —from the shaded light to her soft flesh.

Otherwise, costumes and props are very dull, as if to stimulate the viewer's imagination. Anachronism is also provided by Lancelot embodying the archetypal dashing young hero either as an armor-clad knight or pre-romantic hero with long, curled hair and an ample, creased white shirt. The expressive performance of the actors, their faces constantly exposed in close-ups, their voices literally filling up the space, give the viewer direct access to the mythical characters' quintessential human substance. They are not akin to Rohmer's stiff, ever-smiling actors speaking in monotonous artificial octosyllabic verse in rhymed couplets or the toneless, sententious verbal exchanges preferred by actors hidden in their armors in Bresson, from disabused Lancelot (Luc Simon) to young, uncompromising Guenièvre (Laura Duke Condominas). Variations provide a whole range of human feelings: doubts and existential questions are expressed in the elaborate dialogue between Arthur and aged Merlin who prophesies about his own disappearance in a cavernous, emphatic voice. Dialogue is a mixture of day-to-day language, slang and poetry. Arthur bluntly rails against the Queen, calling her a whore after having been done in by Morgane, but is overheard by Guenièvre, who restores her regal status with a beautiful speech in unrhymed couplets that reveals her vocation. Both witty verbal exchange and casual teasing characterize Merlin and Viviane. The Fisher King (Michel Vitold) asks the Grail Knights the ritual questions in a banal, friendly way, then uses bombast when catechizing his daughter to have her sleep with Lancelot. The latter's diction ranges from the enthusiasm of a fanatical knight to the breathless appeals of the lover, or the madman's sententious lines about the vanity of the world.

Enhancing the actorial presence leaves room for restrained emotional impact. Sexual intercourse between Lancelot and Amythe is indirectly presented by a shot on a white lily as the couple sensuously pull off its petals with fingers or tongue. When Lancelot comes to Guenièvre's chamber at night, the camera pans as he is scrambling out of the window into the room, then swoops on off-screen Guenièvre; the cut to the next scene depicts the lovers' faces awakening in the morning. Pathos is avoided in the entrapment scene when the same cut on Lancelot escaping is replicated at increasing speed to evoke his maddening despair. Unlike Bresson's deconstruction of chivalry through partial views or dismembered knights, fragmented armor works as synecdoche in Llorca. A gauntlet and a sword lying on the Round Table are signs of Mélégant's challenge, which is answered by the whole Arthurian knighthood revived by the mere sight of its reduction to tokens.

Limited theatrical props and set account for this highlighting of characters, as in response to the absence of description of places in medieval romances. Imaginary geography implies a more active role for the viewer, all the more as the set itself is reduced to an alternating red-blue background screen. Its red color is highly evocative when Lancelot and Guenièvre unite on the incandescent background of passion. But the colors are often randomly associated with the episodes, having no graphic dimension, far from the careful aesthetic code of Bresson's abstract color variations on the dark or blank background and the graphic plays of light on the armors (Thompson 301–302). Minimalist props and set stand for natural landscape, as Llorca had done when staging *Twelfth Night* (Paris, 1970), a mere white ribbon standing for the powerful Shakespearean motif of the sea. Thanks to the power of artifice in the theater, should a flower be seen, the viewer is transported into a garden. Even Rohmer's characters, inscribed in a detailed background imitating medieval illuminated manuscripts, are lively puppets moving in stylized models, blue ice standing for a river or sand for moors (Gorgievski, "Réalisme" 207).

Natural, spectacular outdoor locations are rather favored by Anglo-American films, with majestic forests, plains and waterfalls in *Excalibur*, impressive stony valleys in Jerry Zucker's *First Knight* (1995) or rocky mountains and dusty ponds in *Monty Python and the Holy Grail* (1974). The few occurrences in Llorca are rather illusions of natural setting: the reed-covered pond in which young Viviane swims before saving baby Lancelot in a Moses-like episode expresses sensuality, tranquility of nature, with birdsong and a flute. Her primeval magic skills are thus opposed to Merlin's sophisticated arts performed in his alchemical laboratory. The thick, hermetic forest of Lancelot's adventures has an unnatural quality as he is seen riding into it in slow motion. Slow motion strikes the viewer's attention, signaling that one is entering the realm of the marvelous, just the way medieval texts do when a knight is said to ride into a "deep, old" forest before losing his way. Another type of supernatural appears with the outdoor gothic cemetery — its misty surroundings, its creaking gate, its disquieting gravedigger, its magical grave with a hidden staircase that leads down to the Sword Bridge. Finally, the natural cave, in which Lancelot finds refuge and is silhouetted against the light crawling on all fours (a wild beast even his mother has to tame), symbolizes the depth of the human psyche, the subterranean meanders of mental disorder.

Architectural elements are highly stylized, especially because of the absence of long shots or perspective, as in Rohmer's models or even in Bresson's unique low angle shot on the queen's window that gives some sense of proportion. In Llorca, a reverse-shot pattern on Viviane at her window and her son jousting below is repeated with the mother (seen in low angle shot) looking at her son (seen in high angle shot); as the characters have aged between the two patterns, the high and low angle shots underline the passing of time and not the architectural perspective on the lake castle, which is limited to a mere tower emerging from water. The Grail Castle is roughly outlined on the pond, which objectifies the narrative discontinuity between the realm of the Grail and Kamaalot, as knights report when they wonder about the unmeasurable distance they had to travel, as if by sheer magic, to reach the Grail Castle. Only the rather barely furnished rooms of castles can be seen, as if interest lies in the internal, not the external, glamorous aspect of the legend. There is no sordid realism, yet, it contrasts Bresson's fragmented cuts on half-open doors, isolated windows, thresholds, staircases that lead nowhere, and fragile tents — objective correlatives of a fragmented chivalry that cannot piece together the meaning of the quest.

The most interesting stylistic device in Llorca's film is the ellipsis of the image of the Grail, constantly underlined by empty circles as abstract figures of the void. The recurrent motif of the cupped hands holding nothing is a sublimation of the Grail, as women's cupped hands collecting Christ's blood dripping from the cross, Viviane's cupped hands saving baby Lancelot from drowning, or as Amythe's cupped hands in the Grail processions. When the heavy top to the Round Table is rolled into Kamaalot, the circle actually fills the empty space of the screen. Chivalry remains frozen and motionless as the thirteenth seat remains empty. As soon as Galaad is seated, the circle is made complete, and all the knights set out in search of the Grail. Half-circles are reversed images of the cup evoked by the recurrent architectural arches. They create some void below them on the screen, whether in Tintagel, Kamaalot, the Grail Castle or even in the canopy of the cave's roof, framing the characters in a sort of halo. The metaphor of the old bridge (Merlin's own rounded back allows Arthur to reach new realms) turns into a literal screening of Merlin's prophecy when Arthur and Mordret kill each other on an arched bridge. The abstract circle also appears in the cinematic motif of the camera traveling around and suffering Fisher King at night at the beginning of each Grail section. The technique is reminiscent of Rohmer's shot following the Roman soldiers revolving around the cross in the circular room of the Passion Play, but it is part and parcel of Llorca's paradoxical *unscreening* of the perfect geometrical form of the Grail cup. The film has come full circle when Galaad comes back home.

Passive Heroism, Role-Playing

The enigmatic nature of the romance world might also account for Llorca's distancing techniques. His actors are highly expressive but also act in a detached way, as if submitting to the legendary trajectory that they consciously reenact for the viewers. They turn out to be true to the romance hero's characterization. Contrary to an epic hero such as Beowulf or Roland, whose directions are dictated by his will and logical decisions, the romance hero is an errant knight who undergoes marvelous, mysterious adventures. He sets in motion legendary episodes devoid of any realistic justification or cause-and-effect relationships:

> His role is to respond rather than to initiate, to suffer rather than to struggle.

Even where he is the most active he must at the same time passively submit to the larger forces which determine whether he is the hero destined to "achieve" this adventure and which will likewise determine its consequences. The measure of his heroism is his willingness to hazard himself without claiming control over these larger forces — indeed without being able to identify them [Mann 107].

Lancelot for instance submits to "larger forces" as soon as he enters the forest in search of the queen, follows signs such as her comb or listens to Morgane's pieces of advice. There is no interest in modern psychology either, although we understand that Morgane's wicked motivations are dictated by envy. The treatment of the entrapment scene and the public shame of the lovers is revealing. In *Excalibur*, the heroes are close to those of the epic: Arthur immediately reacts to Gawain's accusation of Guinevere's lust and pronounces the sentence of the ordeal that will decide whether the queen is innocent or guilty, all in a logical, chronological way. In Bresson, Arthur seems to be crushed by the pervading sense of guilt and does not react to Gauvain's dire accusations, as if submitting to the "larger forces" that precipitate the fall of chivalry. There is no actual entrapment scene as Lancelot decides not to go to his meeting with Guenièvre, but this decision does not alter the course of events, which would hardly make sense if Bresson's heroes were epic ones. Instead, the queen's blue scarf is forgotten in the forest shed, stolen by Mordred, seen by Lancelot, given to Gauvain and returned to the queen, thus passing from hand to hand as the accusing object and objective correlative of the whole chivalry's guilt (Roussel 145).

Llorca goes even further as there are neither public accusation nor gossips, nor any sign of the court's awareness of Lancelot's breach of decorum and loyalty, as if no reaction was awaited. This important ellipsis also concerns Merlin's prophecies which in the medieval tradition were supposed to warn Arthur of the danger. The viewer must infer from Morgane's scene of jealousy that *she* accused the lovers off-screen: she in fact addresses the viewer when, looking straight into the camera, she decides to avenge herself upon Lancelot, who turned down her unequivocal proposals, and to wage war on Arthur. The entrapment scene in the forest is a private one: no scandal, no shame will follow at court as all the knights have fled to the Grail Quest, allowing the king to face his fate alone. Another important ellipsis concerns the strife and collapse of chivalry, which was central in Bresson's film. Mordred's threatening of Arthur's kingdom is simply mentioned without further details by Viviane to convince Lancelot to leave his cavern, recover from his madness, and help Arthur. This detail reverses Lancelot's sense of guilt (not supporting Arthur would be a sin) and offers some kind of redemption.

Rohmer is also close to the romance passive hero, with Percival's (Fabrice Luchini) repertoire of theatrical looks, dumfounded eyes marveling at and submitting to the course of events like a sleepwalker. But this technique enhances the freshness of Percival's as well as the viewer's discovery of chivalry (Rider 43). Lorca in contrast underlines predestination with the leitmotif of the question sounding almost like a litany: "Do you know what God has created you for?" The prophecies are uttered in a very direct, puzzling way for a modern audience used to suspense, contrary to Boorman's careful and subtle use of indirection and understatement, for instance, when Merlin makes allusions while joking with Arthur. At the beginning of *Les Chevaliers de la table ronde*, mysterious voices (identified only later) inform sleeping Galaad of God's designs. We understand that the accomplishment of this prophecy will follow and constitutes the subject of the film. The Lady of the Lake prophesies that her granddaughter

Viviane will remain a virgin and raise a child; Merlin predicts the foundation of the Round Table; the Fisher King predicts to boy Galaad that he will sit on the Siege Perilous before coming back to the Grail Castle. There is even an instrumental use of predestination, when the Fisher King convinces his daughter she will conceive a son with Lancelot, although she resents cheating him in the guise of Guenièvre, claiming she wants to be loved for herself.

The character's own free will is denied as the interest of the film does not lie in the viewer's empathy for the characters but in experiencing the actors' reenactment of the well-known episodes of the legend, what Umberto Eco calls the pleasure of "reiteration" (Eco 154). Role-playing is highlighted, and the viewer understands that the actors are playing the roles of the powerful mythical models. When aged Viviane (Maria Casarès) looks at herself in a mirror to see how much she has aged, a cut on the mirror reveals the fresh face of young Viviane (Catherine Rétoré). It appears as a convenient narrative device about the passing of time, but it is also a self-reflexive device about role-playing, as it ironically underlines Maria Casarès's own aging and her personal myth as an actress. The film is infused with her past prestigious roles as tragic character in the theater as well as on the screen, from Bresson's *Les Dames du bois de Boulogne* (1945) to her personification of Death in Cocteau's *Le Testament d'Orphée* (1960). Even Alain Cuny's studied diction and dramatic play-acting are strongly reminiscent of his career in the theater, especially in Paul Claudel's plays.

Arthur chooses Guenièvre because she delivers a stunning speech about the Queen's role as a powerful counterpoint to that of the King. He only falls victim to her rhetoric or her perfect role-playing. Lancelot cunningly reminds her of this speech while dying, in order to encourage her to stand by Arthur. Similarly, the Fisher King reminds Lancelot of the necessity of perpetuating the human race, to have one's son complete what one has failed to. He thus assigns to Lancelot his limited role in the legend, as Lancelot's imperfections must be bested by Galaad. Amythe resents playing the part of Guenièvre to seduce Lancelot in the Grail castle, but her revolt against role-playing is short-lived. Coming to Kamaalot, she informs Lancelot that she is with child, which she describes in her turn as necessary and unavoidable.

Many sequences in Llorca's film visually embody the importance of role-playing when the actors are silhouetted against a uniformly lit screen with no setting, moving on a flat, rectilinear plane, as shadow puppets. Such a technique emphasizes role-playing, as the actors are deprived of any substance and flesh, but it departs from the dehumanizing effect of Bresson's blurring of individual outlines. The shadow theater punctuates the motifs of the legend or the arch-motifs of all romances, as the farewell scene between the Duke of Tintagel and his wife Igrayne, just before the fateful intercourse with Uther. The adventurous knight (Galaad's first appearance) is filmed with backlighting, galloping straight in the direction of the fixed camera eye. The viewer is thus submerged by the force of myth, as there is no interest in either action or the knight's trajectory, in which case one might have expected a traveling shot or horizontal pan. When Galaad can be seen etched on a dark background, lying his back against the reassuring tree, the primitive force of the elements can be felt, and there is no interest in the narrative but only in the marvelous itself.

Another instance is the *figure obligée* of the combat between two knights. Lancelot and Mélégant appear as two shadows etched on a black line of crenels on the glowing red screen. In spite of the realistic clanking of swords and the accelerated rhythm of the music creating some kind of suspense, no

Alain Cuny as Merlin (left) and Michel Vitold as the Fisher King waiting in a boat in front of the Grail Castle in Denis Llorca's 1990 film *Les Chevaliers de la table ronde*. (Still courtesy of Les Films du Jeudi.)

bloodbath takes place. The importance of blood and *corporeale* in the almost subliminal fragmented cuts on wounded knights in Bresson, sometimes verging on scenes taken straight out of gore films in Boorman, is here denied to the advantage of role-playing. The mystic function of blood is reserved, as in Rohmer (de la Bretèque 203) to the Grail cup receiving Christ's blood. The repetitive Grail processions display the paper-thin shadows of the female Grail Bearer, the candle bearer, the masked spade holder and an old man slowly moving on an either blue or red screen with a total absence of depth of field. The resulting puppet show is balanced, calm and harmonious, yet unreal and hallucinatory.

The same process is at work in the entrapment scene showing the outlines of the two lovers on a blue screen, mingling with the outlines of a tree — a symbol of the hospitable forest. When the king brandishes his sword, there is no fear for the lovers' flesh (as there is in the same scene in *Excalibur*). In this theater of illusion, there is supposedly no actor's body, but a projection of ephemeral light, which underlines the unattainable status of myth. In the final sequence of the Fisher King and Merlin on a boat with the mere sketch of a castle in the background, the two fragile characters appear as a mirage on water, belonging to a lost realm, a kind of Atlantis momentarily emerged from the depth of the waters, but which can at any time vanish, dissolve into the vaporous, eerie light, back to where it came from, in the land of dreams.

What I called the dramatic compulsion in French adaptations of the Arthurian legend has opposite effects. Llorca's and

Rohmer's characters reenact the legend with self-conscious distance, but their emotional involvement remains intact, attesting the lively appropriation of the legendary heroes' lives. The directors successfully remystify the legend and create empathy with the suffering heroes. Arthur, Lancelot, or Amythe submit to the narrative, however painful the events, and their revolts are short-lived, just as unruffled Perceval impersonates Christ in Rohmer's Passion Play. Intense pleasure is provided thanks to the very process of storytelling as well as the fairy tale ending that profoundly satisfies the audience's needs, with the happy outcome of Galaad's return to the Grail Castle and the open-ended image of Perceval riding off through the woods. Bresson's tragic, demythologizing process leaves no room for satisfaction. Stiffened, depersonalized actors and aesthetic fragmentation convey the impossible escape from the legend's molds as well as the trap in which Lancelot is stuck, his existential sense of guilt, as there is no one to either condemn or redeem him. Bresson's view of crushed humanity is in fact no less didactic than Rohmer's apologetic, if not homiletic story of Perceval's redemption. Llorca comparatively achieves a lighter, more balanced, less biased interpretation of the legendary material, which precisely makes it less provocative and perhaps less daring.

NOTES

1. For representative views of Llorca's film, see: *Les Cahiers du Cinéma* 437 (December 1990): 85; *Les Echos* 9 November 1990; *L'Evénement du Jeudi* 8 November 1990; *Les Fiches du Cinéma* 7 November 1990; *Le Figaro* 7 November 1990; *Positif* 359 (December 1990): 45; *Le Quotidien de Paris* 7 November 1990; *Télérama* 7 November 1990: 48.

WORKS CITED

Attolini, Vito. *Immagini del Medioevo nel cinema.* Bari: Dedalo, 1993.

Barthes, Roland. *Mythologies.* Paris: Seuil, 1957.

de la Bretèque, François. "Le Sang sur l'armure comme motif cinématographique." *Le Sang au Moyen Age.* Cahiers du CRISIMA 4. Montpellier: Université de Montpellier, 1999.

Eco, Umberto. *De Superman au surhomme.* Milan, 1978. Paris: Grasset, 1993.

Estève, Michel. *Robert Bresson.* Paris: Seghers, 1974.

Gorgievski, Sandra. "The Arthurian Legend in the Cinema: Myth or History?" In Marie-Françoise Alamichel, ed. *The Middle Ages after the Middle Ages.* Rochester: Boydell and Brewer, 1997.

_____. "Réalisme, stylisation et parodie dans les films à sujet médiéval des années 1970." In Xavier Kawa-Topor, ed. *Le Moyen Age dans le cinéma européen.* Conques: Centre Européen d'Art et de Civilisation Médiévale, 2001.

Grimbert, Joan Tasker. "Distancing Techniques in Chrétien de Troyes's *Li Contes del Graal* and Eric Rohmer's *Perceval le Gallois.*" *Arthuriana* 10 (Winter 2000): 33–44.

Hoffman, Donald L. "Re-Framing Perceval." *Arthuriana* 10 (Winter 2000): 45–56.

Mann, Jill. "Sir Gawain and the Romance Hero." In Leo Carruthers, ed. *Heroes and Heroines in Medieval English Literature Presented to André Crépin.* Cambridge, Eng.: D. S. Brewer, 1994.

Reader, Keith. *Robert Bresson.* Manchester: Manchester University Press, 2000.

Rider, Jeff, Richard Hull, and Christopher Smith. "The Arthurian Legend in French Cinema: *Lancelot du Lac* and *Perceval le Gallois.* In Kevin J. Harty, ed. *Cinema Arthuriana, Essays on Arthurian Film.* New York: Garland, 1991.

Roussel, François, and Pierre Sivain. "Le dernier acte est sanglant ... *Lancelot du Lac* de Robert Bresson." In Mireille Séguy, ed. *Lancelot.* Paris: Autrement, 1996.

Sineux, Michel. "Le chevalier inexistant." *Positif* 163 (1974): 73–74.

Thompson, Kristin. *Breaking the Glass: Neoformalist Film Analysis.* Princeton: Princeton University Press, 1989.

15

Blank, Syberberg, and the German Arthurian Tradition

ULRICH MÜLLER
(TRANSLATED BY JULIE GIFFIN)

Both Richard Blank's *Parzival* (1980) and Hans-Jürgen Syberberg's *Parsifal* (1981–82) are films based on literary sources: the former on the early thirteenth-century *Parzival* by Wolfram von Eschenbach, and the latter on Richard Wagner's opera, which premiered in 1882.

If the number of extant manuscripts is any evidence of contemporary popularity, then Wolfram's romance, surviving in almost ninety manuscripts, was the most successful courtly poem of the German Middle Ages. Wolfram based his romance on what was probably the last work of Chrétien de Troyes, a poet from northern France who wrote *Perceval*, or *Le Conte du Graal*, under the orders of Count Philip of Flanders. Chrétien's unfinished poem recounts the adventures of two heroes, Perceval and Gauvain.

When Wolfram was commissioned to retell and complete Chrétien's fragment around the year 1200, no one could have foreseen the range, merit, and significance of the result, which would overshadow every other work known at the time. Over the course of many years, Wolfram almost tripled the length of Chrétien's romance (from about 9,200 to 25,000 lines), completed the story in detail, added the early history of Perceval's father, and even gave a preview of the following generation of characters. *Parzival* was by far the longest known romance written in German up to that time.

Though generally faithful to Chrétien's plot, Wolfram changes so many large and small details that his *Parzival* becomes an independent work. It is neither a paraphrase nor a translation. Even his description and interpretation of the Grail are original: his Grail is a mysterious, powerful stone with divine origins, whereas Chrétien represents it as a golden vessel. References to the cup used at the Last Supper or to Christ's blood, references that became so important in the later tradition of the Grail, are completely missing in Wolfram's book, either because he was unaware of these connections (first made in the more or less contemporary *Le Roman de l'Estoire du Graal* by Robert de Boron) or because he rejected them.

Like its source but unlike other courtly romances, Wolfram's poem has two main heroes, whom he calls Parzival and Gawan, and three central scenes of action: King Arthur's court and the realm of the Grail, as in Chrétien, and an original addition, the culturally equal if not superior world of the

Orient. The whole narrative takes place in a magical time and a fantasy world that in many respects mirrors the geography and even the politics of Europe and the Orient.

Unlike Chrétien, who deals with strongly typified and often unnamed characters, Wolfram portrays a huge cosmos, a whole world, and his romance, which covers three generations of characters and events, gives the impression that there are countless characters with distinct personalities or at least personal "histories." The majority of them are related in the most complicated manner by blood, marriage, or political connections.

There is a unique trend in the German reception of the Arthurian legends: the story is retold without any mention of Arthur. Since the revival of interest in Arthurian materials in the early nineteenth century, German-speaking artists and authors have concentrated instead on the story of Parzival and his search for the Grail, and on the story of his son, Lohengrin. There are three reasons for this emphasis: the difficulty of exporting the British-national identification with the legend of King Arthur; the German fixation on other "myths" of the Middle Ages; and the dominating influence of Richard Wagner on the reception of medieval myth in general.

The legend of Arthur and all its ramifications were not unknown to educated Germans at the end of the eighteenth and the beginning of the nineteenth centuries, albeit mostly through French and English versions. There was, however, little interest in these versions. Translations of Wolfram by San Marte (1835–41) and Karl Simrock (1842) were responsible for first stimulating interest in the legend. Richard Wagner (1813–83), who had been working with the Grail material since 1845, had an even stronger and more permanent influence on German Arthuriana. His "Bühnenweihfestspiel" ("Festival of Consecration in a Theater") *Parsifal*, when it premiered in 1882, confirmed the German practice of disregarding Arthur in place of Parzival.

Wagner omits King Arthur and Gawan, central figures in his source, Wolfram's *Parzival* (known to him through the San Marte translation and annotations). Instead, he focuses on the Searcher for the Grail, whom he calls "Parsifal." He reinterprets Wolfram's story, practically turning it upside down. He changes Wolfram's global and well-populated epic into a "Weltanschauung"-drama, one that concentrates on only a few characters. His "Bühnenweihfestspiel" advances the notion that sexual asceticism and the renunciation of the world are of the highest merit. The opera's hero is a searcher who overcomes himself by reducing his instinctual drives. Through asceticism, he gains the power to acquire the Grail and takes on the role of redeemer.

Wagner's central idea, that a searcher can reach his goal through "purity"—"the pure fool, knowing through compassion...." ("durch Mitleid wissend der reine Tor....")—is not found in Wolfram's romance[1]; rather, it is one first found in late medieval versions of the Grail story. This interpretation of the character of Parsifal, which probably reached Wagner through his reading of San Marte's works, came to characterize all later German receptions of the Grail material.

Richard Blank's *Parzival* was first shown on (what was then) West Germany's WDR (Westdeutscher Rundfunk) on 11 November 1980. Since then, it has been rebroadcast several times on the Third Program of ARD (Arbeitsgemeinschaft der öffentlichrechtlichen Rundfunkanstalten der Bundesrepublick Deutschland).[2] While Eric Rohmer in his 1978 film *Perceval le Gallois* attempted an almost word-for-word adaptation of his medieval source, Blank[3] went in the opposite direction: he tried to actualize the medieval work. Like Rohmer, he was ambitious enough to make a film using and telling the *entire* source story.

Two performers, Wolfram Kunkel and Eva Schuchardt, play a majority of the roles in Blank's version. Using Wolfgang Mohr's translation (1977), they act out all the essential parts of Wolfram's second generation of characters. Given that the film is around ninety-two minutes long, this achievement is astonishing. It is also worth noting that Blank's film does not use rapid cuts or high-speed narration. The audience is never made to feel rushed because of the huge amount of material; instead, the director is able to project an "epic pace."

The film takes place partly in an imaginary and timeless Middle Ages, partly in the immediate present. The medieval segments are enacted in a large attic room, which like the prop room of a theater contains a few items indispensable to the story: dummies of horses, coats of arms, and costumes. Not only is the closed-off, windowless attic room reminiscent of a theater prop room, but it also carries associations of a mythical picture of European philosophy and theology: the large "cavern of the memory" as presented and defined by Augustine in his *Confessions*. The plot emerges from this "mythical cave," whose tradition stretches from Plato to Jung, that is, from the collective memory of both the main actors and from their analysis and exposition of Wolfram's text.

Blank explicitly contrasts this "artificial Middle Ages" with the present. Shots from modern-day cities and from the open country repeatedly show the reactions of a modern audience to the plot, and the film several times addresses ecological and environmental issues. Incorporated almost as leitmotifs are scenes in which actor Wolfram Kunkel plays the hurdy-gurdy and sings *lieder* as commentary on the events. The film thus meets the limitations of the television screen. It is not a period film with mass scenes in the style of Hollywood. Rather, the film stresses what the filmmaker saw as a "basic theme despite changed historical and social circumstances." As WDR's short commentary on the film notes: "Struggle and controversy still rule; women are still the main sufferers; human society has still not been realized."

The plot of Wolfram's work, though abridged, is basically unchanged. The film invents no themes that do not exist in the romance. And it stresses two important ideas from Wolfram's work: all humans are fundamentally "related," a constant theme in the romance, and women have special significance as sufferers and as a hope for a better future. Both points are brought together visually at the film's close, when all the important characters come together at the Grail Castle in a huge reconciliation.

Hans-Jürgen Syberberg has been one of the most prolific producers of the "new German Film."[4] His *Parsifal* is a complete adaptation of Wagner's last opera, running almost four hours. For technical and aesthetic reasons, the film was originally supposed to be shown only in especially designed theaters. It has, however, since been shown on television and is also available on videocassette. The director-producer has given a detailed account of his project and its realization in a 1982 book and in subsequent lectures.

Before undertaking *Parsifal*, Syberberg had already dealt with Wagner and his ideology in three previous films: *Ludwig II: Requiem für einen jungfräulichen König* (1972), *Winifred Wagner und die Geschichte des Hauses Wahnfried von 1914–1975* (1975), and *Hitler: Ein Film aus Deutschland* (1977). Syberberg's five-hour documentary about Winifred Wagner, the director of the Bayreuth Festival during the Hitler era,[5] particularly angered some members of the Wagner family. It is unclear whether that anger was a factor in record companies' refusal to allow Syberberg to use existing recordings of *Parsifal* for his film. But Syberberg had conductor Armin Jordan record a new production of the opera for

Erato, one that compares favorably with other recordings of the work.[6] The film itself was made in the Bavaria Ateliers in Munich in 1981. It took only thirty-five days to shoot and had a budget of a little more than three million German marks (about $1.3 million).

Syberberg's *Parsifal* is completely original. He rejected any visual reference to theater and any note of realism. He did not want to make an "opera film" in the usual sense. "I did not make a *Parsifal* as a producer; rather, this *Parsifal* is one by Syberberg and is on film. I used Wagner for it, just as Wagner used the texts of the Middle Ages. Consequently, [the film was] a new creation" (Syberberg, "Filmisches" 76).

Syberberg's *Parsifal* takes place neither in a theater nor at any real site but is set in a place of fantasy, dream, and imagination. The stage floor used in several scenes and segments is a gigantic death mask of Wagner.[7] It is the film's "spiritual home" (Syberberg, *Parsifal* 14).

With two exceptions (Robert Lloyd as Gurnemanz and Aage Haukland as Klingsor), the roles of the opera are here assumed by nonsinging actors and actresses. The synchronization between the music and the film is astonishing; there is never the impression that the actors and actresses are only lip-synching. The achievements of Edith Clever as Kundry and Armin Jordan (the director of the soundtrack) as Amfortas are especially notable. Jordan proves himself to be an impressive and never pretentious actor under Syberberg's direction; Clever, a famous actress on the Berlin Schaubühne, had worked with Syberberg for years, and they are the most fascinating and productive team in German film since Hanna Schygulla and Rainer Werner Fassbinder. Clever's Kundry ranks among the most impressive and most surprising of all interpretations of the role.

The death mask of composer Richard Wagner that serves as the principal setting for Hans-Jürgen Syberberg's 1982 film *Parsifal*. (Still courtesy of the British Film Institute.)

Wagner's *Parsifal* is a highly complicated and suggestive work. In Syberberg's "new creation," this aspect is emphasized through cinematic techniques that challenge the viewer to decode the content and music of the film while recognizing the relationships among its visual puzzles. These puzzles originate in pieces from Wagner's own biography: for example, the disproportionately large image of the composer's coat that appears several times, as well as "pictorial quotes" of Bayreuth, Ravello (where the opera was partly composed), and Venice (where Wagner died). Other signals refer to the effects of the opera; the ideology and politics of the nineteenth and twentieth centuries; Karl Marx, who knew Wagner's work but never met him; the Bavarian king Ludwig II; the Bayreuth Festivals; and National Socialism.[8]

There are also scenes that refer to Wolfram von Eschenbach and the Middle Ages. The viewer must recognize that the Grail throne and Kundry's seat are identical; that the world of the Grail and the world of Klingsor, asceticism and seduction, are like mirror images dependent on each other; that Amfortas and Klingsor suffer from their sexuality; that there are similarities between the "second Parsifal" and the medieval image of Christ; and that in death Amfortas and Kundry represent a medieval ruler and consort as they are shown on old gravestones. Syberberg expects his viewers not only to recognize these references but also to make sense of them.

Surprisingly, Syberberg avoids eroticism, even in the "most-feared scene of this opera" (Syberberg, *Parsifal* 127). This is the "flower girl" scene in the second act. Parsifal and the camera move through a gallery of statue-like girls, accompanied by lively music with seductive overtones and the beat of an "English waltz."[9] It almost seems that Syberberg here attempts to portray a fear of the erotic. One might question whether he stresses the deep structure of Wagner's work too much and the seductive surface too little.

Syberberg's portrayal of Parsifal as androgynous caused much discussion. The role of Parsifal is performed by two impressive novice actors (Michael Kutter and Karin Krick). When Kundry kisses Parsifal, he feels sexual desire for the first time. Accompanying this feeling is the sudden realization of the relation between that desire and Amfortas's guilt, and a female Parsifal separates from the male figure. Both Parsifals, a feminine young man and a masculine young woman, are rejoined only at the film's end. This reunion leads to a scene that is at least partly shocking, when Parsifal sings a duet, as it were, with himself. Syberberg wants to break away from an idea that is generally representative of Wagner's work — "here evil woman, there redeeming man" — by portraying Parsifal as androgynous (Syberberg, *Parsifal* 56).

In a lecture, Syberberg summarized the main characteristics of his film:

> A few words about the things that I in part realized as important in the "Parsifal" movie. First of all, we have a young Parsifal, the like of which has not and could not have been on stage ever before. Furthermore, we have a division of Parsifal, which the stage had never delivered before. There is a type of Kundry that had certainly never been on stage before and probably will not be again for a long time — unless on film: there is also a division of her voice and character. Then there is the ... "separierte Wunde."[10] This ... is incredibly significant. It is possible only when a closeup is possible, as it is with film; on stage, this form would simply be nonexistent. In addition, we had extraordinary voices at our disposal. This results in a clarity — Wagner's demands for distinctness are well known — that simply cannot be delivered on stage [which is characterized by] an eternal "long shot," indistinct speech, faces shrunk to the size of those of dolls.... [This film attempted to] realize things that Wagner could only imagine.... We really could show facial movement, expressions, etc. Therefore, for

Parsifal in both his female (Karin Krick) and male (Michael Kutter) forms arriving at the Chapel of the Grail in Hans-Jürgen Syberberg's 1982 film *Parsifal*. (Still courtesy of the British Film Institute.)

example, we tried in the "Good Friday Spell" to implement all of Wagner's directions and indications: the eye-dialogue of the three people and the gestures fit the music; it did not seem ridiculous. The Grail scene realized in Act I should also be mentioned: we projected an imaginary setting onto that character — something that would also be impossible in theater.... And the projection onto this person makes reference to possibilities that psychoanalysis has introduced into this century, namely: to design a "projection" onto a person in addition to the projection of our ideas [Syberberg, "Filmisches" 67–68].

Syberberg's film has a fascinating power of expression that can be interpreted on many levels. A film of the highest quality, it furthermore is a valuable treatment of a Wagnerian opera, with whose innovative qualities no other screen adaptation (even from Bayreuth) can compare.[11] Occasionally shocking or controversial, it is in all events extraordinarily exciting.

NOTES

1. Even Wagner's image of the Grail differs from Wolfram's. Whereas Wolfram's Grail is a

stone with magical powers, Wagner's Grail follows Robert de Boron's tradition, in which the Grail is the vessel used both at the last Supper and to collect the blood of Christ at the Crucifixion.

2. Thanks to the efforts of Dr. Siegried Schmidt (Salzburg), the Institute for German Studies at the University of Salzburg has a videotape of the film in its possession. The written documents I have at my disposal for the following discussion include an unpublished essay by Annelen Kranefuss, who inspired the film; a short text from WDR; and a few reactions from newspapers.

3. Richard Blank was born in 1939 in Langenfeld in the Rhineland. After receiving his Ph.D. in Philosophy, he wrote radio plays and several books. He also filmed documentaries before switching to the "literary" film. In addition to *Parzival*, he also made *Dracula* and *Peter Schlemihl, der Mann ohne Schatten*. Almost every year since 1978, he has been responsible for the screenplay and direction of a feature-length film (usually made for television). I would like to thank Dr. Blank for a long conversation about his film and his intentions.

4. Syberberg, as quoted in *Opern und Opernfiguren* (1989): "Dr. Hans-Jürgen Syberberg, born on 8 December 1935, in Vorpommern, [in the former] East Germany. Spent childhood in the country until the end of the war; father landowner. Has lived since 1947 in Rostock (Ostsee), where he came into contact with theater, music, and cinema for the first time through films from the Russian Sowexport and DEFA.... He was also in contact with Benno Bresson from Brecht's Berliner Ensemble while in Rostock, and through him received invitation to go to Brecht in Berlin, where he produced his first 8 mm film (*Nach meinem letzten Umzug, Aufnahmen von der Bühne Brechts*, 1953).... Crossed from East to West Berlin in the same year (1953).... Produced over eighty television films... over the course of two years, starting in 1963. Made two-hour film about Fritz Kortner during rehearsals of *Kabale und Liebe*. Produced own films since 1965. Came into contact with Richard Wagner's music through the Ludwig film; plans for a trilogy: *Ludwig* (1972), *Karl May* (1974), *Hitler* (1977) (one hundred years of German and European history)...."

I would like to thank Dr. Syberberg for various conversations about his films and intentions, and I would particularly like to acknowledge his participation in a seminar on German film that was held at the University of Salzburg in the 1988 summer semester and led by Professor Klaus M. Schmidt (Bowling Green State University) and the author.

5. The Englishwoman Winifred Williams Klindworth (1897–1980) married Siegfried, a son of Richard Wagner, in 1915. After his death in 1930, she directed the festivals until the end of World War II. Her close ties with Hitler and National Socialism were incriminating, and she stepped down from her position after the war.

6. The singers for the main roles are Wolfgang Schöne (Amfortas), Hans Tschammer (Titurel), Robert Lloyd (Gurnemanz), Rainer Goldberg (Parsifal), Aage Haugland (Klingsor), and Yvonne Minton (Kundry).

7. The death mask, designed by architect Werner Achmann, consisted of 40 tons of cement; was 15 meters long, 9 meters wide and 4.5 meters high; and cost about 130,000 DM ($58,000.00) to make (Syberberg, *Parsifal* 17).

8. The references to Hitler and National Socialism are recognizable but not obtrusive. The film is thus reminiscent of Syberberg's *Winifred* (1975) and *Hitler* (1977) films, where the producer made the connections between Wagner and National Socialism into a theme. Syberberg does not deal with the accusations of anti–Semitism made against Wagner's *Parsifal*.

9. Wagner's original instruction was "wanting to sound American" ("amerikanisch sein wollend").

10. Amfortas's "separierte Wunde," that is, that his wound is "separated" from his body, is reminiscent of the technique of the Christian votive picture as it is found in places of pilgrimage even today: a faithful and thankful Christ allows his healed body part to be depicted and hung as a picture in or on a church.

11. In the realm of opera films, only Joachim Herz's version of the *Fliegender Holländer* (1964) can match the originality of Syberberg's cinematic techniques; cf. Sirikit Podroschko, "Senta."

WORKS CITED

Müller, Ulrich. "Gral 89: Mittelalter, Moderne Hermetik und die neue Politik der Perestroika: Zu den 'Parzival/Gral-Dramen' von Peter Handke und Christoph Hein." In Irene Burg and others, eds. *Mittelalter-Rezeption IV. Gesammelte Vortäge des Symposions in Lausanne*. Göppingen: Kümmerle, 1991.

———. "Moderne Gral-Questen: Vom Nachleben des 'epischen Mythos' der sinnsuchenden Reise: Fragmentarische Beobachtungen und Bemerkungen zu einigen modernen Dramen und Romanen sowie zu Science Fiction-Filmen von Stanley Kubrick und Andrej Tarkowskij." In Ursula Bieber and Alois Woldan, eds. *Georg Mayer zum 60. Geburtstag* Munich: Otto Sagner, 1991.

———. "Parzival 1980 — auf der Bühne, im Fernsehen und im Film." In Jürgen Kühnel and others, eds. *Mittelalter-Rezeption II*. Gesammelte Vorträge des 2. Salzburger Symposions. Göppingen: Kümmerle, 1982.

———, and Ursula Müller, eds. *Opern und Opernfiguren: Festschrift für Joachim Herz*. Anif, Austria: Müller-Speiser, 1989.

———, and Peter Wapnewski, eds. *Richard-Wagner-Handbuch*. Stuttgart: Kröner, 1986.

———, eds. *Wagner Handbook*. Trans. and ed. John Deathridge. Cambridge: Harvard University Press, 1992.

Podroschko, Sirikit. "Senta, oder *Der Fliegende Holländer* von Joachim Herz: Ein Film nach Richard Wagner (1964)." In Ulrich Müller and Ursula Müller, eds. *Opern und Opernfiguren: Festschrift für Joachim Herz*. Anif, Austria: Müller-Speiser, 1989.

Syberberg, Hans-Jürgen. "Filmisches bei Richard Wagner." In Gerhardt Heldt, ed. *Richard Wagner: Millter zwischen Welten*. Anif, Austria: Müller-Speiser, 1990.

———. *Parsifal: Ein Filmessay*. Munich: Heyne, 1982.

———. *Syberbergs Filmbuch*. Munich: Nymphenburger, 1976.

Wolfram von Eschenbach. *Parzival*. Trans. Wolfgang Mohr. 2nd ed. Göppingen: Kümmerle, 1979.

16

Gawain on Film (The Remake): Thames Television Strikes Back

ROBERT J. BLANCH AND JULIAN N. WASSERMAN

The son of King Lot of Lothian and of King Arthur's sister ("Anna" in Geoffrey of Monmouth, "Morgawse" in Malory), Gawain has, according to Thomas Hahn, represented the central figure in more popular medieval romances than "any other Arthurian (or non–Arthurian) hero" (7). Still, as Hahn points out, such ubiquity "does not, however, endow him with a coherent identity" (3). Frequently portrayed as the knight *par excellence,* especially in early tales, Gawain often attempts to gain self-knowledge through the instrument of *aventures.* Unlike Arthur, who as king must be tied to the locus of the court, Gawain typically enjoys the freedom to explore the margins of the known Arthurian world, thereby encountering giants, Turks, loathly ladies and assorted "carls" who inhabit such regions. As a result of such adventures, Gawain's character sometimes has been as untethered as his person and has undergone a number of contradictory metamorphoses which contrast sharply with the more balanced literary evolutions of his knightly peers. As Keith Busby notes in his "Gawain" entry in *The New Arthurian Encyclopedia*, Gawain can, at least in the corpus of French works, be portrayed as "a real hero, as a somewhat comic figure, or as a true villain." While the English chronicle tradition underscores Gawain's loyal chivalric service and martial valor, the French Arthurian tradition calls attention to the hero's reputation as a lover and as an exemplar of fine manners including courtly *parole*. Yet each tradition counterbalances these virtues with a failing. For the English Gawain, the flaw is rashness; for the French, lechery and pride.[1]

In this essay, we shall explore the ways in which these traditional characterizations of Gawain have been reconfigured in several contemporary cinematic romances, particularly *Knights of the Round Table, Prince Valiant, Monty Python and the Holy Grail, Excalibur, The Sword of Lancelot* and the three attempts to translate *Sir Gawain and the Green Knight* into a feature-length film.[2]

Sir Thomas Malory's treatment of Gawain is particularly crucial to understanding the character as he appears in cinema because it has become *de rigueur* for screenwriters and directors to proclaim that their work is "Based on Sir Thomas Malory's *Le Morte d'Arthur*," whether or not the film demonstrates the slightest connection to that fifteenth-century work. Indeed, *Excalibur*, a film which proudly proclaims its Malorian lineage, seems clearly affected by Tennyson's *Idylls* in its use of light and dark imagery, its animal-like armor affected by Uther and the pre–Arthurian knights (for whom "the beast was ever more and more"[3]), its reconciliation scenes between Arthur and Guinevere, and especially, as we shall see, its portrayal of Gawain. Another post–Malory work whose unannounced sphere of influence on *Excalibur* can be felt is T. H. White's *The Once and Future King*, wherein Malory's torn Gawain becomes decidedly more oafish as one of the dysfunctional Orkneys.

As for Malory's Gawain, following the writer's French sources, Gawain is a conspicuously failed Grail questor. Although Gawain gains stature in his refusal to plot with his brothers Agravayne and Mordred to ensnare Lancelot with the Queen, Gawain's chivalric virtue shines brightest when he refuses to attend the Queen's execution and when he renounces vengeance over the death of Agravayne. Undone through his grief over Lancelot's accidental slaying of Gareth and Geharis, Gawain becomes unrelentingly, self-destructively vengeful. His pure animosity towards a clearly penitent Lancelot casts the latter in a more courteous light as Gawain changes into the reckless warrior of the earlier English chronicle tradition. It is not until his rashness has led him and his men to be slaughtered that he regains a modicum of insight, but by then it is too late for either himself or the society that his thirst for vengeance has brought down. In the end, Malory's Gawain becomes more tragic than villainous, a great knight done in by grief rather than by ambition or worldly desire.

I

With this background established, it is now possible to focus on the conception of Gawain in a number of films. In the 1953 *Knights of the Round Table*, for instance, Gawain appears in no more than a half-dozen scenes, often as a shadowy presence with little or no dialogue. Primarily cast as a symbol of youthful high spirits, he is decidedly more immature than the "serious" knights. At one point we see him attempt to shoot an apple off the head of another comic knight, blaming the misdirected shaft on the poor harping of Gareth.[4] In fact, a minor running joke throughout the first half of the film relies on the affectionate rivalry between Gawain and the even younger Gareth, including youthful roughhousing in the tent during a Valley Forge–like winter as Arthur undertakes his initial campaign to quell the barons' revolt. Later, Gawain simply walks without stopping across the set, from right foreground to left rear, muttering aloud to no one in particular, "The highland mist has rusted [the unseen Gareth's] notes."

Here, as in several medieval works, a number of extratextual references inform the portrait. While Gawain and Gareth continually act out youthful sibling jibes and horseplay, they are never described as brothers although the extratextual presumption seems obvious. Gawain's costume, the only one for a major character to include medievalized long sleeves, seems to imply an awareness of his courtliness. This extratextual acknowledgment of Gawain as a leader in fashion as well as in manners, perhaps, accounts for the peculiar samurai topknot afforded Gawain in *Excalibur* as well, for in both films Gawain, though portrayed differently in each film, seems to possess a unique sense of fashion. In both productions, the extratextual tradition paradoxically informs and defines the character. At the same time, however, this utter dependence on medieval convention allows filmmakers to offer their audiences superficial delineations of Gawain. Rather than being cohesive characters, both Gawains are collections of informed details, the information derived from traditions outside the films themselves.

While such extratextual traditions may be strong enough touchstones to provide some definition of his character, Gawain's position in the romance tradition is flexible enough that he may be used in ways that might surprise those with a knowledge of the Malorian politics of Camelot. Gawain in *Knights of the Round Table* becomes a faithful retainer of Lancelot. Only secondarily is he aligned with Arthur. Throughout the film, Gawain travels with Lancelot, going north with the French knight as he leaves the court to avoid scandal. When Lancelot rides out of his northern castle to harry the Picts, Gawain is left to watch over Elaine, who had also come north as Lancelot's wife. Gawain demonstrates a remarkable flexibility that allows him to play roles as diverse as utility walk-on with a throwaway comic line to a sympathetic listener who allows Elaine to voice her love and concern for her absent husband.

In this film's Gawain, we see his traditional loyalty, but the person to whom he is loyal — Lancelot as opposed to Arthur — has changed. *Knights'* Gawain, as in many versions, is young, but the definition of youth will be seen to change in his various films. Also carried over in *Knights of the Round Table* is the tradition that Gawain is marked by his intimacy with or closeness to women, but the nature of the relationship, in this case to Elaine, has likewise been made over. In short, Gawain remains a set of general qualities — such as loyalty or youth — but without specific content.

Finally, at the end of the film, as Lancelot boldly enters Arthur's court to interrupt the trial of Guinevere and to insist that a "man and woman can love each other with no shame" (it's 1953, and there is no actual adultery), Lancelot is accompanied by several knights, including Gawain, presumably to demonstrate the division of the court into factions. As Lancelot is subsequently exiled, he turns and walks out followed by his retainers. The exit is remarkably quiet. The viewer, however, has to look closely and away from the scene's central character to notice that Gawain does not leave with Lancelot. This detail does undercut the loyalty foregrounded in Gawain's characterization in the film, and Gawain is completely absent from all subsequent scenes. Gawain, his purpose having been fulfilled, simply fades from the narrative. Were Gawain to remain, he would have either to fight alongside Lancelot, vitiating the film's claim to be based on Malory, or to battle against Lancelot, contradicting what little uniformity of character he has in the film.

If *Knights of the Round Table* deviates significantly from Malory in its portrayal of Gawain, some traces of another literary hand are at work here. As we have already noted, T. H. White's *The Once and Future King* seems to provide the model for the young sibling relationship between Gareth and Gawain. In fact, one suspects that White's work, far more popular and accessible than Malory's, especially in the heyday of what might be called the "Robert Taylor era" of Arthurian films, has exerted a significant impact on several productions.

The rather oafish but good-hearted Gawain of Henry Hathaway's 1954 *Prince Valiant* is a case in point.[5] In one of the very few portrayals in which he is neither young nor blonde, Gawain is depicted by Sterling Hayden as someone who misinterprets love and chivalry and who is duped easily by manipulative evildoers. As such, he is largely the foil for Prince Valiant (Robert Wagner), his own squire. Since Gawain adores Valiant's sweetheart, Princess Aleta of Ord (Janet Leigh), he mistakenly believes that she will return his love. And Valiant cannot bear to inform Gawain that both men are attracted to the same woman.

Again, what informs this portrait is what is not within the text of the film proper: the sense of who Gawain is in the wider tradition outside the film. Gawain's reputation as a courtly wooer (as opposed to the devoted and passionate lover, Lancelot) makes *Valiant's* bumbling but sincere Gawain all the more comic. That Gawain cannot escape that reputation is likewise manifest in what is arguably the best informed Arthurian movie ever made, *Monty Python and the Holy Grail* (1975), directed by Terry Gilliam and Terry Jones. Sharply differentiating the aura of chivalric tradition from the "mud, squalor, and death" (Byron and Weis 247–48) of actual life in the Middle Ages, the film skewers the Arthurian legend, including the quest of the Grail, as well as cinematic depictions of the age of knighthood.[6] Gawain's conventional role as a paragon of chivalric valor is, of course, not safe from ridicule. In one brief but memorable scene, Tim the Wizard points out to King Arthur and his band a mysterious cave, "a cave where a vital clue to the grail's whereabouts is located" (Schickel 58). Soon afterward, the small white bunny guarding the cave's entrance is transformed into a killer rabbit, which slays Gawain, its reluctant challenger. Since the rabbit suggests a medieval emblem of lechery and fertility, Gawain's literary reputation as a lover is lampooned in this cinematic battle.[7]

Unlike *Prince Valiant* and *Monty Python*, movies that send up aspects of the Arthurian legend, John Boorman's *Excalibur* (1981) is a serious effort to recapture the epic scope of Arthur's life from birth to death (Ciment, "Deux Entretiens" 20; Ciment, *Boorman* 188) and to unfold, not to reenact, the mythic world of the Arthurian age (Kennedy 31, 33–34). Although Boorman attempts to portray "the whole story of ... [Malory's] *Morte d'Arthur*" (Kennedy 33), the Grail quest section of the movie, at least, is rooted in Weston's *From Ritual to Romance* (Shichtman 41; Ciment, "Deux Entretiens" 19; Ciment, *Boorman* 185).

Although Gawain appears in fewer episodes in *Excalibur* than in *Knights of the Round Table*, those scenes bear far more dramatic weight than in the earlier film. In effect, Boorman has taken the torn Gawain whose grief and wrath represent a major force in the unraveling of Malory's Camelot and tried to condense and capture Gawain's agon in a single scene. While Boorman's cinematic compression clearly points to Gawain's inner turmoil, we are left without any real sense of how the knight came to be divided against himself.

After King Arthur convokes a banquet-meeting of the Round Table, a drunken Gawain (Liam Neeson) rashly discloses both his feelings about Lancelot's worth and his suspicions concerning Guinevere's amorous longings for Lancelot.[8] Although Guinevere forgives Gawain's "hasty words" and implores him to drink wine from Lancelot's cup, thereby cementing once again the bond of friendship between the two knights, Gawain's hand trembles as he seems to be wrestling with some internal conflict. The impetus for the event is clearly Morgana's whispering in Gawain's ear. Perhaps this tormented Gawain torn between Morgana and Arthur constitutes another indication of White's influence, but whether Gawain's reluctance stems from personal affection for Lancelot or from fear of alienating Arthur's most powerful knight, we are unable to guess, for Gawain is without motive. We have not even really seen Gawain in previous scenes to know whether this behavior, both the drunkenness and the accusation, is an aberration. Unable to drink from the cup, Gawain inverts the vessel as though his hand were defying his will. Much like the scene of a naked Lancelot wrestling with his own armor, Gawain's trembling, recalcitrant hand is an emblem of the divided self, but these are intellectual symbols for affective states.

Infuriated by Gawain's accusation, Boorman's Arthur actually begins to rise to defend his wife's honor but checks himself, referring to his superseding obligation as King. What is not noted in this film, however, is Gawain's special relationship with Arthur, a relationship springing from blood ties, fealty, and mutual admiration. Perhaps Boorman presumes that his audience is aware of this tradition, but there is certainly no hint of it within the film. Such unspoken traditions do work in other films, but informing spirits must be summoned if one is to rely on their appearance. Two days after the fateful banquet, Lancelot, "championing the Queen" so as to prove her innocence, then challenges Gawain in the lists. Although Gawain displays his traditional prowess in arms by deftly parrying Lancelot's blows, he is defeated and, begging for mercy, declares the Queen's innocence.

Lancelot has won because he is still technically innocent of adultery, but as he makes a gesture to slay the vanquished Gawain, the Queen's champion collapses and fails to complete the blow since he is innocent only by the letter rather than the spirit of the law. Here one finds the essential conflict between Gawain and Lancelot — the tragic mainspring of the end of Malory's Camelot — writ small rather than in characters of epic proportions. We find no Malorian displaced sun gods waxing and waning as the day goes by. Neither is there a climactic renunciation of revenge over a guilty brother's death nor an obsession with vengeance over two innocent brothers slain by a friend. All of this tension, and with it the tragic cost of Lancelot's actions on his peers, is condensed into Gawain's trembling, perhaps disobedient, hand that overturns the flagon at Arthur's table.

The final scene in *Excalibur* involving Gawain focuses on the search for the Grail, the source of redemption both for the land and for the Round Table.[9] Although Gawain boldly asserts, "We will find the Grail or die!" his end is imminent. Perceval sees a horse riding with a dead man strapped to it. Perceval recognizes the rider and laments Gawain's death at the hands of the villainous Mordred. In the end, then, Boorman's Gawain is the seriously flawed Grail-questor, derived from Chrétien via Malory. Without the heroics of the final stand of the Alliterative *Morte* or even the self-deforming grief of the Gawain of the later Malory, this Gawain is more venial than venereal and is certainly not tragic.

II

It would seem, then, that none of the Malorian grand sweeps of the history of Camelot has afforded Gawain more than a minor role in film, the ephemeral destiny of a famous name that should be present. Surprisingly, Gawain has, until recently, fared little better in the film adaptations of a work in which he is the central character.

Since the appearance of Alain Renoir's landmark 1958 article ("Descriptive Technique" 126–32) on the visual aspects of *Sir Gawain and the Green Knight*, readers have been well aware of the highly cinematic nature of this "best of [English] romances."[10] Yet despite the poem's strong cinematic sensibilities, two films based on the poem — Stephen Weeks's *Gawain and the Green Knight* (1973) and his 1983 remake of virtually the same script, *Sword of the Valiant* — have been laughably inept failures for critics, scholars, and general audiences alike.[11] Still, as Bercilak notes in the poem, "third tyme throwe best" (1680), so we would like to suggest that a third cinematic version — *Gawain and the Green Knight* (Thames 1991) — not only captures the essence of the romance but also may serve as an interesting and useful classroom tool.

Although the 1973 *Gawain and the Green Knight* reproduces faithfully some elements of the original poem — the use of a narrator, gamelike atmosphere, and play rules — Weeks's version reflects too strongly the influence of Jessie L. Weston's *From Ritual to Romance*.[12] In particular, Weeks pays homage to Weston's vision of a pagan vegetation or nature god who yearly rises to fullness and then dies (34–64); the old year thus passes away so that a new year and god can be born.

The ritualistic note of Weeks's film is sounded in the narrator's initial commentary: "This is when pagan gods haunted the world, and good men longed for miracles." Soon after the Green Knight interrupts Arthur's Yuletide festivities, the seasonal aspects of the movie flare into prominence. Wearing green hair and armor, suggestive of youth, freshness, and the rebirth of life in nature, the Knight (Nigel Green) holds merely a staff, but no holly bob, in his hand. This staff, an emblem of the life force, is then twirled by the Knight until the fertile sapling is metamorphosed into an ax. Once the boyish Gawain (Murray Head) agrees to participate in the Knight's "beheading game," he is given a year, not the legalistic year and a day, to find the Green Chapel because he is young. Such an emphasis on immaturity continues with Gawain's departure from Camelot, as the narrator intones, "He left a green youth determined to return a man." The last important example of seasonal symbolism appears in the closing frames of the film. As the Green Knight ages before melting into the ground, he reiterates the movie's underlying fertility myth: "The full cycle of the year is turned. As every green shoot of spring returns to the earth, so return I."[13]

Sword of the Valiant (1983), Stephen Weeks's second adaptation of *Sir Gawain and the Green Knight,* includes a relatively mature cinematic vision and sophisticated special effects.[14] The Weston material is at least toned down enough so that the Green Knight now holds an ax rather than a staff. Still, the fact remains that a major, perhaps overpowering, star (Sean Connery substituted for Nigel Green) plays the Green Knight rather than Gawain, revealing that Weeks's attention is still not fully fixed on Gawain. For all the muting of the Weston material, *Sword of the Valiant* is, however, a mediocre film, like its predecessor fancifully blending the narratives of *Sir Gawain* and Chrétien's *Yvain* with a London version of Hollywood Arthuriana.

Typical of Weeks's treatment is his exclusion in both films of the temptation scenes, the very embodiments of internal tension in the original text, in order to accommodate the material from Chrétien.[15] In fact, the beheading scene and the final denouement between Gawain and the Green Knight are really bookends for the material loosely taken from the French romancer. Besides the fact that, for Chrétien, Gawain is not a particularly sympathetic or even admirable character, Chrétien's characters are primarily one-dimensional figures, who often appear and exit the dreamscape narrative without motive or development.

In his own outlining of the characters, Weeks has chosen to emulate Chrétien.[16] Accordingly, Gawain is remarkably "flat" and is played woodenly in the first case by Murray Head and in the second by former Tarzan Miles O'Keefe, who exudes a kind of earnest oafishness. As the deletion of the temptation scenes and the retention of the beheading contest indicate, peril in both films is, likewise, strictly external, with results that are unfortunate for both the films as a whole and for their central characters as well.

Unfortunately, even the external danger, such as it is, is reduced unintentionally to Monty Python–like comedy. After the Knight departs from Camelot, Arthur praises Gawain for restoring honor to the court, and the Christmas feast then begins in earnest. But Gawain grumbles, "I don't think I'm hungry" in a fashion that seems to indicate that he has never quite understood what transpired and that undermines all pretense to courage as well as to character.[17]

Gawain's foes in the "Yvain section" range from ineptly comic to crabby to annoying, but they are never really dangerous and never really give him a chance to develop. One disarmed opponent takes unfair advantage by picking up the sword that Gawain discards in order to fight him on equal terms. (Gawain's response to being tricked out of his weapon is, "Now that's just dirty!") Attempting to obey a command to shoot Gawain in the back, an archer mistakenly shoots one of his own men while the seneschal who gave the order to shoot says dryly, "Wrong back."

Even more problematic is the function of *Sword*'s mysterious Green Knight. Weeks's decision to convert the green intruder from a moral touchstone, an arbiter who weighs the character of the court and its chivalry, into a cyclical nature god completely undercuts the ethical imperative of the choice between the axe and the holly bob. Nor even is there any tension inherent in the search for the Green Knight who must be located if Gawain is to keep his pledged word since the Green Knight informs Gawain that if Gawain cannot find the Green Knight, the Green Knight will find him.

Moreover, Gawain's acceptance of the challenge is reworked in a fashion that predictably deflates both plot and character. In the fourteenth-century alliterative poem, Gawain is a full knight and the embodiment of the court's values. If he fails, his fault will represent the spiritual bankruptcy of the court. Such a burden is felt keenly by the medieval Gawain because both his knighthood and his court matter to him (and to the reader as well). In both of Weeks's films, however, Gawain is merely a squire and above all else an individual acting alone. In the filmic world of Weeks's Gawains, there are no real obligations, partly because Arthur's court is so petty and, in the end, irrelevant. In both films, little exists beyond the self, and in the case of Gawain, that is a very petty self. This deflation of the once valiant warrior tradition is epitomized by the young knight's borrowed armor, a suit that crushes like tinfoil because, as he learns, it was only ceremonial armor intended for Arthur (Trevor Howard), who is portrayed as an irascible old man who continuously rebukes the court for both its moral decline and expanding bellies.

If Gawain's vaunted military prowess and knightly obligation are minimized, the same is largely true for his reputation as a courtly lover. The romantic material taken from Chrétien is uneven at best and often contradictory in tone and treatment, wavering between the sentimental and the crude. In Chrétien, Yvain, trapped by a portcullis in a gatehouse, is aided by a mysterious maiden, Lunete, who provides the knight with a ring that affords its wearer invisibility. Using the ring, Yvain spies the widow of the man he has just slain and in typical courtly fashion is immediately smitten by her beauty. This situation is fraught with a tension that Chrétien uses to develop his character.

Weeks's alterations, however, are telling. Gawain, likewise trapped, is also aided by young Linet (Cyrielle Claire), but Gawain falls in love with his immediate rescuer, thereby eliminating any character-defining tension generated by a man falling in love with a woman who hates him and who has sworn to take his life. The widow Lyonesse (Lila Kedrova) is not forgotten, however. Cast in the role of the vulgarly over-sexed middle-aged matron, she lusts for the young knight who must comically fend off her advances in a fashion reminiscent of the French romances we have already discussed. Her attraction is obviously purely physical — she surveys his body and comments on its various parts as though buying a horse — because there's no "interior" person to embrace.

III

In contrast, the hallmark of the 1991 Thames Television *Gawain and the Green Knight* is its inclusion of virtually every notable element of the original, even such "non-dramatic" material as the glossing of the pentangle and the castle pared out of paper.[18] The film, however, begins not with Arthur's feast but with the arming and departure chronicled in the second fitt of the poem.

The beheading episode occurs as a

Sean Connery (left) as the Green Knight and Miles O'Keefe as Sir Gawain in Stephen Weeks's 1983 film *Sword of the Valiant*.

series of flashbacks embedded in Gawain's journey through the marches. At first, such a displacement (a lopping off of the head of the tale, as it were) might seem disturbing to devotees of the poem, and yet the unexpected chronological rearrangement serves several purposes, the least of which is to inject a type of temporal circularity that reflects the myriad circles and cycles that are the hallmark of the original. By incorporating the beheading scene into the quest, the screenwriter emphasizes the decapitation's function as a major thematic and structural principle in the narrative rather than as an independent element.

Most importantly, however, the Thames film's presentation of the beheading as a flashback removes the act from the objective world of phenomena and translates it into the subjective, interior world of Gawain's thought.[19] Consider the implications of transferring the simple judgment that the members of the court "were [from an omniscient point of view] in their first age" (54, p. 2)[20] to Gawain's interior monologue. Couched in Gawain's thought, the line may well be interpreted as "they were [to me, Gawain] in their first age." Does the phrase imply that the members of the court never were in their first age but that Gawain erroneously perceived them as such? Has Gawain changed, or has the court changed? Is the phrase a statement of disillusionment? Unlike direct narrative, which possesses the illusion of simply reporting the indisputable, remembrance is overtly a construct, one that calls us to consider among other things the possibility of its falsity as well as psychological forces which determine its re-creation.

In such a light, we might reexamine the differences between the court's and Gawain's adoptions of the green girdle. Surprisingly overlooked by critics is the fact that these views are not two responses to the same stimulus. While Gawain responds to an actual event, the court, of necessity, reacts to Gawain's verbal re-creation of that event. Scholars who fault or praise the court's behavior consistently have assumed that Gawain's recounting of the tale is objective rather than subjective, that the signifier is identical to the signified. This issue is foregrounded by the film's use of flashback.

Situated in memory, Gawain's recapitulation of the Green Knight's entrance in the film thus becomes surreal rather than real. Mouths move without sound. Sounds do not match actions. Figures whirl in slow motion. Furthermore, the Green Knight's first communication is not "language" but a non-linguistic primal scream that implies pure subjectivity rather than rational discourse. When the Green Knight does finally speak, his voice is distorted. His "discourse" does not exist in the rational space between speaker and receiver but, instead, inside the mind, as much the seat of hallucination as perceived fact. The entire picture here is of events sensed or felt, distorted by memory rather than objectively registered in reason.

Indeed, the cinematic focus rests on the relativity of perception rather than on the reality of the perceived. In short, the presentation of the existence of point of view — the decentering of narrative authority — is as much the content of the scenes as the events which are their subjects. For instance, in the early part of the initial challenge, the ax is deliberately kept in the foreground, as though we are seeing the court from the weapon's perspective. The cinematography even includes a shot looking up from the floor which, for a moment, captures the events from the perspective of the Green Knight's severed head. Moments later, we then see the search for the head from the decapitated body's point of view.[21] Most startling of all is the hunt for the boar. Filmed first from what seems like the boar's perspective, the point of view seems to metamorphose into that of the pursuing hounds. Hence for pursuer and pursued, there is no clear, objective truth, simply points of view. The valuation of the hunt does indeed depend on whether one sees it from the boar's or the hounds' point of view. Such multiple perspectives, likewise, serve to enrich the temptation scenes as well.

In many ways, this recasting of the tale as a psychological adventure allows the film to remain true to the poem's larger themes.[22] Consider, for example, the presentation of two of the poem's elements. The film does manage to present the gloss on the pentangle's five fives (625–64, p. 14). However, what in the film begins as an external, spoken prayer quickly becomes internalized. It's a movement from outside to inside that the director presents by playing the exterior of the shield against the interior, here and throughout the film. It's the same movement that is so vividly dramatized as Lady Bercilak pulls the girdle through the slit in her dress. The interior is always the privileged half of the dichotomy.

On the inside of the shield, of course, is the portrait of the Virgin (648–49, p. 14), and Gawain's prayer to her for a place to celebrate Christmas (736–39, p. 16) is internalized, again with interesting results. By including the prayer as part of the subjective world of Gawain's thoughts, the director makes the appearance of the castle (764ff., pp. 16–17), the seeming answer to Gawain's prayer, more enigmatic. Are we still inside Gawain's mind? Is this castle as insubstantial, that is non-phenomenal, as the prayer which beckoned it? Certainly, the presentation of Gawain's arrival reinforces this presumption.

In its dream-like quality and especially in its eerie absence of external language, the highly subjective portrayal of Gawain's arrival at Bercilak's court mirrors his leave-taking from Camelot. In that initial departure, language is kept to a minimum, reduced to Gawain's singularly brief statement, "I must go." All else is gesture. Moreover, the very absence of speech is heightened by the natural sounds which occur in the background. The problem is not that the "mike" is off, for we do, after all, hear the wind hitting the microphone. In this instance, humans, not the world of external nature, are muted. Speech is replaced by gestures, the pointing of hands, and especially the meaningful averting and meeting of gazes, the displaced gaze being a metaphor for much of the film's camera work.

Throughout the film, the camera's lens is often averted. In fact, the film includes a remarkable number of scenes where figures block the camera or are not contained in frames, thereby creating a continual sense of incompleteness, of dealing in synecdoches. Most of all, however, there is a disturbing lack of speech where language becomes an absent presence. That Bercilak's court is a center for direct discourse is made manifest in both the volume and the force of the host's speech as contrasted with the preternaturally silent Gawain. In the first night's entertainment, Bercilak and Gawain participate in a Robin Hood–like battle of quarterstaves with only the host and the staffs producing any sound. Such a painful absence of language in the external world directs us inward and forces us to wonder what are these people thinking. When Bercilak falls progressively more silent after the third exchange, we will be drawn into his inner world as well.

To be sure, the opening scene announces the film's psychological emphasis by having the camera circle Gawain's head. In fact, throughout the film, head shots, often partial, predominate. A recurring visual motif is that of the head in foreground with the subject of thought suitably blurred in the background. At times, that background can be sharply defined as with the image of Lady Bercilak, who is situated behind the foregrounded faces of the host and his guest as they complete the first exchange. But, for the most part, the haziness of the background action evokes for viewers the world of thought rather than the terrain of objectively perceived reality. Significantly, the subjective head shot is discontinued once the Green Knight discloses his identity, only to be revived in the film's final scene wherein Gawain internally distances himself from the court which adopts the green sash as a mark of honor rather than as an emblem of shame. And so the film, beginning where it ended with a close-up of Gawain's head and face, completes another of its visual cycles. But "forme" and "fynisment" (499, p. 11) seldom meet, for our perspective has moved from outside to inside the subject.

Finally, Morgan's treatment in the film constitutes its second major deviation from the original text.[23] Clearly, the director's intent is to protect Morgan from the probing, revealing eye of the camera. In fact, to ensure her ambiguity, the script drops the Green Knight's revelation of her identity, and the credits list her simply as "The Woman in Black." In what is, perhaps, a physical representation of her "marginalization," Morgan is, with only one brief exception, confined to the foreground or background of the scenes in which she appears. In the background scenes, she is a shadow self, an element of the unconscious rather than a hag. But is she the Id or the Superego, the base hag or the ethically beautiful? Significantly, she is never heard to speak. In only one scene does she mouth words, and even then, no sound is heard. While the vast majority of her appearances are as background figure, as we watch the first exchange agreement made between host and guest, Morgan's profile is foregrounded in such a way that she is virtually invisible. In fact, she would most likely go undetected

Jason Durr (left) as Gawain and Malcolm Storry as the Green Knight in John Michael Phillips's 1991 telefilm *Gawain and the Green Knight*. (Still courtesy of Pearson Television Ltd.)

were it not for the strategic blinking of her eye, a movement that causes the viewer to refocus and to detect her framing (and controlling) presence. Morgan may be literally marginalized, but she has become the virtual frame of the tale, both the seen and the unseen hand guiding the action.

To appreciate the cinematic strategy underlying Morgan's portrayal, not as hag, but as shadow self, we must, like the poem, return to our starting point, the problem of the externals of realistic presence. The hag must capture our gaze, while the shadow self must avoid it. The former directs us to the exterior while the latter points to the interior. From the outset it has been clear that this is a film about the interior self. To understand the difference between these two selves, we might consider the film's treatment of the parallel figures of the Green Knight and Bercilak. Implicit in the shape-shifter is the crucial question of exactly whose shape is shifted or, in medieval terms, the difference between "substance" and "accident." Is Bercilak transformed into the Green Knight, or is the reverse the case? Which is the core personality, and which is the ephemeral alter ego? Unlike in the poem, the cinematic representation by its very nature points to a solution. In the film, the Green Knight is so visibly arresting that there is a strong tendency for the viewer's gaze to become fixated on his complex exterior. Because he remains such an exterior presence, there is, as there would be with the equally striking hag, little impetus to direct the viewer inward. In fact, there is no attempt in the film to plumb his psychology. Even whole, the Green Knight is, in effect, headless. On the other hand, Bercilak, as we have already noted, is depicted through both expression and camera angles as a character for whom there are outward signs of an inner life. He seems genuinely pained at Gawain's failures, and one even senses his attachment to his wife and a conflict over her role in Gawain's seduction. In the end, we witness the Green Knight's transformation back into Bercilak, affected in such a way that is less metamorphosis than the peeling away of his decorative green exterior.

Here, then, is the essence of all effective translations, whatever the idioms. This latest film version of *Sir Gawain* is, indeed, remarkably faithful to the details of the original due to the director's direct translation of medieval literary techniques into camera angles and edits, such as borrowing the counterpoint employed by the poet in the temptation/hunt scenes and using flashback rather than linear narrative as a means of recreating the poet's signature circularity. But the film is also much more. This most recent cinematic retelling of *Sir Gawain and the Green Knight* explores and interprets a number of the poem's untapped mysteries and as such represents a worthy complement to a number of recent articles that apply film theory to this most visual of medieval romances.

NOTES

1. For examples of Gawain's depiction in the chronicle tradition, see Geoffrey of Monmouth (241–42, 248, 253); Wace (57, 87–90, 106); and Layamon (213, 219, 221). For illustrations of the French Gawain, see Chrétien de Troyes, *The Story of the Grail* 92–93 and 100; and Busby 394–96.

2. David J. Williams, "Films," lists several films not included in this study.

3. *Idylls of the King*, "The Coming of Arthur," 1.11.

4. Lancelot, in fact, steps in to make the difficult shot on his first try, thereby winning a wager with Gawain. Lancelot's accomplishment thus serves to contrast his serious self-control, skill, and maturity with Gawain's lack of those qualities.

5. Hathaway later disavowed the film; as he stated to Scott Eyman (11), "I don't really care to talk about it.... I did it [*Valiant*] as a personal favor to Darryl [Zanuck]. I didn't particularly care one way or the other, and the picture looked it." The *Time* critique of this film (106) claims that Hathaway and the film's producer (Robert L. Jacks) have captured the "inner mood of stilted boyhood reverie" of the comic strip on which this movie is based and have produced an entertaining story ("all a small boy could ask for").

6. Schickel contends (58) that *Monty Python* "pats down the entire chivalric tradition for bloody and dangerous residual ideas," especially "the gory stupidity of ancient but still potent fancy." Furthermore, according to Schickel, the movie attacks the human penchant for violence.

In his initial review of *Python* (34), Canby claims that the film pokes fun at "the legend, courtly love, fidelity, bravery, costume movies, movie violence and ornithology." Similarly, Canby notes that *Python* parodies "the sound of knighthood," particularly in film treatments of the Arthurian legend ("clanking armor, horses' hoofs").

Later, in his "Film View" on "New Comedies" (2.15), Canby interprets the battle scene at the end of *Python* as "a how-to guide for filmmakers who want to shoot a spectacular battle scene without missing any cliches, the sort that have been made obligatory through the years by 'Ivanhoe,' 'El Cid' and dozens of other solemn epics."

7. Technically, in the Middle Ages, the hare was an emblem. For an explanation of this animal symbolism, see Ferguson 20. For a reference to the symbolic hare in medieval literature, see the Monk's portrait in Chaucer's *General Prologue to the Canterbury Tales*: "of huntyng for the hare/Was al his lust" (I.191–92), as well as the note for I.191 (Chaucer 807).

8. The charge is leveled explicitly against Guinevere as temptress, not against Lancelot.

9. Rooted in Weston's fertility myth theories, the Grail quest of *Excalibur* includes a knight who "must undergo an ordeal of loyalty and patriotism in order to redeem Arthur and the Land" (Shichtman 43).

10. For other studies of the poet's use of visual and spatial techniques, see Renoir ("Progressive Magnification" 245–53) as well as Stanbury ("Space" 476–89 and *Seeing* 96–115). For a recent appraisal of *Gawain* in light of contemporary film theory, see Lowe 67–97.

11. For negative critiques of *Sword*, see Newman 164–65, as well as Nash and Ross, who describe *Sword* as a "muddled adaptation of the classic legend of Sir Gawain and the Green Knight by a director [Stephen Weeks] who had already tried his hand at the tale in 1973." For similar views of *Sword*, see Kevin J. Harty 257 and Williams 389–90.

12. In his *Gawain and the Green Knight*, "an allegory of life where the goal is death" (Berry 7), Weeks attempted to recreate the romantic aura of a pre-Raphaelite painting. According to Weeks, however, once United Artists reshaped the movie into "Walt Disney, a Prince Valiant–type of kids' picture," the resultant film was completely different from what Weeks had envisioned.

13. According to one reviewer, at least, "admirers of the poem in its Tolkien edition will have to wait for a film which captures even a fraction of the original's cryptic complexity" (Baxter 169).

14. Kim Newman, a reviewer of *Sword*, contends (164), however, that this confusing film is not "an improvement over [Weeks's] earlier, purer film."

15. In this respect, Weeks's perspective reveals a misinterpretation of the original text. His cinematic alterations, however, may reflect his awareness of the evolution of medieval romance from an adventure involving knights-errant to a love quest.

16. For a comparison of Weeks's and Chrétien's modes of characterization, see Blanch and Wasserman, "Fear of Flyting."

17. "In order to broaden the appeal of the material, Weeks has opted for a kind of ghastly jokiness ... that turns the film into an unsatisfactory crossbreed of Robin Hood and Monty Python" (Newman 165).

18. This 90–minute film is available for purchase from Princeton-based Films for the Humanities and Sciences.

19. Williams notes that in its emphasis on the psychology the film "responds to something genuinely present in the poem" (392), although Williams clearly has reservations about the use of flashback and does not find the film to be as successful as we do. See 390–92.

20. The standard scholarly edition of *Gawain* is Tolkien-Gordon-Davis. Line and page references to the Borroff translation will appear in our text.

21. On the poem's complex use of perspective in regard to cinematic theory, see Lowe.

22. On the psychological coloring of this medieval romance, see the following sampling of criticism: Brewer, *Symbolic* 72–91; Freeman and Thormann 389–410; Rudnytsky 71–87; and DeRoo 305–24.

23. For brief comments on the film Morgan, see Blanch, Review 126.

WORKS CITED

Baxter, John. Review of *Gawain and the Green Knight*. *Monthly Film Bulletin* 40 (April 1973): 168–69.

Berry, Dave. "Stephen Weeks." *Film* 37 (May 1976): 6–7.

Blanch, Robert J. Review of the Thames Television *Gawain*. *Arthuriana* 8 (Fall 1998): 124–126.

Blanch, Robert J., and Julian N. Wasserman. "Fear of Flyting: The Absence of Internal Tension in *Sword of the Valiant* and *First Knight*." *Arthuriana* 10 (Winter 2000): 15–32.

Borroff, Marie, trans. *Sir Gawain and the Green Knight: A New Verse Translation*. New York: Norton, 1967.

Brewer, Derek. *Symbolic Stories*. Cambridge, Eng.: D. S. Brewer, 1980.

Busby, Keith. *Gauvain in Old French Literature*. Amsterdam: Rodopi, 1980.

_____. "Gawain," entry in Norris J. Lacy, ed. *The New Arthurian Encyclopedia*. New York: Garland Publishing, 1996.

Byron, Stuart, and Elisabeth Weis, eds. *The National Society of Film Critics on Movie Comedy*. New York: Grossman, 1977.

Canby, Vincent. "Film View: New Comedies —

Serious, Farcical, Slapstick." *New York Times* 1 June 1975: 2. 15.

———. Review of *Monty Python and the Holy Grail*. *New York Times* 28 April 1975: 34.

Chaucer, Geoffrey. *The Riverside Chaucer*. Ed. Larry D. Benson and others. 3rd ed. Boston: Houghton Mifflin, 1987.

Chrétien de Troyes. *The Story of the Grail [Perceval]*. Trans. Robert White Linker. 2nd ed. Chapel Hill: University of North Carolina Press, 1960.

———. *Ywain: The Knight of the Lion*. Trans. Robert W. Ackerman and Frederick W. Locke. New York: Ungar, 1957.

Ciment, Michel. "Deux Entretiens avec John Boorman." *Positif* 242 (May 1981): 18–31.

———. *John Boorman*. Trans. Gilbert Adair. London: Faber, 1986.

DeRoo, Harvey. "Undressing Lady Bertilak: Guilt and Denial in *Sir Gawain and the Green Knight*." *Chaucer Review* 27 (1993): 305–24.

Eyman, Scott. "'… I Made Movies …'" *Take One* 5 (February 1976): 6–12.

Ferguson, George. *Signs and Symbols in Christian Art*. New York: Oxford University Press, 1966.

Freeman, Adam, and Janet Thormann. "*Sir Gawain and the Green Knight*: An Anatomy of Chastity." *American Imago* 45 (1988): 389–410.

Geoffrey of Monmouth. *The History of the Kings of Britain*. Trans. Lewis Thorpe. Harmondsworth: Penguin, 1966.

Hahn, Thomas, ed. *Sir Gawain: Eleven Romances and Tales*. Kalamazoo, Mich.: Medieval Institute Publications, 1995.

Harty, Kevin J. *The Reel Middle Ages, American, Western and Eastern European, Middle Eastern and Asian Films About Medieval Europe*. Jefferson, NC: McFarland, 1999.

Kennedy, Harlan. "The World of King Arthur According to John Boorman." *American Film* 6 (March 1981): 30–37.

Krishna, Valerie, trans. *The Alliterative Morte Arthure: A New Verse Translation*. Lanham, Md.: University Press of America, 1983.

Lowe, Jeremy. "The Cinematic Consciousness of *Sir Gawain and the Green Knight*." *Exemplaria* 13 (2001): 67–97.

Malory, Sir Thomas. *Le Morte d'Arthur: The Winchester Manuscript*. Ed. Helen Cooper. New York: Oxford University Press, 1998.

Nash, Jay Robert, and Stanley Ralph Ross. *The Motion Picture Guide, W–Z, 1927–1984*. Chicago: Cinebooks, 1987.

Newman, Kim. Review of *Sword of the Valiant*. *Monthly Film Bulletin* 52 (May 1985): 164–65.

Renoir, Alain. "Descriptive Technique in *Sir Gawain and the Green Knight*." *Orbis Litterarum* 13 (1958): 126–32.

———. "The Progressive Magnification: An Instance of Psychological Description in *Sir Gawain and the Green Knight*." *Moderna Språk* 54 (1960): 245–53.

Review of *Prince Valiant*. *Time* 63 (12 April 1954): 106.

Rudnytsky, Peter L. "'Where th' offense is': Oedipal Temptation in *Gawain*." In Henk Hillenaar and Walter Schönau, eds. *Fathers and Mothers in Literature*. Amsterdam: Rodopi, 1994.

Schickel, Richard. "Legendary Lunacy." *Time* 105 (26 May 1975): 58–59.

Shichtman, Martin B. "Hollywood's New Weston: The Grail Myth in Francis Ford Coppola's *Apocalypse Now* and John Boorman's *Excalibur*." *Post Script* 4 (Autumn 1984): 35–48.

Stanbury, Sarah. *Seeing the Gawain Poet: Description and the Act of Perception*. Philadelphia: University of Pennsylvania Press, 1991.

———. "Space and Visual Hermeneutics in the *Gawain*-Poet." *Chaucer Review* 21 (1987): 476–89.

Tennyson, Alfred, Lord. *Idylls of the King*. Ed. J. M. Gray. New Haven: J. M. Dent, 1983.

Tolkien, J. R. R., and E. V. Gordon, eds. *Sir Gawain and the Green Knight*. 2nd ed. Rev. Norman Davis. Oxford: Clarendon, 1967.

Wace and Layamon. *Arthurian Chronicles*. Trans. Eugene Mason. New York: Dutton, 1962.

Weston, Jessie L. *From Ritual to Romance*. 1920. Garden City, N.Y.: Doubleday, 1957.

White, T. H. *The Once and Future King*. New York: Putnam, 1958.

Williams, David J. "Sir Gawain in Films." In *A Companion to the Gawain-Poet*. Eds. Derek Brewer and Jonathan Gibson. Cambridge, Eng.: D. S. Brewer, 1997.

17

Will the "Reel" Mordred Please Stand Up? Strategies for Representing Mordred in American and British Arthurian Film

MICHAEL A. TORREGROSSA

Unlike the other members of King Arthur's court, Mordred appears in only a handful of the seemingly infinite number of adaptations of the Arthurian legend for film and television. In these adaptations, filmmakers have concentrated on Mordred's adversarial nature and his role as the destroyer of the Arthurian world despite the rich legendary background of his character.[1] While he remains a negative figure in all film adaptations of the Arthurian legend, most films that feature Mordred use various means to redefine his relationship to Arthur without any hint of the incest or parricide found in much of medieval Arthurian literature. Filmmakers either avoid Arthur's possible incest and feature Mordred as the primary villain of the film, or they accept the issue of incest to provide an opportunity for the films' female antagonists to exact their revenge on others.

Although the films discussed in this essay span a period of fifty years and were produced both in the United States and in Great Britain, the majority suggest the repeated nods of filmmakers in general to what today we would call "family values," especially as illustrated initially in the United States by the restrictions of the Hays Code in Hollywood during the 1930s.[2] These films do not always depict Mordred as Arthur's son, and they appear to reflect filmmakers' concerns for family values by ignoring Mordred's incestuous birth and presenting him in a variety of roles, often unrelated to the king whose throne he covets. The earliest representations of Mordred in film give further evidence of the influence of the code in the decision to pit Mordred against the unrelated Lancelot, thus preventing conflict with Arthur. In making such changes to the traditional treatment of Mordred, these films twist the character to fit each filmmaker's conception of Mordred and his role in the narrative.

As Mordred's cinematic character evolves, it becomes confusing to trace his presence in Arthurian film, since filmmakers continue to revise his relationship to Arthur in their various attempts to avoid any display of father-son conflict. In several Arthurian films, the character of Mordred disappears entirely and is replaced by another character, as in Henry Hathaway's *Prince Valiant* (1954), where Arthur's treacherous cousin Brack assumes Mordred's role and allies with the Vikings against the king. A similar approach occurs in George Romero's *Knightriders* (1981), a film that conflates the roles of both Mordred and Morgan Le Fay into a man named Morgan, who bears no familial relation to Billy, the Arthur of the film, but is nonetheless responsible for the initial dissolution of the community of neo-knights. However, unlike Mordred, Romero's Morgan becomes Billy's legitimate successor at the conclusion.

Still other films omit Mordred and substitute one of Arthur's trusted or former knights as his ultimate betrayer. This particular strategy first appears in Nathan Juran's *The Siege of the Saxons* (1963), where Edmund of Cornwall kills Arthur and subsequently tries to take first the king's throne and then his daughter, rather than his queen as in the medieval accounts of Mordred.[3] And, although the Hays Code was in 1968 replaced by the Motion Picture Association of America's current ratings system, several American filmmakers from the 1990s illustrate the continued influence in their films of the ideals embodied by the earlier code by also choosing to replace Mordred. Partially a remake of Mel Damski's 1989 telemovie *A Connecticut Yankee in King Arthur's Court*, Michael Gottlieb's *A Kid in King Arthur's Court* (1995) follows the practice established by *The Siege of the Saxons* and features one of Arthur's most trusted and seemingly loyal knights as the villain of the film. A similar pattern ensues in Jeff Burr's *Johnny Mysto, Boy Wizard* (1996), where the usurper is both a knight and would-be sorcerer. In contrast to these films, the villain of both Jerry Zucker's *First Knight* (1995)[4] and Frederick Du Chau's *Quest for Camelot* (1998) is a former knight of the Round Table, who rebels because his desire for power does not fit into Arthur's vision for Camelot.

Although some filmmakers distance themselves from the less desirable aspects of the medieval representation of Mordred by replacing him with other characters, the majority of Arthurian filmmakers do include Mordred but limit his appearances in their films. Several of these films ignore Mordred's kinship to Arthur entirely and focus instead on his role as villain opposed to the king and his various knights. For example, no blood relationship to Arthur is either stated or implied in Spencer Bennet's fifteen-part serial *The Adventures of Sir Galahad* (1950), apparently the first film to feature Mordred (here Modred) as a character. This film borrows loosely from the medieval tradition and presents Modred as allied with the Saxons, who are Arthur's traditional enemies in such early Arthurian works as the ninth-century *Historia Brittonum* and Geoffrey of Monmouth's *Historia Regum Britanniae*, to kidnap Guinevere. Modred's kidnapping of the queen in this serial recalls his attraction to her in the medieval romances, yet his taking of Guinevere also draws upon another story in medieval Arthurian literature, Guinevere's abduction by King Melwas or Meleagant as featured in Caradoc of Llancarfan's *Vita Gildae* (c. 1130), Chrétien de Troyes's *Le Chevalier de la charrete* (c. 1174–79), and most recently in Jerry Zucker's film, *First Knight*. The final episode of the series depicts Arthur and Modred in combat, where Arthur kills the treacherous knight, but, in contrast to the usual account of their battle, Arthur survives this confrontation.[5]

Mordred's appearance in Richard Thorpe's *Knights of the Round Table* (1953) offers perhaps the most confused account of his relationship with Arthur. Throughout the film, he is in league with Morgan Le Fay, Arthur's half-sister, in an alliance that

Elizabeth Sklar observes has never before been seen in Arthurian literature or film (30–31). In contrast to films that follow, *Knights of the Round Table* is also unique in providing a true motivation for Morgan's desire for the throne. Thorpe deviates from the usual account of her parentage and presents Morgan as Uther Pendragon's daughter, rather than Gorlois', making her the only legitimate heir, since Arthur remains Uther's illegitimate son. Thorpe's Mordred (here also Modred) is an adult about the same age as Arthur, and he appears to be related to Arthur only through Morgan.[6] Modred makes no claim of his own to the throne although he confronts Arthur hoping to secure Morgan's claims.

Unlike Bennet's *The Adventures of Sir Galahad*, Thorpe does not offer any hint of father-son conflict between Arthur and Modred in *Knights of the Round Table*, and he is the first director to feature a confrontation between Lancelot and Modred to replace the more traditional final battle scene between Arthur and Mordred, which Thorpe includes in the narrative of the film but presents off screen. Arthur does not survive long after his battle with Modred, and he orders Lancelot to seek out Modred and destroy him, a request suggestive of the accounts of Lancelot's attacks on Mordred's sons in the Vulgate and post–Vulgate *Le Mort le roi Artu*.

Should anyone think these confused approaches to Mordred were merely a phenomenon of the 1950s, director Russ Mayberry's adaptation of Mark Twain's *A Connecticut Yankee in King Arthur's Court* for Walt Disney Studios as *The Unidentified Flying Oddball* (1979) features a Mordred,

James Mason (left) as Sir Brack and Barry Jones as King Luke in Henry Hathaway's 1954 film *Prince Valiant*.

who like his predecessor in *The Adventures of Sir Galahad*, again appears to bear no kinship at all to Arthur. Here, Mordred replaces Twain's Sagremor as the villain of the film, and he becomes the primary adversary of NASA scientist Tom Trimble and the android HERMES, both filling in for the missing Connecticut Yankee. However, perhaps the strangest rewriting of the legend of Mordred occurs in two recent films. Paul Hunt's *October 32nd* (1992) suggests medieval accounts of Mordred's sons and depicts an older Mordred instructing his adult son Pendragon on how to recover the Sword of Power from Merlin's daughter. Although Pendragon's subsequent killing of Mordred might allude to the traditional depiction of Mordred killing Arthur, the film avoids any reference to Arthur or to the possibility that either Mordred or Pendragon might be related to him. Most recently, Paul Matthews's *Merlin: The Return* (2000) revisits the trend to change the characterization of Mordred by depicting him as sorcerer and the rival of Merlin.[7] Nonetheless this film concludes, much like Bennet's *The Adventures of Sir Galahad*, with Arthur as the survivor of his battle with Mordred.[8]

Although it was not until the 1980s that Mordred would appear as both Arthur's son and nephew, a number of films cast him in one or the other of these roles. Greg Garcia's *Camelot* (1997), originally televised as part of Sony's syndicated series *Enchanted Tales*, recalls Victorian and early twentieth-century versions of the Arthurian legend. This short, animated film is anomalous in treating Mordred as the *legitimate* son of Arthur and his first wife, Morgause of Avalon, and, in a complete reversal of the traditional representation of his character, Garcia's Mordred serves as the voice of legitimacy and morality in the film. Despite this radical alteration in his relationship to Arthur, Mordred still brings about the fall of Camelot, when his insistence that the king punish Lancelot and Guinevere for their adultery leads to war between Arthur and Lancelot. Like many of films discussed here, Garcia's *Camelot* also avoids any suggestion of familial conflict, when, reminiscent of Geoffrey of Monmouth's account of the death of Mordred, Arthur falls in the chaos caused as Mordred leads the forces of Camelot against Lancelot.

Unlike Garcia's *Camelot*, most films that present Mordred as Arthur's son depict him as an illegitimate offspring, although one produced without any hint of the incest found in Arthurian romance or in the minority of films from the late twentieth century. The earlier of these films are also important for their heightened focus on Mordred's hostility towards Lancelot (already noted in *Knights of the Round Table* and Garcia's *Camelot*), which becomes an important tradition in Arthurian film as a method of further distancing Arthur and Mordred from both the king's incest and Mordred's patricide.

The next major confrontation between Mordred (again Modred) and Lancelot appears in the British film *The Sword of Lancelot* (1963) directed by Cornel Wilde. Although film critics have described *The Sword of Lancelot* as groundbreaking for its presentation of the adultery between Lancelot and Guinevere, Wilde too avoids the incest theme. He offers instead an extremely melodramatic Modred as Arthur's illegitimate son, who tells his father of the love between Lancelot and Guinevere hoping to sustain his own tenuous claim to the throne.

Wilde also follows the example set by *Knights of the Round Table* in treating the battle between Arthur and Modred completely off screen. In *The Sword of Lancelot*, Lancelot and Modred face each other sometime after Arthur's death, when Gawain begs Lancelot to return and avenge the king. The ensuing battle is reminiscent of Lancelot's confrontations with Mordred's sons in *Le Mort le roi Artu*, but it also recalls an aspect of Geoffrey of Monmouth's account of the battle between Arthur and Mordred at Camblan, when Modred and Lancelot make speeches to inspire their respective armies. Geoffrey's Mordred encourages his troops by promising them the spoils of war, just as Wilde's Modred urges his men on with the promise of "land and gold and plunder." The Arthur of Geoffrey's narrative inspires his own troops by invoking their honor and bravery, while, in a like manner, Lancelot's words in *The Sword of Lancelot* express his hopes of saving England "from the sword of the tyrant and the ax of the barbarian. From rape and pillage. From injustice and fear."

In contrast to *The Sword of Lancelot*, director Joshua Logan's 1967 film adaptation of the Alan Jay Lerner and Frederick Loewe musical *Camelot* (1960), itself based on T. H. White's *The Once and Future King* (1958), features a more intriguing presentation of Mordred as Arthur's illegitimate son. Logan's Mordred, like the character of the play, appears as the son of Arthur and Queen Morgause of Orkney, here the wife of King Claudius, but, in contrast to the traditional depiction of Morgause, neither she nor her sister, Morgan Le Fay, are blood related to Arthur in either Logan's film or in the original dramatic version of *Camelot*.[9]

Despite the tradition of Mordred as a knight, his primary role in Logan's film is not as a fighter, and, unlike other filmmakers, Logan ignores the cinematic tradition of presenting Mordred in conflict with Lancelot with the exception of a brief confrontation when Mordred catches Lancelot and Guinevere together in the queen's chambers. Mordred does not even fight physically against his father in the film, yet Arthur's words at the conclusion of the film suggest his betrayal by Mordred and the promise of war between father and son in the future.

Complementing the presentation of Arthur in White, Logan's Mordred is a thinker like his father, but, rather than building Camelot, Mordred wants to bring about its destruction. From his initial appearance in Act II of the film, he plots to cause strife between Arthur and Lancelot first by providing proof of Lancelot's adultery with Guinevere and later by goading Arthur into fighting Lancelot in the battle scene that opens and closes the film.

Although family values have continued to remain an influence in Arthurian film, select films of the late twentieth century initiated a new approach to depicting Mordred on film. In films like John Boorman's *Excalibur* (1981), Jud Taylor's *Guinevere* (1994), and Steve Barron's *Merlin* (1998), female characters control the development of Mordred, especially by encouraging his hostility towards Arthur. The pre-

David Hemmings as Mordred in Joshua Logan's 1967 film *Camelot*. (Still courtesy of the British Film Institute.)

sentation of Mordred in these films becomes a means of empowering the female antagonist of each film, since these women set out to construct Mordred as their tool to bring about the destruction of Camelot and the hopes that Arthur might bring peace to a troubled land.

In only a small number of recent films, such as these and Uli Edel's *The Mists of Avalon* (2001), have filmmakers freed themselves from (to borrow from the title of a pioneering article by Norris J. Lacy) the "tyranny of tradition" and presented a more conventional treatment of Mordred's parentage. Beginning with Boorman's R-rated *Excalibur*, filmmakers have discovered that they can present a version of the Arthurian legend designed for a mature audience, and, by accepting Mordred's role as

Arthur's incestuous son, Boorman, Taylor, Barron, and Edel choose to show Arthur's act of incest with his half-sister in graphic detail. *Excalibur* and *Merlin* also deviate from earlier presentations of Mordred in film, since they do not need to develop a strategy for avoiding discord between father and son, such as placing Mordred against Lancelot, because a confrontation between Arthur and Mordred is inevitable given the circumstances of Mordred's conception.

The four films that treat Arthur's incest also transform Mordred's relationship to his father, as they attempt to distance Mordred from his actions in betraying Arthur because his motivations in acting against the king in these films are never his own. Instead, Mordred's hatred towards his father has been instilled in him by his mother, Morgan Le Fay, as in *Excalibur* and *Merlin*; Queen Mab as is the case for *Merlin*; or Morgause as presented in *The Mists of Avalon*. Because of their focus on Merlin's role in Arthur's conception and his continued presence in maintaining Camelot, Boorman, Taylor, and Barron initiate a new version of the Mordred story, one where sibling rivalry leads to the destruction of Camelot and Mordred's role is subsumed as his story becomes just a small part in the larger narrative of the life of Merlin and the mage's struggles with either Morgan Le Fay or Mab. In contrast to these films, *The Mists of Avalon* limits Merlin's role in the narrative, yet it continues to employ the motif of sibling rivalry but moves up one level in Arthur's family tree, when the king's maternal aunt, Morgause, uses Mordred to thwart the plans of her sister Viviane rather than those of Merlin as in the three other films.[10]

Excalibur is the first film to employ Mordred as a tool, and this film highlights the construction of Mordred as the instrument through which his mother, Morgana, seeks to get revenge on Merlin for his role in the conception of her half-brother, Arthur, Merlin's magic having made possible Uther Pendragon's rape of Morgana's mother. Similar to medieval accounts of Merlin's betrayal by the Lady of the Lake, Morgana here seduces Merlin, both the literal and figurative architect of Camelot, and steals from him the Charm of Making, which she uses to frustrate Merlin's plans for Arthur by conceiving Mordred in a scene that essentially reenacts Uther's conception of Arthur upon her mother.

Unlike earlier Arthurian films, where Mordred could not act against his father until their battle nearer the conclusion of the narrative, Boorman's Mordred begins the process of destroying Camelot from the moment he appears on screen as a wailing infant, when, at the instant of Mordred's birth, a bolt of lightning strikes Arthur and, as a result, the land is laid to waste. Raised solely by Morgana, Mordred is filled with hatred for his father, and he and Morgana have already tortured and killed many of Arthur's best knights by the time Mordred grows into manhood.

At last revitalized by the Grail, Arthur and his remaining knights ride out to confront Mordred in battle, but the final victory in *Excalibur* fittingly belongs to Merlin rather than Arthur. On the eve of the battle against Mordred, Arthur, though unconscious, summons Merlin, who returns in spirit form to confront Morgana and reclaim the Charm of Making. Without her magic, Morgana withers into an old hag, whom Mordred kills not realizing that she is his mother. With Morgana's death, Mordred loses his invulnerability, symbolized earlier in the film by her sprinkling of gold dust onto his armor, while Morgana's summoning of the Dragon with the Charm of Making has produced a thick fog, which allows Arthur to come upon Mordred's forces unaware and hide the fact that Mordred's army greatly outnumbers his own.

The theme of revenge also motivates the character of Morgan Le Fay in Taylor's telemovie *Guinevere*, and, like her predecessor in *Excalibur*, Morgan also takes her revenge on Uther and Merlin by seducing Arthur and becoming pregnant with his child. To ensure that their offspring will succeed Arthur as king, Morgan also poisons Guinevere and mistakenly believes that the young queen has miscarried. Unlike other films that present Arthur's incest, Taylor's *Guinevere* vividly presents Arthur's horror in the act. However, Arthur manages to rise above the circumstances that have, in his own words, "defiled" his kingship and left his queen barren. Instead of seeking the death of Morgan's child as in the *Suite du Merlin* or Malory's *Le Morte d'Arthur*, Taylor's Arthur vows that "This island will be my children." Although he has grown old and feeble, Merlin also achieves a victory over Morgan by secreting the child born of Guinevere and Arthur's love to safety on the isle of Anglesey, where she will wait, much like folklore says of Arthur, until Britain has need of her.

More recently, Barron's *Merlin* employs Morgan Le Fay's hatred for her half-brother in reshaping the traditional portrayal of Mordred. However, the conception of Mordred and his use against Arthur in this telemovie is in fact part of a carefully constructed scheme whereby the chthonic deity Mab hopes to thwart Merlin for his refusal to be her champion and bring the people of Britain back to the old pagan religion of the island. Mab attempts to replace Merlin with Mordred, and she uses her magic to show him that she has tricked Arthur into committing incest with his half-sister. Merlin realizes that, in her creation of Mordred, Mab has sown the seed that will tear down all Merlin has built to oppose her schemes. Following Mordred's birth, "Auntie Mab" assists Morgan in raising the child while nurturing the hatred for Arthur he inherits from his mother.

In *Merlin*, as in some earlier films, the confrontation between Arthur and Mordred is brought about by Arthur's unwillingness to punish Lancelot and Guinevere for their indiscretions, while he was away for many years seeking the Holy Grail. Throughout the film, Barron implies that Mordred is only a pawn in Mab's contest with Merlin, and this idea is supported by her symbiotic connection to the young man during his final confrontation with Arthur. As in medieval accounts of their battle, both father and son perish, but, unlike most film versions of the event, Barron adds an unexpected twist to the story. Following this battle, Mab appears and grieves at Mordred's death. As her champion dies, Mab grows weaker, enabling Merlin to defeat her later in the film, in a battle that takes the place of Lancelot's continued struggles with Mordred following the death of Arthur in films such as *Knights of the Round Table* and *The Sword of Lancelot*.

Mordred makes his most recent appearance as Arthur's illegitimate son in the mini-series *The Mists of Avalon* based on the 1982 feminist, neo-pagan retelling of the legend by the late Marion Zimmer Bradley. Edel's *The Mists of Avalon* continues the late twentieth-century approach to presenting Mordred on film, and he follows Bradley's version of Mordred's conception, in which Viviane, the Lady of the Lake of Avalon, uses her niece, Morgaine, and her nephew, Arthur, to produce Mordred. As the offspring of two heirs of the royal line of Avalon, Viviane hopes to employ Mordred as the tool through which she might ensure Arthur's unification of Britain. However, Morgaine rebels against Viviane and seeks support from her aunt Morgause, who has her own plans for Mordred once she learns his parentage.

Near the end of the film, Viviane finally sends Mordred as her champion to Camelot, where Mordred and Morgause set about to weaken Arthur's reign. Unlike the three other films that present Mordred as the incestuous son of Arthur and his half-sister, Edel's Mordred briefly comes into conflict with Lancelot at Camelot, but Edel does not suggest any malice in Mordred's actions against Lancelot nor does Mordred actually fight against him. As in many earlier films, Edel's Arthur is both unable and unwilling to pursue Lancelot and Guinevere, and the king uncharacteristically hands control of the kingdom over to his son. Under Mordred's direction, Camelot becomes, as Viviane soon discovers, a perversion of Avalon. *The Mists of Avalon* next features a verbal battle between Viviane and her sister, which replaces the sorceress confrontation between Merlin and the female antagonist of *Excalibur* or *Merlin*. Viviane denounces Morgause, who is killed when Viviane deflects her blade as Morgause lunges towards her.

Although Morgause is dead, she continues to influence Mordred and the fate of Britain. Mordred attacks Viviane and kills her, and he then leaves Camelot eventually to join the advancing Saxon invasion against his father. Despite Mordred's death at Arthur's hand, the ending of Edel's *The Mists of Avalon* suggests that the villains are in fact the victors. Following the death of the Merlin earlier in the film and now of Viviane, Avalon fades forever into the mists, and, as in Barron's *Merlin*, Arthur's passing brings no hope for the future.[11]

This essay has focused thus far on the development of two competing traditions for representing Mordred in Arthurian film: most films avoid or feign ignorance of Arthur's incest, while only a few accept and subsequently embrace this act. These two trends have in general remained mutually exclusive. However, several films borrow freely from the various options provided by these two strategies for presenting Mordred. Clive Donner's *Arthur the King* (1983), William Kowalchuk's *Camelot: The Legend* (1998) and Damski's *A Connecticut Yankee* are indebted to Boorman's presentation of Morgana and Mordred in *Excalibur* in their use of Mordred as a tool through which

Morgan Le Fay hopes to become the power behind the throne. Yet, unlike *Excalibur*, none of these films treats Arthur's incest, and instead all three filmmakers prefer the earlier tradition of ignoring this relationship. Donner and Kowalchuk present Mordred as Arthur's illegitimate son as in Logan's *Camelot* or Wilde's *The Sword of Lancelot*, while Damski opts for the rarest alternative for representing Mordred on film and depicts him simply as Arthur's nephew.

The Mordred of Donner's *Arthur the King* is weak-willed and easily controlled by his aunt Morgan Le Fay, who incites him to use the growing love between Lancelot and Guinevere as "a dagger" to tear Arthur's "marriage, his Round Table, and his precious kingdom apart." As in Wilde's *The Sword of Lancelot* and Logan's *Camelot*, Donner's Mordred informs Arthur of the queen's infidelity, but the king refuses to listen to what he perceives as Mordred's lies. Meanwhile, Mordred and Agravain, who here makes a rare appearance in Arthurian film, have set a trap for Lancelot and Guinevere. Mordred's visit with his father ends tragically, when Mordred stabs him in the back as they embrace after Arthur forgives Mordred for his accusation against the queen. Mordred then rushes from the room with Excalibur and gleefully proclaims himself king. His first act is to order Agravain to kill Lancelot, for whom he has no further use, but, reminiscent of medieval accounts of Mordred's treachery, he tells Agravain to save Guinevere so she might become his queen.

The two battles that conclude *Arthur the King* also reflect the competing traditions of presenting Mordred in Arthurian film. Throughout the film, Donner follows Boorman's invention of an ongoing battle between Merlin and Morgan Le Fay, and this struggle between the two mages reaches its climax at the end of the film, when, as in *Excalibur*, Merlin reappears in spirit form to destroy Morgan. In addition, *Arthur the*

Will the "Reel" Mordred Please Stand Up? 207

Tom Savini as Morgan in George Romero's 1981 film *Knightriders*.

King partially prefigures Barron's *Merlin* in setting the life of Merlin as the frame through which Donner can tell various episodes from the Arthurian legend. Despite its ties to more recent films, Donner's film also displays a continuity with earlier Arthurian films, such as *Knights of the Round Table* and *Sword of Lancelot*, in its depiction of Lancelot killing Mordred and then maintaining Arthur's legacy by seeking out the "greater good" as Merlin instructs him.

Although an animated comedy, the direct to video *Camelot: The Legend* suggests adult themes, such as those present in *Excalibur*. This film also preserves the hostility between Merlin and Morgan present in both *Excalibur* and *Arthur the King*, since an obese Morgan Le Fay recounts how she used witchcraft to trick the unrelated Arthur into fathering a son. Kowalchuk's Mordred follows the usual pattern for the character on film, as he tries various means to obtain power. Like *Arthur the King*, *Camelot: The Legend* is similar to a number of earlier film treatments of the Arthurian legend, and Kowalchuk pits Mordred in several confrontations with Lancelot, who becomes his enemy after Mordred fails to push Lancelot and Guinevere into falling in love. *Camelot: The Legend* also offers an intriguing twist to Mordred's relationship to Lancelot, when he dons Lancelot's armor to rescue Guinevere following her nontraditional *mock* trial for treason.

In Damski's 1989 made-for-television adaptation of Twain's *Connecticut Yankee*, Mordred again fills the role usually ascribed to Sagremor. Like Kowalchuk and Donner's films, Damski's *A Connecticut Yankee in King Arthur's Court* is transitional in its treatment of Mordred. True to earlier films, Mordred here covets both Arthur's power and his throne, and, despite the presentation of Mordred as Arthur's nephew rather than his son, *A Connecticut Yankee* always places Mordred in direct physical conflict with Lancelot.

As in *Knights of the Round Table* and *The Sword of Lancelot*, it is Lancelot, rather than Arthur, who manages to defeat the traitorous Mordred at the conclusion of the film. However, this film is also similar to those of the late twentieth century that depict Arthur's incest, and like these contemporary films, Mordred's actions against the king in *Connecticut Yankee* are inspired by sibling rivalry in his mother's hatred for her brother, whom she claims has forced her to live in "squalor all these years." In lamenting her fate, Morgan (here Morgana de la Fay) confesses to her imprisoned brother, "My rightful castle should never have been here! My castle should always have been ... Camelot. Soon it will be. My loving son will be on the throne, and you will be dead." Despite Morgana's bravura, Lancelot, of course, saves the day for Arthur and defeats Mordred.

Lancelot's actions in *Connecticut Yankee*, like his presence in *Arthur the King* and *Camelot: The Legend*, thus reestablish the earlier tradition of Mordred on film. The presence of Lancelot in these three films also reinforces the ultimate futility of Morgan Le Fay's plans in late twentieth-century Arthurian films to create a new approach for constructing Mordred, since, as illustrated throughout this essay, all films, which feature Mordred as a character, always balance the scales between good and evil. Returning again to the roots of film censorship, this premise recalls the proscriptions of the Hays Code and its preference for family values in requiring that all films show that "*evil is wrong* and *good is right*" (Vizzard 376). Whether through the actions of Lancelot, Merlin, the various Knights of the Round Table or even Arthur himself, good always triumphs in the "reel" world of Arthurian film.

NOTES

I wish to thank both Professor Kevin J. Harty and Professor Meradith T. McMunn for their continued interest in my research and for their suggestions in revising this essay for publication. I am also grateful to both Professor Harty and Bert Olton for sharing their work on Arthurian film and television. In addition, I thank two of my fellow graduate students at the University of Connecticut: G. William Eggers, for his suggestions during the earliest stages of writing this essay, and Richard Pickering, for providing me with a copy of the Hays Code. Finally, I thank my parents for sitting through repeated viewings of the various films under discussion here and for not complaining *too* much.

1. The figure of Mordred first appears in Arthurian literature in Geoffrey of Monmouth's *Historia Regum Britanniae* (*c.* 1136–38), where he features as Arthur's nephew and as the king's betrayer when he usurps Arthur's crown and attempts to take his wife. The next major development in the legend of Mordred occurs in the French Vulgate (*c.* 1215–40) and post–Vulgate (*c.* 1230–40) cycles of Arthurian romance, but English audiences are most familiar with Thomas Malory's retelling of this material in *Le Morte d'Arthur* (*c.* 1469–70; published 1485). Mordred has a number of adventures in medieval romance, where he appears as Arthur's illegitimate son and nephew, whom Arthur unwittingly sires upon his own half-sister. As in Geoffrey's work, the Mordred of the Arthurian romances also betrays the king, but unlike the earlier narrative, Arthur and Mordred face each other in battle at the conclusion of the cycle romances. For additional information on Mordred, see my on-line bibliography, "The Dark Knight of the Round Table."

2. My application of censorship codes to the discussion of Mordred on film is inspired in part by Sandra Gorgievski's brief discussion of the influence of these codes on *Knights of the Round Table* (157). Similar to my own discussion of Mordred, Jacqueline de Weever touches upon the various approaches to Mordred and to Arthur's incest in *Knights of the Round Table, Camelot, Knightriders* and *Excalibur*, but she does not specifically invoke the influence of censorship codes upon these films.

3. I base all my information on *The Siege of the Saxons* on the plot synopses provided both by Harty and by Jay Robert Nash and Stanley Ralph Ross (Harty 19; Nash and Ross 2912).

4. Despite the absence of traditional characters such as Merlin and Mordred in *First Knight*, Jacqueline Jenkins' reading of the film nevertheless places it into the tradition of presenting Mordred in film. Jenkins suggests that Meleagant (here Malagant) might be seen as Arthur's evil son in conflict with his good son, Lancelot (200, 202–03). As will become apparent as my own discussion

continues, *First Knight* does indeed follow the pattern of earlier Mordred films, such as *Knights of the Round Table* and *The Sword of Lancelot* in pitting Lancelot against Malagant, who like Mordred actively seeks to destroy Arthur and take over Camelot. In addition, the serial *The Adventures of Sir Galahad* also conflates Mordred and Meleagant as the abductor of Guinevere.

5. I base my information on *The Adventures of Sir Galahad* on the detailed plot summary provided by Olton (3–11).

6. Although Thorpe does not specify the exact nature of Morgan's relationship to Mordred in *Knights of the Round Table*, Sklar suggests that Morgan might also be Mordred's half-sister, in addition to Arthur's (31). In contrast to this theory, both Harty and Rebecca A. and Samuel J. Umland claim that Morgan is Mordred's wife (Harty 16; Umland and Umland 77).

7. The presentation of Mordred as a sorcerer here has some precedence in the world of Arthurian comic books, though not in film. The Marvel Comics' universe includes a mage named Modred the Mystic, who, although unrelated to the similarly named Mordred of Arthurian literature, has nonetheless repeatedly battled against Merlin and his modern-day champions. For further details on Modred the Mystic, see both my "*Camelot 3000* and Beyond" and Alan Stewart's *Camelot in Four Colors*.

8. I base all my information on *Merlin: The Return* on that provided both on the official web site of the film and in the review by Stella Bruzzi.

9. Although a familial relationship is specified in T. H. White's *The Once and Future King*, it is not present in either the dramatic or film version of *Camelot* (Lerner and Loewe II.i–v). Therefore, the Umlands are incorrect in their claim that *Camelot* treats the issue of incest to the same degree as Boorman's *Excalibur*, while Alice Grellner appears to have been influenced by the novel in her assertion that Arthur and Morgause are siblings (Umland and Umland 3, 92; Grellner 77).

10. Although developed independently, my theories on the role of Morgan, Mab, and Morgause in *Excalibur*, *Guinevere*, *Merlin*, and *Mists of Avalon* and their relationship to the men of these films are similar to those presented by both de Weever and Sklar. Sklar appears to have been the first to suggest that film treatments of Morgan often shift "the burden of guilt for Camelot's collapse from the masculine to the feminine, from Mordred to Morgan" (31). In addition, she also treats Morgan's "adversarial relationship" to Merlin, a motif that both de Weever and Sara Boyle comment on in their discussions of *Excalibur*.

11. The hopelessness at the end of Arthur's reign in the film version of *The Mists of Avalon* is in direct conflict with Bradley's novel, where Morgaine tells Arthur: "*You did not fail, my brother, my love, my child. You held this land in peace for many years, so that the Saxons did not destroy it. You held back the darkness for a whole generation, until they were civilized men, with learning and music and faith in God, who will fight to save something of the beauty of the times that are past*" (868).

WORKS CITED
(All Internet links were current as of August 2001)

Boyle, Sarah. "From Victim to Avenger: The Women in John Boorman's *Excalibur*." *Avalon to Camelot* 1 (Summer 1984): 42–43.

Bradley, Marion Zimmer. *The Mists of Avalon*. 1982. New York: Ballantine, 1986.

Bruzzi, Stella. "Review of *Merlin: The Return*." *Sight and Sound* 11(January 2001): 55–56.

de Weever, Jacqueline. "Morgan and the Problem of Incest." In Kevin J. Harty, ed. *Cinema Arthuriana: Essays on Arthurian Film*. New York: Garland, 1991.

Gorgievski, Sandra. "The Arthurian Legend in Cinema: Myth or History?" In Marie-Françoise Alamichel and Derek Brewer, eds. *The Middle Ages after the Middle Ages in the English-Speaking World*. Cambridge, Eng.: D. S. Brewer, 1997.

Grellner, Alice. "Two Films That Sparkle: *The Sword in the Stone* and *Camelot*." In Kevin J. Harty, ed. *Cinema Arthuriana: Essays on Arthurian Film*. New York: Garland, 1991.

Harty, Kevin J. "Lights! Camelot! Action!—King Arthur on Film." In Kevin J. Harty, ed. *King Arthur on Film: New Essays on Arthurian Cinema*. Jefferson, N. C.: McFarland, 1999.

Jenkins, Jacqueline. "The Aging of the King: Arthur and America in *First Knight*." In Debra N. Mancoff, ed. *King Arthur's Modern Return*. New York: Garland, 1998.

Lacy, Norris J. "Arthurian Film and the Tyranny of Tradition." *Arthurian Interpretations* 4 (Fall 1989): 75–85.

Lerner, Alan Jay, and Frederick Loewe. "*Camelot*." *Great Musicals of the American Theatre*. Vol. 2. Ed. with intro. and notes by Stanley Richards. Radnor, Penn.: Chilton, 1976.

Merlin: The Return. Peakviewing Transatlantic PLC. http://www.merlinthereturn.com/movie/index.html.

Nash, Jay Robert, and Stanley Ralph Ross. "Siege of the Saxons." *The Motion Picture Guide, S, 1927–1983*. Chicago: Cinebooks, 1987.

Olton, Bert. *Arthurian Legends on Film and Television*. Jefferson, N.C.: McFarland, 2000.

Sklar, Elizabeth S. "Thoroughly Modern Morgan: Morgan le Fey in Twentieth-Century Popular Arthuriana." In Sally K. Slocum, ed. *Popular Arthurian Traditions*. Bowling Green, Ohio: Bowling Green State University Popular Press, 1992.

Stewart, Alan. "*Camelot in Four Colors*, Part 3: Stories featuring unique characters derived from the Arthurian legend." *Camelot in Four Colors: A Survey of the Arthurian Legend in Comics*. 2 June 2001. http://camelot4colors.tripod.com/original.htm#Modred the Mystic.

Torregrossa, Michael A. "*Camelot 3000* and Beyond: An Annotated Listing of Arthurian Comic Books Published in the United States c. 1980–1998. (Revised Edition, May 2000)." *The ARTHURIANA / Camelot Project Bibliographies*. May 2000. University of Rochester. http://www.lib.rochester.edu/camelot/acpbibs/comicbib.htm.

_____. "The Dark Knight of the Round Table: A Bibliographic Guide to Mordred in Arthurian Literature and Popular Culture." *The ARTHURIANA / Camelot Project Bibliographies*. University of Rochester. http://www.lib.rochester.edu/camelot/acpbibs/mordbib.htm.

Umland, Rebecca A., and Samuel J. Umland. *The Use of the Arthurian Legend in Hollywood Film from Connecticut Yankees to Fisher Kings*. Westport, Conn.: Greenwood, 1996.

Vizzard, Jack. "End Note D: A Code to Govern the Making of Motion and Talking Pictures." *See No Evil: Life Inside a Hollywood Censor*. New York: Simon and Schuster, [1970].

18

Filming the Tristan Myth

Meradith T. McMunn

The story of the fatal passion of Tristan and Iseut is one of the best-known legacies of medieval culture.[1] Twentieth-century films are only the latest interpretations of this narrative, which has been set to music, translated from one language into another, from verse to prose, from oral performance to written text, and, most important for our consideration of modern films, from words into visual images. Cinematic recreations of the story use many of the conventions that were also used in the "visual narration" in extensively illustrated medieval romance manuscripts (McMunn 277). A comparison of the visual realizations of the story of Tristan and Iseut, and its underlying myth, in the two periods gives us a more precise understanding of the aesthetic psychology underlying both art forms.

The evidence of medieval literature and art demonstrates that few narratives enjoyed such great popularity throughout the Middle Ages as that of Tristan and Iseut (Loomis and Loomis 42). Although its relationship to the Matter of Britain is tangential, this tragic story had become associated with the Arthurian legends as early as the twelfth century, when the popularity of both the Arthurian tales and the story of Tristan and Iseut was enhanced by their adaptation into the increasingly popular romance genre in the second half of the twelfth century (Loomis 122; Thompson 464). Because the romance is the literary form most closely associated with the legend of Tristan and Iseut, the conventions associated with this genre certainly influenced manuscript painters and, later, filmmakers.

The early manuscripts of these romances were unillustrated or decorated with only a few historiated initials or miniatures.[2] However, by the end of the thirteenth century, manuscripts that contained Tristan and sometimes other Arthurian romances often included extended programs of narrative illustrations.[3] Programs of illustrations of the Tristan romance are also known to have been popular in tapestries and wall paintings from the thirteenth through the fifteenth centuries, though relatively few examples are extant (Loomis and Loomis 42). Ecclesiastical art, including sculpture, wall paintings and misericords at Chester and Lincoln, and domestic objects such as chests, ivory caskets, and mirror cases were also decorated with individual characters or scenes from the Tristan legend.

Though the themes of consuming love and transfiguring death at the heart of the story have lost none of their emotional and aesthetic fascination, the challenge of interpreting the myth cinematically has proved formidable, and those directors who have taken the field have not completed the task to the satisfaction of most critics. Nevertheless, the cinema has been the major artistic medium for the exploration of Arthurian themes, including the Tristan legend, since the middle of the twentieth century (Mancoff 494).

Technical excellence does not necessarily result in artistic success. A big budget did not ensure quality in the products of the medieval scriptorium any more than it does in those of the modern film-production company. In both instances, the artifact may be larger, with more technical refinement and more lavish ornamentation, settings, and costumes, but the intangibles of imagination and artistic impact may still be lacking. The converse is also true of both medieval art and contemporary film. Technical limitations and flawed execution do not necessarily negate the aesthetic effect of creativity and originality.

While the Tristan story was among the earliest filmed works of medieval literature beginning with silent films in 1909, 1911, and 1920 (Harty 264–66), the focus here is on a group of four film versions produced since 1940: *L'Éternel Retour* (1943), directed by Jean Delannoy; *Tristan et Yseult* (1972), directed by Yvan Lagrange; *Lovespell* (1979), directed by Tom Donovan; and *Fire and Sword* (1981), directed by Veith von Fürstenberg.[4] These films demonstrate the considerable variety of approaches to filming this romance, from literal depiction of the narrative to an evocative use of iconic scenes, nearly devoid of narrative continuity.

Fire and Sword (*Feuer und Schwert*), also called *Tristan and Isolde*, directed by Veith von Fürstenberg in 1981, is the most true to the medieval literary sources, and it has the most effective recreation of the medieval period as well. Filmed in color in Ireland, its scenes incorporate actual medieval architecture and natural settings. The film uses chiaroscuro as well as color to create its atmosphere of intimacy and turmoil reminiscent of the work of medieval miniaturists such as René d' Anjou. The title alludes to the dual leitmotifs of passion and violent conflict, love and death, which characterize the Tristan myth. The film opens with the scene of the combat between Morholt and Tristan and ends with that of the lovers' funeral pyre. The story is presented chronologically. Narrative summaries displayed on the screen supply continuity across skips in dramatic time, and the musical score by Robert Lovas provides thematic unity by underlining the scenes of alternating tranquility and conflict and by giving emotional cues.

Tristan and Isolde (Christopher Waltz and Antonia Preser) are well-matched. Neither character predominates. The obvious youth of these actors, as well as the only young Brangane in any of the four films (Christine Wipf), lend credibility to the self-absorption and self-indulgence of Tristan and Isolde, and their sometimes jejune dialogue. Mark (Leigh Lawson) is portrayed as a sympathetic if vacillating man, unable to prevail against the headstrong duo.

Fire and Sword truncates the secondary plot of Tristan and the second Iseut, in some versions called Iseut of the White Hands. In fact, without knowledge of the medieval romance, her presence in the film is somewhat confusing. The film's script retains only the scenes of her rescue from pillaging soldiers by Tristan and of her betrayal of the ailing Tristan with the lie which precipitates his death. In the final scene of the film, the shadowy figures of the grieving Iseut of the White Hands and the faithful Gorvenal watch the blazing funeral pyre of the two lovers on the headland.

Lovespell (1979), alternately titled *Tristan and Isolt*, directed by Tom Donovan, is also relatively faithful to the medieval legend. Filmed in color in Ireland, it emphasizes the Celtic cultural setting of the legend by its score, which uses Irish folk music, its titles, based on the *Book of Kells*, and even Isolt's hawk, which is named for the medieval Irish hero Cuchulain. The script also contains frequent references to Irish history and folklore. Rich colors mark sets and costumes, and scenes are often shot in bright sunlight rather than in the chiaroscuro favored by other Tristan directors.

Kate Mulgrew is cast as Isolt. She matches Richard Burton's Mark in appealing assertiveness and willful intensity. Perhaps in part because of the dynamism of the actors, these two characters dominate the film, shifting the balance away from Tristan (Nicholas Clay). The film's title could well have been "Mark and Isolt." *Lovespell* opens with their meeting in the fields near Isolt's home where she hunts alone with her tercel. Mark orders his companion knight to get the tercel from the unknown girl who "must have stolen it." Her response is a blow with a grouse, which knocks the knight into the nearby stream. The incident may have been suggested by a historical event during the Third Crusade, when Richard the Lionhearted, riding through Calabria with only a single attendant, "rescued" a falcon from a peasant's hut and was chased by the villagers (Runciman 38). Throughout the film, the struggle for control between Mark and Isolt is sometimes friendly but increasingly bitter. She becomes an abused wife, first emotionally and then physically. The once assertive Isolt turns withdrawn and passive.

In the final sequence, Mark brings the mortally wounded Tristan by ship back to Cornwall for the sake of Isolt who is now dying of grief because of his absence. In a reversal of the traditional story, it is Isolt who receives the news that the sails of the ship are white, signifying Tristan's return. As they approach land, Tristan affirms his liaison with the queen, and, in a jealous rage, Mark changes the sails to black, the sign that Tristan is not on board. From the top of the high cliffs, Isolt sees the black sails and falls to her death on the rocks below. Tristan jumps from the ship and swims to shore, but the effort exhausts his remaining strength, though the lovers manage to touch hands as they die on the rocky beach. The final shot of the film is of Mark alone, dressed in red and dominating the visual space, surrounded by the turbulent waves.

The film's attempts at recreating the medieval period conflict with its characterization of Isolt as an independent, freethinking woman and with the intrusive modern psychological motivation and dialogue supplied for all the major characters. The result is a sense of anachronism that makes the medieval settings and costumes seem extraneous. Even actions based on the medieval narrative are placed in a context which undercuts the mythic tragedy, as when Isolt knowingly gives Tristan the love potion to keep him from leaving her. They have earlier consummated their love without need of this magic device.

Tristan and Yseult (1974), directed by the then twenty-one-year-old filmmaker Yvan Lagrange, was filmed in color in Iceland, Morocco, and France. Lagrange also wrote the screenplay and played the role of Tristan, opposite his wife Claire Wauthion, who played Yseult. The film was intended to create "the impression of the theme of the myth — love, eternity, madness, fatality" (Selcer 45). The film does not attempt sequential narration. There is almost no dialogue, and Yseult speaks the only lines. She dominates Tristan just as she controls the two greyhounds which accompany her on a leash in early sequences.

Lagrange uses striking visual images of violence and explicit eroticism to convey the universal mythic dimensions underlying the romance. This is "the naked myth set beyond the anecdotal tradition," according to Jean Marcel, who has given this complex film its most coherent reading to date (244–51). Marcel interprets the principal themes of love and war as the "dreamed aspects" of the reproductive instinct and hunger, respectively. These themes are expressed iconically in static poses: Tristan and Iseult in front of stained-glass windows that depict Adam and Eve, or mimicking a Pietà pose, or in repeated action sequences, such as the one in which Yseult is transformed into a warrior who "kills" Tristan, or an episode in which Yseult, wrapped in cellophane, is carried in Tristan's arms among carcasses hanging in a slaughterhouse. In the final scene, the dead lovers, white roses in their mouths, lie together in a large, bloody beef carcass. This scene is a visual allusion to Delannoy's final scene (see below). The background sound of the sea evokes their first voyage during which they consummated their love (Marcel 251).

L'Éternel Retour (1943), directed by Jean Delannoy from a screenplay by Jean Cocteau, was filmed in and around Nice during the German occupation of France. Of the four films discussed here, it is the only attempt at a modern-dress version of the medieval romance. Though it retains the outline of the medieval story, it has 1940s French settings. On closer examination, however, even the modern settings are more like the archetypal settings of medieval romances ("the castle," "the island") and lack grounding in historical geography.

There is a sensitive use of linguistic sound play to evoke the legendary characters similar to onomatopoetic devices employed in medieval music. Tristan, played by Jean Marais, is called Patrice, and Iseut, played by Madelaine Solange, is called Natalie. The last syllable of each name suggests the first syllable of the name of the character's medieval counterpart. Froissin, the surname of the dwarf Achille and his jealous family, is the same as the name of the medieval dwarf character. Marc, too, retains his legendary name, as does the bully Morolt (Lacy 96).

In this film, Tristan is clearly the dominant character. Camera angles emphasize Marais' chiseled good looks and statuesque heroism. His moods alternate between gaiety and melancholy. His empathy with nature is reflected in his imitation of the nightingale's song and his rapport with his dog, Moulouk.

Because it was shot in black and white, the film's textured lighting serves to isolate the characters within a timeless "otherworld" of emotions and mythical elements. Light and shadow shape the figures, emphasizing their iconic qualities. Even Marais's hair was lightened to match that of Solange and some extraordinary shots of the dwarf are the result of careful lighting and camera angles (Bazin 40; Marais 131–32). The final words of Cocteau's screenplay reiterate this merging of icon and myth. The film closes with the famous shot of the dead lovers on an improvised bier surrounded in light with snow-capped mountains in the background visible through two open arches. "Death has sculpted them, enfolded them, lifted them onto a royal shield. They are alone, enveloped in glory.... And so begins their real life" (Cocteau 99).

To a large extent, the content and aesthetic of any work of visual or verbal art are determined by its intended audience or patron. For example, the marked increase in the production of vernacular illustrated manuscripts beginning in the thirteenth century is usually attributed to the rise in the secular workshops working for lay patrons (Stones 299–300). Christopher de Hamel has suggested that in France the tradition of illustrating literary manuscripts probably began with versions of Arthurian literature (de Hamel 149). Filmmakers, too, are affected by considerations of audience, despite some apparent ambivalence toward the "general audience."

Fire and Sword contains little that would not be easily accessible to the general public. Cocteau has explicitly stated that his goal was a popular rather than a purely artistic or critical success with *L'Éternel Retour* (Cocteau 344). The fact that *Lovespell* was originally intended for television strongly suggests that it, too, was targeted for a popular audience. On the other hand, though Lagrange has not specifically addressed this issue of intended audience in his public state-

Yvan Lagrange as Tristan and Claire Wauthion as Iseult in Lagrange's 1972 film *Tristan et Iseult*. (Still courtesy of the Film Archive of the Museum of Modern Art.)

ments on his film, he has admitted that his deliberate choice of complex imagery and paratactic structure creates an interpretive challenge for the viewer (Selcer 49).

Romances are usually situated in an "elsewhere," and their authors often make up for the lack of a specific geographic location by including a wealth of visual detail. The texts and pictures of most illustrated medieval Tristan romances are notable for their portrayal of architectural spaces, natural settings, clothing, and armor, often depicted in intense, rich colors. The Tristan films likewise use vibrant colors and striking sets and costumes to create a self-contained world, even when these elements may not be historically "correct." Indeed, there are several "Middle Ages" to choose from when setting the romance: a setting suggesting the period of the early Celtic tradition, a thirteenth- or fourteenth-century courtly context, or the late-medieval society of the fifteenth century, centered more in the town than the castle.

The prominence of nature has often been noted as characteristic of romance, where the proclivity for sensory details resulted in frequent descriptions of natural settings. Nature was also used symbolically to explore interior states and psychological relationships. Nature, often sentimentalized, is prominent in medieval manuscript paintings, and this medieval technique translates well into film. For example, animals are used thematically in each of the Tristan and Iseut films to develop characterizations of the principals, as well as to suggest the sometimes changing relationships among the characters. The tercel in *Lovespell*, with its dual associations of independent spirit and loyalty to a single master, has already been mentioned. In *L'Éternel Retour*, the dwarf Achille is both physically and psychologically unnatural as well as hostile to the world of nature. The handsome, gifted Patrice is favored by nature and is responsive to it. The contrasting characters of Patrice and Achille and their fundamental antagonism to each other are defined by contrasting opening shots of the dog that Achille has killed and the affectionate welcome of Patrice by his dog, Moulouk.

Extensively illustrated romances often mix stock and distinctive scenes. Scenes are "distinctive" when they are recognizable as illustrating a particular episode, such as Tristan and Iseut in the forest asleep with a sword between them. Typical stock scenes are those showing two knights or two armies fighting, or two individuals talking—scenes that could illustrate any number of incidents in almost any romance (McMunn 278). Stock scenes may have provided a visual backdrop, like a stage or movie set, which prompted the visual imagination of the medieval reader. These two types of scenes may also be used by the artists in more complex patterns of repetition and interlace.

The cinematic treatments of Tristan employ analogous stock scenes and distinctive scenes, though sometimes treated very differently by their respective directors. For example, the fight between Morolt and Tristan is a mounted combat of two knights with lances and swords in *Fire and Sword*, a recurring battle between two bands of mounted knights in fanciful battle dress whose helmets recall those in the Manasse Codex in Lagrange's film, and the fist-and-knife brawl between Patrice and Morolt in the bar on the island in *L'Éternel Retour*. These stock scenes could come from any number of films made in any number of studios. On the other hand, scenes with Tristan and Iseut drinking the potion or Mark spying on the lovers at the fountain in the garden are distinctive to this particular romance and are immediately recognizable even in a modern-dress adaptation, such as *L'Éternel Retour*.

In these four films, the principal theme is violence and domination. In some films, the nature of the conflict is societal and the personal violence generalized to war (Lagrange and Von Fürstenberg), or the struggle may be between the individuals and society (all four films). The conflict may also be between individuals for dominance in marriage (Von Fürstenberg, Donovan, Cocteau) or in the love relationship (Von Fürstenberg and Lagrange).

Many medieval romances contain an emblematic or iconic use of symbols, such as the love potion, the sword, and the black sails. The use of somewhat static icons contrasts with the equally strong tendency to linear narrative, though there is often an interlacing structure in romance adventure narratives as well. Each of the films under consideration displays a preference for one or the other process, and each film may be located on a continuum from a very literal to a very figural presentation.

Psychological motivation and emotion are prominent in romance narratives. These features are sometimes difficult to convey in manuscript paintings but transfer well to cinematic adaptations, and modern directors, actors, and audiences find them appealing and "contemporary." The linking of psychology and symbolism intensifies the effect of both, providing a rationalized interpretation for less easily accessible mysticism or allegory. The role of the "love potion" in the love affair, or the nature of the relationship between Mark and Iseut, are elements open to a variety of interpretations and permit significantly varied structures in the four films, depending on the characterizations.

Finally, there are the two elements of motion and sound, which are intrinsic to modern films. Though medieval manuscript illustrators portrayed motion, often in a conventionalized manner, and medieval romances were sometimes performed to musical accompaniment, the ability of film as a medium to present visual motion and recorded sound distinguishes the Tristan films as a group from the illustrations in medieval romance manuscripts. Nevertheless, these characteristics are used differently

The final scene from Jean Delannoy's 1943 film *L'Éternel Retour* showing the makeshift bier holding the bodies of Natalie (Madeleine Solange) and Patrice (Jean Marais). (Still courtesy of the Film Archive of the Museum of Modern Art.)

in each of the four cinematic versions of Tristan and Iseut. Both *Fire and Sword* and *Lovespell* are "active" films in which movement is used to enliven the narration but rarely functions on a symbolic level. In *L'Éternel Retour*, the contrast between movement and its absence is used to create a rhythm in the narration and to isolate and intensify key images. In addition to the real-time representation in most of this film, there is a famous sequence that humorously plays on the fact that the film is a recorded artifact. To suggest Achille's haste in leaving Patrice's room, a sequence of "ellipsis in montage" shows a picture, a pack of cigarettes, and a necktie suddenly disappearing from their places (Clifton 151).

Lagrange's technique is even more self-consciously cinematic than those of the other directors. He uses repeated movement ritualistically and hypnotically. Even at static moments, he draws the audience's attention to the movement of hair, hands, and eyes and thus contrasts naturalistic movement with the dreamlike stillness of these scenes, creating emotional and symbolic tension.

Medieval artists often suggested sound visually, portraying the musical notation, human and animal musicians, or singing birds to evoke a sonorous background to their pictures. The musical soundtracks are prominent in all of the Tristan films, but only Yvan Lagrange has used music as a substitute for dialogue. He subtitles his film "*Opéra en scope-couleurs*," and he uses the mesmerizing music performed by the rock group Magma as a leitmotif in scenes of both love and war. The lyrics are deliberately unrecognizable. The driving intensity of the repeated scenes, especially the knights riding in the battle episodes, helps to confirm the haunting ritual-like effect. These repeated scenes function like theme and variations in music or like the *laisses similaires* of medieval *chansons de geste*, with shifts in perspective or setting that occur only after two or three repeats (Marcel 251). The other films, especially *Fire and Sword*, use their musical scores in a more conventional, though still effective, manner to reinforce culture and periodicity, to underline emotions, and to indicate the passage of time.

A consideration here of some of the strategies for visual realization of the story of Tristan and Iseut both in medieval manuscript illustrations and in twentieth-century cinema can tell us much about the creative aesthetic of both the Middle Ages and of our own time.

NOTES

1. Except when referring to a particular film character, I will use the French form of the heroine's name, Iseut.

2. For example, see Paris, Bibliothèque nationale de France, fr. 2186, or Munich, Bayerische Staatsbibliothek, Cgm 51.

3. See for example those in London, British Library Add. 5474, Paris, BnF fr. 750 and fr. 99–100, and Los Angeles, Getty Museum MS Ludwig XV 5. For commentary on the increasing production of secular manuscripts and the increasing use of illustrations, see Alexander 114, Rouse and Rouse 1: 99, Shailor 88–90, and Stones 299–300.

4. Kevin J. Harty, *The Reel Middle Ages*, discusses three silent film versions, and three other films based on or influenced by the legend: *Connemara* (1989); *In the Shadow of the Raven* (1988), alternate titles *I Skugga Hrafnsina* and *The Shadow of the Raven*; and *Trollsyn* (1994), alternate titles *Rypa i justedal* and *Second Sight*. See also Harty's more extended discussion of Ugo Falena's 1911 version in "A Note on Maureen Fries."

WORKS CITED

Alexander, Jonathan J. G. *Medieval Illuminators and Their Methods of Work*. New Haven: Yale University Press, 1992.

Bazin, André. *French Cinema of the Occupation and Resistance*. Trans. Stanley Hochman. New York: Ungar, 1975.

Clifton, N. Roy. *The Figure of Film*. London: Associated University Presses, 1983.

Cocteau, Jean. *Three Screenplays*. Trans. Carol Martin-Sperry. New York: Grossman, 1972.

de Hamel, Christopher. *A History of Illuminated Manuscripts*. 2nd ed. London: Phaidon, 1994.

Harty, Kevin J. *The Reel Middle Ages: American, Western and Eastern European, Middle Eastern and Asian Films About Medieval Europe*. Jefferson, N. C.: McFarland, 1999.

_____, "A Note on Maureen Fries, Morgan le Fay, and Ugo Falena's 1911 Film *Tristano e Isotta*." In Bonnie Wheeler and Fiona Tolhurst, eds. *On Arthurian Women: Essays in Memory of Maureen Fries*. Dallas: Scriptorium Press, 2001.

Lacy, Norris J. "Jean Cocteau." In Norris J. Lacy and others, eds. *The New Arthurian Encyclopedia*. Updated paperback edition. New York: Garland, 1996.

Loomis, Roger Sherman, ed. *Arthurian Literature in the Middle Ages*. Oxford: Clarendon, 1959.

_____, and Laura Hibbard Loomis. *Arthurian Legends in Medieval Art*. New York: Modern Language Association of America, 1938.

McMunn, Meradith. "Translating the Medieval Romance Narrative: From Text to Image in the *Roman de Kanor*." *Romance Languages Annual* 1 (1990): 277–84.

Mancoff, Debra N. "Visual Arts." In Norris J. Lacy and others, eds. *The New Arthurian Encyclopedia*. Updated paperback edition. New York: Garland, 1996.

Marais, Jean. *Mes quatre verités*. Paris: Éditions de Paris, 1957.

Marcel, Jean, "Le Dernière métamorphose de Tristan: Yvan Lagrange (1972)" [originally presented in January 1986 to the Colloque d'Amiens sur le mythe de Tristan]; in the *Actes* of the Colloque. Göppingen: Kümmerle Verlag, 1987; rpt. in Marcel, *Pensées, passions et proses: essais*. Montréal: l'Hexagone, 1992.

Rouse, Richard H. and Mary A. Rouse. *Illiterati et uxorati: Manuscripts and their Makers, Commercial Book Producers in Medieval Paris, 1200–1500*. 2 vols. Turnhout: Harvey Miller, 2000.

Runciman, Steven. *The Kingdom of Acre and the Later Crusades*. Vol. 3 of *A History of the Crusades*. Corr. rpt. Cambridge: Cambridge University Press, 1955.

Scherer, Margaret R. *About the Round Table*. New York: Metropolitan Museum of Art, 1945.

Selcer, Robert. "Yvan Lagrange: Impressions of a Filmmaker." *Tristania* 4 (1979): 44–50.

Shailor, Barbara A. *The Medieval Book*. Toronto: University of Toronto Press, 1991.

Stones, M. Alison. "Manuscripts, Illuminated." In Norris J. Lacy and others, eds. *The New Arthurian Encyclopedia*. Updated paperback edition. New York: Garland, 1996.

Thompson, Raymond H. "Tristan and Isolde." In Norris J. Lacy and others, eds. *The New Arthurian Encyclopedia*. Updated paperback edition. New York: Garland, 1996.

19

Fable *and* Poésie *in Cocteau's* L'Éternel Retour *(1943)*

JOAN TASKER GRIMBERT AND ROBERT SMARZ

for Nicole Passedoit

It is hard today to believe the stir that *L'Éternel Retour* (*The Eternal Return* or *Love Eternal*[1]) caused in occupied Paris upon its release in 1943. Many viewers left the theatre in tears and, reluctant to resume their humdrum existence, lined up for a second screening. Young people swooned over the central couple, Patrice/Tristan and Natalie/Iseult. Both stars launched fashion trends, Jean Marais' Jacquard-like pullover and Madeleine Sologne's straight blond coiffure that Cocteau had created for her. Marais attracted delirious fans who either camped outside the apartment he shared with Cocteau at Palais-Royal or sat in the gardens and gazed up at the star's window (Marais, *Mes Quatre Vérités* 134–36).

Cocteau was delighted with the popularity of a film that he had intended as a bridge between the general public and the small group of connoisseurs attracted to his first and only previous foray into film twelve years before, *Le Sang d'un poète* (*The Blood of a Poet*). The public responded wholeheartedly to the bait that Cocteau had unashamedly set to lure it into the theatre — star-quality actors[2] and a transcendent "myth" made famous by Wagner's 1859 opera, which premiered in 1865, and by Joseph Bédier's best-selling romance, first published in 1900.[3] Indeed, the appeal of the actors and of the celebrated love triangle was so strong that most filmgoers remained unaware of the *poésie cinématographique* with which Cocteau had infused the story. But today's viewers, more or less immune to the outdated charm of the Marais/Sologne duo, have a much greater need to appreciate the film's peculiar poetry.[4]

A large segment of the current audience for *L'Éternel Retour*—at least in the United States—is likely to be composed of medievalists who wish to acquaint their students with an important Arthurian legend. Ideally, students should be aware of how the legend appeared in Béroul's and Thomas's twelfth-century romances and how it was transmuted by Wagner and then adapted by Bédier. But as the complexity of this evolution is daunting, it might be preferable to focus on the two key elements that define Cocteau's transposition of the legend to the screen. On the one hand, Cocteau, whose obsession with death permeated his entire oeuvre, followed Bédier's romanticized version of the legend, but, influenced by Wagner as well, highlighted the theme of death even more. On the other hand, as a counterpoint to the lovers' inexorable progress toward their fated death (*fable*), he sought to introduce his own peculiar form of poetic realism — the intersection of the legend with quotidian reality (*poésie cinématographique*).

Pierre Dubourg has noted: "The transfiguration of the real in *The Eternal Return* is due to the perfect balance achieved between the fable and the modern world.... [T]his story takes place in our time — but how timeless it is.... Incessantly we hesitate between the Middle Ages and the twentieth century."[5] Let us then analyze *L'Éternel Retour* from the perspective that suits it, by considering the film from the standpoint both of the transformed *fable* and of the *poésie cinématographique* created when the legend encounters daily life in the modern world. Perhaps, then, the film, which many today find disappointing, will appear in a very different light.

L'Éternel Retour was directed by Jean Delannoy, and although on occasion Cocteau is cited as co-director, officially he is credited only with "scénario et dialogues." Nevertheless, most critics recognize Cocteau's indelible stamp on the film. Georges Charensol, who considers it one of the four most important films made during the Occupation, asserts that those who saw it in 1943 recognized it as the work of a poet, rather than of the excellent technician that was Delannoy (11–12).[6] For John Russell Taylor, it is "in every respect a Cocteau original" (226). Taylor makes a point of including it in his entry on Cocteau's films in Richard Roud's *Critical Dictionary* of major filmmakers (226), where Delannoy does not make the cut. To be sure, the great critic André Bazin cites Cocteau's screenplay as the weakest element of the film while praising Delannoy's direction and Roger Hubert's camerawork — but only after saying that "to separate the woof from the warp, to sort out Cocteau's errors and Delannoy's merits" seems "a very specious exercise"(38). The attempt to identify Cocteau's specific input does indeed appear futile in this case since, although he wrote that he exercised "only friendly supervision," Cocteau goes on to thank the whole team and elsewhere muses: "What would I have done without Delannoy, who wanted to get on my wavelength and asked me to join him in the cutting and montage; or without Roger Hubert, who filmed through my eyes and my heart?" (*Art of Cinema* 190–92.)[7] Moreover, for a poet and an artist who often reiterated his conviction that in cinema the visual element was primary, it is hard to imagine how Cocteau could have held himself aloof from the shooting of a film that was so dear to his heart and contained so many themes and motifs that are part and parcel of his esthetic. As Dubourg notes: "The lighting, the scenery and props, the sense of grandeur and of night, the close-up shots of essential details, the movement, the rhythm, the play of shadow and light — we will find the same style in all of Cocteau's other films, good or bad."[8]

THE *FABLE*: LOVE AND ESPECIALLY DEATH

"What is remarkable about Cocteau's films," writes Robin Buss, "is their consistency with the rest of his work and fidelity to his personal obsessions" (Cocteau, *Art of Cinema* 10). Buss is referring here to the films that Cocteau actually directed, but as we shall see, *L'Éternel Retour* is very much a part of that oeuvre, one that is, strikingly, "obsessed with the terrible and familiar presence of death, of inseparable death, totally old and totally new, totally new for each of us."[9]

The French are fond of the mythical; they are enamored of complex forms that can be expressed elegantly. Since Wagner, since Bédier, and especially since Denis de Rougemont, they have thought of the Tristan legend as a tale of love and death, Eros and Thanatos inseverably intertwined.[10] Yet as Bédier himself pointed out in his monumental 1902–05 "reconstruction" of the two earliest Old French poems,[11] the medieval Tristan legend is primarily a conflict between love and the law. Although death stalks the lovers from the moment they drink the potion, they do not focus on their ultimate fate. Nor is their attitude toward society the least bit disdainful; on the contrary, they try their best to remain integrated within society and — in Thomas's version at least — bitterly lament the social alienation they experience (Grimbert, "Love, Honor, and Alienation"). Wagner, reworking Gottfried von Strassburg's version of the legend, transformed the threat of death into an actual death wish that the lovers conceive at the beginning of the opera and lovingly caress through to the end. Their social alienation, of which they are fully aware, leaves them singularly unperturbed, and the final *Liebestod*, which Wagner called the "transfiguration," is a transcendent experience that allows them to embrace at last the Night they have sought.

Wagner had reaffirmed the claim the Germans had on the legend owing to the popularity of Gottfried's version, but following the discovery and publication by Francisque Michel of the Old French Tristan poems in 1835–39, Bédier felt justified in repatriating the legend, and his 1900 romance was designed to introduce it to modern French audiences. Nevertheless, he was unable to escape Wagner's powerfully seductive interpretation.[12] The conflict between love and the law is still present in his romance, but the shadow of death hovers much more closely than in the Old French versions and is underscored from the first line of the romance when the narrator asks: "My Lords, if you would hear a high tale of love and death…"[13]— a phrase that Rougemont cites approvingly as the opening sentence of his seminal study (15).

When Cocteau decided to work with the legend, he undoubtedly realized how well it responded — at least in the form Bédier gave it — to his own proclivities. It was, as Stephen Maddux has stated, "a close-to-perfect fit."[14] Joining his own sensibility to Bédier's (and Wagner's), Cocteau amplified still further the theme of death.[15] He did so in several ways: by choosing a setting that cannot be situated in the known world; by depicting the lovers as perfect beings hovering between life and death — and endowed with a guardian angel; by underscoring the poisonous nature of the potion; and by creating veritable "twilight" areas where the frontier between life and death seems most permeable.

The story unfolds in various generic sites: a castle, a boat, a bar, a garage, a mountain retreat, and an island.[16] The characters refer to these places in the singular: *the* island, *the* castle, as if only one existed in the world (Dubourg 181), and just as Iseult the Blonde's Irish roots are effaced, Iseult aux Blanches Mains is uprooted from Britanny, for the second Natalie lives with her brother in *the* garage where Patrice flees following his exile from *the* castle. Thus, the venue that Patrice chooses for his wedding to Natalie II is *the* island, the very one from which he had delivered the first Natalie; he even enlists her guardian Anne to help with the arrangements.

In this apparently insensitive choice, Patrice displays, as Maddux notes, "a sense of symmetry but little of any other kind of sense" (487), but the symmetry does work in a streamlined, mythical vision of the legend. It makes "mythical" sense for the lovers to expire on the very site where they first met and for them to lie "in state" in a "chapel" surrounded by the very sea in which their parents perished, as if returning to the primordial chaos — or waiting to be revived in another guise in the cycle of eternal return.

Just as the setting of the story is amorphous, the main characters do not seem firmly rooted in the world, for Cocteau chose to play down the medieval lovers' rich history. Patrice and Natalie are both orphans, both sets of parents having drowned at sea: they are "enfants de la mer" (children of the sea), as Patrice states. Thus, Natalie, unlike her medieval counterpart, who is an integral part of Irish society, simply lives with her guardian on a nondescript island where she feels out of place.

Patrice is in an analogous situation. Instead of living with his maternal uncle (an important relationship in medieval society), he stands once removed from Marc, who is the husband not of his deceased mother Solange, but of her sister Édith. Gertrude Frossin is the third sister, which makes her son, the evil dwarf Achille/Frocin, Patrice's cousin. Just as King Marc cannot dismiss his barons, neither Marc nor Patrice can evict the Frossins, who "incredibly, are family" (Maddux 481). This complex family tree serves to show how "unmoored" Patrice is, for his relationship with his uncle is not nearly as close as it is in Bédier's version where Marc's love for his nephew — reinforced by important feudal as well as blood ties — keeps him for some time from believing that Tristan is betraying him. In the film, Marc seems all too ready to condemn the pair at the first suggestion of dalliance, although his initial attempt to send Patrice away is supposedly motivated by his fear of gossip and Gertrude's machinations.

Patrice's rootless nature is emphasized when, following his dismissal by Marc, his old friend Lionel/Kaherdin invites him to live at the garage with him and his sister, claiming joyously that they are all "enfants abandonnés" (abandoned children). But the two siblings soon realize that Patrice is incapable of integrating their world. Once Natalie II learns from Anne that Marc's wife is young and beautiful and also called Natalie, she knows Patrice will never marry her. She tells her brother that, even when she is talking to him, he seems invisible and clearly lives in a different world from theirs.

Patrice and Natalie are even endowed with a "guardian angel"—Moulouk/Husdent. The dog actually belonged to Marais, who had found him at the German front in the forest of Compiègne and had brought him home when he was demobilized.[17] Cocteau, thinking that Moulouk meant "angel" in Arabic, believed the dog was Marais's guardian angel (Sprigge and Kihm 150), a role the dog plays — exceedingly well — in the film.[18] He is Patrice's constant companion during the first half of the film where he appears prominently in nearly every scene. He accompanies Patrice on that first fateful trip to the island, and, during the barroom brawl, he can be heard and seen barking excitedly and straining to jump into the fray.

Moulouk is Natalie's guardian angel as well. When Patrice must leave her alone in their mountain retreat, the dog watches over her and follows her and Marc back to the castle, after only the briefest glance backwards. He remains with Natalie — we see him lying on the carpet at the foot of her sickbed — until Patrice's last visit to the castle. Then he breaks free from his leash to accompany his wounded master back to the island, where he will stay by him during the anxious wait for Natalie. At the end of the film, he can be seen curled up next to the overturned boat where the deceased lovers lie and which will eventually be their tomb. In that guise, he is reminiscent of the dog — symbolizing fidelity — that can often be seen at the feet of recumbent figures on medieval sarcophagi.[19]

Cocteau's enduring interest in characters that share an unusually close bond explains why he refashioned the lovers as two beings who are mirror images of each other. He insisted that their hair be an identical pale blond,[20] in order to make them stand out from the Frossin family, and from Lionel and his sister, who are all very dark-haired. The otherworldly perfection of Patrice's and Natalie's beauty is enhanced by their resemblance to statues. Several critics have noted the sculptural quality of

Marais's features,[21] and indeed, at the very moment that Patrice expires, his flesh seems to turn to marble. As Natalie lies down beside him on the overturned boat, which becomes a royal catafalque, the boathouse is transformed into a chapel, and the lovers take on the appearance of marble gisants: "Death has sculpted them, enfolded them, lifted them onto a royal shield. They are alone, enveloped in glory...."(Cocteau, *Three Screenplays* 99).[22]

Sologne, who often wears a long gown featuring regular folds that hang to the floor from her waist, looks at certain moments like a jamb statue of the early Gothic period. The resemblance is especially striking in the scene where Natalie stands erect against the frame of the fireplace in the castle watching Patrice make a fire. Cocteau clearly desired this effect. He reported to Marais from the set of the film: "Sologne was superb yesterday. I've styled her hair so that it is straight and falls very low naturally. She looks like a jamb statue, an odd bird, the ghost of a drowned woman."[23]

Cocteau was very fond of statues, which he plainly associated with death — but death as a state of suspension akin to sleep.[24] Freeman observes that his theater and film sets are "inhabited by statues, hands, arms, severed heads, headless bodies, stone busts, eerie androgynes which could come to life any minute and frequently do."[25] In *Le Sang d'un poète*, the statue-muse and the poet himself are both destroyed and revived phoenix-like, such that each "death," even the bloodiest, seems only provisional. Orphée and Eurydice both die and return to life. And, when at the very end of *L'Éternel Retour* the lover-gisants are laid out on their "tomb" and the narrator intones solemnly that their real life is only beginning, we have the distinct feeling that they are dead only to this world, that they will live on in eternity perhaps as the ideal forms from which other sets of lovers will be incarnated.

This conception of the legend is quintessential Cocteau, but the screenplay has definitely been influenced by Wagner, as can be seen from the way the poet has displaced and transformed the potion scene. In the legend, Tristan and Iseult imbibe the potion while on the boat bound for Cornwall: it is daytime, and when the thirsty pair calls for some wine, Brangaine gives them the love potion by mistake. In Wagner's opera, Isolde asks Brangaine for her flask of potion. Isolde is already in love with Tristan but angry with him both for killing Morolt (her "fiancé" here as in the film) and for appearing to disdain her. Tristan, for his part, is clearly struggling against the attraction he feels so that he can keep his promise to his uncle. Although Brangäne deliberately substitutes the potion for the poison, Isolde and Tristan both believe it is poison and drink it willingly.

Cocteau adopts Wagner's concept of the potion as poison but infuses it with his own sensibility. The corresponding scene occurs during a stormy night when Patrice and Natalie are home alone with Achille. The dwarf, who has found Anne's potion bearing the label "poison" in Natalie's medicine cablinet, pours it into the glasses containing the cocktail that Patrice has prepared. The close-up shot of Achille's hand pouring from the flask labeled "poison" makes the dwarf seem like a maleficent force of fate, an impression reinforced by the thunder and lightning that punctuate the scene. Moreover, after drinking the "poison," the lovers stretch out on the floor in the same position that they will assume on their "tomb," thus underscoring the theme of love and death. Achille's role as an instrument of fate is confirmed later when he inflicts the fatal leg wound from which Patrice will eventually die. The dwarf's very name suggests the man who destroyed Troy, and underscores Patrice's similarity to that other great lover, Paris.[26]

Cocteau was clearly drawn to the legend of Tristan and Iseult because like Wagner he saw in it a metaphoric expression through which he could approach the enigma of death. Speaking of *Orphée*, he wrote: "My moral gait is that of a lame man, with one foot in life and the other in death. Therefore, I am quite naturally drawn to a myth in which life and death meet face to face" (*Cocteau on the Film* 101).[27] In *L'Éternel Retour* the lovers' psychological state must have suggested to him a time and place where one hovers between life and death, between waking and sleeping that is akin to the "Zone" in *Orphée* (Savage 142). Cocteau confessed to a particular affection for the region he describes as "the no man's land of twilight where mysteries thrive" (*Art of Cinema* 156)[28] and where one hovers between life and death.

In *L'Éternel Retour*, access to this twilight world may well be the island where Patrice first discovers his soul mate and nearly dies saving her, and where, mortally wounded again, he will await her at the end, so that together they may embark on a better existence. Surrounded by a calm, mirror-like sea ringed by mountains, the island is regularly bathed in a nacreous light. At the end of the film, when Natalie arrives on the island, it is dawn. The sound of the motor-boat resonates like a heartbeat (Sadoul 82). A white scarf has been fastened to the boat's mast in conformity with Patrice's instructions to Lionel, but Natalie II informs the despairing Patrice that the boat displays the usual red pennant, which they both know is the sign that Natalie is not aboard.[29] When Marc, Lionel, and Natalie II enter the boathouse to discover that both lovers have died, Marc observes, "No one can reach them now" (Cocteau, *Three Screenplays* 99).[30]

Another site that exhibits elements of a no man's land is the modest refuge in the snowy mountains to which the lovers escape after being banned from the castle. The structure's A-frame design suggests not only that this sequence is the apex of their relationship but also that it separates the life they led together in the castle from the one they will live apart. When Moulouk brings Natalie the fur glove signaling Marc's presence nearby, she knows that her life with Patrice is over and that she will return to the castle with her husband. She stands at the doorway and, with great emotion, waves goodbye to Patrice, who exits the frame on the left; almost immediately, Marc's shadow appears to the right of her. Before leaving, she hugs the doorframe lovingly. As she and Marc walk off to the right, the camera pans left, the light reflected on the cabin darkens to dusk, and Patrice approaches from the left. When his birdcall goes unanswered, he exits the frame and can be heard crying out Natalie's name as the camera remains focused on the mountains lit by the setting sun in the distance. The camera pans slowly over the mountains, with the sky occupying no less than three-quarters of the frame, a veritable dreamscape worthy of a Japanese print. The cinematography and the dramatic music anticipate the lovers' final apotheosis on the island.

It might be argued that Patrice and Natalie carry the no man's land within themselves, like the death that Cocteau claims we "marry" at birth and that grows ever more present as we age (*Journals of Jean Cocteau* 200). Of course, in these lovers,

Piéral as the dwarf Achille in Jean Delannoy's 1943 film *L'Éternel Retour*. (Still courtesy of the Film Archive of the Musuem of Modern Art.)

who are ageless, the potion hastens their progression toward their premature death. Once Natalie realizes that Anne's potion has "poisoned" them, she takes on a decidedly somnambular appearance: she is described in the screenplay as heading for Patrice's room as if she were sleepwalking. When she and Patrice are in the mountains, she is plainly ill, and her fear that Patrice will no longer love her if her malady worsens suggests why she allows Marc to take her back. Her decline, which seems precipitous, especially after her return to the castle, remains unexplained — though it is not inexplicable, at least in symbolic or psychological terms (Maddux 486). They have indeed been "poisoned," as Patrice tells Natalie several times, marveling all the while that the experience is wonderful, but Natalie realizes the necessarily ephemeral nature of their happiness.

Patrice seems initially to fare better, thanks largely to his attempt to share in the raucous bonhomie of Lionel and his sister. But to his new friends he appears dreamy and distant, and almost as soon as he agrees to wed Natalie II, his return to the island seems to jog his memory, and his thoughts about his true love leave him inconsolable. Lionel finds him in the Vélo Bar where he has gone in an apparent effort to recapture his past — in vain, since even Morolt has left the scene, swallowed up, like so many others, by a voracious sea. On Patrice's subsequent visit to the castle garden, his worst fears are confirmed: Natalie appears to have shut him out, and his resultant despair is the only explanation for why his calf wound turns out to be fatal. Unlike in the legend, the weapon that inflicts the wound carries no poison, but just as Natalie's physical decline is apparently provoked by her realization that she and her lover will never be able to live their love, Patrice's fatal illness is caused by the appalling belief that the flame of Natalie's love has gone out. The potion has revealed itself to be an insidious poison in that the two actually will themselves to die.

"Poésie de cinéma"

Having examined Cocteau's idiosyncratic conception of the *fable* that he transposed, let us turn now to the *poésie* that the poet-filmmaker injected into the "myth." As a preliminary to our analysis, we can do no better than to note Cocteau's objections to the few changes in the dialogue that the director proposed. He complained to Marais that Delannoy did not seem to realize how the alteration or addition of even one word affected the special rhythm with which Cocteau had imbued the screenplay. For example, toward the end of the film, Natalie does not respond to Patrice's birdcall because she has moved to another room where she cannot hear it. The faithful Moulouk does hear it, and Cocteau has Patrice muse bitterly: "Now I understand. I prefer animals" ("J'ai compris. J'aime mieux les bêtes."), i.e., they at least are faithful! Apparently, Delannoy wanted to change the line to: "She has forgotten everything, everything" ("Elle a tout oublié, tout"), which Cocteau considered banal.[31] Cocteau also objected strenuously to Delannoy's suggestion that Natalie cry out "Patrice!" upon learning that her lover had been shot: "There must be silence" ("Il faut le silence"), he wrote (*Lettres à Jean Marais* 172). Cocteau won this particular battle — and happily so: it is striking to see Natalie, who has suddenly appeared on the stairs "in a white nightgown looking like a ghost," slump silently to the floor.

These details make the film more poetic in Cocteau's understanding of the term. Critics like Sadoul, who say the film's poetic style is outmoded (82), or like Mitry, who complain about the jarring effect of the encounter between the real and the mythical (16), fail to understand that when Cocteau speaks of *poésie de cinéma*, he is referring to the incursion of the modern world or the quotidian into the normally timeless *fable*. He notes that filmgoers generally equate fairy-tales or fables with *évasion* (escape), whereas it is *invasion* that is most effective, for poetry occurs in those moments expressing everyday reality. Cocteau appreciated filmmakers like Bresson and Franju, who "prove to us that film is a medium for realism and lyricism, and that everything depends on the angle from which one observes the spectacles of life — the angle from which they constrain us to share a singular vision of things and emphasize the everyday miracle that lies within them" (*Art of Cinema* 120).[32] Cocteau observed that in *L'Éternel Retour* critics found the lovers' castle suitable to poetry but not the garage,[33] whereas it was precisely in that garage that poetry functioned best (*Journals of Jean Cocteau* 129).

This widely quoted distinction can, however, lead us astray, for the castle, which houses the hilariously dysfunctional Frossin trio, is also the site of the kind of poetry that appealed most to Cocteau. The film begins with a romantic shot of the castle, but almost immediately we see Gertrude talking out the window to the gardener, who holds in his arms the corpse of his dog, whom Achille has shot. Next, the camera takes us inside where Gertrude paces the long corridors in search of her dwarf son, who is hiding from her and making even more mischief, notably in Patrice's room where he steals his cousin's tie and cigarettes. The camera pans around the room in a jerky movement that reflects Achille's darting look, focusing successively on a framed studio-type portrait of Patrice, sent flying off the table, and a package of cigarettes, which disappears as if by magic. Close-up shots of the bug-eyed dwarf accentuate the incongruity between what the viewer expects and what he or she sees. Similarly, the noble shot of Patrice and Natalie on horseback pausing at some distance from the castle before being greeted by Marc contrasts vividly with the frantic snooping of the ignoble Frossins, apprehensive about the likely impact of the newcomer's arrival on their precarious situation in the household.

The clash between the *fable* and the modern world is particularly arresting in the two cases where Patrice and Natalie come close to consummating their love, only to find their idyll shattered by the "invasion" of reality. The stormy evening on which they find themselves (almost) alone in the castle, Achille, whom Patrice first catches stealing Marc's cognac, then insinuates himself into the couple's little party, and — significantly — at the very moment that Patrice is delighting Natalie with his imitation of a nightingale, Achille slips the potion into their drinks. Later, as the two are marveling at the effects of their "cocktail," the dwarf erupts on the scene and tosses the empty bottle labeled "poison" before them.

A similar effect is obtained on the night that Patrice, like a sleepwalker obliviously pursuing his dream, climbs the dark castle stairs to Natalie's tower room. He is illuminated intermittently by the moonlight as he passes each successive *lucarne*,[34] and his relentless, measured climb is intercut with close-ups of Natalie in the grips of some erotic dream. When the lovers are at last reunited and on the verge of consummating their love, their idyll is brutally shattered as lights come on to flood the room. Patrice's desperate glance around him reveals Achille and Gertrude blocking both avenues of escape and Marc looking on sternly from the gallery above before beginning his descent to Natalie's room with a slow, deliberate step that contrasts painfully with Patrice's dreamy ascent. In these two scenes, where the lovers are temporarily enveloped by night, time is abolished for a while until reality intrudes.[35]

To achieve his cinematic poetry, Cocteau favors a "syntax" in which the images are strung together in a way that keeps them from flowing: they are juxtaposed such that each one preserves its own contour.[36] An excellent illustration of this technique is the sequence in the sordid Vélo Bar.[37] In this local island bistro, where Patrice and Natalie first meet, the mythic and the quotidian intersect in an exceptionally striking manner. As Patrice approaches the bar, he hears raucous laughter emanating from it. Glancing in, he finds Morolt, the local drunk, performing what is apparently a daily ritual to the loud, nervous laughter of the islanders. A close-up of Patrice, his radiant blondness contrasting vividly with the dark-haired locals, shows him surveying the scene, then the camera, revealing what he sees, cuts to the giant figure of Morolt standing at the bar hurling glasses of liquor in all directions. Patrice strides into the bar like a gunslinger newly arrived in town, but Morolt quickly recaptures center stage: low camera angles, emphasizing his size and force, chronicle the motion of his long arms, which continue to fling glasses as the cowardly locals laugh weakly.

One glass hits the wall to the right of a beautiful blond woman sitting as still as a statue. This is our first glimpse of Natalie, and it is she who now commands our attention, as indeed she must attract Patrice's gaze. She does not even flinch when the glass strikes the wall but scans the room with utter disgust. Slowly she rises and approaches the bar. She orders Morolt to stop and indicates that it is time to go home. He tries to force her to drink, and when she refuses, he smashes her head down sideways onto the bar next to the glass. The camera frames her in close-up with her hair bathed in the spilled drink. A hand appears from the left of the frame — Patrice's — and grasps the bully's arm, forcing him to remove his grip on Natalie's head and back off.[38] When Patrice orders a cognac, however, Morolt seizes the bottle roughly and refills Natalie's glass, again insisting that she drink. As she raises the glass, trembling, to her lips, Patrice claps his hand firmly over it.

Patrice's intervention arouses Morolt to anger again, and the "duel" begins, despite Natalie's gesture desperately cautioning the newcomer not to intervene. Morolt tries to punch Patrice, who dodges the blow and administers an uppercut, causing the hulk to fall back onto a table, which collapses. A low camera angle underscores the drunk's size as he rises to his full height and lunges headfirst at his adversary. Patrice falls, but Morolt is catapulted over him, landing near the door where he is bombarded with heavy items falling from the shelves above. Patrice drags himself over to the bar and urges Natalie to leave, but Morolt eyes Patrice menacingly and gropes for something in his pocket. Natalie, seeing him hurl his dagger at Patrice, cries out. A series of close-ups show successively the couple's surprise and horror, the victim's face contracted with pain, and the dagger planted deep in his thigh. Morolt climbs back toward the bar, and a medium tracking shot follows the two men both leaning heavily on the counter as they work their way across it from right to left. Patrice, in retreat, suddenly grabs a bottle and smashes it over Morolt's head. Both men slump to the ground unconscious as Natalie springs into action, ordering the bystanders to carry Patrice to her house. Slowly, solemnly, the men bear Patrice out of the bar with Natalie following. The last shot is a tracking close-up of the couple that fate has joined: Patrice's head dangles upside down on the right; Natalie supports it, her face sharing the frame on the left. In the background, the now somber faces of the bystanders, who are lined up as if in the receiving line of a funeral, appear successively in the middle of the frame as the procession leaves the bar.

We have analyzed this sequence in detail both to illustrate the cinematic syntax that Cocteau favored — the connection and clash between disparate images — and to explore the bizarre venue that he chose for Patrice and Natalie's first encounter.

Fable *and* Poésie *in Cocteau's* L'Éternel Retour *(1943)*

Natalie (Madeleine Solange) follows as the wounded Patrice (Jean Marais) is carried from the barroom in Jean Delannoy's 1943 film *L'Éternel Retour*. (Still courtesy of the Film Archive of the Museum of Modern Art.)

Cocteau could have found no better way to drive home the idea that the myth can be reborn at all times and in the most unexpected places. Fate can intervene anywhere, and as Edward B. Savage points out, the bar fits into the loose network of images related to the wheel of fortune (145). The name of the bistro, Vélo Bar, would seem incongruous (since no bikers are in sight) if not for the veiled allusion to fate. Fate is also signified by the stone hand that appears under the title of the film at the very beginning and on which the lines referring to life, love, and luck are prominently displayed. The camera also focuses on hands both in Patrice's fight with Morolt and in the potion scene: just as the close-up of Achille's disembodied hand pouring the poison/potion into the glasses seems to underscore the intervention of fate at that moment, so too does the appearance of Patrice's hand twice to stay Morolt's attempts to make Natalie drink.

That other privileged place of Cocteau's inimitable poetry, Lionel's garage, also displays signs of fortune's wheel. Savage mentions the wall map of France with the routes radiating out from Paris (145). More strikingly, Patrice and Lionel are seen through the wheels of the car they are repairing as they discuss the possibility of Patrice's marrying Natalie II. Patrice has just heard Amédée's false report about how pleased Natalie and Marc were to hear the "rumor" of the wedding, and he is visibly shocked that Natalie's feelings may have changed. In this vulnerable mood, he admits to Lionel that he finds his sister attractive, and though he refuses to make a commitment, he adds somewhat fatalistically: "Things have a way of happening. It's better to let them happen" (Cocteau, *Three Screenplays* 78) and gives one of the wheels a spin (Savage 145).[39]

As Savage rightly cautions, one should not attempt a "symbolic" reading of the film based on these details (143). There was nothing that Cocteau hated more than an overly intellectual approach that, like rationality, like thought even, effectively destroys poetry. Although he believed that, ideally, filmgoers should pay close attention to detail, Cocteau created images that were part of the fabric of daily life. Poetry "happens" when an audience makes connections, even subconsciously, between disparate images. For example, the statues and paintings we see in Marc's castle find their more humble counterparts in Lionel's garage — in the bust in his office that sports a biker's helmet and the pictures of movie stars pasted all over Natalie's bedroom walls. When Gertrude chastises Achille for stealing one of Patrice's ties and demands that he empty his pockets, the objects he places on the table like so many tarot cards — a doorknob, a dead sparrow, a spark plug, a postcard of a pin-up, and an empty pack of cigarettes — make up a collection that is eclectic but not unbelievable, given the dwarf's personality.

At the same time, these objects point to analogous images elsewhere in the film. Achille is a sneak, and one early shot involving him is a close-up of a doorknob slowly turning; three times he is caught eavesdropping. The dead sparrow recalls the dog that Achille shoots at the very beginning of the film, and those two images emphasize the dwarf's perverted sensibility compared to Patrice's positive relationship with animals and nature in general, as demonstrated by his imitation of the nightingale and his close bond with Moulouk.[40] Moulouk himself, notwithstanding our suggestion earlier that he is the couple's guardian angel and connotes fidelity, is so natural that he could be considered simply as an element of the poetry of the quotidian on which Cocteau doted.

Cinematic poetry also results from the clash between sound and image. No doubt the most obvious example of a sound that seems at odds with an image is the loud croaking of frogs routinely heard outside the castle at night. Although the sound is as natural as that of crickets on a summer night, it is discordant in a romantic context. The frogs are heard as Patrice is visited in his room successively by Natalie, warning him about the potion, and by Marc, who finds him gazing dreamily out the window. Their croaking also punctuates the famous garden rendezvous.

Medieval lyric poetry has taught us to expect the song of the nightingale, but the only birdsong we hear is Patrice's imitation, a fact that only underscores the incongruity between *fable* (fiction) and reality. A further irony is that this lovely talent of Patrice's, which recalls Tristan's skill as a musician, works constantly, insidiously, against him. Patrice's first birdcall distracts Natalie and him, allowing Achille to slip the potion into their drinks; the second one alerts the dwarf to Patrice's attempt to summon Natalie for the midnight rendezvous. His two subsequent calls (at the mountain retreat and in his final visit to the garden) fail to reach Natalie's ears, with disastrous results in the second case. In both cases, Natalie's absence seems to indicate that she is determined to forget him.

L'Éternel Retour contains countless instances of the kind of moments that Cocteau considered poetic, and it should be obvious by now that they are to be found not so much in the sequences that recount the *fable* inherited from Bédier as in the myriad details that make up the fabric of daily life in the castle, on the island, and in the garage — details that we owe to an artist who, because of his fondness for the "poetry" of precise things, was pleased to call himself a "cabinetmaker" (Cocteau, *Du Cinématographe* 17, 26, 52).

As we conclude our study of *fable* and *poésie* in a film so redolent of Cocteau's peculiar fragrance, we feel justified in agreeing with John Russell Taylor that *L'Éternel Retour* is indeed "a Cocteau original" (226).

How much better one understands and appreciates the film when, instead of measuring it—as medievalists are wont to do, against the twelfth-century legends or Bédier's version—one views it in the context of Cocteau's life and work, analyzing it in the very manner that he would have wished.

NOTES

1. *Love Eternal* was the title that Cocteau and the producer André Paulvé chose for the English version (Crosland 148–49), but *The Eternal Return* translates better the idea conveyed by the French title and squares with the explanation given at the beginning of the film: "*L'Éternel Retour* ... ce titre, emprunté à Nietzsche, veut dire, ici, que les mêmes légendes peuvent renaître, sans que leurs héros s'en doutent. Éternel retour de circonstances très simples qui composent la plus célèbre de toutes les grandes histoires du coeur" (*The Eternal Return* ... this title, borrowed from Nietzsche, means here that the same legends can be reborn without their heroes' realizing it. Eternal return of very simple circumstances, that make up the most famous of all the great stories of the heart"). All translations from the French, unless otherwise indicated, are our own.

2. Cocteau had originally hoped to have Michèle Morgan play Iseult. Like several French actors and directors, Morgan had left for Hollywood at the beginning of the Occupation (Steegmuller 454). Marais claims that, when he eventually met her, he felt she was the only woman he could have loved with a real love (*Histoires de ma vie* 182). One wonders what kind of chemistry they could have created on the screen.

3. Bédier was a well-known medievalist who researched the two major traditions of the Tristan legend preserved in fragments of twelfth-century poems by Béroul and Thomas de Bretagne. Using later texts written in those two traditions, he attempted to reconstruct Thomas' poem (1902) and published a volume of notes in which he pieced together the more primitive tradition (1905). He also composed a romance in modern French (1900) designed to acquaint the general public with these early versions.

4. Writing in 1965, Georges Sadoul stated that the film's "poetic" style had for a long time seemed as outmoded as Marais' sweaters and Sologne's hairstyle (82).

5. "La transfiguration du réel dans *L'Éternel Retour* est due au parfait dosage de la fable et du monde moderne.... [C]ette histoire se déroule à notre époque—mais comme elle est intemporelle.... Sans cesse on hésite entre le moyen âge et le XXe siècle" (180–81).

6. The other films he cites are Clouzot's *Le Corbeau*, Bresson's *Les Anges du péché*, and Carné's *Les Visiteurs du soir* (11).

7. "Que serais-je devenu sans Delannoy, qui désirait cet échange d'ondes et me demandait de le suivre lorsqu'il montait et mixait les bandes; sans Roger Hubert, qui opérait à travers notre oeil et notre coeur?" (Cocteau, *Du Cinématographe* 157). According to Marais, Cocteau's presence on the set transformed everything—their acting, Delannoy's direction, even the quality of the light (*Histoires de ma vie* 147).

8. "Les éclairages, les arrangements décoratifs, le sens de la grandeur et de la nuit, les détails essentiels en gros plan, le mouvement, le rythme, les jeux de l'ombre et de la lumière, nous retrouverons le même style dans tous les autres films de Cocteau, bons ou mauvais" (194).

9. "Obsédé de la présence familière et terrible de la mort, de l'inséparable mort, toute vieille et toute neuve, toute neuve pour chacun de nous" (Thierry Maulnier, "Avant-propos" in Dubourg iii). Cocteau felt that death was omnipresent, lodged within us from birth and becoming increasingly more visible (*Journals of Jean Cocteau* 200).

10. See Baumgartner 5. Rougemont is primarily responsible for this Romantic view of the legend, which he based on Wagner's opera. On the French love of the metaphysical and the persistence of Rougemont's thesis in French film, see Grimbert, "Truffaut's *La Femme d'à côté* (1981)." See Amengual for a quick survey of how the "myth"—unabashedly defined according to Rougemont's conception—evolved and degenerated in French cinema.

11. See n. 3 above.

12. On the construction and tonality of this romance, see Corbellari's illuminating analysis of Bédier's oeuvre.

13. "Seigneurs, vous plaît-il d'entendre un beau conte d'amour et de mort?" (1)

14. Too perfect, according to Maddux, who argues persuasively that the kinship Cocteau felt with the material accounts for his failure to innovate as much as he did with other stories that he brought to the screen, such as *La Belle et la Bête* (*Beauty and the Beast*) and *Orphée* (*Orpheus*) and for his consequent failure "to work his usual magic" (493–504).

15. Although Cocteau nowhere states that he used Bédier's version, it was the one most available, and Maddux's careful comparison of the screenplay with the romance (478–93) leaves no

doubt that it was his source. Moreover, Rougemont's 1939 study, which relies heavily on Bédier, had just appeared.

16. Contrary to his desire, which was to shoot the film in Brittany, Cocteau had to settle for Nice and Lake Geneva, because the northern coast was too strategically important to the Germans.

17. See Marais, *Histoires de ma vie* 126–27. Marais states that his own pay was poor, but Moulouk was paid handsomely — in red meat, which was expensive and in short supply during the war (147).

18. We are reminded of the guardian angel who comes to take the child (a younger version of the poet) felled by Dargelos' snowball in *Le Sang d'un poète*.

19. Did Cocteau see the stained glass windows recounting the legend that were executed for Harden Grange by Morris and Company in 1862? The final panel, "The Tomb of Tristram and Isolde," designed by Edward Byrne-Jones, shows the lovers as gisants on a tomb guarded by two hounds (Whitaker 196–97).

20. To make sure that Sologne's naturally brown hair and Marais' blond hair came out exactly the same shade, Cocteau had them visit the hairdresser together (Marais, *Histoires de ma vie* 148). They appear to be twins, like the brother and sister in *Les Enfants terribles* (*The Holy Terrors*) and like the poet Orphée linked both to Eurydice and his young rival Cégeste; all these characters sport blond hair.

21. McMunn 173 and Arthur Hoerée in the section "La Critique" following the published French version of the screenplay (47). In his poems to Marais, Cocteau often described the actor's body (and his own) in terms of sculpture; see the poems published at the end of Marais, *Histoires de ma vie*, especially "Les Chevaliers," where Cocteau states that their entwined bodies appear as if sculpted on a tomb (259).

22. "La mort les sculpte, les drape, les hausse sur un pavois royal. Une gloire les isole et les enveloppe" (Cocteau, *L'Éternel Retour* 46). Mitry, who faults the film generally for the uneasy alliance of the real and the mythical, finds this scene magnificent: "The real and the legendary finally come together in the symbol that emanates from it…." ("Le réel et la légende enfin se conjuguent dans le symbole qui en émane…." 165–66).

23. "Sologne était superbe hier. Je la coiffe avec des cheveux plats qui tombent très bas comme ils veulent. Elle a l'air d'une statue de cathédrale, d'un drôle d'oiseau, d'une noyée fantôme" (Cocteau, *Lettres à Jean Marais* 169).

24. Cocteau, speaking of the drawings he made of deceased friends, once said: "Death takes care with its statues. She unwrinkles them" (*Journals of Jean Cocteau* 198). In 1946, Cocteau published *La Mort et les Statues*, a book of photographs of bronze statues removed in 1943 from public places in France and melted down for the war effort. The photographs show the statues heaped in a Paris warehouse, and Cocteau's accompanying text likens their "humiliating" treatment to torture and death.

25. In the introduction to his edition of *Orphée* (xviii).

26. Savage 149. Savage sees Patrice as an amalgam of classical and medieval heroes suggested by various details: the thigh wound (Adonis), his arrival on the scene mounted for the hunt (Hippolytus, who conceived a passion for his mother-in-law), and his ceremonial exit from the bar borne on the shoulders of sailors (Hamlet, Beowulf).

27. "Ma démarche étant celle d'un homme qui boite, un pied dans la vie et un pied dans la mort, il était normal que j'en arrivasse à un mythe où la vie et la mort s'affrontent" (Cocteau, *Entretiens sur le cinématographe* 68).

28. "J'ai toujours aimé 'ce chien-et-loup,' cette pénombre où fleurissent les énigmes" (Cocteau, *Du Cinématographe* 125).

29. The red pennant was inspired by the death of Isadora Duncan who was strangled when what Cocteau called "the long red scarf that hated her" caught in the wheel of her car. In *La Machine infernale*, Jocaste hangs herself with a red scarf, and, in *Les Enfants terribles*, Élizabeth's husband Michael is killed in the same way as Duncan (Sprigge and Kihm 113, 126).

30. "Personne ne peut plus les rejoindre" (Cocteau, *L'Éternel Retour* 46).

31. Eventually, a compromise must have been reached, since Patrice says only: "J'ai compris" (Cocteau, *L'Éternel Retour* 43).

32. "[Qui] nous prouvent que le cinématographe est l'appareil du réalisme et du lyrisme, que tout dépend de l'angle sous lequel les spectacles de la vie s'observent. Angle sous lequel ils nous obligent à partager une vision particulière des choses et nous en soulignent le miracle quotidien" (Cocteau, *Du Cinématographe* 93).

33. "This dream castle, these horse rides, Natalie's long, stylized gowns, her hair worthy of a mythical princess, the love philters — these things are badly suited to stories involving garages, tea rooms, and mechanical break-downs" ("Ce château de rêve, ces chevauchées, les grandes robes stylisées de Natalie, ses cheveux de princesse mythique, les philtres d'amour, tous cela s'intègre mal à des histoires de garage, de salon de thé et de pannes d'auto." (Mitry 165).

34. The sequence, with its haunting effects of clair-obscur, seems — especially in slow motion — to anticipate the progression of Marais/Orphée through the "Zone."

35. See Dubourg's analysis of the role of night (191–93). Night as a refuge for the lovers is an important theme in medieval love poetry, but with Wagner's rendering of the legend, it took on a different resonance, since it signified death as well.

36. "Le cinématographe exige une syntaxe. Cette syntaxe n'est obtenue que par l'enchaînement et par le choc des images entre elles.... Mon premier soin, dans un film, est d'empêcher que les images ne coulent, de les opposer, encastrer et joindre sans nuire à leur relief" (Cocteau, *Entretiens sur le cinématographe* 14).

37. Dubourg identifies this scene and the one in which Natalie and Patrice are playing chess as two passages that demonstrate fully the magical power of the camera when directed by a poet (183). See his excellent analysis of these two scenes (183–85).

38. "Ce geste, qui déclenche le drame et la destinée de quatre personnages, nous est montré en gros plan, énorme photographie d'un détail qui entraîne l'ensemble et dont la gravité ne peut plus échapper au spectateur" ("This gesture, which sets in motion the drama and the destiny of four characters, is shown to us in close-up, an enormous shot of a detail that sums up the entire scene and whose importance is henceforth impressed upon the spectator.") (Dubourg 183).

39. "Les choses ont une façon à elles d'arriver. Laisse les faire" (Cocteau, *L'Éternel Retour* 40).

40. Additionally, the spark plug anticipates Patrice's garage work as a mechanic and his disabling of the car in which Gertrude and Achille are transporting Natalie back toward the island. The picture postcard finds an echo in the photo of Natalie that Anne shows to Natalie II. "Le cinématographe exige une syntaxe. Cette syntaxe n'est obtenue que par l'enchaînement et par le choc des images entre elles.... Mon premier soin, dans un film, est d'empêcher que les images ne coulent, de les opposer, encastrer et joindre sans nuire à leur relief" (Cocteau, *Entretiens sur le cinématographe* 14).

WORKS CITED

Amengual, Barthelémy. *Le Mythe de Tristan et Yseult au cinema*. Alger: Travail et Culture, 1952.

Baumgartner, Emmanuèle. *Tristan et Iseut: de la légende aux récits en vers*. Paris: PUF, 1987.

Bazin, André. *French Cinema of the Occupation and Resistance*. Collected and with an introduction by François Truffaut. Trans. Stanley Hochman. New York: Ungar, 1975.

Bédier, Joseph. *Le Roman de Tristan et Iseut renouvelé par Joseph Bédier*. 1900. Paris: L'Édition d'art H. Piazza, 1946.

———. *Le Roman de Tristan par Thomas*. Paris: S.A.T.F., 1902–05.

Charensol, Georges. "Jean Cocteau et le cinématographe." *Cahiers Jean Cocteau* 3 (1972): 9–16.

Cocteau, Jean. *The Art of Cinema*. Compiled and edited by André Bernard and Claude Gauteur. Trans. Robin Buss. London: Marion Boyars, 1992.

———. *Cocteau on the Film*. Conversations with Jean Cocteau recorded by André Fraigneau. Trans. Vera Traill. New York: Dover, 1972.

———. *Du Cinématographe*. Textes réunis et présentés par André Bernard et Claude Gauteur. Paris: Belfond, 1973.

———. *Entretiens sur le cinématographe*. Édition établie par André Bernard et Claude Gauteur. Postface d'André Fraigneau. Paris: Belfond, 1973.

———. *L'Éternel Retour*. (Screenplay.) *Paris Théâtre* 22 (1950): 22–44.

———. *The Journals of Jean Cocteau*. Ed. and trans. Wallace Fowlie. London: Museum Press, 1956.

———. *Lettres à Jean Marais*. Paris: Albin Michel, 1987.

———. *La Mort et les Statues*. Photographies de Pierre Jahan. Paris: Seghers, 1977.

———. *Orphée. The Play and the Film*. Ed. E. Freeman. Oxford: Blackwell, 1976.

———. *Three Screenplays: L'Éternel Retour, Orphée, La Belle et la Bête*. Trans. Carol Martin-Sperry. New York: Grossman Publishers, 1972.

Corbellari, Alain. *Joseph Bédier: Écrivain et Philologue*. Genève: Droz, 1997.

Crosland, Margaret. *Jean Cocteau*. London: Peter Neville, 1955.

Dubourg, Pierre. *Dramaturgie de Jean Cocteau*. Paris: Bernard Grasset, 1954.

Grimbert, Joan Tasker. "Love, Honor, and Alienation in Thomas's *Roman de Tristan*." In *The Arthurian Yearbook 4*. Ed. Keith Busby. New York: Garland, 1992.

———. "Truffaut's *La Femme d'à côté (1981)*: Attenuating a Romantic Archetype—Tristan and Iseult?" In *King Arthur in Film: New Essays on Arthurian Cinema*. Ed. Kevin J. Harty. Jefferson, N.C.: McFarland, 1999.

Maddux, Stephen. "Cocteau's Tristan and Iseut: A Case of Overmuch Respect." In *Tristan and Isolde: A Casebook*. Ed. Joan Tasker Grimbert. New York: Garland, 1995.

Marais, Jean. *Histoires de ma vie, avec une suite poétique de 115 poèmes inédits de Jean Cocteau*. Paris: Albin Michel, 1975.

———. *Mes Quatre Vérités*. Paris: Éditions de Paris, 1957.

McMunn, Meradith T. "Filming the Tristan Myth: From Text to Icon." In *Cinema Arthuriana: Essays on Arthurian Film*. Ed. Kevin J. Harty. New York: Garland, 1991.

Michel, Francisque. *Tristan, Recueil de ce qui reste des poèmes relatifs à ces aventures composés en anglo-normand et en grec dans les XII et XIII siècles*. London: Pickering; Paris: Techener, 1835–38.

Mitry, Jean. *Histoire du cinéma*. Paris: Jean-Pierre Delarge, 1980.

Rougemont, Denis de. *Love in the Western World* (orig. *L'Amour et l'Occident*, 1939). Trans. Montgomery Belgion. New York: Schocken Books, 1983.

Sadoul, Georges. "*L'Éternel Retour.*" *Dictionnaire des films*. Paris: Seuil, 1965.

Savage, Edward B. *The Rose and the Vine: A Study of the Evolution of the Tristan and Isolt Tale in Drama*. Cairo: American University at Cairo Press, 1961.

Sprigge, Elizabeth, and Jean-Jacques Kihm. *Jean Cocteau: The Man and the Mirror*. New York: Coward McCann, 1968.

Steegmuller, Francis. *Cocteau*. Boston: Little, Brown and Company, 1970.

Taylor, John Russell. "Jean Cocteau." In *Cinema: A Critical Dictionary: The Major Film-makers*. Ed. Richard Roud. New York: Viking Press, 1980.

Wagner, Richard. *Tristan und Isolde*. London: Calder Publications, 1981.

Whitaker, Muriel. *The Legends of King Arthur in Art*. Cambridge, Eng.: D. S. Brewer, 1990.

20

Arms and Armor in Arthurian Films

Helmut Nickel

Among the aspects of Arthurian film that deserve special attention is its treatment of arms and armor. After all, Arthurian films are mainly about knights, and knights would not be knights without their armor. This essay will examine some typical approaches to the subject among these films and try to explain how arms and armor were handled, not only as far as selection of the period style is concerned but also in actual use of weapons in battle and tournament.

In reviewing costume and armor in cinema Arthuriana, one must keep in mind that these films face problems different from those encountered by the average costume drama. Most historical films deal with an exactly datable timespan — say, Imperial Rome for *Ben-Hur* or the fifteenth century for the campaigns of *Henry V* and *Richard III* — and therefore costumes, furniture, and weapons can be designed that should be reasonably accurate for the periods in question, provided that the designers did their research.

Arthurian films, by contrast, are not necessarily bound to such a fixed style period. Actually, the scriptwriter, the director, and the costume designer are free to choose from a timespan of almost a thousand years, if their ambition would call for historical accuracy. Given the legendary nature of the Matter of Britain, though, any flight of fancy concerning costume and setting could be equally well justified.

The version of the tales of King Arthur best known to the general public is Malory's *Le Morte d'Arthur*, written down in the fifteenth century, and for this reason costumes and setting in Late Gothic style might by considered to be appropriate. On the other hand, it is also well known today that the "historical Arthur" would have lived and fought at about the year A.D. 500, and a filmmaker aiming at historical verisimilitude would thus prefer a Dark Age background. Then again, most of the major Arthurian romances were composed during the twelfth and thirteenth centuries, and costume designers might see "around 1200" especially attractive as the right style period, because of its romantic association with the Crusades. All these period styles could be shifted onto an imaginary plane by adding fanciful touches to otherwise quite realistically rendered costumes as *Verfremdungseffekt*, a trick amply used by nineteenth-century illustrators.

The medieval romances of chivalry are legitimate ancestors of both the Western novels and the Western movies, where the Lone Cowboy riding into town is the Questing Knight, the Sheriff and his posse are King Arthur and the companions of the Round Table, the villain in the showdown on Main Street is the Black Knight at the tournament, and the rancher's daughter is the Princess, whose fair hand is the prize at the happy end.

Every moviegoer knows and accepts the "white hats/black hats" rule of the Western horse operas. For the "knights in shining armor" films, the same rules apply in an appropriately modified form. The evil significance of the Black Knight is self-evident[1]; for balance, the Hero, who normally is also the star, not only has to ride a white horse whenever possible, but also has to wear an open-face helmet, in order to make absolutely sure that the audience gets a good look at the star's radiant brow, while the villain is hiding his sinister countenance behind a closed visor. Ever so often, the hero is found fighting through raging battles without benefit of any helmet at all. Such a scene is usually made plausible by a fine touch of realism, when the hero's helmet gets knocked off his head as soon as the battle is under way.

All designers of costumes or armor, even those who rely largely on their own imagination, must necessarily have some models in mind upon which their creations are based. One of the problems with these models is that there are very few actual objects in the field of arms and armor that have survived from the periods in question. Practically ninety-nine percent of existing armor dates from after A.D. 1500. For this reason, a visit to even a major museum can be only of limited help, and therefore book illustrations would be the logical (and also easiest accessible) source for such models. Purists among designers could find their prototypes in the standard reference works of costume and armor, but those searching for the realm of myth and fantasy, if they would be willing to look for inspiration outside of their own imagination, presumably would prefer to glean their inspiration from the glorious illustrations provided by Howard Pyle, Arthur Rackham, Aubrey Beardsley, or N. C. Wyeth. The inspired use of such splendid material would contribute greatly to the success of a film.

Once in a while, a film is straightforwardly based upon fully prescribed pictorial material, which makes it both easy and difficult for the designers, who have to stay faithful to their source but have to use their own imaginations to flesh out the parts not preformed in the prototype. This is the case with *Prince Valiant* (1954), which was an adaptation of the comic-strip classic by Hal Foster. Foster, in his painstakingly precise drawings, had created his own vision of the Middle Ages, which even beyond the circle of his fans is widely taken for medieval reality. The setting of his *Prince Valiant* is as imaginary as his hero himself. Foster created him in the best tradition of medieval minstrels, who kept inventing new heroes and new adventures within the well-known and well-beloved Arthurian framework. This was done to enhance their performances and to catch the attention of their audiences in castle halls and county fairgrounds. The costumes and armor designed by Foster are of a medievalistic nature, vaguely "around 1200," with some highlights from earlier times, such as the Late Roman/Byzantine period, and of course—as would be expected in a story about a prince of Thule—with a generous dose of romantic Viking imagery.

The film designer of *Prince Valiant* faithfully adhered to the style created by Foster, down to such details as the armorial bearings of Sir Gawain (a highly, but quite unheraldically, stylized golden falcon on his green surcoat, doubtlessly chosen to fit the interpretation of Gawain's Welsh name, Gwalchmai, "Hawk of May"). It is interesting that, as far as I know, not one film designer ever made use of the "real" arms of the Knights of the Round Table that can be found recorded in romances, as illuminations in manuscripts, and even as regular rolls of arms from the thirteenth century onward. In all fairness, though, it has to be said that before Pastoureau's *Armorial*, published in 1983 (which mentions non–French material only in passing), reference to Arthurian arms was found mostly in scattered articles in heraldic journals.

The knights at the Great Tournament in *Prince Valiant* wear thirteenth-century-style mail armor with bucket-shaped *heaulms* and flowing armorial surcoats in bright colors. Shields are of the triangular "knightly" type, emblazoned with the champion's heraldic bearings, but Prince Valiant's own shield, with his badge of the red horse's head of Thule, is circular, to hint at his "Viking" heritage. A stickler for technical detail would insist that his shield is structurally closer to that of a Greek hoplite (a heavy-armored citizen soldier of classical antiquity) than to that of a Norseman. (Perhaps this design can be explained as a Mediterranean influence through his association with Aleta, the Queen of the Misty Islands in the Aegean Sea.) Shields in most films are not made of wood covered with leather, as actual medieval shields were, but are stamped out of sheet metal. Such construction has the advantages of faster and less expensive manufacture, of a neat and shiny look, and also of a pleasing acoustic effect, because these metal shields, when hit by sword or mace, give forth a resounding "Bang," instead of the less gratifying dull "Thud" of wood.

The costumes of the invading and marauding Sea Rovers evoke the standard Viking image with shaggy furs and horned helmets; their chieftain, in his conspiratorial meeting with the Black Knight, Sir Brack,[2] has a winged helmet as mark of his rank. (Unfortunately, no archaeologist so far has unearthed a Viking helmet with horns, let alone with wings.)

As light campaign gear, fit equally for battle or quest, Hal Foster's knights are equipped with spiked steelcaps with mail curtains hanging down to protect nape and neck. Because the manufacture of mail is a time-consuming business — it means linking together by hand thousands of tiny rings — the costume designer of the film in what must have been a brilliant brainstorm was able to circumvent considerable labor expenses by simply obtaining a number of *khula-khud*, spiked helmets with camail of a traditional pattern (Robinson, *Oriental Armour* 31–52, 93–115), which were produced en masse in busy family armorers' shops in Persia and India up to the first half of the twentieth century. Made expressly for the tourist trade, they were sold in all the bazaars of the East, and they are still cluttering up antique shops and auction sales. These helmets resemble Foster's noble knightly gear quite admirably, as long as one does not look too closely for tell-tale Oriental features, such as the paired plume-holders on either side of the moveable nasal.

An even more popular Arthurian film has been *Camelot* (1967). Admittedly, one reason for this popularity would be the fact that its model, the Lerner and Loewe musical *Camelot*, has become nostalgically linked with the presidency of John F. Kennedy (Knight 26–31). However, the lavishness of the film's production also guarantees its success. In the unpaginated illustrated souvenir booklet for *Camelot*, the costume designer, John Truscott, states that he "tried to make the film seem sophisticated but with elements which contradict sophistication." Truscott also claims that "materials were collected from all over the world." Though this comment evidently refers to the fabrics for the costumes to be made, it also applies to the armor in a surprising way.

Armor of knights and men-at-arms, a total of 361 suits, was designed to give *Camelot* a "timeless" medieval look, but with generous use of *Verfremdungseffekt*, in order, in the words of director Joshua Logan, to "eliminate all the clichés that have surrounded castle-and-crusade pictures since the beginning of films."

The armor of the men-at-arms, to be seen only more or less on background figures in mass scenes, is vaguely fourteenth-century in style, with mailshirts, iron-studded leather jackets, and simple bassinets. The knights, as befitting their superior status, wear much more elaborate armor. Their articulated arm and leg defenses are also of the type in use since the fourteenth century (Blair 62–67), but the cuirasses and helmets of the main actors, Sir Lionel, Sir Sagramore, Sir Dinadan, and even of King Arthur himself, are derived from Central Asian and Chinese prototypes of the Wei, T'ang, and Ming periods (Robinson, *Oriental Armour* 32, 137–39, 151); a superlative *Verfremdungseffekt* indeed! In particular, Sir Lionel's lamellar helmet with its mask visor is clearly styled after an original of ca. A.D. 500, found in an Avar warrior's grave at Kertch in the Ukraine and now in the Historical Museum, Moscow (Robinson, *Oriental Armour* 55–56; Kirpičnikov 101–02). Presumably in order to make the bumptious Sir Lionel even a little more ridiculous looking, his visor is not hinged at the brow, to fold upward, as it should, but is made to open sideways, like the door of a pot-bellied iron stove.[3]

The bardings and trappings for the noble steeds of the three champions at the tournament, on the other hand, are in sixteenth-century European style. Their horses' chanfrons are magnificently crested: Sir Lionel's with a golden swan with spread wings, Sir Sagramore's with a splendid rack of stag's antlers, and Sir Dinadan's with a huge pair of curling ram's horns. These ram's horns are the clue for where the inspiration for these crests must have come from. Chanfrons with ram's horns as ear protectors are on display in two museums in Madrid. One example is conspicuous as the first in an array of a dozen equestrian figures of knights in full armor, man and horse, in the Great Hall of the Real Armeria, the ancient armory of the kings of Spain (Cortés pl. I and IV); the other has pride of place in the Armor Gallery of the Army Museum (*Museo del Erjecito* 35). Ram's horns as protectors are the *leitmotif* for horse armor made by a prolific Nürnberg armorer, Kunz Lochner (c. 1510–67). The armor in the Army Museum is his work. When *Camelot* was filmed on location in Spain, using real castles in Spain for its scenery (the Castillo de Coca is Camelot; the Alcazar of Segovia is Lancelot's Joyous Guard), the designer seems to have found his inspirations for his horse armor in the Madrid museums. Having decided to adapt the impressive ram's horns for the chanfron crest of Sir Dinadan's charger, it would be only one further step to create the antler rack and the swan crest for the other champions as a "spinoff."

Lancelot's silver armor (he rides a white horse, of course) is topped by his helmet crest of a silver fleur-de-lys — to show not only that he is terribly pure but presumably also that he is French. The same "French" fleur-de-lys, set in a glory of rays, is displayed on his silver shield.[4] This shield has a bouche in its upper dexter corner, a cutout that served as a support for the lance in the charge.

A knight's shield was his main defense in the days of mail armor, which was too flexible to be shock resistant. To make the most out of the shield's protection, knights, especially in the formal combat of the tournament, charged each other left (shield) side against left side, their lances pointing diagonally across their horses' necks.

Unfortunately, fight coordinators in films are generally unaware of the technical function of the shield as a shock breaker. In sword fights, they let their combatants happily flail away, sword clashing against sword (the surest way to ruin a good blade), with their shields held out of the way as a mere ornamental nuisance, and in jousts the combatants all too often point their lances straightforward, meeting their opponents on their right sides unprotected by the ignored shields. Sad to say, in the wayside encounter of Lancelot with King Arthur, and also in his jousts with Sir Lionel and Sir Dinadan, the jousters charge each other right (but wrong) side against right side. Only Sir Sagramore manages to get on the proper side of the tilting barrier, a fine point appreciated by Queen Guinevere.

Another technical point regularly missed by illustrators of knightly tales and fight coordinators alike is that of the broken lance. Inevitably, the loser in the joust falls off his horse ingloriously, his broken lance dangling limply, while the victorious champion's shaft is boldly pointing up — and forward at a triumphant angle — perhaps for us moderns understandable from the point of view of Freudian symbolism, but quite wrong from the technical point. A shattered lance was the best proof that the jouster had hit his opponent with the greatest force possible; a mere glancing blow or a miss would have left the shaft intact. It was a score point recorded by the heralds, whether a jouster broke his lance, even if neither combatant fell. Contemporary depictions invariably show the victor's lance broken, and the loser's intact (Cripps-Day xxvii–xxx; Nickel, "Tournament" 216–17, 248).

In *Camelot*, King Arthur's great sword Excalibur is the sword he drew from the stone, as indicated by the Gothic script etched on its blade: "Whoso Pulleth Out This Sword of the Stone Is Rightwise King Born of All England." The Sword's cruciform hilt vaguely resembles that of a fifteenth-century sword with a grip "of one-hand-and-a-half." In an interesting pattern of mutual influence between the arts, the famous still photo of King Arthur enthroned, his fists clenched around the guard of Excalibur, has been adapted as the cover picture for the third novel, *Arthur*, in Stephen R. Lawhead's Pendragon Cycle (1989). The graphic artist exchanged Richard Harris's frowning brow for a more youthful countenance, and slightly — barely noticeably — altered the appearance of Excalibur by putting a purple gem in its guard, because the novel mentions an "eagle-carved amethyst" on its hilt. The amethyst in Excalibur's hilt has become an established detail, passed on and elaborated upon among Arthurian writers for fifty years, ever since Wart in T. H. White's *The Once and Future King* (1939) pulled at the Sword in the Stone, and "the light all about the churchyard glowed like amethysts."[5]

T. H. White's *The Once and Future King* has been the basis not only of Camelot but also of the Disney version of the story in *The Sword in the Stone* (1963). As an animated film, it is of course subject to rules totally different technically and aesthetically from those films already discussed. Therefore, nobody would expect anything resembling historical accuracy in such an esoteric subject as the arms and armor of the knights meeting at the Tournament toward the end of the picture. It is hard to swallow, though, that the cartoonist quite blithely let the Golden Knight couch his lance with his left hand and carry his round shield in his right![6]

Monty Python and the Holy Grail (1975) is even among satires "in a class by itself" (Lacy and Ashe 281). At first glance, the armor of its knights looks exactly like the medievalistic standard equipment of top-to-toe mail, helmets, and shields. In particular, the armor of King Arthur himself is not noticeably different from that which can be seen on dozens of effigies in dozens of churches and cathedrals all over what used to be Arthur's kingdom of Logres. The gisants of Robert de Vere, Earl of Oxford (d. 1221), or of William Longespée (d. 1228), in Salisbury Cathedral, might well have served as direct models. The jokes, in Monty Python fashion, are in silly details, such as Sir Bedevere's helmet with a visor open like a picture frame, funny armorial bearings like those of the Knight of the Red Herring or of Sir Robin Coeur-de-Poulet, the high-kicking ballet of the knights at Camelot, and of course the outrageous notion of having the knights galumph about on pretend horses. The armor of the Black Knight is probably styled after that of a sculpture of a knightly saint on the façade of Wells Cathedral (Blair 22; Norman 13). It would be interesting to know whether the black cross on the white shield of the knight in the fore of the battle array at Arthur's attack of the Grail Castle was chosen because this was the badge of the Teutonic Knights. This detail could well be one of those sometimes surprisingly subtle Monty Python gags, most likely arranged by Terry Jones, who also happens to be the author of an iconoclastic book about Chaucer's "parfit knyght" and his connection with the Order of the Teutonic Knights (Jones 49).[7]

The French film *Perceval le Gallois* (1978) takes its armor from the twelfth century. Not having seen this film, I know of it only from still photos. Reviewers have, however, praised it highly, because of its beautiful stylization using two-dimensional scenery props to create visual effects like the illuminations in a medieval manuscript (Lacy and Ashe 283). The film designer's puristic use of manuscript illustrations as his models is clearly evident in his treatment of armor. Those mail shirts not yet covered by surcoats, and the huge round-topped shields with simple heraldic charges painted in the Romanesque style of the late twelfth century are taken directly from miniatures in a devotional manuscript, the *Hortus Deliciarum* of the Abbess Herrad von Landsberg (ca. 1185). The precious original, once one of the treasures of the City Library of Strasbourg, was destroyed in a fire when this formidable fortress city was shelled in 1870 during the Franco-Prussian War, we do have carefully made hand-colored lithograph copies of the miniatures from the early nineteenth century (Engelhardt n.p.; Martin 36–39).

Incidentally, when in *Camelot* King Arthur has his talk about Lancelot with King Pellinore,[8] he is toying with two armored puppets, which are so close in style to marionettes shown in one delightful miniature of the *Hortus Deliciarum*, where puppeteers are playing *ludus monstrorum*, that it is hard to think this similarity entirely coincidental (Nickel, "Little Knights" 170–83).

Though *Perceval le Gallois* has been much lauded for how closely it follows Chrétien de Troyes, it seems on the other hand to follow the "white hat" tradition, by letting its title hero ride a white horse, instead of a red sorrel or roan, as he should after he becomes the Red Knight. Very properly, the designer did not give Perceval's charger the flowing trappings so beloved by designers of "castle and crusade" films, because these trappings were not yet in fashion in Chrétien's time (ca. 1170–80). The first representations of knights on horses with trappings are from 1196.

While *Perceval* has its setting in the twelfth century of Chrétien de Troyes, the television series *The Legend of King Arthur* (1979) tries hard to evoke the background of the "historical Arthur" ca. A.D. 500. At times, it succeeds even a little too well in pointing out the rough edges of the Dark Ages; all too often, the Knights of the Round Table look rather more like the Stratford Inn's bane, Larry, his brother Darryl, and his other brother Darryl, from CBS's *Newhart*, than like shining champions at the foremost court of chivalry.

The armor designer for this series gave his knights body armor of the lamellar type, made up of small rectangular iron plates arranged in overlapping rows and laced together with leather straps. This was authentic Dark Age armor, introduced by the steppe tribes that came from the East during the Great Migration period (Robinson, *Oriental Armour* 4–10, 25–27, and *Armour*

The battle between Sylvain Levignac (left) as Anguingueron and Fabrice Luchini as Perceval in Eric Rohmer's 1978 film *Perceval le Gallois*.

of Imperial Rome 163; Kirpičnikov 104–07; Gamber, "Kataphrakten" 7–44). In order to give the armor the "primitive" look appropriate for the Dark Ages, however, the designer seems to have turned these laced-together lamellar cuirasses inside out, so that the strap endings of the lacings dangle loosely (and messily) on the outside for the desired effect.

Primitive starkness was also uppermost in the designer's mind when the film's helmets and shields were created. The helmets with mask visors, cheek pieces, and neck guards are deliberately crude versions of the magnificent original from the fabled Sutton Hoo ship burial of the seventh century (Grohskopf 60ff.; Gamber, "Some Notes" 208–16; Bruce-Mitford 217–80; Nicolle 13). The helmet, now in the British Museum, is richly embellished by an overlay of embossed silver; its crest in shape of a dragon is stretched across the helmet bowl from its brow to the nape of the neck.[9] The helmet's most remarkable element is a visor wrought as a face mask with bristling moustache and garnet-inlaid lips. In the television series, the helmets are of the same type, with visor masks, but of starkly plain dark iron and without any decoration.

Shields in the series are circular, with a central boss sometimes surrounded by five or six smaller bosses that would serve both as reinforcement and as ornamentation. Like the helmets, shields bear no distinguishing marks to tell one from the next. To tell friend from foe by painting shields with such markings was the reason for the rise of heraldry, necessary after the introduction of visored helmets that made faces unrecognizable. For this reason, it is a truly amazing feat that Bors recognizes Lancelot's shield in the bundle that a groom, on Elaine's orders, tries to hide from him.

Arthur's legendary battle standard is a golden dragon; it probably was a windsock-like *draco* (a cavalry ensign of the Late Roman army), with a metal head and a fluttering fabric body (Tatlock 233; Esin 15; Nicolle pl. C; Robinson, *Armour of Imperial Rome* 17). In novels and films alike, Arthur's dragon banner is usually interpreted as a flag with a dragon's image. One of the exceptions is the dragon standard, only fleetingly seen, that is shown in the *Legend of King Arthur* television series. Here it is a sculptured dragon of metal, sitting on a cross-piece on top of a pole, in the style of the eagles and other *signa* of the

Roman legions (Robinson, *Armour of Imperial Rome* 32, 34).

Quite likely, "for some tastes the most successful of the Arthurian films in English is *Excalibur*" (Lacy and Ashe 281). Its ambition is to tell the entire Arthurian story, including the Grail quest, in one fell swoop. It places extraordinary emphasis on the representation of armor, to a degree unusual even among Arthurian films. *Excalibur* in fact indicates the rise, the glory, and the fall of Arthur's kingdom by changes in the appearance of the knights' armor. Not only are the knights in full armor practically all the time — Uther Pendragon keeps his armor on even while he rapes Ygraine, a wry reversal of the hoary old japes about chastity belts — but armor is ingeniously used to convey messages about the deeper meaning underlying the events. Stylistically, the film's armor is, with two exceptions, based on fifteenth-century models, but makes imaginative use of the *Verfremdungseffekt* of fanciful deviations from the traceable prototypes.

In the opening scenes, the kingless interregnum and the no less brutal period of Uther Pendragon's rule are symbolized by warriors in black armor of monstrous shape, with oversize shoulder-pieces and elbow-cops, heavily studded with knobby rivets and wicked spikes. Helmets have bizarre visors of animal forms; Uther Pendragon's own is shaped as the snout of a wild boar. Here symbolism makes a clever play on the term "pig-faced" for this type of pointed visor (Blair 69); with the transformation of his helmet into a realistic boar's snout, Uther Pendragon's unbridled lust, both for power and for Ygraine, is unmistakably expressed in a literal and visual way. By contrast, Duke Gorlois's armor is recognizably based on an existing armor (ca. 1450–60), now in the Historical Museum at Berne, Switzerland (Thomas and Gamber 51; Martin 122). As the wronged husband of Ygraine, Gorlois is the "good guy" and therefore does not qualify for the weirder bizarreries marking the more sinister characters.

After the foundation of the Round Table, the Knights appear in truly "shining armor," beautifully polished and styled in the best tradition of the illustrations of Arthur Rackham, as for instance in his "How Sir Launcelot fought with a fiendly dragon" (Pollard and Rackham pl. 10).[10] Rackham's illustrations inspired entire episodes of the film, such as the hanged knights in the tree (Pollard and Rackham pl. 96) and the climactic last fight at Camlann, derived from "How Mordred was slain by Arthur, and how by him Arthur was hurt to the death" (Pollard and Rackham pl. 16).

The symbolic value of the armor becomes fully evident when the gradual breaking up of the Companionship of the Round Table is demonstrated by the rusting of the armor worn by the questing knights, until Perceval, after the achievement of the Grail, sheds his corroded armor altogether and returns almost naked, dressed only in loose breeches resembling the loincloth of Christ.

Equally, Lancelot's guilty conscience is brought out in the open through the medium of his armor. When resting in the forest, he is attacked and wounded with his own sword by a nightmare enemy, who turns out to be his own still shiny armor come to ghostly life. To demonstrate the fundamental difference between the brutal lust of Uther's rape of Ygraine and the guilty but pure love of Guinevere and Lancelot, armor is deftly utilized as symbolic props. Uther, disguised by Gorlois's armor, ravishes the naked Ygraine, after having ripped the clothes off her body; by contrast, Guinevere joyfully joins Lancelot in the enchanted forest glade, where the lovers embrace in almost chaste nakedness, with Lancelot's armor cast aside, never to be put on again. As a detail borrowed from Gottfried's *Tristan*, where King Mark is still noble and forgiving and not the despicable coward as in Malory (Surles 60–75), Arthur in the only scene in which he rides a white horse finds the guilty lovers asleep in the forest and, with broken heart, plants Excalibur between them, by this token giving up everything worthwhile in his life.

One of the most spectacular scenes in *Excalibur* is the ride of the Knights of the Round Table to meet their destiny at Camlann in a blaze of glory. Their armor shining again, they follow King Arthur on his steed bedecked in golden scale armor, the huge banner of the Dragon floating above. There are few sights more stirring than a knight in sparkling plate armor galloping forth holding aloft a streaming banner of red and gold — and this sight is seen through a screen of apple trees in full bloom.

Interestingly, the scale armor of Arthur's steed is styled after an original cataphract (heavy-armored cavalry) armor found in the Late Roman fortress Dura Europos, Mesopotamia, and now on display in the Higgins Armory Museum, Worcester, Massachusetts. Fragments of such armor have been excavated at Newstead, the site of the Late Roman cavalry fort of Trimontium between Hadrian's and the Antonine Walls; they are now in the National Museum of Antiquities, Edinburgh. This scale armor for horses was introduced by steppe nomads taken into the Late Roman army as auxiliaries from A.D. 175 on.[11] The same steppe nomads, Sarmatians and Alani, introduced their tribal dragon banners as cavalry battle standards into the Roman army (Gamber, "Kataphrakten" 35ff.; Robinson, *Armour of Imperial Rome* 186, 190–95).

Arthur's knights ride to Camlann in shining armor, but the forces of evil, as represented by Mordred's followers, are in dark armor with bizarre elements. Their ensigns are ragged banners topped by skulls, identical to those from the period before Arthur's reign, signaling the lawless times to come.[12] The two glaring exceptions that do not fit the fifteenth century image of armor in *Excalibur* are Mordred's golden helmet and cuirass and the molded breastplate Morgana wears in her last scene of the film.

Mordred's golden helmet with its face mask and embossed curly hair is styled after Late Roman parade helmets in the Oriental fashion (Robinson, *Armour of Imperial Rome* 114–26, and *What Soldiers Wore* 26). One of the three helmets with visor masks found at Newstead might well have been its prototype. Mordred's muscle cuirass is also of Roman pattern (Robinson, *Armour of Imperial Rome* 147). With its embossed nipples, navel, and pectoral and abdominal muscles, it was designed to give the impression of heroic nudity. In antiquity, warriors of the most diverse cultures — Greek, Etruscan, Germanic, Celtic — went into battle naked, believing themselves to be invulnerable by virtue of invocation of the special protection of a deity. In societies where magic actually seems to work, it must have been a mighty deterrent to face such an enemy flaunting his powerful "medicine." More practical fighters, who wanted nothing left to chance with something as important as their own lives, preferred to wear such a muscle cuirass, which had the look of a naked body but gave solid real protection in addition to the magical one. Morgana's words when she is arming Mordred — "No weapon forged by man can harm you, when you wear this armor" — clearly indicate the enchanted quality of this unusual armor. It is only Excalibur, the magic blade from the Lady of the Lake (no man!), returned to Arthur by Guinevere in their reconciliation scene before Camlann, that breaks the spell and kills Mordred.

Morgana's armor, mainly an abbreviated breastplate that looks as if it was designed by and for Cher, covers few of her vital parts and even fewer of her erogenous zones. When wearing it, she weaves her last and fatal spell, indicating thereby that her armor was meant to equal the ritual nakedness of witches. Judging by the expanse of skin exposed, she must have felt supremely

Robert Addie as Mordred in John Boorman's 1981 film *Excalibur*.

confident in its magic defense value, probably against "weapons forged by man," though it proved to be useless against Merlin's greater power that led her into her own trap.

ADDENDUM

After this essay was written and published in 1991, several Arthurian films of importance were made and released. Three of them — *First Knight, The Fisher King*, and *Indiana Jones and the Last Crusade* — are of note in discussing arms and armor in Arthurian film.

The most interesting of the three as far as arms and armor are concerned is *First Knight* (1995). Here, Lancelot is not the son of a king, but a lowly wandering sellsword. As said before, in the main part of this essay, film directors like the ring of blade against blade, and fight coordinators seem to be unaware of the defensive value of shields. Therefore, right at the film's beginning, we see Lancelot lustily whacking away with local champions at a county fair. Again and again, after a whirlwind clash of blades without any regard of the ruination of their edges, he wrests the sword from his opponent's hand and sends it flying. He fervently denies using any tricks, but — unnoticed by the bumpkins at the fair — his sword does have a trick guard with a forward hook to catch an opponent's blade.

The small crowsbows one-handedly wielded like pistols by the bad guys are, of course, without any true medieval models, and their use cheapens the film.

The costumes in *First Knight* were designed in decided Italian style by Costumi dell'Arte of Rome, and the armor was made by Terry English, who also made armor for *Sword of the Valiant* (1982), an attempted reinterpretation of the story of Gawain and the Green Knight. There he recreated credible armor in late fifteenth-century style for Gawain and for most of his opponents (the antlered headdress and leafy elements of the Green Knight's armor excepted). By contrast, the armor worn in battle by the Knights of the Round Table in *First Knight* (breast- and backplates over mail shirts, and ill-fitting arm defenses) is only vaguely medievalistic.

Footsoldiers wear reinforced leather jerkins, spangenhelms, and round shields more or less like those of the Vikings in the *Ancient Warriors* television series. Archers and spearmen in *Sword of the Valiant* wear bascinets, kettlehats, and rivet-studded brigantines; such gear is generally accepted as armor of "medieval" soldiers. (Indeed, these footsoldiers do look strikingly like figurines from the 1969 *Men-at-Arms of the Fourteenth Century* series of Imrie/Risley Miniatures come to life.)

There is, of course, always a considerable amount of artistic liberty to be expected with the costuming in historical, and even more so with pseudo-historical, films, but the "undress" uniform of the Knights of the Round Table in *First Knight*, which they wear when questing or sitting around the Round Table, is something really terrible to behold. One can only hope that the black-and-blue of their tunics was chosen by the Italian designer in all innocence and in ignorance of the English vernacular; their weird trappings certainly do not have anything to do with knightly gear of any period. As token armor for this "undress" uniform, the knights have to wear on their forearms metal tubes that look as if made from tin cans, and on their left shoulders peculiar molded shield shapes that are blank metal for the knights, but decorated in relief with a golden Celtic crowned cross for King Arthur. (This cross is also the device on his blue banner.)

These little shields are presumably a misinterpretation of Italian pictorial sources. The protection of the shoulder joint against heavy blows of sword or mace was a serious technical problem as long as the tough but flexible mail shirt was the only body armor in use. Cup-shaped shoulder guards, probably of *cuir-bouilli*, came into use in the middle of the fourteenth century. At that same time, it became fashionable in Northern Italy to wear surcoats with triangular flaps hanging down from the shoulders. These triangular flaps were somewhat of a shield-shape and, therefore, lent themselves to the display of heraldic charges. It is not clear whether they were reinforced and actually protective armor or were merely decorative. In any case, the very few representations of knights with these elements (Boccia and Coelha figs. 1, 2, 5, 13, 15) show wearers in profile, which might have given the designer the mistaken impression that there was only one "shield" on the left shoulder.

Shortly after *Cinema Arthuriana* was published in 1991, *The Fisher King* appeared on the silver screen. This essay is not the place to review its highly arbitrary interpretation of the Grail story; suffice it to say that the sporadically appearing Red Knight is the only element of the film that has anything to do with arms or armor. This Red Knight, though, is a figment of the imagination of the Grail-seeking Robin Williams, and, as a symbol of the massacre that pushed Williams over the edge, he obviously has no connection whatsoever with his prototype in Chrétien or Wolfram. True to his violent symbolism, his armor is exaggeratedly enhanced by dagged fluttering helmet mantlings and horse trappings that create a flame-like silhouette, in a style reminiscent of the art work of Darrel Sweet and Julek Heller.

Indiana Jones and the Last Crusade is another in that series of adventure films that has done so much to tarnish the image of archaeology. It is a Grail quest revved up by the usual chases to water and land. Near the end of the film, the last surviving Knight Guardian of the Grail makes an appearance in mail armor and surcoat of "around 1200." Somewhat illogically, the clue to the whereabouts of the Grail is provided by an inscription engraved on a crusader's shield in a crypt in Venice (found after Indiana Jones vandalized a medieval marble floor); it goes without saying that the shield is of the sheet metal type, essential for historical films. Armor in the modern military sense is provided by World War I–type tanks clattering around, supposedly in 1938. Indiana Jones's competitors in the search for the Grail are the Nazis, who are on the quest for purposes of Evil. Their use of the badge of Rommel's World War II Afrikakorps is rather premature for 1938.

Finally, there is the 1994 educational film *Knights and Armor*, made for the A&E Television Network. The historical armor shown here is from the best European collections, the Hofrüstkammer of Vienna, the Landeszeughaus of Graz, and the Wallace Collection of London among them. There is in the film the obligatory reference to King Arthur and his Knights of the Round Table. In one of the film's spirited fighting scenes, a reenactment in mail with "Norman" helmets and "Norman" shields, the shields are properly used as shock breakers and are actually emblazoned with the arms of Arthurian knights from the "Armagnac Armorial," Sir Calogrenant (*gules, a serpent or*) and Sir Galegantin of Wales (*per pale of or and sable, a lion vert overall*). Too bad, though, that these "Norman" shields are of sheet metal, and that Sir Galegantin wields his trusty sword in his left hand and his shield in his right. That he is bested in this fight shows, although unintentionally I am sure, the danger of neglecting the niceties of proper medieval combat.

The Mists of Avalon, Marian Zimmer Bradley's feminist retelling of the Arthuriad, came to television in the summer of 2001. As essentially macho subjects, arms and armor play a relatively subordinate role in the telefilm, and, as is too often the case with medievalistic films (see the latest remake of *Henry V*), those responsible for costuming have no clue about the niceties of knightly combat. This, in blissful ignorance of the accepted rules of chivalry, the left-handed Lancelot is picked for the role of the best knight of them all.

Spaced out over the telefilm's four hours, there are three major battles, two ambushes, and three swordfights. The script makes constant reference to the rescue of British-Roman civilization from the barbarism of the always bellicose Saxons, who are represented as shaggy savages clad in rough tunics and animal hides and fur. The civilized Christian Roman-Britons wear standard Hollywood early medieval garb, but interestingly, the true British "of the Old Religion" gambol around their Beltane fires half-naked in animal skins with horned and feathered headdresses. By strange coincidence, in the spring of 2001, Univision aired a Spanish-language costume drama, *Ramona*, where "Yaqui mission Indians" did almost identical war-dances in almost identical outfits.

In *The Mists*, the Saxons bear round shields with bosses (quite historical as familiar from Viking films) and wear little armor, and mercifully no horned or winged helmets. Their weapons are swords (although none of their eponymous *seaxes*), spears, and axes. In particular, one huge double-axe makes a repeatedly spectacular (albeit totally unhistoric) appearance. Saxon battle ensigns are tattered skins mounted on rickety sticks and painted with Pictish clan symbols. (The murals of stag and boar seen in the sacred places of the "Old Religion" are copied from reliefs on the silver cauldron found at Gundestrup in Denmark.)

The Roman-British elite warriors, such as Arthur's knights, wear neat leather armor reinforced with small metal plates, riveted on in the manner of Victorian misinterpretations of "Norman" mail armor represented in the Bayeux Tapestry. For ceremonial wear, Arthur has a "Roman" armor of breastplate and skirt straps. Men-at-arms have to do with plain leathers with sewn on washers. Helmets are simply conical; some have "Norman" style nasals. The most elaborate helmet belongs to Duke Gorlois and is styled after the visor helmets found in the Viking age Swedish royal burial mounds at Vendel and Valsgaerde. The helmet serves as Uther's disguise for the seduction of Igraine after he kills Gorlois and takes his armor. Shields are oval, in the late Roman style, with central bosses, but in most sword combats, the champions prefer to fight without them. (The ring of the blade is still more dramatic than the dull thud against a wooden shield.)

Castle architecture and women's costumes are more or less "Norman." Interestingly, the only credible "Norman" armor with conical helmets with nasals and with "Norman" shield of pointed almond-shape is worn by two toy knights with which Morgaine and Arthur play as children. These puppets are evidently inspired by the figurines that King Arthur toys with in *Camelot* during his talk with King Pellinore mentioned above: they are derived from the miniature *ludus monstrorum* in the twelfth century manuscript *Hortus Deliciarum*, where two puppeteers stage just such a fight using puppets (Nickel, "Little Knights" 170–83).

Shields in *The Mists* lack any markings

Edward Atterton as Arthur (left) and Michael Vartan as Lancelot in Uli Edel's 2001 mini-series *The Mists of Avalon*. (Still courtesy of Turner Network television.)

to indicate heraldry. To indicate they are Christian, the Roman-Britons do carry a banner with the Chri-Rho labarum. The dragon emblems of Uther and Arthur are displayed golden on red banners or blue as tattoos on their sword arms. Some of the dragon banners are on crossbeams similar to Roman vexilla, but most are mounted (upright with a short bracing rod on top) like sashimono of Japanese samurai, a detail that raises some interesting questions about transcontinental cultural influences in the so-called Dark Ages. Excalibur is first a cross on a stone altar. It is changed into a gleaming sword by an apparition of the Lady of the Lake in Arthur's hour of need during one of the battle scenes, and after Camlann, when it is thrown into the Lake of Avalon by Morgaine, in midair it turns into a blindlingly radiant cross — as the Mists of Avalon lift forever.

In conclusion, it can be said — not surprisingly — that the ways to approach the subject of arms and armor in Arthurian films are as many as there are costume designers, but that a blending of historical realism and fantasy seems to be the most successful, insofar as it corresponds to the image of the "knight in shining armor" every Arthurian carries in his or her heart.

Appendix

One of the first educational films ever made, *A Visit to the Armor Galleries*, was a project done in 1923 by Bashford Dean, Curator of the Department of Arms and Armor, The Metropolitan Museum of Art, New York, and his assistant and eventual successor, Stephen V. Grancsay. This film attempted to dispel popular myths about armor that existed already before they became cast in concrete by Laurence Olivier's *Henry V* and the television series about Henry VIII, where knights are hoisted into their saddles with derricks.

Armor is heavy, as can be expected from its being made of iron, but it is not so heavy that a knight would be unable to get up when thrown to the ground. A mailshirt with long sleeves weighs about twenty-five pounds; a full cap-à-pie plate armor of the fifteenth century, not more than sixty-five pounds. This weight, if properly "custom-made" and fitted to the body, represents no encumbrance for a well-trained man. In the armor film, the "knight" in fifteenth-century Burgundian armor gets up on his steed for a ride in Central Park (with the Belvedere Castle as an appropriate backdrop; the skyline was not yet cluttered up with high-rises), falls to the ground and gets up again, all unaided, though he had no previous training.

Terry Jones, in his *Chaucer's Knight* (273–74), states that in the filming of *Monty Python and the Holy Grail* most of the knights wore "imitation chain-mail made out of knitted wool, which was uncomfortable enough, but Graham Chapman, as King Arthur, wore a genuine metal chain-mail coif and found the weight of it unbearable for more than short periods." He also remarks that during the making of Eric Rohmer's film *Perceval le Gallois* "real chain-mail" was used. From my own experience, I can say that though a mailshirt is heavy it can be worn without major discomfort for hours, if this is done with a proper undergarment, a padded and quilted acton or pourpoint, which would prevent chafing on pressure points. It is also important to wear a tight sword-belt to take up the drag of the loose-hanging skirts, and to minimize the weight on the shoulders. Part of the problem with Graham Chapman's coif was that it was hanging loosely over the shoulders, with its full weight pulling down from the top of the head. Original coifs were cunningly tailored to fit around head, neck, and shoulders so as to distribute the weight; a padded skullcap was worn under the coif against the painful pressure of the steel rings (and catching of hair).

One designer of theatrical costumes in Berlin had "mail" made out of cheap brown-paper string in use after World War II, knitted with extra-thick needles by a group of nice old ladies whom his atelier had under contract. For the proper metallic effect, these shirts were dyed black and brushed with silver paint. Helmets and breastplates were hammered out of aluminum. Aluminum was also the material for the armor worn by Ingrid Bergman in her *Joan of Arc*. This armor in its entirety and the prototypes for the helmets and body defenses worn by the other "knights" were manufactured by the late Leonard Heinrich, then armorer of the Metropolitan Museum (one of the great moments in the Department of Arms and Armor was when Ingrid Bergman came for measurements and fittings). "White" medieval armor was highly polished, and Master Heinrich did wonders with the aluminum elements. It turned out, however, that they were too dazzling under the lights, and — alas — had to be dulled.

Armor's main drawback is not so much that it is heavy as that it is hot. Wearing a quilted acton against the chafing of the metal elements, and a closed helmet in summer temperature, can be trying indeed, quite aside from the heat of the metal under the sun's rays. For the tournaments staged as part of annual summer community events at The Cloisters (the medieval branch of the Metropolitan Museum in upper Manhattan's Fort Tryon Park), we therefore had "mailshirts" made out of silver lamé, covered with colorful surcoats to eliminate the need for breastplates; shields of masonite; and helmets of fiberglass cast from originals in the Museum's collections. Because of this lack of body armor, "safety" lances — slim cones of rolled-up brown paper, slipped onto thin mailing tubes for handles — were used to be aimed against the shields only. The jousts were done by John Franzreb, the stuntman who broke the Round Table in *Camelot* by jumping his horse onto it. He was, incidentally, also the White Knight in the old Ajax cleanser commercials. Ajax's white horse did participate in the Cloisters tournaments too, though not as a charger in the jousts, but — for reasons of advanced age — as the palfrey of the Lady of the Lake.

NOTES

Acknowledgements: For generously given assistance in locating material for this essay, I would like to express my thanks to my friend and colleague, Karl Katz, Consultant for Film and Television, and to Nadine Covert, Program for Art on Film, at New York's Metropolitan Museum of Art. Special thanks are due to Terry Geesken, Film Stills Archive, Museum of Modern Art, New York.

1. There are of course exceptions to this rule. In the film *The Black Knight* (1954), the Black Knight is the hero. The occasional Black Knight as a "good guy" goes back to the Black Knight in *Ivanhoe*, who turns out to be Richard Coeur-de-Lion in disguise, and lastly to the real-life Black Prince, Edward, Prince of Wales (1330–76), who is considered, at least in English-speaking circles, to be the Flower of Chivalry.

2. A still photo of Sir Brack at the Tournament was used for the back-cover illustration of the paperback edition of the fifteenth-century romance of chivalry *Tirant lo Blanc*, by Joannot Martorell and Marti Joan de Galba, translated by David H. Rosenthal (New York: Warner 1984).

3. Helmet visors opening sideways are a standard element in Howard Pyle's illustrations of *Otto of the Silver Hand* (1888). Here, though, they are not supposed to be used humorously, because they are found on the helmets of both the "good guys" and "bad guys."

4. Interestingly enough, the fleur-de-lys (which for us is the heraldic figure par excellence) does not occur in any of the fictitious arms attributed to the Knights of the Round Table before the eighteenth century.

5. The amethyst in Excalibur's hilt occurs also in Rosemary Sutcliff's *Sword at Sunset* (1963), Sanders Anne Laubenthal's *Excalibur* (1973), and Stephen R. Lawhead's *Arthur* (1989).

6. One of the questions invariably asked at any guided tour of the Armor Galleries or after a lecture is "What happened if a knight was left-handed?" There seems to be no answer to this problem; all armor that I know of was designed for the conventional combat with the opponents charging each other left (shield) side against left side. Even the sixteenth-century stalwart, Götz von

Berlichingen "of the Iron Hand," had himself an artificial right hand made after he lost his right hand in battle, rather than fight with his left. However, in the collections of the Metropolitan Museum's Department of Arms and Armor, there is one seventeenth-century Polish saber made for a left-hander.

7. One of the climactic events in "castle and crusader" dramas is a duel between knights fighting with two-handed swords, though these swords were strictly foot soldiers' weapons of the sixteenth century. Even in carefully researched films, such as *Joan of Arc*, with Ingrid Bergman, for which the Armor Shop of the Metropolitan Museum furnished prototypes for helmets and body armor (in aluminum), the fight coordinator could not resist the temptation to slip in such a duel. Therefore, the two-handed swords clashing away in the encounter with the Black Knight at the ford in *Monty Python* are practically unavoidable.

8. King Pellinore, with his bald head, flowing mustaches, and befuddled manner, is obviously modeled after the White Knight in Lewis Carroll's *Through the Looking-Glass*, as illustrated by John Tenniel. The spikes of the horse's armor and the horse-headed visors of the White Knight's and the Red Knight's helmets are like some armor to be found in *Excalibur*.

9. The armor found at Sutton Hoo corresponds in detail—parade lorica, circular shield, dragon-crested helmet—to the description that Geoffrey of Monmouth gives of Arthur's in his arming before the battle of Badon (*History* ix, 4) indicating that Geoffrey must have had some "ancient book" as his source for Dark Age arms. Armor in Geoffrey's own time (ca. 1136) was quite different with mailshirts, triangular shields, and crestless helmets.

10. Rackham's illustrations seem to have been the source for the costumes in NBC's 1989 Christmas telefilm, *A Connecticut Yankee in King Arthur's Court*, with Keshia Knight Pulliam, the cute kid from *The Cosby Show*, as the Yankee who teaches karate and other black arts to Queen Guinevere and her ladies.

11. Of the 8,000 Sarmatians serving in the Roman army as the first heavy armored auxiliary cavalry, 5,500 were sent to North Britain to fight Picts, attached to the Legio VI Victrix, whose *praefectus* was a certain Lucius Artorius Castus. As late as A.D. 428, a kibbutz-like settlement of Sarmatian veterans is documented at Ribchester, Lancashire. These Sarmatians had the *draco* as their tribal battle ensign and worshiped a sword thrust upright in the ground as an image of their war god.

12. The armor, A 78, in the Waffensammlung, Vienna, Austria, with its helmet sporting a mask visor shaped as an eagle's beak and batwing side elements, seems to have been the inspiration for some armors of the sinister characters at Uther's time, and also for some of Mordred's followers. On the other hand, Arthur's knights, in their "shining armor," have similar, non-functional batwing elements attached to their visors. Perhaps the costume designer got his inspirations from the catalogue of the Innsbruck exhibition of 1954, the only publication in which the "Gorlois" and the "batwing" helmets are illustrated together (Thomas and Gamber 51, ill. 1; 67–68, ill. 48 and 49).

WORKS CITED

Blair, Claude. *European Armour*. London: Batsford, 1959.

Boccia, Lionello G., and Eduardo T. Coelho. "Colaccio Beccadelli: An Emilian Knight of about 1340." In Robert Held, ed. *Armors and Armor Annual*. Northfield, Ill.: Digest Books, 1973.

Bruce-Mitford, Rupert. "The Sutton Hoo Helmet-Reconstruction and the Design of the Royal Harness and Swordbelt." *Journal of the Arms and Armour Society* 10 (1982): 217–80.

Combs, Carl. *Camelot*. New York: National Publishers, 1967. [Souvenir booklet.]

Cortés, Javier. *Guia Illustrada de la Real Armeria de Madrid*. Madrid: Blass, 1950. [Museum guide.]

Cripps-Day, Francis Henry. *The History of the Tournament in England and in France*. London: Quarich, 1918.

Engelhardt, Christian Moritz. *Der Herrad von Landsberg, Äbtissin von Honberg und Odilienberg im Elsass, Hortus Deliciarum*. Stuttgart and Tübingen, 1818. [Portfolio.]

Esin, Emel. "Tös und Moncuk." *Central Asiatic Journal* 16 (1972): 14–37.

Gamber, Ortwin. "Kataphrakten, Clibanarier, Normannenreiter." *Jahrbuch der Kunsthistorischen Sammlungen zu Wien* 64 (1968): 7–44.

——. "Some Notes on the Sutton Hoo Military Equipment." *Journal of the Arms and Armour Society* 10 (1982): 208–16.

Grohskopf, Bernice. *The Treasure of Sutton Hoo*. New York: Atheneum, 1970.

Harty, Kevin J. "Cinema Arthuriana: A Bibliography of Selected Secondary Materials." *Arthurian Interpretations* 3 (Spring 1989): 119–37.

——. "Cinema Arthuriana: A Filmography." *Quondam et Futurus* 7 (Spring 1987): 5–8.

——. "Cinema Arthuriana: Translations of the Arthurian Legend to the Screen." *Arthurian Interpretations* 2 (Fall 1987): 95–113.

Jones, Terry. *Chaucer's Knight: The Portrait of a Medieval Mercenary*. New York: Methuen, 1980.

Kirpičnikov, A. N. "Russische Waffen des 9.-15.

Jahrhunderts" *Waffen- und Kostümkunde* 2 (1986): 85–129.

Knight, W. Nicholas. "Lancer: Myth-Making and the Kennedy 'Camelot.'" *Avalon to Camelot* 2 (1986): 26–31.

Lacy, Norris J., and Geoffrey Ashe. *The Arthurian Handbook*. New York: Garland, 1988.

Martin, Paul. *Waffen und Rüstungen — von Karl dem Grossen bis zu Ludwig XIV*. Frankfurt am Main: Umschau, 1967.

Museo del Ejercito. Madrid, n.d. [Museum guide.]

Nickel, Helmut. "The Little Knights of the Living Room Table." *Metropolitan Museum Bulletin* 25 (1966): 170–83.

_____. "The Tournament: An Historical Sketch." In Howell Chickering and Thomas H. Seiler, eds. *The Study of Chivalry*. Kalamazoo: Western Michigan University, 1988.

Nicolle, David. *Arthur and the Anglo-Saxon Wars*. London: Osprey, 1984.

Norman, Vesey A. B. *Arms and Armor*. New York: Putnam, 1964.

Pastoureau, Michel. *Armorial des Chevaliers de la Table Ronde*. Paris: Léopard d-Or, 1983.

Pollard, Alfred W., and Arthur Rackham. *The Romance of King Arthur and His Knights of the Round Table*. 1917. rpt. New York: Weathervane, n.d.

Robinson, H. Russell. *The Armour of Imperial Rome*. New York: Scribner, 1975.

_____. *Oriental Armour*. London: Jenkins, 1967.

_____. *What Soldiers Wore on Hadrian's Wall*. Newcastle upon Tyne: Graham, 1976.

Surles, Robert L. "Mark of Cornwall: Noble, Ignoble, Ignored." *Arthurian Interpretations* 3 (Spring 1989): 60–75.

Tatlock, J. S. P. "The Dragon of Wessex and Wales." *Speculum* 8 (April 1933): 223–35.

Thomas, Bruno, and Ortwin Gamber. *Die Innsbrucker Plattnerkunst*. Innsbruck: Museum Ferdinandeum, 1954. [Exhibition catalogue.]

21

Cinema Arthuriana: A Comprehensive Filmography and Bibliography

KEVIN J. HARTY

This filmography and bibliography provides information on cinematic versions of the legend of King Arthur released between 1904 (the Edison film of Wagner's *Parsifal*) and 2001 (the Turner Network telefilm of Marion Zimmer Bradley's *The Mists of Avalon*). General studies of cinema Arthuriana appear first, followed by an alphabetical listing of individual films by main and alternate titles. Entries in the listing include the film's title, date of production or release, country of production or original release, director, screenwriter(s), production company or distributor, alternate title(s), and cast. For some films, especially the earliest silent films, surviving records do not always contain all of this information. I then provide a comprehensive list of reviews and additional discussions of each film. The most up-to-date printed source for information on the availability of films on videotape, laser disc, or DVD remains *The Video Source Book*, which is revised annually. In addition, there are multiple on-line sources for information about the availability of films for purchase or rental in any of these formats.

As with the films discussed in the initial overview to and elsewhere in this collection of essays, I take a fairly conservative view of what constitutes cinema Arthuriana. (Bert Olton, whose *Arthurian Legends on Film and Television* is cited throughout below, is less literal-minded than I, and his reference guide, therefore, also includes films in which there are only vague or implied Arthurian connections.) My principal criterion for inclusion is simple: a film must have a major, clear relation to the legend of Arthur in some form. I do not, therefore, include the *Star Wars* trilogy, even though a number of critics (especially in the area of popular culture) have seen the relationship between Luke Skywalker and Obi Wan Kanobi as analogous to that between Arthur and Merlin. Nor do I include anthology films, such as the insipid *Stuck on You* from Troma, a company known for its off-the-wall productions, in which there is a brief sketch involving Arthur and Guinevere and their unsuccessful attempt (with sword and mace) to solve their marital difficulties. I do, however, include films such as *The Mighty* and *The Sixth Sense*, where the legend of Arthur plays a key role in healing the central characters from their psychological traumas.

General Studies of Cinema Arthuriana

Armengual, Barthélemy. *Le Mythe de Tristan et Yseult au cinéma.* Algiers: Travail et culture, 1952.

Andrew, Geoff. "Of Saints and Sinners: Screening the Medieval World." *National Film Theatre Programme* [London] March 2000: 10–22.

Armstrong, Richard B., and Mary Willems Armstrong. *Encyclopedia of Film Themes, Settings, and Series.* Jefferson, N.C.: McFarland, 2000.

Attolini, Vito. *Immagini del Medioevo nel cinema.* Bari: Edizioni Dedalo, 1993.

Beatie, Bruce A. "Arthurian Films and Arthurian Texts: Problems of Reception and Comprehension." *Arthurian Interpretations* 2 (Spring 1988): 65–78.

de la Bretèque, François Amy. "La Figure de chevalier errant dans l'imaginaire cinématographique." In Daniel Poirion, ed. *Le Moyen Age dans le théâtre et le cinéma français.* Cahiers de l'Association Internationale des Études Françaises 47 (May 1995). Paris: Société d'Édition les Belles Lettres, 1995.

_____. "Le Moyen Age du cinéma français 1940–1987." In M. Perrin, ed. *Dire le moyen age hier et aujourd'hui.* Laon: Université Picardie, 1987.

_____. "Présence de la littérature française du Moyen Age dans le cinéma français." *Cahiers de recherches médiévales* 2 (1996): 155–65.

_____. "Le Regard du cinéma sur le moyen age." In Michel Pastourneau, ed. *Le Moyen age aujourd'hui.* Cahiers du Léopard 7. Paris: Le Léopard D'or, 1998.

_____, ed. *Le Moyen Age au Cinéma.* Cahiers de la cinémathèque 42–43 (Summer 1985): 1–188. [Special issue.]

Driver, Martha, ed. *Medieval Period in Film: Film & History* 29. 1–2 (1999): 1–90; 29. 3–4 (1999): 1–100. [Two special double issues.]

Durand, Jacques. "La Chevalerie à l'écran." *Avant-scène du cinéma* 221 (1 February 1979): 29–40.

Farrell, Eleanor M. "King Arthur 'Lite': Dilution of Mythic Elements in Arthurian Film." *Mythlore* 22 (Winter 1999): 55–65.

Gentry, Francis G. "König Artus und das amerikanische Selbstverständnis: Artus-filme aus Hollywood." In Kurt Gamerschlag, ed. *Moderne Artus-Rezeption 18.–20. Jahrhundert.* Göppingen: Kümmerle Verlag, 1991.

Giavarini, Laurence. "Signes et symboles, spectacle et représentation: l'aura du moyen age au cinéma." In Michèle Gally, ed. *La Trace médiévale et les écrivains d'aujourd'hui.* Paris: Presses Universitaires de France, 2000.

Giesen, Rolf. "Artus im phantastischen Film." In Kurt Gamerschlag, ed. *Moderne Artus-Rezeption 18.–20. Jahrhundert.* Göppingen: Kümmerle Verlag, 1991.

Gorgievski, Sandra. "The Arthurian Legend in Cinema: Myth or History?" In Marie-Françoise Alamichel and Derek Brewer, eds. *The Middle Ages After the Middle Ages in the English-Speaking World.* Cambridge, Eng.: D. S. Brewer, 1997.

_____. "Vingt ans de production arthurienne dans le monde anglophone (1970–1990)." *Bulletin des Anglicistes Médiévistes* 53 (Summer 1998): 55–74.

Halsall, Albert W. "Camelot: paradigmes narratifs modernes d'un modele ideologique médiéval." In M. Perrin, ed. *Dire le moyen age hier et aujourd'hui.* Laon: Université Picardie, 1987.

Harty, Kevin J. *Arthurian Film.* [The Arthuriana-CAMELOT Project Bibliographies.] http://www.lib.rochester.edu/camelot/acpbibs/harty.htm

_____. "Cinema Arthuriana: A Bibliography of Selected Secondary Materials." *Arthurian Interpretations* 3 (Spring 1989): 119–37.

_____. "Cinema Arthuriana: A Filmography." *Quondam et futurus* 7 (Spring 1987): 5–8; 7 (Summer 1987): 18.

_____. "Cinema Arthuriana: Translations of the Arthurian Legend to the Screen." *Arthurian Interpretations* 2 (Fall 1987): 95–113.

_____. "Film Treatments of the Legend of King Arthur." In Valerie M. Lagorio and Mildred Leake Day, eds. *King Arthur Through the Ages.* New York: Garland, 1990.

_____. "Parsifal and Perceval on Film: The Reel Life of a Grail Knight." In Arthur Groos and Norris J. Lacy, eds. *Perceval/Parsifal: A Casebook.* New York: Routledge, 2002.

_____. *The Reel Middle Ages: American, Western and Eastern European, Middle Eastern and Asian Films About Medieval Europe.* Jefferson, N.C.: McFarland, 1999.

_____, ed. *Cinema Arthuriana, Essays on Arthurian Film.* New York: Garland, 1991.

_____, ed. *King Arthur on Film, New Essays on Arthurian Cinema.* Jefferson, N.C.: McFarland, 1999.

Holly, Linda Tarte. "Medievalism in Film: The Matter of Arthur, A Filmography." In Jürgen Kühnel and others, eds. *Mittelalter-Rezeption III.* Göppingen: Kümmerle, 1988.

Kawa-Topor, Xavier, ed. *Le Moyen age vu par le cinéma européen.* Le Cahiers de Conques 3 (October 2000). Conques: Centre Européen d'Art et de Civilisation Médiévale, 2001

Lacy, Norris J. "Arthurian Film and the Tyranny of Tradition." *Arthurian Interpretations* 4 (Fall 1989): 75–85.

_____, ed. *The New Arthurian Encyclopedia*. Updated paperback edition. New York: Garland, 1996.

_____, and Geoffrey Ashe (with Debra N. Mancoff). *The Arthurian Handbook*. 2nd ed. New York: Garland, 1997.

Lagorio, Valerie M. "King Arthur and Camelot, U.S.A. in the Twentieth Century." In Bernard Rosenthal and Paul E. Szarmach, eds. *Medievalism in American Culture*. Binghamton, N.Y.: Medieval & Renaissance Texts & Studies, 1989.

Lefébure du Bus, Olivier. "La Table ronde et ses chevaliers." *Séquences* 177 (March-April 1995): 51–52.

Lupack, Alan, and Barbara Tepa Lupack. *King Arthur in America*. Cambridge, Eng.: D. S. Brewer, 1999.

Lupack, Alan, and Kevin J. Harty, eds. *Screening Camelot: Further Studies of Arthurian Cinema*. *Arthuriana* 10 (Winter 2000): 1–86. [Special issue.]

MacCurdy, Marian. "Bitch or Goddess: Polarized Images of Women in Arthurian Films and Literature." *Platte Valley Review* 18 (Winter 1990): 3–24.

Miller-Avrich, Charlene, and Virginia Blanton-Whetsell, eds. *Medieval Women in Film: Medieval Feminist Newsletter* Subsidia Series 1 (2000): 1–68. [Special issue.]

Moran, Daniel. "A Guide to Arthurian Films." In *CliffsNotes*: *White's The Once and Future King*. New York: Hungry Minds, 2000.

Mourier, Maurice, and Michel Mesnil. "Moyen Age et cinéma: solutions françaises." In M. Perrin, ed. *Dire le moyen age hier et aujourd'hui*. Laon: Université Picardie, 1987.

Olton, Bert. *Arthurian Legends on Film and Television*. Jefferson, N.C.: McFarland, 2000.

Parish, James Robert, and Don E. Stanke. *The Swashbucklers*. New Rochelle, N.Y.: Arlington House, 1976.

Richards, Jeffrey. "From Christianity to Paganism: The New Middle Ages and the Values of 'Medieval' Masculinity." *Cultural Values* 3 (April 1999): 213–34.

_____. *Swordsmen of the Screen from Douglas Fairbanks to Michael York*. London: Routledge, 1977.

Roberts, Adam. *Silk and Potatoes, Contemporary Arthurian Fantasy*. Amsterdam: Rodopi, 1998.

Salda, Michael N. "'What's Up, Duke?' A Brief History of Arthurian Animation." In Kevin J. Harty, ed. *King Arthur on Film, New Essays on Arthurian Cinema*. Jefferson, N.C.: McFarland, 1999.

Savage, Edward B. *The Rose and the Vine, A Study of the Evolution of the Tristan and Isolt Tale in Drama*. Cairo: American University at Cairo Press, 1961.

Tarpley, Fred. "King Arthur on Film." In William E. Tanner, ed. *The Arthurian Myth of Quest and Magic, A Festschrift in Honor of Lavon B. Fulwiler*. Dallas: Caxton's Modern Arts Press, 1993.

Torregrossa, Michael. "Merlin Goes to the Movies: The Changing Role of Merlin in Cinema Arthuriana." *Film & History* 29. 3–4 (1999): 54–65.

Umland, Rebecca A., and Samuel J. Umland. *The Use of Arthurian Legend in Hollywood Film From Connecticut Yankees to Fisher Kings*. Westport, Conn.: Greenwood, 1996.

Wehrhahn, Jürgen. "König Artus und die Ritter der Tafelrunde." *Retro* 12 (November-December 1981): 5–13.

Williams, David. "Medieval Movies." *Yearbook of English Studies* 20 (1990): 1–32.

_____. "Sir Gawain in Films." In Derek Brewer and Jonathan Gibson, eds. *A Companion to the Gawain-Poet*. Cambridge, Eng.: D. S. Brewer, 1997.

Wood, Michael. "The Magic of Merlin." *Radio Times* [London] 3–9 April: 33–36.

FILMOGRAPHY AND BIBLIOGRAPHY OF REVIEWS AND ADDITIONAL DISCUSSIONS OF INDIVIDUAL FILMS

The Adventures of Sir Galahad (1950)

United States; dir. Spencer G. Bennet; screenplays by George H. Plympton, Lewis Clay, and David Mathews; Columbia Pictures Serials
Cast: William Fawcett, Lois Hall, Nelson Leigh, George Reeves

REVIEWS:
Monthly Film Bulletin 18 (March 1951): 231.
Motion Picture Herald 178 (14 January 1950): Product Digest Section 155. *To-day's Cinema* 2 February 1951: 10; 9 February 1951: 12.

ADDITIONAL DISCUSSIONS:
Barbour, Alan. *Cliffhanger*. New York: A & W, 1979.

_____. *The Serials of Columbia*. Kew Gardens, N.Y.: Screen Facts, 1967.

Catalog of Holdings of the American Film Institute Collection and the United Artists Collection at the Library of Congress. Washington, D.C.: American Film Institute, 1978.

Cline, William C. *In the Nick of Time*. Jefferson, N.C.: McFarland, 1984.

Harmon, Jim, and Donald F. Glut. *The Great Movie Serials*. Garden City, N.Y.: Doubleday, 1972.

Harty, Kevin J. *The Reel Middle Ages: American, Western and Eastern European, Middle Eastern and Asian Films About Medieval Europe*. Jefferson, N.C.: McFarland, 1999.

Henderson, Jan Alan. "The Life and Times of Honest George." *Film Fax* 11 (June-July 1988): 40–45, 51.

Kinnard, Roy. *Fifty Years of Serial Thrills*. Metuchen, N.J.: Scarecrow, 1983.

Olton, Bert. *Arthurian Legends on Film and Television*. Jefferson, N.C.: McFarland, 2000.

Richards, Jeffrey. *Swordsmen of the Screen from Douglas Fairbanks to Michael York*. London: Routledge, 1977.

Shipley, Glenn. "Spencer Gordon Bennet." *Views and Reviews* 2 (Fall 1969): 6–21.

Weiss, Ken, and Ed. Goodgold. *To Be Continued*. New York: Crown, 1972.

Arthur of the Britons (1975)
See *King Arthur, the Young Warlord* (1975)

Arthur the King (1982)
United States and Great Britain; dir. Clive Donner; screenplay by J. David Wyles; Martin Poll Productions and Comworld Films for CBS
Alternate title: *Merlin and the Sword*
Cast: Candace Bergen, Rupert Everett, Rosalyn Landor, Malcolm McDowell, Liam Neeson, Patrick Ryecart, Philip Sayer, Ann Thornton, Edward Woodward

REVIEWS:
Chicago Tribune 26 April 1985: 5. 5. *Courier-Journal* [Louisville, Ky.] 25 April 1985: 66. *Daily News* [New York] 26 April 1985: 74. *Hollywood Reporter* 26 April 1985: 12. *New York Times* 26 April 1985: 3. 30. *TV Guide* 20 April 1985: A-144. *Variety* 8 May 1985: 162.

ADDITIONAL DISCUSSIONS:
Harty, Kevin J. *The Reel Middle Ages: American, Western and Eastern European, Middle Eastern and Asian Films About Medieval Europe*. Jefferson, N.C.: McFarland, 1999.

Marill, Alvin H. *Movies Made for Television, 1964–1986*. New York: Zoetrope, 1987.

Olton, Bert. *Arthurian Legends on Film and Television*. Jefferson, N.C.: McFarland, 2000.

Schobert, Walter, and Horst Shäfer, eds. *Fischer Film Almanach 1987*. Frankfurt am Main: Fischer Taschenbuch, 1987.

Torregrossa, Michael. "Merlin Goes to the Movies: The Changing Role of Merlin in Cinema Arthuriana." *Film & History* 29. 3–4 (1999): 54–65.

Arthur, Warlord of the Britons (1975)
See *King Arthur, The Young Warlord* (1975)

Arthur's Quest (2000)
Great Britain; dir. Neil Mandt; screenplay by Lance W. Dressen, Clint Hutchinson, Gregory Poppen; Sky International Films
Cast: Zach Gallagan, Arye Gross, Katie Johnston, Eric Olsen, Catherine Oxenberg

REVIEW:
Cable Guide [Great Britain] May 2001: 68.

ADDITIONAL DISCUSSION:
Olton, Bert. *Arthurian Legends on Film and Television*. Jefferson, N.C.: McFarland, 2000.

Artus, Merlin a Prchlici (1995)
Czech Republic; dir. Vera Simková-Plivová; screenplay by Katerina Priscáková; Ateliéry Zlin
Cast: Veronika Filipová, Veronika Jeniková, Valerie Kaplanová, Pavel Novy

REVIEW:
Filmovy prehled 10 (1995): 5–6.

The Black Knight (1954)
Great Britain; dir. Tay Garnett; screenplay by Alec Coppel; Warwick-Columbia Pictures
Cast: Richard Adam, Harry Andrews, Bill Brandon, Anthony Bushnell, Peter Cushing, Alan Ladd, Jean Lodge, Patricia Medina, Andre Morell, Patrick Troughton

REVIEWS:
America 92 (27 November 1954): 259. *Catholic World* 179 (September 1954): 466. *Commonweal* 61 (19 November 1954): 188. *Film Daily* 21 October 1954: 6. *Harrison's Reports* 23 October 1954: 120. *Hollywood Reporter* 9 November 1954: 3. *Kinematograph Weekly* 26 August 1954: 21–22. *Monthly Film Bulletin* 21 (October 1954): 147. *Motion Picture Herald* 197 (23 October 1954): Product Digest Section 185. *National Parent-Teacher* 49 (January 1955): 38. *New York Times* 29 October 1954: 27. *Newsweek* 44 (15 November 1954): 112. *Sign* 35 (October 1954): 33. *Time* 64 (8 November 1954): 110. *To-day's Cinema* 25 August 1954: 10. *Variety* 8 September 1954: 6.

ADDITIONAL DISCUSSIONS:
Beylie, Claude, and others "Les 44 films de Tay Garnett." *Ecran* 57 (April 1977): 28–38; 58 (May 1977): 40–45.

Garnett, Tay, and Fredda Dudley Valling. *Light Up Your Torches and Pull Up Your Tights*. New Rochelle, N.Y.: Arlington House, 1973.

Halliwell, Leslie. "Putting a Name to the Place." *TV Times* [London] 14–21 February 1987: 34.

Harty, Kevin J. *The Reel Middle Ages: American, Western and Eastern European, Middle Eastern and Asian Films About Medieval Europe.* Jefferson, N.C.: McFarland, 1999.

Henry, Marilyn, and Ron De Sourdis. *The Films of Alan Ladd.* Secaucus, N.J.: Citadel, 1981.

Lupack, Alan. "An Enemy in Our Midst: *The Black Knight* and the American Dream." In Kevin J. Harty, ed. *Cinema Arthuriana, Essays on Arthurian Film.* New York: Garland, 1991. [Rpt. above.]

Nash, Jay Robert, and Stanley Ralph Ross. *The Motion Picture Guide, A–B, 1927–1983.* Chicago: Cinebooks, 1985.

Olton, Bert. *Arthurian Legends on Film and Television.* Jefferson, N.C.: McFarland, 2000.

Richards, Jeffrey. *Swordsmen of the Screen from Douglas Fairbanks to Michael York.* London: Routledge, 1977.

Umland, Rebecca A., and Samuel J. Umland. *The Use of Arthurian Legend in Hollywood Film from Connecticut Yankees to Fisher Kings.* Westport, Conn.: Greenwood, 1996.

Viviani, Christian. "Tay Garnett, 1898–1977." *Avant-scène du cinéma* 245 (1 April 1980): 97–128.

The Boy Merlin (1978)

Great Britain; dir. Vic Hughes; screenplay by Anne Carlton and Stewart Farrar; Thames Television Productions

Alternate title: *Shadows*

Cast: Cassandra Harris, Donald Houston, Margaret John, Ian Rowlands, Archie Tew, Rachel Thomas

REVIEWS:

Television Today 19 October 1978: 18. *TV Times* [Great Britain] 7–13 October 1978: 59.

Camelot (1967)

United States; dir. Joshua Logan; screenplay by Alan Jay Lerner; Warner Bros.–Seven Arts Productions

Cast: Richard Harris, David Hemmings, Lionel Jeffries, Laurence Naismith, Franco Nero, Vanessa Redgrave, Estelle Winwood

REVIEWS:

America 117 (11 November 1967): 582–83. *Bianco e nero* 29 (May–June 1968): 161–63. *Christian Century* 10 January 1968: 52–53. *Columbia* [New Haven] 47 (November 1967): 29. *Commonweal* 87 (17 November 1967): 207. *Daily Cinema* 17 November 1967: 6. *Extension* [Chicago] 62 (January 1968): 38. *Film Daily* 26 October 1967: 3, 6. *Film Facts* 10 (15 November 1967): 280–81. *Film Quarterly* 21 (Spring 1968): 56. *Films and Filming* 14 (November 1967): 15–17; 14 (January 1968): 22. *Films in Review* 18 (December 1967): 649–50. *Harper's* 236 (January 1968): 81–82. *Hollywood Reporter* 25 October 1967: 3, 14. *Kinematograph Weekly* 18 November 1967: 10, 18. *Le Monde* 17–18 March 1968: 17. *Monthly Film Bulletin* 35 (January 1968): 3. *Motion Picture Herald* 237 (1 November 1967): Product Digest Section 737. *National Review* 20 (27 February 1968): 199–201. *New York Times* 26 October 1967: 54. *Newsweek* 70 (6 November 1967): 90. *Saint Anthony Messenger* 75 (March 1968): 8. *Senior Scholastic* 91 (14 December 1967): 21. *Sign* 47 (October 1967): 45. *Tablet* [London] 18 November 1967: 1208; 4 December 1982: 1222. *Time* 90 (3 November 1967): 100. *Times* [London] 16 November 1967: 8. *Variety* 25 October 1967: 6. *Vogue* 150 (December 1967): 175.

ADDITIONAL DISCUSSIONS:

Borgzinner, Jon. "The Shining Pageant of Camelot." *Life* 63 (22 September 1967): 70–86.

Bouineau, Jean-Marc. *Les 100 chefs-d'œuvre du film musical.* Alleur, Belgium: Marabout, 1989.

Combs, Carl. *Camelot: The Movie Souvenir Book.* New York: National, 1968.

Elley, Derek. *The Epic Film.* London: Routledge, 1984.

Grellner, Alice. "Two Films That Sparkle: *The Sword in the Stone* and *Camelot.*" In Kevin J. Harty, ed. *Cinema Arthuriana, Essays on Arthurian Film.* New York: Garland, 1981. [Rpt. above in revised form.]

Harty, Kevin J. *The Reel Middle Ages: American, Western and Eastern European, Middle Eastern and Asian Films About Medieval Europe.* Jefferson, N.C.: McFarland, 1999.

Hirschhorn, Clive. *The Hollywood Musical.* New York: Crown, 1981.

———. *The Warner Brothers Story.* New York: Crown, 1979.

Kaplan, Phillip. J [with the Editors of *Consumer Guide*]. *The Best, Worst & Most Unusual: Hollywood Musicals.* New York: Beekman House, 1983.

Knee, Allan, ed. *Selections from Idylls of the King and Camelot.* New York: Dell, 1967.

Krafsur, Richard P., ed. *The American Film Institute Catalog of Feature Films 1961–1970.* New York: Bowker, 1976.

Larkin, Colin. *The Virgin Encyclopedia of Stage and Film Musicals.* London: Virgin Books, 1999.

Lightman, Herb A. "Capturing on Film the Mythical Magic of *Camelot.*" *American Cinematographer* 49 (January 1968): 30–33.

Logan, Joshua. *Movie Stars, Real People, and Me.* New York: Delacorte, 1978.
Maeder, Edward. *Hollywood and History, Costume Design in Film.* Los Angeles: Los Angeles County Museum of Art, 1987.
Matthew-Walker, Robert. *From Broadway to Hollywood.* London: Sanctuary Publishing, 1996.
Medved, Harry, and Michael Medved. *The Golden Turkey Awards.* New York: Perigee, 1980.
_____. *The Hollywood Hall of Shame.* New York: Perigee, 1984.
Moran, Daniel. "A Guide to Arthurian Films." In *CliffsNotes: White's The Once and Future King.* New York: Hungry Minds, 2000.
Nash, Jay Robert, and Stanley Ralph Ross. *The Motion Picture Guide, C–D, 1927–1983.* Chicago: Cinebooks, 1985.
Olton, Bert. *Arthurian Legends on Film and Television.* Jefferson, N.C.: McFarland, 2000.
Parish, James Robert, and Michael R. Pitts. *The Great Hollywood Musical Pictures.* Metuchen, N.J.: Scarecrow, 1992.
Redgrave, Vanessa. *Vanessa Redgrave, An Autobiography.* New York: Random House, 1994.
Schroth, Evelyn. "Camelot: Contemporary Interpretation of Arthur in 'Sens' and 'Matière.'" *Journal of Popular Culture* 17 (Fall 1983): 31–43.
Simon, John. *Movies into Film.* New York: Dell, 1971.
Smith, Gus. *Richard Harris, Actor by Accident.* London: Robert Hale, 1990.
Umland, Rebecca A., and Samuel J. Umland. *The Use of Arthurian Legend in Hollywood Film from Connecticut Yankees to Fisher Kings.* Westport, Conn.: Greenwood, 1996.
White, T. H. "What It's Like to Be Translated into 'Camelot'." *Vogue* 137 (15 February 1961): 43, 116–117.

Camelot (1982)
United States; dir. Marty Callner; screenplay by Alan Jay Lerner; HBO Television
Cast: Richard Backus, Meg Bussert, Richard Harris, Barrie Ingham, Robert Muenz, James Valentine

REVIEWS:
Films in Review 33 (November 1982): 567–69. *Hollywood Reporter* 24 September 1982: 30. *New York Times* 24 September 1982: C27. *Screen International* 25 September 1982: 6. *Women's Wear Daily* 15 September 1982: 42.

ADDITIONAL DISCUSSIONS:
Ashley, Franklin. "They Haven't Heard the Last of Richard Harris." *TV Guide* 25 September 1982: 27–29.

Harty, Kevin J. *The Reel Middle Ages: American, Western and Eastern European, Middle Eastern and Asian Films About Medieval Europe.* Jefferson, N.C.: McFarland, 1999.
Olton, Bert. *Arthurian Legends on Film and Television.* Jefferson, N.C.: McFarland, 2000.
Smith, Gus. *Richard Harris, Actor by Accident.* London: Robert Hale, 1990.

Les Chevaliers de la table ronde (1990)
France; dir. Denis Llorca; screenplay by Denis Llorca and Philippe Viadèles; Les Films du Jeudi
ALTERNATE TITLE: *The Knights of the Round Table*
Cast: Maria Casarès, Alain Cuny, Mireille Delcroix, Alain Macé, Catherine Rétoré, Michel Vitold

REVIEWS:
Année du cinéma 15 (1991): 216. *Cahiers du cinéma* 437 (November 1990): 85. *Film français* 16 October 1990: 13. *Image et son* 465 (November 1990): 29. *Positif* 359 (January 1991): 44–45. *Revue du cinéma* [La Saison cinématographique] Hors série 37 (1990): 27. *Studio* [Paris] 43 (November 1990): 24.

ADDITIONAL DISCUSSIONS:
Harty, Kevin J. *The Reel Middle Ages: American, Western and Eastern European, Middle Eastern and Asian Films About Medieval Europe.* Jefferson, N.C.: McFarland, 1999.
Heymann, Danièle, and Pierre Murat. *L'Année du cinéma 1991.* Barcelona: Almann-Lévy, 1991.
Les Films français. Paris: Unifrance International Film, 1990.
Leguèbe, Éric. *Cinéguide 2001.* Paris: Omnibus: 2000.
Tous les films 1990. Paris: Éditions Chrétiens-Médias, 1991.

A Connecticut Yankee (1931)
United States; dir. David Butler; screenplay by William Conselman; Fox Film Corporation
Cast: Frank Albertson, William Barnum, Mitchell Harris, Brandon Hurst, Myrna Loy, Maureen O'Sullivan, Will Rogers

REVIEWS:
Bioscope 1 April 1931: 18–19. *Cinema, Video & Cable Movie Digest* 1 (August 1991): 64. *Film Daily* 12 April 1931: 32. *Film Spectator* 11 (25 April 1931): 11. *Harrison's Reports* 11 April 1931: 58. *Illustrated London News* 20 June 1931: 1052, 1074. *Motion Picture Herald* 21 March 1931: 39. *National Board of Review Magazine* 6 (April 1931): 15. *New York Times* 11 April 1931: 17; 4 May 1936: 16. *New Yorker* 7 (18 April 1931): 75,

77. *Outlook and Independent* 157 (15 April 1931): 539. *Photoplay* 29 (April 1931): 48. *Picturegoer Weekly* NS 13 (22 August 1931): 29. *Retro* 12 (November–December 1981): 20–23. *Rob Wagner's Script* 5 (30 May 1931): 10–11. *Time* 17 (20 April 1931): 28. *Variety* 15 April 1931: 20, 33.

ADDITIONAL DISCUSSIONS:

Fetrow, Alan G. *Sound Films, 1927–1939.* Jefferson, N.C.: McFarland, 1992.

The Film Index: A Bibliography. Vol. 1: The Film as Art. 1941. rpt. White Plains, N.Y.: Kraus International, 1988.

Fries, Maureen. "How to Handle a Woman, or Morgan at the Movies." In Kevin J. Harty, ed. *King Arthur on Film: New Essays on Arthurian Cinema.* Jefferson, N.C.: McFarland, 1999.

Hall, Mordaunt. "An Arlis Sans Monocle." *New York Times* 19 April 1931: 8. 5.

Hanson, Patricia King, ed. *The American Film Institute Catalog of Motion Pictures Produced in the United States, Feature Films, 1931–1940.* Berkeley: University of California Press, 1993.

Harty, Kevin J. "Camelot Twice Removed: *Knightriders* and the Film Versions of *A Connecticut Yankee in King Arthur's Court.*" In Kevin J. Harty, ed. *Cinema Arthuriana, Essays on Arthurian Film.* New York: Garland, 1991. [Rpt. above in revised form.]

_____. *The Reel Middle Ages: American, Western and Eastern European, Middle Eastern and Asian Films About Medieval Europe.* Jefferson, N.C.: McFarland, 1999.

Korsilibas-Davis, James, and Myrna Loy. *Being and Becoming.* London: Bloomsbury, 1987.

Leonard, William Tolbert. *Theatre: Stage to Screen to Television.* Metuchen, N.J.: Scarecrow, 1981.

Nash, Jay Robert, and Stanley Ralph Ross. *The Motion Picture Guide, C–D, 1927–1983.* Chicago: Cinebooks, 1985.

Nowlan, Robert A., and Gwendolyn Wright Nowlan. *Cinema Sequels and Remakes, 1903–1987.* Jefferson, N.C.: McFarland, 1989.

Olton, Bert. *Arthurian Legends on Film and Television.* Jefferson, N.C.: McFarland, 2000.

Parish, James Robert, and William T. Leonard. *The Funsters.* New Rochelle, N.Y.: Arlington House, 1979.

Quirk, Lawrence J. *The Films of Myrna Loy.* Secaucus, N.J.: Citadel, 1980.

Rollins, Peter G. *Will Rogers, A Bio-Bibliography.* Westport, Conn.: Greenwood, 1984.

Sterling, Bryan B., ed. *The Will Rogers Scrapbook.* New York: Grosset & Dunlap, 1976.

_____, and Frances N. Sterling. *Will Rogers in Hollywood.* New York: Crown, 1984.

Umland, Rebecca A., and Samuel J. Umland. *The Use of Arthurian Legend in Hollywood Film from Connecticut Yankees to Fisher Kings.* Westport, Conn.: Greenwood, 1996.

"Will Rogers and King Arthur." *New York Times* 29 March 1931: 8. 7.

A Connecticut Yankee (1954)

United States; dir. Fiedler Cook; screenplay by George Roy Hill; Kraft Theatre for ABC
Cast: Edgar Bergen, Sally Gracie, Victor Jory, Jack Livesey, Carl Reiner, Joey Walsh

REVIEW:

Variety 14 June 1954: 30.

ADDITIONAL DISCUSSION:

Harty, Kevin J. *The Reel Middle Ages: American, Western and Eastern European, Middle Eastern and Asian Films About Medieval Europe.* Jefferson, N.C.: McFarland, 1999.

A Connecticut Yankee (1955)

United States; dir. Max Liebman; screenplay by William Friedberg, Neil Simon, and Will Glickman; Max Liebman Productions for NBC
Cast: Eddie Albert, Janet Blair, John Conte, Leonard Elliott, Boris Karloff, Gale Sherwood

REVIEW:

Variety 16 March 1955: 35.

ADDITIONAL DISCUSSIONS:

Buehrer, Beverley B. *Boris Karloff, A Bio-Bibliography.* Westport, Conn.: Greenwood, 1993.

Harty, Kevin J. *The Reel Middle Ages: American, Western and Eastern European, Middle Eastern and Asian Films About Medieval Europe.* Jefferson, N.C.: McFarland, 1999.

Hummel, David. *The Collector's Guide to the American Musical Theatre.* Metuchen, N.J.: Scarecrow, 1984.

Nollan, Scott Allen. *Boris Karloff, A Critical Account of His Screen, Stage, Radio, Television, and Recording Work.* Jefferson, N.C.: McFarland, 1991.

Richard Rodgers Fact Book (with Supplement). New York: Lynn Farnol Group, 1968.

Shanley, J. P. "Nothing to Be Scared About." *New York Times* 6 March 1955: 2. 13.

Terrace, Vincent. *Encyclopedia of Television Series, Pilots and Specials, 1937–1973.* New York: Zoetrope, 1986.

_____. *Television Specials.* Jefferson, N.C.: McFarland, 1995.

A Connecticut Yankee at King Arthur's Court (1920)

United States; dir. Emmett J. Flynn; screenplay

by Bernard McConville; Fox Film Corporation

Cast: Charles Clary, Adele Farrington, Carl Formes, Herbert Fortier, Charles Gordon, William MacDonald, Harry C. Meyers, William V. Mong, George Siegmann, Pauline Starke, Rosemary Theby

REVIEWS:

Exceptional Photoplays 1 (March 1921): 2, 7; 1 (November 1921): 3, 8, 12. *Exhibitor's Trade Review* 12 February 1921: 1065. *Harrison's Reports* 12 February 1921: 26. *Life* 77 (5 May 1921): 652. *Motion Picture News* 12 February 1921: 1383. *New York Times* 15 March 1921: 14. *Photoplay* 20 (June 1921): 51. *Times* [London] 15 May 1921: 6. *Variety* 28 January 1921: 40. *Wid's Daily* 6 February 1921: 3.

ADDITIONAL DISCUSSIONS:

Connelly, Robert. *The Motion Picture Guide, Silent Film 1910–1936.* Chicago: Cinebooks, 1986.

The Film Index: A Bibliography. Vol. 1: The Film as Art. 1941. rpt. White Plains, N.Y.: Kraus International, 1988.

Hamilton, James Shelley. "Five Pictures." *Exceptional Photoplays* 1 (November 1921): 3, 8, 12.

Hanson, Patricia King, ed. *The American Film Institute Catalog, Feature Films 1911–1920.* Berkeley: University of California Press, 1988.

Harty, Kevin J. "Camelot Twice Removed: *Knightriders* and the Film Versions of *A Connecticut Yankee in King Arthur's Court.*" In Kevin J. Harty, ed. *Cinema Arthuriana, Essays on Arthurian Film.* New York: Garland, 1991. [Rpt. above in revised form.]

_____. *The Reel Middle Ages: American, Western and Eastern European, Middle Eastern and Asian Films About Medieval Europe.* Jefferson, N.C.: McFarland, 1999.

Leonard, William Tolbert. *Theatre: Stage to Screen to Television.* Metuchen, N.J.: Scarecrow, 1981.

Munden, Kenneth W., ed. *The American Film Institute Catalog, Feature Films 1921–1930.* New York: Bowker, 1971.

O'Dell, Scott. *Representative Photoplays Analyzed.* Hollywood, Calif.: Institute of Authorship, 1924.

"Special Service Section on 'A Connecticut Yankee in [sic] King Arthur's Court.'" *Motion Picture News* 26 February 1921: 1673–82.

A Connecticut Yankee in King Arthur's Court (1949)

United States; dir. Tay Garnett; screenplay by Edmund Beloin; Paramount Pictures

Charles Clary as King Arthur in Emmett J. Flynn's 1920 film *A Connecticut Yankee at King Arthur's Court.* (Still courtesy of the Film Archive of the Museum of Modern Art.)

Cast: William Bendix, Bing Crosby, Virginia Field, Rhonda Fleming, Sir Cedric Hardwicke, Joseph Vitale, Murvyn Vye, Richard Webb, Henry Wilcoxon

REVIEWS:

America 81 (16 April 1949): 96–97. *Collier's* 123 (19 March 1949): 36, 73. *Commonweal* 50 (22 April 1949): 48. *Cosmopolitan* 126 (April 1949): 12–13, 92. *Extension* 44 (July 1949): 40. *Film Daily* 24 February 1949: 6. *Good Housekeeping* 128 (April 1949): 303. *Harrison's Reports* 26 February 1949: 35. *Hollywood Reporter* 21 February 1949: 3. *Monthly Film Bulletin* 16 (3 March 1949): 48. *Motion Picture Herald* 174 (26 February 1949): Product Digest Section 4513. *New Republic* 31 (18 April 1949): 31. *New York Times* 8 April 1949: 31. *New Yorker* 25 (16 April 1949): 965. *Newsweek* 33 (18 April 1949): 89. *Photoplay* 35 (April 1949): 22. *Revue du cinéma* [La Saison cinématographique] Hors série 30 (1948–1949): 212. *Rotarian* 75 (August 1949): 42. *Scholastic* 54 (13 April 1949): 25. *Senior Scholastic* 54 (13 April 1949): 25. *Sign* 28 (March 1949): 45. *Time* 53 (25 April 1949): 99–100. *Times* [London] 21 March 1949: 7. *To-day's Cinema* 4 February 1949: 11. *Variety* 23 February 1949: 10. *Woman's Home Companion* 76 (April 1949): 10–11.

ADDITIONAL DISCUSSIONS:

Beylie, Claude, and others "Les 44 films de Tay Garnett." *Ecran* 57 (April 1977): 27–38; 58 (May 1977): 40–45.

Bookbinder, Robert. *The Films of Bing Crosby.* Secaucus, N.J.: Citadel, 1977.

Fries, Maureen. "How to Handle a Woman, or Morgan at the Movies." In Kevin J. Harty, ed. *King Arthur on Film, New Essays on Arthurian Cinema.* Jefferson, N.C.: McFarland, 1999.

Garnett, Tay, and Fredda Dudley Balling. *Light Up Your Torches and Pull Up Your Tights.* New Rochelle, N.Y.: Arlington House, 1973.

Hanson, Patricia King, ed. *The American Film Institute Catalog of Motion Pictures Produced in the United States, Feature Films, 1941–1950.* Berkeley: University of California Press, 1999.

Harty, Kevin J. "Camelot Twice Removed: *Knightriders* and the Film Versions of *A Connecticut Yankee in King Arthur's Court.*" In Kevin J. Harty, ed. *Cinema Arthuriana, Essays on Arthurian Film.* New York: Garland, 1991. [Rpt. above in revised form.]

_____. *The Reel Middle Ages: American, Western and Eastern European, Middle Eastern and Asian Films About Medieval Europe.* Jefferson, N.C.: McFarland, 1999.

Hirschhorn, Clive. *The Hollywood Musical.* New York: Crown, 1981.

Leonard, William Tolbert. *Theatre: Stage to Screen to Television.* Metuchen, N.J.: Scarecrow, 1981.

Maeder, Edward. *Hollywood and History, Costume Design in Film.* Los Angeles: Los Angeles County Museum of Art, 1987.

Nash, Jay Robert, and Stanley Ralph Ross. *The Motion Picture Guide, C–D, 1927–1983.* Chicago: Cinebooks, 1985.

Nathan, Paul S. "Books into Films." *Publisher's Weekly* 153 (1 May 1948): 1907.

Nowlan, Robert A., and Gwendolyn Wright Nowlan. *Cinema Sequels and Remakes, 1903–1987.* Jefferson, N.C.: McFarland, 1989.

Olton, Bert. *Arthurian Legends on Film and Television.* Jefferson, N.C.: McFarland, 2000.

Osberg, Richard H., and Michael E. Crow. "Language Then and Language Now in Arthurian Film." In Kevin J. Harty, ed. *King Arthur on Film, New Essays on Arthurian Cinema.* Jefferson, N.C.: McFarland, 1999.

Osterholm, J. Roger. *Bing Crosby, A Bio-Bibliography.* Westport, Conn.: Greenwood, 1994.

Thomas, Bob. "Tay Garnett: A Man for All Films." *Action* 7 (September-October 1972): 12–16.

Umland, Rebecca A., and Samuel J. Umland. *The Use of Arthurian Legend in Hollywood Film from Connecticut Yankees to Fisher Kings.* Westport, Conn.: Greenwood, 1996.

Viviani, Christian. "Tay Garnett, 1898–1977." *Avant-scène du cinéma* 245 (1 April 1980): 97–128.

Wachhorst, Wyn. "Time-Travel Romance on Film: Archetypes and Structures." *Extrapolation* 25 (Winter 1984): 340–59.

A Connecticut Yankee in King Arthur's Court (1952)

United States; dir. Franklin Schaffner; screenplay by Alvin Sapinsley; Westinghouse Studio One for CBS

Cast: Loretta Day, Robert Duke, Boris Karloff, Berry Kroeger, Salem Ludwig, Thomas Mitchell

DISCUSSIONS:

Gianakos, Larry James. *Television Drama Series Programming: A Comprehensive Chronicle, 1947–1959.* Metuchen, N.J.: Scarecrow, 1980.

Harty, Kevin J. *The Reel Middle Ages: American, Western and Eastern European, Middle Eastern and Asian Films About Medieval Europe.* Jefferson, N.C.: McFarland, 1999.

Kim, Erwin. *Franklin J. Schaffner.* Metuchen, N.J.: Scarecrow, 1985.

Olton, Bert. *Arthurian Legends on Film and Television.* Jefferson, N.C.: McFarland, 2000.

Osberg, Richard H., and Michael E. Crow. "Language Then and Language Now in Arthurian Film." In Kevin J. Harty, ed. *King Arthur on Film, New Essays on Arthurian Cinema.* Jefferson, N.C.: McFarland, 1999

A Connecticut Yankee in King Arthur's Court (1970)

Australia; dir. Zoran Janjic; screenplay by Michael Robinson; Air Programs International

Cast: (The voices of) Orson Bean, Ron Haddrick, Barbara Llewellyn, John Llewellyn, L. Ostrich, Brenda Senders

REVIEW:

Daily News [New York] 27 November 1970: 63.

ADDITIONAL DISCUSSIONS:

Harty, Kevin J. *The Reel Middle Ages: American, Western and Eastern European, Middle Eastern and Asian Films About Medieval Europe.* Jefferson, N.C.: McFarland, 1999.

Salda, Michael N. "'What's Up, Duke?' A Brief History of Arthurian Animation." In Kevin J. Harty, ed. *King Arthur on Film, New Essays on Arthurian Cinema.* Jefferson, N.C.: McFarland, 1999.

Wollery, George. *Animated TV Specials.* Metuchen, N.J.: Scarecrow, 1989.

A Connecticut Yankee in King Arthur's Court (1978)

United States; dir. David Trapper; screenplay

by Stephen Dick; PBS Once Upon a Classic and WQED (Pittsburgh)
Cast: Richard Basehart, Roscoe Lee Browne, Frederick Coffin, Tovah Feldshuh, Paul Rudd, Dan Shor

REVIEWS:
Christian Science Monitor 22 May 1978: 23. *New York Post* 23 May 1978: 32.

ADDITIONAL DISCUSSIONS:
Harty, Kevin J. *The Reel Middle Ages: American, Western and Eastern European, Middle Eastern and Asian Films About Medieval Europe.* Jefferson, N.C.: McFarland, 1999.
Marill, Alvin H. "The Television Scene." *Films in Review* 35 (November 1984): 570–71.
"Recycling Mark Twain." *TV Guide* 20 May 1978: 11.

A Connecticut Yankee in King Arthur's Court (1989)

United States; dir. Mel Damski; screenplay by Paul Zindel; Consolidated and Schaeffer Karpf Productions in association with NBC
Cast: Rene Auberjonois, Huge E. Blick, Michael Gross, Whip Hubley, Jean Marsh, Keshia Knight Pulliam, Emma Samms

REVIEWS:
Baltimore Sun 18 December 1989: 1B, 2B. *Boston Herald* 18 December 1989: 49. *Chicago Sun-Times* 18 December 1989: 33. *Chicago Tribune* 18 December 1989: 2. 5. *Christian Science Monitor* 13 December 1989: 10. *New York Post* 18 December 1989: 60. *New York Times* 3 December 1989: 2. 33; 18 December 1989: 2. 4. *Newsday* 18 December 1989: 2. 10. *TV Guide* 16 December 1989: 53, 120. *Variety* 20 December 1989: 48.

ADDITIONAL DISCUSSIONS:
Byrne, Bridget. "A Little 'Yankee' Ingenuity Spices Up Modern Tale." *Chicago Tribune TV Week* 17 December 1989: 3, 15.
Harty, Kevin J. "Camelot Twice Removed: *Knightriders* and the Film Versions of *A Connecticut Yankee in King Arthur's Court.*" In Kevin J. Harty, ed. *Cinema Arthuriana, Essays on Arthurian Film.* New York: Garland, 1991. [Rpt. above in revised form.]
_____. *The Reel Middle Ages: American, Western and Eastern European, Middle Eastern and Asian Films About Medieval Europe.* Jefferson, N.C.: McFarland, 1999.
Knutzen, Eirik. "Michael Gross in a Royal Role." *Philadelphia Inquirer TV Week* 17 December 1989: 4–5.
Lipson, Eden Ross. "A Sparse Harvest of Sugarplum Viewing." *New York Times* 3 December 1989: 2. 33, 48.

Olton, Bert. *Arthurian Legends on Film and Television.* Jefferson, N.C.: McFarland, 2000.
Sklar, Elizabeth S. "Twain for Teens: Young Yankees in Camelot." In Kevin J. Harty, ed. *King Arthur on Film, New Essays on Arthurian Cinema.* Jefferson, N.C.: McFarland, 1999.
Thompson, Raymond H. "The Ironic Tradition in Arthurian Film Since 1960." In Kevin J. Harty, ed. *Cinema Arthuriana, Essays on Arthurian Film.* New York: Garland, 1991. [Rpt. above.]
Umland, Rebecca A., and Samuel J. Umland. *The Use of Arthurian Legend in Hollywood Film from Connecticut Yankees to Fisher Kings.* Westport, Conn.: Greenwood, 1996.

Connemara (1989)

France; dir. Louis Grospierre; screenplay by Louis Grospierre; Lapaca Productions
Cast: Charley Boorman, Bernard-Pierre Donnadieu, Deirdra Donnelly, Brigitte Marvine, Maurice O'Donoghue, Daragh O'Malley, Steven Rekap, Jean-Pierre Rives, Hervé Schmitz

DISCUSSIONS:
de la Bretèque, François Amy. "Présence de la littérature française du Moyen Age dans le cinéma français." *Cahiers de recherches médiévales* 2 (1996): 155–65.
Les Films français. Paris: Unifrance International Film, 1989.
Harty, Kevin J. *The Reel Middle Ages: American, Western and Eastern European, Middle Eastern and Asian Films About Medieval Europe.* Jefferson, N.C.: McFarland, 1999.
Tous les films 1990. Paris: Éditions Chrétiens-Médias, 1991.

Il Cuore e la spada (1998)

Italy; dir. Fabrizio Costa; screenplay by Lucio De Caro; Canale 5
Alternate title: *Tristan und Isolde, Eine Liebe für die Ewigkeit*
Cast: Ralf Bauer, Léa Bosco, Joachim Fuchsberger, Mandala Tayde

REVIEWS:
Frankfurter Allgemeine 17 May 1999: 50. *La Stampa* 22 November 1998: 25, 27. *TAZ* [Berlin] 12 May 1999: 16.

ADDITIONAL DISCUSSION:
Müller, Ulrich, and Werner Wunderlich. "The Modern Reception of the Arthurian Legend." In W. H. Jackson and S. A. Ranawake, eds. *The Arthur of the Germans.* Cardiff: University of Wales Press, 2000.

The Eternal Return (1943)

See *L'Éternel retour* (1943)

L'Éternel retour (1943)

France; dir. Jean Delannoy; screenplay by Jean Cocteau; Discina International Films

Alternate titles: *The Eternal Return* and *Love Eternal*

Cast: Yvonne De Bray, Jean Marais, Jean Murat, Piéral, Madeleine Sologne, Roland Toutain

REVIEWS:

Christian Century 26 April 1950: 548. *Cinema* 66 (13 February 1946): 20. *Commonweal* 47 (13 February 1948): 448. *Film français* 23 October 1943: 9. *Kinematograph Weekly* 21 February 1946: 25. *Listener* 10 April 1986: 32. *Monthly Film Bulletin* 13 (28 February 1946): 22–23. *New Statesman and Nation* 31 (23 February 1946): 136–37. *New York Times* 5 January 1948: 15. *New Yorker* 23 (17 January 1948): 62. *Newsweek* 31 (19 January 1948): 89. *Rotarian* 76 (June 1950): 37. *Sight and Sound* NS 4 (August 1994): 62. *Theatre Arts* 32 (February 1948): 44. *Time* 51 (19 January 1948): 102. *Variety* 17 December 1948: 8, 22.

ADDITIONAL DISCUSSIONS:

Armengual, Barthélemy. *Le Mythe de Tristan et Yseult au cinéma.* Algiers: Travail et culture, 1952.

Auden, W. H. *The Dyer's Hand.* London: Faber, 1963.

Bardèche, Maurice, and Robert Brasillach. *Histoire du cinéma.* Rev. ed. 2 vols. Givors: Martel, 1953–54.

Bazin, André. *French Cinema of the Occupation and Resistance: The Birth of A Critical Esthetic.* Trans. Stanley Hochman. New York: Ungar, 1981.

Bernard, André, and Claude Gauteur, eds. *Jean Cocteau, The Art of Cinema.* Trans. Robin Buss. London: Marion Boyars, 1992.

Bertin-Maghit, Jean-Pierre. "*L'Éternel retour*: un choix idologique." *CinemAction* 65 (September 1992): 142–51.

Beylie, Claude. *Cocteau.* Supplement to *L'Avant-scène du cinéma* 56 (February 1966). Paris: Anthologie du cinéma, 1966.

Bianchi, Pietro, and Franco Berutti. *Storia del cinema.* 2nd ed. Rome: Garzanti, 1959.

"Brillantes premières à Vichy et à Paris de 'L'Éternel retour.'" *Film français* 23 October 1943: 7.

Christensen, Peter. "Jean Cocteau and Jean Delannoy's *L'Éternel Retour*: The Nietzsche Connection." *Tristania* 19 (1998): 93–116.

Cocteau, Jean. "L'Équipe de 'L'Éternel retour.'" In *Œuvres complètes.* 11 vols. Geneva: Marguerat, 1946–51.

———. "*L'Éternel retour.*" In *Œuvres complètes.* 11 vols. Geneva: Marguerat, 1946–51.

———. *Three Screenplays.* Trans. Carol Martin-Sperry. New York: Grossman, 1972.

de la Bretèque, François Amy. "Le Moyen Age du cinéma français 1940–1987." In M. Perrin, ed. *Dire le moyen age hier et aujourd'hui.* Laon: Université Picardie, 1987.

———. "Présence de la littérature française du Moyen Age dans le cinéma français." *Cahiers de recherches médiévales* 2 (1996): 155–65.

Delmas, Christian. "Jean Cocteau et la jeunesse sous le gouvernement de Vichy." *Littératures* [Montréal] 5 (1990): 19–30.

Les Éternels du Cinéma Français (1930–1960). Paris: La Fondation Gan pour le Cinéma, 1988. [Festival catalogue.]

Fraigneau, André. *Cocteau on the Film: Conversations with Jean Cocteau.* Trans. Vera Traill. (With a new introduction by George Amberg.) New York: Dover: 1972.

Hackett, Hazel. "The French Cinema During the Occupation." *Sight and Sound* 15 (Spring 1946): 1–3.

Hommage à Jean Marais. Paris: Musée de la Vie romantique, 1999. [Festival and exhibition catalogue.]

Kaitting, Mary Lou. "L'Espace dans l'oeuvre cinématographique de Jean Cocteau." *Littératures* [Montréal] 5 (1990): 167–80.

"Legion Bans French Film." *New York Times* 29 March 1948: 18.

Maddux, Stephen. "Cocteau's *Tristan and Iseut*: A Case of Overmuch Respect." In Joan Tasker Grimbert, ed. *Tristan and Isolde, A Casebook.* New York: Garland, 1995.

Magill, Frank N., ed. *Magill's Survey of Cinema: Foreign Language Films.* Englewood Cliffs: N.J.: Salem, 1985.

Manvell, Roger. "Films of the Quarter." *Sight and Sound* 15 (Spring 1946): 24–27.

Marais, Jean. *Mes quatres verités.* Paris: Éditions de Paris, 1957.

McMunn, Meradith T. "Filming the Tristan Myth: From Text to Icon." In Kevin J. Harty, ed. *Cinema Arthuriana, Essays on Arthurian Film.* New York: Garland, 1991. [Rpt. above in revised form.]

Nash, Jay Robert, and Stanley Ralph Ross. *The Motion Picture Guide, E–G, 1927–1983.* Chicago: Cinebooks, 1986.

"Of Local Origin." *New York Times* 19 July 1948: 11.

Olton, Bert. *Arthurian Legends on Film and Television.* Jefferson, N.C.: McFarland, 2000.

Paris, James Reid. *The Great French Films.* Secaucus, N.J.: Citadel, 1983.

Sadoul, Georges. *Dictionary of Films.* Trans. Peter Morris. Berkeley: University of California Press, 1972.

Savage, Edward B. *The Rose and the Vine, A Study of the Evolution of the Tristan and Isolt Tale in Drama*. Cairo: American University at Cairo Press, 1961.

Steegmuller, Francis. *Cocteau, A Biography*. Boston: Little, Brown, 1970.

Topart, Robert. "*L'Éternel retour.*" In *Analyses des films*. Paris: Institut des Hautes Études Cinématographiques, [1948].

Tulard, Jean. *Guide des Films*. Rev. ed. Paris: Éditions Robert Laffont, 1997.

Vialle, Gabriel. "Trois visages de Jean Cocteau." *Image et son* 214 (1968): 183–96.

Whitehall, R. E. "Such Stuff as Dreams Are Made Of." *Film Quarterly* [London] Summer 1947: 26–29.

Excalibur (1981)

United States; dir. John Boorman; screenplay by John Boorman and Rospo Pallenberg; Orion Pictures

Cast: Robert Addie, Gabriel Byrne, Nicholas Clay, Cherie Lunghi, Helen Mirren, Nigel Terry, Nicol Williamson

REVIEWS:

24 Images 10 (September 1981): 71–72. *Amis du film et de la télévision* 301–02 (July-August 1981): 15. *Cahiers du cinéma* 326 (July-August 1981): 61–62. *Casablanca* 7–8 (July-August 1981): 79. *Celuloide* 331 (January 1982): 15–18. *Christian Century* 27 May 1981: 619; 29 July 1981: 774–76. *Christian Science Monitor* 23 April 1981: 19. *Ciné Revue* 20 (14 May 1981): 5. *Cinefantastique* 11 (Summer 1981): 13; 11 (Fall 1981): 47. *Cinéma* [Paris] 270 (June 1981): 112–13. *Cinema Canada* 75 (July 1981): 34. *Cinema nuovo* 31 (February 1982): 49–50. *Cinema Papers* 34 (September-October 1981): 399–401. *Contemporary Review* 240 (February 1982): 103. *Continental Film and Video Review* 28 (July 1981): 6–10. *Contracampo* 28 (March 1982): 65. *Ecran fantastique* 19 (1981): 66–67. *Film a doba* 30 (January 1984): 43–45. *Film en televisie* 290–91 (July-August 1981): 14–15. *Film Journal* 84 (6 April 1981): 13–14. *Film og kino* 49.4 (1981): 143–44. *Film und Fernsehen* 14 (November 1986): 24. *Filmcritica* 32 (August 1981): 349–51; 33 (January 1982): 20–24. *Filmfaust* 24 (October-November 1981): 28. *Filmihullu* 6 (1981): 35. *Films* 1 (June 1981): 26–30; 1 (July 1981): 36–37. *Films in Review* 32 (July 1981): 377. *Furrow* [Ireland] 32 (August 1981): 541. *Hablemos de cine* 18 (May 1982): 91–92. *Hollywood Reporter* 6 April 1981: 2. *Jeune cinéma* 136 (July-August 1981): 41–44. *Kosmorama* 27 (June 1981): 98. *Levende billeder* 7 (October 1981): 63. *Los Angeles Times* 27 March 1981: 6. 1–2; 5 April 1981: Calendar 28; 17 June 1981: Calendar 1, 6. *Listener* 9 July 1981: 61; 27 February 1986: 30. *Maclean's* 94 (27 April 1981): 50. *Mademoiselle* 87 (August 1981): 62, 64. *Marriage and Family Living* 63 (July 1981): 30. *Medien + Erziehung* 26.1 (1982): 19–22. *Month* [Series 2] 14 (August 1981): 281. *Monthly Film Bulletin* 48 (June 1981): 112. *Motion Picture Product Digest* 15 April 1981: 87. *Mythlore* 31 (Spring 1982): 29–30. *Nation* 232 (16 May 1981): 612. *New Leader* 64 (4 May 1981): 17. *New Statesman* 102 (3 July 1981): 22. *New York* 14 (13 April 1981): 50–52. *New York Post* 10 April 1981: 43. *New York Times* 10 April 1981: 3. 11; 10 May 1981: 2. 13. *New Yorker* 57 (20 April 1981): 146–51. *Newsday* 10 April 1981: 27. *Newsweek* 97 (13 April 1981): 82. *Positif* 242 (May 1981): 16–17. *Prevue* 44 (February-March 1981): 34–37. *Revue du cinéma* [La Saison cinématographique] Hors série 25 (1981): 132–33. *Rolling Stone* 14 May 1981: 36–37. *Saint Anthony Messenger* 89 (June 1981): 6. *San Francisco Chronicle* 10 April 1981: 64. *Screen International* 11 July 1981: 15. *Segnocinema* 2 (December 1981): 58. *Skoop* 17 (August 1981): 14–15; 17 (September-October 1981): 58. *Soho News* [New York] 15 April 1981: 55. *Starburst* 35 (1981): 16–19. *Sunday Times* [London] 5 July 1981: 40. *Sunday Times* [London] *Magazine* 28 June 1981: 36. *Tablet* [London] 235 (11 July 1981): 675. *Time* 117 (13 April 1981): 96. *Times* [London] 28 June 1981: 36; 3 July 1981: 11. *Times* [London] *Literary Supplement* 17 July 1981: 812. *Variety* 8 April 1981: 18. *Village Voice* 15 April 1981: 51. *Washington Post* 10 April 1981: F 1 and Weekend 17. *Women's Wear Daily* 10 April 1981: 8.

ADDITIONAL DISCUSSIONS:

"The Art of *Excalibur*." *Starburst* 38 (1981): 20–21.

Bartone, Richard C. "Variations on Arthurian Legend in *Lancelot du Lac* and *Excalibur*." In Sally Slocum, ed. *Popular Arthurian Traditions*. Bowling Green, Ohio: Bowling Green University Popular Press, 1992.

"Boorman and the Arthurian Legend." *Photoplay* 31 (November 1980): 40–41.

Borie, Bertrand. "Entretien avec John Boorman." *Ecran fantastique* 19 (1981): 6–8.

――――. "Table ronde autour d'*Excalibur*." *Ecran fantastique* 20 (1981): 70–72.

Bouineau, Jean-Marc, and Alain Charlot. *Les 100 chefs-d'œuvre du film fantastique*. Alleur, Belgium: Marabout, 1989.

Boyle, Sarah. "From Victim to Avenger: The Women in John Boorman's *Excalibur*." *Avalon to Camelot* 1 (Summer 1984): 42–43.

Brode, Douglas. *The Films of the Eighties*. New York: Citadel, 1990.

Brüne, Klaus, ed. *Lexikon des Internationalen Films*. Reinbek bei Hamburg: Rowohlt, 1987.

Burns, E. Jane. "Nostalgia Isn't What It Used to Be: The Middle Ages in Literature and Film." In George Slusser and Eric S. Rabkin, eds. *Shadows of the Magic Lamp, Fantasy and Science Fiction in Film*. Carbondale: Southern Illinois University Press, 1985.

Canby, Vincent. "Of a Hit, A Series and the Word." *New York Times* 10 May 1981: D 13.

Chandès, Gérard. "Lancelot dans *Excalibur* de John Boorman." In Ulrich Müller, and others, eds. *Lancelot*. Göppingen: Kümmerle, 1984.

Ciment, Michel. "Deux entretiens avec John Boorman." *Positif* 242 (May 1981): 18–31.

_____. *John Boorman*. Trans. Gilbert Adair. London: Faber, 1986.

Cine para leer 1981. Bilboa: Mensajero, 1982.

Clegg, Cynthia. "The Problem of Realizing Romance in Film: John Boorman's *Excalibur*." In George Slusser and Eric S. Rabkin, eds. *Shadows of the Magic Lamp, Fantasy and Science Fiction in Film*. Carbondale: Southern Illinois University Press, 1985.

Decampo, M., and F. Vega. "John Boorman habla de 'Excalibur.'" *Casablanca* 7–8 (July-August 1981): 52–53, 56–57.

de la Bretèque, François. "L'Épée dans le lac, 'Excalibur' de John Boorman ou les aléas de la puissance." *Cahiers de la cinémathèque* 42–43 (Summer 1985): 91–96.

_____. "Une 'Figure obligé' du film de chevalerie: le tournoi." *Cahiers de la cinémathèque* 42–43 (Summer 1985): 21–26.

de Weever, Jacqueline. "Morgan and the Problem of Incest." In Kevin J. Harty, ed. *Cinema Arthuriana, Essays on Arthurian Film*. New York: Garland, 1981. [Rpt. above in revised form.]

D'Heur, J. M. and J. De Groeve. "Arthur, Excalibur and the Enchanter Boorman." *Studia in honorem prof. M. de Riquer, III*. Barcelona: Quaderns Crema, 1988.

"Dossier: *Excalibur*." *Positif* 247 (October 1981): 29–43.

Dubost, Francis. "Merlin et le texte inaugural." *Cahiers de la cinémathèque* 42–43 (Summer 1985): 85–89.

Filme 1981/84. Dülmen: Katholisches Institut für Medieninformation, 1985.

Foury, Marie-Hélène. "*Excalibur* de J. Boorman: Quête originelle d'un imaginaire contemporain 1980." In Xavier Kawa-Topor, ed. *Le Moyen age vu par le cinéma européen*. Le Cahiers de Conques 3 (October 2000). Conques: Centre Européen d'Art et de Civilisation Médiévale, 2001.

Fries, Maureen. "How to Handle a Woman, or Morgan at the Movies." In Kevin J. Harty, ed. *King Arthur on Film, New Essays on Arthurian Cinema*. Jefferson, N.C.: McFarland, 1999.

Haller, Robert. "*Excalibur* and Innovation." *Field of Vision* 13 (Spring 1985): 2–3.

Harty, Kevin J. "Parsifal and Perceval on Film: The Reel Life of a Grail Knight." In Arthur Groos and Norris J. Lacy, eds. *Perceval/Parsifal: A Casebook*. New York: Routledge, 2002.

_____. *The Reel Middle Ages: American, Western and Eastern European, Middle Eastern and Asian Films About Medieval Europe*. Jefferson, N.C.: McFarland, 1999.

Holley, Linda Tarte. "Medievalism in Film." *Southeastern Medieval Association Newsletter* 9. 2 (1983–1984): 13–17.

"Interview with Alex Thompson." *American Cinematographer* 63 (May 1982): 452, 491–493, 504–506.

"John Boorman Talks About *Excalibur*." *Film Directions* 4. 15 (1981): 16–19.

Jones, Leslie. "Stone Circles and Tables Round: Representing the Early Celts in Film and Television." In Amy Hale and Philip Payton, eds. *New Directions in Celtic Studies*. Exeter: University of Exeter Press, 2000.

Just, Lothar R., ed. *Das Filmjahr '81/82*. Munich: Filmland Presse, 1981.

Kemp, Philip. "Gone to Earth." *Sight and Sound* 11 (January 2001): 22–26.

Kennedy, Harlan. "The World of King Arthur According to John Boorman." *American Film* 6 (March 1981): 30–37.

Krzywinska, Tanya. *A Skin for Dancing In: Possession, Witchcraft and Voodoo in Film*. Trowbridge, Wiltshire: Flicks Books, 2000.

Lacy, Norris J. "Arthurian Film and the Tyranny of Tradition." *Arthurian Interpretations* 4 (Fall 1989): 75–85.

_____. "Mythopoeia in *Excalibur*." In Kevin J. Harty, ed. *Cinema Arthuriana, Essays on Arthurian Film*. New York: Garland, 1981. [Rpt. above.]

MacCurdy, Marian. "Bitch or Goddess: Polarized Images of Women in Arthurian Films and Literature." *Platte Valley Review* 18 (Winter 1990): 3–24.

Magill, Frank N., ed. *Magill's Cinema Annual 1982, The Films of 1981*. Englewood Cliffs, N.J.: Salem, 1982.

_____. *Magill's Survey of Cinema: English Language Films*. Second Series. Englewood Cliffs, N.J.: Salem, 1981.

Miller, Barbara D. "'Cinemagicians': Movie Merlins of the 1980s and 1990s." In Kevin J. Harty, ed. *King Arthur on Film, New Essays on*

Arthurian Cinema. Jefferson, N.C.: McFarland, 1999.

Moran, Daniel. "A Guide to Arthurian Films." In *CliffsNotes White's The Once and Future King.* New York: Hungry Minds, 2000.

Nash, Jay Robert, and Stanley Ralph Ross. *The Motion Picture Guide, E–G, 1927–1983.* Chicago: Cinebooks, 1986.

Neff, Joanne Moliver. "Translating Malory into Film: Misogyny in Boorman's *Excalibur.*" *"A Ful Noble Knyght": A Medieval Newsletter Devoted to the Life and Art of Sir Thomas Malory* 1 (Fall 1999): 1–4.

Nickel, Helmut. "Arms and Armor in Arthurian Film." In Kevin J. Harty, ed. *Cinema Arthuriana, Essays on Arthurian Film.* New York: Garland, 1981. [Rpt. above in revised form.]

Olton, Bert. *Arthurian Legends on Film and Television.* Jefferson, N.C.: McFarland, 2000.

Open, Michael. "The Dynamic Principle of Fantasy." *Film Directions* 4. 15 (1981): 20–21.

Osberg, Richard H., and Michael E. Crow. "Language Then and Language Now in Arthurian Film." In Kevin J. Harty, ed. *King Arthur on Film, New Essays on Arthurian Cinema.* Jefferson, N.C.: McFarland, 1999.

Piccardi, Adriano. "*Excalibur* di John Boorman." *Cineforum* 21 (October 1981): 39–46.

———. *John Boorman.* Florence: La Nuova Italia, 1982.

Pietzsch, Ingeborg. "Gewalt für Jugend zugelassen?" *Film und Fernsehen* 11 (1986): 24.

Polinien, Gilles. "Le Nouveau John Boorman." *Ecran fantastique* 18 (1981): 42–43.

Purdon, Liam O., and Robert J. Blanch. "Hollywood's Myopic Medievalism: *Ecalibur* [sic] and Malory's *Morte d'Arthur.*" In Sally Slocum, ed. *Popular Arthurian Traditions.* Bowling Green, Ohio: Bowling Green University Popular Press, 1992.

Rafferty, Terrence. "A Very English Risk Taker in a Play-It-Safe World." *New York Times* 25 February 2001: 2. 23, 32.

Rooney, Phillip J. "The Quest Elements in the Films of John Boorman." Ph.D. Dissertation. University of Nebraska-Lincoln, 1989.

Ross, Philippe. "L'heroïc fantasy." *Revue du cinéma* 386 (September 1983): 69–79.

Schaefer, Hans Joachim, and others. *Besonders Wertvoll: Langfilme 1981/1982.* Wiesbaden: Filmbewertungsstelle, 1983.

Shictman, Martin B. "Hollywood's New Weston: The Grail Myth in Francis Ford Coppola's *Apocalypse Now* and John Boorman's *Excalibur.*" *Post Script* 4 (Autumn 1984): 35–49.

Stanbrook, Alan. "Is God in Showbusiness Too? The First Twenty-five Years of John Boorman, Our Most Anti-materialist Director." *Sight and Sound* 59 (Autumn 1990): 259–63.

Strick, Philip. "John Boorman's Merlin." *Sight and Sound* 49 (Summer 1980): 168–71.

Tessier, Max. "Entretien avec John Boorman (sur *Excalibur*)." *Revue du cinéma* 363 (July-August 1981): 31–34.

———. "*Excalibur.*" *Revue du cinéma* 362 (June 1981): 19–23.

Torregrossa, Michael. "Merlin Goes to the Movies: The Changing Role of Merlin in Cinema Arthuriana." *Film & History* 29. 3–4 (1999): 54–65.

Tous les films 1981. Paris: Éditions O.C.F.C., 1982.

Umland, Rebecca A., and Samuel J. Umland. *The Use of Arthurian Legend in Hollywood Film from Connecticut Yankees to Fisher Kings.* Westport, Conn.: Greenwood, 1996.

Vaines, Colin. "Magic Moments." *Screen International* 252 (2–9 August 1980): 15.

Verniere, James. "The Technology of Style: An Interview with John Boorman." *Filmmakers Monthly* 14 (June 1981): 22–29.

Whitaker, Muriel. "Fire, Water, Rock: Elements of Setting in *Excalibur.*" In Kevin J. Harty, ed. *Cinema Arthuriana, Essays on Arthurian Film.* New York: Garland, 1981. [Rpt. above in revised form.]

Williams, David. "Sir Gawain in Films." In Derek Brewer and Jonathan Gibson, eds. *A Companion to the* Gawain-*Poet.* Cambridge, Eng.: D. S. Brewer, 1997.

Yakir, Dan. "The Sorcerer." *Film Comment* 17 (May-June 1981): 49–53.

The Excalibur Kid (1998)
United States; dir. James Head; screenplay by Antony Anderson; Canarom Productions for Castel Films
Cast: Natalie Eester, Mak Fyfe, François Klanfer, Jason McSkimming, Francesca Scorsone

DISCUSSIONS:
Dempsey, John. "Direct-to-Kidsvids." *Daily Variety* 23 June 1998: 573.

Olton, Bert. *Arthurian Legends on Film and Television.* Jefferson, N.C.: McFarland, 2000.

Excalibur, The Raising of the Sword (1982)
Great Britain; dir. Dorian Cowland; screenplay by Dorian Cowland; Whaddon Boys Club Film Unit
Cast: Adrian Lester and the Members of the Whaddon Boys Club

DISCUSSION:
"Sword Play." *Movie Maker* 17 (February 1983): 90–91.

La Femme d'à côté **(1981)**
See *The Woman Next Door* (1981)

Feuer und Schwert **(1981)**
See *Fire and Sword* (1981)

Fire and Sword **(1981)**
Germany; dir. Veith von Fürstenberg; screenplay by Veith von Fürstenberg; Genée and von Fürstenberg Filmproduktion
Alternate titles: *Feuer und Schwert* and *Die Legende von Tristan und Isolde*
Cast: Peter Firth, Leigh Lawson, Walo Lüönd, Antonia Presser, Christoph Waltz

REVIEWS:
Continental Film and Video 29 (November 1981): 18. *Das Fernsehspiel im ZDF* 44 (March-May 1984): 43–46. *Film-dienst* 35 (26 January 1982): 16–17. *Film-echo Filmwoche* 47–48 (28 August 1981): 18. *Film und Fernsehen* 12. 7 (1984): 35. *Kino* [Germany] 4 (August 1981): 33. *Month* 14 (November 1981): 388. *Variety* 10 June 1981: 18.

ADDITIONAL DISCUSSIONS:
Brüne, Klaus, ed. *Lexikon des Internationalen Films*. Reinbek bei Hamburg: Rowohlt, 1987.
Filme 1981/84. Dülmen: Katholisches Institut für Medieninformation, 1985.
Harty, Kevin J. *The Reel Middle Ages: American, Western and Eastern European, Middle Eastern and Asian Films About Medieval Europe*. Jefferson, N.C.: McFarland, 1999.
Helt, Richard C., and Marie E. Helt. *West German Cinema Since 1945: A Reference Handbook*. Metuchen, N.J.: Scarecrow, 1987.
Just, Lothar R., ed. *Das Filmjahr '82/83*. Munich: Filmland Presse, 1983.
Kerdelhue, Alain. "'Feuer und Schwert,' lecture materielle du mythe." In Ulrich Müller, and others, eds. *Tristan et Iseut, mythe europeen et mondial*. Göppingen: Kümmerle, 1987.
Kino 81. Munich: Export-Union des deutschen Films [1982].
McMunn, Meradith T. "Filming the Tristan Myth: From Text to Icon." In Kevin J. Harty, ed. *Cinema Arthuriana, Essays on Arthurian Film*. New York: Garland, 1991. [Rpt. above in revised form.]
Rockett, Kevin, ed. *The Irish Filmography*. Dublin: Red Mountain Media, 1996.
Schaefer, Hans Joachim, and others. *Besonders Wertvoll: Langfilme 1981/1982*. Wiesbaden: Filmbewertungsstelle Wiesbaden, 1983.

First Knight **(1995)**
United States; dir. Jerry Zucker; screenplay by William Nicholson; Columbia Pictures
Cast: Sean Connery, Ben Cross, Liam Cunningham, Richard Gere, Julia Ormond, Christopher Villiers

REVIEWS:
Arthuriana 5 (Fall 1995): 137–40. *Atlanta Constitution* 7 July 1995: P6, P9. *Boston Globe* 7 July 1995: 27. *Boston Herald* 7 July 1995: S3. *Chicago Sun-Times* 7 July 1995: Weekend Plus 37. *Chicago Tribune* 7 July 1995: Friday B, C. *Christian Science Monitor* 7 July 1995: 12. *Daily Mail* [London] 7 July 1995: 44–45. *Daily News* [Los Angeles] 7 July 1995: L12. *Daily News* [New York] 7 July 1995: 35. *Daily Telegraph* [London] 7 July 1995: 24. *Empire* 74 (August 1995): 30. *Entertainment Weekly* 276 (26 May 1995): 36; 283 (14 July 1995): 34–35. *EPD Film* 12 (September 1995): 49–50. *Evening Standard* [London] 6 July 1995: 32, 41. *Film Journal* 98 (August-September 1995): 30. *Film Review* 297 (August 1995): 64. *Films in Review* 46 (September-October 1995): 56–57. *Financial Times* [London] 6 July 1995: Arts 23. *Globe and Mail* [Toronto] 7 July 1995: C3. *Guardian* [London] 6 July 1995: 6. *Independent* [London] 9 July 1995: Critics 26. *Independent on Sunday* [London] 9 July 1995: 26. *Los Angeles Times* 7 July 1995: Calendar 1. *Maclean's* 108 (7 July 1995): 57. *Mail on Sunday* [London] 9 July 1995: 27. *Movieline* 6 (May 1995): 46–47; 7 (September 1995): 37. *New York* 28 (17 July 1995): 49. *New York Post* 7 July 1995: 41. *New York Times* 7 July 1995: C10. *New Yorker* 71 (17 July 1995): 84–85. *Newsday* 7 July 1995: B2–B3. *Newsweek* 126 (10 July 1995): 56. *Observer* [London] 9 July 1995: Review 7. *People Weekly* 44 (10 July 1995): 14. *Philadelphia Daily News* 7 July 1995: 29. *Philadelphia Inquirer* 7 July 1995: Weekend 3. *Positif* 416 (October 1995): 38. *Realms of Fantasy* 1 (June 1995): 16–24. *San Francisco Chronicle* 7 July 1995: Weekend 3. *San Francisco Examiner* 7 July 1995: C3. *Screen International* 21 July 1995: 15. *Sight and Sound* NS 5 (August 1995): 49–50. *Soundtrack* 55 (September 1995): 19. *Studio* [Paris] 101 (July-August 1995): 18. *Sunday Express* [London] 9 July 1995: Magazine 33. *Sunday Telegraph* [London] 9 July 1995: 6. *Sunday Times* [London] 9 July 1995: 10. 6. *Time* 146 (17 July 1995): 58. *Time Out* [London] 5 July 1995: 22–23. *Times* [London] 6 July 1995: 33. *Times* [London] *Educational Supplement* 14 July 1995: SS16. *Today* [London] 7 July 1995: 36–37. *Toronto Star* 7 July 1995: B7. *USA Today* 7 July 1995: D1. *Variety* 26 June 1995: 78, 85. *Village Voice* 11 July 1995: 45. *Wall Street Journal* 7 July 1995: A8. *Washington Post* 7 July 1995: Weekend 36.

ADDITIONAL DISCUSSIONS:
Blanch, Robert J., and Julian N. Wasserman.

"Fear of Flyting: The Absence of Internal Tension in *Sword of the Valiant* and *First Knight*." *Arthuriana* 10 (Winter 2000): 15–32.

"Blending Traditional Skills with Computer Technology." *In Camera* Spring 1995: 3.

Brett, Anwar. "First Knight: No Nerves." *Film Review* 298 (September 1995) 62–65.

Fhaner, Beth A., and Christopher P. Scanlon, eds. *Magill's Cinema Annual 1996*. Detroit: Gale, 1996.

Fisher, Bob. "Camelot in Shadows." *American Cinematographer* 76 (July 1995): 56–64.

Grant, Steve. "Knights to Remember." *Time Out* [London] 5 July 1995: 22–23.

Greenberg, Adam. "First Knight." *In Camera* 26 (Spring 1995): 1–4.

Harty, Kevin J. *The Reel Middle Ages: American, Western and Eastern European, Middle Eastern and Asian Films About Medieval Europe*. Jefferson, N.C.: McFarland, 1999.

Jenkins, Jacqueline. "First Knights and Common Men: Masculinity in American Arthurian Film." In Kevin J. Harty, ed. *King Arthur on Film, New Essays on Arthurian Cinema*. Jefferson, N.C.: McFarland, 1999.

Levich, Jacob, ed. *The Motion Picture Guide, 1996 Annual (The Films of 1995)*. New York: Cinebooks, 1996.

Miller, Barbara D. "'Cinemagicians': Movie Merlins of the 1980s and 1990s." In Kevin J. Harty, ed. *King Arthur on Film, New Essays on Arthurian Cinema*. Jefferson, N.C.: McFarland, 1999.

Moran, Daniel. "A Guide to Arthurian Films." In *CliffsNotes: White's The Once and Future King*. New York: Hungry Minds, 2000.

"'Oh! What a Night It Was, It Really Was, Such a Night!'" *In Camera* Spring 1995: 12.

Olton, Bert. *Arthurian Legends on Film and Television*. Jefferson, N.C.: McFarland, 2000.

Pearce, Garth. "... And the horse you rode in on." *Empire* 74 (August 1995): 72–77, 79.

Schwam-Baird, Shira. "King Arthur in Hollywood: The Subversion of Tragedy in *First Knight*." [The Southeastern Medieval Association] *Medieval Perspectives* 14 (1999): 202–13.

Tirard, Laurent. "Richard Gere." *Studio* [Paris] 101 (July-August 1995): 74–77.

Umland, Rebecca A., and Samuel J. Umland. *The Use of Arthurian Legend in Hollywood Film from Connecticut Yankees to Fisher Kings*. Westport, Conn.: Greenwood, 1996.

The Fisher King (1991)

United States; dir. Terry Gilliam; screenplay by Richard LaGravanese; Tri-Star Pictures

Cast: Jeff Bridges, Michael Jeter, Amanda Plummer, Mercedes Ruehl, Robin Williams

REVIEWS:
24 Images 58 (November-December 1991): 69. *American Film* 16 (September-October 1991): 50–51. *American Spectator* 21 (November 1991): 41. *Atlanta Constitution* 27 September 1991: E1; 26 March 1992: G11. *Billboard* 104 (23 May 1992): 49. *Boston Globe* 19 September 1991: Arts and Film 86; 20 September: Arts and Film 37. *Boxoffice* November 1991: R-78. *Cahiers du cinéma* 448 (October 1991): 74. *Chicago Sun-Times* 20 September 1991: Weekend Plus 47. *Chicago Tribune* 20 September 1991: 7C. *Christian Century* 30 October 1991: 1009. *Christian Science Monitor* 20 September 1991: 12. *Cineaste* 18 (December 1992): 46–47. *Cinefantastique* 22 (February 1992): 55. *Cinefex* 54 (May 1993): 93–94. *Cinema, Video & Cable Movie Digest* 1 (October 1991): 10. *City Limits* [London] 7 November 1991: 25. *Commentary* 92 (November 1991): 50. *Daily Mail* [London] 8 November 1991: 34. *Daily Telegraph* [London] 7 November 1991: 18. *Empire* 30 (December 1991): 20–21. *Entertainment Weekly* 84 (20 September 1991): 84; 111 (27 March 1992): 78–80. *EPD Film* 8 (November 1991): 38. *Evening Standard* [London] 7 November 1991: 41. *Film a doba* 38 (Summer 1991): 118–20. *Film en televisie* 415 (December 1991): 14–15. *Film Journal* 94 (October-November 1991): 57–58. *Filmcritica* 42 (November 1991): 507–09. *Filmihullu* 1 (1992): 44; 2 (1992): 40–43. *Filmrutan* 34 (January-February 1992): 44–46. *Films in Review* 43 (January-February 1992): 44–46. *Financial Times* [London] 7 November 1991: 19. *Guardian* [London] 7 November 1991: 29. *Hollywood Reporter* 10 September 1991: 9, 11. *Independent* [London] 8 November 1991: 18. *Independent on Sunday* [London] 10 November 1991: 22. *Interview* 21 (October 1991): 38. *Kino* [Bulgaria] September 1992: 20–23. *Kosmorama* 38 (Spring 1992): 57. *Library Journal* 117 (15 April 1992): 136. *Los Angeles Times* 20 September 1991: Calendar 1, 15. *Maclean's* 104 (30 September 1991): 69. *Mail on Sunday* [London] 10 November 1991: 39. *Le Monde* 7 October 1991: 15. *Morning Star* [London] 8 November 1991: 7. *National Catholic Reporter* 18 October 1991: 16. *National Review* 44 (20 January 1992): 62. *New Republic* 205 (21 October 1991): 27. *New Statesman and Society* 4 (8 November 1991): 30. *New York* 24 (30 September 1991): 60. *New York Post* 30 September 1991: 31 *New York Times* 20 September 1991: C10; 22 September 1991: 2. 13. *Newsday* 20 September 1991: Weekend 82. *Newsweek* 118 (23 September 1991): 57. *Observer* [London] 10 November 1991: 56. *People Weekly* 36 (23 September 1991): 16. *Philadel-*

phia Daily News 27 September 1991: 51. *Philadelphia Inquirer* 27 September 1991: Weekend 3. *Positif* 368 (October 1991): 47. *Premiere* [United States] 11 (September-October 1991): 10–13. *Première* [France] 175 (October 1991): 26. *Reader* [Chicago] 27 September 1991: 14. *Revue du cinéma* 475 (October 1991): 24–26. *Revue du cinéma* [La Saison cinématographique] Hors série 39 (1991): 46. *Rolling Stone* 17 October 1991: 99. *San Francisco Chronicle* 27 September 1991: D-1, D-15. *San Francisco Examiner* 27 September 1991: D-1. *Screen International* 11 October 1991: 53–54. *Séquences* 155 (November 1991): 82–83. *Sight and Sound* NS 1 (November 1991): 42–43; NS 2 (November 1992): 60; NS 3 (January 1993): 61. *Spectator* 267 (9 November 1991): 62. *Starburst* 158 (November 1991): 38–40. *Studio* [Paris] 54 (October 1991): 6. *Sun* [London] 8 November 1991: 22. *Sunday Express* [London] 10 November 1991: 62. *Sunday Times* [London] 10 November 1991: 6. 8–9. *Time* 138 (23 September 1991): 68. *Time Out* [London] 6 November 1991: 19. *Times* [London] 7 November 1991: 19. *Times* [London] *Literary Supplement* 22 November 1991: 17. *Today* [London] 8 November 1991: 23, 26. *TV Guide* 28 March 1992: 25. *United Church Observer* [Canada] 55 (January 1992): 44. *USA Today* 20 September 1991: 5D. *Variety* 16 September 1991: 89–90. *Video Magazine* 16 (April 1992): 44–45. *Video Watchdog* 13 (September-October 1992): 50–51. *Village Voice* 1 October 1991: 70. *Vogue* 181 (September 1991): 284. *Wall Street Journal* 19 September 1991: A12. *Washington Post* 20 September 1991: B1; Weekend 53. *Western Mail* [Great Britain] 9 November 1991: 6. *What's On In London* 6 November 1991: 84.

ADDITIONAL DISCUSSIONS:

Andrew, Geoff. "Grail Force." *Time Out* [London] 23 October 1991: 18–21.

Ashbrook, John. *Terry Gilliam*. Harpenden, Herts: Pocket Essentials, 2000.

Blair, Ian. "Manhattan Knights." *Chicago Tribune* 22 September 1991: Arts 6–7.

Blanch, Robert J. "The Fisher King in Gotham: New Age Spiritualism Meets the Grail Legend." In Kevin J. Harty, ed. *King Arthur on Film, New Essays on Arthurian Cinema*. Jefferson, N.C.: McFarland, 1999.

Bouineau, Jean-Marc. *Le Petit Livre de Terry Gilliam*. Rev. ed. Garches: Spartorange, 1996.

Calhoun, John. "The Fisher King." *Theatre Crafts* 25 (April 1991): 40–44, 54–59.

Chevassu, François, and Lucie Desanglois. "Entre audace et prudence: le plus anglais des americains." *Revue du cinéma* 475 (October 1991): 24–26.

Christie, Ian, ed. *Gilliam on Gilliam*. London: Faber and Faber, 1999.

Dougan, Andy. *Robin Williams*. London: Orion House, 1999.

"Eye on ... Opening Nights." *Harper's Bazaar* 124 (September 1991): 186.

Fleischer, Leonore. *The Fisher King*. New York: Signet, 1991. [Novelization.]

Forestier, François. "Robin Williams." *Première* [France] 175 (October 1991): 86–87.

Frankel, Martha. "The Ladies' Man." *Movieline* 7 (April 1996): 74–78, 89.

Gelman-Waxman, Libby. *If You Ask Me*. New York: St. Martin's, 1994.

Gill, Andy. "Mercedes Ruehl: *The Fisher King*." *Empire* 36 (June 1992): 44–45.

Goldman, Steve. "King of Comedy." *Sunday Times* [London] 3 November 1991: 6, 11.

Das große Kino und Video Jahrbuch '92. Munich: ProVideo Verlag, 1992.

Grove, Martin A. "Hollywood Report." *Hollywood Reporter* 5 September 1991: 5; 26 September 1991: 5; 27 September 1991: 12.

Haas, Christine. "Terry Gilliam." *Première* [France] 175 (October 1991): 88.

Harty, Kevin J. "*The Fisher King*: A List of Critical Reviews and Other Discussions." In Keith Busby, ed. *The Arthurian Yearbook III*. New York: Garland, 1993.

_____. "Parsifal and Perceval on Film: The Reel Life of a Grail Knight." In Arthur Groos and Norris J. Lacy, eds. *Perceval/Parsifal: A Casebook*. New York: Routledge, 2002.

Heisner, Beverly. *Production Design in Contemporary American Film*. Jefferson, N.C.: McFarland, 1997.

Hoffman, Donald L. "Re-Framing Perceval." *Arthuriana* 10 (Winter 2000): 45–56.

Homan, Richard L. "The Everyman Movie, Circa 1991." *Journal of Popular Film and Literature* 25 (Spring 1997): 21–30.

James, Caryn. "'The Fisher King' Is Wise Enough to Be Wacky." *New York Times* 22 September 1991: 2. 13.

Johnson, Kim Howard. "Tales of the Fisher King." *Starlog* 171 (October 1991): 47–51, 69.

Keogh, Peter. "Happy Grails to You." *Chicago Sun-Times* 22 September 1991: Show 6.

Kokino, Keith. "From Clown Prince to Fisher King." *Mediascene Prevue* 22 (May-August 1991): 18–19.

LaGravenese, Richard. *The Fisher King, The Book of the Film*. New York: Applause, 1991. [Screenplay.]

Lavoignat, Jean-Pierre. "La Quête du fou: une interview de Robin Williams." *Studio* [Paris] 54 (October 1991): 69–74.

Magid, Ron. "The Fisher King's Logistical

Knight-Mare." *American Cinematographer* 72 (December 1991): 70–77.
Magill, Frank N., ed. *Magill's Cinema Annual 1992, A Survey of the Films of 1991*. Pasadena, Calif.: Salem Press, 1992.
Matthews, Jack. "On Movies Still a Rebel, Terry Gilliam Mellows Out." *Newsday* 29 September 1991: Fanfare 5.
McCabe, Bob. *Dark Knights & Holy Fools: The Art and Films of Terry Gilliam*. New York: Universe, 1999.
McCarthy, Robert E. *Secrets of Hollywood Special Effects*. Boston: Focal Press, 1992.
Miller, Barbara D. "'Cinemagicians': Movie Merlins of the 1980s and 1990s." In Kevin J. Harty, ed. *King Arthur on Film, New Essays on Arthurian Cinema*. Jefferson, N.C.: McFarland, 1999.
Miller-Monzon, John, ed. *Motion Picture Guide, 1992 Annual (The Films of 1991)*. New York: Baseline, 1992.
Mills, Bart. "Fantasy vs. Reality Amid the Madness." *San Francisco Chronicle* 22 September 1991: Datebook 19.
Morgan, David. "And Now for Something Completely Different...." *Empire* 30 (December 1991): 86–88, 91–93.
_____. "Terry Gilliam: The Millimeter Interview." *Millimeter* 19 (March 1991): 43–53.
_____. "They're Getting a Terry Gilliam Film." *Los Angeles Times* 24 June 1990: Calendar 5.
Olton, Bert. *Arthurian Legends on Film and Television*. Jefferson, N.C.: McFarland, 2000.
Osberg, Richard H. "Pages Torn From the Book: Narrative Disintegration in Gilliam's 'The Fisher King.'" In Leslie J. Workman and Kathleen Verduin, eds. *Medievalism in England II*. Studies in Medievalism 1995. Cambridge, Eng.: D. S. Brewer, 1996.
_____, and Michael E. Crow. "Language Then and Language Now in Arthurian Film." In Kevin J. Harty, ed. *King Arthur on Film, New Essays on Arthurian Cinema*. Jefferson, N.C.: McFarland, 1999.
Perry, George. "The Quest for Identity." *Sunday Times* [London] 10 November 1991: 6. 8–9.
Persons, Don. "The Fisher King." *Cinefantastique* 21 (June 1991): 4–5.
Powers, John. "Alive Again." *Sight and Sound* NS 1 (November 1991): 6.
Ryan, James. "Plummer Finally Finds a Role in Hollywood." *Boston Globe* 22 September 1991: A10.
Sanello, Frank. "The Hairiest Man in Hollywood." *Empire* 30 (December 1991): 89–90.
Sante, Luc. "Odd Woman In." *Movieline* 11 (April 1991): 40–42, 78, 85.
Schmidt, Klaus M. "'I Got the Power!—Forgive Me!' Ein Paket fürs dritte Jahrtausend: Terry Gilliam's *Fisher King* und die Parzival-Geschichte." In Ulrich Müller, ed. *Im Sechsten Jahr des Drachen*. Göppingen: Kümmerle Verlag, 2000.
Sheehan, Henry. "The King of Fairy Tales." *Boston Globe* 22 September 1991: A7, A9.
Sternberg, Doug. "Tom's a-cold: Transformation and Redemption in *King Lear* and *The Fisher King*." *Literature/Film Quarterly* 23 (July 1994): 160–69.
Stukator, Angela. "'Soft Males,' 'Flying Boys,' and 'White Knights': New Masculinity in *The Fisher King*." *Literature/Film Quarterly* 25 (July 1997): 214–21.
Thomas, Bob. "Hollywood Finally Embraces Terry Gilliam." *Chicago Sun-Times* 2 October 1991: 2. 4.
Tous les films 1991. Versailles: Éditions Chrétiens-Médias, 1992.
Umland, Rebecca A., and Samuel J. Umland. *The Use of Arthurian Legend in Hollywood Film from Connecticut Yankees to Fisher Kings*. Westport, Conn.: Greenwood, 1996.
Wallace, David. "'The Fisher King's' Catch." *Los Angeles Times* 24 September 1991: Calendar 1.
Willman, Chris. "Tilting at Windmills." *Los Angeles Times* 19 September 1991: Calendar 1.
Winer, Linda. "Getting Radical About Comedy." *Newsday* 23 September 1991: 2. 49.

Four Diamonds (1995)
United States; dir. Peter Werner; screenplay by Todd Robinson; The Disney Channel
Cast: Jayne Brook, Kevin Dunn, Thomas Guiry, Sarah Rose Karr, Christine Lahti

REVIEWS:
Arthuriana 6 (Summer 1996): 115–18. *Chicago Tribune* 6 August 1995: TV Week 3. *Daily News* [New York] 12 August 1995: 48. *Daily Variety* 8 August 1995: 16. *Detroit Free Press* 23 August 1995: 5E. *Hollywood Reporter* 11 August 1995: 35. *New York Times* 11 August 1995: B14. *People Weekly* 14 August 1995: 15. *TV Guide* 12 August 1995: 69, 74. *USA Today* 11 August 1995: 3D.

ADDITIONAL DISCUSSIONS:
Delsite, Alison. "Son's Death Led to Therapy of Fund Raising." *The Patriot* [Harrisburg, Penn.] 21 February 1994: B1.
Harty, Kevin J. *The Reel Middle Ages: American, Western and Eastern European, Middle Eastern and Asian Films About Medieval Europe*. Jefferson, N.C.: McFarland, 1999.
_____. "The Return to Camelot on Page and Screen: Chris Millard's 'Four Diamonds.'" In

Thomas Guiry as Sir Millard in Peter Werner's 1995 telefilm *Four Diamonds*. (Still courtesy of The Disney Channel.)

Debra N. Mancoff, ed. *King Arthur's Modern Return*. New York: Garland, 1998.

Gawain and the Green Knight (1973)

Great Britain; dir. Stephen Weeks; screenplay by Stephen Weeks and Philip Green; United Artists and Sancrest Films

Cast: Nigel Green, Robert Hardy, Murray Head, Ronald Lacey, Davil Leland, Ciaran Madden, Anthony Sharp

REVIEW:

Monthly Film Bulletin 40 (April 1973): 168–69.

ADDITIONAL DISCUSSIONS:

Berry, Dave. "Stephen Weeks." *Film* 37 (May 1976): 6–7.

Berry, David. *Wales and Cinema, The First Hundred Years*. Cardiff: University of Wales Press, 1994.

Blanch, Robert J., and Julian N. Wasserman. "Gawain on Film." In Kevin J. Harty, ed. *Cinema Arthuriana, Essays on Arthurian Film*. New York: Garland, 1991. [Rpt. above in revised form.]

Elley, Derek. *The Epic Film*. London: Routledge, 1984.

Harty, Kevin J. *The Reel Middle Ages: American, Western and Eastern European, Middle Eastern and Asian Films About Medieval Europe*. Jefferson, N.C.: McFarland, 1999.

Nash, Jay Robert, and Stanley Ralph Ross. *The Motion Picture Guide, E–G, 1927–1983*. Chicago: Cinebooks, 1986.

Pirie, David. "New Blood." *Sight and Sound* 40 (Spring 1971): 73–75.

Richards, Jeffrey. *Swordsmen of the Screen from Douglas Fairbanks to Michael York*. London: Routledge, 1977.

Umland, Rebecca, and Sam Umland. "The Long Happy Film Life of Stephen Weeks." *Video Watchdog* 60 (June 2000): 4–6.

———. "The Short, Unhappy Film Life of Stephen Weeks." *Video Watchdog* 59 (May 2000): 32–39.

Williams, David. "Sir Gawain in Films." In Derek Brewer and Jonathan Gibson, eds. *A Companion to the Gawain-Poet*. Cambridge, Eng.: D. S. Brewer, 1997.

Woods, Linda, ed. *The British Film Catalogue, 1971–1981*. London: BFI, 1983.

Gawain and the Green Knight (1991)

Great Britain; dir. John Michael Phillips; screenplay by David Rudkin; Thames Television

Cast: Jason Durr, Marie Francis, Valerie Gogan, Tommy Searroll, Malcolm Storry, Marc Warren

REVIEWS:

Arthuriana 8 (Fall 1998): 124–26. *Independent* [London] 4 January 1991: 14. *Scotsman* [Edinburgh] 4 January 1991: 23.

ADDITIONAL DISCUSSIONS:

Olton, Bert. *Arthurian Legends on Film and Television*. Jefferson, N.C.: McFarland, 2000.

Williams, David. "Sir Gawain in Films." In Derek Brewer and Jonathan Gibson, eds. *A Companion to the Gawain-Poet*. Cambridge, Eng.: D. S. Brewer, 1997.

Ginevra (1992)

Germany; dir. Ingemo Engström; screenplay by Ingemo Engström; Theuring-Engström Productions

Cast: Michèle Addala, Christian Koch, Serge Maggiani, Amanda Ooms, Zacharias Preen, Gerhard Theuring, Diego Wallraff

REVIEWS:

Berlinale Journal 3 (15 February 1992): 18. *Filmdienst* 47 (24 May 1994): 20. *Filmwärts* 23 (August 1992): 80. *Variety* 16 March 1992: 60.

ADDITIONAL DISCUSSIONS:

Dokumentation: 42. Internationale Filmfestspiele Berlin [13.–24. February 1992]. Berlin: Berlin International Film Festival, 1992.

Official Catalogue: Edinburgh International Film Festival [15–30 August 1992]. Edinburgh: Edinburgh International Film Festival, 1992.

Girl Slaves of Morgana Le Fay (1971)
See *Morgane et ses Nymphes* (1971)

The Grail (1915)
United States; dir. William Worthington; screenplay by L. V. Jefferson; Laemmle Films
Cast: Anna Little, Herbert Robinson, William Worthington

REVIEWS:
Bioscope 2 September 1915: supplement vii. *Moving Picture World* 3 July 1915: 66.

Guinevere (1994)
United States; dir. Jud Taylor; screenplay by Ronni Kern; Lifetime Television Productions
Cast: Brid Brennan, Sheryl Lee, Donald Pleasance, Noah Wyle

REVIEWS:
Times-Picayune [New Orleans] 1 May 1994: TV4. *TV Guide* 7 May 1994: 67, 76.

ADDITIONAL DISCUSSIONS:
Harty, Kevin J. *The Reel Middle Ages: American, Western and Eastern European, Middle Eastern and Asian Films About Medieval Europe.* Jefferson, N.C.: McFarland, 1999.
Olton, Bert. *Arthurian Legends on Film and Television*. Jefferson, N.C.: McFarland, 2000.
Torregrossa, Michael. "Merlin Goes to the Movies: The Changing Role of Merlin in Cinema Arthuriana." *Film & History* 29. 3–4 (1999): 54–65.

I Skugga Hrafnsina (1988)
See *In the Shadow of the Raven* (1988)

In the Shadow of the Raven (1988)
Iceland; dir. Hrafn Gunnlaugsson; screenplay by Hrafn Gunnlaugsson; Sandrews Film Productions
Alternate titles: *I Skugga Hrafnsina* and *The Shadow of the Raven*
Cast: Reine Brynolfsson, Tinna Gunnlaugsdottir, Egil Olafsson, Sune Maangs, Helgi Skulason

REVIEWS:
Boston Globe 24 May 1990: 84. *Chaplin* 219 (December 1988): 308–09. *Daily News* [New York] 12 July 1991: 55. *Filmrutan* 31.4 (1988): 35–36. *Hollywood Reporter* 9 October 1990: 11, 151. *New York Post* 12 July 1991: 29. *New York Times* 13 July 1991: 12. *Newsday* 12 July 1991: 71. *San Francisco Chronicle* 31 August 1990: E7. *San Francisco Examiner* 31 August 1990: C7. *Variety* 19 October 1988: 249, 255. *Village Voice* 23 July 1991: 63. *Washington Post* 18 January 1991: Weekend 40; 19 January 1991: C11.

ADDITIONAL DISCUSSIONS:
Cowie, Peter, ed. *Le Cinéma des pays nordiques*. Paris: Centre Georges Pompidou, 1990.
_____, ed. *Variety International Film Guide 1989*. New York: Zoetrope, 1988.
_____, ed. *Variety International Film Guide 1990*. Hollywood, Calif.: Samuel French, 1989.
Fridgeirsson, Asgeir. "The Bishop and the Actor." *Iceland Review* 29.3 (191): 37–40.
Hansen, Peter Risby. "Blandt vildmænd, drøommere og barske businessfolk." *Kosmorama* 184 (Summer 1988): 43–47.
Harty, Kevin J. *The Reel Middle Ages: American, Western and Eastern European, Middle Eastern and Asian Films About Medieval Europe.* Jefferson, N.C.: McFarland, 1999.
Icelandic Films 1979–1988. Reykjavik: Icelandic Film Fund, 1988.
Jónsdóttir, Solveig K. "Once Upon a Time in the North." *Iceland Review* 25.4 (1987): 4–11.
The Motion Picture Guide: 1989 Annual (The Films of 1988). Evanston, Ill.: Cinebooks, 1989.
Swedish Film Institute Film Catalogue. Stockholm: Swedish Film Institute, 1989.

Indiana Jones and the Last Crusade (1989)
United States; dir. Steven Spielberg; screenplay by Jeffrey Boam; Lucasfilm and Paramount Pictures
Cast: Sean Connery, Alison Doody, Denholm Elliott, Harrison Ford, Julian Glover, River Phoenix, John Rhys-Davies

REVIEWS:
24 Images 44–45 (Fall 1989): 100–01. *L'Actualité* 14 August 1989: 69. *America* 160 (17 June 1989): 591. *American Spectator* 22 (August 1989): 73. *Antiquity* 64 (March 1990): 157. *Atlanta Constitution* 24 May 1989: C1. *Boston Globe* 24 May 1989: 53, 59. *Cahiers du cinéma* 424 (October 1989): 51–52. *Chatelaine* 30 (August 1989): 25. *Christian Science Monitor* 9 June 1989: 15. *Christianity Today* 8 September 1989: 70. *Cinefantastique* 20 (November 1989): 98–99, 118. *Cinéma* [Paris] 460 (October 1989): 27–28. *City Limits* [London] 22 June 1989: 19. *Commonweal* 116 (14 July 1989): 403. *Cosmopolitan* 207 (August 1989): 73. *Daily Mail* [London] 27 June 1989: 3. *Daily Mirror* [London] 30 June 1989: 28. *Daily News* [New York] 24 May 1989: 37. *Daily Telegraph* [London] 29 June 1989: 16. *EPD Film* 6 (September 1989): 24–25. *Evening Standard* [London] 29 June 1989: 32–33. *Film* [Italy] 1 (September-October 1989): 1–2. *Film Comment* 25 (July-August 1989): 9–11. *Film en televisie* 389 (October 1989): 25. *Filmcritica* 399 (November 1989): 575–81. *Filmihullu* 6–7 (1989): 46. *Filmrutan*

32.4 (1989): 30. *Films and Filming* 417 (July 1989): 40–41. *Financial Times* [London] 29 June 1989: 23. *Guardian* [London] 29 June 1989: 21. *Hollywood Reporter* 19 May 1989: 4, 13. *Independent* [London] 29 June 1989: 15. *Insight* 5 (5 June 1989): 57. *Kino* [Bulgaria] 2 (February 1991): 28–32. *Kino* [Poland] 271 (January 1990): 42–43. *Listener* 29 June 1989: 40. *Los Angeles Times* 25 May 1989: B8. *Maclean's* 102 (5 June 1989): 56. *Mail on Sunday* [London] 2 July 1989: 14. *Monthly Film Bulletin* 56 (July 1989): 198–200. *Morning Star* [London] 30 June 1989: 8. *Nation* 248 (19 June 1989): 862. *National Catholic Reporter* 25 August 1989: 13. *New Republic* 200 (19 June 1989): 28–29. *New Statesman and Society* 2 (30 June 1989): 15. *New York* 22 (5 June 1989): 58–59. *New York Native* 29 May 1989: 25. *New York Post* 24 May 1989: 31. *New York Press* 9 June 1989: 13. *New York Times* 24 May 1989: 3. 15; 14 January 1990: 2. 32. *New Yorker* 65 (12 June 1989): 103–05. *Newsday* 24 May 1989: 2. 2; 1 June 1989: 2. 13. *Newsweek* 113 (29 May 1989): 69. *Le Nouvel observateur* 19 October 1989: 12. *People Weekly* 31 (5 June 1989): 13. *Positif* 344 (October 1989): 70–71. *Premiere* 9 (June-July 1989): 12–19. *Revue du cinéma* 453 (October 1989): 14–16. *Rolling Stone* 15 June 1989: 31. *Saint Anthony Messenger* 97 (July 1989): 6. *Screen International* 3 June 1989: 21. *Segnocinema* 40 (November 1989): 36–37. *Séquences* 141–42 (September 1989): 107–08. *Sight and Sound* NS 3 (January 1993): 59. *Skrien* 169 (December 1989–January 1990): 67. *Starburst* 11 (July 1989): 24–25. *Sun* [London] 27 June 1989: 15. *Sunday Express* [London] 2 July 1989: 19. *Sunday Times* [London] 2 July 1989: C9. *Time* 133 (19 May 1989): 82. *Time Out* [London] 21 June 1989: 34. *Times* [London] 29 June 1989: 21. *Today* [London] 30 June 1989: 30. *Variety* 24 May 1989: 25; 31 May 1989: 27. *Video Review* 10 (March 1990): 51. *Village Voice* 30 May 1989: 89. *Wall Street Journal* 25 May 1989: A16. *Washington Post* 26 May 1989: WW41. *Western Mail* [Great Britain] 1 July 1989: 13. *What's On In London* 21 June 1989: 63.

ADDITIONAL DISCUSSIONS:

Aronstein, Susan. "'Not Exactly a Knight': Arthurian Narrative and Recuperative Politics in the *Indiana Jones* Trilogy." *Cinema Journal* 34 (Summer 1995): 3–30.

Briggs, Nicholas. "Licensed to Crusade." *Starburst* 130 (June 1989): 8–11.

———. "Producing the Hero." *Starburst* 131 (July 1989) 16–19.

Brode, Douglas. *The Films of Steven Spielberg.* New York: Citadel Press, 1995.

Brown, Christine, and Lynne C. Boughton. "The Grail Quest as Illumination." *Journal of Interdisciplinary Studies* 9.1–2 (1997): 39–62.

Canby, Vincent. "Spielberg's Elixir Shows Signs of Mature Magic." *New York Times* 18 June 1989: 2. 15–16.

Eisenberg, Adam. "Father, Son and the Holy Grail." *Cinefex* 40 (November 1989): 46–67.

Gelman-Waxman, Libby. *If You Ask Me.* New York: St. Martin's, 1994.

Gómez, Pablo. *En Busca del Héroe Perdido, Guia no Oficial del Arqueólogo Henry Jones, Jr.* Valencia: Carena Editors, 1999.

"Great New Indy Special Effects." *Popular Mechanics* 166 (July 1989): 18.

Grebe, Coralee. "Raiders of the Myths." *Cinefantastique* 19 (May 1989): 7, 58.

Griffin, Nancy. "Manchild in the Promised Land." *Premiere* 2 (June 1989): 86–94.

Heuring, David. "Effects Maestros Put Buckle in Indy's Swash." *American Cinematographer* 70 (December 1989): 66–74.

———. "Indiana Jones and the Last Crusade." *American Cinematographer* 70 (June 1989): 57–66.

Iaccino, James F. *Jungian Reflections with the Cinema, A Psychological Analysis of Sci-Fi and Fantasy Archetypes.* Westport, Conn.: Praeger, 1998.

Indiana Jones and the Last Crusade. [Hollywood, Calif.]: Paramount, 1989. [Production handbook.]

James, Caryn. "It's a New Age for Father-Son Relationships." *New York Times* 9 July 1989: 2. 11–12.

Jones, Alan, and Coralee Grebe. "Indiana Jones and the Last Crusade." *Cinefantastique* 19 (May 1989): 6–7, 61.

MacGregor, Ron. *Indiana Jones and the Last Crusade.* New York: Penguin, 1989. [Novelization.]

Miller, Barbara D. "'Cinemagicians': Movie Merlins of the 1980s and 1990s." In Kevin J. Harty, ed. *King Arthur on Film, New Essays on Arthurian Cinema.* Jefferson, N.C.: McFarland, 1999.

The Motion Picture Guide: 1990 Annual (The Films of 1989). Evanston: Cinebooks, 1990.

Olton, Bert. *Arthurian Legends on Film and Television.* Jefferson, N.C.: McFarland, 2000.

Osberg, Richard H., and Michael E. Crow. "Language Then and Language Now in Arthurian Film." In Kevin J. Harty, ed. *King Arthur on Film, New Essays on Arthurian Cinema.* Jefferson, N.C.: McFarland, 1999.

Royal, Susan. "*Indiana Jones and the Last Crusade:* An Interview with Harrison Ford." *American Premiere* 9 (June-July 1989): 12–19.

Shichtman, Martin B. "Whom Does the Grail

Serve? Wagner, Spielberg, and the Jewish Issue of Appropriation." In Debra N. Mancoff, ed. *The Arthurian Revival, Essays on Form, Tradition, and Transformation.* New York: Garland, 1992.

Smith, Jane. "Indiana Jones and the Big Spiel." *Detroit News* 19 June 1989: 1C, 3C.

Summerfield, Thea. "Reading a Motion Picture: Why Steven Spielbreg Should Read the *Roman van Walewein.*" In Bart Besamusca and Erik Kooper, eds. *Arthurian Literature XVII: Originality and Tradition in the Middle Dutch Roman van Walewein.* Cambridge, Eng.: D. S. Brewer, 1999.

Tous les films 1989. Paris: Éditions Chrétiens-Médias, 1990.

Umland, Rebecca A., and Samuel J. Umland. *The Use of Arthurian Legend in Hollywood Film from Connecticut Yankees to Fisher Kings.* Westport, Conn.: Greenwood, 1996.

Vaz, Mark Cotta, and Shinji Hata. *From Star Wars to Indiana Jones.* San Francisco: Chronicle Books, 1994.

White, Armond. "Keeping Up With the Joneses." *Film Quarterly* 25 (July-August 1989): 9-11.

Woodward, Richard B. "Meanwhile, Back at the Ranch." *New York Times* 21 May 1989: 2. 1, 16.

Isolde (1989)

Denmark; dir. Jytte Rex; screenplay Jytte Rex; Norsk Film Production and the Danish Film Institute

Cast: Claus Flygare, Kim Jansson, Pia With

REVIEWS:

Kosmorama 35 (Summer 1989): 10-11. *Variety* 29 March 1989: 17. *Washington Post* 8 June 1990: Weekend 54.

ADDITIONAL DISCUSSIONS:

Catalogue of the American Film Institute and Los Angeles Film Festival. Los Angeles: American Film Institute and Los Angeles Film Festival, 1996.

Cowie, Peter, ed. *Variety International Film Guide 1990.* Hollywood, Calif.: Samuel French, 1989.

Johnny Mysto, Boy Wizard (1996)

United States; dir. Jeff Burr; screenplay by Benjamin Carr; Kushner-Locke Productions for Paramount Pictures

Cast: Ian Abercrombie, Toran Caudell, Jack Dooner, Russ Tamblyn

DISCUSSION:

Olton, Bert. *Arthurian Legends on Film and Television.* Jefferson, N.C.: McFarland, 2000.

A Kid in King Arthur's Court (1995)

United States; dir. Michael Gottlieb; screenplay by Michael Part and Robert L. Levy; Walt Disney Pictures

Cast: Joss Ackland, Paloma Baeza, Daniel Craig, Art Malik, Ron Moody, Thomas Ian Nicholas, David Tysall, Kate Winslet

REVIEWS:

Arthuriana 6 (Summer 1996): 115-18. *Boston Globe* 11 August 1995: 49. *Boston Herald* 11 August 1995: S6. *Daily News* [New York] 11 August 1995: 56. *Film Journal* 98 (October-November 1995): 33. *Hollywood Reporter* 11 August 1995: 10, 35. *Los Angeles Times* 11 August 1995: F4. *New York Post* 11 August 1995: 42. *New York Times* 11 August 1995: C16. *Newsday* 11 August 1995: B5. *Philadelphia Daily News* 11 August 1995: 51. *Philadelphia Inquirer* 11 August 1995: Weekend 5. *San Francisco Chronicle* 11 August 1995: C3. *San Francisco Examiner* 11 August 1995: D6. *Starburst* 228 (August 1997): 62. *Toronto Star* 11 August 1995: D7. *Variety* 14 August 1995: 55, 59. *Washington Post* 11 August 1995: F6; Weekend 41.

ADDITIONAL DISCUSSIONS:

Fhaner, Beth A., and Christopher P. Scanlon, eds. *Magill's Cinema Annual 1996.* Detroit: Gale, 1996.

Harty, Kevin J. *The Reel Middle Ages: American, Western and Eastern European, Middle Eastern and Asian Films About Medieval Europe.* Jefferson, N.C.: McFarland, 1999.

Levich, Jacob, ed. *The Motion Picture Guide, 1996 Annual (The Films of 1995).* New York: Cinebooks, 1996.

Mazer, Anne. *A Kid in King Arthur's Court.* New York: Disney Press, 1995. [Novelization.]

Olton, Bert. *Arthurian Legends on Film and Television.* Jefferson, N.C.: McFarland, 2000.

Sklar, Elizabeth S. "Twain for Teens: Young Yankees in Camelot." In Kevin J. Harty, ed. *King Arthur on Film, New Essays on Arthurian Cinema.* Jefferson, N.C.: McFarland, 1999.

Torregrossa, Michael. "Merlin Goes to the Movies: The Changing Role of Merlin in Cinema Arthuriana." *Film & History* 29. 3-4 (1999): 54-65.

Umland, Rebecca A., and Samuel J. Umland. *The Use of Arthurian Legend in Hollywood Film from Connecticut Yankees to Fisher Kings.* Westport, Conn.: Greenwood, 1996.

Kids of the Round Table (1995)

Canada; dir. Robert Tinnell; screenplay by David Sherman; Melenny Productions and Telefilm Canada

Cast: Michael Ironside, Malcolm McDowell, Johnny Morina, Ren Simard

REVIEWS:
L'Express [Montréal] 9 December 1995: C1, C2.
Variety 22 May 1995: 109.

ADDITIONAL DISCUSSIONS:
Olton, Bert. *Arthurian Legends on Film and Television*. Jefferson, N.C.: McFarland, 2000.
Torregrossa, Michael. "Merlin Goes to the Movies: The Changing Role of Merlin in Cinema Arthuriana." *Film & History* 29. 3–4 (1999): 54–65.

King Arthur (1980)
See *Le Roi Arthur* (1980)

King Arthur and the Siege of the Saxons (1963)
See *The Siege of the Saxons* (1963)

King Arthur; or, The Knights of the Round Table (1910)
See *Il Re Artù e i cavalieri della tavola rotonda* (1910)

King Arthur, the Young Warlord (1975)
Great Britain; dir. Sidney Hayers, Patrick Jackson, and Patrick Sasdy; screenplay by Terence Feely and Robert Banks Stewart; Heritage Enterprises
Alternate titles: *Arthur of the Britons* and *Arthur, Warlord of the Britons*
Cast: Brian Blessed, Peter Firth, Michael Gothard, Oliver Tobias, Jack Watson

REVIEWS:
TV Times [Great Britain] 2–8 December 1972: 55; 9–15 December 1972: 57; 16–29 December 1972: 45; 30 December 1972–5 January 1973: 41; 6–12 January 1973: 39; 13–19 January 1973: 39; 20–26 January 1973: 43; 27 January–2 February 1973: 45; 3–9 February 1973: 37; 10–16 February 1973: 45; 17–23 February 1973: 43; 8–14 September 1973: 55; 15–21 September 1973: 55; 22–28 September 1973: 57; 29 September –5 October 1973: 57; 6–12 October 1973: 57; 13–19 October 1973: 55; 20–26 October 1973: 53; 27 October–2 November 1973: 53; 3–9 November 1973: 57; 10–16 November 1973: 60; 17–23 November 1973: 51; 24–30 November 1973: 57.

ADDITIONAL DISCUSSIONS:
Escourt, Peter. "Arthur, Warlord of the Britains." *TV Times* [Great Britain] 2–8 December 1972: 14–16.
Harty, Kevin J. *The Reel Middle Ages: American, Western and Eastern European, Middle Eastern and Asian Films About Medieval Europe*. Jefferson, N.C.: McFarland, 1999.
Olton, Bert. *Arthurian Legends on Film and Television*. Jefferson, N.C.: McFarland, 2000.

"Star of the Month: Oliver Tobias." *TV Times* [Great Britain] 9–15 December 1972: 40–41.
Vahimagi, Tise. *An Illustrated Guide to British Television*. London: Oxford University Press, 1994.
The Video Source Book 1997. 18th ed. Detroit: Gale, 1996.

King Arthur Was a Gentleman (1942)
Great Britain; dir. Marcel Varnel; screenplay by Marriott Edgar and Val Guest; Gainsborough Films
Cast: Arthur Askey, Max Bacon, Evelyn Dall, Vera Frances, Peter Graves, Anne Shelton, Jack Train

REVIEWS:
Kinematograph Weekly 10 December 1942: 14.
Monthly Film Bulletin 9 (31 December 1942): 153. *Motion Picture Herald* 150 (16 January 1942): Product Digest Section 1114. *To-day's Cinema* 4 December 1942: 5.

ADDITIONAL DISCUSSIONS:
Askey, Arthur. *Before Your Very Eyes*. London: Woburn, 1975.
Everson, William K. "Arthur Askey." *Films in Review* 37 (March 1986): 169–75.
Murphy, Robert. *Realism and Tinsel, Cinema and Society in Britain 1939–1948*. 1989. rpt. London: Routledge, 1992.
Nash, Jay Robert, and Stanley Ralph Ross. *The Motion Picture Guide, H–K, 1927–1983*. Chicago: Cinebooks, 1985.
Olton, Bert. *Arthurian Legends on Film and Television*. Jefferson, N.C.: McFarland, 2000.
Quinlan, David. *British Sound Films, The Studio Years 1928–1959*. Totowa, N.J.: Barnes and Noble, 1984.
Seaton, Roy, and Roy Martin. "Gainsborough in the Forties." *Films and Filming* 333 (June 1982): 13–20.

A Knight in Camelot (1998)
United States; dir. Roger Young; screenplay by Joe Wiesenfeld; Rosemont Productions in association with Walt Disney Television
Cast: Robert Addie, Paloma Baeza, James Coombes, Amanda Donohoe, Simon Fenton, Whoopi Goldberg, Ian Richardson, Michael York

REVIEWS:
Arthuriana 9 (Spring 1999): 167–69. *Buffalo News* 8 November 1998: TV 8. *Daily News* [New York] 8 November 1998: Vue 6. *Entertainment Weekly* 457 (6 November 1998): 68. *Houston Chronicle* 7 November 1998: 7. *Los Angeles Times* 7 November 1998: F21. *New York Times* 7 November 1998: 15B. *TV Guide* 7 No-

vember 1998: 105, 121. *USA Today* 6 November 1998: 13E. *Variety* 2 November 1998: 36. *Washington Post* 8 November 1998: TV Week Y3.

ADDITIONAL DISCUSSIONS:
Bobbin, Jay. "Test Your Camelot IQ." *Arizona Republic* 8 November 1998: TV 47.
Grose, Thomas K. "A 'Knight' to Remember: Making Whoopi Fit into Camelot." *USA Today* 5 November 1998: 3D.
Hall, Steve. "Whoopi Still Feels Victim of Ageism." *Indianapolis Star* 4 November 1998: E7.
Olton, Bert. *Arthurian Legends on Film and Television*. Jefferson, N.C.: McFarland, 2000.

Knightriders (1981)

United States; dir. George Romero; screenplay by George Romero; Laurel Entertainment and United Films
Cast: Cynthia Adler, Brother Blue, Christine Forrest, Ed Harris, Amy Ingersoll, Gary Lahti, Tom Savini, Warner Shook, Patricia Tallman

REVIEWS:
Boxoffice 4 May 1981: 82–84. *Christian Science Monitor* 23 April 1981: 19. *Cineaste* 11.3 (1981): 31–33. *Ecran fantastique* 19 (1981): 68. *Film Journal* 84 (20 April 1981): 13–14. *Filme* [Germany] 10 (July-August 1981): 52. *Films and Filming* 334 (July 1982): 38. *Los Angeles Times* 9 April 1981: Calendar 1, 5. *Motion Picture Production Digest* 20 May 1981: 96. *Nation* 232 (16 May 1981): 612–13. *New Leader* 67 (4 May 1981): 17–18. *New York* 14 (27 April 1981): 64. *New York Post* 17 April 1981: 31. *New York Times* 17 April 1981: C8. *New Yorker* 57 (18 May 1981): 147–51. *Newsday* 17 April 1981: 2. 7. *Newsweek* 97 (13 April 1981): 82. *Perfect Vision* 6 (23 October 1994): 140. *Rolling Stone* 28 May 1981: 51–52. *Screen International* 14 June 1980: 18. *Soho News* [New York] 15 April 1981: 55, 61. *Time* 117 (27 April 1981): 54–55. *Variety* 8 April 1981: 20. *Village Voice* 15 April 1981: 15.

ADDITIONAL DISCUSSIONS:
Blanch, Robert J. "George Romero's *Knightriders*: A Contemporary Arthurian Romance." *Quondam et futurus* 1 (Winter 1991): 61–69.
Burke-Block, Candace. "The Film Journal Interviews George Romero on *Knightriders*." *Film Journal* 84 (4 May 1981): 25.
Gagne, Paul R. *The Zombies That Ate Pittsburgh: The Films of George Romero*. New York: Dodd, Mead, 1987.
Harty, Kevin J. "Camelot Twice Removed: *Knightriders* and the Film Versions of *A Connecticut Yankee in King Arthur's Court*." In Kevin J. Harty, ed. *Cinema Arthuriana, Essays on Arthurian Film*. New York: Garland, 1991. [Rpt. above in revised form.]
Heimel, Cynthia. "The Living Dead Ride Again." *New York* 13 (21 July 1980): 46–48.
Just, Lothar, ed. *Das Filmjahr '81/82*. Munich: Filmland Presse, 1981.
Kael, Pauline. *Taking It All In*. New York: Holt, Rinehart and Winston, 1984.
Martin, Bob. "Knightriders." *Fangora* 12 (1981): 17–19, 66–67.
Miller, Barbara D. "'Cinemagicians': Movie Merlins of the 1980s and 1990s." In Kevin J. Harty, ed. *King Arthur on Film, New Essays on Arthurian Cinema*. Jefferson, N.C.: McFarland, 1999.
Murray, Raymond. *Images in the Dark, An Encyclopedia of Gay and Lesbian Film and Video*. Rev. ed. New York: Plume, 1996.
Nash, Jay Robert, and Stanley Ralph Ross. *The Motion Picture Guide, H–K, 1927–1983*. Chicago: Cinebooks, 1986.
Olton, Bert. *Arthurian Legends on Film and Television*. Jefferson, N.C.: McFarland, 2000.
Parish, James Robert. *Gays and Lesbians in Mainstream Cinema*. Metuchen, N.J.: Scarecrow, 1993.
Seligson, Tom. "George Romero: Revealing the Monsters Within Us." *Twilight Zone* 1 (August 1981): 12–17.
Umland, Rebecca A., and Samuel J. Umland. *The Use of Arthurian Legend in Hollywood Film from Connecticut Yankees to Fisher Kings*. Westport, Conn.: Greenwood, 1996.
Weldon, Michael. *The Psychotronic Encyclopedia of Film*. New York: Ballantine, 1983.
Yakir, Dan. "Knight After Knight with George Romero." *American Film* 6 (May 1981): 42–45, 69.

Knights of the Round Table (1953)

Great Britain; dir. Richard Thorpe; screenplay by Talbot Jennings, Jan Lustig, and Noel Langley; MGM
Cast: Felix Aylmer, Stanley Baker, Anne Crawford, Mel Ferrer, Ava Gardner, Maureen Swanson, Robert Taylor

REVIEWS:
America 90 (16 January 1954): 407. *Catholic World* 178 (March 1954): 460. *Celuloide* 331 (January 1982): 15–18. *Commonweal* 59 (29 January 1954): 427–28. *Extension* 48 (March 1954): 4. *Farm Journal* 78 (March 1954): 94. *Film Daily* 23 December 1953: 6. *Films and Filming* 5 (June 1963): 37. *Films in Review* 5 (February 1954): 90–91. *Harrison's Reports* 26 December 1953: 208. *Kinematograph Weekly* 20 May 1951: 19–20. *Library Journal* 79 (15 January 1954): 139. *Life* 36 (25 January 1954):

The marriage of Arthur (Mel Ferrer) and Guinevere (Ava Gardner) in Richard Thorpe's 1953 film *Knights of the Round Table*.

108–10. *Look* 17 (29 December 1953): 34. *Los Angeles Herald Examiner* 5 September 1980: D6. *Monthly Film Bulletin* 21 (July 1954): 100–01. *Motion Picture Herald* 193 (26 December 1953): Product Digest Section 2117. *National Parent-Teacher* 48 (March 1954): 38. *New Statesman and Nation* 47 (22 May 1954): 661. *New York Times* 8 January 1954: 17. *New Yorker* 29 (19 January 1954): 85–86; 62 (10 February 1992): 23. *Newsweek* 43 (18 January 1954): 88. *Picturegoer* 12 June 1954: 20. *Saturday Review* 37 (16 January 1954): 32. *Scholastic* 64 (3 February 1954): 27. *Sign* 33 (February 1954): 64. *Spectator* 192 (21 May 1954): 613–14. *Tatler* 212 (26 May 1954): 462. *Time* 63 (26 April 1954): 112. *Times* [London] 14 May 1954: 8; 15 May 1954: 12. *Today* 9 (March 1954): 14. *To-day's Cinema* 13 May 1954: 7–8. *Variety* 23 December 1953: 6.

ADDITIONAL DISCUSSIONS:
Carr, Robert E., and R. M. Hayes. *Wide Screen Movies.* Jefferson, N.C.: McFarland, 1988.
de la Bretèque, François Amy. "La Figure de chevalier errant dans l'imaginaire cinématographique." In Daniel Poirion, ed. *Le Moyen*

Age dans le théatre et le cinéma français. (Cahiers de l'Association Internationale des Études Françaises 47 [May 1995].) Paris: Société d'Édition les Belles Lettres, 1995.

_____. "Le Table ronde au far-west: 'Les Chevaliers de la table ronde' de Richard Thorpe (1953)." *Cahiers de la cinémathèque* 42–43 (Summer 1985): 97–102.

Dietz, Howard. "The Anomalous Sir Thomas Malory." *New York Times* 10 January 1954: 2. 5.

Fowler, Karin J. *Ava Gardner, A Bio-Bibliography.* New York: Greenwood Press, 1990.

Fraser, George MacDonald. *The Hollywood History of the World.* New York: Morrow, 1988.

Harty, Kevin J. *The Reel Middle Ages: American, Western and Eastern European, Middle Eastern and Asian Films About Medieval Europe.* Jefferson, N.C.: McFarland, 1999.

Hudgins, Morgan. "Logistics of a Bivouac on the Liffy River." *New York Times* 22 November 1953: 2. 5.

Knights of the Round Table, A Souvenir Booklet. New York: Al Greenstone, 1954.

Knights of the Round Table, A Story of King Arthur. London: Ward, Lock, 1954. [Novelization.]

Lambert, Gavin. "Actor on CinemaScope." *Sight and Sound* 23 (October-December 1953): 70.

Nash, Jay Robert, and Stanley Ralph Ross. *The Motion Picture Guide, H–K, 1927–1983.* Chicago: Cinebooks, 1986.

Olton, Bert. *Arthurian Legends on Film and Television.* Jefferson, N.C.: McFarland, 2000.

Quirk, Lawrence J. *The Films of Robert Taylor.* Secaucus, N.J.: Citadel, 1975.

Richards, Jeffrey. *Swordsmen of the Screen from Douglas Fairbanks to Michael York.* London: Routledge, 1977.

Smith, Gary A. *Epic Films.* Jefferson, N.C.: McFarland, 1991.

Umland, Rebecca A., and Samuel J. Umland. *The Use of Arthurian Legend in Hollywood Film from Connecticut Yankees to Fisher Kings.* Westport, Conn.: Greenwood, 1996.

Wayne, Jane Ellen. *Robert Taylor.* New York: St. Martin's, 1987.

Williams, David. "Sir Gawain in Films." In Derek Brewer and Jonathan Gibson, eds. *A Companion to the* Gawain-*Poet.* Cambridge, Eng.: D. S. Brewer, 1997.

The Knights of the Round Table (1990)
See *Les Chevaliers de la table ronde* (1990)

Knights of the Square Table; or, The Grail (1917)
United States; dir. Alan Crosland; screenplay by James Austin Wilder; Edison Films

Cast: Thomas Blake, Yale Boss, Andy Clark, Paul Kelly, George Romaine, James Austin Wilder

REVIEWS:
Moving Picture World 4 August 1917: 849; 11 August 1917: 955–56. *New York Dramatic Mirror* 4 August 1917: 18. *Scouting* 5 (15 July 1917): 11. *Wid's* 26 July 1917: 474.

ADDITIONAL DISCUSSIONS:
"Boy Scout's Endorsement." *New York Dramatic Mirror* 25 August 1917: 26.

Hanson, Patricia King, ed. *The American Film Institute Catalog of Motion Pictures Produced in the United States, Feature Films, 1911–1920.* Berkeley: University of California Press, 1988.

Harty, Kevin J. "*The Knights of the Square Table*: The Boy Scouts and Thomas Edison Make an Arthurian Film." *Arthuriana* 4 (Winter 1994): 313–23.

Horowitz, Rita, and Harriett Harrison. *The George Kleine Collection of Early Motion Pictures in the Library of Congress, A Catalog.* Washington, D.C.: Library of Congress, 1980.

"Praise for Scout Film." *New York Dramatic Mirror* 4 August 1917: 24.

Knutzy Knights (1954)
United States; dir. Edward Bernds; screenplay by Edward Bernds; Columbia Pictures and Screen Gems

Alternate title: [Remake with stock footage of] *Square Heads of the Round Table* (1948)

Cast: The Three Stooges

REVIEW:
Today's Cinema 3 November 1954: 10.

ADDITIONAL DISCUSSIONS:
DeMichael, Tom. *Love Those Stooges.* Barrington, Ill.: Superior Promotions, 1993.

Fleming, Michael. *The Three Stooges, An Illustrated History.* New York: Random House, 1999.

Forrester, Jeffrey. *The Stooge Chronicles.* Chicago: Contemporary Books, 1981.

Howard, Moe. *Moe Howard & the 3 Stooges.* Secaucus, N.J.: Citadel Press, 1977.

Kurson, Robert. *The Official Three Stooges Encyclopedia.* Chicago: Contemporary Books, 1998.

Lenburg, Jeff, and others. *The Three Stooges Scrapbook.* Secaucus, N.J.: Citadel Press, 1982.

Okuda, Ted. *The Columbia Comedy Shorts, Two-Reel Hollywood Film Comedies, 1933–1958.* Jefferson, N.C.: McFarland, 1986.

Olton, Bert. *Arthurian Legends on Film and Television.* Jefferson, N.C.: McFarland, 2000.

***Lancelot and Elaine* (1909)**
See *Launcelot and Elaine* (1909)

***Lancelot and Guinevere* (1963)**
See *The Sword of Lancelot* (1963)

***Lancelot du Lac* (1974)**
France; dir. Robert Bresson; screenplay by Robert Bresson; Mara Films
Alternate title: *Lancelot of the Lake.*
Cast: Vladimir Antolek-Oresek, Humbert Balsan, Laura Duke Condominas, Luc Simon

REVIEWS:
Amis du film et de la télévision 224 (May 1975): 16–17. *Audience* 84 (June 1975): 5–6. *Avant-scène du cinéma* 408–09 (January-February 1992): 102–08. *Cinefantastique* 4 (Summer 1975): 37. *Cinéma* [Paris] 190–91 (September-October 1974): 273–75. *Cinema nuovo* 33 (September-October 1974): 366–68. *Cinéma pratique* 134–35 (November-December 1974): 224–26. *Cinéma Quebec* 4 (May 1975): 34–35. *Ecran* 29 (October 1974): 57–59. *Ekran* 12 (1974): 88–93. *Empire* 65 (November 1994): 40. *Études* [Paris] 341 (November 1974): 593–95. [British] *Federation* [of Film Societies] *News* 33 (December 1975): 5. *Film* 22 (January 1975): 3; 23 (December 1975): 4. *Film Comment* 35 (July-August 1999): 46–48. *Film en televisie* 239 (April 1977): 38. *Film français* 6 September 1974: 14. *Film Review* [London] November 1994: 22. *Filmcritica* 25 (May 1974): 162–63. *Filmkritik* 19 (August 1975): 378–80. *Filmrutan* 17 (1974): 136–37. *Hollywood Reporter* 7 October 1974: 17. *Image et son* 285 (June-July 1974): 29; 291 (December 1974): 98–102; 292 (January 1975): 2–3. *Independent Film Journal* 75 (14 May 1975): 10. *Listener* 18 September 1975: 381. *Los Angeles Times* 26 August 1975: 4. 12. *Monthly Film Bulletin* 42 (September 1975): 199–200. *New Statesman* 90 (5 September 1975): 287. *New York* 8 (19 May 1975): 80. *New York Times* 1 October 1974: 33; 5 June 1975: 50. *New Yorker* 51 (9 June 1975): 117–18. *Newsweek* 84 (14 October 1974): 131–33. *Partisan Review* 41 (1974): 581. *Positif* 162 (October 1974): 55–57; 163 (November 1974): 71–74. *Revue du cinéma* 291 (December 1974): 98–102. *San Francisco Chronicle* 19 February 1977: 35. *Sight and Sound* 43 (Summer 1974): 128–30; NS 4 (November 1994): 62. *Skoop* 11 (March 1975): 34–35. *Sunday Times* [London] 23 October 1994: 10. 54; 17 November 1974: 35; 4 January 1976: 36; 31 August 1975: 24; 7 September 1975: 36. *Tablet* [London] 229 (13 September 1975): 869. *Take One* 4 (December 1974 [for September-October 1973]): 34. *Téléciné* 214 (January 1977): 13–14. *Thousand Eyes* 2 (March 1977): 7. *Time Out* [London] 19 October 1994: 64. *Times* [London] 20 October 1994: 37; 14 November 1974: 14; 5 September 1975: 7. *Variety* 12 June 1974: 24. *Village Voice* 31 October 1974: 10.

ADDITIONAL DISCUSSIONS:
Aristarco, Guido, ed. *Guida a al film*. Milan: Fabbri Editori, 1979.
Armes, Roy. "Film Theory and Practice." *London Magazine* 15 (April-May 1975): 96–101.
Baby, Yvonne. "Metal Makes Sounds: An Interview with Robert Bresson." (Trans. Nora Jacobson.) *Field of Vision* 13 (Spring 1985): 4–5.
Bartone, Richard C. "Variations on Arthurian Legend in *Lancelot du Lac* and *Excalibur*." In Sally K. Slocum, ed. *Popular Arthurian Traditions*. Bowling Green, Ohio: Bowling Green State University Popular Press, 1992.
Bergan, Ronald, and Robyn Karney. *Bloomsbury Foreign Film Guide*. Rev. ed. London: Bloomsbury, 1992.
Bertin-Maghit, Jean-Pierre. "De L'ecran à la classe: *Lancelot du lac* de Robert Bresson." *Pédagogie* 31 (February 1976): 53–64.
Buchka, Peter, and others. *Robert Bresson*. Munich: Hanser, 1978.
Codell, Julie F. "Decapitation and Deconstruction: The Body of the Hero in Robert Bresson's *Lancelot du Lac*." In Debra Mancoff, ed. *The Arthurian Revival, Essays on Form, Tradition, and Transformation*. New York: Garland, 1992.
Comuzio, Ermanno. "Robert Bresson." *Cineforum* 134 (July 1974): 537–53.
Crotta, Bruno. "Lancelot du Lac: La guerre, le simulcare de la vertu." *Camera/Stylo* 5 (January 1985): 83–86.
Cugier, Alphonse. "'Lancelot du lac' de Robert Bresson: Le Moyen âge revisité ou la dimension tragique de xxe siècle." *Cahiers de la cinémathèque* 42–43 (Summer 1985): 119–24.
de la Bretèque, François. "Une 'Figure oblige' du film de chevalrie: le tournoi." *Cahiers de la cinémathèque* 42–43 (Summer 1985): 91–96.
Delmas, J. "Lancelot du lac: Robert Bresson et ses armures." *Jeune cinéma* 82 (November 1974): 19–24.
Dempsey, Michael. "Despair Abounding: The Recent Films of Robert Bresson." *Film Quarterly* 34 (Fall 1980): 2–15.
"Entretien avec Robert Bresson." *Unifrance Film* 45 (December 1957): 1–3.
Estève, Michel. *Cinéma et condition humaine*. Paris: Albatros, 1978.
———. *Robert Bresson*. Rev. ed. Paris: Seghers, 1974.
Ferrero, Adelio. *Bresson*. Florence: La Nuova Italia, 1976.

Gauville, Hervé. "Lancelot du sang." *Camera/Stylo* 5 (January 1985): 100–03.

Gorgievski, Sandra. "Réalisme, stylisation et parodie dans le film à sujet médiéval des années 1970." In Xavier Kawa-Topor, ed. *Le Moyen age vu par le cinéma européen.* Le Cahiers de Conques 3 (October 2000). Conques: Centre Européen d'Art et de Civilisation Médiévale, 2001.

Hanlon, Lindley. *Fragments: Robert Bresson's Film Style.* Rutherford, N.J.: Fairleigh Dickinson University Press, 1986.

Harty, Kevin J. *The Reel Middle Ages: American, Western and Eastern European, Middle Eastern and Asian Films About Medieval Europe.* Jefferson, N.C.: McFarland, 1999.

Jutkewitsch, Sergej. "Die 'Cinematographie'" des Robert Bresson (3): Ein politischer Regisseur." *Film und Fernsehen* 11 (1983): 45–49.

"*Lancelot du lac,* un film de Robert Bresson." *Avant-scène du cinéma* 155 (February 1975): 46–50.

Le Dantec, Mireille Latil. "Lancelot." *Cinématographe* 10 (November-December 1974): 38–42.

Margetts, John. "Robert Bressons 'Lancelot du lac': Monotonie und Depression." In Jürgen Kühnel and others, eds. *Mittelalter-Rezeption II.* Göppingen: Kümmerle, 1982.

Micciché, Lino. "Bresson: La Scrittura di una situazione interiore." *Cinema sessanata* 97–98 (May-August 1974): 27–34.

Nash, Jay Robert, and Stanley Ralph Ross. *The Motion Picture Guide, L–M, 1927–1983.* Chicago: Cinebooks, 1986.

Olton, Bert. *Arthurian Legends on Film and Television.* Jefferson, N.C.: McFarland, 2000.

Oudart, Jean-Pierre. "Un Pouvoir qui ne pense, ne calcule, ni ne juge?" *Cahiers du cinéma* 258–59 (July-August 1975): 36–41.

Paquette, Jean-Marcel. "La Dernière métamorphose de Lancelot." *Cahiers de la cinémathèque* 42–43 (Summer 1985): 113–18.

———. "La Dernière métamorphose de Lancelot: Robert Bresson." In Ulrich Müller and others, eds. *Lancelot.* Göppingen: Kümmerle, 1984.

Prédal, René. "Poétique de Robert Bresson: expression plastique et approche de l'indicible dans *Lancelot du lac*." *Recherches et travaux* [University Stendahl] 37 (1989): 103–16.

———, and others. "Dossier: Robert Bresson." *Cinéma* [Paris] 294 (June 1983): 3–32.

Pruitt, John. "Robert Bresson's *Lancelot du lac.*" *Field of Vision* 13 (Spring 1985): 5–9.

Quandt, James, ed. *Robert Bresson.* Toronto: Cinematheque Ontario, 1998.

Reader, Keith. *Robert Bresson.* Manchester: Manchester University Press, 2000.

Rider, Jeff, and others. "The Arthurian Legend in French Cinema: *Lancelot du Lac* and *Perceval le Gallois.*" In Kevin J. Harty, ed. *Cinema Arthuriana, Essays on Arthurian Film.* New York: Garland, 1981. [Rpt. above in revised form.]

Robert Bresson. Madrid: Filmoteca nacional, 1977.

Roud, Richard, ed. *Cinema, A Critical Dictionary.* New York: Viking, 1980.

Roussel, François, and Pierre Sivan. "Le dernier acte est sanglant ... *Lancelot du Lac* de Robert Bresson." In Mireille Séguy, ed. *Lancelot.* Paris: Éditions Autrement, 1996.

Schrader, Paul. "Robert Bresson, Possibly." *Film Comment* 13 (September-October 1977): 26–30.

Sémolué, Jean. "Lancelot du lac." *Téléciné* 191–92 (September-October 1974): 23–26.

Sloan, Jane. *Robert Bresson, A Guide to References and Resources.* Boston: Hall, 1983.

Targe, André. "Ici l'espace naît du temps." *Camera/Stylo* 5 (January 1985): 87–99.

Thomas, Nicholas, ed. *International Dictionary of Films and Filmmakers—Vol. 2: Directors.* 2nd ed. Chicago: St. James, 1991.

Thompson, Kristin. *Breaking the Glass: Neoformalist Film Analysis.* Princeton: Princeton University Press, 1989.

Tinazzi, Giorgio. *Il Cinema di Robert Bresson.* Venice: Marsilo, 1976.

———. "'Lancelot du lac': a proposito di Bresson." *Cinema e cinema* 2 (April-July 1975): 83–92.

Torri, Bruno. "Bresson: lo stile e la grazia." *Cinema sessanata* 97–98 (May-August 1983): 20–23.

Tulard, Jean. *Guide des Films.* Rev. ed. Paris: Éditions Robert Laffont, 1997.

Walters, John. "Guilty Pleasures." *Film Comment* 19 (July-August 1983): 20–23.

Williams, Alan. "On the Absence of the Grail." *Movietone News* 47 (January 1976): 10–13.

Williams, David. "Sir Gawain in Films." In Derek Brewer and Jonathan Gibson, eds. *A Companion to the* Gawain-*Poet.* Cambridge, Eng.: D. S. Brewer, 1997.

Lancelot: Guardian of Time (1999)
United States; dir. Rubian Cruz; screenplay by Patricia Monville; Alpine Pictures
Cast: Leonard Auclair, Adam Carter, Claudia Christian, John Saxon, Marc Singer

DISCUSSION:

Olton, Bert. *Arthurian Legends on Film and Television.* Jefferson, N.C.: McFarland, 2000.

Lancelot of the Lake **(1974)**
See *Lancelot du Lac* (1974)

Launcelot and Elaine **(1909)**
United States; dir. Charles Kent; screenplay by Charles Kent (?) based on the poem by Alfred, Lord Tennyson; Vitagraph
Alternate title: *Lancelot and Elaine*
Cast: W. Blackton, Leo Delaney, Charles Kent, Paul Panzer, Florence Turner

REVIEWS:

Bioscope 27 January 1910: 53; 25 December 1913: supplement xxi; 15 January 1914: supplement xxxi. *Moving Picture World* 23 October 1909: 565; 27 November 1909: 759, 773. *New York Dramatic Mirror* 20 November 1909: 16.

ADDITIONAL DISCUSSIONS:

The Film Index: A Bibliography. Vol. 1: The Film as Art. 1941. rpt. White Plains, N.Y.: Kraus International, 1988.
Harty, Kevin J. *The Reel Middle Ages: American, Western and Eastern European, Middle Eastern and Asian Films About Medieval Europe*. Jefferson, N.C.: McFarland, 1999.
"Launcelot and Elaine." *Vitagraph Bulletin* 1–15 November 1909: n.p. [film 949].
"Notes of the Trade." *Moving Picture World* 25 September 1909: 409; 6 November 1909: 604; 13 November 1909: 672.
Savada, Elias. *The American Film Institute Catalog of Motion Pictures Produced in the United States: Film Beginnings, 1893–1910*. Metuchen, N.J.: Scarecrow, 1995.
Slide, Anthony, ed. *Selected Film Criticism 1896–1911*. Metuchen, N.J.: Scarecrow, 1982.

The Legend of Gawain and the Green Knight **(1983)**
See *Sword of the Valiant* (1983)

Die Legende von Tristan und Isolde **(1981)**
See *Fire and Sword* (1981)

The Light in the Dark **(1922)**
United States; dir. Clarence Brown; screenplay by William Dudley Pelley; Associated First National Pictures
Alternate title: *The Light of Faith*
Cast: Lon Chaney, Theresa Maxwell Conover, Hope Hamilton, E. K. Lincoln, Dorothy Walters

REVIEWS:

Kinematograph Weekly 10 May 1923: 68. *Motion Picture News* 9 September 1922: 1295. *Moving Picture World* 9 September 1922: 128. *Variety* 1 September 1922: 42.

ADDITIONAL DISCUSSIONS:

Blake, Michael F. *A Thousand Faces*. Vestal, N.Y.: Vestal Press, 1995.

Munden, Kenneth W., ed. *The American Film Institute Catalog, Feature Films 1921–1930*. New York: Bowker, 1971.
O'Dell, Scott. *Representative Photoplays Analyzed*. Hollywood, Calif.: Institute of Authorship, 1924.
Olton, Bert. *Arthurian Legends on Film and Television*. Jefferson, N.C.: McFarland, 2000.
Pelley, William Dudley. *The Door to Revelation*. Asheville, N.C.: Pelley Publishers, 1939.

The Light of Faith **(1922)**
See *The Light in Dark* (1922)

Love Eternal **(1943)**
See *L'Éternel retour* (1943)

Lovespell **(1979)**
See *Tristan and Isolt* (1979)

Lucinda's Spell **(1998)**
United States; dir. Jon Jacobs; screenplay by Jon Jacobs; Zero Pictures
Cast: Shannah Bettz, Ajx Davis, Christina Fulton, Leon Herbert, Jon Jacobs, Alix Koromzay

REVIEWS:

Daily News [New York] 10 September 1999: 59. *Entertainment Weekly* 566 (27 October 2000): 95. *New York Post* 10 September 1999: 56. *New York Times* 10 September 1999: E10. *Variety* 22 June 1998: 54. *Village Voice* 14 September 1999: 146. *Washington Times* 28 September 2000: M24.

The Magic Sword: Quest for Camelot **(1998)**
See *Quest for Camelot* (1998)

Merlin **(1992)**
See *October 32nd* (1992)

Merlin **(1998)**
United States; dir. Steve Barron; screenplay by Ed Khmara and David Stevens; Hallmark Entertainment for NBC
Cast: Daniel Brocklebank, Helena Bonham Carter, Paul Curran, Lena Headey, Sam Neill, Isabella Rossellini, Miranda Richardson, Jeremy Sheffield, Martin Short

REVIEWS:

Arizona Republic 24 April 1998: D1. *Arthuriana* 8 (Winter 1998): 174–76. *Atlanta Journal and Constitution* 26 April 1998: Arts 1L. *Boston Globe* 24 April 1998: D1; 26 April 1998: Television Week 4. *Boston Herald* 24 April 1998: 59. *Chicago Sun-Times* 24 April 1998: 47; 26 April 1998: TV Prevue 4. *Chicago Tribune* 24 April 1998: Tempo 1. *Christian Science Monitor* 24 April 1998: B7. *Daily News* [New York] 23 April 1998: 104. *Dallas Morning News* 26 April

1998: 1C. *Denver Post* 23 April 1998: E1. *Entertainment Weekly* 428 (24 April 1998): 60–61. *Hollywood Reporter* 23 April 1998: 9, 12. *Houston Chronicle* 23 April 1998: Houston 1; 26 April 1998: Television 3. *Los Angeles Times* 25 April 1998: F1, F19. *Milwaukee Journal Sentinel* 26 April 1998: 2. *New York* 31 (27 April 1998): 63. *New York Times* 24 April 1998: B1, B26. *Newsday* 26 April 1998: TV Plus 3. *Philadelphia Daily News* 24 April 1998: 79. *Philadelphia Inquirer* 22 April 1998: C1, C9. *Rocky Mountain News* 26 April 1998: 5D, F4. *Sacramento Bee* 26 April 1998: Encore 3. *San Diego Union-Tribune* 26 April 1998: Entertainment 6. *San Francisco Chronicle* 24 April 1998: D1, D9. *Seattle Times* 26 April 1998: TV 2. *St. Louis Post-Dispatch* 26 April 1998: D4, TV 3. *Times-Picayune* [New Orleans] 26 April 1998: TV Focus T9. *Toronto Star* 26 April 1998: F8; Starweek 11. *TV Guide* 25 April 1998: 44, 123. *USA Today* 24 April 1998: 8E, 9E. *Variety* 27 April 1998: 43. *Washington Post* 26 April 1998: G1, G10.

ADDITIONAL DISCUSSIONS:
Baldwin, Kristen. "Mini Theories." *Entertainment Weekly* 424 (27 March 1998): 18–19.
Bickley, Claire. "The Magic of Merlin." *Toronto Sun TV Magazine* 26 April 1998: 3.
Bradley, Marion Zimmer. "The Once and Future Merlin." *TV Guide* 25 April 1998: 42–44.
Hoge, Warren. "Visual Wizardry Beyond Merlin's Dreams." *New York Times* 26 April 1998: 13.4.
Khmara, Ed, and David Stevens. *Merlin: The Shooting Script*. New York: Newmarket Press, 1998.
King, Susan. "Wizards and Gnomes with Heart." *Los Angeles Times* 26 April 1998: TV Week 3.
Krzywinska, Tanya. *A Skin for Dancing In: Possession, Witchcraft and Voodoo in Film*. Trowbridge, Wiltshire: Flicks Books, 2000.
Mills, Nancy. "Half-Mortal Merlin Full of Heart." *Chicago Tribune TV Week* 26 April–2 May 1998: 3, 31.
Olton, Bert. *Arthurian Legends on Film and Television*. Jefferson, N.C.: McFarland, 2000.
Tonks, Paul. "The Emperor Jones." *Film Score Monthly* 3 (September 1998): 25–29.
Tumposky, Ellen. "The Original Wiz Kid." *Daily News Vue* [New York] 26 April–2 May 1998: 5, 54.
Wilkinson, Alec. "Magic Kingdom." *TV Guide* 25 April 1998: 38–41.
Winslow, Harriet. "'Merlin': Magic for May." *Washington Post TV Week* 26 April–2 May 1998: 7, 58.
Wood, Michael. "The Magic of Merlin." *Radio Times* [London] 3–9 April: 33–36.

Merlin and the Sword (1982)
See *Arthur the King* (1982)

Merlin of the Crystal Cave (1991)
Great Britain; dir. Michael Darlow; screenplay by Steve Bescoby; Noel Gay Television for BBC1
Cast: Don Henderson, Robert Powell, Kim Thomson, George Winter

REVIEW:
Times [London] 7 December 1991: Weekend 16.

ADDITIONAL DISCUSSIONS:
O'Kelly, Lisa. "The Making of a Legend." *Radio Times* [London] 16 November 1991: 43–44.
Olton, Bert. *Arthurian Legends on Film and Television*. Jefferson, N.C.: McFarland, 2000.

Merlin, or The Gold Rate (1982)
See *Merlin, ou le cours de l'or* (1982)

Merlin, ou le cours de l'or (1982)
France; dir. Arthur Joffé; screenplay by Arthur Joffé; Dune Films in collaboration with TFI Productions
Alternate title: *Merlin, or The Gold Rate*
Cast: Simone Carle, Dominique Pinon

REVIEWS:
Screen International 29 May 1982: 1. *Unifrance Film* 10 (June 1982): 25.

Merlin: The Return (2000)
Great Britain; dir. Paul Matthews; screenplay by Paul Matthews; Tanmarsh Communications in association with Peakingview Transatlantic Productions
Cast: Patrick Bergin, Tia Carrere, Julie Hartley, Rik Mayall, Adrian Paul, Craig Sheffer, Byron Taylor

REVIEWS:
Daily Mail [London] 22 December 2000: 52. *Daily Record* [London] 22 December 2000: Features 52. *Empire* 139 (January 2001): 65. *Film Review* 601 (January 2001): 32. *Independent* [London] 24 December 2000: Features 3. *Mail on Sunday* [London] 24 December 2000: 70. *Mirror* [London] 23 December 2000: Features 36; 29 December 2000: Features 6. *Observer* [London] 24 December 2000: Reviews 13. *Scotsman* [Edinburgh] 21 December 2000: 12. *Sight and Sound* 11 (January 2001): 55–56. *Times* [London] 23 December 2000: 44. *Variety* 15 January 2001: 62.

ADDITIONAL DISCUSSIONS:
"Sheer Wizardry." *Screen Africa* January 1999: 8.
Thomas, Ceri. "Dream Factory." *Exposure* [Great Britain] Spring 1999: 8–9.

Merlin's Shop of Magical Wonders **(1996)**
United States; dir. Kenneth J. Berton; screenplay by Kenneth J. Berton; Berton Productions and Monarch Home Video
Cast: Ernest Borgnine, Mark Hurtado, George Milan, Patricia Sansone, Bunny Summers, John Terrance

REVIEW:
Arthuriana 8 (Fall 1998):126–28.

ADDITIONAL DISCUSSIONS:
Grant, Edmond, ed. *The Motion Picture Guide, 1997 Annual (The Films of 1996)*. New York: CineBooks, 1997.
Olton, Bert. *Arthurian Legends on Film and Television*. Jefferson, N.C.: McFarland, 2000.

The Mighty **(1998)**
United States; dir. Peter Chelsom; screenplay by Charles Leavitt; Miramax Films and Scholastic/Simon Fields Productions
Cast: Gillian Armstrong, Kieran Culkin, James Gandolfini, Elden Henson, Jennifer Lewis, Meat Loaf, Joe Perrino, Gena Rowlands, Harry Dean Stanton, Sharon Stone

REVIEWS:
Arthuriana 9 (Spring 1999): 165–67. *Boston Globe* 12 September 1998: A18. *Cahiers du cinéma* 531 (January 1999): 71. *Daily News* [New York] 9 October 1998: 53. *Empire* 124 (October 1999): 143. *Entertainment Weekly* 454 (16 October 1998): 58. *Filmbulletin* 219 (December 1998): 39–41. *Film Comment* 34 (November-December 1998): 76–77. *Film Score Monthly* 4 (January 1999): 36. *Los Angeles Times* 9 October 1998: Calendar 2. *Movieline* 9 (November 1998): 39; 10 (June 1999): 91. *New York Post* 9 October 1998: 47. *New York Times* 9 October 1998: E14. *Newsday* 9 October 1998: Weekend B7. *Newsweek* 132 (19 October 1998): 81. *Positif* 449–50 (July-August 1998): 103. *Premiere* 12 (November 1998): 29. *Screen International* 11 April 1998: 8. *Sight and Sound* 9 (January 1999): 50–51. *Time Out* [New York] 8 October 1998: 93. *Toronto Star* 9 October 1998: C7. *Toronto Sun* 9 October 1998: 67. *USA Today* 9 October 1998: 6E. *Variety* 25 May 1998: 60.

ADDITIONAL DISCUSSIONS:
Banks, Michelle, ed. *Magill's Cinema Annual 1999*. Detroit: Gale, 1999.
Olton, Bert. *Arthurian Legends on Film and Television*. Jefferson, N.C.: McFarland, 2000.
Philbrick, Rodman. *The Mighty*. New York: Scholastic, 1998. [Rpt. of the 1993 novel, *Freak the Mighty*, with stills from the film.]

The Mists of Avalon **(2001)**
United States; dir. Uli Edel; screenplay by Gavin Scott; Turner Network Television
Cast: Joan Allen, Edward Atterton, Michael Byrne, Caroline Goodall, Anjelica Huston, Julianna Margulies, Samantha Mathis, Hans Matheson, Michael Vartan

REVIEWS:
Arthuriana 11 (Fall 2001): 121–22. *Atlanta Constitution* 14 July 2001: 5C. *Baltimore Sun* 14 July 2001: 1D. *Boston Globe* 13 July 2001: C12. *Boston Herald* 15 July 2001: Arts & Life 67; Television 6. *Chicago Daily Herald* 13 July 2001: Time Out 29. *Christianity Today* 9 July 2001: 55–56. *Daily News* [Los Angeles] 15 July 2001: L5. *Daily News* [New York] 13 July 2001: 120. *Daily Variety* 12 July 2001: 11. *Entertainment Weekly* 604 (13 July 2001): 65–66. *LA Weekly* 15 July 2001: TV-O. *Mythprint* 38 (August 2001): 7. *New Times* [Los Angeles] 12 July 2001: Arts V. *New York* 34 (16 July 2001): 66. *New York Post* 13 July 2001: 105. *New York Times* 13 July 2001: E25. *Newsday* 15 July: TV Plus 3. *Plain Dealer* [Cleveland] 15 July 2001: 11I. *Philadelphia Inquirer Magazine* 15 July 2001: 31. *Pittsburgh Post-Gazette* 15 July 2001: TV 5. *Rolling Stone* 2 August 2001: 72. *San Francisco Chronicle* 13 July 2001: C1. *Star Tribune* [Minneapolis] 13 July 2001: 6E. *Time Out* [New York] 303 (July 2001): 117. *TV Guide* 14 July 2001: 10, 92. *US Weekly* 335 (16 July 2001): 64. *USA Today* 13 July 2001: 2E. *Washington Post* 14 July 2001: C8; 15 July 2001: Y3.

ADDITIONAL DISCUSSIONS:
Calhoun, John. "Parting the Mists: Creating Fog for an Arthurian TV Movie." *Entertainment Design* 35 (July 2001): 5.
Clark, John. "Who Needs Chivalry?" *Los Angeles Times* 15 July 2001: Calendar 5.
Dawidziak, Mark. "Huston Dons the Crown of Avalon." *Plain Dealer* [Cleveland] 15 July 2001: 11I.
Durbin, Karen. "Ladies of the Lake." *TV Guide* 14 July 2001: 16–17, 35.
_____. "Rites of Passage." *TV Guide* 14 July 2001: 12–15.
Goldman, Michael. "Get Misty." *Millimeter* 29 (May 2001): 13.
Hodges, Ann. "From the Mists." *Houston Chronicle* 15 July 2001: Television 2.
Keveney, Bill. "Into the 'Mists.'" *USA Today* 13 July 2001: 1E-2E.
Kuklenski, Valerie. "Frankly 'Avalon.'" *Daily News* [Los Angeles] 12 July 2001: L5.
Levesque, John. "A Woman's Realm." *Seattle Post-Intelligencer* 13 July 2001: E1.
Marsh, Norma. "Play Misty for Me." *Times-Picayune* [New Orleans] 15 July 2001: Books 6.
Mayer, Peter. "Visions in the Mists." *Emmy* 23 (August 2001): 48–53.

Nelson, Resa. "Television." *Realms of Fantasy* 7 (August 2001): 12–16.
Olexa, Keith. "The Other Side of Camelot." *Starlog* 289 (August 2001): 72–76.
Rohna, Virginia. "Playing a Villain Was the Hook." *The Record* [Bergen County, N.J.] 13 July 2001: 51.
Weintraub, Joanne. "Sisters of the Sword." *Milwaukee Journal Sentinel* 10 July 2001: 1E.

Moero Arthur (1980)
See *Le Roi Arthur* (1980)

Monty Python and the Holy Grail (1975)
Great Britain; dir. Terry Gilliam and Terry Jones; screenplay by Graham Chapman, John Cleese, Terry Gilliam, Eric Idle, Terry Jones, and Michael Palin; Python Pictures
Cast: Graham Chapman, John Cleese, Terry Gilliam, Eric Idle, Terry Jones, Michael Palin

REVIEWS:
America 132 (31 May 1976): 428–29. *Amis du film et de la television* 238 (March 1976): 6–7. *APEC: Revue Belge du cinéma* 13 (April 1976): 38–39. *Arts and Entertainment* 7 (July 1992): 23. *Boston Herald* 14 June 2001: 49; 15 June 2001: S21. *Boston Globe* 15 June 2001: C6. *Cineaste* 7 (Fall 1975): 14–18. *Cinefantastique* 4 (Fall 1975): 39. *Cineforum* 159 (November 1976): 717–19. *Cinéma* [Paris] 205 (January 1976): 143. *Commonweal* 102 (6 June 1975): 182. *Daily News* [New York] 15 June 2001: 63. *Film en televisie* 226 (March 1976): 31. *Film Review* 25 (June 1975): 8–9. *Films and Filming* 21 (May 1975): 40. *Films Illustrated* 4 (May 1975): 326. *Hollywood Reporter* 13 March 1975: 18. *Image et son* 301 (December 1975): 117. *Independent Film Journal* 75 (30 April 1975): 13–14. *Jeune cinéma* 93 (March 1976): 29–30. *Listener* 10 April 1975: 480. *Los Angeles Times* 23 July 1974: 4. 1; 15 June 2001: Calendar 16. *Monthly Film Bulletin* 42 (April 1975): 84–85. *Motion Picture Herald* 14 May 1975: Product Digest Section 94. *New Republic* 172 (24 May 1975): 20. *New Statesman* 89 (4 April 1975): 489. *New York* 8 (5 May 1975): 76. *New York Times* 28 April 1975: 34; 1 June 1975: 2. 15. *New Yorker* 51 (5 May 1975): 115–17. *Newsday* 15 June 2001: B6. *Newsweek* 85 (19 May 1975): 90–91. *Penthouse* 6 (August 1975): 37–39. *Positif* 171–72 (July-August 1975): 68. *Revue du cinéma* 301 (December 1975): 117; 309–10 (October 1976): 247–48. *Rolling Stone* 19 June 1975: 16. *Saturday Review* 2 (31 May 1975): 44–45. *Time* 105 (26 May 1975): 58. *Time Out* [New York] 299 (14 June 2001): 81. *Times* [London] 10 May 1975: 9. *Variety* 19 March 1975: 32. *Video Watchdog* 17 (May-June 1993): 61–64. *Village Voice* 5 May 1975: 81–82. *Vogue* 165 (July 1975): 30.

ADDITIONAL DISCUSSIONS:
Abel, Christian, and others. "Entretien: Monty Python." *Revue du cinéma* 351 (June 1980): 74–81.
Ashbrook, John. *Terry Gilliam*. Harpenden, Herts: Pocket Essentials, 2000.
Bishop, Ellen. "Bakhtin, Carnival and Comedy: The New Grotesque in Monty Python and the Holy Grail." *Film Criticism* 15 (Fall 1990): 49–64.
Blanch, Robert J., and Julian N. Wasserman. "Gawain on Film." In Kevin J. Harty, ed. *Cinema Arthuriana, Essays on Arthurian Film*. New York: Garland, 1991. [Rpt. above in revised form.]
Bouineau, Jean-Marc. *Le Petit Livre de Terry Gilliam*. Rev. ed. Garches: Spartorange, 1996.
Boyce, Charles. "The Man Who Wasn't King." *Arts & Entertainment Magazine* 7 (July 1992): 20–23.
Burde, Mark. "Monty Python's Medieval Masterpiece." In Keith Busby, ed. *The Arthurian Yearbook III*. New York: Garland, 1993.
Burns, E. Jane. "Nostalgia Isn't What It Used to Be: The Middle Ages in Literature and Film." In George Slusser and Eric S. Rabkin, eds. *Shadows of the Magic Lamp, Fantasy and Science Fiction in Film*. Carbondale: Southern University of Illinois Press, 1985.
Byron, Stuart, and Elisabeth Weiss, eds. *Film Comedy*. New York: Grossman, 1977.
Christie, Ian, ed. *Gilliam on Gilliam*. London: Faber and Faber, 1999.
Day, David D. "Monty Python and the Medieval Other." In Kevin J. Harty, ed. *Cinema Arthuriana, Essays on Arthurian Film*. New York: Garland, 1991. [Rpt. above in revised form.]
Garel, A. "A propos du Monty Python." *Image et son* 304 (March 1976): 21–26.
Garrett, Stephen. "Burn Him!" *Time Out* [New York] 299 (14 June 2001): 168.
Gorgievski, Sandra. "Le Mythe comme objet de déconstruction dans Monty Python and the Holy Grail." In Raphaëlle Costa de Beauregard and others, eds. *Le Cinéma et ses objects*. Poitiers: La Licorne: 1997.
———. "Réalisme, stylisation et parodie dans le film à sujet médiéval des années 1970." In Xavier Kawa-Topor, ed. *Le Moyen age vu par le cinéma européen*. Le Cahiers de Conques 3 (October 2000). Conques: Centre Européen d'Art et de Civilisation Médiévale, 2001
Gow, Gordon. "'he said with incredible arrogance....'" *Films and Filming* 212 (December 1974): 12–17.

Harty, Kevin J. *The Reel Middle Ages: American, Western and Eastern European, Middle Eastern and Asian Films About Medieval Europe.* Jefferson, N.C.: McFarland, 1999.

King, Loren. "And Now for More of Something Completely Different." *Boston Globe* 17 June 2001: G9.

Magill, Frank N., ed. *Magill's Survey of Cinema: English Language Films.* Second Series. Englewood Cliffs, N.J.: Salem, 1981.

McCabe, Bob. *Dark Knights & Holy Fools: The Art and Films of Terry Gilliam.* New York: Universe, 1999.

McCall, Douglas L. *Monty Python: A Chronological Listing of the Troupe's Creative Output, and Articles and Reviews about Them, 1969–1989.* Jefferson, N.C.: McFarland, 1991.

Meuwese, Martine. "De Animatie van Margedecoratie in *Monty Python and the Holy Grail.*" *Madoc: tijdschrift over de Middeleeuwen* [The Netherlands] 12.1 (1998): 2–13.

Monty Python and the Holy Grail (Book). New York: Methuen, 1977 [Screenplay and related documents.].

Moran, Daniel. "A Guide to Arthurian Films." In *CliffsNotes: White's The Once and Future King.* New York: Hungry Minds, 2000.

Murray, Raymond. *Images in the Dark, An Encyclopedia of Gay and Lesbian Film and Video.* Rev. ed. New York: Plume, 1996.

Nash, Jay Robert, and Stanley Ralph Ross. *The Motion Picture Guide, L–M, 1927–1983.* Chicago: Cinebooks, 1986.

Nickel, Helmut. "Arms and Armor in Arthurian Film." In Kevin J. Harty, ed. *Cinema Arthuriana, Essays on Arthurian Film.* New York: Garland, 1991. [Rpt. above in revised form.]

Olton, Bert. *Arthurian Legends on Film and Television.* Jefferson, N.C.: McFarland, 2000.

Osberg, Richard H., and Michael E. Crow. "Language Then and Language Now in Arthurian Film." In Kevin J. Harty, ed. *King Arthur on Film, New Essays on Arthurian Cinema.* Jefferson, N.C.: McFarland, 1999.

Perry, George. *Life of Python.* London: Pavilion Books, 1983.

Rubenstein, Lenny. "The Wondrous Return of the Wacky Monty Python's Flying Circus." *Cineaste* 7 (Fall 1975): 15–18.

Sigoloff, Marc. *The Films of the Seventies.* Jefferson, N.C.: McFarland, 1984.

Thompson, Raymond H. "The Ironic Tradition in Arthurian Film Since 1960." In Kevin J. Harty, ed. *Cinema Arthuriana, Essays on Arthurian Film.* New York: Garland, 1991. [Rpt. above.]

Umland, Rebecca A., and Samuel J. Umland. *The Use of Arthurian Legend in Hollywood Film from Connecticut Yankees to Fisher Kings.* Westport, Conn.: Greenwood, 1996.

Vigouroux-Frey, Nicole. "Vingt ans après ... Sacré Graal! ou L'humor des Monty Python (1974)." *Humoresques* 6 (February 1995): 115–27.

Weinkauf, Gregory. "Have at You!" *New Times* [Los Angeles] 14 June 2001: M.

Whipp, Glenn. "The Full Monty: The Story of the Writing of the Film That Says 'Ni'!" *Daily News* [Los Angeles] 14 June 2001: L3.

Morgane et ses Nymphes (1971)

France; dir. Bruno Gantillon; screenplay by Bruno Gantillon; Sofracima

Alternate title: *Girl Slaves of Morgana Le Fay*

Cast: Dominique Delpierre, Michèle Perello, Mireille Saunin

REVIEWS:

Cinefantastique 3 (Autumn 1973): 39. *Film français* 9 April 1971: 10. *Unifrance Film* 81 (1972): n.p.

The Morte d'Arthur (1984)

Great Britain; dir. Gillian Lynne; screenplay by Gillian Lynne abridged from Sir Thomas Malory's *Le Morte d' Athur*; BBC2

Cast: John Barton, Jeremy Brett, Anton Dolin, Nickolas Grace, Barbara Keller, David Robb

REVIEWS:

Daily Express [London] 7 May 1984: 15. *Daily Telegraph* [London] 7 May 1984: 13. *Evening Standard* [London] 24 April 1984: 21. *Guardian* [London] 27 April 1984: 21. *Listener* 3 May 1984: 31. *New Statesman* 98 (11 November 1984): 30–31. *Sunday Telegraph* [London] 13 May 1984: 15. *Sunday Times* [London] 13 May 1984: 54. *Television Today* 21 April 1984: 19. *Times* [London] 7 May 1984: 15. *Times* [London] *Educational Supplement* 11 May 1984: 25. *Times* [London] *Literary Supplement* 18 May 1984: 552.

ADDITIONAL DISCUSSIONS:

Harty, Kevin J. *The Reel Middle Ages: American, Western and Eastern European, Middle Eastern and Asian Films About Medieval Europe.* Jefferson, N.C.: McFarland, 1999.

Totten, Eileen. "The Knight's Tale." *Radio Times* [London] 5 May 1984: 8–9.

The Natural (1984)

United States; dir. Barry Levinson; screenplay by Phil Dusenberry and Roger Towne; Columbia Tri-Star Productions

Cast: Kim Basinger, Wilfred Brimley, Glenn Close, Robert Duvall, Barbara Hershey, Robert Prosky, Robert Redford

REVIEWS:

America 150 (23 June 1984): 493. *Christian Century* 30 May 1984: 563–64. *Cineaste* 13 (October 1984): 45–46. *Cineforum* 24 (November 1984): 77. *Cinéma* [Paris] 310 (October 1984): 39. *Cinématographe* 103 (September-October 1984): 54. *City Limits* [London] 19 October 1984: 22. *Commonweal* 111 (15 June 1984): 373–74. *Daily News* [New York] 11 May 1984: Friday 5. *Film en televisie* 329 (October 1984): 12–13. *Films and Filming* 357 (June 1984): 42; 361 (October 1984): 44. *Films in Review* 35 (August-September 1984): 427. *Hollywood Reporter* 7 May 1984: 8; 21 June 1984: 14. *Horizon* 27 (April 1984): 52–53. *Jeune cinéma* 162 (November 1984): 42–43; 163 (December 1984–January 1985): 34–35. *Kosmorama* 30 (December 1984): 206–09. *Los Angeles Times* 11 May 1984: Calendar 1. *Maclean's* 97 (21 May 1984): 65. *Millimeter* 12 (May 1984) 84–86. *Monthly Film Bulletin* 51 (November 1984): 337–38. *Motion Picture Digest* 11 (30 May 1984): 94. *Nation* 238 (2 June 1984): 682–83. *National Review* 36 (13 July 1984): 51–52. *New Leader* 67 (11 June 1984): 21. *New Republic* 190 (11 June 1984): 24–25. *New Statesman* 108 (19 October 1984): 36–37. *New York* 17 (21 May 1984): 94–95. *New York Native* 4 June 1984: 24. *New York Post* 11 May 1984: 19. *New York Times* 1 April 1984: 5. 2; 6 May 1984: 2. 1, 17; 11 May 1984: C8; 14 June 1984: C17. *New Yorker* 60 (28 May 1984): 100–01. *Newsweek* 103 (28 May 1984): 77. *Observer* [London] 21 October 1984: 22. *Photoplay* 35 (November 1984): 16–17, 20. *Positif* 286 (December 1984): 67–69. *Revue du cinéma* 397 (August 1984): 30–31. *School Update* 117 (7 September 1984): 27–28. *Screen International* 6 October 1984: 18. *Segnocinema* 4 (September 1984): 53; 5 (January 1985): 71. *Soundtrack* 3 (September 1984): 25–26. *Sport Magazine* 75 (May 1984): 108. *Sports Illustrated* 60 (7 May 1984): 71. *Time* 123 (14 March 1984): 91. *Time Out* [London] 18 October 1984: 49. *Variety* 9 May 1984: 10. *Village Voice* 22 May 1984: 57. *Vogue* 174 (May 1984): 75. *Women's Wear Daily* 11 May 1984: 7.

ADDITIONAL DISCUSSIONS:

Curtin, Kevin Thomas. "*The Natural*: Our Iliad and Odyssey." *Antioch Review* 43 (Spring 1985): 225–41.

Desowitz, Bill. "Tri-Star's First Production Either Loved or Hated; Mixed Feelings Rare." *Hollywood Reporter* 23 May 1984: 6.

Griffith, James. *Adaptations as Imitations, Films from Novels*. Newark: University of Delaware Press, 1997.

———. "Say It Ain't So: *The Natural*." *Literature/Film Quarterly* 19 (July 1991): 157–63.

Krey, Robert, and Michael Haney. "Caleb Deschanel, ASC, and *The Natural*." *American Cinematographer* 66 (April 1985): 58–63.

Saperstein, Jeffrey. "Irony and Cliché: Malamud's *The Natural* In the 1980s." *Literature/Film Quarterly* 24 (January 1996): 84–87.

Silberman, Rob. "Mr. Smith Goes to the Ballpark." *Jump Cut* 31 (March 1986): 5–6.

Turchi, Peter. "Roy Hobbs' Corrected Stance: An Adaptation of *The Natural*." *Literature/Film Quarterly* 19 (July 1991): 150–56.

Umland, Rebecca A., and Samuel J. Umland. *The Use of Arthurian Legend in Hollywood Film from Connecticut Yankees to Fisher Kings*. Westport, Conn.: Greenwood, 1996.

The New Adventures of a Connecticut Yankee in King Arthur's Court (1987)

See *Novye priklučhenia janke pri dvore Korola Artura* (1987)

Novye priklučhenia janke pri dvore Korola Artura (1987)

Soviet Union; dir. Viktor Gres; screenplay by Viktor Gres; Dovzhenko Studios

Alternate title: *The New Adventures of a Connecticut Yankee in King Arthur's Court*

Cast: Albert Filozov, Evdokia Ghermanova, Mark Gres, Alexander Kaidanovsky, Sergei Koltakov, Anastasia Vertinskaya

REVIEWS:

Iskusstvo kino 3 (March 1989): 87–91. *Soviet Film* 4 (April 1989): 18–19.

ADDITIONAL DISCUSSIONS:

Harty, Kevin J. *The Reel Middle Ages: American, Western and Eastern European, Middle Eastern and Asian Films About Medieval Europe*. Jefferson, N.C.: McFarland, 1999.

The Motion Picture Guide, 1989 Annual (The Films of 1988). Evanston, Ill.: Cinebooks, 1989.

"On the Spot Report." *Soviet Film* 6 (1987): 18–19.

October 32nd (1992)

Great Britain; dir. Paul Hunt; screenplay by Nick McCarty; October 32nd Productions and United Film Makers

Alternate title: *Merlin*

Cast: Nadia Cameron, James Hong, Richard Lynch, Ted Markland, Peter Phelps, John Stone, Rodney Wood

REVIEW:

Variety 22 June 1992: 45–46.

The hall of the Grail King in Edwin S. Porter's 1904 film *Parsifal*. (Still courtesy of the Library of Congress.)

ADDITIONAL DISCUSSIONS:

Fries, Maureen. "How to Handle a Woman, or Morgan at the Movies." In Kevin J. Harty, ed. *King Arthur on Film, New Essays on Arthurian Cinema*. Jefferson, N.C.: McFarland, 1999.

Klisz, Anjanelle M. *The Video Source Book*. Detroit: Gale Research, 1995.

Pallot, James, ed. *The Motion Picture Guide, 1995 Annual (The Films of 1994)*. New York: Cinebooks, 1994.

Parsifal (1904)

United States; dir. Edwin J. Porter; screenplay by Edwin J. Porter (?) from the opera by Richard Wagner; Edison Films

Cast: Adelaide Fitz-Allen and Robert Whittier

REVIEWS:

National Gallery of Art Film Calendar [Washington, D.C.] Summer 1993: n.p. *New York Clipper* 12 November 1904: 895. *Optical Lantern and Cinematograph Journal* 1 (1905): 52.

ADDITIONAL DISCUSSIONS:

Bush, W. Stephen. "The Possibilities of Synchronization." *Motion Picture World* 2 September 1911: 607–08.

Catalogue of Educational Motion Picture Films. Chicago: George Kleine, 1910.

The Film Index: A Bibliography. Vol. 1: The Film as Art. 1941. rpt. White Plains, N.Y.: Kraus International, 1988.

Harty, Kevin J. "The Arthurian Legends on Film: An Overview." In Kevin J. Harty, ed. *Cinema Arthuriana, Essays on Arthurian Film*. New York: Garland Publishing, 1991. [Rpt. above in revised form.]

_____. "Parsifal and Perceval on Film: The Reel Life of a Grail Knight." In Arthur Groos and Norris J. Lacy, eds. *Perceval/Parsifal: A Casebook*. New York: Routledge, 2002.

_____ *The Reel Middle Ages: American, Western and Eastern European, Middle Eastern and Asian Films About Medieval Europe*. Jefferson, N.C.: McFarland, 1999.

Musser, Charles. *Before the Nickelodeon*. Berkeley: University of California Press, 1991.

_____. *History of the American Cinema 1: The Emergence of Cinema: The American Screen to 1907*. New York: Scribner's, 1990.

Niver, Kemp R. *The First Twenty Years, A Segment of Film History*. Los Angeles: Locare Research Group, 1968.

_____. *Motion Pictures from the Library of Congress Paper Print Collection, 1894–1912*. Berkeley: University of California Press, 1967.

"Parsifal." *Edison Films* July 1906: 50–53.

Savada, Elias. *The American Film Institute Catalog of Motion Pictures Produced in the United*

States, Film Beginnings, 1893–1910. Metuchen, N.J. Scarecrow Press, 1995.

Spears, Jack. "Edwin S. Porter." *Films in Review* 21 (June-July 1970): 327–54.

Parsifal (1912)

Italy; dir. Mario Caeserini; screenplay by Arrigo Frusta; Ambrosio Films

REVIEWS:

Bisocope 30 October 1913: 427; 27 November 1913: 811–13. *Kinematograph Monthly Record* 20 (December 1913): 59–60. *Moving Picture World* 28 December 1912: 1307–08.

ADDITIONAL DISCUSSIONS:

The Film Index: A Bibliography. Vol. 1: The Film as Art. 1941. rpt. White Plains, N.Y.: Kraus International, 1988.

Harty, Kevin J. *The Reel Middle Ages: American, Western and Eastern European, Middle Eastern and Asian Films About Medieval Europe.* Jefferson, N.C.: McFarland, 1999.

Jarratt, Vernon. *The Italian Cinema.* London: Falcon, 1951.

Lephrohon, Pierre. *The Italian Cinema.* Trans. Roger Greaves and Oliver Stallybrass. New York: Praeger, 1972.

Weinberg, Herman G., ed. *Fifty Years of Italian Cinema.* Rome: Carlo Bestetti-Edizioni d'Arte, 1955.

Parsifal (1953)

Spain; dir. Daniel Mangrane; screenplay by Francesco Naranjo; Cine-Español

Cast: Gustavo Rojo and Ludmilla Tcherina

REVIEW:

Film français 448 (13 November 1953): 20.

ADDITIONAL DISCUSSION:

Harty, Kevin J. *The Reel Middle Ages: American, Western and Eastern European, Middle Eastern and Asian Films About Medieval Europe.* Jefferson, N.C.: McFarland, 1999.

Parsifal (1982)

Germany; dir. Hans-Jürgen Syberberg; screenplay by Gretl Zeilinger from the opera by Richard Wagner; Gaumont-TMS

Cast: Edith Clever, Aage Haugland, Armin Jordan, Karin Krick, Michael Kutter, Robert Lloyd, Martin Speer

REVIEWS:

24 Images 19 (Winter 1983–1984): 13–14. *L'Acualité* 9 February 1984: 89. *Avant-scène du cinema* 338 (July-August 1982): 51–55. *Casablanca* 19–20 (July-August 1982): 56. *Ciné Revue* 21 (20 May 1982): 44. *Cinéma* [Paris] 283–284 (July-August 1982): 95. *Cinema nuovo* 32 (August-October 1983): 8–9. *Cinématographe* 79 (June 1982): 71–72. *Continental Film and Video Review* 29 (August 1982): 44–45; 30 (May 1983): 10–11. *Ecran fantastique* 25 (1982): 19–20. *Études* [Paris] 357 (August-September 1982): 235–37. *Film Journal* 86 (18 February 1983): 41. *Films* 3 (June 1983): 34. *High Fidelity and Musical America* 33 (June 1983): [between] 80 and 83 [18–20]. *Hollywood Reporter* 11 March 1983: 34. *Image et son* 374 (July-August 1982): 78–80. *Los Angeles Times* 20 July 1983: 6. 3. *Monthly Film Bulletin* 50 (May 1983): 137–38. *New Republic* 188 (14 February 1983): 24–26. *New York* 16 (31 January 1983): 54–56. *New York Times* 23 January 1983: 1. 46; 11 February 1984: 3. 8. *Newsweek* 101 (31 January 1983): 54–56. *Opera* [England] 34 (June 1983): 686–88. *Opera News* 47 (12 March 1983): 42–43. *Positif* 259 (September 1982): 65–66. *Revue du cinéma* (La Saison cinématographique) Hors serie 26 (1982): 251–52. *San Francisco Chronicle* 23 April 1983: 33. *Séquences* 115 (January 1984): 40–42. *Sunday Times* [London] 3 April 1983: 39. *Tablet* [London] 237 (16 April 1983): 357. *Time* 121 (24 January 1983): 84. *Time Out* [London] 25 March 1983: 12–13; 29 December 1993: 135. *Times* [London] 26 March 1983: 11; 31 March 1983: 10. *Times* [London] *Literary Supplement* 8 April 1983: 352. *Variety* 26 May 1982: 16; 9 February 1983: 18. *Video Review* 11 (September 1990): 11. *Village Voice* 22 February 1983: 60; 3 February 1987: 41–42. *Wagner News* 22 (April-May 1983): 11–15. *Washington Post* 7 December 1984: Weekend 39.

ADDITIONAL DISCUSSIONS:

"Beim 'Parsifal' keine Konfrontationem." *Kino-Information* 8 (22 April 1982): 5.

Bianciotti, Hector. "Le Sourire de Parsifal." *Le Nouvel observateur* 26 December 1981: 70–72.

Bonnet, Jean-Claude, and Michel Celemski. "Entretien avec Hans-Jürgen Syberberg." *Cinématographe* 78 (May 1982): 12–19.

Borie, Bertrand. "Entretien avec Hans-Jürgen Syberberg." *Ecran fantastique* 25 (1982): 20–21.

Citron, Marcia J. *Opera on Screen.* New Haven: Yale University Press, 2000.

Dénes, Zoltai. "Opera és film." *Filmvilág* 29 (January 1986): 2–5.

Ellero, Robert, and others. "Conversazione con Hans-Jürgen Syberberg." *Cinema e cinema* 10 (January-March 1983): 66–69.

"A Golden Age of German Cinema." *Continental Film and Video Review* 29 (September 1982): 40–42.

"Hans-Jürgen Syberberg on His New Film 'Parsifal.'" *Kino* 1 (February 1982): 15.

Harty, Kevin J. "Parsifal and Perceval on Film:

The Reel Life of a Grail Knight." In Arthur Groos and Norris J. Lacy, eds. *Perceval/Parsifal: A Casebook*. New York: Routledge, 2002.

_____. *The Reel Middle Ages: American, Western and Eastern European, Middle Eastern and Asian Films About Medieval Europe*. Jefferson, N.C.: McFarland, 1999.

Henahan, Donal. "The Wagnerian Enigma and Mystique Live On." *New York Times* 13 February 1983: 2. 1, 15.

Hoffman, Donald L. "Re-Framing Perceval." *Arthuriana* 10 (Winter 2000): 45–56.

Holloway, Ronald. "Exhibition Formula for Syberberg's 'Parsifal' Follows 'Epic' Scenario." *Variety* 20 October 1982: 33.

Just, Lothar R., ed. *Das Filmjahr '82/83*. Munich: Filmland Presse, 1983.

Kleis, John Christopher. "The Arthurian Dilemma: Faith and Works in Syberberg's *Parsifal*." In Kevin J. Harty, ed. *King Arthur on Film, New Essays on Arthurian Cinema*. Jefferson, N.C.: McFarland, 1999.

Larsen, Jan Kornum. "Tyskland — et vintereventyr." *Kosmorama* 30 (April 1984): 18–25.

László, Földényi F. "Az üdvkeresés terhe." *Filmvilág* 29 (January 1986): 13–16.

Lévi-Strauss, Claude. "Od Chrétiena de Troyesa do Richarda Wagnerja." *Ekran* 8. 6 (1983): 9–13.

Magill, Frank N., ed. *Magill's Cinema Annual 1983*. Englewood Cliffs, N.J.: Salem, 1984.

Müller, Ulrich. "Blank, Syberberg, and the German Arthurian Tradition." In Kevin J. Harty, ed. *Cinema Arthuriana, Essays on Arthurian Film*. New York: Garland, 1991. [Rpt. above.]

Nash, Jay Robert, and Stanley Ralph Ross. *The Motion Picture Guide, N–R, 1927–1983*. Chicago: Cinebooks, 1986.

Nattiez, Jacques. *Wagner Androgyne*. Princeton: Princeton University Press, 1993.

Olton, Bert. *Arthurian Legends on Film and Television*. Jefferson, N.C.: McFarland, 2000.

Porter, Andrew. "Musical Events: By Comparison Made Wise." *New Yorker* 59 (21 February 1983): 112–16, 119.

Sainderichen, Guy-Patrick. "Voyage à Munich." *Cahiers du cinéma* 331 (January 1982): 22–29.

Socci, Stefano. "*Parsifal*, film-opera dell'avvenire." *Filmcritica* 381–83 (January-February 1988): 7–13.

Stanbrook, Alan. "The Sight of Music." *Sight and Sound* 56 (Spring 1987): 132–35.

Syberberg, Hans-Jürgen. "Filmisches bei Richard Wagner." In Gerhard Heldt, ed. *Richard Wagner: Mittler zwischen Zeiten*. Anif, Austria: Müller-Speiser, 1990.

_____. "'nur der Kranke hält es aus.'" *Medium* 12 (April 1982): 27–29.

_____. "'ohne Neugier und Lust und Informationsredlichkeit.'" *Medium* 12 (September-October 1982): 78–80.

_____. *Parsifal, ein Filmessay*. Munich: Heyne, 1982.

_____. "'Vorführen braucht soviel Energie und Phantasie wie Machen.'" *Medium* 12 (December 1982): 31–33.

_____. "'wir sollen den anderen ins Gesicht spuken.'" *Medium* 12 (July 1982): 40–41.

Tambling, Jeremy. *Opera, Ideology and Film*. New York: St. Martin's, 1987.

Tous les films 1982. Paris: Éditions Chrétiens-Médias, 1983.

Vollemanns, Kees, and Agnes Schreiner. "Hans-Jürgen Syberberg." *Skrien* 131 (October-November 1983): 4–8.

Vrdlovec, Zdenko. "Kaj zmore glas." *Ekran* 8. 6 (1983): 4–8.

Parzival (1980)

West Germany; dir. Richard Blank; screenplay by Richard Blank from Wolfram von Eschenbach's poem; West Deutchse Rundfunk

Cast: Wolfram Kinkel and Eva Schuchardt

DISCUSSIONS:

Harty, Kevin J. *The Reel Middle Ages: American, Western and Eastern European, Middle Eastern and Asian Films About Medieval Europe*. Jefferson, N.C.: McFarland, 1999.

Müller, Ulrich. "Blank, Syberberg, and the German Arthurian Tradition." In Kevin J. Harty, ed. *Cinema Arthuriana, Essays on Arthurian Film*. New York: Garland, 1991. [Rpt. above.]

_____. "Parzival 1980–auf der Bühne, im Fernsehem und im Film." In Jürgen Kühnel and others, eds. *Mittelalter-Rezeption II*. Göppingen: Kümmerle, 1982.

_____. "Wolfram, Wagner, and the Germans." In Will Hasty, ed. *A Companion to Wolfram's Parzival*. Columbia, S.C.: Camden House, 1999.

Wagemann, Anke. *Wolframs von Eschenbach "Parzival" im 20. Jahrhundert*. Göppingen: Kümmerle, 1998.

Perceval (1978)

See *Perceval le gallois* (1978)

Perceval le gallois (1978)

France; dir. Eric Rohmer; screenplay by Eric Rohmer; Gaumont-Les Films du Losange

Alternate title: *Perceval*

Cast: Marie-Christine Barrault, Arielle Dombrasie, André Dussollier, Marc Eyraud, Fabrice Luchini

REVIEWS:
Amis du film et de la télévision 272 (January 1979): 18; 275 (April 1979): 33. *Cahiers du cinéma* 299 (April 1979): 41–46. *Christian Science Monitor* 16 November 1978: 16. *Cinema nuovo* 290–91 (August–October 1984): 61–62. *Cinemateca revista* 39 (November 1983): 79. *Cinématographe* 44 (February 1979): 11–15. *Continental Film Review* 25 (August 1978): 16–17. *Ecran* 76 (15 January 1979): 71–72. *Études* [Paris] 350 (April 1979): 541–45. *Film a doba* 25 (February 1979): 110. *Film en televisie* 294 (November 1981): 33. *Film Quarterly* 33 (Winter 1979–1980): 49–52. *Films in Review* 76 (January 1979): 53–54. *Hollywood Reporter* 12 October 1978: 1. *Image et son* 334 (December 1978): 109–12. *Jeune cinéma* 116 (December 1978): 28–31. *Nation* 227 (11 November 1978): 520. *New Leader* 61 (6 November 1978): 19–20. *New Republic* 179 (21 October 1978): 30–31. *New York Times* 6 October 1978: n.p. *Newsweek* 92 (30 October 1978): 95. *Penthouse* 10 (February 1979): 45–47. *Positif* 216 (March 1979): 74. *San Francisco Chronicle* 24 January 1979: 49. *Segnocinema* 13 (May 1984): 68. *Shakespeare on Film Newsletter* 8 (April 1984): 5, 9. *Studies* [Dublin] 91 (Summer 1982): 193. *Tablet* [London] 233 (December 1979): 1188. *Take One* 7 (January 1979): 9–10. *Télérama* 1517 (10–16 February 1979): 86–89. *Time* 114 (20 November 1978): 104. *Time Out* [London] 8–15 January 1992: 143. *Times* [London] 14 November 1979: 10. *Variety* 13 September 1978: 36. *Village Voice* 23 October 1978: 23.

ADDITIONAL DISCUSSIONS:
Adair, Gilbert. "Rohmer's Perceval." *Sight and Sound* 47 (Autumn 1978): 230–34.
Amiel, Mireille. "Des Arts, des armes et des lois...." *Cinéma* [Paris] 242 (February 1979): 8–10.
Angeli, Giovanna. *Eric Rohmer*. Milan: Moizzi Editore, 1979.
_____. "Perceval le Gallois d'Eric Rohmer et ses sources." *Cahiers de l'Association Internationale des Etudes Françaises* 47 (1995): 33–48.
Beatie, Bruce. "The Broken Quest: The 'Perceval' Romances of Chrétien de Troyes and Eric Rohmer." In Debra Mancoff, ed. *The Arthurian Revival, Essays on Form, Tradition, and Transformation*. New York: Garland, 1992.
Bergan, Ronald, and Robyn Karney. *Bloomsbury Foreign Film Guide*. Rev. ed. London: Bloomsbury, 1992.
Botermans, J. "De lange weg can Eric Rohmer." *Mediafilm* 142 (Spring 1983): 2–11.
Burns, E. Jane. "Nostalgia Isn't What It Used to Be: The Middle Ages in Literature and Film." In George Slusser and Eric S. Rabkin, eds. *Shadows of the Magic Lamp, Fantasy and Science Fiction in Film*. Carbondale: Southern Illinois University Press, 1985.
Callahan, Leslie Abend. "*Perceval le Gallois*: Eric Rohmer's Vision of the Middle Ages." *Film & History* 29. 3–4 (1999): 46–53.
Cinéma français. Paris: Unifrance Film, 1978.
Cormier, Raymond J. "Rohmer's Grail Story: Anatomy of a French Flop." *Yale French Review* 5 (Winter 1981): 391–96.
Crisp, C. H. *Eric Rohmer: Realist and Moralist*. Bloomington: Indiana University Press, 1988.
de la Bretèque, François Amy. "Le Moyen Age du cinéma français 1940–1987." In M. Perrin, ed. *Dire le moyen age hier et aujourd'hui*. Laon: Université Picardie, 1987.
_____. "Présence de la littérature française du Moyen Age dans le cinéma français." *Cahiers de recherches médiévales* 2 (1996): 155–65.
Delevaud, Gilles, and Jacques Montaville. "Entretien avec Eric Rohmer." *Education 2000* 18–20 (March 1981): 85–90.
Detassis, Piera. "Perceval di Eric Rohmer." *Cineforum* 234 (May 1984): 47–44.
"Dossier film: *Perceval*." *Cinéma francçais* 21 (1978): 37–42.
Douin, Jean-Luc. "Entretien avec Eric Rohmer; 'Perceval,' C'est Buster Keaton au moyen âge." *Télérama* 1517 (10–16 February 1979): 90–91.
"Eric Rohmer." *Cahiers du cinéma* 400 (October 1987): supplement 44–45.
"Eric Rohmer Talks about the Concept of 'Perceval.'" *Continental Film Review* 26 (June 1979): 16–17.
"Eric Rohmer's *Perceval le gallois*." *Avant-scène du cinéma* 221 (1 February 1979): 9–64. [Screenplay.]
Fieschi, Jacques. "Un Innocence mortelle." *Avant-scène du cinéma* 221 (1 February 1979): 4–6.
Filme 1981/1984. Dülmen: Katholisches Institut für Medieninformation, 1985.
Fisher, Lucy. "Roots: The Medieval Tale as Modernist Cinema." *Field of Vision* 9–10 (Winter-Spring 1980): 21–25, 33.
Gorgievski, Sandra. "Réalisme, stylisation et parodie dans le film à sujet médiéval des années 1970." In Xavier Kawa-Topor, ed. *Le Moyen age vu par le cinéma européen*. Le Cahiers de Conques 3 (October 2000). Conques: Centre Européen d'Art et de Civilisation Médiévale, 2001
Grimbert, Joan Tasker. "Aesthetic Distance in Rohmer's *Perceval le Gallois*." In Maud S. Walther, ed. *Proceedings of the Purdue University Fifth Annual Conference on Film October*

30–November 1, 1980. West Lafayette, Ind.: Purdue University, 1980.

⸺. "Distancing Techniques in Chrétien de Troyes's *Li Contes del Graal* and Eric Rohmer's *Perceval le Gallois*." *Arthuriana* 10 (Winter 2000): 33–44.

Harty, Kevin J. "Parsifal and Perceval on Film: The Reel Life of a Grail Knight." In Arthur Groos and Norris J. Lacy, eds. *Perceval/Parsifal: A Casebook*. New York: Routledge, 2002.

⸺. *The Reel Middle Ages: American, Western and Eastern European, Middle Eastern and Asian Films About Medieval Europe*. Jefferson, N.C.: McFarland, 1999.

Hoffman, Donald L. "Re-Framing Perceval." *Arthuriana* 10 (Winter 2000): 45–56.

Huchet, Jean-Charles. "Mereceval." *Litterature* 40 (1980): 69–84.

Jourdat, Alain. "L'Espace comme support d'un récit romanesque." *Technicien du film* 272 (15 Jul–15 September 1979): 8–11.

Just, Lothar R., ed. *Das Filmjahr 1984*. Munich: Filmland Presse, 1984.

Larsen, Jan Jorum. "Virkeligehd og vindmller." *Kosmorama* 28 (August 1982): 104–15.

Magill, Frank N., ed. *Magill's Survey of Cinema: Foreign Language Films*. Englewood Cliffs, N.J.: Salem, 1985.

Magny, Joël, and Dominique Rabourdin. "Entretien avec Eric Rohmer." *Cinéma* [Paris] 242 (February 1979): 11–19.

⸺. *Eric Rohmer*. Paris: Rivages, 1986.

⸺. "Eric Rohmer ou la quête du graal." *Cinéma* [Paris] 242 (February 1979): 20–23.

Mancini, Michele. *Eric Rohmer*. Florence: La Nuova Italia, 1983.

Marty, Joseph. "'Perceval le gallois' d'Eric Rohmer, un itinéraire roman." *Cahiers de la cinémathèque* 42–43 (Summer 1985): 125–32.

⸺. "'Perceval le gallois': un symbolisme de l'alliance chrétienne." In Michael Estève, ed. *Eric Rohmer 2*. Paris: Minard, 1986.

Milne, Tom. "Rohmer's Seige Perilous." *Sight and Sound* 50 (Summer 1981): 192–95.

Movshovitz, Howard P. "Rohmer's *Perceval*: Narrative Time and Space in Medieval Literature and Film." In Maud S. Walther, ed. *Proceedings of the Purdue University Fifth Annual Conference on Film October 30–November 1, 1980*. West Lafayette, Ind.: Purdue University, 1980.

Olton, Bert. *Arthurian Legends on Film and Television*. Jefferson, N.C.: McFarland, 2000.

Rider, Jeff, and others. "The Arthurian Legend in French Cinema: *Lancelot du Lac* and *Perceval le Gallois*." In Kevin J. Harty, ed. *Cinema Arthuriana, Essays on Arthurian Film*. New York: Garland, 1991. [Rpt. above in revised form]

Rohmer, Eric. "Note sur la traduction et sur le mise en scène de 'Perceval.'" *Avant-scène du cinéma* 221 (1 February 1979): 6–7.

Roud, Richard, ed. *Cinema, A Critical Dictionary*. New York: Viking, 1980.

Smith, Sarah W. R. "Rohmer's *Perceval* as Literary Criticism." In Maud S. Walther, ed. *Proceedings of the Purdue University Fifth Annual Conference on Film October 30–November 1, 1980*. West Lafayette, Ind.: Purdue University, 1980.

Sterritt, David. "Rohmer's Thoughts About Perceval." *Christian Science Monitor* 27 December 1978: 18.

Tesich-Savage, Nadja. "Rehearsing the Middle Ages." *Film Comment* 14 (September-October 1978): 50–56.

Tulard, Jean. *Guide des Films*. Rev. ed. Paris: Éditions Robert Laffont, 1997.

Williams, David. "Sir Gawain in Films." In Derek Brewer and Jonathan Gibson, eds. *A Companion to the* Gawain-*Poet*. Cambridge, Eng.: D. S. Brewer, 1997.

Williams, Linda. "Eric Rohmer and the Holy Grail." *Literature/Film Quarterly* 11 (April 1983): 71–82.

Prince Valiant (1954)

United States; dir. Henry Hathaway; screenplay by Dudley Nichols; 20th Century–Fox

Cast: Brain Aherne, Donald Crisp, Sterling Hayden, Janet Leigh, James Mason, Victor McLaglen, Robert Wagner

REVIEWS:

America 91 (24 April 1954): 117–19. *Catholic World* 179 (May 1954): 142–43. *Commonweal* 60 (16 April 1954): 41. *Film Daily* 2 April 1954: 6. *Films in Review* 5 (May 1954): 241–42. *Harrison's Reports* 3 April 1954: 55. *Hollywood Reporter* 2 March 1954: 3. *Kinematograph Weekly* 6 May 1954: 16. *Library Journal* 79 (15 April 1954): 766. *Life* 36 (25 January 1954): 108–10. *Look* 17 (29 December 1953): 34–35. *Monthly Film Bulletin* 21 (July 1954): 85–86. *Motion Picture Herald* 3 April 1954: 30; 10 April 1954: Product Digest Section 2254–55. *National Parent-Teacher* 48 (June 1954): 38. *New Statesman and Nation* 47 (1 May 1954): 598. *New York Times* 7 April 1954: 40. *New Yorker* 30 (April 1954): 93–94. *Newsweek* 43 (19 April 1954): 106–07. *Sign* 33 (May 1954): 62. *Tatler* 212 (12 May 1954): 356. *Time* 63 (12 April 1954): 106. *Times* [London] 3 May 1954: 9.

Today 9 (June 1954): 14. *To-day's Cinema* 29 April 1954: 6. *Variety* 7 April 1954: 6.

ADDITIONAL DISCUSSIONS:

Brownell, William H., Jr. "Comics Come Alive." *New York Times* 1 November 1953: 2. 7.

Buckley, Michael P. "James Mason." *Films in Review* 45 (January-February 1994): 6–13; 45 (March-April 1994): 20–34.

Canham, Kingsley. "Henry Hathaway: A Filmography." *Focus on Film* 7 (1971): 28–35.

de la Bretèque, François Amy. "La Figure de chevalier errant dans l'imaginaire cinématographique." In Daniel Poirion, ed. *Le Moyen Age dans le théatre et le cinéma français.* Cahiers de l'Association Internationale des Études Françaises 47 (May 1995). Paris: Société d'Édition les Belles Lettres, 1995.

Eyman, Scott. "'... I made Movies ...'" *Take One* 5 (February 1976): 6–12.

Fuchs, Wolgang J. "Prinz Eisenherz." *Jugend, Film, Fernsehen* 19.3 (1975): 183–84.

Harty, Kevin J. "The Arthurian Legends on Film: An Overview." In Kevin J. Harty, ed. *Cinema Arthuriana, Essays on Arthurian Film.* New York: Garland Publishing, 1991. [Rpt. above in revised form.]

———. *The Reel Middle Ages: American, Western and Eastern European, Middle Eastern and Asian Films About Medieval Europe.* Jefferson, N.C.: McFarland, 1999.

Hirschhorn, Clive. *The Films of James Mason.* London: LSP, 1975.

Hofstede, David. *Hollywood and the Comics.* N.p.: Zanne-3, 1991.

Kaminsky, Stuart M. "Legend of the Lost." *Velvet Light Trap* 14 (Winter 1975): 25–29.

Nash, Jay Robert, and Stanley Ralph Ross. *The Motion Picture Guide, N–R, 1927–1983.* Chicago: Cinebooks, 1986.

Nogueira, Rui. "Henry Hathaway." *Focus on Film* 7 (1971): 11–27.

Olton, Bert. *Arthurian Legends on Film and Television.* Jefferson, N.C.: McFarland, 2000.

Reid, John H. "The Best Second Fiddle." *Films and Filming* 9 (November 1962): 14–16.

Richards, Jeffrey. *Swordmen of the Silver Screen from Douglas Fairbanks to Michael York.* London: Routledge, 1977.

Screen Stories Annual. New York: Dell, 1954.

Smith, Gary A. *Epic Films.* Jefferson, N.C.: McFarland, 1991.

Sweeney, Kevin. *James Mason, A Bio-Bibliography.* Westport, Conn.: Greenwood, 1999.

Williams, David. "Sir Gawain in Films." In Derek Brewer and Jonathan Gibson, eds. *A Companion to the* Gawain-*Poet.* Cambridge, Eng.: D. S. Brewer, 1997.

Prince Valiant (1997)

Germany, Great Britain, Ireland, United States; dir. Anthony Hickox, Michael Frost Beckner, and Carsten Lorenz; screenplay by Anthony Hickox; Constantin Films

Cast: Edward Fox, Katherine Heigl, Thomas Kretschmann, Udo Kier, Joanna Lumley, Stephen Moyer, Gavan O'Herlihy, Ron Perlman, Ben Pullen

REVIEWS:

Arthuriana 8 (Fall 1998):126–28. *Cahiers du cinéma* 516 (September 1997): 82. *Daily Mail* [London] 19 December 1997: 41. *Daily Record* [London] 19 December 1997: 22. *Daily Telegraph* [London] 19 December 1997: 22. *Empire* 103 (January 1998): 42. *EPD Film* 14 (August 1997): 46. *Film Review* [London] January 1998: 21. [Rpt. *Film Review Yearbook* 1997/98: 76.] *Filmecho/Filmwoche* 27 (5 July 1997): 51; 29 (19 July 1997): 38. *Independent* [London] 19 December 1997: 9; 20 December 1997: 20. *Independent on Sunday* [London] 21 December 1997: 2. 8. *Kino* [Germany] 3 (1996): 11. *Le Monde* 7 August 1997: 20; 15 August 1997: 9. *Neon* 13 (January 1998): 92. *Observer* [London] 21 December 1997: Review 12. *Positif* 439 (September 1997): 48. *Première* [France] 246 (September 1997): 28. *Sight and Sound* 8 (January 1998): 52. *Sunday Telegraph* [London] 21 December 1997: Sunday 9. *Sunday Times* [London] 21 December 1997: 7. 26. *Time Out* [London] 17 December 1997: 111. *Times* [London] 18 December 1997: 34. *Toronto Star* 16 March 1998: E7. *Toronto Sun* 16 March 1998: Entertainment 5.

ADDITIONAL DISCUSSIONS:

Delrio, Martin. *Prince Valiant.* New York: Avon, 1998. [Novelization.]

Jones, Alan. "Prince Valiant." *Cinefantastique* 29 (March 1998): 53–53.

Olton, Bert. *Arthurian Legends on Film and Television.* Jefferson, N.C.: McFarland, 2000.

Shäfer, Horst, and Walter Schobert, eds. *Fischer Film Almanach 1998.* Frankfurt am Main: Fischer Taschenbuch, 1998.

Quest for Camelot (1998)

United States; dir. Frederik Du Chau; screenplay by Kirk De Micco; Warner Bros.

Alternate title: *The Magic Sword: Quest for Camelot*

Cast: (The voices of) Pierce Brosnan, Gabriel Byrne, Andrea Corr, Celine Dion, Cary Elwes, John Gielgud, Jessalyn Gilsig, Eric Idle, Gary Oldman, Steve Perry, Don Rickles, Jane Seymour, Bryan White, Jaleel White

REVIEWS:

Arizona Republic 15 May 1998: D1. *Atlanta Journal and Constitution* 15 May 1998: 10P. *Boston Globe* 15 May 1998: D5. *Boston Herald* 15 May 1998: S4. *Chicago Sun-Times* 15 May 1998: 31NC. *Chicago Tribune* 15 May 1998:

Friday A. *Ciné-live* 15 (July-August 1998): 88. *Cinema* [Germany] 242 (July 1998): 128. *Cinemascape* 4 (May-June 1998): 32–33. *Daily News* [New York] 15 May 1998: 56. *Dallas Morning News* 15 May 1998: 1C. *Denver Post* 15 May 1998: E3. *Detroit News* 15 May 1998: D3. *Empire* 110 (August 1998): 46. *Entertainment Weekly* 433 (22 May 1998): 48. *Gazette* [Montréal] 15 May 1998: D5. *Hollywood Reporter* 12–18 May 1998: 20. *Houston Chronicle* 15 May 1998: Weekend 1. *Independent* [London] 23 July 1998: 11. *Irish Times* [Dublin] 24 July 1998: 13. *Los Angeles Times* 15 May 1998: Calendar 2. *Mirror* [London] 24 July 1998: 7. *New York Post* 15 May 1998: 52, 58. *New York Times* 15 May 1998: E10. *Newsday* 15 May 1998: B7. *Ottawa Citizen* 15 May 1998: F3. *People* 49 (25 May 1998): 34. *Philadelphia Inquirer* 15 May 1998: Weekend 3, 10. *San Francisco Chronicle* 15 May 1998: C3. *Screen International* 15 May 1998: 24. *Seattle Times* 15 May 1998: F6. *Sight and Sound* 8 (August 1998): 50–51. *Time* 151 (11 May 1998): 74. *Times* [London] 23 July 1988: 36. *USA Today* 15 May 1998: 9E. *Variety* 11 May 1998: 58. *Washington Post* 15 May 1998: D5; Weekend 56–57.

ADDITIONAL DISCUSSIONS:
Banks, Michelle, ed. *Magill's Cinema Annual 1999.* Detroit: Gale, 1999.
Gardner, J. J. *Quest for Camelot.* New York: Scholastic, 1998. [Novelization.]
Kulik, Nancy. *Quest for Camelot: The Battle for Camelot.* New York: Scholastic, 1998. [Novelization.]
_____. *Quest for Camelot: The Search for Excalibur.* New York: Scholastic, 1998. [Novelization.]
Lyons, Mike. "Animating Arthur: An Interview with *Quest for Camelot* Director Frederik Du Chau." *Animato* 39 (Spring 1988): 40–42.
_____. "*Quest for Camelot.*" *Cinefantastique* 30 (June 1998): 16–17.
Olton, Bert. *Arthurian Legends on Film and Television.* Jefferson, N.C.: McFarland, 2000.
Patrick, James. *Quest for Camelot.* New York: Scholastic, 1998. [Novelization.]
Peters, Jenny. "The Quest for Success." *Animation Magazine* 67 (May 1998): 6–8, 58, 60.
Quest for Camelot. Miami: Warner Bros. Publications, 1998. [Vocal selections.]
Weinberger, Kimberly. *Quest for Camelot.* New York: Scholastic, 1998. [Novelization.]

The Quest of the Holy Grail (1915)
United States; D. W. Griffith; screenplay by D. W. Griffith; Triangle Productions

DISCUSSIONS:
"Film Flashes." *Variety* 28 May 1915: 16.
"Griffith to Make Holy Grail Picture." *Moving Picture World* 1 May 1915: 769.
Harty, Kevin J. *The Reel Middle Ages: American, Western and Eastern European, Middle Eastern and Asian Films About Medieval Europe.* Jefferson, N.C.: McFarland, 1999.
Stern, Seymour. *An Index to the Creative Work of David Wark Griffith. Part II: The Art Triumphant. (b) Triangle Productions: 1915–1916.* Special Supplement to *Sight and Sound.* London: British Film Institute, 1946.

Il Re Artù e i cavalieri della tavola rotonda (1910)
Italy; dir. Giuseppe de Liguoro; screenplay by Arrigo Frusta (?) from Sir Thomas Malory's *Le Morte d'Arthur* (?); Milano Films
Alternate title: *King Arthur; or, The Knights of the Round Table*

REVIEW:
Bisocope 15 September 1910: 39.

ADDITIONAL DISCUSSIONS:
Bernardini, Aldo. *Archivo del cinema italiano. Volume 1. Il cinema muto 1905–1931.* Rome: ANICA, 1991.
D'Heur, J. M. and J. De Groeve. "Arthur, Excalibur and the Enchanter Boorman." *Studia in honorem prof. M. de Riquer, III.* Barcelona: Quaderns Crema, 1988.
Harty, Kevin J. *The Reel Middle Ages: American, Western and Eastern European, Middle Eastern and Asian Films About Medieval Europe.* Jefferson, N.C.: McFarland, 1999.
Prolo, Maria Adriana. *Storia del cinema muto italiano.* Milan: Poligono Società Editrice, 1951.

Le Roi Arthur (1980)
Japan; dir. Masayuki Akehi; screenplay by Masayuki Akehi; Toei Doga
Alternate titles: *King Arthur* and *Moero Arthur*

DISCUSSIONS:
Baricordi, Andrea, and others. *Anime: A Guide to Japanese Animation (1958–1988).* Trans. Adeline D'Opera. Montréal: Protoculture, 2000.
Leguèbe, Éric. *Cinéguide 2001.* Paris: Omnibus, 2000.

Seaview Knights (1994)
Great Britain; dir. Richard Kurti; screenplay by Richard Kurti and Bev Doyle; Seaview Knights Productions and Stranger Than Fiction Films
Cast: Sarah Alexander, James Bolam, Clive Darby, Anita Dobson, Andrew Durant, Bob Flag, Neil Hildegard, Steven Osborne

REVIEWS:
Arthuriana 8 (Fall 1998): 126–28. *Variety* 13 June 1994: 62.

ADDITIONAL DISCUSSIONS:

"In Camera Production News: New Starts." *Moving Pictures International* 1 July 1993: 27.

Olton, Bert. *Arthurian Legends on Film and Television*. Jefferson, N.C.: McFarland, 2000.

"Production Report." *Screen International* 9 July 1993: 17.

Thynne, Jane. "£500 Can Buy Slice of the Action in a New British Film." *Daily Telegraph* [London] 16 June 1993: 7.

The Shadow of the Raven (1988)
See *In the Shadow of the Raven* (1988)

Shadows (1978)
See *The Boy Merlin* (1978)

The Siege of the Saxons (1963)
Great Britain; dir. Nathan Juran; screenplay by Jud Kinberg and John Kohn; Columbia Pictures

Alternate title: *King Arthur and the Siege of the Saxons*

REVIEWS:

Daily Cinema 24 July 1963: 10. *Film Daily* 8 August 1963: 4. *Films and Filming* 9 (September 1963): 24. *Hollywood Reporter* 22 August 1963: 3. *Kinematograph Weekly* 25 July 1963: 31–32. *Monthly Film Bulletin* 30 (September 1963): 133. *Motion Picture Herald* 230 (4 September 1963): Product Digest Section 884. *Variety* 21 August 1963: 17.

ADDITIONAL DISCUSSIONS:

Chibnall, Bernard, and Michael Moulds, eds. *The British National Film Catalogue*. London: British National Film Catalogue, 1963.

Harty, Kevin J. *The Reel Middle Ages: American, Western and Eastern European, Middle Eastern and Asian Films About Medieval Europe*. Jefferson, N.C.: McFarland, 1999.

Nash, Jay Robert, and Stanley Ralph Ross. *The Motion Picture Guide, S, 1927–1983*. Chicago: Cinebooks, 1987.

Olton, Bert. *Arthurian Legends on Film and Television*. Jefferson, N.C.: McFarland, 2000.

Umland, Rebecca A., and Samuel J. Umland. *The Use of Arthurian Legend in Hollywood Film From Connecticut Yankees to Fisher Kings*. Westport, Conn.: Greenwood, 1996.

Sir Galahad of Twilight (1914)
United States; dir. William D. Taylor; screenplay by William D. Taylor (?); American Film Manufacturing Company

Cast: Vivian Rich, Jack Richardson, Harry Van Meter

REVIEWS:

Bioscope 3 December 1914: supplement i. *Moving Picture World* 7 November 1914: 789

The Sixth Sense (1999)
United States; dir. M. Night Shyamalan; screenplay by M. Night Shyamalan; Buena Vista release of a Hollywood Pictures Spyglass Entertainment Production

Cast: Mischa Barton, Toni Collette, Glenn Fitzgerald, Trevor Morgan, Bruce Norris, Haley Joel Osment, Donnie Wahlenberg, Olivia Williams, Bruce Willis

REVIEWS:

Arizona Republic 6 August 1999: D1. *Atlanta Journal and Constitution* 6 August 1999: 11P. *Baltimore Sun* 6 August 1999: 1E. *Boston Globe* 6 August 1999: D8. *Boston Herald* 6 August 1999: S13. *Chicago Sun-Times* 6 August 1999: Weekend Plus 32. *Christian Science Monitor* 6 August 1999: 15. *Cine & Media* [Belgium] 5 (1999): 16–18. *Daily Mail* [London] 4 November 1999: 25. *Daily News* [Los Angeles] 6 August 1999: 54. *Daily News* [New York] 6 August 1999: 59. *Daily Telegraph* [London] 5 November 1999: 24. *Empire* 126 (December 1999): 18; 132 (June 2000): 126; 134 (August 2000): 122. *Entertainment Weekly* 13 August 1999: 50; 31 March 2000: 47. *Evening Standard* [London] 4 November 1999: 31. *Fangoria* 193 (June 2000): 52. *Filmecho/Filmwoche* 33 (21 August 1999): 24. *Film Review* 588 (December 1999): 20–21; Special Issue 33 (2000–01): 92. *Film tutti i film della stagione* 43 (January-February 2000): 46–48. *Financial Times* [London] 4 November 1999: 20. *Guardian* [London] 5 November 1999: 2. 5. *Houston Chronicle* 6 August 1999: Arts 7. *Independent* [London] 5 November 1999: 11. *Independent of Sunday* [London] 7 November 1999: Culture 3. *Legend* [Great Britain] 30 (2000): 33–34. *Los Angeles Times* 6 August 1999: Calendar 10. *Mail on Sunday* [London] 7 November 1999: 70. *Le Monde* 5 January 2000: 25. *Movieline* 11 (February 2000): 109. *Music from the Movies* 25 (Winter 1999): 34. *National Review* 16 (30 August 1999): 53–54. *New York Post* 6 August 1999: 43. *New York Times* 6 August 1999: E14. *New Yorker* 75 (23 August 1999): 200–02. *Newsday* 6 August 1999: B6. *Observer* [London] 7 November 1999: Review 7. *People Weekly* 52 (16 August 1999): 33. *Positif* 468 (February 2000): 42–43. *Premiere* [United States] 13 (January 2000): 35–36. *Première* [France] 275 (January 2000): 53. *Rolling Stone* 19 August 1999: 128. *San Francisco Chronicle* 6 August 1999: C1. *San Francisco Examiner* 6 August 1999: C3. *Seattle Times* 6 August 1999: F1. *Screen International* 13 August 1999: 50. *Sight and Sound* 9 (November 1999): 54–55; 10 (May 2000): 65. *Starburst* 255 (November

1999): 60–61; 266 (October 2000): 85. *Sun* [London] 6 November 199: 53. *Sunday Observer* 7 November 1999: 7. *Sunday Telegraph* 7 November 1999: 10. *Télérama* 5 January 2000: 28. *Time* 154 (61 August 1999): 70. *Time Out* [London] 3 November 1999: 84. *Times* [London] 4 November 1999: 46; 6 November 1999: Features 3. *Total Film* 33 (November 1999): 14. *TV Guide* 1 April 2000: 51. *USA Today* 6 August 1999: 10E. *Variety* 2 August 1999: 33–34. *Village Voice* 10 August 1999: 70. *Washington Post* 6 August 1999: Style 1; Weekend N4. *Washington Times* 6 August 1999: C16.

ADDITIONAL DISCUSSIONS:
Aberry, James. "The Sixth Sense." *Shivers* 72 (December 1999): 8–11.
Argent, Daniel. "An Interview with M. Night Shyamalan." *Creative Screenwriting* 6 (September-October 1999): 41–46.
———. "The Sixth Sense." *Creative Screenwriting* 6 (September-October 1999): 38–40.
Atkinson, Michael. "Ten Best Actors." *Movieline* 11 (March 2000): 62–69.
Cummings, Jean, and Astrid Schon. "Little Man Osment." *Starburst* 256 (December 1999): 48–53.
D'Antonio, Michael. "The Unguarded Heart." *Written By* 4 (March 2000): 16–23.
Doherty, Thomas. "Horror Classic." *Cinefantastique* 31 (February 2000): 61–62.
Flynn, Gillian, and Will Lee. "Sixth Heaven." *Entertainment Weekly* 502 (10 September 1999): 18–19.
Harty, Kevin J. "Looking for Arthur in All the Wrong Places: A Note on M. Night Shyamalan's *The Sixth Sense*." *Arthuriana* 10 (Winter 2000): 57–62.
Heuring, David, and others. "Impeccable Images." *American Cinematographer* 6 (June 2000) 74–109.
Horn, John. "Triumph of the Willis." *Premiere* 13 (January 2000): 35–36.
Naughton, John. "Child's Play." *Empire* 126 (December 1999): 88–98.
Nayman, Ira. "The Man Who Wasn't There." *Creative Screenwriting* 8 (March-April 2001): 57–60.
Nocenti, Annie. "Writing and Directing *The Sixth Sense*: A Talk with M. Night Shyamalan." *Scenario* 5.4 (2001): 51–57, 184–87.
"Reel News: Making Sense of It All." *Empire* 128 (February 2000): 46–47.
Reese, Presley. "The Sixth Sense." *Cinefantastique* 31 (February 2000): 61–62.
Rynning, Roald. "Sixth Heaven." *Film Review* 588 (December 1999): 60–63.

"Sense and Sensibility." *Fangoria* 187 (October 1999): 40–42, 82.
Shyamalan, M. Night. "The Sixth Sense." *Scenario* 5.4 (2001): 12–50. [Screenplay.]

The Spaceman and King Arthur (1979)
See *The Unidentified Flying Oddball* (1979)

Square Heads of the Round Table (1948)
See *Knutzy Knights* (1954)

Summer of the Falcon (1979)
See *Tristan and Isolt* (1979)

The Sword in the Stone (1963)
United States; dir. Wolfgang Reitherman; screenplay by Wolfgang Reitherman; Walt Disney Productions
Cast: (The voices of) Norman Alden, Sebastian Cabot, Junius Matthews, Alan Napier, Ricky Sorenson, Karl Swenson, Martha Wentworth

REVIEWS:
America 110 (11 January 1964): 55. *Commonweal* 79 (13 December 1963): 350. *Daily Cinema* 4 December 1963: 8. *Extension* 58 (December 1963): 8. *Film Daily* 3 October 1963: 14. *Film Facts* 6 (9 December 1963): 286–87. *Films and Filming* 10 (January 1964): 25–26; 352 (January 1984): 42–43. *Furrow* [Ireland] 15 (August 1964): 539. *Hollywood Reporter* 2 October 1963: 3. *Kinematograph Weekly* 5 December 1963: 9. *Los Angeles Times* 26 March 1983: 5. 7. *Monthly Film Bulletin* 31 (February 1964): 22. *Motion Picture Herald* 230 (16 October 1963): Product Digest Section 913–14. *New Republic* 149 (21 December 1963): 29–30. *New York Times* 26 December 1963: 33. *Photoplay* 21 (January 1964): 21. *Tablet* [London] 217 (14 December 1963): 1362. *Times* [London] 12 December 1963: 15. *Variety* 2 October 1963: 6.

ADDITIONAL DISCUSSIONS:
Bär, Willi, and Hans Jürgen Weber, eds. *Fischer Film Almanach 1980*. Frankfurt am Main: Fischer, 1980.
Carey, Mary. *The Sword in the Stone*. Racine, Wisc.: Whitman, 1963. [Novelization.]
Duchène, Alain, and Odile Houen. "Merlin l'enchanteur ou le désenchantment." *Banctitre* 40 (April 1984): 33–35.
Frank, Thomas, and Ollie Johnston. *Disney Animation: The Illusion of Life*. New York: Abbeville, 1981.
Fries, Maureen. "How to Handle a Woman, or Morgan at the Movies." In Kevin J. Harty, ed. *King Arthur on Film, New Essays on Arthurian Cinema*. Jefferson, N.C.: McFarland, 1999.

Grant, John. *Encyclopedia of Walt Disney Animated Characters.* New York: Harper, 1987.

Grellner, Alice. "Two Films That Sparkle: *The Sword in the Stone* and *Camelot.* " In Kevin J. Harty, ed. *Cinema Arthuriana, Essays on Arthurian Film.* New York: Garland, 1991. [Rpt. above in revised form.]

Harty, Kevin J. *The Reel Middle Ages: American, Western and Eastern European, Middle Eastern and Asian Films About Medieval Europe.* Jefferson, N.C.: McFarland, 1999.

Jackson, Kathy Merlock. *Walt Disney, A Bio-Bibliography.* Westport, Conn.: Greenwood, 1993.

Johnston, Ollie, and Frank Thomas. *The Disney Villain.* New York: Hyperion, 1993.

Krafsur, Richard P., ed. *The American Film Institute Catalog of Feature Films, 1961–1970.* New York: Bowker, 1976.

Leebron, Elizabeth, and Lynn Gartley. *Walt Disney, A Guide to References and Resources.* Boston: Hall, 1979.

Matlin, Leonard. *The Disney Films.* Rev. ed. New York: Crown, 1984.

Moran, Daniel. "A Guide to Arthurian Films." In *CliffsNotes*: *White's The Once and Future King.* New York: Hungry Minds, 2000.

Nash, Jay Robert, and Stanley Ralph Ross. *The Motion Picture Guide, S, 1927–1983.* Chicago: Cinebooks, 1987.

Olton, Bert. *Arthurian Legends on Film and Television.* Jefferson, N.C.: McFarland, 2000.

Plas, Marc. "'Merlin l'enchanteur' de Walt Disney: du roman médiéval au conte de fées." *Cahiers de la cinémathèque* 42–43 (Summer 1985): 103–04.

Torregrossa, Michael. "Merlin Goes to the Movies: The Changing Role of Merlin in Cinema Arthuriana." *Film & History* 29. 3–4 (1999): 54–65.

Umland, Rebecca A., and Samuel J. Umland. *The Use of Arthurian Legend in Hollywood Film From Connecticut Yankees to Fisher Kings.* Westport, Conn.: Greenwood, 1996.

The Sword of Lancelot (1963)

Great Britain; dir. Cornel Wilde; screenplay by Cornel Wilde; Emblem Productions

Alternate title: *Lancelot and Guinevere*

Cast: Brian Aherne, George Baker, Mark Dingham, Michael Meacham, Jean Wallace, Cornel Wilde

REVIEWS:

America 108 (27 April 1963): 623. *Commonweal* 78 (6 September 1963): 539. *Daily Cinema* 3 May 1963: 5. *Film Daily* 29 April 1963: 8. *Film Facts* 6 (10 October 1963): 211–12. *Films and Filming* 9 (July 1963): 24. *Hollywood Reporter* 29 April 1963: 3. *Monthly Film Bulletin* 30 (June 1963): 87. *Motion Picture Herald* 229 (15 May 1963): Product Digest Section 809. *New York Times* 10 October 1963: 49. *Newsweek* 62 (28 October 1963): 97. *Sign* 42 (June 1963): 42. *Times* [London] 2 May 1963: 6. *Variety* 1 May 1963: 6.

ADDITIONAL DISCUSSIONS:

Chibnall, Bernard, and Michael Moulds, eds. *The British National Film Catalogue.* London: British National Film Catalogue, 1963.

Coen, John. "Producer/Director Cornel Wilde." *Film Comment* 6 (Spring 1970): 53–61.

Gow, Gordon. "Survival!" *Films and Filming* 17 (October 1970): 4–10.

Harty, Kevin J. *The Reel Middle Ages: American, Western and Eastern European, Middle Eastern and Asian Films About Medieval Europe.* Jefferson, N.C.: McFarland, 1999.

Kaminsky, Stuart M. "Getting Back to Basics with Cornel Wilde." *Take One* 5 (October 1976): 22–24.

Krafsur, Richard P., ed. *The American Film Institute Catalog of Feature Films, 1961–1970.* New York: Bowker, 1976.

Lancelot and Guinevere. London: Rank Film Distributors [1963]. [Press book.]

Luciano, Patrick. *With Fire and Sword, Italian Spectacles on American Screens 1958–1968.* Metuchen, N.J.: Scarecrow, 1994.

Nash, Jay Robert, and Stanley Ralph Ross. *The Motion Picture Guide, S, 1927–1983.* Chicago: Cinebooks, 1987.

Olton, Bert. *Arthurian Legends on Film and Television.* Jefferson, N.C.: McFarland, 2000.

Parish, James Robert, and Don E. Stanke. *The Swashbucklers.* New Rochelle, N.Y.: Arlington House, 1976.

Richards, Jeffrey. *Swordsmen of the Screen from Douglas Fairbanks to Michael York.* London: Routledge, 1977.

Smith Gary. *The Epic Film.* Jefferson, N.C.: McFarland, 1991.

Umland, Rebecca A., and Samuel J. Umland. *The Use of Arthurian Legend in Hollywood Film From Connecticut Yankees to Fisher Kings.* Westport, Conn.: Greenwood, 1996.

Sword of the Valiant (1983)

Great Britain; dir. Stephen Weeks; screenplay by Stephen Weeks; Cannon Films

Alternate title: *The Legend of Gawain and the Green Knight*

Cast: Cyrielle Claire, Sean Connery, Peter Cushing, Trevor Howard, Miles O'Keefe

REVIEWS:

Cinefantastique 15 (May 1985): 53. *Monthly Film Bulletin* 52 (May 1985): 164–65. *Philadelphia Inquirer* 3 December 1984: 8E. *Star-*

burst 70 (June 1984): 24–25. *Variety* 5 December 1984: 17. *Western Mail* [England] 27 July 1985: 19.

ADDITIONAL DISCUSSIONS:
Berry, David. *Wales and Cinema, The First Hundred Years.* Cardiff: University of Wales Press, 1994.
Blanch, Robert J., and Julian N. Wasserman. "Fear of Flyting: The Absence of Internal Tension in *Sword of the Valiant* and *First Knight*." *Arthuriana* 10 (Winter 2000): 15–32.
_____. "Gawain on Film." In Kevin J. Harty, ed. *Cinema Arthuriana, Essays on Arthurian Film.* New York: Garland, 1991. [Rpt. above in revised form.]
Dupuis, Jean Jacques. *Sean Connery.* Paris: Veyrier, 1986.
Harty, Kevin J. *The Reel Middle Ages: American, Western and Eastern European, Middle Eastern and Asian Films About Medieval Europe.* Jefferson, N.C.: McFarland, 1999.
Jackson, Paul. "Please Don't Scratch the Walls." *Western Mail* [England] 4 December 1982: 7.
Munn, Michael. *Trevor Howard, The Man and His Films.* London: Robson, 1989.
Nash, Jay Robert, and Stanley Ralph Ross. *The Motion Picture Guide, W–Z, 1927–1984.* Chicago: Cinebooks, 1987.
Olton, Bert. *Arthurian Legends on Film and Television.* Jefferson, N.C.: McFarland, 2000.
Parker, John. *Sean Connery.* London: Gollancz, 1993.
Pfeiffer, Lee, and Philip Lisa. *The Films of Sean Connery.* New York: Citadel, 1993.
Sellers, Robert. *The Films of Sean Connery.* New York: St. Martin's, 1990.
Tanitch, Robert. *Sean Connery.* London: Chapmans, 1992.
Umland, Rebecca, and Sam Umland. "The Long *Happy* Film Life of Stephen Weeks." *Video Watchdog* 60 (June 2000): 4–6.
_____. "The Short, Unhappy Film Life of Stephen Weeks." *Video Watchdog* 59 (May 2000): 32–39.
Williams, David. "Sir Gawain in Films." In Derek Brewer and Jonathan Gibson, eds. *A Companion to the Gawain-Poet.* Cambridge, Eng.: D. S. Brewer, 1997.

Tennessee Ernie Ford Meets King Arthur (1960)
United States; dir. Lee J. Cobb; screenplay by Roland Kibbee; Ford Startime for NBC
Cast: Danny Arnold, John Dehner, Robert Emhardt, Tennessee Ernie Ford, Alan Mowbray, Vincent Price, Addison Richards, Alan Young

REVIEW:
Variety 18 May 1960: 39.

ADDITIONAL DISCUSSIONS:
Gianakos, Larry James. *Television Drama Series Programming: A Comprehensive Chronicle, 1959–1975.* Metuchen, N.J.: Scarecrow, 1978.
Harty, Kevin J. *The Reel Middle Ages: American, Western and Eastern European, Middle Eastern and Asian Films About Medieval Europe.* Jefferson, N.C.: McFarland, 1999.
"Rivals Dethrone Tenn. Ernie's 'King' in Ratings' Race." *Daily Variety* 12 May 1960: 11.
Terrace, Vincent. *Encyclopedia of Television Series, Plots and Specials 1937–1973.* New York: Zoetrope, 1986.
_____. *Television Specials.* Jefferson, N.C.: McFarland, 1995.

To Parsifal (1963)
United States; dir. Bruce Baillie; screenplay by Bruce Baillie; Canyon Cinema Co-op
Cast: Bruce Baillie

REVIEW:
Harbinger 1 (July 1967): 27–28.

ADDITIONAL DISCUSSIONS:
Bragin, John. "The Work of Bruce Baillie." In Gregory Battock, ed. *The New American Cinema.* New York: Dutton, 1967.
"Bruce Baillie: An Interview." *Film Comment* 7 (Spring 1971): 24–32.
Curtis, David. *Experimental Cinema.* New York: Delta, 1971.
Nygren, Scott. "Myth and Bruce Baillie's *To Parsifal*." *Field of Vision* 13 (Spring 1985): 3–4.
Olton, Bert. *Arthurian Legends on Film and Television.* Jefferson, N.C.: McFarland, 2000.
Polt, Harriet. "The Films of Bruce Baillie." *Film Comment* 2 (Fall 1964): 50–53.
Sitney, Alan P. "Bruce Baillie and the Lyrical Film." In Annette Michelson, ed. *New Forms in Film.* Montreux, Switz.: Corbaz, 1974.
"Special Section: The Films of Bruce Baillie." *Harbinger* 1 (July 1967): 15–36.
Whitehall, Richard. "An Interview with Bruce Baillie." *Film Culture* 47 (Summer 1969): 16–20.

Tortilla Flat (1942)
United States; dir. Victor Fleming; screenplay by John Lee Mahin and Benjamin Glazer; MGM
Cast: John Garfield, Hedy Lamarr, Sheldon Leonard, Frank Morgan, Akim Tamiroll, Spencer Tracy

REVIEWS:
Commonweal 36 (12 June 1942): 6. *Film Daily* 22 April 1942: 9. *Hollywood Reporter* 22 April

1942: 3. *Kinematograph Weekly* 25 June 1942: 30. *Life* 12 (1 June 1942): 39–41. *Motion Picture Exhibitor* 6 May 1942: 1002. *Motion Picture Herald* 25 April 1942: Product Digest Section 621–22. *New Republic* 106 (1 June 1942): 766. *New York Times* 22 May 1942: 27. *New Yorker* 18 (23 May 1942): 63. *Newsweek* 19 (1 June 1942): 66. *Photoplay* 21 (July 1942): 6. *Theatre Arts* 26 (June 1942): 398. *Time* 39 (18 May 1942): 84. *Times* [London] 12 October 1942: 8. *Today's Cinema* 19 June 1942: 7, 12. *Variety* 22 April 1942: 8.

ADDITIONAL DISCUSSIONS:
Beaver, James N. *John Garfield, His Life and Films*. New York: A. S. Barnes, 1978.
Burrows, Michael. *John Steinbeck and His Films*. St. Austell, Cornwall: Formative Film Series Publications, 1971.
Deschner, Donald. *The Complete Films of Spencer Tracy*. New York: Citadel, 1968.
Gelman, Howard. *The Films of John Garfield*. Secaucus, N.J.: Citadel, 1975.
Hanson, Patricia King, ed. *The American Film Institute Catalog of Motion Pictures Produced in the United States, Feature Films, 1941–1950*. Berkeley: University of California Press, 1999.
Hayashi, Tetsumaro, ed. *Steinbeck and the Arthurian Theme*. Muncie, Ind.: John Steinbeck Society of America and Ball State University, 1975.
King, Alison. *Spencer Tracy*. New York: Crescent Books, 1992.
McGrath, Patrick J. *John Garfield*. Jefferson, N.C.: McFarland, 1993.
Millichap, Joseph R. *Steinbeck and Film*. New York: Ungar, 1983.
Olton, Bert. *Arthurian Legends on Film and Television*. Jefferson, N.C.: McFarland, 2000.
Owens, Louis. "Camelot East of Eden." *Arizona Quarterly* 38 (Autumn 1982): 203–16.
Scheer, Ronald D. "Steinbeck Into Film: *Tortilla Flat*." *West Virginia University Bulletin* 26 (August 1980): 30–36.
Young, Christopher. *The Films of Hedy Lamarr*. Secaucus, N.J.: Citadel, 1978.

Tristan and Isolda (1911)
See *Tristano e Isotta* (1911)

Tristan and Isolt (1979)
Ireland; dir. Tom Donovan; screenplay by Claire Labine; Clar Productions
Alternate titles: *Lovespell* and *Summer of the Falcon*
Cast: Richard Burton, Nicholas Clay, Cyril Cusack, Geraldine Fitzgerald, Kate Mulgrew

REVIEW:
Irish Times [Dublin] 29 September 1981: 10.

ADDITIONAL DISCUSSIONS:
Alpert, Hollis. *Burton*. Toronto: Paper Jacks, 1987.
Harty, Kevin J. *The Reel Middle Ages: American, Western and Eastern European, Middle Eastern and Asian Films About Medieval Europe*. Jefferson, N.C.: McFarland, 1999.
Lacy, Norris J. "*Lovespell* and the Disinterpretation of a Legend." *Arthuriana* 10 (Winter 2000): 5–14.
McMunn, Meradith T. "Filming the Tristan Myth: From Text to Icon." In Kevin J. Harty, ed. *Cinema Arthuriana, Essays on Arthurian Films*. New York: Garland, 1991. [Rpt. above in revised form.]
Olton, Bert. *Arthurian Legends on Film and Television*. Jefferson, N.C.: McFarland, 2000.
Rockett, Kevin, ed. *The Irish Filmography*. Dublin: Red Mountain Media, 1996.
Singer, Michael, ed. *Film Directors, A Complete Guide*. Beverly Hills: Lone Eagle, 1987.
Steverson, Tyrone. *Richard Burton, A Bio-Bibliography*. Westport, Conn.: Greenwood, 1992.
Tobin, Yann. "Ce soir, je ferai pleurer le public." *Positif* 236 (December 1984): 11–15.
Willis, John. *Screen World*. [Vol. 33, for 1981.] New York: Crown, 1982.

Tristan et Iseult (1972)
France; dir. Yvan Lagrange; screenplay by Yvan Lagrange; Film du Soir
Cast: Yvan Lagrange and Claire Wauthion

REVIEWS:
Cinéma [Paris] 187 (May 1974): 138. *Ecran* 25 (May 1974): 68. *Image et son* 284 (May 1974): 103–04; 288–89 (October 1974): 364–65. *Kino* [Poland] 9 (January 1974): 60–61. *Téléciné* 188 (May 1974): 27. *Variety* 18 July 1973: 14.

ADDITIONAL DISCUSSIONS:
de la Bretèque, François Amy. "Le Moyen Age du cinéma français 1940–1987." In M. Perrin, ed. *Dire le moyen age hier et aujourd'hui*. Laon: Université Picardie, 1987.
Harty, Kevin J. *The Reel Middle Ages: American, Western and Eastern European, Middle Eastern and Asian Films About Medieval Europe*. Jefferson, N.C.: McFarland, 1999.
Marcel, Jean. *Pensées, passiones et proses*. Montréal: L'Hexagone, 1992.
McMunn, Meradith T. "Filming the Tristan Myth: From Text to Icon." In Kevin J. Harty, ed. *Cinema Arthuriana, Essays on Arthurian Film*. New York: Garland, 1991. [Rpt. above in revised form.]
Paquette, Jean-Marcel. "Le Derniere metamorphose de Tristan: Yvan Lagrange (1972)." In Ulrich Müller, and others, eds. *Tristan et*

Iseut, mythe europeen et mondial. Göppingen: Kümmerle, 1987.

Payen, Jean Charles. "Le *Tristan et Iseult* de Lagrange comme un anti–Tristan." *Tristania* 4 (May 1979): 51–56.

Selcer, Robert W. "Yvan Lagrange: Impressions of a Filmmaker." *Tristania* 4 (May 1979): 44–50.

Tulard, Jean. *Guide des Films.* Rev. ed. Paris: Éditions Robert Laffont, 1997.

Vialle, Gabriel. "Musique, la quatrième dimension." *Image et son* 29 (December 974): 10–12.

Tristan et Yseult (1909)

France; dir. Albert Capellani; screenplay by Michel Carré; Pathé Frères, S.C.A.G.L.
Cast: Paul Capellani and Stacia Napierkowska

DISCUSSIONS:

de la Bretèque, François Amy. "Présence de la littérature française du Moyen Age dans le cinéma français." *Cahiers de recherches médiévales* 2 (1996): 155–65.

Harty, Kevin J. *The Reel Middle Ages: American, Western and Eastern European, Middle Eastern and Asian Films About Medieval Europe.* Jefferson, N.C.: McFarland, 1999.

Mitry, Jean. *Filmographie universelle: tome deuxième. Primitifs et précurseurs 1895–1915. Première partie: France et Europe.* Paris: IDHEC, 1964.

Tristan et Yseult (1911)

See *Tristano e Isotta* (1911)

Tristan et Yseut (1920)

France; dir. Maurice Mariaud; screenplay by Franz Toussaint; Nalpas Films
Cast: Sylvio de Pedrelli, Frank Heurs, Andre Lionel
Alternate title: *Tristram and Isolda*

REVIEW:

Kinematograph Weekly 24 November 1921: 73–74.

ADDITIONAL DISCUSSIONS:

Abel, Richard. *French Cinema, The First Wave, 1915–1926.* Princeton: Princeton University Press, 1984.

Bardèche, Maurice, and Robert Brasillach. *Histoire du cinéma.* Rev. ed. 2 vols. Givors: Martel, 1953–1954.

de la Bretèque, François Amy. "Présence de la littérature française du Moyen Age dans le cinéma français." *Cahiers de recherches médiévales* 2 (1996): 155–65.

Fescourt, Henri. *La Foi et les montagnes.* Paris: Montel, 1959.

Harty, Kevin J. *The Reel Middle Ages: American, Western and Eastern European, Middle Eastern and Asian Films About Medieval Europe.* Jefferson, N.C.: McFarland, 1999.

Landry, Lionel. "La Reconstruction historique." *Cinémagazine* 3 (14 September 1923): 368.

Tristan und Isolde (1981)

See *Fire and Sword* (1981)

Tristan und Isolde, Eine Liebe für die Ewigkeit (1998)

See *Il Cuore e la spada* (1998)

Tristana (1970)

Spain; dir. Luis Buñuel; screenplay by Luis Buñuel; Epoca Film
Cast: Antonio Casas, Catherine Deneuve, Jésus Fernández, Lola Gaos, Franco Nero, Fernando Rey, Vincente Soler

REVIEWS:

Cahiers du cinéma 225 (November-December 1970): 58–60. *Celuloide* 13 (February 1970): 14–17, 147. *Cineforum* 260 (December 1986): 35–40. *Cinéma* [Paris] 9 (July-August 1970): 22–23. *Cinema 2002* 37 (March 1978): 82–83. *Cinema nuovo* 23 (September-October 1970): 377; 24 (March-April 1971): 116–19. *Cinestudio* 84 (April 1970): 33–34. *Daily News* [New York] 22 September 1970: 77. *Evening News* [Newark, N.J.] 21 September 1970: 14. *Film Heritage* 7 (Winter 1971–1972): 1–9. *Film Quarterly* 24 (Winter 1970–1971): 52–53. *Films and Filming* 18 (January 1972): 58–59. *Hollywood Reporter* 24 September 1970: 8. *Image et son* 240 (June-July 1970): 128–29. *Life* 69 (6 November 1970): 11. *Lumière du cinéma* 10 (December 1977): 72–75. *Monogram* 5 (1974): 19–20. *Monthly Film Bulletin* 454 (November 1971): 226; 456 (January 1972): 23. *Morning Telegraph* [New York] 22 September 1970: 3. *New York* 3 (28 September 1970): 55. *New York Post* 22 September 1970: 73. *New York Times* 21 September 1970: 54; 27 September 1970: 2. 1, 3. *New Yorker* 46 (26 September 1970): 123–24. *Newsweek* 76 (12 October 1970): 112. *Observer* [London] 3 October 1971: 35. *Positif* 254–55 (May 1982): 86–87. *Revue du cinéma* 470 (April 1991): 46. *Saturday Review* 53 (3 October 1970): 50. *Séquences* 180 (September-October 1995): 43. *Sight and Sound* 40 (Spring 1971): 103; NS 3 (August 1993): 62. *Skrien* 149 (September-October 1986): 16–17. *Télérama* 8 March 1995: 109. *Time* 96 (23 September 1970): 74. *To-day's Cinema* 15 October 1971: 8. *Variety* 8 April 1980: 16. *Village Voice* 15 October 1970: 53, 55. *Women's Wear Daily* 22 September 1970: 20.

ADDITIONAL DISCUSSIONS:
Baxter, John. *Buñuel*. London: Fourth Estate, 1994.
Buache, Freddy. *The Cinema of Luis Buñuel*. Trans. Peter Graham. London: Tantivity Press, 1973.
Buñuel, Luis. "Tristana." *Avant-scène du cinéma* 110 (January 1971): 7–54. [Screenplay.]
_____. *Tristana*. Trans. Nicholas Fry. New York: Simon and Schuster, 1971. [Screenplay.]
Dongan, Christine. "Tristana." *Cahiers de la cinémathèque* 38–39 (Winter 1984): 168–76.
Durgnat, Ray. "Tristana." *Film Comment* 10 (September-October 1974): 54–62.
Edwards, Gwynne. *Indecent Exposures: Buñuel, Saura, Erice and Almodóvar*. London: Marion Boyars, 1995.
Eidsvik, Charles. "Dark Laughter, Buñuel's *Tristana* (1970)." In Andrew Horton and Joan Magretta, eds. *Modern European Filmmakers and the Art of Adaptation*. New York: Ungar, 1981.
Girad, R. "Tristana." *Film Heritage* 7 (Winter 1971–72): 1–9.
Grossvogel, David. I. "Buñuel's Obsessed Camera: *Tristana* Dismembered." *Diacritics* 2 (Spring 1972): 51–56.
Hedges, I. "Substitutionary Narration in the Cinema?" *Sub-stance* 9 (1974): 45–57.
Hoffman, Donald L. "Tristan la Blonde: Transformations of Tristan in Buñuel's *Tristana*." In Kevin J. Harty, ed. *King Arthur on Film, New Essays on Arthurian Cinema*. Jefferson, N.C.: McFarland, 1999.
Mellen, Joan. *Women and Their Sexuality in the New Film*. London: Davis-Poynter, 1974.
Miller, Beth. "From Mistress to Murderess: The Metamorphosis of Buñuel's *Tristana*." In Beth Miller, ed. *Women in Hispanic Literature: Icons and Fallen Idols*. Berkeley: University of California Press, 1983.
Nash, Jay Robert, and Stanley Ralph Ross. *The Motion Picture Guide, T–V, 1927–1984*. Chicago: Cinebooks, 1987.
Olton, Bert. *Arthurian Legends on Film and Television*. Jefferson, N.C.: McFarland, 2000.
"[Dossier on] *Tristana*." *Cahiers du cinéma* 223 (August 1970): 5–28.
Tulard, Jean. *Guide des Films*. Rev. ed. Paris: Éditions Robert Laffont, 1997.

Tristano e Isotta (1911)
Italy; dir. Ugo Falena; screenplay by Ugo Falena (?); Il Film d'arte italiana, S.A.P.F.
Cast: Francesca Bertini, Bianca Lorenzoni, Serafino Mastracchio, Giovanni Pezzinga
Alternate titles: *Tristan and Isolda* and *Tristan et Yseult*

REVIEW:
Bioscope 28 September 1911: supplement v.
ADDITIONAL DISCUSSIONS:
Bousquet, Henri. *Catalogue Pathé des années 1896 à 1914: 1910–1911*. Paris: Henri Bousquet, 1994.
de la Bretèque, François Amy. "Présence de la littérature française du Moyen Age dans le cinéma français." *Cahiers de recherches médiévales* 2 (1996): 155–65.
Harty, Kevin J. "A Note on Maureen Fries, Morgan le Fay, and Ugo Falena's 1911 Film *Tristano e Isotta*." In Bonnie Wheeler and Fiona Tolhurst, eds. *On Arthurian Women: Essays in Memory of Maureen Fries*. Dallas: Scriptorium Press, 2001.
_____. *The Reel Middle Ages: American, Western and Eastern European, Middle Eastern and Asian Films About Medieval Europe*. Jefferson, N.C.: McFarland, 1999.

Tristram and Isolda (1920)
See *Tristan et Yseut* (1920).

The Unidentified Flying Oddball (1979)
United States; dir. Russ Mayberry; screenplay by Don Tait; Walt Disney Productions
Alternate title: *The Spaceman and King Arthur*
Cast: Jim Dale, Dennis Dugan, John Le Mesurier, Ron Moody, Kenneth More, Sheila White

REVIEWS:
Boxoffice 6 August 1979: 20. *Columbia* [New Haven] 59 (October 1979): 41. *Ecran fantastique* 11 (1979): 7. *Film Bulletin* 48 (September 1978): Review-D. *Films Illustrated* 8 (July 1979): 412. *Independent Film Journal* 82 (September 1979): 14, 55. *Monthly Film Bulletin* 46 (July 1979): 154–55. *Screen International* 198 (14–21 July 1979): 18. *Tablet* [London] 233 (28 July 1979): 730. *Variety* 18 July 1979: 16.

ADDITIONAL DISCUSSIONS:
Crume, Vic. *The Unidentified Flying Oddball*. New York: Scholastic Book Services, 1979. [Novelization.]
Hardy, Phil, ed. *Science Fiction, The Aurum Film Encyclopedia*. London: Aurum, 1992.
Harty, Kevin J. "Camelot Twice Removed: *Knightriders* and the Film Versions of *A Connecticut Yankee in King Arthur's Court*." In Kevin J. Harty, ed. *Cinema Arthuriana, Essays on Arthurian Film*. New York: Garland, 1991. [Rpt. above in revised form.]
_____. *The Reel Middle Ages: American, Western and Eastern European, Middle Eastern and Asian Films About Medieval Europe*. Jefferson, N.C.: McFarland, 1999.

Just, Lothar R., ed. *Das Filmjahr '80/81.* Munich: Filmland Presse, 1981.

Nash, Jay Robert, and Stanley Ralph Ross. *The Motion Picture Guide 1927–1983, Volume 8, T–V.* Chicago: Cinebooks, 1987.

Olton, Bert. *Arthurian Legends on Film and Television.* Jefferson, N.C.: McFarland, 2000.

Simon, Heather. *The Spaceman and King Arthur.* London: New English Library, 1979. [Novelization.]

Thompson, Raymond H. "The Ironic Tradition in Arthurian Films Since 1960." In Kevin J. Harty, ed. *Cinema Arthuriana, Essays on Arthurian Film.* New York: Garland, 1991. [Rpt. above.]

Tous les films 1981. Paris: Éditions O.C.F.C., 1982.

Umland, Rebecca A., and Samuel J. Umland. *The Use of Arthurian Legend in Hollywood Film From Connecticut Yankees to Fisher Kings.* Westport, Conn.: Greenwood, 1996.

Vaines, Colin. "King Arthur's Yankee Enters the Space Age." *Screen International* 5 August 1978: 10–11.

Willis, Donald C. *Horror and Science Fiction Films II.* Metuchen, N.J.: Scarecrow, 1982.

The Woman Next Door (1981)

France; François Truffaut; screenplay by François Truffaut; Les Films di Carrosse–TFI/UA
Alternate title: *La Femme d'à côté*
Cast: Fanny Ardant, Michele Baumgartner, Gerard Depardieu, Henri Garcin, Veronique Silver

REVIEWS:

Cahiers du cinéma 329 (November 1981): 51–52. *Casablanca* 17 (May 1982): 51–52. *Chaplin* 36.3 (1982): 141–42, 144. *Christian Science Monitor* 22 October 1981: 18. *Cine revue* 61 (September 1981): 18–21. *Cineaste* 12.1 (1982): 56–57. *Cineforum* 22 (January-February 1982): 43–48. *Cinéma* [Paris] 274 (October 1981): 98–99. *Cinéma de France* 58 (September-October 1981): 15, 23. *Cinema nuovo* 31 (June 1982): 45–46. *Cinemateca Revista* 38 (May 1983): 55, 57. *Cinématographe* 73 (December 1981): 85. *Continental Film and Video Review* 28 (12 October 1981): 14–15. *Contracampo* 29 (April–June 1982): 65. *Daily News* [New York] 12 October 1981: 37. *Film a doba* 31 (July 1985): 404–05. *Film français* 20 March 1981: 14. *Film og kino* 50 (July 1982): 257–58. *Films* [Great Britain] 2 (March 1982): 32–33. *Films and Filming* 329 (February 1982): 32. *Films in Review* 33 (March 1982): 172. *Hollywood Reporter* 20 October 1981: 2. *Iskusstvo kino* 12 (December 1983): 149–52. *Jeune cinéma* 138 (November): 37–38. *Listener* 28 January 1982: 27–28. *Monthly Film Bulletin* 49 (February 1982): 27. *Nation* 233 (7 November 1981): 484. *New Leader* 64 (16 November 1981): 17. *New Republic* 185 (11 November 1981): 24–25. *New Statesman* 103 (22 January 1982): 22–23. *New York* 14 (2 November 1981): 60. *New York Post* 9 October 1981: 48. *New York Times* 9 October 1981: C8; 11 October 1981: 2. 19, 24; 18 October 1981: 2. 1, 30; 30 October 1981: C8. *Newsweek* 98 (19 October 1981): 92. *Observer* [London] 24 January 1982: 28. *Pic Biz* 20 (July-August 1981): 3. *Positif* 248 (November 1981): 59–61. *Revue du cinéma* 366 (November 1981): 31–34. *San Francisco Chronicle* 17 December 1981: 82. *Segnocinema* 2 (March 1982): 56. *Séquences* 27 (April 1982): 25–26. *Sight and Sound* 5 (October 1995): 67. *Skoop* 18 (June 1982): 35. *Skrien* 121 (September 1982): 7. *Stills* 1 (Winter 1982): 92. *Sunday Times* [London] 24 January 1982: 40. *Time* 118 (2 November 1981): 115. *Times* [London] 22 January 1982: 11. *Times* [London] *Literary Supplement* 12 February 1982: 160. *Variety* 30 September 1981: 22. *Village Voice* 14 October 1981: 47. *Women's Wear Daily* 12 October 1981: 20.

ADDITIONAL DISCUSSIONS:

Allen, Don. *Finally Truffaut.* New York: Beaufort Books, 1985.

Chutkow, Paul. *Depardieu.* London: HarperCollins, 1994.

Collet, Jean *François Truffaut.* Paris: Lherminier, 1985.

DeFornai, Oreste. *I Film di François Truffaut.* Rome: Gremes Editore, 1990.

Grimbert, Joan Tasker. "Truffaut's *La Femme d'à côté* (1981): Attenuating a Romantic Archetype — Tristan and Iseult?" In Kevin J. Harty, ed. *King Arthur on Film, New Essays on Arthurian Cinema.* Jefferson, N.C.: McFarland, 1999.

Guérif, François. *François Truffaut.* Paris: Edilig, 1988.

Insdorf, Annette. *François Truffaut.* Rev. ed. New York: Cambridge University Press, 1994.

Le Berre, Carole. *François Truffaut.* Paris: Cahiers du cinéma, 1993.

Nicholls, David. *François Truffaut.* London: Batsford, 1993.

Olton, Bert. *Arthurian Legends on Film and Television.* Jefferson, N.C.: McFarland, 2000.

Truffaut, François. "*La Femme d'à côté.*" *Avant-scène du cinéma* 389 (February 1990): 1–93. [Screenplay and special issue.]

Waltz, Eugene P. *François Truffaut, A Guide to References and Resources.* Boston: G.K. Hall, 1982.

Ymadawiad Arthur (1994)

Wales; dir. Marc Evans; screenplay by Marc Evans; S4C for BBC Wales

Cast: Toni Carrol, Gillian Eusa, Moriajis Thomas, Nia Samuel, Yland Williams

REVIEW:
Screen International 11 August 1995: xii.

ADDITIONAL DISCUSSION:
Olton, Bert. *Arthurian Legends on Film and Television*. Jefferson, N.C.: McFarland, 2000.

A Young Connecticut Yankee in King Arthur's Court (1995)

Canada; dir. R. L. Thomas; screenplay by Frank Encarnacao and R. L. Thomas; Filmline International and Images Television International

Cast: Paul Hopkins, Jack Langedijk, Nick Mancuso, Philippe Ross, Theresa Russell, Polly Shannon, Michael York

REVIEWS:
Arthuriana 6 (Summer 1996): 115–18. *Globe and Mail* [Toronto] 1 June 1995: C1.

ADDITIONAL DISCUSSIONS:
Adilman, Sid. "Singer Sells New Album on Computer Network." *Toronto Star* 24 1994: C5.

Harty, Kevin J. *The Reel Middle Ages: American, Western and Eastern European, Middle Eastern and Asian Films About Medieval Europe*. Jefferson, N.C.: McFarland, 1999.

Olton, Bert. *Arthurian Legends on Film and Television*. Jefferson, N.C.: McFarland, 2000.

Quill, Greg. "CBC Critics Best Heed a Warning from U.S." *Toronto Star* 1 June 1995: B8.

Sklar, Elizabeth S. "Twain for Teens: Young Yankees in Camelot." In Kevin J. Harty, ed. *King Arthur on Film, New Essays on Arthurian Cinema*. Jefferson, N.C.: McFarland, 1999.

Index

Abbey, Edwin Austin 10
Addie, Robert: stills 48, 244
The Adventures of Sir Galahad 14, 200–2, 254–55
Akehi, Masayuki 17
Alani 243
Albert, Eddie 12
Alexander Nevsky 51
Allen, Joan 28; still 62
Alliterative *Morte Arthure* 189
America Faces Communism 67
American dream 64–70
Anglo-Saxon Chronicle 137
Antolek, Vladmir: still 152
armor in Arthurian film 235–51
arms in Arthurian film 235–51
Around the World in Eighty Days 145
Arthur (novel by Lawhead) 239
Arthur of the Britons see *King Arthur, The Young Warlord*
Arthur the King 22, 206–8, 255
Arthur, Warlord of the Britons see *King Arthur, The Young Warlord*
Arthurian Propaganda see Pochoda, Elizabeth T.
Arthur's Quest 29, 255
Askey, Arthur 12–13; still 13
Atterton, Edward 28; still 247
Augustine, St. 179

Baden-Powell, Robert Lord 9
Baillie, Bruce 16
Baker, Joe Don 86; still 82
Bara, Theda 28
Barron, Steve 26, 44–53, 203–6
Barthes, Roland 170
Barton, John 22
Basinger, Kim 86
Bayreuth Festival 179–82; see also Wagner, Richard
Beardsley, Aubrey 236
Beaumont, Francis 137
Beckett, Samuel 169–70
Bédier, Joseph 8, 220–34
Beloin, Edmond 100
Ben-Hur (film) 235
Bennet, Spencer 14, 200–2
Beowulf 172
Berger, Thomas 110

Bergman, Ingrid 249
Bernard, Patrick: still 152
Béroul 220–21
Berreur, François 164
Beyond the Fringe 136
Biskind, Peter 70
The Black Knight 15–16, 17, 64–70, 255–56; still 68
Blank, Richard 20, 177–79
The Blood of the Poet see *Le Sang d'un poète*
Book Delivery Room (Boston Public Library) 10
Book of Hours 144
Book of Kells 212
Boorman, John 21, 26, 28, 34–63, 104–6, 151–52, 163–64, 169, 188–89, 203–6
Boorman, Katrina 46
Borgnine, Ernest 25
Boston Public Library 10
The Boy Merlin 22, 256
Boy Scouts 9
Bradley, Marion Zimmer 26–27, 61–63, 205; see also The Mists of Avalon (novel and telefilm)
Braunberger, Pierre 163
Brecht, Bertolt 145, 147
Bresson, Robert 19, 136–38, 149–62, 163, 166, 170, 172, 227
Brimley, Wilford 85–86
Brione, Benoit 164
Brown, Clarence 10
Brut 54
Buckley, Keith: still 48
Buñuel, Luis 18
Burne-Jones, Edward 170
Burr, Jeff 200
Burton, Kenneth J. 25
Burton, Richard 20, 213
Butler, David 11
Byrne, Gabriel 46

Calvino, Italo 143
Camelot (1967 film) 17–18, 56, 64, 74, 118, 121–26, 202–3, 206, 237–40, 256–57; stills frontispiece, 124, 203
Camelot (1982 film) 257
Camelot (animated short) 202

Camelot (Broadway musical) 17–18, 61, 114, 202–3
Camelot: The Legend 206–8
Capellani, Albert 8
Captains Courageous 75
Caradoc of Llancarfan 200
Caravaggio, Michaelangelo da 170
Carmina Burana 48
Carter, Helena Bonham 49
Caserini, Mario 8
Cassenti, Frank 150
Caxton, William 66–67, 71–72, 139; see also Malory, Sir Thomas
Centre Dramatique National de Franche-Comté (Besançon) 163
Chaney, Lon 10
Chaplin, Charlie 11, 98
Chapman, Graham 114, 129, 133, 139, 248; still 139
Chapman, Vera 26
Charlemagne 65
Charles I, King of England 25
Chaucer, Geoffrey 134, 141
Chelsom, Peter 25
Le Chevalier de la charette 200
Les Chevaliers de la table ronde (film by Llorca) 23, 163–76, 257; stills 166, 175
Chrétien de Troyes 20, 45, 64, 85, 110, 115, 144–46, 149–62 passim, 164, 169, 177–79, 188, 190–91, 200, 240, 245; see also *Le Chevalier de la charette*; *Le Conte du Graal*; *Yvain*
Claire, Cyrielle 191
Clary, Charles: still 259
Clay, Nicholas 213; still 40
Cleese, John 114, 127–28, 132, 140
Clemens, Samuel see Twain, Mark
Clever, Edith 180
Close, Glenn 86–92
Cobb, Lee J. 12
Cocteau, Jean 14, 174, 214, 220–34; see also *L'Éternel Retour*
Communism 64–70 passim
Communist threat to America, the Arthurian legend and 64–70 passim
Condominas, Laura Duke 170; still 154

303

Index

Confessions see Augustine, St.
A Connecticut Yankee (1931 film) 11, 99–100, 257–58
A Connecticut Yankee (1954 telefilm) 12, 258
A Connecticut Yankee (1955 telefilm) 12, 258
A Connecticut Yankee (stage musical) 11
A Connecticut Yankee at King Arthur's Court (1920 film) 10–11, 97–99, 258–59; stills front cover, 99, 259
A Connecticut Yankee in King Arthur's Court (1949 film) 11–12, 13, 64, 100–1, 259–60
A Connecticut Yankee in King Arthur's Court (1952 telefilm) 12, 260
A Connecticut Yankee in King Arthur's Court (1970 animated feature) 260
A Connecticut Yankee in King Arthur's Court (1978 telefilm) 12, 260–61
A Connecticut Yankee in King Arthur's Court (1989 telefilm) 12, 101–2, 110, 113–14, 117, 200, 207–8, 261
A Connecticut Yankee in King Arthur's Court (novel by Twain) 64, 70, 96–104, 107, 110, 201; *see also* multiple film adaptations and stage musical
Connemara 23, 261
Connery, Sean 19, 190; stills 24, 192
Conselman, William 99
Le Conte du Graal 20, 115,149–62 passim, 177; *see also* Chrétien de Troyes
Contes Moraux 155
Cook, Fielder 12
Coppel, Alex 65, 67
Cornishmen *see* Cornwall
Cornwall 7–29, 64–70; *see also* Tristan and Isolde, legend of
Cortazar, Julio 143
Costumes *see* arms in Arthurian film; armor in Arthurian film
Cowland, Dorian 21
Cromwell (film) 26
Crosby, Bing 11, 13, 64, 100–1
Crusades 235
Cuchulain 212
Cuny, Alain: stills 166, 175
Il Cuore e la spada 261
A Curious Dream 97
Curran, Paul: still 50

Dall, Evelyn: still 13
Les Dames du bois de Boulogne 175
Damski, Mel 12, 101–2, 110, 113–14, 117, 200, 206–8
Dante 130
Darmon, Nadine 164
Dean, Bashford 248

Degas, Edgar 170
Delannoy, Jean 14, 150, 212, 220–34; *see also L'Éternel Retour*
de la Tour, Bernard 150
de la Tour, George 170
de Liguoro, Giuseppe 9
Dennis, Arthur: still 10
Deschanel, Caleb 86, 89
Diner 80
Donner, Clive 22, 206–7
Donovan, Tom 20, 212, 216
Dostoevski, Feodor 163
Du Chau, Frederik 26, 200
Dugan, Dennis: still 113
Durr, Jason: still 195
Dusenberry, Phil 86
Duvall, Robert 85–86

Eco, Umberto 7, 29, 174
Edel, Uli 61–63, 203–6
Edison, Thomas 7–8, 9
Eisenstein, Sergei 51
The Elephant Man 28
Eliot, T. S. 16, 45
Encarnacao, Frank 102
Enchanted Tales 202
Engström, Ingemo 22
Equus (film) 28
Etchverry, Michel: still 157
The Eternal Return see *L'Éternel Retour*
L'Éternel Retour 14, 150, 212, 214–218, 220–34, 262–63; stills 217, 225, 229
Excalibur (1981 film) 21, 26, 34–63, 104, 106, 151–52, 164, 168–69, 171, 173, 175, 185–86, 203–4, 242–44, 263–65; stills 36, 40, 48, 58, 244
Excalibur (the sword) 13–14, 17, 24–26, 80–92; *see also Excalibur* (1981 film)
The Excalibur Kid 29, 265
Excalibur, The Raising of the Sword 21, 265

Fair Unknown: medieval legend of 16
Fairbanks, Douglas 11
Falena, Ugo 8
Fassbinder, Rainer Werner 180
Fawlty Towers 132
La Femme d'à côté see *The Woman Next Door*
Ferrer, Mel: still 276
Feuer und Schwert see *Fire and Sword*
Fiorentino, Rosso 170
Fire and Sword 20–21, 212, 266
First Knight 23–24, 26, 171, 200, 244–45, 266–67
The Fisher King, legend of 23, 80–92, 163–76; *see also The Fisher King* (1991 film) and the film versions of *Parsifal*

The Fisher King (1991 film) 23, 38, 246, 267–69
Fleming, Rhonda 100
Fleming, Victor 74–77
Flynn, Emmett J. 10–11, 98
Ford, Harrison: still 24
Foster, Hal 25–26
Four Diamonds (1995 film) 25, 269–70; still 270
"Four Diamonds" (short story) *see Four Diamonds* (1995 film)
Four Diamonds Fund *see Four Diamonds* (1995 film)
Fox, Edward 26
Franju, Georges 227
Franklin, Benjamin 65
Fransworth, Richard 86
Franzreb, John 249
Freak the Mighty 25; see also *The Mighty*
From Ritual to Romance see Weston, Jessie L.
Fudge, Alan 87

Galdós, Benito Peréz 18
Gantillo, Bruno 20
Garcia, Greg 202
Gardner, Ava: still 276
Garfield, John 13, 74–77; still 76
Garnett, Tay 11, 64–70, 100–1
Gawain and the Green Knight (1973 film) 18–19, 189–91, 270
Gawain and the Green Knight (1991 telefilm) 19, 191–96, 270; still 195
Geisweiller, Gilles 164
Geoffrey of Monmouth 49, 54, 63, 141, 200, 202; *see also Historia Regum Britanniae*
Gere, Richard 23–24
Gielgud, John 49
Gilliam, Terry 23, 114, 131, 140–144, 188; still 139
Ginvera 22, 270
Girl Slaves of Morgana Le Fay see *Morgane et ses Nymphes*
Gladiator (film) 131
Godard, Jean Luc 136
Goldberg, Whoopi 13, 103; still 103
Gottfried von Strassburg 222
Gottleib, Michael 12–13, 102, 200
The Grail *see* The Holy Grail
The Grail (1915 film) 9, 271
Grancsay, Stephen V. 248
Green, Nigel 190
Gres, Viktor
Griffith, D. W. 9–10
Grospierre, Louis 22
Gross, Michael 12, 102
Guinevere (1994 telefilm) 22, 203–5, 271
Guiry, Thomas: still 270
Gunnlauggson, Hrafn 21

Hardwicke, Sir Cedric 100
Harris, Ed: still 106
Harris, Richard 121, 239; still frontispiece
Hart, Lorenz 11
Hathaway, Henry 187, 200; see also Prince Valiant (1954 film)
Hauer, Rutger 49
Haukland, Aage 180
Hayden, Sterling 187
Hayes Code 199–210
Head, Murray 190
Hemmings, David: still 203
Henry V (film) 20, 235, 246
Herod, King 137
Herrad von Landesberg 240
Hershey, Barbara 86–92
Hickox, Anthony 25–26
Historia Brittonum 200
Historia Regum Britanniae 34, 49, 54, 200; see also Geoffrey of Monmouth
History of the Kings of Britain see *Historia Regum Britanniae*
Hitler: Ein Film aus Deutschland 179
The Holy Grail 9–10, 19–20, 23, 38–39, 80–92, 163–78, 188
Hood, Robin 17, 20
Hortus Deliciarum 240
Howard, Trevor 19, 191
Hubert, Roger 221
Hughes, Vic 22
Hugo, Victor 163
Hunt, Paul 24, 201
Huston, Anjelica 28; still 62

I Skugga Hrafnsina see *In the Shadow of the Raven*
Idle, Eric 114
The Idylls of the King 34, 44–53, 121, 185–86; see also Tennyson, Alfred Lord
In the Shadow of the Raven 21, 271
Indiana Jones and the Last Crusade 23, 245, 271–73; still 24
Ingersoll, Amy: still 106
Invasion of the Body Snatchers 69–70
Iron John 24
Isolde see Tristan and Isolde, legend of
Isolde (1989 film) 22, 273
Ivanhoe (film) 104

Jacobs, Jon 26
Joan of Arc (film) 249
Joffe, Arthur 21
Johnny Mysto, Boy Wizard 200, 273
Jones, Barry: still 201
Jones, James Earl 52
Jones, Terry 114, 129, 188, 248
Jordan, Armin 179–80
Juran, Nathan 17, 200

Karloff, Boris 12

Kedrova, Lila 191
Kennedy, John F. 121, 237
Kent, Charles 8–9
The Kid (Chaplin film) 11, 98
A Kid in King Arthur's Court 12, 102, 200, 273
Kids of the Round Table 25, 274
King Arthur (1980 film) see *Le Roi Arthur*
King Arthur and His Knights (by Knowles) 25
King Arthur and the Siege of the Saxons see *The Siege of the Saxons*
King Arthur; or, The Knights of the Round Table see *Il Re Artù e i cavalieri della tavola rotonda*
King Arthur, The Young Warlord 19–20, 274
King Arthur Was a Gentleman 13–14, 274; still 13
Kings (film by Llorca) 163
The King's Damosel 26
A Knight in Camelot 13, 103–4, 274–75; still 103
Knight of the Burning Pestle 137
Knightriders 21, 56, 97–98, 104–7, 200, 275; stills 106, 207
Knights and Armor (television series) 245–46
Knights of the Round Table (1953 film) 15, 185–87, 200–2, 205, 207–8, 275–76; still 276
Knights of the Round Table (1990 film) see *Les Chevaliers de la table ronde*
Knights of the Square Table; or, The Grail 9, 277; still 10
Knowles, Sir James 25
Knutzy Knights 14, 277; see also *Squareheads of the Round Table*
Kowalchuk, William 206–7
Krick, Karin 181; still 182
Kunkel, Wolfram 179
Kurit, Richard 24
Kutter, Michael 181; still 182

Ladd, Alan 64–70 passim; still 68
Lagrange, Yvan 18, 150, 212–17; still 215
Lamarr, Hedy 74–77
Lancelot and Elaine see *Launcelot and Elaine*
Lancelot and Guinevere see *The Sword of Lancelot*
Lancelot du Lac 19, 136, 138, 149–62, 163, 278–79; stills 152, 154
Lancelot: Guardian of Time 29, 279
Lancelot of the Lake see *Lancelot du Lac*
The Last of the Mohicans (film) 131
The Laud Manuscript 137
Launcelot and Elaine (film) 8–9, 280
"Launcelot and Elaine" (poem by Tennyson) 8–9

Lawhead, Stephen 239
Layamon 54
Legend of Gawain and the Green Knight see *Sword of the Valiant*
The Legend of King Arthur (1979 television series) 240–42
Die Legende von Tristan und Isolde see *Fire and Sword*
Legion of Decency 14
Leigh, Janet 187
Lerner, Alan Jay 61, 114, 121–26, 202–3
Levinson, Barry 22–23, 80–95
Levignac, Sylvain: still 241
Levy, Robert 102
Liebman, Max 12
The Light in the Dark 10, 280
The Light of Faith see *The Light in the Dark*
Llorca, Denis 23, 163–76
Lloyd, Robert 180
Loewe, Frederick 61, 114, 121–26, 202–3
Logan Joshua, 17–18, 206–8, 237–38
Love Eternal see *L'Éternel Retour*
Lovespell 212–13, 214–217; see also *Tristan and Isolt* (1979 film)
Lowell, James Russell 70
Loy, Myrna 11, 99
Luchini, Fabrice 150–51, 173; stills 157, 241
Lucinda's Spell 26, 280
Ludwig II, King of Bavaria 179, 181
Ludwig II: Requiem für einen jungfraülichen König 179
Lumley, Joanna 26
Lunghi, Cherie 46; still 40

Mabinogi 60
Macbeth 169
Macé, Alain 164; still 166
Madame Mim see Mim, Madame
Maddux, Stephen 222, 223
The Magic Sword: Quest for Camelot see *Quest for Camelot*
Mahin, John Lee 74–77
Major, John 24
Malamud, Bernard 12, 22–23, 80–95, 102; see also *The Natural* (film and novel)
Malory, Sir Thomas 9, 16, 21, 22, 34–43, 44–45, 54, 64, 66–67, 71–73, 85, 96, 105–7, 123, 133, 137, 139–41, 151–52, 164, 185–86, 187, 188, 205, 235; see also *Le Morte d'Arthur*
Mangrane, Daniel 8
Mantle, Burns 98
Marais, Jean 220–34 passim; stills 217, 229
Marguilies, Julianna 28; still 62
Mariaud, Maurice 8
Mark, King of Cornwall see Tristan and Isolde, legend of

Marlowe, Christopher 136
Marx, Karl 182
Mason, James: still 201
Matheson, Hans 28
Mathis, Samantha 28
Matthew, Paul 26, 202
Mayberry, Russ 12, 101, 201
McConville, Bernard 98
McGavin, Darien 86, 88
Le Médicin malgré lui 169
Medina, Patricia 65
Merlin (1992 film) see *October 32nd*
Merlin (1998 telefilm) 26, 44–53, 203, 205, 206–7, 280–81; still 50
Merlin and the Sword see *Arthur the King*
Merlin of the Crystal Cave 281
Merlin, or The Gold Rate see *Merlin, ou le cours de l'or*
Merlin, ou le cours de l'or 21, 281
Merlin: The Return 26, 202, 281
Merlin's Shop of Magical Wonders 25, 281–82
Meyers, Harry C. 11, 97–99; still 99
Michel, Francisque 222
The Mighty 25, 252, 282
Millard, Chris 25
Mim, Madame 17, 119–21; still 121
Mirren, Helen 46; still 58
Les Misérables (film by Llorca) 163
The Mists of Avalon (novel by Bradley) 26–27, 252
The Mists of Avalon (2001 telefilm) 26–27, 61–63, 203–6, 245–46, 252, 282–83; stills 62, 247
Mitchell, Thomas 12
Mitry, Jean 226–27
Moero Arthur (animated Japanese television series) 17; see also *Le Roi Arthur*
Mohr, Wolfgang 179
Molière 169
Monty Python and the Holy Grail 19, 101, 110, 114–117, 127–48, 171, 185, 188–89, 239–40, 248, 283–84; stills 116, 133, 139, 146
Monty Python troupe 19, 127–48, 185, 188, 190
Monty Python's Flying Circus 114, 127–35
Moody, Ron 12
Morgane et ses Nymphes 20, 284
Le Mort le roi Artu 16, 19, 149–50, 201–2
Le Morte d'Arthur 9, 21–22, 34–45, 54, 64, 66–67, 71–73, 96, 105–7, 123, 137–41, 151, 185–88, 235; see also Malory, Sir Thomas
The Morte d'Arthur (1984 telefilm) 22, 284
Mulgrew, Kate 213
Mussett, Charles: still 10

My Fair Lady (musical) 18
My Night at Maud's 151

National Socialism 179–84
The Natural (film) 22–23, 80–95, 284–85; stills 82, 91
The Natural (novel by Malamud) 12, 80–95, 102
Neeson, Liam 188
Neill, Sam 26, 49–52; still 50
Nero, Franco 18, 121, 122; still 124
New Adventures of a Connecticut Yankee in King Arthur's Court see *Novye prikluchenia janke pri dvore Korola Artura*
Newhart (television series) 240
Night of the Living Dead 104
Novye prikluchenia janke pri dvore Korola Artura 12, 285

October 32nd 24, 201, 285–86
O'Keefe, Miles 190; still 192
Olivier, Lawrence 19
The Once and Future King 17–18, 54, 56, 64, 105, 186, 187, 202–3, 239; see also White, T. H.
L'Orage en colère brise la voix de la forêt 164
Orff, Carl 48
Orphée 225
Osment, Haley Joel: still 27
O'Sullivan, Maureen 11, 99

Palin, Michael 114, 129, 131
Pallenberg, Rospo 28, 34
The Parker Manuscript 137
Parsifal (1904 film) 7–8, 252, 286–87; still 286
Parsifal (1912 film) 8, 287
Parsifal (1953 film) 8, 287
Parsifal (1982 film) 8, 177, 179–84, 287–88; stills 180, 182
Parsifal (opera) 7–8; see also film versions; Wagner, Richard
Part, Michael 102
Parzival (1980 film) 20, 288
Parzival (medieval romance) 177–79; see also film version; Wolfram von Eschenbach
Peet, Bill 118–19
Pendragon Cycle see Lawhead, Stephen
Perceval (1978 film) see *Perceval le Gallois*
Perceval (romance by Chrétien de Troyes) 144–46; see also Chrétien de Troyes; *Le Conte du Graal*; *Perceval le Gallois*
Perceval le Gallois 19, 23, 64, 149–62, 178, 248, 288–90; stills 157, 241
Philbrick, Rodman 25
Philip, Count of Flanders 177
Phillips, John Michael 19, 191–96;

see also *Gawain and the Green Knight* (1991 telefilm)
Piéral: still 225
Pochoda, Elizabeth T. 106–7
Porter, Edwin S. 7–8
The Possessed (film) 163
Prévaud, Jean-François 164
Prince Valiant (1997 film) 25–26, 291
Prince Valiant (comic strip) 25–26, 236; see also Foster, Hal; 1954 and 1997 films
Prince Valiant (1954 film) 15, 185, 187–88, 200, 236–37, 290–91; still 201
Prose Merlin 49
Prosky, Robert 86, 88
Pulliam, Keshia Knight 12, 102
Pyle, Howard 9, 66, 236

Quest for Camelot 26, 200, 291–92
The Quest of the Holy Grail (unrealized 1915 film) 9–10, 292
Queste del Saint Graal 34, 114, 137, 140, 142, 143, 145–46

Rackham, Arthur 236, 242
Rauf Coilyear 65
Il Re Artù e i cavalieri della tavola rotonda 9, 292
The Real Inspector Hound 137
Redford, Robert 22–23, 85–92; still 91
Redgrave, Vanessa 121, 122; still 124
Reeves, George 14
Reitherman, Wolfgang 110, 118–21
René d'Anjou 212
Renoir, Alain 189
Rétoré, Catherine 164, 174
Rex, Jytte 22
Rich, Robert 87
Richard I, King of England 17
Richard III (film) 235
Richardson, Miranda 49
Robert de Boron 140, 177
Robin Hood see Hood, Robin
Robin Hood's Merry Men 73
Rodgers, Richard 11
Rodgers, Will 11, 99
Rohmer, Eric 20, 64, 149–62, 163–76, 178, 248
Le Roi Arthur 17, 292
Roland 172
Roman de Brut 54–55
Le Roman de l'Estoire du Graal 177
Romero, George 21, 56, 97, 98, 104–7
Rosellini, Isabella 49
Royal Shakespeare Company 22
Rudkin, David 19

San Marte 178
Le Sang d'un poète 220, 224

Index

Saracens 64–70
Sarmatians 243
Savini, Tom: still 207
Sayre, Nora 68
Schaffner, Franklin 11–12
Schuchardt, Eva 179
Schygulla, Hanna 180
Scott, Gavin 28
Seaview Knights 24, 292–93
The Second Shepherd's Play 141
The Shadow of the Raven see *In the Shadow of the Raven*
Shadows see *The Boy Merlin*
Shakespeare, William 169
Shearer, Douglas 13
Short, Martin 49
Shyamalan, M. Night 28–29
The Siege of the Saxons 17, 200, 293
Simková-Plívová, Vera 25
Simon, Luc 170; still 152
Simorck, Karl 178
Sir Galahad of Twilight 9, 292
Sir Gawain and the Green Knight (medieval romance) 18–19, 54–64, 168, 185, 189–96
The Sixth Sense 28–29, 252, 293–94; still 27
Snow White 139
Solange, Madeleine 220–34; stills 217, 229
The Spaceman and King Arthur see *The Unidentified Flying Oddball*
Spielberg, Steven 23
Square Heads of the Round Table 14; see also *Knutzy Knights*
Stanek, Lou 96–97
Star Wars 252
Steinbeck, John 13, 71–79
Stoppard, Tom 137
Storry, Malcolm: still 195
The Story of King Arthur and His Knights see Pyle, Howard
Stuck on You 252
Suite du Merlin 49, 205
Summer of the Falcon see *Tristan and Isolt*
Swift, Jonathan 134
The Sword in the Stone (1963 animated film) 17, 64, 110–12, 117, 118–26, 239, 294–95; stills 120, 121
The Sword in the Stone (novel) 110–12, 117, 118–26; see also *The Once and Future King*; White, T. H.
The Sword of Lancelot 16–17, 64, 185, 202–6, 295; still 16
Sword of the Valiant 64, 189–91, 244, 295–96; still 192
Syberberg, Hans-Jürgen 8, 20, 177, 179–84

Tait, Don 101
Tale of Sir Thompas 141
Tamiroff, Akim: still 76
Taylor, John Russell 221, 230
Taylor, Jud 22, 203, 204–5
Taylor, Robert 104, 187
Tennesee Ernie Ford Meets King Arthur 12, 296
Tennyson, Alfred Lord 8–9, 10, 34, 44–54, 121, 133, 185–86
Terry, Nigel 45; still 36
Le Testament d'Orphé 174
Teutonic Knights 240
Thames Television 19, 22, 185–98
Theby, Rosemary 98; still 99
Thomas (medieval poet) 220, 222
Thomas, R. L. 13, 102
Thorpe, Richard 55–56, 200–1
The Three Stooges 14
Tinnell, Robert 25
To Parsifal 16, 296
Tortilla Flat (1942 film) 13, 71–79, 296–97; still 76
Tortilla Flat (novel) 13, 71–79
Towne, Robert 86
Tracy, Spencer 13, 74–77; still 76
Tristan and Isolda (1911 film) see *Tristano e Isotta*
Tristan and Isolde, legend of 20–22, 141, 144, 211–34; see also film versions
Tristan and Isolt (1979 film) 20, 297
Tristan et Iseult (1972 film) 18, 297–98
Tristan et Yseult (1909 film) 8, 298
Tristan et Yseult (1911 film) see *Tristano e Isotta*
Tristan et Yseult (1972) 212, 213–14; still 215
Tristan et Yseut (1920 film) 8, 298
Tristan und Isolde (1981 film) see *Fire and Sword*
Tristan und Isolde (opera) 8, 37; see also film versions of the legend
Tristan und Isolde, Eine Liebe für die Ewigkeit see *Il Cuore e la spada*
Tristana 18, 298–99
Tristano e Isotta (1911 film) 8, 299
Tristram and Isolda (1920 film) see *Tristan et Yseut*
Truffaut, François 22
Truscott, John 237
Twain, Mark 64, 70, 73, 96–104, 107, 110, 201, 207–8; see also *A Connecticut Yankee in King Arthur's Court* (film versions and novel)
Twelfth Night (film by Llorca) 171

The Unidentified Flying Oddball 12, 101, 110, 112–34, 117, 201, 299–300; still 113

Van Ness, Jon 90
Varnel, Marcel 13–14
Vartan, Michael 28; still 247
Verfremdungseffekt 235, 237, 242
Vialèles, Philipe 163
"Vision of Sir Launfal" 70
A Visit to the Armor Galleries (film) 248
Vita Merlini 54, 63
Vitold, Michel 171; still 175
von Fürstenberg, Veith 20, 212, 216
Vulgate Cycle 34, 114, 137, 140, 142, 143, 145–46, 201

Wace 54–55
Wagner, Richard 7–8, 37, 45, 48, 61, 168, 177–84, 220–34, 252; see also *Parisfal* (films and opera); *Tristan und Isolde* (films and opera)
Wagner, Robert 187
Wagner, Winifred 179
Waiting for Godot 169–70
Warner, Sylvia Townsend 122
The Wasteland (poem) 16
Wauthion, Claire 213; still 215
Weeks, Stephen 18–19, 189–91
Werner, Peter 25
Weston, Jessie L. 21, 45, 189–90
White, Sheila: still 113
White, T. H. 17–18, 54, 56, 64, 105, 110, 118–26, 186, 187, 188, 202–3, 239; see also *The Once and Future King*; *The Sword in the Stone*
Wiesenfield, Joe 103
Wilde, Cornel 16–17, 104, 202, 206
Wilder, James A. 9
Williams, Robin 245
Williamson, Nicol 46, 52; still 58
Winifred Wagner und die Geschicte des Haues Wahnfried von 1914-1975 179
Wolfram von Eschenbach 20, 45, 177–79, 245
The Woman Next Door 22, 300
Woolley, Persia 22
Worthington, William 9
Wyeth, N. C. 236

Ymadawiad Arthur 24–25, 300–1
York, Michael 13
York Mystery Cycle 137
Young, Roger 103
A Young Connecticut Yankee in King Arthur's Court 12, 102, 301
Yvain (medieval romance) 190–91

Zindel, Paul 102
Zucker, Jerry 23–24, 171, 200

www.ingramcontent.com/pod-product-compliance
Lightning Source LLC
Chambersburg PA
CBHW081540300426
44116CB00015B/2694